T0205769

Lecture Notes in Computer Science

Lecture Notes in Artificial Intelligence   14514

Founding Editor

Jörg Siekmann

Series Editors

Randy Goebel, *University of Alberta, Edmonton, Canada*
Wolfgang Wahlster, *DFKI, Berlin, Germany*
Zhi-Hua Zhou, *Nanjing University, Nanjing, China*

The series Lecture Notes in Artificial Intelligence (LNAI) was established in 1988 as a topical subseries of LNCS devoted to artificial intelligence.

The series publishes state-of-the-art research results at a high level. As with the LNCS mother series, the mission of the series is to serve the international R & D community by providing an invaluable service, mainly focused on the publication of conference and workshop proceedings and postproceedings.

Minghui Dong · Jia-Fei Hong · Jingxia Lin ·
Peng Jin
Editors

Chinese Lexical Semantics

24th Workshop, CLSW 2023
Singapore, Singapore, May 19–21, 2023
Revised Selected Papers, Part I

 Springer

Editors
Minghui Dong 🆔
Institute for Infocomm Research
Singapore, Singapore

Jia-Fei Hong 🆔
National Taiwan Normal University
Taipei, Taiwan

Jingxia Lin 🆔
Nanyang Technological University
Singapore, Singapore

Peng Jin 🆔
Leshan Normal University
Leshan, China

ISSN 0302-9743   ISSN 1611-3349 (electronic)
Lecture Notes in Artificial Intelligence
ISBN 978-981-97-0582-5   ISBN 978-981-97-0583-2 (eBook)
https://doi.org/10.1007/978-981-97-0583-2

LNCS Sublibrary: SL7 – Artificial Intelligence

This Springer imprint is published by the registered company Springer Nature Singapore Pte Ltd.
The registered company address is: 152 Beach Road, #21-01/04 Gateway East, Singapore 189721, Singapore

Paper in this product is recyclable.

Preface

The 2023 Chinese Lexical Semantics Workshop (CLSW 2023) was organized by the Chinese Language Information Processing Society (COLIPS) of Singapore, in collaboration with the National University of Singapore (NUS) and Nanyang Technological University (NTU). We were proud to contribute once more to the field of Chinese lexical semantics. COLIPS was established in 1988, dedicated to advancing research in computer processing of Chinese and other Asian languages. In 2004, COLIPS hosted the 5th Chinese Lexical Semantics Workshop (CLSW) in Singapore. In 2008 and 2016, we successfully held the CLSW conference in Singapore again. This year marked the 4th time that CLSW was held in Singapore.

During this conference, we scheduled four keynote presentations that covered various research areas. First, Xu Jie from the Chinese Language and Literature Department of the University of Macau presented on the categorization of negation in Chinese. Next, Dong Minghui from the Agency for Science, Technology, and Research (A*STAR) explored the application of language models in Chinese semantic research. The third presentation was delivered by Su Qi from the School of Foreign Languages at Peking University, sharing research on culture and cultural history conducted under data-driven approaches. Lastly, Du Jingjing from Xiamen University presented the research achievements of the Chinese elementary education standardized version's lexical semantics. These keynote presentations added more academic highlights to the conference.

This conference predominantly showcased in-person presentations, signifying the first significant event since the end of the pandemic. Regrettably, certain authors couldn't join us physically due to various reasons. Nevertheless, we made concerted efforts to keep in touch with remote participants, ensuring their active engagement through online platforms for discussions and interactions. Regardless of the mode of participation, every attendee enriched this conference with their distinctive perspectives and experiences. The enthusiastic involvement in the presentation and discussion sessions fostered a profound exchange of ideas and knowledge, creating a truly inspiring and collaborative academic gathering.

We received a total of 215 paper submissions for this conference. The review work was done using the Microsoft CMT3 system, with a double-blind review process. Each paper was reviewed by 3 reviewers. Scores were given for three major aspects: (1) Impact of the work on society and the research domain. (2) The technical correctness of the work, such as supported by data and other proof. (3) The clarity of the presentation, meaning whether the paper clearly describes the work.

The review scores were further evaluated by 3 program chairs, and decisions were made based on the review scores and the discussions among program chairs when disputes arose among reviewers. After rigorous evaluation and selection, we arranged 113 paper presentations, including 79 oral presentations and 34 poster presentations, covering a wide range of research topics in Chinese lexical semantics. We are grateful for the hard work and contributions of all the authors.

October 2023

Minghui Dong
Jia-Fei Hong
Peng Jin
Jingxia Lin

Organization

Conference Chair

Dong, Minghui   Institute for Infocomm Research, A*STAR, Singapore

Program Committee Chairs

Hong, Jia-Fei   Taiwan Normal University, Taiwan
Jin, Peng   Leshan Normal University, China
Lin, Jingxia   Nanyang Technological University, Singapore

Advisory Committee

Diao, Yanbin   Beijing Normal University, China
Hong, Jia-Fei   Taiwan Normal University, Taiwan
Hsieh, Shu-Kai   Taiwan University, Taiwan
Huang, Chu-Ren   Hong Kong Polytechnic University, China
Ji, Donghong   Wuhan University, China
Jin, Peng   Leshan Normal University, China
Liu, Meichun   City University of Hong Kong, China
Lu, Qin   Hong Kong Polytechnic University, China
Qu, Weiguang   Nanjing Normal University, China
Su, Xinchun   Xiamen University, China
Sui, Zhifang   Peking University, China
Lua, Kim Teng   Chinese and Oriental Languages Information Processing Society, Singapore
Wu, Jiun-Shiung   Taiwan Chung Cheng University, Taiwan
Xu, Jie   University of Macau, China
Zan, Hongying   Zhengzhou University, China
Zhang, Yangsen   Beijing Information Science and Technology University, China
Zhuo, Jing-Schmidt   University of Oregon, USA

Organizing Chairs

Lin, Jingxia   Nanyang Technological University, Singapore
Tan, Xiaowei   National University of Singapore, Singapore
Yuan, Min   National University of Singapore, Singapore

Finance Chairs

Wang, Lei   Huawei and COLIPS, Singapore
Wu, Yan   Institute for Infocomm Research, A*STAR, Singapore

Publication Chairs

Su, Qi   Peking University, China
Tang, Xuri   Huazhong University of Science and Technology, China

Contents – Part I

Lexical Semantics

A Study on Native Mandarin Speakers' Homogeneity of Degree Adverbs
and Adjectives 3
Huichen S. Hsiao, Yunhan Wang, and Anwei Yu

Assessing Lexical Psycholinguistic Properties in Mandarin Discourse
Production by Patients with Aphasia 11
Juqiang Chen and Hui Chang

Research on the Interactive Elements and Functions of Live Streaming
Sales Language ——Take "*Hao Bu Hao*" as an Example 23
Hanmeng Li and Xin Kou

Chinese Optatives: A Preliminary Study 34
Jiun-Shiung Wu and Chih-Hsuan Chung

The Semantic Features and Pragmatic Functions of Cantonese
Quasi-Demonstrative Type Quantifier *di1*: A Comparison
with Demonstratives *ne1* and *go2* 46
Xiyue Huang

A Comparative Study of the General Classifier *Gè* and Its Near-Synonyms
in Modern Chinese——Taking *Gè, Zhǒng,* and *Jiàn* as Examples 60
Jingying Rui and Jia-Fei Hong

The Semantic Analysis of *Zhexia*: From the Perspectives of Spatial
Metaphor, Subjectivity and Discourse Function 74
Jung-Jung Kang and Chia-Rung Lu

Sociolinguistic Aspects of Popular Abbreviations in Hong Kong Cantonese 90
Ken Siu-kei Cheng and Ka-wai Ho

The Semantic Features and Construal Mechanisms of the Expectational
Negative Adverb *Kong* in Mandarin 101
Jinghan Zeng and Yulin Yuan

The Formation Features and Structural Mechanism of Modern Chinese
"$V_{cooking}$+N" Structure 116
Yuqi Shen and Jiapan Li

Classifiers of Mandarin Alphabetical Words with Character-Alphabet
Structure 130
   Xinlan Zhao, Yu-Yin Hsu, and Chu-Ren Huang

Feasibility of Direct Language Transfer of the Verb "to Eat"
from Cantonese to Mandarin 146
   Ka-Hang Leung and Jia-Fei Hong

The Usage and Standardization of Function Words in Legislative Chinese
Language Overseas: A Case Study of Auxiliary Words in the Civil Code
of Macao 160
   Linqian Bai, Lei Zhang, and Shanshan Yang

The Licensing Contexts of Polarity-Sensitive Adverb *Sǐhuó* ('no matter
what'): A Force-Dynamic Analysis 173
   Yifa Xu

The Influence of Neologisms from Mainland China on Changes
in the Lexical Semantics of Hong Kong Cantonese 187
   Yike Yang and Ho Kuen Ho

Research on the Semantic Collocations of Mental Verbs and the Generative
Mechanisms of Polysemy: The Generative Lexicon 196
   Weili Wang, Jianshe Zhou, and Kai Zhang

Profiling the Mandarin Physical Contact Verbs with *ná, wò, chí* and *zhuā*
Using Collocational, Syntactic and Discourse Features 211
   Qian Zhong and Tianqi He

Temporal *Hái* in Mandarin Chinese Revisited: A Presuppositional Account 225
   Chih-Hsuan Chung and Jiun-Shiung Wu

A Study on Semantic Shift of Uncivilized Words in Bullet-Screen
Comments 239
   Juanjuan Fan and Jianguo Yang

A Multiple Correspondence Analysis on the Adverbial Uses of the Chinese
Color Term *Bai* 'White' 254
   Jinmeng Dou, Meichun Liu, and Zhuo Zhang

The Semantic Interpretation of Implicit Negative Compound Nouns 266
   Enxu Wang and Xiaoqing Lv

Semantic Preferences of *Biran* and *Yiding*: A Distinctive Collexeme
Analysis of Chinese Near-Synonymous Constructions of "Mod + Verb" 278
  Zhuo Zhang, Meichun Liu, and Jinmeng Dou

Zero Anaphora Errors and the Restriction Rules of Zero Anaphora
in Discourse for Middle and Senior International Students 288
  Hao You

A Cognitive Semantic Analysis of the Spatial Dimension Adjective
"Deep/Shallow" from the Perspective of Lexical Typology 302
  Jia Yi and Bing Qiu

A Study on the Restraining Factors and Its Acting Forces of Selected
Components of Chinese Abbreviations 317
  Yaolin Feng

On the Verb *Huaiyi* with Passive Voice in Hong Kong-Style Chinese 332
  Hantao Xu

The Semantic Characteristics of the Counter-Expectation Adverbs
"Făn'ér" and "Ohiryo" in Chinese and Korean from the Perspective
of Comparison 343
  Qingcong Shan

A Cognitive Approach to the Semantic Change of the Polysemy *gàng*
'Wooden Bar' 358
  Hongzhu Wang and Yin Zhong

An Analysis of One-Dimensional Adjectives from the Perspective
of Lexical Semantic Typology 370
  Chaeri Kim

Semantic Analysis of the Tool-Meaning Quasi-Affixes "*Jī, Qì, Yí* and *Jì*" 386
  Ao Sun

A Study of Adding Psychological Feeling into the Model of Synaesthesia
at the Morpheme Level in Modern Chinese 400
  Han Wen and Shuwen Zheng

Analysis of the Form and Meaning in Collocation of Chinese "V + Color"
Verb-Object Compounds 415
  Junping Zhang, Qi Zhu, and Ting Zhu

The Effect of Working Memory Capacity on the Figurative Language
Processing of Chinese Second Language Learners 426
   Xun Duan and Xingsan Chai

A Study on the Use and Integration of the Network Buzzword '*Rùn*' 440
   Quan Li

A Semantic Analysis of *Suffocate* Verbs 454
   Shaoming Wang and Shan Wang

From Blame to Exclamation: On the Lexicalization Mechanism
and Syntactic-Semantic Function of Cross-Layer Sequence Form "guài
zhǐ guài" 466
   Xuting Zhan

A Research on the Manchu-Chinese Bilingual Comparative Characteristics
of the *Yu Zhi Zeng Ding Qing Wen Jian* Dictionary 480
   Yao Zhang

A Study on the Combination of the "Artificial/Natural" Semantics
in the Chinese NN Attributive-Head Compounds 495
   Tengteng Du and Jiapan Li

Author Index 511

Contents – Part II

Computational Linguistics and Natural Language Processing

Teaching Chinese Pattern Extraction and Its Knowledge Base Construction
for Specific Domain Texts 3
    Zuntian Wei, Weiming Peng, Jihua Song, Shaodong Wang,
    and Mengyu Zhao

Probability Distribution of Dependency Distance of Mongolian Nouns 15
    Dulan and Dabhurbayar

The Use and Evolution of Colors in Written Chinese Since the Late Qing
Dynasty 27
    Yiwei Xu and Gaoqi Rao

A Study of Identification of Chinese VO Idioms with Statistical Measures 42
    Xueyi Wen, Yi Li, Yuanbing Zhao, and Hongzhi Xu

Sensory Features in Affective Analysis: A Study Based on Neural Network
Models 52
    Yuhan Xia, Qingqing Zhao, Yunfei Long, and Ge Xu

Corpus Construction of Critical Illness Entities and Relationships 61
    Kunli Zhang, Chenghao Zhang, Wenxuan Zhang, and Hongying Zan

Research on the Structure of Pediatric Epilepsy Electronic Medical
Records Based on Transfer Learning 76
    Yu Song, Pengcheng Wu, Dongming Dai, Kunli Zhang,
    Chenghao Zhang, Hengxing Zhang, Xiaomei Liu, and Jie Li

Semantic and Phonological Distances in Free Word Association Tasks 91
    Marc Allassonnière-Tang, I.-Ping Wan, and Chainwu Lee

Suffix ʔɐ51 in Zhangzhou: An Interdisciplinary Explorations 101
    Yishan Huang

Does Bert Know How 'Virus' Evolved: Tracking Usage Changes
in Chinese Textual Data 116
    Jing Chen, Le Qiu, Bo Peng, and Chu-Ren Huang

The Evolution of "X huà" in the Press Since the Late Qing Dynasty 126
   Xingyu Hu, Zilin Yi, and Gaoqi Rao

Distribution of Motifs in Mongolian Word Length 139
   Lingxiong Bao, Dahubaiyila, and Wuyoutan

Construction of Knowledge Base of Non-Core Argument Based on Serial
Verb Construction 153
   Shufan Zhou, Guirong Wang, Gaoqi Rao, and Endong Xun

The Application of Chinese Word Segmentation to Less-Resourced
Language Processing 173
   Meng-hsien Shih

Research on Automatic Summary Method for Futures Research Reports
Based on TextRank 180
   Yingjie Han, Tengfei Chen, Xiaodong Ning, and Heguo Yang

Automatic Question Generation for Language Learning Task Based
on the Grid-Based Language Structure Parsing Framework 192
   Tian Shao, Zhixiong Zhang, Yi Liu, Gaoqi Rao, and Endong Xun

Corpus Linguistics

What Factors Can Facilitate Efficient Propagation of Chinese
Neologisms–A Corpus-Driven Study with Internet Usage Data 209
   Menghan Jiang, Kathleen Ahrens, and Chu-Ren Huang

COVID-19 Related Expressions and Their Correlation with the Pandemic:
An Internet-Based Study 216
   Jia-Fei Hong and Jia-Ni Chen

Chinese Inter-clausal Anaphora in Causal Relation—A Corpus Study 234
   Shunting Chen

Corpus-Based Study on the Evolution of the Lexical Phonetic Forms
from Old Chinese to Middle Chinese 243
   Bing Qiu

A Corpus-Based Study of Lexical Chunks in Chinese Academic Discourse:
Extraction, Classification, and Application 257
   Qihong Zhou and Li Mou

Gender Variation in Mix-Gender Conversations in the Semi-institutional
Discourse: The Case of Talk Show 274
    Xin Luo, Parti Gábor, and Chu-Ren Huang

A Comparative Study of Computational Linguistics Terminology
in English Papers by Chinese and American Scholars 286
    Yonghui Xie, Wei Huang, and Erhong Yang

Native Speakers' Judgment of the Epistemic Evidentiality of Synonym
Verbs of "Think" in Mandarin: A Corpus-Based Study of Renwei, Yiwei,
Juede, Kaolü, and Xiang 301
    Yaoru Ye and Yu-Yin Hsu

Investigating Acoustic Cues of Emotional Valence in Mandarin Speech
Prosody - A Corpus Approach 316
    Junlin Li and Chu-Ren Huang

Corpus-Based Analysis of Lexical Features of Mongolian Language
Policy Text 331
    Annaer and Dahubaiyila

Offensiveness Analysis of Chinese Group Addressing Terms and Dataset
Construction 342
    Shucheng Zhu and Ying Liu

Let's Talk About Business: A Corpus-Based Study of 'Business' Related
Near-Synonyms and Their Teaching in Chinese as a Second Language 357
    Yin Zhong and Yujing Rao

Differences in Word Collocations of "*Jǐnzhāng*" in Cross-Strait Chinese 377
    Yi-Jia Lin and Jia-Fei Hong

A Corpus-Based Comparative Study on the Semantics and Collocations
of *meili* and *piaoliang* 393
    Ka Hei Szeto and Yike Yang

Development of a Chinese Tourism Technical Word List Based on Corpus
Analysis 406
    Yue Xu, Wei Wei, and Zhimin Wang

General Linguistics

A Preliminary Study on Japanese CSL Learners' Acquisition of Mandarin
Potential Expressions 423
    Anwei Yu and Huichen S. Hsiao

On the Discourse Functions of *Biede Bushuo* Based on Pragma-Dialectical
Theory 435
  Si Chen and Lue Huang

X-Copying as Metalinguistic Negation in Chengdu Chinese 447
  Jiajuan Xiong

Duration Phrases as Fake Nominal Quantifiers: A Functional Account
with Corpus Evidence 458
  Xiaopei Zhang and Meichun Liu

A Study on the Position of Preposition-Objects Structures in Kongzijiayu 469
  Yonghong Ke

A Structural Priming Study of the Information Function of the Chinese *Ba*
Construction 486
  Bingxian Chen and Yu-Yin Hsu

A Case Study of a Preschool Child's Compliment Expression Based
on Schema Theory 498
  Siqi Xie

Author Index 515

Lexical Semantics

A Study on Native Mandarin Speakers' Homogeneity of Degree Adverbs and Adjectives

Huichen S. Hsiao[(✉)] ⓘ, Yunhan Wangⓘ, and Anwei Yuⓘ

Department of Chinese As a Second Language, National Taiwan Normal University, Taipei, Taiwan

{huichen.hsiao,yunhan.wang,yu.anwei}@ntnu.edu.tw

Abstract. This study aims to investigate whether scale and polarity affect the semantic acceptability of native Mandarin speakers in terms of the collocation between degree adverbs and adjectives via a native corpus analysis and a forced-choice language sense task administered to native Mandarin speakers from Taiwan. The preliminary results of the acceptability judgment task indicate that most absolute adjectives are context-independent and can stably collocate with degree adverbs, which align with the corpus study results. However, some factors were found to affect the semantic acceptability of native Mandarin speakers, such as context, subjective differences and cognitive asymmetry.

Keywords: Scalarity · Polarity · Degree Adverb-Adjective Collocations

1 Introduction

Historically, many of the studies on the collocation of adverbs and adjectives have been conducted on English, but not many researchers have probed the situation of degree adverbs and adjectives in Mandarin. For instance, Paradis [1, 2] utilized a spoken corpus and classified adjectives in English as "scalar," "extreme," or "limit" based on gradability and boundedness. Paradis [1, 2] found that "scalar" adjectives are unbounded antonym pairs (e.g., long/short) that collocate with "scalar modifiers," while "extreme" and "limit" adjectives more often collocate with "reinforcing totality modifiers." Furthermore, Paradis [2] argued that the above factors affect the configurational harmony of collocation patterns between adverbs and adjectives. Based on these patterns, Kennedy [3] proposed the use of "Mutual Information" (MI) to measure the strength of the bond between members of these two parts of speech. Kennedy [3] discovered that adverbs and adjectives exhibit systematic collocation patterns; e.g., 'absolutely' tends to collocate with adjectives used hyperbolically, such as 'fantastic.'

In the case of Mandarin, the majority of early studies have been on the classifications of adverbs and adjectives based on scalar structure, i.e., whether the terms could be used to make comparisons, and Wang [4] classified adverbs and adjectives as "relative" or "absolute" based on these criteria. In turn, Han [5] investigated the collocations between adverbs of differing degrees and adjectives and found that absolute adverbs of low degree (i.e., *yǒudiǎn* "a little bit") collocate more often with adjectives with negative

M. Dong et al. (Eds.): CLSW 2023, LNAI 14514, pp. 3–10, 2024.
https://doi.org/10.1007/978-981-97-0583-2_1

polarity and relative adverbs of low degree often collocate with adjectives with positive polarity (i.e., *yǒudiǎn nán* "a little bit difficult;" *gèng hǎo* "better"). However, the above scholars did not verify their findings via corpus data or questionnaires administered to native speakers. Therefore, the present study aims to investigate the collocations between Mandarin degree adverbs and adjectives based on the classification system that Wang [4] proposed by calculating the MI score between different adverbs and adjectives based on Kennedy [3] and then administering an acceptability judgment task to native Mandarin speakers.

2   Materials and Methods

The present study utilizes an acceptability judgment task in the form of a forced-choice task to investigate the collocations between Mandarin degree adverbs with different scalar structures and adjectives of differing polarity. Detailed information is described below.

2.1 Pilot Study

The pilot study was used to choose the adverbs and adjectives utilized in the main study via inputting the command "X_Dfa*" into the Corpus of Contemporary Taiwanese Mandarin 2019 (COCT 2019) [6] to search for the degree adverbs that most often collocate with adjectives while exhibiting an MI score of 4.7 or above. According to the adverbs classification of Wang [4], we have selected four high-frequency degree adverbs that belong to different levels of relative or absolute adverbs when combined with adjectives as the focus of this experiment. Adverbs of the same degree and lower frequency were excluded. To test the effects of polarity and scalarity on native speaker collocations, adjectives were chosen as antonym pairs with differing polarity, based on Shi [7], and five pairs of absolute and relative adjectives were chosen respectively to act as experimental materials, according to Paradis [2] and Kennedy & McNally [8], and the terms chosen have the capacity to act as both predicates and attributives according to Hsu [9]. In addition, results containing negative adverbs (i.e., *bù*, *méi* "no") were removed to control for subjectivity. Tables 1 and 2 below show the materials chosen.

Table 1. Adverbs Chosen for the Main Study with Ranking of MI Score

Ranking of MI in Corpus	Degree Adverb	Percentage	Ranking of MI in Corpus	Degree Adverb	Percentage
2	*tài* "too/ so"	17.27%	7	*yǒudiǎn* "a little bit"	2.16%
5	*zuì* "most"	3.28%	8	*gèng* "more"	2.01%

Table 2. Adjectives Chosen for the Main Study

Presumed Scalarity	Polarity	
	Positive Polarity	Negative Polarity
Absolute Adjectives	*mǎnyì* "satisfied"	*shīwàng* "disappointed"
	zhèngquè "correct"	*bú duì* "incorrect"
	qīngchǔ "clear"	*yíhuò* "doubtful"
	wǎnzhěng "complete"	*cánquē* "incomplete"
	zhēnshí "real"	*xūjiǎ* "fake"
Relative Adjectives	*yánjǐn* "strict"	*cǎoshuài* "rash"
	ānjìng "quiet"	*chǎonào* "noisy"
	yǒnggǎn "brave"	*dǎnqiè* "timid"
	qīngsōng "relaxed"	*mánglù* "busy"
	fàngxīn "relieved"	*dānxīn* "worried"

2.2 Participants

A total of 103 native Mandarin speakers from Taiwan without background in linguistics were recruited to participate in the experiment. Among them were 27 males and 76 females[1] with an average age of 22.18 years old.

2.3 Procedure

The forced-choice task was formatted as a survey administered via Surveycake. Each question contained a question and two possible responses. The responses contained a collocation of "degree adverb-positive/negative adjective"; e.g., *yǒudiǎn ānjìng/ yǒudiǎn chǎonào* "a little bit quiet/ a little bit noisy," and participants were instructed to choose the response that they felt was most natural as fast as possible. Participants that submitted overly similar responses were eliminated before data analysis.

---

[1] Gender was not found to have any significant effect on the results.

2.4 Materials

The experimental materials utilized in this study were randomly organized via Latin Square Design, and no materials were repeated. The target questions were made up of combinations of the adverbs in Table 1 and the adjectives in Table 2, with a total of 80 combinations formatted as 40 questions. The filler questions consisted of adverb-adjective collocations not included in Tables 1 and 2. Each individual's survey included a total of 15 questions, including a practice question, target questions and filler questions (10*4/3 + 1 = 15). An example of a target question is shown below in Fig. 1.

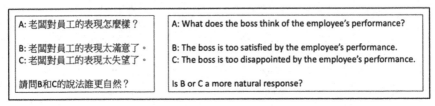

Fig. 1. Example of Target Question and its Translation in English

3   Results and Discussion

According to the results of the forced-choice task and the Mutual Information results found in COCT 2019, we found several collocation patterns. First, the experimental results are consistent with the corpus. The effect of boundedness in the forced-choice task can be seen clearly in this group (cf. Table 3). Second, the proportion of one of the antonym pairs in the experiment is higher and differs from the MI score found in the corpus. In this situation, context becomes a key factor in the lexical choices of native Mandarin speakers.

From the results of the forced-choice task (as shown in Table 3), negatives are lower-bounded. They can be used only with absolute degree adverbs, whereas positives show transcendence in the experimental results and are therefore judged to be unbounded and can be used with relative degree adverbs. For instance, the participants tended to pair *zhèngquè* "correct" with relative degree adverbs and *búduì* "incorrect" with absolute adverbs, indicating that the *búduì* "incorrect" has greater boundedness according to the participants 'perception. The correlation was also verified from the corpus results, with a higher MI score for *zhèngquè* "correct" paired with relative degree adverbs and a lower MI score for *búduì* "incorrect" when paired with relative degree adverbs. Comparing the MI score with the experimental results in the horizontal row of the table, we can see that the participants also preferred the higher MI score pairings, which verifies that participants could judge the collocation between degree adverbs and adjectives via configurational harmony in the absence of context [10].

In the below section, we observed that the context or the cognitive asymmetry of polarity has an effect on the results. Concrete performance is one of the antonyms in the experiment, is higher than another, and differs in the MI score from the corpus. We

Table 3. The experimental results are consistent with the corpus.

		Absolute Adverb		Relative Adverb	
		tài "too/so"	*yǒudiǎn* "a little bit"	*zuì* "most"	*gèng* "more"
Forced- Choice Task Results (Mutual Information score)	*zhèngquè* "correct"	45.00% (-0.21)	0.00% (/)^2	82.00% (3.08)	86.00% (5.41)
	búduì "incorrect"	55.00% (-0.56)	100.00% (4.41)	18.00% (-4.58)	14.00% (/)
	zhēnshí "real"	30.00% (1.59)	0.00% (0.36)	95.00% (3.89)	83.00% (5.32)
	xūjiǎ "fake"	70.00% (3.12)	100.00% (4.87)	5.00% (1.17)	17.00% (/)
	yánjǐn "strict"	8.00% (1.14)	6.00% (/)	62.00% (3.53)	75.00% (6.89)
	cǎoshuài "rash"	92.00% (6.44)	94.00% (6.19)	38.00% (0.58)	25.00% (/)
	fàngxīn "relieved"	42.00% (0.53)	3.00% (0.67)	58.00% (1.37)	91.00% (5.30)
	dānxīn "worried"	58.00% (2.82)	97.00% (6.77)	42.00% (3.59)	9.00% (2.16)

separate the data into two different kinds. First, is that participants reasonably to the positive adjective in the result. Second, the participants tend to use negative adjectives in the result, which is also different from the corpus data.

According to Table 4, participants tended to use positive adjectives, and few differed from the corpus results. First, this result may be related to cognitive asymmetry, as negative adjectives generally do not have an actual onset and cannot be measured. Therefore, native Mandarin speakers tend to use positive adjectives in this case.

Moreover, the participants viewed sentences containing positive terms as a more natural collocation in the task. For example, 93.00% of the participants considered *gèng* "more" to be more natural with the positive term *yǒnggǎn* "brave" as opposed to negative *dǎnqiè* "timid". Looking at this phenomenon from the perspective of Lin [11], the participants may think that the negative *dǎnqiè* "timid" has no real starting point in the scale. Hence, native Mandarin speakers prefer the positive term *yǒnggǎn* "brave" as a sentence preposition in their forced-choice task. In addition, participants' subjectivity towards adjectives also influenced the experiment's results. For example, in the case of the word pair *ānjìng-chǎonào* "quiet-noisy," the participants considered *ānjìng* "quiet," which is usually considered a positive adjective as opposed to *chǎonào* "noisy," to naturally collocate with the degree adverb *yǒudiǎn* "a little bit"(*yǒudiǎn ānjìng* "a little bit quiet": 79%). This result is inconsistent with the trend in the collocation of

---

^{2} The slash "/" used in Tables 3, 4 and 5 indicates that no data was found.

Table 4. The proportion of positive adjectives are higher than negatives

		Absolute Adverb		Relative Adverb	
		tài "too/ so"	*yǒudiǎn* "a little bit"	*zuì* "most"	*gèng* "more"
Forced-Choice Task (Corpus /Mutual Information)	*wǎnzhěng* "complete"	85.00% (−1.70)	14.00% (/)	97.00% (4.42)	94.00% (5.32)
	cánquē "incomplete"	15.00% (0.73)	86.00% (5.12)	3.00% (/)	6.00% (/)
	yǒnggǎn "brave"	83.00% (0.81)	20.00% (/)	76.00% (4.42)	93.00% (4.66)
	dǎnqiè "timid"	17.00% (3.87)	80.00% (8.05)	24.00% (0.65)	7.00% (5.32)
	ānjìng "quiet"	48.00% (3.80)	79.00% (1.84)	67.00% (2.26)	73.00% (3.81)
	chǎonào "noisy"	52.00% (4.81)	21.00% (3.30)	33.00% (2.01)	27.00% (/)

the degree adverb *yǒudiǎn* "a little bit," which usually collocates with negative words [5]. Each individual has different criteria for defining a sound or an environment as *ānjìng* "quiet" or *chǎonào* "noisy." Hence, *ānjìng* "quiet" is not a positive term for some people, but rather a neutral or negative term.

Table 5. The proportion of negative adjectives are higher than positive

		Absolute Adverb		Relative Adverb	
		"too/ so"	*yǒudiǎn* "a little bit"	*zuì* "most"	*gèng* "more"
Forced-Choice Task (Corpus/Mutual Information)	*mǎnyì* "satisfied"	27.00% (1.10)	0.00% (2.07)	75.00% (3.17)	33.00% (3.72)
	shīwàng "disappointed"	73.00% (7.32)	100.00% (2.76)	25.00% (−0.17)	67.00% (3.87)
	qīngchǔ "clear"	44.00% (2.72)	3.00% (/)	34.00% (3.39)	64.00% (4.81)
	yíhuò "doubtful"	56.00% (/)	97.00% (6.80)	66.00% (−1.95)	36.00% (5.31)
	qīngsōng "relaxed"	36.00% (2.86)	15.00% (1.41)	41.00% (2.99)	44.00% (5.14)
	mánglù "busy"	64.00% (4.37)	85.00% (0.18)	59.00% (3.70)	56.00% (3.72)

From the result of the forced-choice task, in this pairing, the participants chose negative terms more often than positive ones. For example, as shown in Table 5, the percentage of participants collocating *shīwàng* "disappointed" with degree adverbs was higher than *mǎnyì* "satisfied"; 73% and 67% of participants believed *tài shīwàng* "too/so disappointed" and *gèng shīwàng* "more disappointed" are more natural collocations, respectively. Moreover, *yǒudiǎn* "a little bit" collocated *shīwàng* "disappointed" most frequently at 100%. According to the MI score from the corpus, *tài shīwàng* "too/so disappointed" is 7.32, ranking first, and *yǒudiǎn shīwàng* "disappointed" ranked third. Similar to the experimental results, participants should be more inclined to use *mǎnyì* "satisfied" with *zuì* "most".

However, in this group, some results do not match the corpus MI results. Taking the second group *yíhuò* "doubtful" and *qīngchǔ* "clear" for example, the results show that the participants tended to collocate *yíhuò* "doubtful" with *yǒudiǎn* "a little bit." In addition, they were more likely to pair *zuì* "most" with *yíhuò* "doubtful" over *qīngchǔ* "clear" (*yíhuò* "doubtful" = 66%; *qīngchǔ* "clear" = 34%). However, according to the MI score from the corpus, the MI score of *yíhuò* "doubtful" paired with *zuì* "most" was -1.95, implying that participants should be more inclined to choose *qīngchǔ* "clear." This may be related to the context of the forced-choice task, which makes participants more likely to choose *yíhuò* "doubtful."

4 Conclusion

In sum, this study implemented a forced-choice task to investigate the collocations of Mandarin degree adverbs and adjectives via the language sense of native Mandarin speakers. Based on the cross-comparison of experimental results and data from the corpus, we found several interesting phenomena from the results. First, some adjectives are context-independent and show stable and harmonious collocations with degree adverbs, which can be categorized as absolute adjectives and are mostly lower-bounded. Second, some factors were observed in the experimental results that influenced the participants' judgments, which in turn made the results of the forced-choice task differ from the ranking of the MI score in the corpus. These factors include, but are not limited to, (1) context, where the subject and prepositional components in the context influence the subjects' judgments. For example, according to Wu and Li [12], their results also indicate that the polarity sensitivity of minimal degree words is not solely determined by semantics; one must also consider pragmatics and frequency when making polarity determinations; (2) subjective differences, where each person has a different definition of the adjective in their mental lexicon, e.g., some people consider *ānjìng* "quiet" to be positive term, while others consider it to be negative; (3) cognitive asymmetry, where the range of magnitudes in which certain positive words can be used in a context is larger, making the frequency of 'degree adverb + positive term' higher. Although we observed different kinds of influence in the study, the influence of age, gender, region, and other aspects previously mentioned by scholars on the composition and collocation of 'degree adverb-adjective' remains to be discussed and can serve as a possible direction for further research in the future.

Acknowledgments. This research was supported by National Science and Technology Council (NSTC) research grants (MOST 110–2410-H-003–040-) & (NSTC 111–2410-H-003 -085-). We would like to express our gratitude to Professor Chu-Ren Huang and the anonymous reviewers for their valuable suggestions on this study. All errors are of course our sole responsibility.

References

1. Paradis, C.: Degree Modifiers of Adjectives in Spoken British English. Lund University Press, Lund (1998)
2. Paradis, C.: Adjectives and boundedness. Cognitive. Linguistics **12**(1), 47–65 (2001)
3. Kennedy, G.: Amplifier collocations in the British National Corpus: implications for English language teaching. TESOL Q. **37**(3), 467–487 (2003)
4. Wang, L.: Modern Chinese grammar [Zhongguo xiandai hanyu yufa]. The Commercial Press, Beijing (1985). (in Chinese)
5. Han, Y.-S: Degree adverbs in modern Chinese [Xiandai hanyu de chengdu fuci]. Chin. Lang. Learn. [Hanyu xuexi], **2**, 12–15 (2000). (in Chinese)
6. Research Center for Translation, Compilation and Language Education: Corpus of Contemporary Taiwanese Mandarin 2019. National Academy for Educational Research (2019)
7. Shi, Y.-Z: Forms and Motivations of Chinese Grammar [Yufa de xingshi he liju]. Jiangxi Education Publishing House, Nanchang (2001). (in Chinese)
8. Kennedy, C., McNally, L: Scale structure, degree modification, and the semantics of gradable predicates. Language **81**(2), 345–381 (2005)
9. Hsu, H.-H: Collocation and Applications of Chinese Verb Classification [Hanyu dongci fenlei de jufa dapei yu jiaoxue yingyong]. Master's thesis, Taiwan Normal University, Taipei (2009). (in Chinese)
10. Todelo, A., Sassoon, G. W: Absolute vs. relative adjectives-variance within vs. between individuals. In: Ashton, N., Chereches, A., Lutz, D. (eds.) Proceedings from Semantics and Linguistic Theory, vol. 21, pp. 134–154 (2011)
11. Lin, J.-W: Issues in Chinese adjectival and nominal predicates: Semantic analyses and the teaching of Chinese [Xingrongci weiyuju ji mingci weiyuju de yixie wenti: tan yuyi fenxi yu huayu jiaoxue]. Chuugoku Gogaku [Zhongguo Yuxue] **267**, 1–23 (2020). (in Chinese)
12. Wu, Z., Li, L: Polarity sensitivity of minimal degree adverbs in modern Chinese. In: Lu, Q., Gao, H. (eds.) Chinese Lexical Semantics. CLSW 2015. LNCS, vol. 9332, pp. 361–368. Springer, Cham (2016). https://doi.org/10.1007/978-3-319-27194-1_36

Assessing Lexical Psycholinguistic Properties in Mandarin Discourse Production by Patients with Aphasia

Juqiang Chen[✉] and Hui Chang

School of Foreign Languages, Shanghai Jiao Tong University, No. 800 Dongchuan Road, Minhang District, 200240 Shanghai, People's Republic of China
{juqiang.c,ch9647}@sjtu.edu.cn

Abstract. Due to its high ecological validity, oral discourse production has been increasingly recognized as an important source for assessing language deficits in patients with aphasia (PWA). The present study investigated lexical psycholinguistic properties, such as concreteness, imageability and familiarity, in Mandarin PWA discourse via large-scale psycholinguistic norms. We found that PWA used more concrete, imageable and familiar words than the control group and there were variations among different task types. These findings suggest that psycholinguistic lexical properties need to be incorporated into current aphasia discourse assessment frameworks in addition to lexical variability and grammatical categories.

Keywords: Psycholinguistic Norms · Concreteness · Imageability · Familiarity · Aphasia · Mandarin Chinese

1 Introduction

Patients with aphasia (PWA) have varying degrees of difficulties in retrieving words during discourse production. Assessing their word-finding deficits has been a central issue for both aphasia research and clinical practices. However, most previous studies examined only English PWA discourse production with a focus on grammatical properties. Those few studies that analyzed Mandarin discourse measured lexical diversity only. Psycholinguistic norms have been primarily used in selecting stimuli for lexical decision or naming tasks, but recently their use has been extended to quantifying second language lexical development [1–3] and diachronic semantic change in language use [4–8]. The present study aims to apply these psycholinguistic norms in assessing lexical properties in Mandarin PWA discourse.

1.1 Assessing Lexical Knowledge and Usage

Assessing lexical knowledge has long been an important theme in applied linguistics. Different theoretical constructs have been proposed. Lexical richness, for example, has

M. Dong et al. (Eds.): CLSW 2023, LNAI 14514, pp. 11–22, 2024.
https://doi.org/10.1007/978-981-97-0583-2_2

been conceptualized as a multidimensional overarching term to indicate lexical knowledge and usage in discourse, which encompasses different components, such as lexical variation, lexical density, lexical sophistication [9]. Lexical variation (or diversity) refers to the range of a person's vocabulary in language use. Many indices have been developed to quantify lexical diversity, most of which are derived from type token ratios (TTR), that is, the number of different word (types) divided by the total number of words (tokens) in a given text. On the other hand, lexical density refers to the ratio of lexical/content (as opposed to grammatical/function) words to the total words in a text. In both cases, only word information of the text in question, i.e., either frequencies of types/tokens or those of word class, is considered.

In contrast, lexical sophistication or rareness, measures the difficulty of words and is operationalized as the proportion of relatively unusual or advanced words in the text [10]. Unusual or advanced words are defined with reference to their frequencies from a large corpus. In this sense, information external to the text is used. However, it is argued that measures of lexical diversity, density and sophistication generally focus on surface level lexical variables and could not reveal deeper level word knowledge [2]. To investigate the depth of lexical knowledge, second language (L2) researchers utilized psycholinguistic word information, such as concreteness, imageability, meaningfulness, and familiarity, in the hope of characterizing lexical development in L2 oral discourse [1–3]. These measures were selected because they were reported to affect L2 lexical learning/processing [11, 12].

1.2 Analysis of PWA Discourse Production

Analyzing discourse production has gained an increasingly important role in aphasia research due to its high ecological validity. Three major clusters of measures have been used in previous research: (1) measures related to language productivity (e.g., sample length, lexical diversity, speech fluency, word finding behaviours); (2) measures related to information content (e.g., cohesion, lexical, semantic/conceptual, schema-related measures); (3) measures related to grammatical complexity (e.g., morphological, word class, syntactic measures)[13].

Several multi-measure systems have been established to standardize linguistic assessment of discourse, such as Quantitative Production Analysis (QPA)[14], the Northwestern Narrative Language Analysis (NNLA) system [15] and the Shewan Spontaneous Language Analysis (SSLA)[16]. Automated computer programs were developed for some of them, such as QPA (i.e., C-QPA) [17] and NNLA [18, 19].

In most of these systems, lexical variables are based on either word types/tokens frequencies or grammatic category frequencies. The former mainly characterizes lexical diversity while the latter is related to lexical density.

Admittedly, these studies revealed important lexical/grammar deficits of PWA [20, 21]. They cannot uncover deeper level word knowledge which requires information external to the texts, which can be provided by psycholinguistic norms.

1.3 Lexical Psycholinguistic Properties

Lexical psycholinguistic properties, such as concreteness, familiarity and imageability, have been studied for a long time in psycholinguistic research, in which these features correlate with accuracy and speed of lexical processing and retrieval in healthy adults' naming or lexical decision. Although previous studies have successfully applied these measures in characterizing lexical development in L2 learners' oral discourse, they have been largely ignored in PWA discourse studies to date.

Concreteness refers to how perceptible and tangible the mental representation of a word is. For example, the word "desk", which can be perceived via direct, sensual experiences, is more concrete than the word "idea" which needs to be explained by other words. Concrete words are more easily retrieved and processed than abstract words. Many theories have been proposed to account for this effect. The dual-code theory [22] argues that concrete words are represented in dual systems, i.e., both verbal and imagery systems, whereas abstract words solely in a verbal system, without an imagery representation. Thus, abstract words are more difficult to process than concrete words. Alternatively, the contextual availability theory posits that contextual information can benefit the comprehension process and high availability of contextual information in concrete words results in its processing advantage over abstract words [23]. In addition, clinical research has shown selective impairments of concrete versus abstract words. Patients with Alzheimer's disease showed more difficulties in abstract than concrete word retrieval and/or processing whereas those with semantic dementia show more severe impairments in concrete than abstract words [24–26]. Thus, word concreteness may help to reveal cognitive mechanisms underlying different brain diseases.

Imageability refers to how easy it is to construct a mental image of a word. Imageability scores can quantify the capacity to activate mental images of things or events. If a word or concept can trigger a mental image more quickly and easily, it is easier to retrieve and process. It was found that patients with Parkinson's disease were more accurate and faster in naming nouns than verbs and their noun-verb difference was higher than the control. This difference can be partially accounted for by word imageability [27]. It should be noted that imageability and concreteness can be overlapped for some words. However, differences exist between the two properties in that objects rarely experienced (e.g., armadillo) are concrete but not always highly imageable [28, 29] and some highly imageable words can be somewhat abstract (e.g., the word traffic is not very concrete, but can trigger strong mental pictures).

Familiarity indicates how familiar words are to adults. Although word familiarity scores are associated with word (printed) frequency, some research argues that words of the same low frequency are not always equally (un)familiar to subjects and familiarity better predicted word recognition latencies than frequency [30]. Word frequency depends on the relationship of the target item to a larger corpus whereas familiarity norms reflect word distribution patterns in spoken data with a bias toward natural exposure [31]. In some extreme cases, low frequency words can be rated with a relatively high familiarity. Clinical research has found that word familiarity can predict naming accuracy for patients with chronic post-stroke aphasia and performance was better in response to familiar than unfamiliar words [32].

1.4   The Present Study

The present study utilized existing Mandarin Chinese psycholinguistic norms to examine deeper level lexical knowledge in PWA discourse. Three measures, i.e., concreteness, imageability, familiarity, were selected to reveal potential word retrieval deficits in Mandarin PWA discourse with reference to the control group.

2   Method

2.1   Data

We used data from the Mandarin section of the AphasiaBank [33, 34]. The Mandarin protocol kept the five sections (i.e., Greetings, Picture Description, Story Narrative, Procedural Discourse, Free Speech) as in the original English protocol with modifications to some specific tasks. The *Cinderella* story in Story Narrative section was replaced by two culturally familiar stories: *The tortoise and the hare* and *Cry of wolf*. In addition, the *Peanut butter and jelly sandwich* Procedural Discourse task was replaced with the description of *Egg ham fried rice*. The four picture description tasks, i.e., *Broken window, Refused umbrella, Cat rescue, Flood*, remain the same as the original. Details regarding the administration of these tasks and transcription of discourse samples can be found at the AphasiaBank website (https://aphasia.talkbank.org/protocol/languages/Mandarin/).

We selected all the seven semi-spontaneous discourse tasks out of the three major task categories, i.e., Picture Description, Story Narrative, Procedural Discourse, for assessing PWA lexical psycholinguistic properties and for examining task variations.

Transcripts of 12 PWAs, who were diagnosed by WAB-R [35] with anomic aphasia, were retrieved from the AphasiaBank database (see Table 1). There are a few additional transcripts for other subtypes in the database, but they are so small in number and were not included in the analysis below. Transcripts from 46 control speakers were selected from the control group of Mandarin native participants in the same database. Their data served as a baseline for comparison with PWA productions. There were no significant differences between the PWA and the control group in terms of age.

Table 1. Demographic information for all individuals. F = Female; M = Male; AQ = Aphasia Quotient

Group	Gender	n	Age (yrs)		WAB AQ		Time since stroke (months)	
			M	SD	M	SD	M	SD
Control	F	26	49.6	11.3	–	–	–	–
	M	20	51.9	11.9	–	–	–	–
PWA	F	6	44.8	17.2	80.9	10.8	8.3	7.5
	M	6	47.3	6.0	86.0	8.6	6.8	4.4

2.2 Psycholinguistic Norms

To maximize the overlap between lexical items in the psycholinguistic norms and the words in our corpus, we selected four large-scale norms among several existing norms [36–39]. There is only one large-scale norm for single-character words, and it contains ratings for all three measures. Three additional norms from three different studies were used for multi-character words, one for each psycholinguistic property (See Table 2). In other words, two norms were used for each psycholinguistic property, one for single-character words and the other for multi-character words. It should be noted that single-character norms from Liu were rated by the same group of participants whereas other norms were rated by participant groups in each study.

Table 2. Psycholinguistic norms of Mandarin Chinese.

Psycholinguistic properties	Source	lexicon	Rating scale
Concreteness	Liu 2007	2390 single-character	1 = abstract 7 = concrete
	Xu & Li 2020	9877 two-character words	1 = very concrete 5 = very abstract
Imageability	Liu 2007	2390 single-character	1 = difficult to image 7 = easy to image
	Su 2022	10426 two-character words	1 = difficult to image 7 = easy to image
Familiarity	Liu 2007	2390 single-character	1 = unfamiliar 7 = familiar
	Su 2022	20275 two-character, 1231 three-character, 2819 four-character	1 = unfamiliar 7 = familiar

2.3 Data Processing

In the present study, we used several state-of-the-art natural language processing and modelling packages in *R* [40] to analyse the Mandarin Chinese data instead of the Computerized Language Analysis (CLAN) program. The *R* packages maximise the efficiency and reproducibility of data analysis with a highly integrated workflow.

First, we extracted different tasks from the transcripts. Then, we used functions in the *stringr* package with regular expressions to filter out annotations such as repetition and pauses. Only transcriptions of clear speech were kept. Third, we tokenised the transcriptions via *jiebaR* package, which uses dynamic programming to find the most probable combination based on the word frequency. We also manually checked the results and modified user-defined dictionary to improve tokenisation accuracy.

Each word in transcripts were matched with a lexical item in the norms if exists. Each matched word was counted only one time regardless of how many times it was used. Then we calculated the means of each psycholinguistic measure per participant per task.

3 Results

Given that the two norms for each psycholinguistic property were rated by different groups of people, we ran separate *t*-tests for each norm (single-character vs. multiple-character norms) and each task (see Table 3).

3.1 Concreteness

Our results (see Table 3 and Fig. 1) indicate that single-character words in PWA discourse were significantly more concrete than those in the control group for the *Cat rescue*

Table 3. Statistical results of comparisons between PWA and the controls across psycholinguistic norms and discourse tasks. Pic = Picture description; Proc = Procedural discourse; S = Story narrative. Single = Single-character norm; Multiple = Multi-character norm. * = significant.

Measures	Norms	task	t	df	p
Concreteness	Single	Pic-CatRescue	−2.69	15.4	0.01*
		Pic-Flood	−0.34	13.66	0.736
		Pic-Umbrella	−2.01	11.75	0.068
		Pic-Window	−1.6	13.01	0.133
		Proc-FriedRice	0.49	11.51	0.634
		S-CryWolf	0.06	13.58	0.953
		S-TortoiseHare	−1.04	12.66	0.319
	Multiple	Pic-CatRescue	4.65	17.18	< .001*
		Pic-Flood	2.34	10.85	0.04*
		Pic-Umbrella	2.67	12.7	0.019*
		Pic-Window	1.41	12.42	0.182
		Proc-FriedRice	2.09	12.05	0.058
		S-CryWolf	2.22	13.18	0.044*
		S-TortoiseHare	2.42	12.11	0.032*
Imageability	Single	Pic-CatRescue	−0.82	14.81	0.428
		Pic-Flood	−1.07	15.34	0.301
		Pic-Umbrella	−2.32	11.26	0.04*
		Pic-Window	−2.39	15.23	0.03*
		Proc-FriedRice	0.09	11.56	0.932
		S-CryWolf	0.14	17.32	0.888
		S-TortoiseHare	−0.51	16.09	0.615
	Multiple	Pic-CatRescue	−2.97	12.73	0.011*
		Pic-Flood	−0.69	10.74	0.506
		Pic-Umbrella	−2.09	11.47	0.06
		Pic-Window	−2.5	11.88	0.028*
		Proc-FriedRice	−1.81	11.56	0.097
		S-CryWolf	−0.84	13.14	0.418

(continued)

Table 3. (*continued*)

Measures	Norms	task	t	df	p
		S-TortoiseHare	−1.45	11.73	0.173
Familiarity	Single	Pic-CatRescue	−1.01	13.47	0.33
		Pic-Flood	−1.43	13.88	0.175
		Pic-Umbrella	−2.18	16.25	0.044*
		Pic-Window	−0.34	13.4	0.742
		Proc-FriedRice	−0.42	11.71	0.68
		S-CryWolf	−1.36	13.92	0.194
		S-TortoiseHare	2.13	14.13	0.05*
	Multiple	Pic-CatRescue	−0.38	12.25	0.71
		Pic-Flood	−1.94	13.64	0.073
		Pic-Umbrella	−2.18	12.97	0.048*
		Pic-Window	−0.21	13.6	0.84
		Proc-FriedRice	−1.85	12.76	0.088
		S-CryWolf	−2.04	11.87	0.064
		S-TortoiseHare	−0.7	12.36	0.5

picture description task. On the other hand, multi-character words in PWA were also significantly more concrete than those in the control group for the *Cat rescue, Flood and Refused umbrella* picture descriptions and the two story-telling tasks, *Cry wolf* and *Tortoise and hare*. Note that the two concreteness norms have different scales and 1 indicates extremely abstract in the single-character norm and extremely concrete in the multi-character norm.

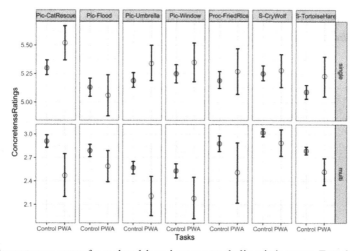

Fig. 1. Concreteness scores for each task based on two psycholinguistic norms. Error bars indicate 95% confidence intervals around the mean.

3.2   Imageability

Our results show that single-character words in PWA discourse were significantly higher in imageability than those in the control for the *Refused umbrella* and *Broken window* picture descriptions, suggesting that PWA used words that are easier to form mental image (see Table 3 and Fig. 2). Similarly, multi-character words in PWA discourse were also significantly higher in imageability than those in the control group for the picture description of *Cat rescue*, *Refused umbrella* (marginally significant) and *Broken window*.

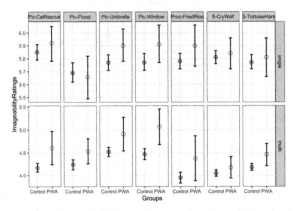

Fig. 2.   Imageability scores for each task based on two psycholinguistic norms. Error bars indicate 95% confidence intervals around the mean.

3.3   Familiarity

Our results demonstrate that both single-character and multi-character words in the *Refused umbrella* picture description task produced by PWA were significantly higher

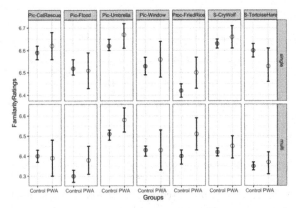

Fig. 3.   Familiarity scores for each task based on two psycholinguistic norms. Error bars indicate 95% confidence intervals around the mean.

in familiarity than those by the control group, suggesting that PWA tended to use more familiar words in the task (see Table 3 and Fig. 3). However, the single-character words in the *Tortoise and the hare* story narrative task by PWA were significantly lower in familiarity than those by the control group, suggesting the complexity of interplay between task types and lexical psycholinguistic properties.

4 Discussion

In the present study we examined three psycholinguistic lexical properties, namely concreteness, imageability and familiarity, in Mandarin PWA discourse production using existing large-scale norms. In general, PWA discourse showed distinctive patterns in these lexical properties compared with the control group.

First, the words PWA used in picture descriptions and story narratives but not the procedural discourse were significantly more concrete than the control group, consistent with previous findings about patients with Alzheimer's disease [24–26]. Given that abstract words are generally more difficult to retrieve and process in psycholinguistic experiments, we speculate that PWA were more inclined to use concrete words in their discourse production to reduce cognitive load.

Second, Mandarin PWA used words with higher imageability than controls in picture descriptions but not procedural discourse nor story narratives. We speculate that the picture description task strongly activated words with more imageable mental representations in PWA whereas healthy controls were less affected by the pictures, which they used only as a guide for constructing their description.

Third, word familiarity effects were observed in picture descriptions and story narratives. Mandarin PWA tended to use words with high familiarity compared with the control group, suggesting that these highly familiar words were better retained in their mental lexicon and were easier to retrieve in discourse production.

Fourth, there were variations of psycholinguistic lexical property effects both within and across task types. Picture description tasks were generally better at revealing the selected psycholinguistic lexical property differences between PWA and the controls than story narratives, which in turn were more revealing than the procedural discourse task. Within the picture description tasks, multi-picture tasks, such as the *Refused umbrella* task, and the *Broken window* task were generally more revealing than the single-picture task, i.e., the *Flood* picture.

There are some limitations of the present study. First, we used two norms for each psycholinguistic measure from different studies, which prevented us from constructing a unifying model to statistically compare psycholinguistic property differences between single-character and multi-character words. Second, although we had selected large-scale norms, these norms did not cover all the lexical items in the discourse production. Future research could utilize state-of-the-art semantic similarity algorithm [41] to complement psycholinguistic norms with the ability to bypass the coverage issues [42].

5   Conclusion

In conclusion, PWA used more concrete, imageable and familiar words in discourse production than the control group, indicating their deficits in using abstract, less imageable and less familiar lexical items. Psycholinguistic norms in this case provided us with sought-after evidence about the deficits of deeper level lexical knowledge in PWA. Such measures need to be incorporated into current aphasia discourse assessment frameworks in addition to surface lexical features, such as lexical diversity and density.

Acknowledgments. Project funded by the Project of Humanities and Social Sciences Fundation of the Ministry of Education of PRC (23YJC740002), a China National Committee for Terminology in Science and Technology (CNTERM) Annual Grant, YB2022019 and a China Postdoctoral Science Foundation Grant, 2022M712098.

References

1. Crossley, S.A., Skalicky, S.: Examining lexical development in second language learners: an approximate replication of Salsbury, Crossley & McNamara (2011). Lang. Teach. **52**, 385–405 (2019). https://doi.org/10.1017/S0261444817000362
2. Salsbury, T., Crossley, S.A., McNamara, D.S.: Psycholinguistic word information in second language oral discourse. Second. Lang. Res. **27**, 343–360 (2011). https://doi.org/10.1177/026 7658310395851
3. Berger, C.M., Crossley, S.A., Kyle, K.: Using native-speaker psycholinguistic norms to predict lexical proficiency and development in second-language production. Appl. Linguis. **40**, 22–42 (2019). https://doi.org/10.1093/applin/amx005
4. Hills, T.T., Adelman, J.S.: Recent evolution of learnability in American English from 1800 to 2000. Cognition **143**, 87–92 (2015). https://doi.org/10.1016/j.cognition.2015.06.009
5. Hollis, G., Westbury, C., Lefsrud, L.: Extrapolating human judgments from skip-gram vector representations of word meaning. Q. J. Exp. Psychol. **70**, 1603–1619 (2017). https://doi.org/10.1080/17470218.2016.1195417
6. Snefjella, B., Généreux, M., Kuperman, V.: Historical evolution of concrete and abstract language revisited. Behav. Res. **51**, 1693–1705 (2019). https://doi.org/10.3758/s13428-018-1071-2
7. Li, Y., Siew, C.S.Q.: Diachronic semantic change in language is constrained by how people use and learn language. Mem. Cogn. **50**, 1284–1298 (2022). https://doi.org/10.3758/s13421-022-01331-0
8. Li, Y., Hills, T.T.: Language patterns of outgroup prejudice. Cognition **215**, 104813 (2021) https://doi.org/10.1016/j.cognition.2021.104813
9. Lu, X.: The relationship of lexical richness to the quality of ESL learners' oral narratives. Mod. Lang. J. **96**, 190–208 (2012). https://doi.org/10.1111/j.1540-4781.2011.01232_1.x
10. Read, J.: Assessing vocabulary. Cambridge Univ. Press, Cambridge (2000)
11. Ellis, N.C., Beaton, A.: Psycholinguistic determinants of foreign language vocabulary learning. Lang. Learn. **43**, 559–617 (1993). https://doi.org/10.1111/j.1467-1770.1993.tb00627.x
12. Crossley, S., Salsbury, T., McNamara, D.: Measuring L2 lexical growth using hypernymic relationships. Lang. Learn. **59**, 307–334 (2009). https://doi.org/10.1111/j.1467-9922.2009.00508.x

13. Bryant, L., Ferguson, A., Spencer, E.: Linguistic analysis of discourse in aphasia: a review of the literature. Clin. Linguist. Phon. **30**, 489–518 (2016). https://doi.org/10.3109/02699206. 2016.1145740

14. Saffran, E.M., Berndt, R.S., Schwartz, M.F.: The quantitative analysis of agrammatic production: procedure and data. Brain Lang. **37**, 440–479 (1989). https://doi.org/10.1016/0093-934 X(89)90030-8

15. Thompson, C.K., Shapiro, L.P., Tait, M.E., Jacobs, B.J., Schneider, S.L., Ballard, K.J.: A system for the linguistic analysis of agrammatic language production. Brain Lang. **51**, 124–129 (1995)

16. Shewan, C.M.: Expressive language recovery in aphasia using the Shewan Spontaneous Language Analysis (SSLA) system. J. Commun. Disord. **21**, 155–169 (1988). https://doi.org/10. 1016/0021-9924(88)90003-2

17. Fromm, D., et al.: A comparison of manual versus automated quantitative production analysis of connected speech. J. Speech Lang. Hear. Res. **64**, 1271–1282 (2021). https://doi.org/10. 1044/2020_JSLHR-20-00561

18. Fromm, D., MacWhinney, B., Thompson, C.K.: Automation of the northwestern narrative language analysis system. J. Speech Lang. Hear. Res. **63**, 1835–1844 (2020). https://doi.org/ 10.1044/2020_JSLHR-19-00267

19. Hsu, C.-J., Thompson, C.K.: Manual versus automated narrative analysis of agrammatic production patterns: the northwestern narrative language analysis and computerized language analysis. J. Speech Lang. Hear. Res. **61**, 373–385 (2018). https://doi.org/10.1044/2017_J SLHR-L-17-0185

20. Fergadiotis, G., Wright, H.H., West, T.M.: Measuring lexical diversity in narrative discourse of people with aphasia. Am. J. Speech Lang. Pathol. **22**, S397–408 (2013). https://doi.org/10. 1044/1058-0360(2013/12-0083)

21. Lai, Q., Jiang, Z., Chen, Z., Deng, B., Zhou, L., Lin, F.: Exploratory analysis of discourses in subjects with anomic aphasia and health controls based on Mandarin AphasiaBank. Chin. J. Rehabil. **34**, 507–512 (2019)

22. Paivio, A.: Mental representations: a dual coding approach. Clarendon Press, Oxford (1990)

23. Schwanenflugel, P.J., Harnishfeger, K.K., Stowe, R.W.: Context availability and lexical decisions for abstract and concrete words. J. Mem. Lang. **27**, 499–520 (1988). https://doi.org/10. 1016/0749-596X(88)90022-8

24. Catricalà, E., Della Rosa, P.A., Plebani, V., Vigliocco, G., Cappa, S.F.: Abstract and concrete categories? Evidences from neurodegenerative diseases. Neuropsychologia **64**, 271–281 (2014). https://doi.org/10.1016/j.neuropsychologia.2014.09.041

25. Joubert, S., et al.: Comprehension of concrete and abstract words in semantic variant primary progressive aphasia and Alzheimer's disease: A behavioral and neuroimaging study. Brain Lang. **170**, 93–102 (2017). https://doi.org/10.1016/j.bandl.2017.04.004

26. Hoffman, P., Jefferies, E., Lambon Ralph, M.A.: Ventrolateral prefrontal cortex plays an executive regulation role in comprehension of abstract words: convergent neuropsychological and repetitive TMS evidence. J. Neurosci. **30**, 15450–15456 (2010). https://doi.org/10.1523/ JNEUROSCI.3783-10.2010

27. Bayram, E., et al.: The effect of Subthalamic nucleus deep brain stimulation on verb and noun naming in Turkish-Speaking Parkinson's disease patients. Brain Lang. **212**, 104865 (2021). https://doi.org/10.1016/j.bandl.2020.104865

28. Paivio, A., Yuille, J.C., Madigan, S.A.: Concreteness, imagery, and meaningfulness values for 925 nouns. J. Exp. Psychol. **76**, 1–25 (1968). https://doi.org/10.1037/h0025327

29. Bird, H., Franklin, S., Howard, D.: Age of acquisition and imageability ratings for a large set of words, including verbs and function words. Behav. Res. Methods Instrum. Comput. **33**, 73–79 (2001). https://doi.org/10.3758/BF03195349

30. Gernsbacher, M.A.: Resolving 20 years of inconsistent interactions between lexical familiarity and orthography, concreteness, and polysemy. J. Exp. Psychol. Gen. **113**, 256–281 (1984). https://doi.org/10.1037//0096-3445.113.2.256

31. Stadthagen-Gonzalez, H., Davis, C.J.: The Bristol norms for age of acquisition, imageability, and familiarity. Behav. Res. Methods **38**, 598–605 (2006). https://doi.org/10.3758/BF0319 3891

32. Alyahya, R.S.W., Halai, A., Conroy, P., Lambon-Ralph, M.: The relationship between the multidimensionality of aphasia and psycholinguistic features. Aphasiology **32**, 5–6 (2018). https://doi.org/10.1080/02687038.2018.1486374

33. MacWhinney, B., Fromm, D., Forbes, M., Holland, A.: AphasiaBank: methods for studying discourse. Aphasiology **25**, 1286–1307 (2011). https://doi.org/10.1080/02687038.2011. 589893

34. MacWhinney, B., Fromm, D.: AphasiaBank as BigData. Semin. Speech Lang. **37**, 010–022 (2016). https://doi.org/10.1055/s-0036-1571357

35. kertesz, A.: Western Aphasia Battery-Revised. Pearson, San Antonio, TX (2006)

36. Liu, Y., Shu, H., Li, P.: Word naming and psycholinguistic norms: chinese. Behav. Res. Methods **39**, 192–198 (2007). https://doi.org/10.3758/BF03193147

37. Xu, X., Li, J.: Concreteness/abstractness ratings for two-character chinese words in MELD-SCH. PLoS ONE **15**, e0232133 (2020). https://doi.org/10.1371/journal.pone.0232133

38. Su, Y., Li, Y., Li, H.: Imageability ratings for 10,426 Chinese two-character words and their contribution to lexical processing. Curr. Psychol. **42**, 23265–23276 (2022). https://doi.org/ 10.1007/s12144-022-03404-4

39. Su, Y., Li, Y., Li, H.: Familiarity ratings for 24,325 simplified Chinese words. Behav. Res. **55**(1), 1–14 (2022). https://doi.org/10.3758/s13428-022-01878-5

40. R Core Team: R: A language and environment for statistical computing. , Vienna, Austria (2018)

41. Jin, P., Qiu, L., Zhu, X., Liu, P.: A hypothesis on word similarity and its application. In: Su, X. and He, T. (eds.) Workshop on Chinese Lexical Semantics, pp. 317–325. Springer International Publishing, Cham (2014). https://doi.org/10.1007/978-3-319-14331-6_32

42. Sun, K., Lu, X.: Assessing lexical psychological properties in second language production: a dynamic semantic similarity approach. Front. Psychol. **12**, 672243 (2021)

Research on the Interactive Elements and Functions of Live Streaming Sales Language ——Take *"Hao Bu Hao"* as an Example

Hanmeng Li[(✉)] [ORCID] and Xin Kou [ORCID]

School of Literature, Shandong University, Jinan 250100, Shandong, China
LHM19588930730@163.com

Abstract. This paper starts from the expression function of the high-frequency construction "hao bu hao (Ok?)" in live streaming sales. By classifying and analyzing the structure from the perspective of context and multimodal discourse, the paper finally summarizes four interactive functions of the tag question "hao bu hao (Ok?)" in the specific context of live streaming sales, i.e. seeking recognition, holding the turn, maintaining attention and emphasizing the key points. This paper further demonstrates the diachronic subjectification process of tag questions such as "hao bu hao (Ok?)": the question degree weakens and gradually evolves into discourse marker. The emphasis function can distinguish the key information, which is a supplement to the interaction function of tag questions in previous studies. Besides, it should be noted that several interactive functions of "hao bu hao (Ok?)" are not contradictory, and only one "hao bu hao (Ok?)" is likely to show multiple functions at the same time.

Keywords: Hao Bu Hao (Ok?) · Live Streaming Sales · Interaction Function · Multimodal · Discourse Analysis

1 Introduction

In recent years, e-commerce live broadcasting has emerged as a novel consumer model within the Internet economy. Several renowned anchors have gained prominence, accumulating substantial wealth. E-commerce live broadcasting significantly diverges from the traditional brick-and-mortar sales model, as anchors frequently employ distinctive and persuasive language styles to stimulate the audience into making purchases.

However, the predominant focus of current research on e-commerce live broadcasting lies within the realms of communication and marketing. There exists considerable scope for further investigation into the language employed in live-streaming sales. Within this domain, numerous unexplored opportunities await researchers. A more profound exploration of the characteristics of live sales language, the influencing factors, and its correlation with consumer behavior will augment our comprehension of this dynamic field. This understanding is not only pivotal for e-commerce practitioners and marketing experts but also exerts a positive influence on consumer shopping experiences and market trends.

M. Dong et al. (Eds.): CLSW 2023, LNAI 14514, pp. 23–33, 2024.
https://doi.org/10.1007/978-981-97-0583-2_3

Upon scrutinizing the live broadcast corpus, this study has identified "hao bu hao (Ok?)" as one of the top three high-frequency phrases (structures) shared by several anchors in their live-streaming sales language. Given that the corpus encompasses three anchors with distinct styles, it can be inferred that the frequent use of "hao bu hao (Ok?)" is not merely a personal linguistic habit but a favored syntactic pattern within the specialized language genre of live broadcasting. Consequently, this study proposes that an in-depth examination of this construction will contribute to unveiling the stylistic nuances of live broadcasting and the realization mechanism of its stylistic function.

The syntactic structure of "hao bu hao (Ok?)" has been thoroughly examined by previous scholars. According to [1], "hao bu hao (Ok?)" has undergone a process of temporal defamiliarization, transitioning from the position of the predicate in the sentence to the end of the sentence, leading to its grammaticalization. This evolution has progressed through four successive stages, culminating in the construction developing into a function word that intensifies the tone of negativity.

Additionally, [2] has proposed that the tag question form "hao bu hao" can be categorized into four types based on its functional interpretation in specific contexts. These categories include true questions used to solicit opinions, weak questions employed for seeking approval, false questions employed to diminish the strength of a statement, and non-questions utilized to express the discourse marker of a refuting tone. For instance:

(1) *"Uncle Qian," Ruixuan whispers,"Go home and eat something, ok?" The old man refused without hesitation, "No!"* (Lau Shaw, *The Yellow Storm*).
(2) *It's a limited edition, 100ml oversized bottle limited edition, ok? Is that clear?* (Jaqi Lee 20220522).

Example (1) shows the true questioning usage of "hao bu hao (Ok?)". Example (2) shows the use of "hao bu hao (Ok?)" in the language of live-streaming sales, where the questioning tone has disappeared, demonstrating a unique expressive function that cannot be incorporated into the existing explanatory framework at present.

In addition, "hao bu hao (Ok?)", as a kind of tag question, has a certain interactive function. The interactive function of tag questions has also attracted much attention in the academic community. [3] pointed out that "seeking verification" and "asking for permission" are the two basic discourse functions of tag questions. [4] discussed the discourse function of "Right?" in conversation. [5] examined the interactional function of "Isn't it?" in natural spoken language, and explored the effects of the position of the turn sequence position and the speaker's cognitive state on the interactional function of "Isn't it?".

The categorization of "hao bu hao (Ok?)" has been comprehensive, but there's a gap in researching its non-question interactive aspect. Prior studies on tag questions mostly focus on face-to-face conversations, neglecting the linguistic context of live streaming sales. Our data reveals that the frequent use of "hao bu hao (Ok?)" in live-streaming sales is not random.

Expanding on past research, this paper uses discourse and multi-modal analysis to explore the interactive function of "hao bu hao (Ok?)" in live streaming. It emphasizes the emerging interactive role of "hao bu hao (Ok?)" and its pragmatic interpretation in this unique setting, aiming to understand how language contributes to interaction and consumption stimulation.

2   Selection and Processing of Corpus

This study is based on a 9.5-h corpus consisting of five live playback videos. We selected five Taobao live broadcasts of three head anchors on the list of famous live carriers--Li Jiaqi, Lie'er Baby, and Chen Jie (Kiki), and used IFLYREC's "video to text conversion" tool to transcribe the live playback videos into text, and then manually proofread them to obtain a text corpus of 190,607 words.

2.1   High-Frequency Word Search and Discourse Analysis

In this study, we first used the Wordlist function in corpus retrieval software AntConc 4.1.2 to retrieve features and statistics of the live-streaming sales corpus. After searching, it was found that "hao bu hao (Ok?)" ranked first, second and third in the high-frequency word (structure) lists of the three anchors, with a total of 280 occurrences in all the corpora. Afterwards, the Concordance function was used to locate the word "hao bu hao (Ok?)", and the preceding and following segments were extracted and categorized for the next step of analysis.

2.2   Multimodal Discourse Analysis

In addition to high-frequency word retrieval, this paper uses the annotation tool ELAN to build a corpus of these videos for multimodal discourse analysis of the dynamic

Table 1. Top 10 high frequency words (structures) for Jiaqi Li, Kiki and Lie'er Baby

| Rank | Jiaqi Li20200522 | | Kiki20200628 | | Lie'er Baby20201106 | |
	Type	Frequency	Type	Frequency	Type	Frequency
1	**hao bu hao (Ok?)**	**96**	right	36	right	89
2	milliliter	71	**hao bu hao (Ok?)**	**22**	ok	19
3	ok	43	share	11	**hao bu hao (Ok?)**	17
4	yuan	32	ok	9	yes	13
5	Jiaqi's studio	28	I	5	link	10
6	yes	25	a	4	yuan	7
7	discount	24	Are you ready?	4	number	6
8	buy	21	Isn't it	4	discount coupon	6
9	right	18	yes	4	put the link on	5
10	month	17	baby	3	a	5

discourse of live-streaming videos. First, the video corpus is separated into MP4 and WAV format audio, and then the WAV format audio is imported into ELAN along with the video for the annotation of body movements, facial expressions, gestures and mood.

3   Pre- and Post-segment Analysis of "Hao Bu Hao (Ok?)"

"hao bu hao (Ok?)" appeared 280 times in the five live broadcasts, and the position of "hao bu hao (Ok?)" in the language of the live broadcasts has a certain degree of regularity, so this study randomly selected 108 examples of the corpus, and further analyzed the pre- and post-statement of "hao bu hao (Ok?)".

3.1   Pre-segment

After analyzing and summarizing the pre-segments of the tag question "hao bu hao (Ok?)" in the language of live-streaming sales, it was found that there are five main categories of its subject: requesting attention to receive coupons, activity introduction, process preview, teaching methods and product recommendations. Specific data are summarized in the Tables 1, 2, 3 below:

Speech Act Category. Through the analysis of the table, it can be found that the proportion of pre-segment belonging to the three subject categories of "hao bu hao (Ok?)" requesting attention to receive coupons, activity introduction and process preview is the largest, accounting for a total of 76.85%, and the following example sentences (3, 4 and 5) correspond to these three types respectively:

(3) *The red button above your head, please pay more attention to Jiaqi Live, ok?*
(4) *The Tmall store price is 199 a piece, Jiaqi will do a second sale of 149 a piece for you, ok?*
(5) *Jiaqi Live will give you seconds at 3:00, ok?*

These three types of segmental subject matter are distinguished from the other two by the fact that they are "speech acts", which have a performative meaning and can be regarded as a strong directive act by the anchor to the audience to ask for acceptance of his or her own opinion or suggestion. The three situations under the category of speech act are

Table 2. Types of subjects and usage frequency (proportions) of pre-segments of " hao bu hao (Ok?)"

Types	Speech Act			Nonverbal Behavior	
	requesting attention to receive coupons	activity introduction	process preview	teaching methods	product recommendations
frequency (proportions)	27 cases (25%)	34 cases (31.48%)	22 cases (20.37%)	7 cases (6.48%)	18 cases (16.67%)

closely related to the activities and processes of the live broadcast and require immediate interaction and cooperation from the audience. Out of the Cooperative Principle, in order to ensure the smooth progress of the live broadcast process, the audience will generally make after receiving this message to the relevant page to pay attention to the coupon, to give advice on the strength of the activity or ready to buy the purchase and other feedback behavior.

Nonverbal Behavior Category. Pre-segment passages in the teaching methods and product recommendation categories are more oriented towards the presentation of objective facts with no or very weak sense of exertion. For example:

(6) *Just hold it like this in reverse and then use water to rinse it out a little faster, ok?*
(7) *Because it doesn't have silicone, it's going to make your hair fluffy right after you wash it, ok?*

In example (6), the anchor explains a quick rinse of hair removal cream, and example (7) explains the ingredients and efficacy of the shampoo, without requiring the listener to respond substantively to this in the live stream, and even if a response is given, it is only necessary to give a feedback signal that this information has been received.

3.2 Post-segment

There are two main types of the post-segment of the tag question "hao bu hao (Ok?)". One is to repeat the previous text, and the other is to change the topic. In addition, there is also a special category in Li Jiaqi's live broadcast language- "Is it clear?".The specific data are as follows:

Repeat the Previous Text. In the category of repetition, the sentences before and after the additional question "hao bu hao (Ok?)" are slightly different in word formation, but they convey exactly the same message. Example sentences are as follows:

(8) *Jiaqi is doing seconds of 149 a piece for you guys, ok? 149 a piece of lip serum for you guys.*
(9) *Come on let's go straight to the link, ok? Prepare for the link.*

In example (8), the preceding and following segments of "hao bu hao (Ok?)" are stating the active price of the lip essence in the live broadcast, while in example (9), the anchor is repeatedly reminding the listeners of the links to the products that will be on the shelves, so it is categorized as a repetition of the preceding text.

Table 3. Types of subjects and usage frequency (proportions) of post-segments of " hao bu hao (Ok?)"

Types	Repeat the Previous Text	"Is it clear?"	Change the Topic
frequency (proportions)	28 cases (25.93%)	8 cases (7.41%)	72 cases (66.67%)

Request for Feedback. "Is it clear?" accounts for a smaller percentage. In this kind of sentences, it can be assumed that the semantic meaning of "is it good" and "is it clear" are the same, both of them are confirming to the listener whether the information they conveyed in the previous sentence has been received and inviting the listener to recon-firm the information. For example:

(10) *89 for 220 ml is the lowest price ever for a single gram of Black Essence, number one, ok? Is that clear? Only 50,000 girls can buy it.*

In example (10), the anchor begins by stating the magnitude of the event, and adverbs of degree such as "ever, lowest" are used several times to show the importance of this piece of information. Two questions are then used to confirm that the listener has understood the discount and to request feedback from the listener.

Change the Topic. The total number of post-segment of the tag question "hao bu hao (OK?)" belonging to the category of topic change is 72, which is the largest number, accounting for 66.67%. For example:

(11) *It's under 50% off, a 49% off HELENA event, ok? Head over to the red button above and follow us live for more.*
(12) *Let's just shoot for one of the most practical colors in black, hurry up and buy it, ok? Come on, we actually have one more goodie to share with you today, a super pop from our little Austin.*

In example (11), the anchor first states the discount of the product with the tag question "hao bu hao (Ok?)", and then changes the topic to ask listeners to pay attention to the live broadcast. In example (12), the anchor switches from urging to place an order to recommending another product. Between the two distinct topics, the anchor pauses only briefly, relying mainly on "hao bu hao (Ok?)" to connect the two sentences.

4   A Multimodal Discourse Analysis of "Hao Bu Hao (Ok?)"

Modality refers to the channels and media of communication, including language, technology, images, colors, music and other symbol systems. Discourse that uses two or more modalities at the same time is called "multimodal discourse". Live streaming is essentially a kind of economic behavior with multimodal language interaction as the core pivot for the purpose of commodity trading [6]. [7] demonstrate the need for multimodal learning for stance detection and developed models that utilize three different modalities, including text, speech and visual signals,the results show that multimodal information indeed improve the dialogue stance detection to some extent. The live-streaming sales video is a typical multimodal discourse, and this study focuses on the segment in which the anchor sends out the tag question of "hao bu hao (Ok?)", and conducts a multimodal discourse analysis in terms of mood, facial expression, gestures, and body movements to further analyze the role of "hao bu hao (Ok?)"in the interactive process of the anchor guiding the listener to put shopping into practice.

In this study, the three anchors' live playback videos with a total duration of 3 h and 10 min were selected from the corpus, and a total of 108 dynamic discourse segments containing the tag question of "hao bu hao (Ok?)" were analyzed. The analysis results are shown in the following table:

Table 4. Results of multimodal analysis of "hao bu hao (Ok?)" in five pre-segment subjects[1]

Types	Speech Act			Nonverbal Behavior	
	requesting attention to receive coupons(27 cases)	activity introduction(27 cases)	process preview(27 cases)	teaching methods(27 cases)	product recommendations(27 cases)
ML	0(0%)	0(0%)	1(2.94%)	1(14.29%)	0(0%)
MH	9(33.33%)	11(32.35%)	9(40.91%)	4(57.14%)	5(27.78%)
MF	22(78.57%)	28(82.35%)	20(90.91%)	5 (71.43%)	13(72.22%)
MP	2(7.14%)	4(11.76%)	1(4.55%)	2(28.57%)	5(27.78%)
GP	3(10.71%)	7(20.59%)	1(4.55%)	0(0%)	3(16.67%)
GU	5(17.86%)	9(26.47%)	2(9.09%)	1(14.29%)	5(27.78%)
GC	2(7.14%)	3(8.82%)	3(13.64%)	0(0%)	0(0%)
FR	7(25%)	17(50%)	8(36.36%)	4(57.14%)	8(44.44%)
FS	5(17.86%)	4(11.76%)	2(9.09%)	3(42.86%)	4(22.22%)
FC	5(17.86%)	1(2.94%)	2(9.09%)	0(0%)	1(5.56%)
BC	1(3.57%)	0(0%)	3(13.64%)	0(0%)	1(5.56%)
MH	9(33.33%)	11(32.35%)	9(40.91%)	4(57.14%)	5(27.78%)

Table 4 shows the collocation between various types of multimodal information and specific semantic information, in which speech interaction shows the speaker's interaction intention through the speaker's tone intensity and speech rate. Expressive features are often related to specific social behaviors and social purposes, such as the "raised eyebrow" expression is often an effective way to enhance the interaction between the speaker and the listener. Anchors' questioning tone accompanied by eyebrow-raising behaviors are actually drawing the audience's attention, confirming to the listener whether the message has been received, or anticipating the listener's response to his or her question. In terms of action interaction, gestures and body shifts can also convey important interactional information. [8] points out that image symbols in multimodal discourse can also express meaning and are as multifunctional as linguistic symbols, and explains them as the three functions of representation, interaction, and composition, respectively. Movements away from or close to the camera have a great impact on the interactive function.

Based on the above information, we can further discuss and verify the important pragmatic value of "hao bu hao (Ok?)" in the live-streaming sales interaction.

---

[1] See appendix for description of labeling symbols.

4.1 Seek Recognition

In the pre-sentence segmental analysis of "hao bu hao (Ok?)", the speech act category belongs to "asking without doubt". The anchor's use of the question form of the tag question "hao bu hao (Ok?)" is aimed at seeking common ground rather than evidence. That is to say, he expects the audience to accept the suggestion and cooperate with the interaction, not to get the real response from the audience to this question, so he cannot form a strict "question-answer" adjacency pair. Although "hao bu hao (Ok?)" has the form of a question, it has no doubt about the meaning. In the speech interactions of multimodal analysis, the accelerated speech rate of "hao bu hao (Ok?)" also supports the conclusion that the questioning meaning of "hao bu hao (Ok?)" has disappeared or been weakened. Comparing the data in Table 4, the speeding up of "hao bu hao (Ok?)" is significantly higher than the slowing down of "hao bu hao (Ok?)".

[3] believe that in conversational communication, the speaker verifies or confirms the correctness of the transmitted information or evaluation to the listener through tag questions, and when both parties to the communication (through language and context) judge that the speaker has a high degree of certainty of a certain piece of information, the tag questions develop from the seeking of confirmation to the seeking of the hearing and listening to the two sides of the same point of view, in order to ensure that the smooth progress of the conversation function. In the live broadcasting room, the initiative to formulate activity rules and promote the sales process is almost completely in the hands of the anchor, the amount of information held by the anchor is also much larger than the audience, when the amount of power and awareness of the anchor state is higher than the audience, the function of "hao bu hao (Ok?)" is transformed into seeking recognition.

4.2 Hold the Turn

When the latter part of "hao bu hao (Ok?)" changes the topic, "hao bu hao (Ok?)" often plays the role of holding the turn and filling the gap in thinking. Liu Hong proposes two criteria for measuring the turn: one is whether the speaker is continuous, whether there is silence at the end of a grammatical-semantic completion sequence. If there is silence, then the speaker's words have more than one turn. The second is whether a role reversal between speaker and hearer has occurred. If it occurs, it marks the end of one talk round and the beginning of the next [9]. In the language environment of the live studio, the anchor's language is very fast-paced and the sales process is tightly interconnected, lacking the silent time required for a single person to switch talk turns. Since viewers cannot directly vocalize in the live broadcast but can only interact with the anchor through pop-up comments, the anchor needs to continuously act as a session sender to ensure the smooth flow of the live broadcast process, as well as to facilitate the interaction between the seller and the consumer in the segment of selling goods.

[10] mentioned that Richards categorized the strategies for holding a turn as follows: strategies for continuing a turn, strategies for holding a turn, and strategies for giving a turn. The strategy for holding a turn is to indicate that the speaker still has something to say. In order to hold a turn, there are the following techniques that can be used. Using some of the word items that Sachs called "utterance incompletor", such as *but, and, however,* and other connectives. Using "incompletion maker" such as *since when* to

indicate to the listener that there are at least two more clauses before the first possible end. In the case of a speaker who has not thought about what to say, but does not want to give up his turn of speaking, the "hesitation filler" is used to buy time for themselves in order to keep the turn of speech, such as: *er, well, um, You know, let me see*, etc.

In the specific context of the live-streaming sales,the conversion of the topic category "hao bu hao (Ok?)" can be regarded as a kind of hesitation filler, is a kind of strategy anchor used to hold the turn. At this time, the anchor will also be accompanied by eye avoidance, away from the camera's expression and action, "hao bu hao (Ok?)" can make up for the blank thinking of the conversion of the topic, the anchor to win the time to think, but also alleviate the hard and awkward of the sudden change of the topic, so that the live process is more fluent and natural.

4.3 Maintain Attention

In the context of live broadcasting rooms, where interactions play a crucial role, it's important to consider how linguistic elements like "hao bu hao (Ok?)" can serve various functions. When we categorize the pre-sentence segment of "hao bu hao (Ok?)" as a form of non-verbal behavior, it undergoes a transformation in terms of its informational role. In this context, its traditional information-seeking function disappears entirely. Instead, it takes on a new role, primarily aimed at maintaining the attention of the listener.

Live-streaming sessions in these scenarios often extend over prolonged periods, and the anchor must continuously gauge the audience's engagement throughout the narration. To achieve this, [11] suggests an effective technique: incorporating occasional questions within continuous declarative sentences. This strategic use of question clauses, like "hao bu hao (Ok?)," serves to consistently prompt the audience's active participation, thereby enhancing the overall interactivity of the conversation.

Moreover, it's worth noting that during this interaction, the question clause "hao bu hao (Ok?)" is frequently accompanied by a range of non-verbal cues from the anchor. These may include expressions such as raising eyebrows, gesturing with hands, pointing to products, or moving closer to the camera. These multimodal signals work in tandem with the linguistic element to convey to the audience that the interaction is not a one-sided monologue but rather a dynamic engagement. This combination of linguistic and non-verbal cues is an effective strategy employed by the anchor to signal their intent to maintain the audience's attention and participation throughout the live-streaming session.

4.4 Emphasizing the Key Points

Compared with the traditional face-to-face natural conversation, "hao bu hao (Ok?)" also shows a new expression function in the context of live-streaming sales--emphasize.

In previous studies, grammatical emphasis is usually realized by adverbs of tone, such as "*indeed, absolutely, obviously*". If there is something to be emphasized in daily communication or speech, we may use the following methods: 1. Emphasize by changing the speed of speech; 2. Emphasize by repetition; 3. Emphasize by contrast; 4. Emphasize by questioning or rhetorical questioning.

When the meanings of the statements before and after "hao bu hao (Ok?)" are exactly the same, i.e., when the phrase after "hao bu hao (Ok?)" belongs to the category of repeating the previous text, the anchor is actually emphasizing the importance of this piece of information by repeating the strategy, which is similar to the way street vendors appeal to people to buy by repeatedly shouting out the key features of commodities. Similar to street vendors who call on people to buy goods by repeatedly shouting the key features of the goods, "hao bu hao (Ok?)" also plays the role of emphasizing the message in this case. As in example (7) above, the anchor repeatedly reminds listeners of the link to the product that will be on the shelves because he expects them to click on the link to buy the product, which is directly related to the anchor's core interest--company profits. "hao bu hao (Ok?)" is immediately followed by "Is it clear?", two interrogative clauses used in conjunction, also emphasize the important information in the previous sentence. In the multimodal analysis, it is found that in these two types of tag questions, "hao bu hao (Ok?)" is accompanied by the phenomenon of the anchor's voice rising and clapping, which is also an important evidence that "hao bu hao (Ok?)" plays an emphasizing function.

Anchors use "hao bu hao (Ok?)" to play the function of emphasizing for two reasons, one is to maintain the attention of the listener, and the other is to distinguish important information. Unlike natural conversations in which both participants change their turns and alternate their voices, anchors in live broadcasting contexts, as the only voice messenger, output a large amount of information in one direction, making it difficult for listeners to recognize the importance of various types of information. Under such a premise, the anchor will use "hao bu hao (Ok?)" and other expressions and actions to help listeners distinguish the key points, especially those related to the anchor's personal interests, such as "request attention" and "process preview ".

5   Conclusion

This paper focuses on the expression function of the high-frequency word "hao bu hao (Ok?)" in the language of live streaming sales. By classifying and analyzing the structure from the perspective of context and multimodal discourse, we finally summarizes four interactive functions of the tag question "hao bu hao (Ok?)" in the specific context of live streaming sales: seeking recognition, holding the turn, maintaining attention and emphasizing the key points. This paper further demonstrates the diachronic subjectification process of tag questions such as "hao bu hao (Ok?)": the question degree weakens and gradually evolves into discourse marker. The emphasis function can distinguish the key information, which is a supplement to the interaction function of tag questions in previous studies. It should be noted that several interactive functions of "hao bu hao (Ok?)" are not contradictory, and only one "hao bu hao (Ok?)" is likely to show multiple functions at the same time.

On the one hand, this study adds yet another example of the non-questioning usage of question forms in interaction. On the other hand, while previous research on interaction function mainly focuses on face-to-face communication, this paper discusses more complex online interaction scenarios and integrates multimodal discourse analysis methods, moving from two-dimensional discourse analysis to three-dimensional discourse analysis, and from static research to dynamic research, which makes the interpretation of the interaction function of "hao bu hao (Ok?)" more comprehensive and accurate.

Appendix. Multimodal Annotation Transcription Examples

Mood	ML	Loudness decrease
	MH	Loudness increases
	MF	Faster speech
	MP	Longer tone
Gesture	GP	Pointing to goods
	GU	Raise one's hand
	GC	Clapping
Facial Expression	FR	Raise eyebrows
	FS	Looking back at the audience
	FC	Avoid with one's eyes
Body Movement	BC	Move closer to the camera
	BF	Away from the camera

References

1. Peng, J., Fu, K.: The weaking effect of Haobuhao. J. Hanjiang Normal Univ. **02**, 73–74 (2008)
2. Yu, G., Yao, Y.: A pragmatic research on the expressional function of hao bu hao and its process of formation. Linguist. Sci. **06**, 625–632 (2009)
3. Gao, H., Zhang, W.: The functions of tag questions in chinese: an interactional analysis. Lang. Teach. Linguist. Stud. **05**, 45–52 (2009)
4. Liang, D.: The pragmatic function of *duiba* in conversation. Contemp. Rhetoric **01**, 50–53 (2006)
5. Yao, S., Tian, M.: The interactional function of *shiba* and its epistemic status in Chingese daily conversation. Lang. Teach. Linguist. Stud. **06**, 47–59 (2020)
6. Wang, Y., Pan, D.: Research on multimodal interaction in Taobao live streaming. Chin. J. Lang. Policy Plann. **03**, 34–46 (2022)
7. Hu, M., Liu, P., Wang, W., Zhang, H., Lin, C.: MSDD: A Multimodal Language Dateset for Stance Detection. In: Su, Q., Xu, G., Yang, X. (eds.) Chinese Lexical Semantics. CLSW 2022, LNCS, vol. 13495, pp. 112–124. Springer, Cham (2023)
8. Wei, Q.: On the overall meaning construction of multimodal discourse - a discourse analysis based on a multimodal media discourse. J. Tianjin Foreign Stud. Univ. **06**, 16–21 (2008)
9. Liu, H.: Conversation Structure Analysis. Peking University Press, Beijing (2004)
10. Lu, L.: Turn-talking: speech-exchange system in English conversation. J. Shenzhen Univ. (Humanities and Social Sciences) **03**, 118–121 (2003)
11. Li, Z.: Discourse marking function of several question clauses - and a little view on the depiction of discourse marking function. Contemp. Rhetoric **02**, 36–42 (2013)
12. Grice, H.P.: Logic and Conversation. Academic Press, New York (1975)

Chinese Optatives: A Preliminary Study

Jiun-Shiung Wu(✉) ⓘ and Chih-Hsuan Chung

Institute of Linguistics, National Chung Cheng University, Minhsiung, Chiayi County 621301,
Taiwan
Lngwujs@ccu.edu.tw, joanne109@alum.ccu.edu.tw

Abstract. In this paper, we argue that *jiù hǎo le* 'JIU nice Prc' is a fixed expression and functions as an optative operator. This operator induces a partial ordering of possible worlds based on the likelihood of a proposition being true. Moreover, the operator presents a proposition *p* true in a lower world on the ordering and presupposes ¬*p*, which is true in a higher world. An optative reading is derived through the interaction between the literal meaning of *jiù hǎo le* 'JIU nice Prc' and presentation of a proposition true in a lower world of the partial ordering. Moreover, a Chinese optative contributes to the interpretation of discourse in the following way: it *cause*s another situation, which can be present or not in the discourse. An Segmented Discourse Representation Theoretic account is proposed for the Chinese optative operator to capture the complicated information an optative sentence can express and its contribution to the interpretation of discourse. Finally, it is proposed that *jiǎshè/jiǎrú* 'hypothetically/if' are not compatible with an optative while *yàoshì/rúguǒ* are because the former two present a proposition which presumably cannot be realized as a fact, while the latter two present a condition, which has no problem being realized as a fact. A proposition presumably unable to be realized as a fact is inherent contradictory with a wish because a wish is to bring about an event.

Keywords: Optative · Partial ordering · Presupposition · Segmented Discourse Representation Theory · Chinese

1 Introduction

[1] defines sentence mood as "an aspect of linguistic form conventionally linked to the fundamental conversation functions with semantic/pragmatic theory." (p 122) The major types of sentence mood under inquiry are declarative, imperative and interrogative, as presented in Chapter 3 in [1]. In this paper, the focus is on optatives in Mandarin Chinese (henceforth, Chinese). [2] discusses the optative mood in Classical Greek, one of whose functions is to denote wish (pp. 204–207). Along similar lines, [3] states that "[o]ptative utterances express a wish, regret, hope or desire without an overt lexical item that means *wish, regret, hope,* or *desire.*" (p 13).

In Chinese, there is a construction which expresses the speaker's wish without explicitly using verbs such as *xīwàng* 'to hope, to wish'. See below.

© The Author(s), under exclusive license to Springer Nature Singapore Pte Ltd. 2024
M. Dong et al. (Eds.): CLSW 2023, LNAI 14514, pp. 34–45, 2024.
https://doi.org/10.1007/978-981-97-0583-2_4

(1) a. (Yàoshì) zǎo   tīng   bàma-de   huà   jiù   hǎo   le.
     (if)   early   listen.to   parent-ASSO[1] words   JIU   nice   Prc
     'Lit. If I had listened to my parents earlier, it would have been nice!'
     'If only I had listened to my parents!'

  b. (Rúguǒ) wǒ   nēng ràng   tāmen   liǎojiě   wǒ-de
     (if)   1st.SG   can   make   3rd.PL   understand   1st.SG-ASSO
     guāndiǎn   jiù   hǎo   le .
     view.point   JIU   nice   Prc
     'Lit. If I could make my viewpoint understood, it would be nice!'
     'If only I could make my viewpoint understood!'

As shown in (1), these two sentences both express the speaker's wishes. In (1a), the speaker wishes that (s)he had listened to his/her parents earlier, while in (1b) the speaker wishes that (s)he had been able to make his/her viewpoint understood. However, even though these two sentences denote optative readings, there is no verb such as *xīwàng* 'to hope, to wish' in them.

In addition, while *rúguǒ/yàoshì* 'if' are compatible with an optative, *jiǎshè/jiǎrú* 'hypothetically, if' are not. See the examples below.

(2) Yàoshì/rúguǒ/*jiǎrú/jiǎshè   yì   nián qiáng   gàosù
    If/   if   /hypothetically/hypothetically one   year before   tell
    tāmen   jiù   hǎo   le.
    3rd.PL   JIU   nice   Prc
    'If only we had told them one year before!'

As shown in (2), *yàoshì/rúguǒ* 'if' are fine in a Chinese optative, but *jiǎrú/jiǎshè* 'hypothetically, if' are not.

In this paper, three issues are addressed. First of all, since there is no verb expressing an optative reading, where does an optative reading in sentences such as (1a, b) and (2) come from? Second, is *jiù hǎo le* 'JIU nice Prc' in Chinese optatives compositional, i.e. a phrase, or a fixed construction for optatives? Third, why are *yàoshì/rúguǒ* 'if' acceptable in Chinese optatives but *jiǎrú/jiǎshè* 'hypothetically, if' are not?

This paper is organized as follows. Section 2 is a critical review of previous literature on English optatives such as [3–5]. In Sect. 3, we present our analysis and address the three questions raised above. Section 4 concludes this paper.

2 Literature Review

[3, 4] pay attention to what is referred to as *independent if-optatives*, contrasted with optative conditional, and further suggest that, in English, independent *if*-optatives should be distinguished from optative conditions. See below.

(3) a. Independent *if*-optative
     If only it would snow!
  b. Optative conditional
     If only it would snow, things would be good.

(3a) is an independent *if*-optative, where *if* and *only* together produce optativity. (3b) is a conditional, consisted of an antecedent and a consequent, where the antecedent is structurally identical to an independent *if*-optative. [6] points out that the antecedent such as (3b) still expresses optativity even though it is embedded in a conditional. Furthermore, he also points out that the distinction between independent *if*-optatives and optative conditionals are called for because the former cannot function as an embedded clause, while the latter can.

[4] basically suggests the following. Even though particles such as *but, just, only*, etc. seems obligatory in *if*-optatives, they do not participate in the compositional semantics of *if*-optatives. Instead, they function as a pragmatic cue that helps to identify an optative interpretation.

[4] proposes *Utilize Cues* (informal) as follows:

(4) a. If a marked use of an ambiguous utterance can be made more salient by adding certain element (e.g. particles, interjections, intonational tunes) to this utterance, the addition of one (or more than one) such element is obligatory. Such elements qualify as *cues* for the respective utterance use. (p93)
   b. The requirement above can be obviated if the intended utterance use is independently prominent in the utterance context. (p93)

The *Utilize Cues* (4) function in the following way. Given an *if*-clause, e.g. *if it would snow*, it is ambiguous between as an antecedent to a conditional or an optative. According to (4a), in order to make an optative interpretation salient, some element needs to be used. This is why particles such as *only* are required in an optative, but this obligotoriness does not mean that these particles result in an optative interpretation.

As for how particles such as *only* make an optative reading more salient, [3] suggests that *only* identifies a proposition which is lower on a salient scale (p15). Suppose the following scenario. The weather forecast says that, for tomorrow, raining is more likely than being cloudy, which is in turn more likely than being sunny. That is, a scale as the one below is given:

(5)

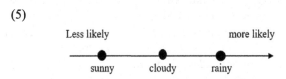

The semantic function of *only* in an optative is to select a position lower in the scale. In terms of the weather condition, based on the scale in (5), it is generally the case that the lower the better. This is how particles such as *only* can contribute to optativity, even though they do not semantically express an optative interpretation. Let's take *if only it were sunny today* as an example. This *if*-optative has two possible interpretations: first, a conditional reading and second an optative reading, where the former is natural and the latter is marked. The particle *only* indicates that the proposition is lower on a scale such as (4). A conditional reading does not require such a lower-on-a-scale reading and therefore *only* biases toward an optative reading. Given that what is generally wished for is, in some sense, in reverse proportion to the likelihood scale (5), the lower-on-a-scale reading of *only* induces an optative reading.

The major problem with the account of [4] as presented above is that it is not constrained enough. The same idea of a scale and of identification of a point less on the scale applies to other constructions, such as *lián ... dōu* construction in Chinese. Let's see how a scale of such type can account for *lián ... dōu* construction.

(6) a. Tā   lián   yì   bǎi   kuài   dōu bù   kěn   jiè.
    3rd.SG even   one   hundred   dollar   DOU not   willing lend
    'He was not willing to lend me even (as little as) 100 dollars.'

   b.

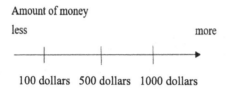

The scale in (6b), which is very similar to (5), can explain the interpretation of (6a).[1] (6a) basically says the following: he is not willing to lend (me) even (as little as) 100 dollars, and implies that he is much less likely to lend (me) more than 100 dollars. The sentence identifies a less amount on the scale and this behavior is very similar to *only* identifying a point less likely on a scale of likelihood such as (5). Does (6a) express an optative reading? Obviously not. Therefore, a scale alone, such as (5) and (6b), cannot be the whole answer to an optative reading.

The second potential problem is why an *if* clause is ambiguous between a conditional and an optative. While an *if* clause naturally functions as (the antecedent of) a conditional, yet it is rather opague why an *if* clause can serve as an optative. The third potential problem is with the function of *only*. While *only* naturally identifies the one on the lower end of the scale (5) due to its semantics of *limited amount of something*, it is not clear why *only* can render a marked use more salient, as suggested in (4a).

[5] provides another account for English optatives. To begin with, she suggests that *if only!* is a conditional, based on two observations, contra [6]. First, two *if only!* constructions can be coordinated, such as in (7). And, second, the consequent can always be recovered, such as (8).

(7) A: I can't believe the picnic went so poorly!
   B: If only Meg had brought a corkscrew and if only Jim had made a decent salad!
                                                              (= Ex. 13, p121)
(8) A: If only I were taller.
   B: Then your desires wouldn't have become true either.
                                                              (= Ex. 14, p122)

In order to explain the optative reading, [5] suggests that *if only* construction involves reversed topicality, that is, in an optative, the antecedent, i.e. the *if* clause, is the focus,

---

[1] Please refer to [7] for a detailed examination for *lián ... dōu* among others.

whereas the consequent is the topic. Moreover, she utilizes *immediate question under discussion* (IQuD) as proposed in [8] to account for the optative interpretation. IQuD basically is to model the speaker's intention. [5] suggests that, given an optative (*if only* α, β), its IQuD is as follows:

(9) How do we bring β about? Or, how would we have brought β about?

As pointed out in [5], compared to a normal conditional *if* α, β, α is the topic and β the focus, contrary to the case of optative *if only!* construction. The IQuD for a normal condition is: what α can bring about or what α could have brought out?

In Sect. 5.3, [5] relies on [9]'s explanation for the function of conventional focus sensitive lexical items, such as *only*, *at least*, etc., to account for the role of *only* in *if only!* construction. [9] states three points about *only* and *at least*, presented below.

(10)   a. The function of exclusives such as *only* is to say that the strongest true answer to the IQuD is weaker than some expected answer. (p 42)
        b. A sentence with *only* expresses a presupposition that the strongest true alternatives in the IQuD are *at least* as strong as the prejacent. (p77)
        c. The descriptive of a sentence with *only* states that the strongest true alternatives in the IQuD are *at most* as strong as the prejacent. (p 251)

[5] uses the following example to explain how (10) works. Given a scenario as follows: John had a job interview this morning. He drove there but his car broke down. John called Tom, a mechanic friend, but by the time he got the car running it was too late for John to make it. Tom uttered:

(11) If *only* I had arrived earlier!

So, what role does *only* play in this *if only!* optative? It induces a hierarchy of alternatives based on likelihood as follows:

(12)   a. John drove his car more carefully.   [+likely]
        b. Tom arrived earlier and fixed his car.
        c. Tom fixed the car faster.
        d. Tom went out and bought a new car.   [−likely]

The four sentences in (12) are alternatives functioning as potential answers to the IQuD *How do we bring β about*, where β stands for the proposition *John would have gotten to the interview on time*. According to (10a), the strongest true answer to the IQuD is weaker than some expected answer, and therefore (12a), which is the most likely alternative, is ruled out. According to (10b), there is a presupposition expressing that the strongest true alternatives in the IQuD are *at least* as strong as the prejacent. This statement rules in (12b-d) as possible answers to the IQuD because everyone of the three, serving as the answer to the IQuD, i.e. the prejacent, has an alternative at least as strong as the answer. According to (10d), the strongest true alternatives in the IQuD are *at most* as strong as the prejacent. This requirement rules out (12c, d). If one of these two serves as the answer to the IQuD, i.e. the prejacent, there is always an alternative, i.e. (12b), which is stronger than the prejacent. Only (12b) is the appropriate answer because, given the fact that (12a) has been excluded, (12b) as a prejacent does not have an alternative stronger than it and hence the requirement is satisfied the strongest true alternatives in the IQuD are *at most* as strong as the prejacent.

A recap. [5] suggests that an optative is an answer to the IQuD such as (9) and the IQuD serves as a type of goal. A proposition answering the IQuD is to fulfill the goal. A proposition which fulfils the goal is desired, compared to the other propositions, a desirability reading for optatives is derived. And, the function of *only* is accounted for.

The major problem with [5]'s account is that the IQuD account is not constrained enough. In fact, [5] provides counter-example to her IQuD account to the *if only!* construction.

(13) John: How would I get to the supermarket?
      Bill: Walk south and turn right to the next street.   = Ex. 21 (p 127)

As pointed out in [5], John's utterance in (13) is a *goal-oriented* question, which is also the function of an IQud for the *if only!* construction. As a matter of fact, it can function as an IQuD for an optative *if only!* sentence such as *if only I had walked south and turned right to the next street!* So, how can we distinguish the time when an imperative is used for an answer and the time when an optative *if only!* sentence is provided as an answer?

As the critical reviews on [3–5] point out, the previous literature on English optatives cannot provide a satisfactory account for English optatives, let along Chinese ones. Therefore, Chinese optatives call for further examination.

3   Partial Ordering of Possibility, Lower Possibility and Optativity

Before discussing optativity, we would like to examine the status of *jiù hǎo le* 'JIU nice Prc'. From (1) and (2), we can find that *jiù hǎo le* 'JIU nice Prc' appears in all Chinese optatives. So, the first question is whether *jiù hǎo le* 'JIU nice Prc' is a fixed construction or a phrase, which is formed by means of compositionality. We argue that *jiù hǎo le* 'JIU nice Prc' is a fixed construction because *hǎo* 'nice', though gradable, cannot be modified by *hěn* 'very' when *jiù hǎo le* 'JIU nice Prc' is present in an optative. See below.

(14) a. (Yàoshì) zǎo   tīng   bàma-de   huà   jiù (*hěn) hǎo
          (if)   early   listen.to parent-ASSO words JIU (*very) nice
          le.
          Prc
          'If only I had listened to my parents!'
      b. Yǒu de   chī jiù (hěn)   hǎo   le.
          Have asso eat jiu (very) good Prc
          'It is good enough to have food to eat.'

As we can see from (14b), when *jiù hǎo le* 'JIU nice Prc' is compositional, and expresses that something is good enough, the gradability of *hǎo* 'nice' remains and *hǎo* 'nice' can be modified by degree modifiers such as *hěn* 'very'. On the other hand, when *jiù hǎo le* 'JIU nice Prc' appears in an optative, such as (14a), *hěn* 'very' is not allowed. That is, *jiù hǎo le* 'JIU nice Prc' in an optative is a fixed construction so that the gradability of *hǎo* 'nice' is lost, and optativity is induced non-compositionally. The construction *jiù hǎo le* 'JIU nice Prc' is referred to as the Chinese optative operator.

Moreover, from (1) and (2), repeated below as (15) and (16) for the sake of discussion, we can find that *jiù hǎo le* 'JIU nice Prc' in an optative induces a partial ordering based on likelihood.

(15) a. (Yàoshì) zǎo   tīng   bàma-de   huà   jiù   hǎo le.
          (if)   early   listen.to   parent-ASSO words JIU   nice Prc
          'If only I had listened to my parents!'

     b. (Rúguǒ) wǒ   néng ràng   tāmen   liǎojiě   wǒ-de
          (if)   1st.SG   can make   3rd.PL   understand   1st.SG-ASSO
          guāndiǎn jiù   hǎo le .
          view.point JIU   nice Prc
          'If only I could make my viewpoint understood!'

(16) Yàoshì/rúguǒ/*jiǎrú/jiǎshè   yì   nián qiáng gàosù
      If/   if /hypothetically/hypothetically one year before tell
      tāmen   jiù   hǎo le.
      3rd.PL   JIU   nice Prc
      'If only we had told them one year before!'

(17) Partial ordering on possible worlds based on likelihood

      $w_1 < w_2 < w_3 < \ldots < w_n < \ldots$

      ⟶

      low   high

(17) is a partial ordering on possible worlds based on how likely a proposition is true. $w_1 < w_2$ stands for that a proposition true in w_1 is less likely to be realized as true than the one in w_2.

An optative presupposes that a negative version of the proposition in the optative is actually the one that is true. For (15a), the presupposition is that the speaker had not listened to his/her parents. Given the two proposition, *I had listened to my parents* and *I had not listened to my parents*, the former, i.e. the one presented in the optative, is true in a possible world lower on the ordering (17), whereas the latter, that is, the presupposition, is true in a possible world in a higher world on the ordering. This ordering is based on the speaker's knowledge about the likelihood of (s)he having listened to his/her parents in the real world. There might be different degrees of *listening to one's parents*, which would be true in worlds between the one where the prejacent is true and the one where the presupposition is true.

Along the same lines, (15b) presupposes that the speaker cannot make his/her viewpoint understood. And, just like (15a), the prejacent *I could make my viewpoint understood* is true in a world lower on the ordering, while the presupposition is true in a world higher on the ordering for (16). This ordering is based on the likelihood of (s)he being able to make his/her viewpoint understood in the real world. The presupposition is that it is not possible to tell them (something) one year before. The prejacent in (16) is true in a world lower on the ordering and the presupposition in a world higher.

Given the above analysis, it is argued that the Chinese optative operator induces a partial ordering on possible worlds according to how likely a proposition can be realized as true. The optative operator presents, as its prejacent, a proposition p true in a lower world and presupposes $\neg p$, which is true in a higher world.

While the above generalization account for how a partial ordering based on likelihood helps the optative operator identify a proposition as its prejacent, yet, the partial ordering alone cannot explain where an optative reading comes from. Its significant contribution is to spell out that the prejacent in an optative is true in a lower world, while the presupposition is true in a higher world. So, where does an optative reading come from? We argue that an optative reading comes form the interplay of the literal meaning *jiù hǎo le* 'JIU nice Prc' and that fact that it identifies a proposition true in a lower world on a partial ordering. The reasoning is as follows. *Jiù hǎo le* 'JIU nice Prc' literally means that something is/would be good. Under unmarked circumstances, a proposition which is true in a higher world on a partial ordering is more preferable because it takes less effort to be realized and therefore such a proposition "is/would be good'. However, *jiù hǎo le* 'JIU nice Prc' in an optative picks up a proposition which is less likely to be true in the real world. While there are many ways to render such a proposition good, one of the major and most common ways is for the speaker to wish for the proposition to become true, even though the proposition is on the lower end of the ordering. This is how an optative reading is derived.

One issue involving the above analysis is whether *jiù hǎo le* 'JIU nice Prc' in Chinese optatives presents a counterfactual.[2] In English, counterfactuals are expressed by past tense in conditionals. Chinese is not an inflectional language and verbs are not marked, except for aspect, and therefore it is still under debate whether counterfactual is part of the Chinese grammar or Chinese simply expresses counterfactual readings, e.g. [13–15], etc.

If we take a conservative stand and adopt the position that Chinese can express counterfactual reading, leaving the issue aside whether counterfactual is part of Chinese grammar, we can find that *jiù hǎo le* 'JIU nice Prc' in Chinese opatives presents a proposition with a counterfactual reading.

Let's look at (15a). The sentence actually tells us that the speaker did not listen to his/her parents. That is, the proposition *zǎo tīng bàma-de huà* 'I had listened to my parents early' is contradictory to the fact and hence the whole sentence in (15a) gets a counterfactual reading.

So, where does this counterfactual reading come from? We would like to propose that the counterfactual reading of a Chinese optative comes from the partial ordering induced by *jiù hǎo le* 'JIU nice Prc'. As argued above, *jiù hǎo le* 'JIU nice Prc' induces a partial ordering of possible worlds according to how likely a proposition can be realized to be true. Moreover, this optative construction presents a proposition true in a lower world on the ordering. Since such a proposition is less likely to be realized as true, but the optative construction presents this proposition, accordingly a Chinese optative tends to get a counterfactual reading.

Given that, one question immediately arises: can a Chinese optative get a non-counterfactual reading? That is, can a Chinese optative describe a situation that is not contradictory to the fact? The answer is positive. See the example below.

---

[2] Some might refer to counterfactual as subjunctive. Here, we do not discuss issue. Please refer to [10, 11, 12] for semantics of counterfactuals or subjunctives. Interested readers are also refer to Chapter 5 of [2] for a cross-linguistic examination on subjunctives.

(18) Suīrán   wǒ   bù   zhīdào   Lǎozhāng míngtiān lái-bù-lái,
      although 1ˢᵗ.SG not   know   Laozhang tomorrow come-not-come,
      bùguò rúguǒ tā   néng   lái   jiù   hǎo le.
      but   if   3ʳᵈ.SG can   come   JIU   nice Prc
      'Although I do not know whether he will come tomorrow, yet, it would be
      nice if he could come.'

In (18), the *bùguò* 'but' clause is an optative. However, since the *although* clause clearly states that the speaker has no idea whether Laozhang will come tomorrow and therefore *he can come tomorrow* is not a counterfactual because there is no fact yet. The above discussion suggests that a *jiù hǎo le* 'JIU nice Prc' optative can, but not necessarily, express a counterfactual reading.

One might ask how a partial ordering based on likelihood is possible for the optative in (18) if there is no fact existing yet. Our response is as follows. The partial ordering of possibility does not have to, while it can, rely on facts. The partial ordering for (18) orders possible worlds according to the speaker's evaluation of the likelihood of the proposition *Laozhang will/can come tomorrow*.

Now, let's turn our attention to (16), where *rúguǒ/yàoshì* 'if' are compatible with a Chinese optative, whereas *jiǎrú/jiǎshè* 'hypothetically, if' are not. We propose that this grammatical distinction is due to the following reading. Morphologically, *jiǎrú* and *jiǎshè* both include *jiǎ*, which in Chinese means *fake/false*. That is, although *jiǎrú* and *jiǎshè* can function as discourse connectives[3], a proposition they present is marked with a feature such as *hypothesis*, while a proposition presented by *rúguǒ/yàoshì* 'if' is marked with a feature such as *condition*. A hypothesis presumably is not and cannot be realized as a fact, while a condition has no problem being realized as a fact. An optative expresses a wish, which potentially can be realized. Therefore, *jiǎrú* and *jiǎshè* are not compatible with Chinese optatives.

An interim summary. The Chinese optative operator *jiù hǎo le* 'JIU nice Prc' induces a partial ordering of possible worlds according to the likelihood of a proposition being true. The operator identifies a proposition p in a lower world as its prejacent and presupposes $\neg p$, which is true in a higher world. An optative reading is derived through the interaction of the literal meaning of the Chinese optative operator and the identification of a proposition true in a lower world on the partial ordering.

The last issue is how the optative reading is formalized. While the above account works for a Chinese optative syntactically and semantically, one important aspect is not taken into consideration: its dynamic semantics. A Chinese optative has a contextual effect, which can be explicitly or implicitly manifested in the discourse. See examples below.

---

[3] Please note that it is still under debate whether Chinese has the syntactic category *conjunction*. It is well-noted that *yīnwèi* 'because' and *suǒyǐ* 'so' are often used in the same sentence. In this paper, following [16, 17], we use *discourse connectives* to indicate those lexical items which connects two sentences/clauses, and ignore whether they are conjunctions or not.

(19) a. (Yàoshì) zǎo   tīng   bàma-de   huà   jiù   hǎo   le.
          (if)   early   listen.to parent-ASSO words   JIU   nice Prc
          jīntiān   jiù   bù huì zhème cǎn   le.
          today   JIU   not will so   miserable Prc
          'If only I had listened to my parents! I wouldn't be so miserable today.'

(20) A: (Yàoshì) zǎo   tīng   bàma-de   huà   jiù   hǎo   le.
          (if)   early   listen.to parent-ASSO words   JIU   nice Prc
          'If only I had listened to my parents!'
      B: Zěnme   shuō?
          how   say
          'Why?'
      A: jīntiān   jiù   bù huì zhème cǎn   le.
          today   JIU   not will so   miserable Prc
          'I wouldn't be so miserable today.'

As we can see from (19), a consequence can be added to follow a Chinese optative. What is worth noting is: when an optative stands alone, such as in (20 A), one can actually inquire about this consequence, such as (20 B). From (19) and (20), we can find that an optative tends to be in a causal relationship with another situation in the same discourse and, if this situation is not present in the discourse, it can be inquired upon. Therefore, we can argue that, following the ideas of rhetorical relations and rhetorical structure proposed in [18], an optative has a *cause*$_D$ relationship (p.204–207) with another situation in the same discourse, which can be explicit or implicit in the discourse. A *cause*$_D$ relationship indicates that an optative is connected to another sentence/clause by rhetorical relation *Result*. That is, if α is an optative and β is in a *cause*$_D$ relationship with α, then *Result*(α, β), which means that the result of α is β.

Therefore, we propose a Segmented Discourse Representation Theory (for short, SDRT) proposed in [18] for a Chinese optative as follows:

(21)

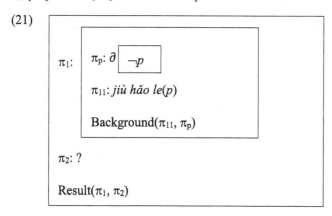

The Segmented Discourse Representation Structure (SDRS) (21) says the following. p is the prejacent in a Chinese optative. π_{11} represents the optative with p as its prejacent. As argued above, an optative presupposes the negative version of its prejacent. In the SDRS above ∂ stands for a presupposition and the presupposition is $\neg p$. As suggested in p 239 of [18], a presupposition is usually attached to a clause inducing the presupposition by *Background* and hence $Background(\pi_{11}, \pi_p)$. π_1 represents the SDRT consisting of the optative, its presupposition and the rhetorical relation that connects them. To put it in a different way, although a Chinese optative is only a sentence, it actually expresses complicated information and π_1 in the SDRS captures the complicated information expressed by the optative.

Moreover, an optative *causes* another situation in the same discourse, which is explicit or implicit in the discourse. In the SDRS above, π_2 stands for this situation and the question mark ? means that this situation is underspecified and needs to be resolved as the discourse progresses. Because an optative *causes* another situation, the result of the optative is the situation, represented as $Result(\pi_1, \pi_2)$.

To sum up, in this section, We argue for the following points. First, *jiù hǎo le* 'JIU nice Prc' is a fixed construction for Chinese optatives. It is referred to as the Chinese optative operator. Second, for *jiù hǎo le(p)*, where *p* is the prejacent of an optative, the optative presupposes $\neg p$. Third, the operator induces a partial ordering of possible worlds based on how likely a proposition can be realized as true. It presents a proposition true in a lower world, while its presupposition is true in a higher world. Fourth, it is argued that an optative reading comes from the interaction between the literal meaning of *jiù hǎo le* 'JIU nice Prc' and presentation of a proposition true in a lower world. Fifth, a Chinese optative has a dynamic semantics: it is connected to another situation, which can be explicit or implicit in the discourse, by rhetorical relation *Result*. Finally, *jiǎshè/jiǎrú* cannot occur in a Chinese optative but *rúguǒ/yàoshì* can because the former two take a proposition marked with features such as *hypothesis*, which presumably is not and cannot be realized as a fact and hence cannot be wished for to come true, contra what an optative inherently denotes.

4   Conclusion

In this paper, we examine Chinese optatives. In Chinese, proposition plus *jiù hǎo le* 'jiu nice Prc' can express the speaker's wish even though such a sentence does not include any lexical item which denote *wish, hope, desire*, etc. *Jiù hǎo le* 'jiu nice Prc' is argued to be a fixed construction and referred to as the Chinese optative operator. The operator induces a partial ordering of possible worlds based on how likely a proposition is realized to be true. It presents, as its prejacent, a proposition true in a lower world on the ordering, and presupposes, which is the negative version of the prejacent, true in a higher world. It is argued that an optative reading is derived in the following way. *Jiù hǎo le* 'jiu nice Prc' literally means that something is/would be better. Identifying a proposition true in a lower world on a partial ordering based on likelihood means that a proposition which is less likely to be true is presented. One way to render such a proposition "better/preferable" is to wish for it to be true. In addition, the contribution of an optative to the discourse is that it *causes* another situation, which is implicit or explicit in the discourse. An SDRT-style dynamic semantics is proposed for the Chinese optative operator to capture the semantic contribution of an optative to the discourse. Finally, the phenomenon that *jiǎishè/jiǎrú* 'hypothetically/if' are not compatible with Chinee optatives while *rúguǒ/yàoshì* 'if' is explained as follows. *Jiǎshè/jiǎrú* present a proposition marked with *hypothesis*, which presumably is not and cannot be realized as a fact, while *rúguǒ/yàoshì* present one with *condition*, which has no problem being realized as a fact. A wish is not compatible with a proposition which is not and cannot be realized as a fact because of inherent contradiction between a wish and such a proposition.

Acknowledgements. The research reported here is part of the projected finally funded by Ministry of Science and Technology under the grant number MOST 111-2410-H-194-045. I thank my part-time research assistants Chi-Hsun Chung and Hsin-yen Lu for their help in this project. I am especially grateful to Chi-Hsun Chung, the second author of this paper, for her insight in the issues under discussion here.

References

1. Portner, P.: Mood. Oxford Studies in Semantics and Pragmatics 5. Oxford University Press, Oxford (2018)
2. Palmer, F.R.: Mood and Modality, 2nd edn. Cambridge University Press, Cambridge (2001)
3. Groze, P.G.: On the Grammar of Optative Constructions. Ph.D. dissertation. MIT, Boston (2011)
4. Groze, P.G.: Optative markers as communicative cues. Nat. Lang. Seman.Seman. **16**, 89–115 (2014)
5. Biezma, M.: Optatives: deriving desirability from scalar alternatives. In: Proceedings of Sin & Bedeutung, vol. 15, pp. 117–132. Saarland University (2011)
6. Rifkin, J.: If only if only were if plus only. In: Proceedings of CLS 36-1, pp. 369–384. Chicago Linguistic Society (2000)
7. Hole, D.: Focus and Background Marking in Mandarin Chinese. Routledge, London (2003)
8. Roberts, C.: Information Structure in Discourse: Towards an Integrated Formal Theory of Pragmatics. OSU Working Papers in Linguistics 49, 91–136 (1996)
9. Beaver, D., Clark, B.: Sense and Sensitivity: How Focus Determines Meaning. Wiley-Blackwell, Malden (2008)
10. Lewis, D.: Counterfactuals. Blackwell, Malden (1973)
11. Farkas, D.: On the semantics of subjunctive complements. In: Hirschbueleter, P., Koerner, K. (eds.) Romance Languages and Modern Linguistic Theory, pp. 69–104. John Benjamin, Armsterdam (1992)
12. Kratzer, A.: Partition and revision: the semantics of counterfactuals. J. Philos. Logic **10**, 201–216 (1981)
13. Eifrin, H.: The Chinese counterfactual. J. Chin. Linguist. **16**(2), 193–218 (1988)
14. Yong, Q.: Typological stage of counterfactuals in Chiense. In: Proceedings of PACLIC 27, pp. 329–338. Taipei, National Chengchi University (2013)
15. Jiang, Y.: On the counterfactual readings of Chinese conditionals. In: Studies and Investigation of Chinese Grammar, pp. 257–271. Commercial Publishing, Beijin (2000)
16. Wu, J.: On the dynamic semantics of *Fǒuzé* and *Bùrán* in mandarin Chinese. In: Dong, M., Gu, Y., Hong, J. (eds.) Chinese Lexical Semantics: 22nd Workshop, CLSW 2021, Revised Selected Papers, pp. 319–331. Springer, Switzerland (2022). https://doi.org/10.1007/978-3-031-06703-7_24
17. Wu, J.: On the two discourse connectives *Fǒuzé* and *Bùrán* in mandarin Chinese: an SDRT account. Taiwan J. Linguist. **21**(1) (2023)
18. Asher, N., Lascarides, A.: Logics of Conversation. Cambridge University Press, Cambridge (2003)

The Semantic Features and Pragmatic Functions of Cantonese Quasi-Demonstrative Type Quantifier *di1*: A Comparison with Demonstratives *ne1* and *go2*

Xiyue Huang[✉]

School of Chinese Language and Literature, Beijing Normal University, Beijing 100875, China
huangxiyue@mail.bnu.edu.cn

Abstract. The Cantonese collected quantifier *di1* exhibits a demonstrative use within the quantifier-noun construction, which results from the grammaticalization of the quantifier *di1*. It can be regarded as a quasi-demonstrative quantifier. While this phenomenon of using quantifiers independently exists in many southern Chinese dialects, there is a limited description of the semantics and pragmatic functions of the Cantonese quasi-demonstrative quantifier *di1*. This paper compares *di1* with two basic demonstratives in Cantonese, *ne1* and *go2*, to describe the semantic features, referential properties, and pragmatic functions of *di1*. The fundamental conclusion is that *di1* does not convey the meaning of distance, but it carries an indefinite plural meaning and functions similarly to neutral demonstratives. Therefore, in Cantonese, *di1* is a neutral quasi-demonstrative. Regarding referential properties, *di1* falls under the category of indeterminate expressions, and its identifiability, referentiality, and generic/individual depend on the context. From a pragmatic perspective, *di1* not only shares functions with *ne1* and *go2*, such as indicating discourse referents, direct speech pointing, deixis, and identification but also can mark topics.

Keywords: Quasi-demonstrative quantifier · 啲[di1] · Cantonese demonstratives · Semantic features · Pragmatic functions

1 Introduction

Sheng et al. (2016) distinguishes two types of definite quantifier-noun constructions: quasi-article-type and quasi-demonstrative-type. The quasi-article-type quantifier-noun construction is one in which the quantifier functions similarly to a definite article. In Cantonese, most quantifier-noun constructions fall into this category. On the other hand, the quasi-demonstrative-type quantifier-noun construction is one in which the quantifier serves a function similar to demonstratives. Sheng (2017) further categorizes the quasi-demonstrative-type quantifier-noun constructions into distance-quasi-demonstrative-type and neutral-quasi-demonstrative-type, distinguished by whether the quantifier within the structure can express distance. Based on the theoretical framework of Sheng (2016 & 2017), this paper analyzes the quantifier *di1* within the quantifier-noun construction.

© The Author(s), under exclusive license to Springer Nature Singapore Pte Ltd. 2024
M. Dong et al. (Eds.): CLSW 2023, LNAI 14514, pp. 46–59, 2024.
https://doi.org/10.1007/978-981-97-0583-2_5

In Cantonese, *ne1* and *go2* are considered typical demonstratives (Zhang 1972; Matthews & Yip 1994), while *di1* is primarily viewed as a quantifier (Zhang 1972; Tang 2005). However, through an examination of spoken Cantonese data, it becomes evident that *di1* also possesses demonstrative functions within quantifier-noun constructions and can, in certain contexts, replace *ne1* and *go2*. Although some scholars have suggested that *di1* can be considered a demonstrative (Peng 2006), this paper contends that *di1* falls into the category of a "neutral-quasi-demonstrative" quantifier. Given the absence of a systematic exploration of quasi-demonstrative quantifiers such as *di1*, as well as basic demonstratives *ne1* and *go2*, this paper will describe the semantic features and pragmatic functions of *di1* through a comparison with demonstratives *ne1* and *go2*, to fill the research gap.

The Cantonese data used in this paper primarily comes from extended dialogues with native Cantonese speakers we recorded. Additionally, three Cantonese corpora were consulted: the PolyU Corpus of Spoken Chinese: Cantonese, the Hong Kong Cantonese Corpus (referred to as HKCancor when citing data), and A Linguistic Corpus of Mid-20th Century Hong Kong Cantonese.

2 Semantic Features of *ne1*, *go2* and *di1*

In all languages, there are at least two different demonstratives used to indicate objects at different distances: one for objects proximate to the deictic center and another for objects distal from the deictic center [7]. In the Cantonese demonstrative system, we use *ne1* for proximal reference, and *go2* for distal reference, while *di1* does not indicate distance. According to Diessel (1999), demonstratives carry deictic features including distance, visibility, and height, as well as qualitative features providing classification information about the referred objects, such as quantity, animacy, gender, and so on. For basic demonstratives in Mandarin and other Chinese dialects, the deictic features are the most salient, and they typically lack qualitative features. Generally, additional elements are needed to express the qualities of the referred objects. Existing grammatical resources provide substantial information about *ne1* and *go2*, so this section will offer a more concise description of these two demonstratives while focusing more on *di1*.

2.1 *ne1* and *go2*

ne1 serves as the basic demonstrative in Cantonese and requires pairing with a quantifier for reference [4]. For example, "呢件衫[ne1gin6 saam1]" (this shirt) cannot omit the quantifier to become "呢衫[ne1saam1]". Aside from the pronunciation *ne1*, *ne1* also has three phonetic variants: *li1*, *lei1* and *yi1*. For instance, "ne1 di1" (these) can also be pronounced as "lei1 di1" [4]. This is perhaps the result of nasal [n] becoming [l] and subsequently being dropped.

Regarding spatial distance, *ne1* is generally used to indicate objects closer to the deictic center, making it a proximal demonstrative in Cantonese (Gao 1980; Zhan 2004). It is analogous to "this" in English [4] and "zhe" in Chinese. For instance, in (1), "呢邊[ne1 bin1] (this side)" indicates the side closer to the speaker. In (2), "呢處[ne1 cyu2] (here)" points to the location where the speaker is situated. Essentially, *ne1* is used for direct reference to nearly any individual or place in the discourse context.

(1) 我哋喺呢邊, 你兩個去嗰邊搵下嘞!(Movie "A Thousand Ways to Snatch the God of Wealth", 1962)

We're over here, you two go over there and take a look!

(2) 呢處就營業部, 工場就喺二樓, 我帶你去睇吓咧!(Movie "The Standard Husband", 1965)

Here is the sales department, and the factory is on the second floor. Let me take you to have a look!

go2 is often considered the counterpart to *ne1*, used to indicate objects that are distant from the deictic center. It functions as the distal demonstrative in Cantonese [8], akin to "that" in English [4] and "na" in Mandarin. In (3), "嗰度[go2 dou6](there)" suggests Inner Mongolia, which can be inferred from the context.

(3) 因為其實我哋去嗰度係學樂器。 (The most unforgettable experience_ informant13)

Because actually, we went there to learn musical instruments.

In terms of spatial distance, *ne1* and *go2* can be combined with quantifiers to refer to near or far singular entities. When combined with the collective quantifier *di1*, *ne1 di1* and *go2 di1* can refer to near or far plural entities. "呢排[ne1 paai4]" indicates a relatively recent time, close to the present discourse, while "嗰陣[go2 zan6]" refers to a time that is before or after the current discourse, similar to "that time" or "then".

2.2 di1

The basic usage of *di1* is as an indefinite quantifier, indicating "some" or "a little", such as "高翻啲[gou1 faan1 di1] (a bit taller)" in (4), and "一啲[jat1 di1] (some)" in (5). Some scholars have also singled out the usage of "adjective + di1" [10], considering the *di1* after an adjective, like in (4), signifies "a bit", while the *di1* in "呢啲[ne1 di1]" and "一啲[jat1 di1]" implies "some" and falls under the category of fuzzy quantifiers. Additionally, when *di1* modifies a nominal element that functions as the object of the sentence, it is typically recognized as a qualifier glossed as some or a bit, rather than a demonstrative. As seen in (6):

(4) 呢條柱高翻啲囉噃。 (Tang 2015:124)

This pillar is a bit taller, huh.

(5) 我已經畀過一啲意見佢哋啦。 (Peng 2006:112)

I've already given some advice to them.

(6) 我而家趕住去雷太屋企打牌, 一陣間你同阿表叔出去, 睇下邊間酒樓, 搵啲嘢食下喇, 吓! (Movie "The Standard Husband", 1965)

I'm in a hurry to go to Uncle Lei's house to play cards. In a while, you and Uncle Biao go out, check out which restaurant, and find some food, okay?

In terms of its demonstrative usage, some scholars have different views. Zhang (1972) and Matthews & Yip (1994) argue that the omission of demonstratives before *di1* allows it to function as a demonstrative. Peng (2006) acknowledges variations in the demonstrative strength of *di1* but maintains that it can function as a demonstrative, which can be viewed as the result of the grammaticalization of the quantifier *di1*. From this, *di1* possessed the demonstrative function in modern Cantonese, which has evolved from a quantifier, resulting from the loss of the preceding demonstrative. As Diessel (1999) points out, when a demonstrative is dropped, the lexical item it was associated with may assume a deictic function, which is an important means of generating new demonstratives.

Although *di1* does exhibit functions similar to demonstratives within the quantifier-noun construction, especially the most basic deictic function, we still consider that *di1* cannot be regarded as a true demonstrative, for three main reasons: First, it lacks inherent distance meaning which is the most basic characteristic in demonstratives. Importantly, *di1* inherently carries a fuzzy quantity meaning, limiting it to refer to uncertain or uncountable entities, such as "啲細菌[di1 sai3 kwan2](that bacteria)", "啲茶[di1 caa4](that tea)", as seen in (7). Second, *di1* cannot co-occur with true demonstratives like *ne1* and *go2*. Third, while *di1* serves a demonstrative role in the definite quantifier-noun construction, it leans more towards functioning as a quantifier, akin to "some" in English, within the indefinite quantifier-noun construction. Therefore, according to the definition from Sheng (2017), it is better to be categorized as a quasi-demonstrative quantifier.

(7) 你咳咗啲微菌入晒啲茶道, 噉我飲咗你杯茶, 咪即係我都要變肺癆?!(Movie "Spring in the Palace", 1966)

You coughed that bacteria into that tea. if I drink your tea, will I get tuberculosis too?

The demonstrative use of *di1* in the quantifier-noun construction is closely intertwined with its characteristics as a quantifier. In real language usage, the boundaries between the two functions of *di1* are not always clear-cut. For instance, in (8), *di1* can be understood as a quantifier meaning "a little bit" or as a demonstrative "that". The two functions are the results of different stages of the grammaticalization of *di1*, namely, the use as an indefinite quantifier, and then possessed the use as a demonstrative (Peng 2006). To avoid ambiguity, the examples discussed in the following text are instances where *di1* exhibits clear demonstrative use.

(8) 咁你有無學到啲蒙古語呀?(The most unforgettable experience_ informant13)

Have you learned a little bit/that Mongolian?

3 Referential Properties of the Noun Phrase Modified by *ne1*, *go2* and *di1*

The functioning of demonstratives or demonstrative-like quantifiers in language is constrained by their semantic features, and their selection mechanism in actual language use is related to their referential properties. Therefore, before analyzing the pragmatic functions of *ne1*, *go2*, and *di1*, it is essential to establish their respective referential property. In discussions about Chinese reference, Chen (1986) introduced five sets of concepts, including definite and indefinite, referential and non-referential, identifiable and non-identifiable, specific and non-specific, and generic and individual. Among these, definite and indefinite belong to the realm of grammar. In the other four sets, which are within the realm of semantics and pragmatics, identifiable/non-identifiable primarily focuses on whether the hearer can associate the reference with entities in the real-world context, while the remaining three sets are mainly defined from the perspective of the speaker's cognition. In Mandarin Chinese, demonstratives like "zhe", "na", and their plural forms "zhe xie" and "na xie" are considered definite [11]. However, the quasi-demonstrative-type plural quantifier *di1* in Cantonese exhibits distinct characteristics. The referential attributes of *ne1*, *go2*, and *di1* in Cantonese will be examined from three perspectives: identifiability, referentiality, and generic/individual. Since specific/nonspecific only pertains to non-identifiable or indefinite elements, some scholars argue that there is no need to distinguish between them [12], thus this section will not delve into these concepts.

3.1 The Referents in Discourse

In discourse, referents can be entities or propositions [13]. In Cantonese, *ne1*, *go2*, and *di1* can refer to entities, as exemplified earlier, but they can also refer to propositions. For instance, in (9), "啲經歷[di1 ging1 lik6] (those experiences)" refers to the experiences mentioned earlier, which are the experiences of going on a trip with your mom, the experiences of things like "not letting you do this, not letting you do that".

(9) 即係我哋呢代嘅媽媽係好傳統嘅, 你同佢哋去旅行呢, 佢哋好……呢樣又唔畀你做, 嗰樣又唔畀你做㗎。……但係嗰次呢, 咁啱大家差唔多年紀, 幾位女士呢, 大家原來啲經歷差唔多, 所以大家好盡情咁去玩, 所以就玩得好開心囉!(The most unforgettable experience_informant15)

It's just that the mothers of our generation are quite traditional. When you travel with them, they are very… they won't let you do this, they won't let you do that. But that time, coincidentally, everyone was of a similar age. There were several girls, and our past experiences were quite similar. So, we all had a great time playing, and we had a lot of fun!

3.2 Identifiability

Identifiability describes the psychological representation of a referent in the listener's cognition. It pertains to whether the listener can establish a connection between the reference and the referent. The term identifiable refers to a situation in which the speaker believes that the listener can form a connection between the noun phrase and the referent, or the speaker can select a specific referent based on the context during speech. The other term unidentifiable, on the other hand, denotes the opposite scenario. These two aspects can be expressed through grammatical means involving definiteness or indefiniteness. Apart from these two categories, there are indeterminate expressions, whose identifiability cannot be determined from a lexical or morphology perspective.

In Chinese, demonstratives like "zhè", "nà", "zhè xiē", and "nà xiē" are often considered means of expressing identifiable [14]. In Cantonese, *ne1* and *go2* both can be used to indicate identifiable referents. However, "identifiable" does not necessarily mean that the listener can identify the referent, partial identification is sufficient for a listener to be considered identifiable [11]. For example, in (10), "呢班人[ne1 baan1 jan4](these people)" can be identified as the generation influenced by the TV show "Super Trio Series", without the need for specifying individuals. Meeting the "curiosity principle" is enough for identifiability.

(10) 有啲係《獎門人》蘇格蘭場, 個啲又影響咗一代人, 20年30年後, 呢班人都仲係識唸啲啲無謂嘅字。(Interview_2)

Some people were from the Scottish version of the "Super Trio Series", and that influenced a generation of people, twenty or thirty years later, these people still know how to read these meaningless words.

When comparing *ne1* and *go2* with *di1*, it becomes apparent that *ne1* and *go2* are associated with identifiable, while *di1* is considered an indeterminate expression. In the context of Chinese languages, indeterminate expressions can be categorized as bare nouns and cardinality expressions [15]. Given that *di1* itself carries the feature of plural quantity, it results in the noun phrase it modifies behaving as if they are part of a cardinality expression. For instance, in (11), "啲人[di1 jan4](those people)" is unidentifiable. In (12), "啲滑水梯[di1 waat6 seoi2 tai1](those water slides)" refers back to the water slides mentioned previously and is identifiable.

(11) 你唔畀啲人鬧你皆廢, 唔係鬧我, 係咪。(Interview_2)

You didn't let those people harass you; it's not that they harassed me, is it?

(12) 咁同埋佢啲滑水梯真係夠晒高囉! (The most unforgettable experience_informant15)

And those water slides are indeed very tall!

It can be observed that the identifiability of demonstratives *ne1* and *go2*, as well as the quasi-demonstrative-type quantifier *di1*, differs to some extent. Noun phrases modified by *ne1* and *go2* fall under the category of identifiable, while *di1* is characterized by its plural quantifier nature, causing the noun phrases it modifies to be considered indeterminate expressions, that is, its identifiability determined by the objects mentioned earlier in the discourse or the context.

3.3 Referentiality

In the context of reference, the noun phrase to indicate the entity in the real world is considered referential, while those that might refer to existing entities are non-referential [16]. Du Bois (1980) proposed two methods to identify referentiality: the ability to refer back to previously mentioned objects, namely whether is an anaphor, and whether is sensitive to singularity or plurality. Based on these principles, the noun phrases modified by the Cantonese demonstratives *ne1* and *go2* are generally referential. For example, "呢套戲[ne1 tou3 hei3] (this movie)" in (13) can enter into the discourse's anaphoric chains. However, non-referential situations can arise, such as when *ne1* and *go2* co-occur to indicate a distinctive meaning, as seen in (14) with "呢個[ne1 go3] (this)" and "嗰個[go2 go3] (that)".

(13) 你話如果拍完呢套戲, 我同美儀都講, 嗰啲師奶一定喊死嘅, 宜家唔係師奶喊, 連登仔都喊, 嗰到恐怖, 皆宜個係喜出望外咯。(Interview_2)

You said that after filming this movie, Meiyi and I both thought that those housewives would be in tears. Now, it's not just the housewives crying; even the schoolboys are crying, to that extent, we can say it's a happy surprise.

(14) 梗係冇啦, 以訛傳訛嘅, 吹得就吹, 呢個吹完嗰個就抄嘅。(Interview_2)

Of course not. It's all hearsay, just blow it up. Once this is blown, that's copied.

The noun phrase modified by the quasi-demonstrative quantifier *di1* can be either referential or non-referential, characterized by uncertainty, and its referentiality depends on contextual cues. This is primarily due to the indefinite quantifier nature of *di1*, which mostly modifies entities with uncertain quantities. Wang (2006) posits that when the modified noun phrase refers to individual entities with distinct features, such as people, books, etc., as in (15), *di1* can be both referential and non-referential. In such cases, *di1* can function both as a demonstrative and a quantifier. However, when the entities are referred to without distinct characteristics, like meat, rocks, etc., they can only be interpreted as non-referential, as in (16) with "啲豬肉[di1 zyu1juk6](this pork)". In such cases, removing the "啲" in front of the noun phrase would not change the meaning of the sentence. Therefore, the referentiality of *di1* is more uncertain than that of *ne1* and *go2*, thus when the referent of *di1* is definite, it functions like a demonstrative, but in indefinite contexts, it serves as a quantifier.

(15) 啲人就話我坐不定啊, 整蠱人啊, 過度活躍啊。(Interview_2)

Those people said I couldn't sit still, was very naughty, and being overly active.

(16) 啲豬肉幾多錢啊?(Conversation_1)

How much is (this) pork?

3.4　Generic/Individual

The term generic refers to the reference to an entire category, characterized by non-individuation, a lack of extension, and typically employing property-level predicates [18]. The term individual, on the other hand, involves reference to one or more individuals within a category. Generic and individual are both cognitive concepts related to the speaker and intersect with the concepts of definiteness and indefiniteness.

The Cantonese demonstratives *ne1*, *go2*, and the quasi-demonstrative-type quantifier *di1* are frequently used for individual reference. The only difference when used for individual reference is that *ne1* and *go2* can refer to either one individual or multiple individuals, while *di1* can only indicate multiple individuals due to its inherent plural meaning. *ne1* and *go2* often combine with collective quantifiers to indicate generic reference, as in "呢種/嗰種[ne1 zung2/go2 zung2] (this type/that type)" or "呢類/嗰類[ne1 leui6/go2 leui6] (this kind/that kind)", as shown in (17), while *di1* can directly modify the noun phrase to denote a category, as seen in "啲劇本[di1 kek6 bun2] (those scripts)" in (18).

In Cantonese, *di1* is more commonly used for denoting generic references, this is attributed to two main factors. First, the inherent plural meaning of *di1* aligns with the characteristics of generic reference, which generally excludes individuality. Therefore, in languages such as English, plural nouns are often preferred to denote generic references [18]. Second, *di1* falls under the category of indeterminate encoding, a common feature for generic reference in Chinese languages. The ambiguity arises from the fact that when using *di1* for reference, it directly proceeds a noun phrase, regardless of whether it's a generic or individual reference. For instance, "啲學生[di1 hok6 saang1] (that students)" can refer either to a specific group of students or to students in the generic sense. Consequently, distinguishing between generic and individual references denoted by *di1* largely depends on the context and its relationship with the predicate.

(17) 誒, 呢種藥, 嗯, 我睇好嘢嚟㗎! 補身有益㗎! (Movie "Lover in Disguise",1965)

Oh, this type of medicine, I think it's good stuff! It's beneficial for the body!

(18)　　其實我話如果啲劇本你係到咧, 自自然然就會push你跟住嗰個情緒去。(Interview_2)

I think that if those scripts are well-crafted, they will naturally immerse you in that kind of emotion.

3.5 Summary

In summary, when modifying the quantifier-noun construction, *di1* can, like *ne1* and *go2*, refer to entities or propositions. However, due to the semantic meaning of the plural quantity of *di1* and its lack of distance distinction, it exhibits different referential properties compared to *ne1* and *go2*. The references denoted by *ne1* and *go2* are identifiable, while *di1* falls into the category of indeterminate encoding, its identifiability determined by prior context or discourse. *ne1* and *go2* are often referential, whereas *di1* carries an inherent uncertainty in reference, necessitating contextual cues for clarification. Moreover, *di1* is more frequently employed for generic reference compared to *ne1* and *go2*. Consequently, *di1* possesses distinct referential properties from *ne1* and *go2*, and to some extent, it complements them in terms of referential functions.

4   Pragmatic Functions of Cantonese Quasi-Demonstrative Quantifier *di1* and Demonstratives

Demonstratives are generally categorized into situational and non-situational uses. In Halliday's classification, situational use corresponds to exophoric reference, which primarily serves the purpose of connecting discourse to the external world, the non-situational use, termed endophoric reference, primarily functions in maintaining discourse continuity and can be further divided into anaphora and cataphora (Halliday 2004). Fillmore (1982) categorized the non-situational functions into text reference, shared vs. unshared knowledge, serial order, and others. Building upon these scholars' work, Himmelmann (1996) mainly based his categorization of demonstratives on their discourse functions, dividing them into situational use, discourse deictic use, tracking use, and recognitional use. This section will describe the pragmatic functions of Cantonese demonstratives *ne1*, *go2*, and the quasi-demonstrative quantifier *di1* within Himmelmann's framework. It is worth noting that situational use falls under the category of exophoric reference, while the others fall under endophoric reference.

4.1   Situational Use

Situational use of demonstratives serves the function of indicating entities present in the discourse context and is typically associated with deictic reference [21]. Deictic reference can be categorized into spatial and temporal deictic reference [22]. Spatial deictic reference concerns entities located in the immediate environment and can be aided by gestures, eye contact, and other non-verbal cues. As mentioned earlier, in Cantonese, *ne1* and *go2* respectively refer to proximal and distal entities, while the use of *di1* for proximity or distance depends on the context. Regarding temporal deictic reference, *ne1* can be used to indicate the current time, whereas *go2* can be employed to refer to a past or future time, see examples (19) and (20), while *di1* does not have a temporal deictic function.

(19) 何止今晚呀？我呢排都係噉㗎嘞! (Movie "Standard Husband", 1965)
Not just tonight, but this period has been like this!

(20) 我嗰日搭巴士，爭你一毫子呢，我聽日還返畀你，吓!(Movie "Incarnate Lover", 1965)

I took the bus that day, and owe you a dime; I'll give it back to you tomorrow!

4.2 Discourse Deictic Use

Discourse deictic use is to indicate the proposition or event mentioned in the discourse. This can be seen as an instance of what Lyons (1977) termed "impure text deixis", referred to as "textual use" by Fang (2002). In this usage, demonstratives may refer to a clause or an entire narrative. Similar to situational use, there is no antecedent referent. However, the key distinction between tracking use and recognitional use lies in the fact that it always refers to adjacent discourse segments in deictic use [21]. In Cantonese, *ne1*, *go2*, and *di1* can all be used for discourse deixis.

The noun phrase as discourse deictic use can also indicate a time in the discourse. This function differs from temporal deixis in situational use, as the latter refers to the actual time of the speech event, while discourse deixis refers to moments within the narrated events. Due to the semantic constraints of *di1*, it cannot indicate time in discourse deixis. However, *ne1* and *go2* have no such limitation, as exemplified in (21) with "呢個時候[ne1 go3 si4 hau6] (this moment)".

(21)   大師兄嬌喘一聲倒在外賣仔嘅懷裡，   喺呢個時候，   大師兄眼如微絲……(Movie "Rumble King", 1994)

Big brother gasped and fell into the arms of the delivery boy, at this moment, big brother's eyes were like fine silk…

4.3 Tracking Use

Tracking use, also known as anaphoric or co-referential use [21], involves referring back to objects or entities previously mentioned in the discourse to help the listener trace preceding information. According to Chen's (1986) framework of Chinese anaphoric forms, demonstratives primarily combine with nominal constituents to form nominal anaphora. Building upon this framework, Xu (2005) further subdivides nominal anaphora into co-referential and associative anaphora. Associative anaphora, in this context, refers to an anaphoric reference that lacks an antecedent and relies on a preceding word within the discourse that serves as the antecedent [25]. This includes cases of both cataphora and linked references. Xu (2005) noted that associative anaphora does not necessarily provide significant assistance in tracking previous information, instead, it often serves the progression of the discourse. Therefore, when identifying the tracking use of demonstratives in this paper, the primary consideration is whether they help in tracing objects introduced in earlier discourse, including instances of both cataphora and linked reference. Cantonese demonstratives *ne1*, *go2*, and *di1* can all form nominal phrases in the discourse for anaphoric reference, as exemplified in (22)–(24).

(22) 初初我第二日已經拍喊戲, 過場係我去翻舊樓, 發覺係已經唔屬於我哋嘅了呢層樓, 其實都係我當年嘅錯, 落錯車, 搞到你哋樣。(Interview_2)

Originally, I was shooting a crying scene the next day. That scene was when I returned to the old building. I found that this floor no longer belonged to us. It was all my fault from back then, getting on the wrong bus, which led to you (referring to the protagonist's wife) being like this.

(23) 第一次帶團去印尼, 睇咪阿素波咪同我講, "啊子民啊, 我細妹想同我一齊去, 不過佢張機票呢我出, 我自己出嘅, 佢可以去服侍我, 幫我睇頭睇尾嘅。但係佢識彈古箏, 你不如當畀個節目佢彈下啦!" 點知去到機場, 嚇到我哇!嗰個古箏我唔知係點嘅嘛初初, 一睇個古箏, 好似個棺材仔咁大。(interview_4)

The first time I led a group to Indonesia, Bo said to me, "Zi Man, my little sister wants to come with me, but I will pay for her flight. I want her to take care of me, look after this and that. However, she can play the Chinese zither. Why don't you give her a program to perform?" Little did I know, when we got to the airport, I was shocked! I had no idea what that Chinese zither was like, when I saw that zither, it was almost as big as a coffin.

(24) 同埋係, 譬如, 都有滑水梯咁樣, 四個人一齊玩, 同你一個人係唔同嘅, 總之四個一齊玩, 好熱鬧, 大家一齊嗌, 因為唔知邊個落水先, 係落水嗰個係慘啲。……咁同埋佢啲滑水梯真係夠晒高囉!(The most unforgettable experience_informant15)

Moreover, for example, there are slides, when four people play together, it's different from playing alone. In any case, playing with four people is lively. Everyone yells together because they don't know who will fall into the water first. The one who falls into the water is in for a harder time… And these slides are tall!

4.4 Recognitional Use

In the recognitional use, the referent is identified according to the shared interactive history or common experiences between the speaker and the listener, rather than relying on the discourse context or preceding segments for identification. The referent in this context is typically introduced, but also be a non-tracking referent which has been mentioned earlier [11]. This usage is primarily employed to introduce a referent with relatively low identifiability, a referent that might not have been mentioned in the preceding text or context but is mutually recognized by both the speaker and the listener [24].

The crucial distinction between the reference for recognitional use and tracking use is that the former do not occupy a central position within the topic. Their continuity in the discourse is not mandatory. However, when the listener encounters difficulties in identification, the speaker can provide supplementary descriptions of the referent. Cantonese demonstratives $ne1$, $go2$ and $di1$ can all function as a reference for recognitional use. For instance, in (25), the speaker presumes that the listener knows that the school the speaker attended in their childhood was an elite school, with students hailing from relatively affluent family backgrounds, so "啲闊太[di1 kwaau3 taai3] (those affluent ladies)" is used to refer to those student's mother.

(25) 皆我帶去面試, 我見到其它啲闊太係走廊到, 點樣練好一點。(Interview_2)

So, I took my child for an interview, and I saw those affluent ladies in the hallway, (thinking about) how to better prepare.

4.5 Topic Marker

In addition to the four functions mentioned above, *di1* also serves an extended function as a topic marker, akin to the usage of "zhe" in Mandarin. Demonstratives used as topic markers introduce objects that are first encountered in the conversation and are non-anaphoric [24]. For instance, in (26) "啲工作[di1 gung1 zok3] (that work)" is a topic. In such cases, using the more identifiable "呢啲[ne1 di1]" or "嗰啲[go2 di1]" instead of *di1* would be unsuitable. Fang (2002) suggests that demonstratives functioning as topic markers are an extension of situational use, they aim at transforming unknown information into known information or making an already definite element appear "like" a definite noun. But *ne1* and *go2*, as observed in our corpus, do not exhibit this function as topic markers. This difference may be related to the relatively pronounced generic function of *di1*, much like how "zhe" in Beijing Mandarin and "ge" in Suzhou dialect serve both generic and topic-marking functions [18]. Nevertheless, compared to Beijing Mandarin's "zhe" with its prominent topic-marking function, the topic-marking role of *di1* is not as prominent, mainly because *di1* can only be used before nouns and not before verbal phrases.

(26) 啲工作咧, 有時候真係冇必要做得太認真。(Conversation_2)

As for that work, sometimes, there's no need to take it too seriously.

4.6 Summary

In summary, *di1*, apart from its inability to indicate time in situational use and discourse deictic use, shares four pragmatic functions with Cantonese's two primary demonstratives, *ne1* and *go2*. These functions encompass situational use, discourse deictic use, tracking use, and recognitional reference. Additionally, *di1* can also function as a topic marker. Based on the analysis of four oral narrative discourses and three representative dialogues from the PolyU Corpus of Spoken Chinese: Cantonese, the distribution of these three demonstratives' their functions in discourse is outlined in Table 1.

Table 1. The pragmatic function of *ne1*, *go2* and *di1*.

	ne1	go2	di1	Total
Situational use	5	14	0	19
Discourse deictic use	6	25	2	33
Tracking use	7	20	10	37
Recognitional use	2	13	6	21
Topic marker	0	0	3	3
Total	20	72	21	113

Two particular observations are noteworthy. First, in the seven discourse examples, *di1* does not appear as situational use. This is not because *di1* cannot be used for direct deixis in spoken discourse but possibly due to its lack of distance semantics, which leads to the need for higher interactivity and immediacy for *di1* to frequently occur in situations where both conversational participants interact extensively. Also, due to the semantic meaning in the plural quantity of *di1*, it cannot refer to singular entities, places, or times within discourse. The second notable point is that, within the existing corpus, only *di1* serves the role of a topic marker.

5   Conclusion and Further Discussion

There is no doubt that *di1* has the demonstrative function in the quantifier-noun construction, which exhibits not only the basic deictic function but also the ability, akin to *ne1* and *go2*, to refer to entities and propositions in discourse. However, *di1* is still fundamentally a quantifier, and its inherent collective quantifier properties significantly influence its demonstrative function within the quantifier-noun construction: on one hand, the semantic feature in the plural quantity of *di1* makes the noun phrase modified by *di1* can only denote plural referents while precluding it from referring to locations and times. On the other hand, this characteristic imbues its referent identification with uncertainty, thereby accentuating its pronounced generic reference function. From a pragmatic perspective, *di1*, like *ne1* and *go2*, seamlessly fulfills the functions of situational use, discourse deictic use, tracking use, and recognitional use, and it can even serve as a topic marker. Therefore, overall, *di1* can be regarded as a quasi-demonstrative-type quantifier, and it exhibits distinct characteristics in terms of semantic features, referential properties, and pragmatic functions compared to the proximal *ne1* and distal *go2*.

Semantics, pragmatics, and syntax are three aspects that influence the choice between the demonstrative-quantifier-noun construction or the quantifier-noun construction. For *di1* and *go2*, the primary influencing factor is their semantic meaning in distance. As for the selection mechanism of *di1* in discourse, based on existing linguistic data and the semantic and pragmatic characteristics of it, the following inferences can be made:

1) Due to the semantic meaning in the plural quantity of *di1*, there may be a tendency for it to gradually take over when referring to objects with an indefinite or unclear quantity. The distribution of referents with quantity meaning in the collected 7 discourse data reflects this point (see Table 2). Related to this is the preference for *di1* when the referent is a category, i.e., as a generic reference.

Table 2. Expression of Quantity by *ne1*, *go2*, and *di1* in Discourse.

	Singular	Plural (countable)	Plural (uncountable)	Total
ne1	14	1	5	20
go2	28	1	17	46
di1	/	/	22	22

2) *di1* is essentially a quantifier and lacks inherent distance meaning. Therefore, when a speaker refers to objects without emphasizing distance, they may tend to use *di1*.

3) In the construction of quantifier-noun, the referentiality of *di1* is not clearly defined, and compared to *ne1* and *go2*, it is more natural and common when used as a nonreferential reference. Therefore, when the referent is not very clear, there is a tendency to use *di1*. For example, in (27), "啲人[di1 jan4] (those people)" is non-specific, and it is not clear which people are referred to. If "呢啲人[ne1 di1 jan4](these people)" or "嗰啲人[go2 di1 jan4](those people)" were used in this context, it would make the referent scope clearer, which might not align with the intended semantics.

(27) 視帝我真係冇所謂嘅, 係啊, 你畀我又冇所謂, 你唔畀<u>啲人</u>鬧你皆廢, 唔係鬧我, 係咪。(Interview_2)

As for the award, I really don't care. Yeah, it doesn't matter to me if you give it to me. If you don't give me the award, <u>those people</u> will just trouble you, not me, right?

4) From a pragmatic perspective, when the referent simultaneously serves a topical function, there may be a preference for choosing *di1*, which prominently exhibits its generic reference function, as the topic marker.

References

1. Sheng, Y., Tao, H., Jin, C.: The quasi-article type and the quasi-demonstrative type: two types the quasi-article type and the quasi-demonstrative type: two types of definite CL-NP constructions in the Shaoxing dialect of Chinese. Linguist. J. [Yuyanxue Luncong] (01), 30–51 (2016). (in Chinese)
2. Sheng, Y.: The definite classifier-noun constructions in chinese dialects: universality and diversity. Contemp. Linguist. [Dangdai Yuyanxue] **19**(2), 181–206 (2017). (in Chinese)
3. Zhang, H.: Research on Hong Kong Cantonese Grammar. The Chinese University of Hong Kong Press, Hong Kong (1972). (in Chinese)
4. Matthews, S., Yip, V.: Cantonese: A Comprehensive Grammar. Routledge, London (1994)
5. Tang, S.: Lecture Notes on Cantonese Grammar. The Commercial Press, Hong Kong (2015). (in Chinese)
6. Peng, X.: Notes on plural structural particle di1 in Cantonese. Dialects [Fangyan] (02), 112–118 (2006). (in Chinese)
7. Diessel, H.: Demonstratives: Form, Function and Grammaticalization. John Benjamins Publishing Company, Amsterdam/Philadelphia (1999)
8. Gao, H.N.: Research on Guangzhou Dialect. The Commercial Press, Hong Kong (1980). (in Chinese)
9. Zhan, B.: Overview of the Guangdong Dialect. Jinan University Press, Guangzhou (2004). (in Chinese)
10. Zhang, Q., Tang, S.: Commonality and differences: a study on noun phrases in Cantonese. Lang. Linguist. [Yuyan Ji Yuyanxue] **15**(5), 733–760 (2014). (in Chinese)
11. Chen, P.: Referent introducing and tracking in Chinese narratives. Ph.D. dissertation, UCLA (1986)
12. Wang, H.: My views on functional grammar reference classification. Teach. Chinese World Lang. [Shijie Hanyu Jiaoxue] (02), 16–24+2 (2004). (in Chinese)
13. Lambrecht, K.: Information Structure and Sentence Form. Cambridge University Press, New York (1994)
14. Zhou, S.: Research on information structure of Chinese sentences: from topic prominence to focus prominence. Ph.D. dissertation, Beijing Normal University (2005). (in Chinese)
15. Chen, P.: Identifiability and definiteness in chinese. Linguistics **42**(6), 1129–1184 (2004)

16. Wang, H.: Conditions for the generation of referential uncertainty. Lang. Res. [Yuwen Yanjiu] (03), 31–37 (2006). (in Chinese)
17. Du Bois, J.W.: Beyond definiteness: the trace of identity in discourse. In: Chafe, W.L. (ed.) The Pear Stories: Cognitive Cultural and Linguistic Aspects of Narrative Production, pp. 203–274. Albex Publishing Corporation, Norwood (1980)
18. Liu, D.: Semantic and syntactic properties of kind-denoting elements in Chinese. Chinese Lang. [Zhongguo Yuwen] (05), 411–422+478–479 (2002). (in Chinese)
19. Halliday, M.A.K.: An Introduction to Functional Grammar, 3rd edn. Arnold, London (2004)
20. Fillmore, C.J.: Towards a descriptive framework for spatial deixis. In: Jarvella, R.J., Klein, W. (eds.) Speech, Place and Action: Studies in Deixis and Related Topics, pp. 31–59. Wiley, London (1982)
21. Himmelmann, N.P.: Demonstratives in narrative discourse: a taxonomy of universal uses. In: Barbara, A.F. (ed.) Study in Anaphora. John Benjamins, Amsterdam/Philadelphia (1996)
22. Chen, Y.: A Typological Study of Chinese Demonstratives. China Social Sciences Press, Beijing (2010). (in Chinese)
23. Lyons, J.: Semantics. Cambridge University Press, Cambridge (1977)
24. Fang, M.: On the grammaticalization of Zhe in Beijing mandarin: from demonstrative to definite article. Chin. Lang. [Zhongguo Yuwen] (04), 343–354 (2002). (in Chinese)
25. Xu, J.: A study of modern Chinese anaphora. Chin. Lang. [Zhongguo Yuwen] (03), 195–204+287 (2005). (in Chinese)
26. Jiang, L., Zhang, Y., Guan, J., Du, Z.: Construction and implementation of the quantifier-noun collocation knowledge base for proofreading based on multiple knowledge sources. In: Liu, P., Su, Q. (eds.) Chinese Lexical Semantics, pp. 593–602. Springer, Heidelberg (2013). https://doi.org/10.1007/978-3-642-45185-0_62

A Comparative Study of the General Classifier *Gè* and Its Near-Synonyms in Modern Chinese——Taking *Gè*, *Zhǒng*, and *Jiàn* as Examples

Jingying Rui[1] 🆔 and Jia-Fei Hong[2(✉)] 🆔

[1] School of Humanities, Minjiang University, Fuzhou, China
RaisingRui@mju.edu.cn
[2] Department of Chinese as a Second Language, Taiwan Normal University, Taipei, Taiwan
Jiafeihong@ntnu.edu.tw

Abstract. As the only general classifier in modern Chinese, the attribute of *Gè* (个) inevitably leads to semantic overlap with other classifiers resulting in misuse, which is worthy of further research. This study conducts a comparative analysis of *Gè* and its near-synonyms, *Zhǒng* (种) and *Jiàn* (件), based on corpus research. It shows that *Gè* and *Jiàn* have co-occurrence contexts when measuring nouns about events, but the use of *Gè* is usually limited to colloquial language, while *Jiàn* is applicable to both colloquial and written language. The noun *Shìjiàn* (事件) 'event' is usually modified by *Gè* not by *Jiàn*. There is no semantic overlap between *Gè* and *Zhǒng* and they cannot be used interchangeably. Some nouns can appear simultaneously in the *Num/RNum+Gè/Zhǒng+N* structure, and choosing which classifier is only determined by quantitative or categorical concepts they expressed.

Keywords: Classifier · Semantics · *Gè* · *Zhǒng* · *Jiàn*

1 Introduction

The General classifier *Gè* is omnipresent and versatile in everyday spoken communication in modern Chinese. It can refer to both people and things and is found not only in literary works dominated by written language but also in popular media and daily conversations dominated by spoken language. According to the Modern Chinese Balanced Corpus Word Frequency Table by the National Language Commission of Mainland China[1], *Gè* and *Zhǒng* are the two most frequently used classifiers. *Gè* ranks 21st in word frequency among all Chinese vocabulary, with a cumulative frequency of 20.0794, while the classifier *Zhǒng* ranks 24th with a cumulative frequency of 20.9808. Similarly,

---

[1] National Language Commission of Mainland China's Modern Chinese Balanced Corpus Word Frequency Table download link: http://corpus.zhonghuayuwen.org/ (retrieved on May 20, 2023).

M. Dong et al. (Eds.): CLSW 2023, LNAI 14514, pp. 60–73, 2024.
https://doi.org/10.1007/978-981-97-0583-2_6

in the Modern Chinese Corpus Word Frequency Statistics for Taiwan[2], *Gè* and *Zhǒng* are also the two most frequently used classifiers. *Gè* ranks 6th in word frequency among all Chinese vocabulary, with a cumulative frequency of 11.658, and the classifier *Zhǒng* ranks 29th with a cumulative frequency of 21.763. These two corpora are representative and commonly used modern Chinese language databases for both sides of the Taiwan Strait. *Gè* is the top-ranked classifier in both corpora, highlighting its significant role in modern Chinese classifiers.

Being the only General classifier in modern Chinese, the attribute of universal associated with *Gè* inevitably leads to situations of semantic overlap with other specific classifiers. According to the Chinese Word Sketch Thesaurus[3], the Thesaurus retrieval results (Fig. 1) show that *Gè*, *Zhǒng*, *Wèi* (位), *Míng* (名), *Jiàn*, and other classifiers can all be considered synonyms of *Gè* with overlapping or similar meanings in certain contexts.

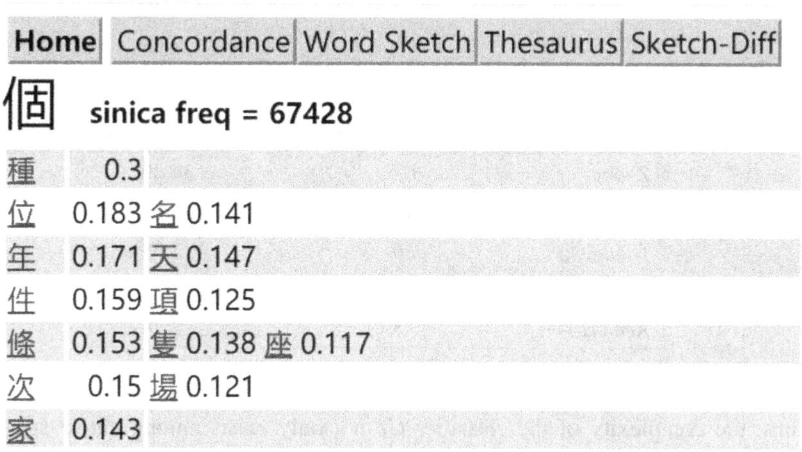

Fig. 1. Thesaurus retrieval results for *Gè* in CWS

The use of classifiers is highly complex [1], which implies that native speakers may occasionally misuse them in actual language communication. For example:

(1) **另外   一个 是 作者 的 心态 问题**, 他 在 写作 的 时候, 没有 Lìngwài yígè shì zuòzhě de xīntài wèntí, tā zài xiězuò de shíhou, méiyǒu 应有 的 责任感, **只是   把 其   当做   个人   情绪   发泄**yīngyǒu de zérèngǎn, zhǐshì bǎ qí dàngzuò gèrén qíngxù fāxiè**的   一个 方式**。

de yígè fāngshì.

---

[2] Taiwan Modern Chinese Corpus Word Frequency Statistics link: https://elearning.ling.sinica. edu.tw/cwordfreq.html (retrieved on May 20, 2023).

[3] Chinese Word Sketch Thesaurus introduction and link: https://wordsketch.ling.sinica.edu.tw/ (retrieved on May 21, 2023).

Another one is the author's state of mind. When he wrote, he did not have the due sense of responsibility, just as a way to vent personal emotions. (微博语料, BCC 语料库)

This sentence is an instance from the native speaker corpus, where the expression *Yígè fāngshì* (一个方式) is not accurate; the appropriate classifier should be *Zhǒng*. From this, it can be seen that the distinction between *Gè* and other near-synonymous classifiers in the contemporary linguistic environment, as well as whether native speakers can clearly differentiate and accurately distinguish between *Gè* and its near-synonyms, is a topic worthy of further exploration.

Through an examination of classifier errors in the HSK Dynamic Composition Corpus 2.0[4], it was found that among all the classifiers that were erroneously used as *Gè* when other classifiers should have been used, *Zhǒng* and *Jiàn* ranked first and second, respectively, accounting for a total of 60%. The detailed distribution is shown in the following table (Table 1):

Table 1. Top 5 classifier errors in the HSK Dynamic Composition Corpus 2.0

Order	Classifier	Quantity	Proportion
1	*Zhǒng*	62	34.4%
2	*Jiàn*	46	25.6%
3	*Diǎn* (点)	6	3.33%
4	*Shǒu* (首)	6	3.33%
5	*Rèn* (任)	5	2.78%

Thus, the complexity of the classifier *Gè* not only exists among native speakers but also appears in various errors made by learners when using *Gè* for communication in international Chinese education [2]. Hence, understanding the commonalities and individualities in the use of different classifiers, aiding international students in mastering the usage of *Gè* and its near-synonyms, is also worthy of consideration and exploration.

2   Literature Review

Regarding the grammatical classification of *Gè*, there are generally two viewpoints in academia. One perspective regards *Gè* as a classifier without other grammatical explanations [3–5]. In this view, the usage of *Gè* as a classifier gradually expands with language development, giving rise to structures such as $V^5+Gè+V$ and $V+Gè+N$. Another perspective holds that, besides its role as a classifier, *Gè* also has non-classifier usages [6–10]. The grammaticalization of *Gè* essentially involves a gradual shift from its classifier

---

[4] HSK Dynamic Composition Corpus 2.0 introduction and link: http://hsk.blcu.edu.cn/ (retrieved on May 21, 2023).

[5] V = verb.

usage to non-classifier usage. However, this process lacks clear boundaries, leading to a situation of semi-classifier, semi-auxiliary. This study primarily focuses on the nominal classifier and individual classifier usages of *Gè*, where the basic syntactic structure is: *Num/RNum*[6]*+Gè+N*. While the noun in this structure can be omitted in certain contexts, the classifier *Gè* cannot be omitted [11].

Through investigation, it has been found that most of the comparative and analytical studies on the Chinese classifier *Gè* and its near-synonyms focus on differences and similarities in scope, linguistic style, and emotional nuances, particularly when compared with person-specific classifiers like Wei, Ming, and Yuan. Some scholars affirm that *Gè* has the broadest scope of referring to people, is more commonly used in spoken language, and conveys a neutral emotional tone [12–14]. However, a few scholars contest the neutral tone of *Gè*, asserting that its specific emotional tone is determined by the subjective consciousness of the speaker [15]. While a plethora of error instances related to *Gè*, *Jiàn*, and *Zhǒng* have been identified from the errors made by international students, there remains a significant research gap in distinguishing among these three classifiers. To date, there has been no specific comparative study. Given this research background and the exploration of relevant literature, the following research questions have been formulated: What semantic features does *Gè* exhibit as a General individual classifier in the structure *Num/RNum+Gè+N*? What are the differences and similarities in usage between *Gè* and the near-synonyms *Jiàn* and *Zhǒng*?

3   Research Methods

To ensure objectivity in the research findings, this study predominantly relies on authentic language corpus data to verify its viewpoints. The primary source of data is the BLCU Chinese Corpus (BCC), a corpus of native speaker language usage. Additionally, this study utilizes the Chinese Wordnet[7], a lexical semantic knowledge base, to compare and analyze the semantic meanings of relevant classifiers.

3.1   BLCU Chinese Corpus

The BCC corpus comprises approximately 15 billion characters, covering various fields such as newspapers (2 billion), literature (3 billion), microblogs (3 billion), technology (3 billion), comprehensive (1 billion), and Classical Chinese (2 billion). Encompassing both written and spoken Language, it is a comprehensive corpus that provides a comprehensive reflection of contemporary Chinese Language use in society. The corpus is equipped with a fuzzy retrieval function that allows corpus retrieval based on combinations of parts of speech. For instance, a search with the key phrase m Gè n yields results as shown in Fig. 2.

Here, *m* represents numerals (including round numbers), *n* represents nouns, and *m Gè n* corresponds to all instances of the *Num/RNum+Gè+N* structure in the corpus.

---

[6] RNum = round number.

[7] Introduction to Chinese Wordnet and Website: https://lope.linguistics.ntu.edu.tw/cwn2/ (Retrieved on: December 23, 2023).

Fig. 2. Example of BCC Corpus Retrieval

3.2   Chinese Wordnet

The differentiation and expression of word meanings must be established on a sound foundation of lexical semantics theory and ontology architecture. The Chinese Wordnet is a knowledge base that provides comprehensive distinctions of Chinese word meanings (senses) and lexical semantic relations. Since 2003, this database system has gradually refined definitions of word sense distinctions and ways to express word sense knowledge, combining recent research achievements.

This study will combine the semantic classifications within the corpus to divide the meanings of the classifier *Gè* and its near-synonyms *Jiàn* and *Zhǒng*. On this basis, a detailed semantic analysis will be conducted. Using *Gè* as an example, the retrieval result from the Chinese Wordnet is shown in Fig. 3.

Fig. 3. Example of Chinese Wordnet Retrieval

4 Comparative Analysis of Classifiers *Gè*, *Jiàn*, and *Zhǒng*

According to the retrieval results from the Chinese Word Sketch Thesaurus, *Zhǒng* and *Jiàn* have overlapping usage with *Gè* when paired with nouns that refer to objects. They can appear in the same structural and linguistic context. Through an examination of classifier errors in the HSK Dynamic Composition Corpus and the TOCFL Learner Corpus[8], it has been observed that Chinese learners often misuse or interchange *Gè* with both *Jiàn* and *Zhǒng*. Hence, this section will conduct a comparative study on these two sets of easily confused classifiers.

4.1 Semantic Distribution of Classifier *Gè*

Concerning the semantic distribution of the classifier *Gè*, this section will primarily utilize the Chinese Wordnet as a research tool to focus on the semantic features of the classifier. The analysis of *Gè* will primarily rely on the semantic classification provided by the Chinese Wordnet. According to the retrieval results from the Chinese Wordnet, *Gè* can be divided into *Gè1* and *Gè2* based on different semantic categories, as shown in Fig. 4.

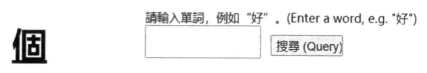

個

請輸入單詞，例如 "好" 。(Enter a word, e.g. "好")

搜尋 (Query)

個¹ 《ㄜˋ 有4個詞義。

個² 《ㄜˋ 有7個詞義。

Fig. 4. Retrieval Results of *Gè* in Chinese Wordnet

Among them, *Gè1* represents the non-classifier usages of *Gè*, including nouns, adjectives, adverbs, etc., with a total of 4 meanings. *Gè2* encompasses the classifier usages of *Gè* and its degrammaticalized adverb usages, totaling 7 meanings. The detailed distribution of the classifier meanings and example sentences is as follows:

Gè2 meaning 1: Classifier, counting individual concrete objects. For example:

(2) 各校　应　辅导　学生　依照　七个　项目　来　申请　工读
　　Gèxiào yīng fǔdǎo xuéshēng yīzhào qīgè xiàngmù lái shēnqǐng gōngdú 实施 计划。
　　shíshī jìhuà.
　　Schools should instruct students to apply for the work-study implementation plan in accordance with the seven items.

---

[8] Introduction to TOCFL Learner Corpus Retrieval System and Website: http://tocfl.itc.ntnu.edu.tw:8080/ (Retrieved on: May 21, 2023).

Gè2 meaning 2: Classifier, counting specific abstract nouns. For example:

(3) 当   我 得到 这么   一个 体验, 喜悦 油然 从 中 而 来。
Dāng wǒ dédào zhème yígè tǐyàn, xǐyuè yóurán cóng zhōng ér lái.
When I have such an experience, joy comes naturally from it.

Gè2 meaning 3: Classifier, counting time. For example:

(4) 再 过 两个 星期, 第 二十一   次   院士 会议 将 在 南港
Zài guò liǎnggè xīngqī, dì èrshíyī cì yuànshì huìyì jiāng zài Nángǎng 本院 举行。
běnyuàn jǔxíng.
The 21st meeting of Academicians will be held in two weeks' time at Nangang.

Gè2 meaning 4: Classifier, counting units of approximate quantities for specific objects. For example:

(5) 才 走 个 几步 他 的 额头 上   就   渗出   汗珠。
Cái zǒu gè jǐbù tā de étóu shàng jiù shènchū hànzhū.
After only a few steps, beads of sweat seeped from his forehead.

Among all the meanings of *Gè2*, meanings 1, 2, 3, and 4 are identified as classifier usages, while meanings 5, 6, and 7 are adverb usages. Although meaning 4 is recognized as a classifier usage, its syntactic manifestation has already exhibited a trend of grammaticalization. In the phrase *Zǒugè jǐbù* (走个几步), the *Gè* is not in a classifier-noun structure but serves as a complement marker. It bears resemblance to meaning 6, indicating a stage in the grammaticalization process. Its usage persists in modern Chinese. Among the meanings conforming to the scope of this study (individual classifier usage), *Gè* has three meanings: *Gè2* meaning 1, measuring independent specific objects; *Gè2* meaning 2, measuring specific abstract nouns; and *Gè2* meaning 3, measuring time.

4.2 Comparative Analysis of *Gè* and *Jiàn*

In the Chinese Wordnet, *Jiàn* is divided into *Jiàn1* with a total of 10 usages (as shown in Fig. 5). Among these, *Jiàn* meanings 2, 4, 6, 8, and 10 are classifier usages. Their detailed classifications are as follows:

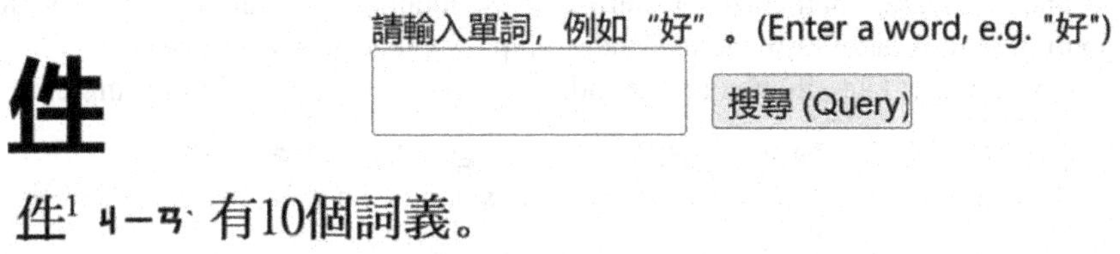

性

請輸入單詞, 例如 "好" . (Enter a word, e.g. "好")

搜尋 (Query)

件¹ ㄐㄧㄢˋ 有10個詞義。

Fig. 5. Retrieval Results of Jiàn in Chinese Wordnet

Classifier meaning 2: Counting units of clothing or accessories. For example:

(6) 在 他 保存 的 十四件 服饰 中,皇帝 穿 的 龙袍 就
Zài tā bǎocún de shísìjiàn fúshì zhōng, huángdì chuān de lóngpáo jiù 多达 七件

。

duōdá qījiàn。

Of the 14 pieces of garments he preserved, seven were dragon robes.

Classifier meaning 4: Counting units of machine components. For example:

(7) 另外 还 需要 一件 耗材 才 能 使用,该 耗材
Lìngwài hái xūyào yíjiàn hàocái cái néng shǐyòng, gāi hàocái.
为何
wéihé?
It requires one more consumable to use it. What is that consumable?

Classifier meaning 6: Counting units of written documents.

(8) 可以 在 一件 申请书 中 申请 多类 商品 或 服务Kěyǐ zài
yíjiàn shēnqǐngshū zhōng shēnqǐng duōlèi shāngpǐn huò fúwù.商标。
Shāngbiāo
Multiple types of goods or service trademarks can be applied for in one application.

Classifier meaning 8: Counting units of individual items of the same kind. For example:

(9) 任何 天才 , 他 一生 的 作品 中,真正 有 价值 的Rènhé tiāncái,
tā yìshēng de zuòpǐn zhōng, zhēnzhèng yǒu jiàzhí de 只有 四五件。

zhīyǒu sìwǔjiàn.

For any genius, only four or five of his life's works are really valuable.

Classifier meaning 10: Counting units of events. For example:

(10) 历来 飞行伞 的 失事 比率,是 滑翔翼 的 五 至 六倍,
Lìlái fēixíngsǎn de shīshì bǐlǜ , shì huáxiángyì de wǔ zhì liùbèi,
平均 每年 发生 十件 以上。
píngjūn měinián fāshēng shíjiàn yǐshàng.
For many times in the past, the crash rate of flying parachutes was five to six times that of gliders, with an average of more than ten accidents per year.

Among the five usages above, except for meaning 10, the others are mostly used to modify specific nouns with clear scope, and they are rarely prone to misuse. In the case of meaning 10, *Jiàn* is used to measure nouns about events, which may bear similarity or overlap with the usage of *Gè2* meaning 2 in modifying specific abstract nouns, as shown in the examples:

(11) 我 人生 中 最 幸运 的 两件 事情,一件 是 时间是 时间 Wǒ
rénshēng zhōng zuì xìngyùn de liǎngjiàn shìqíng, yíjiàn shì shíjiān终于 将 我 对 你
的 爱情 消耗殆尽,另 一件 是zhōngyú jiāng wǒ duì nǐ de àiqíng xiāohàodàijìn,
lìng yíjiàn shì

很久很久 以前 有 一天 我 遇见 你。

hěnjiǔhěnjiǔ yǐqián yǒu yìtiān wǒ yùjiàn nǐ.

There are two luckiest things in my life, one is that time has finally exhausted my love for you, and the other is that one day I met you a long time ago. (微博语料, BCC 语料库)

(12) 作为 国家 领导人, **你们 的 历史责任 就是 要 在 一百 件**Zuòwéi guójiā lǐngdǎorén, nǐmen de lìshǐ zérèn jiùshì yào zài yìbǎi jiàn **事情 中 除去 九十九件 不能 成 的事情**, 找出 那 shìqing zhōng chúqù jiǔshíjiǔjiàn bùnéng chéng de shìqing, zhǎochū nà **一件 能成 的 来。** yíjiàn néngchéng de lái.

As the leader of the country, your historical responsibility is to remove 99 things out of a hundred things that cannot be done, and find out which one can be done. (超新星纪元/刘慈欣, BCC 语料库)

(13) 在 故事 中, **几个 事件 可以 同时 发生**, 但是 话语 必须 把 Zài gùshì zhōng, jǐgè shìjiàn kěyǐ tóngshí fāshēng, dànshì huàyǔ bìxū bǎ **它们 一件 一件 地 叙述 出来**; tāmen yíjiàn yíjiàn de xùshù chūlái;

In a story, several events can occur at the same time, but the words must narrate them one by one; (科技文献, BCC 语料库)

(14)

今天 看了 罗大佑 那期 的《康熙来了》 突然 想起 一个事......Jīntiān kànle luódàyòu nàqī de kāngxīláile tūrán xiǎngqǐ yígèshì.

Today, I watched Luo Dayou's issue of Kangxi is Coming and suddenly remembered something... (微博语料, BCC 语料库)

In all four sentences above, *Gè* and *Jiàn* both modify nouns indicating events, and there is a possibility of interchangeability in usage. For instance, in example (11), *Yígè shìjiàn* (一个事件) can also be expressed as *Yíjiàn shìjiàn* (一件事件) following native speaker conventions. However, this does not imply that *Gè* and *Jiàn* can be used interchangeably when measuring units of events. Based on a comparison and integration of the language data, this study attempts to summarize the patterns of *Gè* and *Jiàn* in the *Num/RNum+Gè/Jiàn+N* structure as follows:

1. *Jiàn* can be used in written and spoken language, while *Gè* is generally only used in spoken language.

Taking the noun *shìqíng* (事情) 'event' as an example, the retrieval results from the BCC corpus show that there are a total of 6580 instances of *Num/RNum+Jiàn+shìqíng* in various domains, including literature, newspapers, technology, microblogs, etc. On the other hand, there are only 319 instances of *Num/RNum+Gè+shìqíng*, which is significantly fewer than *Num/RNum+Jiàn+shìqíng*. Furthermore, almost all of the instances of *Num/RNum+Gè+shìqíng* are concentrated in the realm of microblogs, indicating that this usage is prevalent in internet colloquial language and rarely appears in literature and technology-related fields.

Based on the word cloud comparison results in the BCC corpus, the word cloud distribution of *Num/RNum+Jiàn+shìqíng* is much richer compared to *Num/RNum+Gè+shìqíng*. The detailed distributions are illustrated in Fig. 6 and 7.

Fig. 6. Word Cloud Distribution of *Num/RNum+Jiàn+shìqíng*

Fig. 7. Word Cloud Distribution of *Num/RNum+Gè+shìqíng*

In conclusion, when measuring nouns about events, compared to *Gè*, *Jiàn* exhibits certain limitations in terms of usage scope. *Jiàn* can be used in both written and spoken language, while *Gè* is generally limited to spoken language.

2. Preceding the noun *Shìjiàn* with Multiple *Gè*

Although the scope of *Gè* in measuring nouns about events is not as extensive as that of Jiàn, there is one exception based on the characteristic of avoiding repetition in Chinese language. This exception is the noun *Shìjiàn* (事件). The choice between *Gè* and *Jiàn* before events is not semantically related but rather influenced by Chinese rhythm and expression habits. Throughout history, Chinese has exhibited the linguistic feature of avoiding repetitive words. For example, phrases like *Tónggān gòngkǔ* (同甘共苦) 'go through thick and thin together' rather than *Tónggān tóngkǔ* (同甘同苦) and *ěryú wǒzhà* (尔虞我诈) 'deceive and blackmail each other' instead of *ěrzhà wǒzhà* (尔诈我诈) exemplify this phenomenon. In the BCC corpus, there are only 17 instances of *Num/RNum+Jiàn+Shìjiàn*, while there are 385 instances of *Num/RNum+Gè+Shìjiàn*, significantly more than the former. In summary, the semantic characteristics of *Gè* and *Jiàn* when measuring nouns about events are as follows:

Gè:　　**[+ expressing abstract nouns representing events]**　　**[- formal language]**
　　　　[+ spoken language]　　**[+ *Shìjiàn*]**
Jiàn:　　**[+ expressing abstract nouns representing events]**　　**[+ formal language]**
　　　　[+ spoken language]　　**[- *Shìjiàn*]**

Furthermore, *Gè* has continuously derived some more vague usages during its process of grammaticalization. Some usages include the expression *Gè+shì/shìqíng*, for example:

(15) 只是　看到　一句 "跟你说个事", 不知 为何 我 就有了 不详 的 Zhǐshì kàndào yíjù *gēnnǐshuōgèshì*, bùzhī wèihé wǒ jiùyǒule bùxiáng de 预感。
yùgǎn.
Just seeing the phrase tell you something, for some reason I had a sense of foreboding. (人民日报海外版**2016**年**10**月**17**日, BCC 语料库)

(16) 至于　沈祥福　是否　能够　出任　国家队　主教练,　　　　这个Zhìyú shěnxiángfú shìfǒu nénggòu chūrèn guójiāduì zhǔjiàoliàn, zhège 事情 不是 属于 我 的 业务 范围。shìqing búshì shǔyú wǒ de yèwù fànwéi.
As for whether Shen Xiangfu can become the head coach of the national team, this matter is not my business scope. (人民日报海外版**2002**年**06**月**11**日, BCC 语料库)

In the above two examples, *Gè* is respectively an adverb *Gè* and a demonstrative pronoun after *Gè*, and it is not the focus of this study. However, it cannot be denied that it is precisely the presence of such usages that leads learners to confusion in the usage of *Gè*. Due to their highly similar structures, learners might expand the usage of *Gè* in the *Num/RNum+Gè+N* structure beyond its appropriate scope, thus resulting in misuse errors.

4.3　Comparative Analysis of *Gè* and *Zhǒng*

In the Chinese Wordnet, *Zhǒng* is divided into *Zhǒng1*, *Zhǒng2*, and *Zhǒng3* based on different categories of meanings (as shown in Fig. 8). Among these, *Zhǒng1* meaning 9 is the classifier usage of *Zhǒng*, representing the unit for counting categories of things, for example:

(17) 五色鸟　全身　计有 五种　颜色, 身体 为 翠绿色。
Wǔsèniǎo quánshēn jìyǒu wǔzhǒng yánsè, shēntǐ wéi cuìlǜsè.
The five-colored bird has five colors and an emerald green body.

(18) 民主　是 一种　生活　的 方式, 生活 的 习惯。
Mínzhǔ shì yìzhǒng shēnghuó de fāngshì, shēnghuó de xíguàn.
Democracy is a way of living, a habit of living.

From the perspective of semantic distribution, *Gè* does not have the function of measuring categories of things. Even when measuring specific abstract nouns, it still emphasizes the individual entity itself. *Zhǒng*, on the other hand, lacks the usage of measuring individual objects and time. Therefore, there is no semantic overlap between

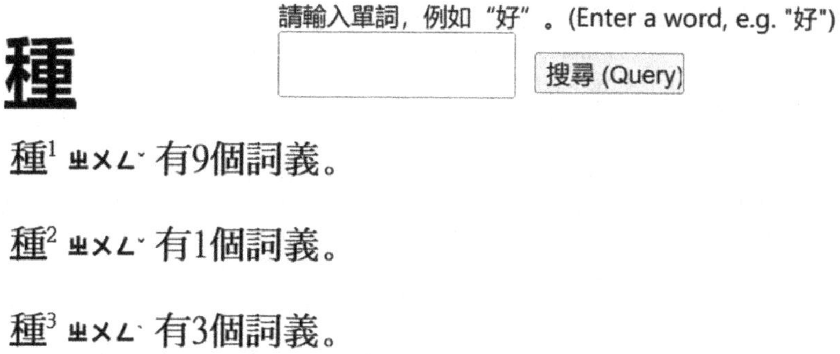

種

種¹ ㄓㄨㄥˇ 有9個詞義。

種² ㄓㄨㄥˇ 有1個詞義。

種³ ㄓㄨㄥˇ 有3個詞義。

Fig. 8. Retrieval Results of Zhŏng in Chinese Wordnet

Gè and *Zhŏng*. However, based on noun collocations, some nouns can appear in both the *Num/RNum+Gè/Zhŏng+N* structures, for example:

(19) 他　根本　不看　房间里　的　画，一　坐下　就　抓起　两个　苹果，Tā gēnběn búkàn fángjiānlǐ de huà, yí zuòxià jiù zhuāqǐ liǎnggè píngguǒ, 咔啦咔啦　咬光　了　一个，又　接上　吃　第二个。kālākālā yǎoguāng le yígè, yòu jiēshàng chī dìèrgè

He didn't look at the paintings in the room at all, and as soon as he sat down, he grabbed two apples, clicked and bit off one, and then ate the second. (张炜/你在高原, BCC 语料库)

(20) 对了，我　早上　拿了　两种　苹果　（蛇果、富士）　在他Duìle, wǒ zǎoshang nále liǎngzhŏng píngguǒ (shéguǒ, fùshì) zài tā 面前，本来　打算　给 他吃 蛇果，他 之前　爱吃 蛇果。miànqián, běnlái dǎsuàn gěi tāchī shéguǒ, tā zhīqián àichī shéguǒ.

By the way, I took two kinds of apples (Red Delicious and Fuji) in front of him in the morning, and I was going to give him Red Delicious, he used to love Red Delicious. (微博, BCC 语料库)

In example (19), *Liǎnggè píngguǒ* (两个苹果) expresses the apples as individual entities, where Ping Guo refers to independent objects. On the other hand, in example (20), *Liǎngzhŏng píngguǒ* (两种苹果) emphasizes the category of apples, specifically selecting two types from all categories. Hence, the choice between the classifier *Gè* and *Zhŏng* before the same noun depends on whether the concept being expressed is related to measurement or categorization.

Furthermore, similar to the confusion with the classifier *Jiàn*, due to the vagueness of *Gè* in its grammaticalization process, some sentences expressing categorization concepts may still exhibit the expression *Gè+Noun*, for example:

(21)

德勒斯登人　用　这个　方式　取得 充分　的 空气　与 阳光Délèsīdēngrén yòng zhège fāngshì qǔdé chōngfèn de kōngqì yǔ yángguāng.

In this way, the people of Dresden obtained sufficient air and sunlight. (吉耶勒卢普/明娜, BCC 语料库)

(22) 我先   说个   玩法 —— 咱们   一人 三枪，你 一枪，我 一枪。 Wǒxiān
shuōgè wánfǎ ——zánmen yìrén sānqiāng, nǐ yìqiāng, wǒ yìqiāng.
        I'll start with a game - let's shoot three shots per person, you one shot, I shoot.
(冯骥才/神鞭, BCC 语料库)

Although the categories of nouns need to be measured in both example (21) and example (22), the demonstrative pronoun *Gè* and adverb *Gè* after the demonstrative pronoun break the restriction of the original classifier in the numeral-noun structure, broadening their usage. This to some extent can cause difficulties in learners' comprehension and lead to errors.

5   Conclusion

Based on the retrieval results from relevant corpora, the individual classifier *Gè* that falls within the scope of this study has three meanings. These meanings respectively count independent objects, abstract nouns, and time. In the process of comparing synonyms, this research discovered that there is a semantic overlap between *Gè* and *Jiàn* in some contexts when measuring nouns about events. However, the usage of *Gè* is typically confined to spoken language, while *Jiàn* is applicable to both spoken and written language. The noun *Shìjiàn* is generally modified by *Gè* and not by *Jiàn*. In contrast, *Zhǒng* and *Gè* are distinctly different from each other in terms of semantics, despite sharing similar syntactic structures and the possibility of modifying the same nouns. Their expressed meanings are completely different and cannot be used interchangeably. Learners' confusion in using these three classifiers is partially attributed to the vagueness of *Gè*, which expands the applicable scope of its collocated nouns. Learners subjectively apply these usages to the *Num/RNum+Gè+N* structure, thus resulting in errors.

In summary, the preliminary conclusions regarding the semantic comparison of *Gè*, *Jiàn*, and *Zhǒng* can be drawn as follows:

1. When measuring nouns about events, *Jiàn* has a broader scope than *Gè* and can be used in both spoken and written language.
2. When preceding the noun *Shìjiàn*, *Gè* is used more frequently than *Jiàn*.
3. Compared to *Gè*, *Zhǒng* emphasizes the category of things.
4. Compared to *Zhǒng*, *Gè* emphasizes the quantity of individual entities.
5. The additional vague usages of *Gè* expand its applicable scope to collocated nouns, leading to confusion and misuse when compared with *Jiàn* and *Zhǒng*.

This research pioneers a semantic comparison of the classifiers *Gè*, *Jiàn*, and *Zhǒng*, moving beyond the conventional focus on classifiers referring to people. It aims to provide a more comprehensive understanding of the similarities and differences between the classifier *Gè* and other synonymous classifiers when referring to non-human entities. Due to the lack of relevant literature and research methods as references, this article unavoidably has certain research limitations. Criticisms and corrections are welcome, and further in-depth analyses and discussions on distinguishing *Gè* from its synonymous classifiers can be conducted based on this foundation.

References

1. Yuan, X., Lin, J.: Classifiers in Singapore Mandarin Chinese: a corpus-based study. In: Dong, M., Lin, J., Tang, X. (eds.) CLSW 2016. LNCS, vol. 10085, pp. 65–75. Springer, Cham (2016). https://doi.org/10.1007/978-3-319-49508-8_7
2. Li, Y.: Error analysis of chinese classifier Gè, and position noun Gè. Henan: Unpublished Master's Thesis, Anyang Normal University (2020). (in Chinese)
3. Zhao, Y.R.: Spoken Chinese Grammar. Commercial Press, Beijing (1979). (in Chinese)
4. Zhu, D.X.: Grammar Lecture Notes. Commercial Press, Beijing (1982). (in Chinese)
5. Shao, J.M.: Analysis of the verb+*Gè*+adjective/verb structure—discussion with comrade You Rujie. Chin. Learn. **2**, 50–54 (1984). (in Chinese)
6. Song, Y.Z.: Classifier Gè and particle Gè. Logic Lang. Learn. (6), 44 (1993). (in Chinese)
7. Zhou, M.Q.: Ephemeral characteristics of Chinese classifier *Gè*. J. Chin. Lang. Lit. **1**, 41–44 (2002). (in Chinese)
8. Zhang, Y.S.: From classifier to particle: a *Gè* analysis of the grammaticalization process of *Gè* construction. Contemp. Linguist. **5**(3), 193–205 (2003). (in Chinese)
9. Wang, L.Q.: *Gè*: from classifier to particle. J. Zhoukou Norm. Univ. **24**(3), 117–121 (2007). (in Chinese)
10. Chen, Z.G.: Syntactic analysis of the generalization of *Gè* usage. Lang. Transl. (Chin.) **3**, 29–31 (2007). (in Chinese)
11. Rui, J.Y.: Exploring the Num+*Gè*+N structure of Chinese classifier *Gè* based on corpora. Res. Chin. Lang. Teach. **17**(3), 53–82 (2020). (in Chinese)
12. Li, Y.Z.: Comparative study of the semantic features of *Gè* construction with classifier *Gè* and position noun yuan. J. Chin. Lang. Lit. **16**, 116–118 (2007). (in Chinese)
13. Yu, Y.: Discussion on classifier *Gè* and position. J. Suzhou Univ. **24**(1), 54–56 (2009). (in Chinese)
14. Fan, S.M., Chen, W.L.: Syntax and semantic differentiation of the classifier Gè, noun, and position in reference to people. Mod. Chin. (Lang. Res. Edn.) **3**, 34–36 (2010). (in Chinese)
15. Lv, H.M.: Comparative study of the usage of classifier *Gè* and position. Times Lit. (Second Half Mon.) **8**, 208–210 (2011). (in Chinese)

The Semantic Analysis of *Zhexia*: From the Perspectives of Spatial Metaphor, Subjectivity and Discourse Function

Jung-Jung Kang[⊠] 🆔 and Chia-Rung Lu 🆔

Graduate Institute of Linguistics, National Taiwan University, Taipei 10617, Taiwan
ms0797899@gmail.com, chiarung@ntu.edu.tw

Abstract. *"Zhèxià* 這下*"* is a lexical item with unique functions, despite its relatively low frequency. Its typical usages include phrases such as *zhèxià wǒ sǐ-dìng le* (這下我死定了) and *zhèxià cǎn le* (這下慘了), which demonstrate that it is used in specific contexts and implies the speaker's mood. This study discusses *zhèxià* from both lexical-semantic and pragmatic perspectives. Firstly, the rationale behind the presence of *zhèxià* in modern Chinese is explored through lenses of spatial metaphor and semantic extension. This explains why *zhèxià* exists in modern Chinese, while the combinations of other demonstratives with other spatial morphemes do not (e.g., *"zhè* 這{*shàng* 上/*qián* 前/*hòu* 後}"). Secondly, the discourse functions of *zhèxià* is discussed through collocation analysis and close investigation of its role in connecting clauses.

Keywords: *Zhèxià* · Spatial metaphor · Semantic prosody · Discourse function · Modality

1 Introduction

While the surface structure of *zhèxià* is composed of a demonstrative and a spatial word, Zhang, Fang and Zang suggest that it is not a phrase with a combination of two meaningful units, but rather a fixed lexicon with its own distinct meaning that can be used independently within a sentence [1]. Previous scholars have generally believed that *zhèxià* carries both temporal meaning and discourse-connecting functions [1–4]. However, so far there have been only a few discussions on *zhèxià* in Chinese Linguistics field, and many aspects are still left to be further explored and elaborated upon. For example, one question that arises is why Chinese only emerges the lexicon with proximal demonstrative, but leaves a gap of the distal demonstrative use, *nàxià* 那下? On another note, why does the lexicon incorporate the combination of a demonstrative with the downward direction *"xià"*, but not include the combination of other directions such as *qián* 前, *hòu* 後, *shàng* 上? Do these questions pertain to the metaphorical change and different degrees of grammaticalization of these morphemes? Additionally, what are some special functions of *zhèxià* in pragmatic use?

These issues will be discussed from semantic, pragmatic, and the concepts of "perspective".

M. Dong et al. (Eds.): CLSW 2023, LNAI 14514, pp. 74–89, 2024.
https://doi.org/10.1007/978-981-97-0583-2_7

2   Literature Review

2.1   The Meanings and Usage of Spatial Terms in Chinese: A Review of *shàng, xià, qián,* and *hòu*

"*Shàng, xià, qián, hòu*" are two sets of spatial words that have opposite directions. These words have undergone a semantic shift from concrete to abstract meanings, and from spatial to temporal meanings through metaphor. However, due to human cognitive and communication needs, the degrees of grammaticalization of the four spatial words are not entirely symmetrical, which leads to their different meanings and syntactic functions in modern Chinese.

According to the dictionaries and previous scholars, the prototypical meanings of *shàng* and *xià* are spatial, while *qián* and *hòu* are derived from the sense of motion. Furthermore, these words follow different semantic expansion paths. *Shàng* and *xià* undergo two changes from their original spatial meaning: **first to temporal** and **second to motion**, while *qián* and *hòu* primarily follow the path **from motion to spatial and then to temporal**. The following will discuss each lexicon and its semantic shift path with examples.

Firstly, following the "spatial to temporal" path, *shàng* and *xià* developed the temporal meaning of "earlier" and "later" (e.g. *shàngzhōu* 上週: last week; *xiàzhōu* 下週: next week). Then, *xià* further developed a temporal sense related to "the short period near the observer" (e.g. "*yǎnxià* 眼下: at this moment"; "*shíxià*時下: nowadays") through spatial metaphor [5], whereas *shàng* did not acquire the opposite sense.

Secondly, *shàng* and *xià* evolved unsymmetrical words following the path of spatial to motion, as summarized below [6, 7]:

Shàng: "to move upward (as a verb)" (*shànglóu* 上樓: to go upstairs) > "an upward movement (as a complement)" (*páshàng* 爬上: to climb up) "to go, arrive at" (*shàngjiē* 上街: take to the streets) > "to start" (*míshàng* 迷上: to fall in love with something) > "to achieve a state" (*suǒshàng* 鎖上: on locked)

Xià: "to move downward (as a verb)" (*xiàlóu* 下樓: to go downstairs) > "a downward movement (as a complement)" (*fàngxià* 放下: to put down) "to leave" (*xiàbān* 下班: to get off work) > "one time of an action (as a verbal quantifier)" (*dǎ yīxià* 打一下: a hit) > "small amount" (*yánjiū yīxià* 研究一下: to do some research)

The summary indicates that as language develops over time, there is an increasing asymmetry between the two lexicons. For example, *shàng* lacks counterparts for "the verbal quantifier" use and "a small amount of time"; *xià* has no corresponding terms for "to go, arrive at", "to start", and "to achieve a state".

Qián and *hòu* extend their meanings along the path of motion > spatial > temporal. Different from *shàng* and *xià*, their prototypical meanings are motion but not spatial—that is, *qián* denotes the act of moving forward, while *hòu* expresses the meaning of "to walk behind or to walk slowly". Their spatial senses, specifically the concepts of "front" and "back," extended from the motion expressions. Subsequently, the temporal senses of "earlier" and "later" developed from the spatial meanings [8, 9]. In short, the semantic extension and examples of *qián* and *hòu* in chronological order can be summarized as follows:

Qián: "to move forward" (*wèisuōbùqián* 畏縮不前: to cringe) > "front" (*qiánmén* 前門: front door) > "earlier" (*qiántiān* 前天: the day before yesterday).

Hòu: "to walk behind or to walk slowly" (*xiānláihòudào* 先來後到: (to do something) in sequence) > "back" (*hòumén* 後門: back door) > "later" (*hòutiān* 後天: the day after yesterday).

In conclusion, after examining the semantic changes of *shàng*, *xià*, *qián*, and *hòu*, we can infer that the uniqueness of *zhèxià* is likely related to the spatial metaphor of *xià*. Additionally, the fact that Mandarin Chinese lacks the expressions of *zhèshàng*, *zhèqián*, *zhèhòu* appears to result from differences in how these spatial terms have undergone semantic changes and expansions.

2.2   A Review of Zhang, Fang, and Zang (2018): the Discourse Function of *zhèxià*

So far, only a study by Zhang, Fang, and Zang (2018) focuses on exploring *zhèxià* from the perspective of discourse marker [1]. They consider the discourse function of *zhèxià* contains "narrator-hiding connection" and "narrator-revealing connection." The former connects two events in a sequence or cause-and-effect relationship without any personal evaluation from the narrator. On the other hand, the latter use of *zhèxià* forces the clause to be independent of the main storyline and implies the narrator's evaluation, judgment, and speculation. Furthermore, the collocations with the "narrator-revealing" function of *zhèxià* also convey a subjective tone. For example, it often co-occurs with (1) evaluative expressions, *hǎo le* 好了 (great), *wán le* 完了 (to be doomed), (2) the modal adverb *kě* 可 to convey the speaker's expectation, and (3) *le2*[1] to show the interaction between the speaker/narrator and the listener/reader [10].

Additionally, the authors calculate the distribution of *zhèxià* in different styles of speech, and discover that it is predominantly used in novels, followed by colloquial discourse, and less commonly used in news. However, we contend that the authors' conclusion regarding the lower frequency of *zhèxià* in spoken language is potentially flawed, as it may be influenced by the corpus they have chosen; in addition, the novels include many dialogues, which can also be counted as the colloquial form. Therefore, it may not be accurate for the authors to claim that *zhèxià* is less common in spoken language.

Finally, we argue that Zhang, Fang, and Zang's study can be improved in a specific way. Since their discussions mainly focus on *zhèxià*'s "textual" functions based on the data drawn from stories but the function of spoken discourse had not been analyzed, this study will extend the discussion from a pragmatic perspective. The main point is to expand the understanding of the meanings and functions of *zhèxià*, which could be beneficial for teaching Chinese as a foreign language.

---

[1] Lu (1999): *le*1 is the post-verbal particle, which expresses the perfection of an action; *le*2 is sentence-final particle used to complete a sentence, which usually indicates a change of state [19].

3 Research Method

3.1 Data Sources

This study utilizes both qualitative and quantitative methods. The qualitative analysis of the corpus primarily uses the "sinica" and "gigaword2all" corpora of the Chinese Word Sketch system (CWS), comprising a total of 577 instances of *zhèxià*. Additionally, for the collocation analysis, to ensure the statistical validity of the results, apart from the aforementioned data, we also collect the data from the Contemporary Chinese Corpus of Peking University (CCL) and the "newspaper" section of the Beijing Language University Corpus (BCC), resulting in a total of 4132 instances of data (including CWS corpus).

3.2 Theoretical Frameworks

Firstly, the article applies Tao's (1999) discourse mode to classify the corpus data in order to elucidate the lexical gap of *nàxià*. The following lists the three discourse modes proposed by Tao [11]:

1. Interactive mode: Involving communication and dialogue between two or more speakers.
2. Story mode: Narration without dialogue, where a speaker primarily tells a story.
3. Intermediate mode: Positioned between interactive and story modes, where a speaker mainly restates events or a person's statement.

Secondly, a collocation analysis is employed to discuss the semantic prosody and pragmatic function of *zhèxià*, including the contextual usage and mood. "Semantic prosody" refers to the sentimental connotation of a word, typically classified as positive, negative, or neutral [12–15]. Partington defined semantic prosody as "Connotational coloring beyond single word boundaries [14]", this suggests that words are influenced by their surrounding context. Hence, scholars have investigated semantic prosodies by examining collocations in extensive datasets. Additionally, identifying a word's "collocability" discerns whether the joint occurrence of two terms stems from linguistic conventions or emerges randomly.

Figure 1 outlines the step-by-step approach of collocation analysis carried out in this study.

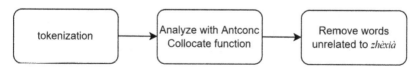

Fig. 1. Collocation Analysis Process

First, we employed the jiebaR package to tokenize the corpus data. Second, the tokenized data was fed into Antconc, where it underwent analysis utilizing the "Collocate" function. To tailor the analysis specifically to our context, we customized the application settings. The window span was set as 0 positions to the left and 8 positions to the right of the node word. Typically, in collocation studies, the usual span for node words is four to five words, but it may be insufficient in the analysis of lexical entries that have conjunction function [16]. Therefore, we extended the span to 8 words to capture a more comprehensive linguistic context.

Furthermore, the results were set to be sorted by the Effect criterion. In the context of Antconc, the Effect criterion indicates the collocability between two words, with a higher value suggesting a stronger association, which elucidates the close relationship between the words.

In the final step, words with less association with *zhèxià*, such as personal pronouns, particles, and those appearing to be on different syntactic levels, are excluded from the collocation test as they provide limited information.

4   Result and Discussion

4.1   The Discourse Modes of *zhèxià*

The first analysis categorizes the CWS corpus data into three discourse modes. Before presenting the result, the following provided examples of *zhèxià* in the three respective modes.

Firstly, sentence (4-1) presents *zhèxià* being used in an interactive context, which is a scene of the main speaker Fàn Yuàn communicating with his father-in-law, Fàn Kuāng Fū.

(4-1)   *zhèxià* in interactive mode

那	天	早上，	剛剛	在	學校	入	黨	的	范願
Nà	*tiān*	*zǎoshàng*	*gānggāng*	*zài*	*xuéxiào*	*rù*	*dǎng*	*de*	*Fàn Yuàn*
That	day	morning	just	at	school	enter	party	NOM	Fàn Yuàn

擁	著	姐姐、	姐夫	來		到	父母	跟	前：
yōng	*zhe*	*jiějiě* 、	*jiěfū*	*lái*		*dào*	*fùmǔ*	*gēn*	*qián*
hug	PRG-P	sister	brother.in.law	come		to	parent	foot	front

「爸爸，	姐姐	給	您	領回	個	黨員	女婿，
bàbà ·	*jiějiě*	*gěi*	*nín*	*lǐng.huí*	*ge*	*dǎngyuán*	*nǚxù*
father	sister	for	you	take.back	CLF	party.member	son.in.law

這下	您	該	高興	了	吧。」	范匡夫
zhèxià	*nín*	*gāi*	*gāoxìng*	*le*	*ba*	*Fàn Kuāng Fū*
zhèxià	you	should	happy	PFV	FP	Fàn Kuāng Fū

笑	著	點點頭。
xiào	*zhe*	*diǎndiǎntóu*
laugh	PRG-P	nod.head

"That morning, just after becoming a party member at school, Fàn Yuàn came to his parents with his older sister and brother-in-law. He said to his father, "Dad,

sister has brought you a party member son-in-law. **Now** you should be happy."
Fàn Kuāng Fū smiled and nodded."

Secondly, sentence (4-2) is a paragraph in which a narrator recounts the tale of a
chef; as a result, the usage of *zhèxià* in this example can be interpreted as being employed
in a narrative mode.

(4-2) *zhèxià* in story mode

他	好奇地	到	餐廳	的	操作間	一	看 ,
tā	hàoqíde	dào	cāntīng	de	cāozuòjiān	yī	kàn
3SG	curiously	to	restaurant	ASSOC	kitchen	one	look

沒想到		廚師	們	都	是	自己	在	北京	飯店
méixiǎngdào		chúshī	men	dōu	shì	zìjǐ	zài	běijīng	fàndiàn
out.of.expectation		chef	PL	all	C/F	own	at	Beijing	hotel

帶	過	的	徒弟 。	這下	樂壞	了
dài	guò	de	túdì	zhèxià	lèhuài	le
lead	EXP	NOM	apprentice	*zhèxià*	overjoy	PFV

這	位	特級	烹飪	技師
zhè	wèi	tèjí	pēngrèn	jìshī
this	CL	special.class	cooking	chef

"Curiously, he went to take a look at the restaurant's kitchen area, only to find out
that the chefs were all apprentices he had trained himself at a hotel in Beijing. This
truly delighted the accomplished master chef."

Thirdly, sentence (4-3) demonstrates a narrator restating the speech of the character
Zhèng Zé Shì and the restatement does not directly appear in a dialogue. Therefore, in
this example, *zhèxià* is considered to be used in an intermediate mode.

(4-3) *zhèxià* in intermediate mode

前晚　　他　吃　麻辣鍋 ，　昨天　　中午　　大　啖　大閘蟹 ，

Qiánwǎn　tā　chī　málàguō　zuótiān　zhōngwǔ　dà dàn　dàzháxiè
last.night　3SG　eat　spicy.pot　yesterday　noon　　big eat　hairy.crab

晚上　　還　要　「進攻」　　牛肉麵 。　因　　火氣

wǎnshàng　hái　yào　jìngōng　niúròumiàn　yīn　huǒqì
evening　still　want　offense　beef.noodles　because internal.heat

太大　而　鬧　牙　疼　的　　鄭則士 ，　笑　　說

tài　dà　ér　nào　yá　téng de　ZhèngZéShì　xiào　shuō
too　big　so　suffer　tooth　hurt　NOM　ZhèngZéShì　laugh　say

自己　這下　能　把　拍　戲　瘦　　下來　的　　體重 ，

zìjǐ　zhèxià　néng　bǎ　pāi　xì　shòu　xiàlái　de　tǐzhòng
self　zhèxià　can　BA　shoot film　thin　down　NOM　weight

再　　給　吃　　回來　了 ！

zài　gěi　chī　huílái　le
again　to　eat　back　CRS

"Last night, he had spicy hot pot, at noon yesterday he feasted on a large hairy crab, and in the evening, he was even planning to "offense" a bowl of beef noodles. Zhèng ZéShì, who has a toothache due to internal heat, laughed and said that the weight previously lost from filming and can now all be gained back by eating!"

Figure 2 presents the result of categorizing the corpus data into these three discourse modes.

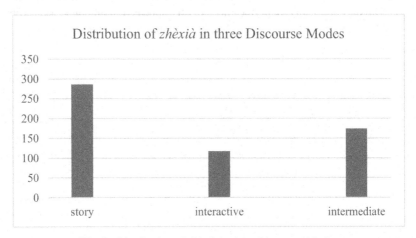

Fig. 2. Distribution of *zhèxià* in three Discourse Modes

Figure 2 illustrates that *zhèxià* primarily appears in story mode contexts (286 tokens), followed by intermediate mode (174 tokens), and with interactive mode having the lowest frequency (117 tokens). Two main insights can be observed from this result.

Firstly, *zhèxià* is used to indicate "a situation" within the same discourse mode, rather than cross modes. According to [11], if the referent is in the same discourse mode, there is generally no restriction on using *zhè* or *nà*; however, in a cross-discourse mode context (e.g. in an interactive mode pointing to a referent in the story world), only *nà* is deemed acceptable ([11], pp. 82–86). In this way, the above three instances of *zhèxià* all present that the speaker describes a situation in a single speech scene, but not an event in a different time and space.

Secondly, the fact that the frequency distribution of *zhèxià* is story mode > intermediate mode > interactive mode appears to echo the finding of Zhang, Fang, and Zhang [1], which presents that *zhèxià* is used more in novels and less in colloquial discourse. However, there is a notable distinction in our findings. The instances from CWS all indicate that *zhèxià* is used in the speaker's monologue, marking the speaker's own evaluation, rather than serving to interact with an interlocutor. This does not indicate that, as in [1]'s conclusion, *zhèxià* is more of a written form and less colloquial (pp. [1] 90–92). The language being used in novels can still be colloquial, especially in the speech of a character. Specifically, in the CWS data, 50% (291 tokens) of the instances of *zhèxià* appear in characters' speech.

4.2 Possible Reasons for the Lexical Gap of *nàxià*

The previous section suggests that *zhèxià* indicates a situation closely related to the speaker, whether in terms of time, space, or mental state. This links to the question of why Chinese lacks a distal demonstrative lexeme "*nàxià*". We believe that it is due to the usage differences between *zhè* and *nà*, as well as people's habitual choice of them in different discourse modes. The following summarizes the distinctions between *zhè* and *nà* in discourse modes from Tao (1999) [11] and Fang (2002) [17] (Table 1).

Table 1. Discourse Functions of *zhè* and *nà*

	這 *zhè*:	那 *nà*
Usage type[a]	Usually a "**situational use**", referring to an object within the speech scene, also known as "exophoric"	Usually a "**tracking use**", referring to an object previously introduced in the preceding text, also known as "anaphoric" or "coreferential" reference

(*continued*)

Table 1. (*continued*)

	這 *zhè*:	那 *nà*
Discourse mode	Used for indicating an object within the **same** discourse context	Used for indicating a farther object in the same discourse modes or an object in **different** discourse modes. Only "*nà*" can be used for the latter purpose. For instance, in interactive modes to refer to objects within a narrative mode

[a]Himmelmann (1994) proposed four types of functions for demonstratives in natural discourse: situational use, textual use, tracking use, and recognitional use [11].

Based on the information provided above, possible explanations for the question can be inferred:

1. "*Zhè*" indicates the time, situation, or object at the moment of speech, while *xià* (下) can denote the temporal-spatial proximity to the speaker. These two lexicons are naturally collocated.
2. "*Nà*" points to an object further in time or space, or within a different discourse mode. *Nà* can also refer to a more distant object within the same space; however, from the "temporal" aspect, *nà* can only indicate a certain time in the past or future, according to its one-dimensional nature [18]. Consequently, pairing *nà* with *xià* contradicts its nature.
3. In Chinese, both *dāngxià* (當下) and *nàshí* (那時) can be used to indicate distant time. Thus, there is no necessity for the emergence of *nàxià*.

4.3 Possible Reasons for the Lexical Gap of *zhèshàng, zhèqián, zhèhòu*

Another question to be addressed is the absence of *zhè* with other spatial words like *qián*, *hòu*, and *shàng*. According to [2, 17], and [3], two possible reasons can be identified to explain this phenomenon.

1. The morphemes that can follow demonstratives have selective restrictions.
   Demonstratives *zhè* typically precede morphemes that possess nominal characteristics [17]. Therefore, only *xià* can be chosen by demonstratives, as *xià* has the verbal quantifier use and can function as a pronoun.
2. "yī + predicate" construction (" 一 + 謂語 " 構式).
   Zhèxià is believed to derive from "*zhè yí xià* 這一下" [2, 3], which is related to the "yī + predicate" construction. In the dictionary *Modern Chinese 800 Words* (現代漢語八百詞), the construction "yī + predicate" is defined as "to reach a certain

result or conclusion through a quick action" ([19], p. 600). For example, in sentence (4-4), "*yī jiǎnchá*" demonstrates that as soon as the doctor examined, he found the subject had pneumonia.

(4-4) (Lu, 1999: p. 600)

醫生	一	檢查，	果然	是	肺炎。
Yīshēng yī		*jiǎnchá* ·	*guǒrán*	*shì*	*fèiyán*
Doctor	one	examine	absolutely	C/F	pneumonia

"As the doctor examined, they found it was indeed pneumonia."

[17] specified that this construction is easily preceded by a demonstrative to indicate a certain action ([17], p. 345). For example,

(4-5) (Fang, 2002: p. 346)

你	這	一	哭，	所有	問題	都	解決	了。
nǐ	*zhè*	*yī*	*kū* ·	*suǒyǒu*	*wèntí*	*dōu*	*jiějué*	*le*
2SG	this	one	cry	all	problem	all	solve	PFV

"With your cry, all the problems have been resolved."

In Sect. 2.1 of this study, we mentioned that *xià* developed the usage of complement, meaning "small amount", which is grammatically and semantically compatible with the structure of the "*yī* + predicate" construction. As a result, it can naturally fit into the construction, becoming "*zhè yí xià*". Subsequently, the numeral *yī* was dropped due to bleach in meaning and for the sake of pronunciation economy.

In sum, these two reasons provide grammatical explanations for the emergence of *zhèxià* and account for the absence of terms featuring other spatial lexicons.

5   The Semantic Prosody and Discourse Function of *zhèxià*

5.1   Collocation Analysis and Semantic Prosody

This section displays the result of collocation analysis and discusses the semantic prosody of *zhèxià*. Table 5-1 presents the top 22 collocations of *zhèxià*.

Firstly, Table 2 top 22 collocations of *zhèxià*. illustrates that the predicates frequently collocate with *zhèxià* are verbs or adjectives expressing mental attitudes[2]. This indicates that *zhèxià* often appears in contexts with subjective attitudes. Second, the presence of a (+) or (−) mark beside each word represents its positive or negative connotation. In this table, 16 out of 22 words are negative, indicating that *zhèxià* tends to have negative prosody. On the other hand, fewer tokens of *zhèxià* co-occur with positive words, such

---

[2] "Mental attitude adjectives (心理態度動詞)" is a term coined by [20]. This category is distinct from the typical mental adjective (心理動詞), such as *juédé* (覺得), *pà* (怕), *xǐhuān* (喜歡), *ài* (愛), *dānxīn* (擔心), because mental attitude adjectives do not take an object in grammar.

Table 2. Top 22 collocations of *zhèxià*

Ranking	Type	Effect Value	Freq	Ranking	Type	Effect Value	Freq
1	kě kǔ 可苦(-)	2.64	11	12	jí huài 急壞(-)	2.012	37
2	quán wán 全完(-)	2.503	13	13	rè nào 熱鬧(+)	1.947	34
3	dà huò 大禍(-)	2.387	12	14	nán zhù 難住(-)	1.904	35
4	rě nǎo 惹惱(-)	2.383	23	15	zāo 糟(-)	1.833	22
5	xià huài 嚇壞(-)	2.322	15	16	huài 壞(-)	1.813	44
6	kě hǎo 可好(+/-)	2.289	50	17	tǒng 捅(-)	1.779	23
7	lè huài le 樂壞了(+)	2.268	34	18	zěn me bàn 怎麼辦(-)	1.756	28
8	wán le 完了(-)	2.195	21	19	míng bái 明白(+)	1.657	69
9	wán dàn 完蛋(-)	2.181	20	20	kě hǎo le 可好了(+/-)	1.602	53
10	mǎ fēng wō 馬蜂窩(-)	2.072	23	21	jí 急(-)	1.532	25
11	má fán 麻煩(-)	2.025	28	22	fàng xīn 放心(+)	1.198	51

as "*lè huài le* (wild with joy), *rènào* (bustling), *fàngxīn* (relieve), which convey positive emotion on a whole (refer to example 5-4 for a more comprehensive context). Third, *kě hǎo/kě hǎo le* (great) are positive expressions in surface, but are tagged with (±), meaning that they can denote admiration and irony. The following sentences exemplify the two tones respectively.

(5-1) *kěhǎo* expresses admiration

在	烤制	工藝	上	他	也	有	新	招數，
zài	*kǎozhì*	*gōngyì*	*shàng*	*tā*	*yě*	*yǒu*	*xīn*	*zhāoshù*
At	roast	craft	aspect	3SG	also	have	new	trick

除了	洋蔥，	他	還	增添	了	幾	味
chúle	*yángcōng*	*tā*	*hái*	*zēngtiān*	*le*	*jǐ*	*wèi*
additional.to	onion	3SG	also	add	PFV	other	taste

新	佐料。	這下	可好，	他	的	烤品
xīn	*zuǒliào*	*zhèxià*	*kěhǎo*	*tā*	*de*	*kǎopǐn*
new	dressing	zhèxià	good	3SG	GEN	roasted.good

香	而不	膩，	脆	而	不	生，
xiāng	*ér bù*	*nì*	*cuì*	*ér*	*bù*	*shēng*
aromatic	but	NEG oily	crispy	but	NEG	raw

那	個	味道	真	叫	一絕，	妙不可言
nà	*gè*	*wèidào*	*zhēn*	*jiào*	*yījué*	*miàobùkěyán*
that	CL	taste	really	call	exceptional	beyond.words.

"In roasting techniques, he also has some new techniques. In addition to onions, he has added several new seasonings. **Now**, his roasted goods are not only fragrant without being greasy, but also crispy without being raw. That flavor is truly extraordinary, indescribably wonderful."

(5-2) *kěhǎo* expresses irony

可	誰	知，	錢	迷	心竅，
Kě	*shéi*	*zhī，*	*qián*	*mí*	*xīnqiào*
But	who	know	money	confuse	consciousness

主人	還	想	賺	得	更	多，
zhǔrén	*hái*	*xiǎng*	*zuàn*	*dé*	*gèng*	*duō*
host	still	want	earn	CSC	more	more

就	偷偷	在	我們	的	毛	裡	加	進	些	棉花。
jiù	*tōutōu*	*zài*	*wǒmen*	*de*	*máo*	*lǐ*	*jiā*	*jìn*	*xiē*	*miánhuā*
just	secret	at	1PL	GEN	fur	in	add	in	some	cotton

這下	可好，	被	人	發現	了，
zhèxià	*kěhǎo*	*bèi*	*rén*	*fāxiàn*	*le ·*
zhèxià	good	BEI	people	discover	CRS

嘩啦嘩啦	四面八方	全	退貨。
huálāhuálā	*sìmiànbāfāng*	*quán*	*tuìhuò*
ONOM	in.all.direction	all	return

"But who knows, money obsessed his consciousness. The host wanted to earn more so he secretly filled cotton into our fur. **Now** it is discovered, everyone is returning the goods in a rush."

In sentence (5-1), the phrase "*zhèxià kě hǎo*" is the speaker's conclusion to the subject's new roasting recipe. The context shows that it is a strong appreciation to his skill. On the contrary, in sentence (5-2), the same phrase is used ironically to depict a dishonest businessman facing the consequences of selling defective goods.

5.2 The Discourse Function and Mood

The previous section employed a quantitative method and revealed the negative semantic prosody of *zhèxià*. Nevertheless, this provides less linguistic insights. As Wu (2018) argued, "...the effect of a lexical entry on the inter-sentential relation, plays a significant role in accurately and completely understanding the semantics of the lexical entry. [21]" As a result, this section further discusses its discourse function and modality of *zhèxià*.

First, the speaker uses *zhèxià* to express a mood of anticipation and emphasis. Second, in terms of its discourse function, *zhèxià* gives a clue of "*Result*" rhetorical relation [22], which links two clauses, establishing a background condition in the first clause and an anticipated outcome in the subsequent clause. The condition introduced by *zhèxià* carries a negative implicit meaning, and the result it accompanies may be either negative or positive. *Zhèxià* serves to amplify the gap between the situation in the past and the current (or the gap between the mental expectation and the actual result). Sentence (5-3) and (5-4) are two examples:

(5-3) Negative condition → negative result

這	支	短片		內容	是	一	名	英挺
Zhè	*zhī*	*duǎnpiàn*		*nèiróng*	*shì*	*yī*	*míng*	*yīngtǐng*
This	CL	short.filme		content	C/F	one	CL	handsome

的	男性	年輕	官員	在	海關	巡視，
de	*nánxìng*	*niánqīng*	*guānyuán*	*zài*	*hǎiguān*	*xúnshì*
NOM	male	young	official	at	custom	patrol

以	國語	要求	一	名	外形	邋遢	男子，
yǐ	*guóyǔ*	*yàoqiú*	*yī*	*míng*	*wàixíng*	*lātā*	*nánzǐ*
use	Chinese	require	one	CL	appearance	shabby	male

打開	行李	檢查，	結果	發現	男子	違法	攜帶
dǎkāi	*xínglǐ*	*jiǎnchá*	*jiéguǒ*	*fāxiàn*	*nánzǐ*	*wéifǎ*	*xidài*
open	luggage	inspect	result	discover	male	illegal	carry

象牙	入	關，	此時		男子	以	台語
xiàngyá	*rù*	*guān*	*cǐshí*		*nánzǐ*	*yǐ*	*táiyǔ*
ivory	enter	custom	this.moment		male	use	Taiwanese

輕	嘆「	這下	慘	了！」
qīng	*tàn*	*zhèxià*	*cǎn*	*le*
low	cry	*zhèxià*	screw	CRS

"This short film depicts a young, upright male official conducting customs inspection in Mandarin. He requests a scruffy-looking man to open his luggage for inspection. The result reveals that the man is illegally carrying ivory into the country. At this moment, the man sighs in Taiwanese, "**Now**, I'm doomed!"

(5-4) Negative condition → positive result

在	備受	媒體	負面	報導，	並	傳出
Zài	*bèishòu*	*méitǐ*	*fùmiàn*	*bàodǎo*	*bìng*	*chuánchū*
at	suffer	media	negative	report	and	come.out

與	導演	拉斯馮提爾		吵架	之後，	這	位	首	次
yǔ	*dǎoyǎn*	*lāsīféngtíěr*		*chǎojià*	*zhīhòu*	*zhè*	*wèi*	*shǒu*	*cì*
with	director	Lars Von Trier		quarrel	after	this	CL	first	time

擔任	女	主角	的	熱門	音樂	另類	歌星
dānrèn	*nǚ*	*zhǔjiǎo*	*de*	*rèmén*	*yīnyuè*	*lìnglèi*	*gēxīng*
work.as	female	lead.role	NOM	popular	music	alternative	singer

這下	可	真	揚眉吐氣。
zhèxià	*kě*	*zhēn*	*yángméitǔqì*
zhèxià	certain	really	feel.proud

"Amidst a barrage of negative media coverage and rumors of a disagreement with director Lars Von Trier, this popular music artist, who is taking on the role of a female lead for the first time, can finally feel proud of herself."

Firstly, both sentences present anticipations within their respective *zhèxià* clauses. Specifically, in sentence (5-3), "*zhèxià cǎn le!*" (**Now**, I'm doomed) suggests that the speaker expects the consequence he is about to face. Moving on to sentence (5-4), the phrase "*zhèxià kě zhēn yángméitǔqì*" conveys the speaker's (who is the narrator of this content) anticipation that the actress must be proud of herself.

Secondly, sentence (5-3) presents a typical use of *zhèxià*, which connects a negative condition and a negative result. The condition is a man passed through customs with illegal ivory and was discovered by a coast guard. As a result, the man cried out "*zhèxià cǎn le!*" (I'm doomed). On the other hand, sentence (5-4) describes a Demark superstar who went through bitter experiences and finally was rewarded as the best female actress at the Festival de Cannes. The condition implies a negative event, which was the actress having quarrels with the director Lars Von Trier. However, she ultimately achieved the title of the best actress. The clause "*zhèxià kě zhēn yángméitǔqì*" is the speaker's subjective comment on the actress, which highlights a significant disparity between the condition and the result.

6   Conclusion

The discussion in this study provides insights into the emergence of the lexical unit *zhèxià* in contemporary Mandarin Chinese. The absence of the corresponding use of "*zhè+shàng/qián/hòu*" in vocabulary is intricately intertwined with the spatial metaphors and selection constraints of demonstrative pronouns. Additionally, the gap of the lexical unit *nàxià* may be attributed to inherent disparities between the demonstrative pronouns "*zhè*" and "*nà*", as well as the speaker's habitual choice between the two in discourse.

Furthermore, the collocation analysis and observation of the clausal relationships reveal that *zhèxià* exhibits a high degree of subjectivity and frequently co-occurs with words denoting subjective attitudes. The modality expressed by *zhèxià* typically reflects the speaker's anticipation and emphasizes the psychological gap caused by the result of a negative condition.

References

1. Zhang, W.X., Fang, D., Zhang, Y.Y.: Yǔtǐ shìjiǎo xià "zhèxià" de huàyǔ biāojì gōngnéng jí qí jiāoxué tàntǎo [On the discourse marker function of "Zhexia" and its teaching from the genre perspective]. Chin. Lang. Learn. **5**, 85–96 (2018). (in Chinese)
2. Li, Z.J.: "Zhèxià" de piānzhāng gōngnéng [The discourse function of zhexia]. Chin. Teach. World **4**, 56–63 (2007). (in Chinese)
3. Jin, G.T.: Yě tán "zhèxià" hé "zhèhuì" biǎo shíjiān guānxì piānzhāng gōngnéng de chǎnshēng [Study on the temporal discourse function of Zhexia and Zhehui]. Wuhan Univ. Technol. (Soc. Sci. Edn.) **21**(3), 438–441 (2008). (in Chinese)
4. Chang, F.C.: Zhǐliàng duǎnyǔ "zhèxià" yánjiū [A Study on the Phrase Refers to the Amount of "Zhexia"] (MA). Liaoning University (2016). (in Chinese)

5. Zhang, H.: "Shàng/xià" yǔyì yǎnhuà de rènzhī kǎochá [To explore the semantic evolution of "Shang/Xia" from cognitive angle] (MA). Huazhong Univ. Sci. Technol. (2004). (in Chinese)
6. Su, I.W., Liu, H.M.: Metaphorical extension and lexical meaning. In: Proceedings of the 13th Pacific Asia Conference on Language, Information and Computation, pp. 63–74. National Cheng Kung University, Taiwan (1999)
7. Shan, B.S., Xiao, L.: "Xià" de yǔfǎhuà lìchéng [The Diachrony about "Xia"]. J. Changchun Norm. Univ. (Humanit. Soc. Sci.) **28**(2), 75–80 (2009). (in Chinese)
8. Wang, Li.: Hànyǔ fāngwèi cí "qián、hòu、lǐ、wài" yánjiū [A Study of Chinese Spatial Prepositions qián, hòu, lǐ, wài] (MA) Henan University (2005). (in Chinese)
9. Wu, F.X.: Hànyǔ fāngsuǒ cíyǔ "hòu" de yǔyì yǎnbiàn [Semantic evolution of the Chinese spatial preposition hòu]. Stud. Chin. Lang. **6**, 494–506 (2007). (in Chinese)
10. Wang, H.J., Li, R., Yue, Y.: Héshí yòng "le 2"?——jiān lùn huà zhǔ xiǎnshēn de zhǔguān jìn jù hùdòng shì yǔtǐ [When to Use "le2"? A Discussion on Close Intersubjective Style of Speech]. Collection of Linguistic Studies, vol. 40. The Commercial Press, Beijing (2009). (in Chinese)
11. Tao, H.Y.: The grammar of demonstratives in mandarin conversational discourse: a case study. J. Chin. Linguist. **27**(1), 69–103 (1999)
12. Sinclair, J.: Corpus, Concordance, Collocation. Oxford University Press, Oxford (1991)
13. Stubbs, M.: Text and Corpus Analysis: Computer Assisted Studies of Language and Culture. Blackwell, Oxford (1996)
14. Partington, A.: Patterns and Meanings – Using Corpora for English Language Research and Teaching. John Benjamins, Amsterdam, Philadelphia (1998)
15. Louw, B.: Contextual prosodic theory: bringing semantic prosodies to life. Heffer Chris & Sauntson Helen, pp. 48–94 (2000)
16. Wu, Z., Lan, X.J.: The semantic prosody of "*Youyu*": evidence from corpora. In: Hong, J.F., Zhang, Y., Liu, P. (eds.) CLSW 2019. LNCS, vol. 11831, pp. 654–660. Springer, Cham (2020). https://doi.org/10.1007/978-3-030-38189-9_66
17. Fang, M.: Zhǐshì cí "zhè" hé "nà" zài běijīnghuà zhōng de yǔfǎhuà [The grammaticalization of the demonstratives Zhe and Na In Beijing Mandarin]. Stud. Chin. Lang. **4**, 343–356 (2002). (in Chinese)
18. Comrie, B.: Tense. Cambridge University Press, Cambridge (1985)
19. Lu, S.X.: Xiandai Hanyu Babai Ci. The Commercial Press, Beijing (1999). (in Chinese)
20. Miao, J.: Xīnlǐ tàidù xíngróng cí [The mental attitude adjectives]. Rev. Res. Chin. Lit. **5**, 32–37 (2007). (in Chinese)
21. Wu, J.S.: Temporal behavior of temporal modifiers and its implications:. In: Wu, Y., Hong, J.F., Su, Q. (eds.) CLSW 2017. LNCS, vol. 10709, pp. 86–96. Springer, Cham (2018). https://doi.org/10.1007/978-3-319-73573-3_7
22. Jasinskaja, K., Elena, K.: Rhetorical relations. In: Gutzmann, D., Matthewson, L., Meier, C., Rullmann, H., Zimmermann, T.E. (eds.) The Wiley Blackwell Companion to Semantics, pp. 1–29 (2020). https://doi.org/10.1002/9781118788516.sem061

Sociolinguistic Aspects of Popular Abbreviations in Hong Kong Cantonese

Ken Siu-kei Cheng[(✉)] and Ka-wai Ho

The Hong Kong Polytechnic University, Hung Hom, Hong Kong
`ken.cheng@polyu.edu.hk`

Abstract. This paper aims to study certain popular abbreviations in Hong Kong Cantonese in recent years from a sociolinguistic perspective so as to understand their characteristics and uniqueness. It was found that these abbreviations come from different languages and regions, and different strategies such as Cantonese romanization acronym and translation of foreign languages into Chinese characters were used in the process of abbreviation. In terms of grammar, they are mainly composed of adverb-verb and verb-object structures, and the part of speech may change in some cases. Some abbreviations also have rhetorical effects related to homonyms or taboos. These abbreviations are mastered by younger generations and are mostly used in informal domains. The main consideration for adopting abbreviations is of practical concern as well as their function of "insider communication". Respondents rated Cantonese abbreviations as overall positive.

Keyword: Hong Kong Cantonese · Abbreviations · Contraction Strategies · Domain

1 Introduction

Different scholars hold slightly different views about the abbreviations and their related concepts (cf. Yu [9]; Chen [2]). This paper is based on the definition of Yu [9] and refers to the discussion of Guo [4] before positing some conditions. Yu [9] postulates, the abbreviation of words is a name for commonly used polyphonic words, phrases, or in some fixed forms, in which some of the partial forms represent the whole in the development of diachronics, under the premise that the meaning remains unchanged, it becomes a basic unit of discourse. In this regard, two limiting conditions for abbreviations are proposed here:

(1) An abbreviation must have a relatively fixed full form that corresponds to it;
(2) An abbreviation must shorten or omit certain linguistic units of the full form.

For example, in Hong Kong Cantonese, 狗衝 *gau2 cong1*[1] is generally used to describe "like a dog rushing forward blindly" (Lai [7]). It is also interpreted as "males

---

[1] The Cantonese romanization scheme "Jyutping" of the Linguistic Society of Hong Kong [6] is adopted throughout the whole paper.

M. Dong et al. (Eds.): CLSW 2023, LNAI 14514, pp. 90–100, 2024.
https://doi.org/10.1007/978-981-97-0583-2_8

rushing toward a subject stimulated by the outside world like a dog" (5.Hong Kong Internet Encyclopedia Website [5]). Nevertheless, these are merely explanations and not fixed full forms, which do not meet condition (1), so they cannot be considered abbreviations. Furthermore, such as the popular term 姜糖 *goeng1tong2*, although there is a relatively fixed full name (姜濤粉絲 *goeng1 tou4 fan2 si1* "Fans of Keung To[2]"), the word 糖 *tong2* in that term is not abbreviated from the linguistic unit of the full form, which does not meet condition (2), and therefore it cannot be considered an abbreviation, it is just a nickname or alias. There is also a numeral generalized statement, like 雙失 *soeng1 sat1*"dual loss" (失學兼失業 *sat1 hok6 gim1 sat1 jip6* "dropping out of school and unemployed"). Chen [2] and Wu [8] consider it a kind of abbreviation, but Guo [4] holds a negative stance. According to the above-mentioned limiting conditions, this paper agrees with the latter view. There is no corresponding linguistic unit for 雙 *soeng1* in the full statement 失學兼失業 *sat1 hok6 gim1 sat1 jip6*; likewise, similar expressions like 三國 *saam1 gwok3* "Three Kingdoms" (魏 *ngai6*, 蜀 *suk6*, 吳 *ng4*), 五常 *ng5 soeng4* "Five Constant Virtues" (仁 *jan4*, 義 *ji6*, 禮 *lai5*,智 *zi3*, 信 *seon3* "Benevolence, Righteousness, Propriety, Wisdom, Fidelity"), none of them have adopted any linguistic unit from the complete statement, so they do not meet condition (2). This paper does not consider these as abbreviations but refers to them as general terms.

Based on the definition and limiting conditions mentioned above, this paper has collected some examples of popular abbreviations in Hong Kong Cantonese from the observation of the media, the internet, and daily communication. Observations and analysis have been conducted from different perspectives to understand its uniqueness as well as users' views and attitudes.

2 Some Characteristics of Popular Abbreviations in Hong Kong Cantonese

Based on the aforementioned definition, we collected 30 examples of Hong Kong Cantonese abbreviations through the observation of people's daily communication and different channels such as the media and the internet, for further exploration[3]. Furthermore, we have used WisersOne news database to search for the occurrences of these abbreviations in all major and minor newspaper media and web media throughout Hong Kong in the past five years to confirm that these terms are widely used among the public. These abbreviations can be divided into general, traffic, society, politics, entertainment, swear words, food and drink, and video games, as shown below:

---

[2] Keung To (姜濤), Hong Kong male artist, singer and actor, currently a member of the Hong Kong boy band MIRROR.

[3] Referencing web resources include: Trendy Expression Dictionary (https://hkdic.my-helper. com/), "Google Hong Kong 2021 Search" Trendy Expression List (https://trends.google. com.hk/trends/yis/2021/HK/), 2021 Yahoo search "Top Ten Trendy Expressions" ranking list (https://ynews.page.link/VbQy), etc.

Table 1. The abbreviations studied in this paper

No.	Abbreviation	Full form	Meaning	Category
1.	世一 sai3 jat1	世界第一 sai3 gaai3 dai6 jat1	The best in the world	General
2.	LM	留名 lau4 ming4	Leave a name	General
3.	盲反 maang4 faan2	盲目反對 maang4 muk6 faan2 deoi3	Blind opposition	General
4.	脫單 tyut3 daan1	脫離單身 tyut3 lei4 daan1 san1	Get rid of being single	General
5.	中同 zung1 tung4	中學同學 zung1 hok6 tung4 hok6	Secondary school class-mate	General
6.	八半 baat3 bun3	八點半 baat3 dim2 bun3	Eight thirty (8:30)	General
7.	PM	Private Message	Private Message	General
8.	巴迷 baa1 mai4	巴士迷 baa1 si2 mai4	Bus fan	Traffic
9.	巴總 baa1 zung2	巴士總站 baa1 si2 zung2 zaam6	Bus terminal	Traffic
10.	港女 gong2 neoi2	香港女性 hoeng1 gong2 neoi5 sing3	Hong Kong girls	Society
11.	醉駕 zeoi3 gaa3	醉酒後駕駛 zeoi3 zau2 hau6 gaa3 sai2	Drink and drive	Society
12.	藥駕 joek6 gaa3	濫藥後駕駛 laam6 joek6 hau6 gaa3 sai2	Drug and drive	Society
13.	法援 faat3 wun4	法律援助 faat3 leot6 wun4 zo6	Legal aid	Society
14.	綜援 zung1 wun4	綜合援助 zung3 hap6 wun4 zo6	Comprehensive Social Security Assistance	Society
15.	企跳 kei2 tiu3	企圖跳樓 kei5 tou4 tiu3 lau2	Attempt to jump off a building	Society
16.	港豬 gong2 zyu1	香港豬民 hoeng1 gong2 zyu1 man4	Hong Kong "Pig", i.e. politically apathetic individuals	Politics
17.	和理非非 wo4 lei5 fei1 fei1	和平、理性、非暴力、非粗口 wo4 ping4 lei5 sing3 fei1 bou6 lik6 fei1 cou1 hau2	Peace, Rationality, Nonviolence, No Swear Words	Politics
18.	逃恥 tou4 ci2	《逃避可恥但有用》 tou4 bei6 ho2 ci2 daan6 jau5 jung6	"The Evasion Is Shameful But Useful", a TV drama	Entertainment
19.	神劇 san4 kek6	神級劇集 san4 kap1 kek6 zaap6	Epic drama	Entertainment
20.	膠劇 gaau1 kek6	硬膠劇集 ngaang6 gaau1 kek6 zaap6	Crap drama	Entertainment
21.	網紅 mong5 hung4	網絡紅人 mong5 lok3 hung4 jan4	Internet influencer	Entertainment

(continued)

Table 1. (*continued*)

No.	Abbreviation	Full form	Meaning	Category
22.	鏡粉 geng3 fan2	MIRROR[4]粉絲 *MIRROR fan2 si1*	Fan of MIRROR, a music group	Entertainment
23.	爵屎 zoek3 si2	呂爵安[5]FAN屎 *leoi5 zoek3 on1 fen1 si2*	Fan of Edan Lui	Entertainment
24.	嚫模 leng1 mou4	嚫妹模特兒 *leng1 mui1 mou4 dak6 ji4*	Young female model	Entertainment
25.	CLS	黐撚線 *ci1 lan2 sin3*	Go crazy	Swear words
26.	JM9	做乜鳩 *zou6 mat1 gau1*	What the hell	Swear words
27.	SLS	笑撚死 *siu3 lan2 sei2*	Dying of laughter	Swear words
28.	珍奶 zan1 naai5	珍珠奶茶 *zan1 zyu1 naai5 caa4*	Bubble milk tea	Food & drink
29.	FF	Final Fantasy	Final Fantasy	Video games
30.	GG	Good Game	It's Over	Video games

We first collected popular examples and then tried to categorize them. We did not deliberately pursue an equal number of examples for each category, but it does not affect the analysis in the paper. Below we will preliminarily analyze some characteristics of these abbreviations from the perspectives of sources, abbreviation strategies, syllables, grammar, and rhetoric.

2.1 Sources

These popular abbreviations come from different sources. In terms of language, some are derived from Japanese (such as 逃げるは恥だが役に立つ "Escape is shameful, but it is useful," abbreviated as 逃げ恥 "Escape is shame" and then referred to as 逃恥 *tou4 ci2*), and from English (such as "Final Fantasy" is abbreviated as "FF," and "Private Message" is abbreviated as "PM"); in terms of regions, some are derived from Mainland China (such as 網絡紅人 *mong5 lok3 hung4 jan4* are abbreviated as 網紅 *mong5 hung4*, and 脫離單身 *tyut3 lei4 daan1 san1* is abbreviated as 脫單 *tyut3 daan1*), Taiwan (such as 珍珠奶茶 *zan1 zyu1 naai5 caa4* is abbreviated as 珍奶 *zan1 naai5*), and of course there are ones from Hong Kong itself (such as MIRROR 粉絲 *MIRROR fan2 si1* are abbreviated as 鏡粉 *geng3 fan2*, and 嚫妹模特兒 *leng1 mui1 mou4 dak6 ji4* is abbreviated as 嚫模 *leng1 mou4*).

2.2 Abbreviation Strategies

In terms of abbreviation strategies (referring to Wu [8]), they can be mainly divided into: First, extracting Chinese characters (such as 和平、理性、非暴力、非粗口 *wo4 ping4 lei5 sing3 fei1 bou6 lik6 fei1 cou1 hau2* abbreviated as 和理非非 *wo4 lei5 fei1 fei1*); second, using the initial of Cantonese romanization (such as 黐撚線 *ci1 lan2 sin3* abbreviated as CLS); third, substituting with numeric homophones (like 做乜鳩 *zou6 mat1 gau1* abbreviated as JM9); fourth, translating foreign languages into monosyllabic Chinese characters (like MIRROR 鏡粉 *MIRROR fan2 si1* abbreviated as 粉絲 *geng3 fan2*).

2.3 Syllable Characteristics

The characteristics can primarily be categorized as follows: First, disyllabic abbreviations (such as 神級劇集 *san4 kap1 kek6 zaap6* abbreviated as 神劇 *san4 kek6*); second, trisyllabic abbreviations (like 笑撚死 *siu3 lan2 sei2* abbreviated as SLS); third, quadrisyllabic abbreviations (like 和平、理性、非暴力、非粗口 *wo4 ping4 lei5 sing3 fei1 bou6 lik6 fei1 cou1 hau2* abbreviated as 和理非非 *wo4 lei5 fei1 fei1*). As mentioned in Chen & Luo [1], the most easily found abbreviations are disyllabic, followed by trisyllabic, and the fewest are quadrisyllabic.

2.4 Grammatical Features

In terms of grammatical features, most abbreviations retain the word classes or sentence elements of the full form, such as nouns: 中學同學 *zung1 hok6 tung4 hok6* abbreviated as 中同 *zung1 tung4*, and 八點半 *baat3 dim2 bun3* abbreviated as 八半 *baat3 bun3*; Verbs: 盲目反對 *maang4 muk6 faan2 deoi3* abbreviated as 盲反 *maang4 faan2*, and 脫離單身 *tyut3 lei4 daan1 san1* abbreviated as 脫單 *tyut3 daan1*. However, there are also exceptions, mostly when nouns are converted into verbs. For instance, Final Fantasy is originally the name of a video game, which is a noun, but when abbreviated as FF in Hong Kong Cantonese it becomes a verb meaning excessive fantasy (such as "唔好FF咁多啦 *m4 hou2 FF gam3 do1 laa1*", which means "Don't fancy too much"); similarly, Private Message is a noun, but after being abbreviated to PM in Cantonese, it acts like a transitive verb (like "記得PM我 *gei3 dak1 PM ngo5*" "Remember to send me a PM").

From the perspective of grammatical structure, full forms of different grammatical structures have examples of abbreviations, such as the joint structure 和平、理性、非暴力、非粗口 *wo4 ping4 lei5 sing3 fei1 bou6 lik6 fei1 cou1 hau2* abbreviated as 和理非非 *wo4 lei5 fei1 fei1*), modifier-head structure 神級劇集 *san4 kap1 kek6 zaap6* abbreviated as 神劇 *san4 kek6*, 盲目反對 *maang4 muk6 faan2 deoi3* abbreviated as 盲反 *maang4 faan2*), predicate-object structure 脫離單身 *tyut3 lei4 daan1 san1* abbreviated as 脫單 *tyut3 daan1*, 做乜鳩 *zou6 mat1 gau1* abbreviated as JM9), predicate-complement structure (笑撚死 *siu3 lan2 sei2* abbreviated as SLS), and subject-predicate structure (腦內補完 *nou5 noi6 bou2 jyun4* "Finish in mind" abbreviated as 腦補 *nou5 bou2*, which is out of the above list). There are also examples of entire sentences being abbreviated, like《逃避可恥但有用》 *tou4 bei6 ho2 ci2 daan6 jau5 jung6* abbreviated into 逃恥 *tou4 ci2*. However, the modifier-head and predicate-object structures are the most common.

2.5   Rhetorical Effect

Some abbreviations also have rhetorical effects. The first is homophonic puns (Chin [3]) like the abbreviation 爵屎 *zoek3 si2*, being the homophone of 雀屎 *zoek3 si2* "bird droppings," which can also harmonize with 爵士 *zoek3 si6* "nobility"; and another one is 香港居民 hoeng1 gong2 geoi1 man4 "Hong Kong residents" homophonically pronounced in Mandarin as 香港豬民 "Hong Kong pig people" (the Mandarin pronunciation of 居 *jū* "reside" is similar to the pronunciation of 豬 *zyu1* "pig" in Cantonese), meaning politically apathetic individuals, which is further abbreviated as 港豬 *gong2 zyu1*.

Moreover, euphemisms are also a type of rhetoric. In the abbreviation strategy, many of those using Cantonese romanization initials as abbreviations or numeric homophones as substitutes (see Sect. 2.2.) fall into the category of swear words. For instance: 撚 *lan2* in 黐撚線 *ci1 lan2 sin3* and 笑撚死 *siu3 lan2 sei2*, and 鳩 *gau1* in 做乜鳩 *zou6 mat1 gau1* are all swear words, in their abbreviations the phonetic initial "L" and numeric homophone "9" are employed respectively to avoid using the vulgar language.

3   Sociolinguistic Findings

This paper also attempts to explore the characteristics of these abbreviations at the pragmatics or socio-psychological level. This section collects data through an online questionnaire. The questionnaire data was collected via Google Forms from December 10–17, 2021. The sample size was 132 individuals, all Cantonese speakers and people who have lived in Hong Kong for at least ten years and/or whose native families communicate in Cantonese. Males and females respectively make up 45.5% (60 respondents) and 54.5% (72 respondents) of the sample; in terms of age groups, 15.1% (20 respondents) are 11–20 years old, 25.8% (34 respondents) are 21–30 years old, 21.9% (34 respondents) are 31–40 years old, 34.1% (34 respondents) are 41–50 years old, and only 3.1% (4 respondents) are over 51 years old.

3.1   Analysis by Age Group

The first part of the questionnaire asks which of the abbreviations listed in Fig. 1 are recognizable to the respondents. The following compares the recognition rates of these abbreviations among different age groups[4]:

---

[4] There were only 4 people over the age of 51 in the sample, and they were excluded from the age group analysis.

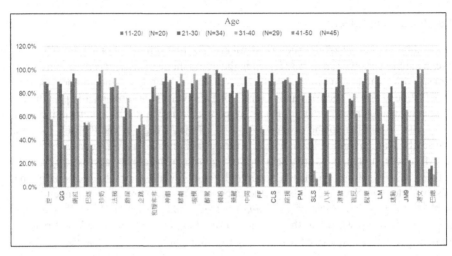

Fig. 1. Recognition of different abbreviations (comparison across age groups)

From the above figure, it can be seen that overall, the younger generation (30 years old and above) has a higher recognition rate of these abbreviations (average recognition rate of 83%); the second is the 31–40 age group (average recognition rate of 79.9%), and the 41–50 age group's grasp of these abbreviations is significant lower (average recognition rate of 64.5%).

Upon closer observation, it can be found that those with similar mastery rates across age groups are generally more formal abbreviations, like 醉駕 *zeoi3 gaa3* (the difference between different age groups is no more than 2.1%), 綜援 *zung1 wun4* (the difference between different age groups is no more than 4.2%); for newer abbreviations, like "SLS," there are significant differences between the groups, and the mastery level decreases with age (11–20 years old: 80%; 21–30 years old: 41.2%; 31–40 years old: 13.8%; 41–50 years old: 6.7%). From this, it can be inferred that new abbreviations are often derived from the youngest group, and then gradually spread to the older groups.

3.2   Analysis by Domain

The second part of the questionnaire proposed five different scenarios: communication with families, communication with friends, chatting online, examinations, and job interviews, corresponding respectively to five domains: family, friendship, entertainment, education, and work. It asked whether the respondents would use each of the abbreviations listed in Table 1 in those scenarios (either verbal or written usage), and sought to understand the reasons for using or not using abbreviations in those scenarios. The following compares the usage rates of these abbreviations in different domains:

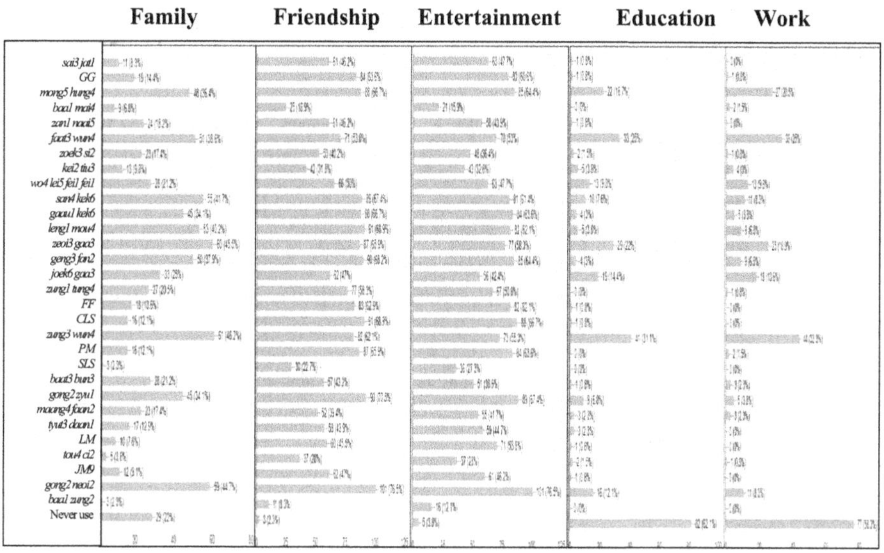

Family	Friendship	Entertainment	Education	Work

Fig. 2. The usage of different abbreviations (comparison across domains)

From Fig. 2, it can be seen that the abbreviations examined in this paper are mostly used in informal domains. It is most common among friends (friendship domain) and in online chats (entertainment domain). Among the 30 abbreviations examined, there are 26 abbreviations used by 30% or more of the respondents in each case, and there are 16 abbreviations used by more than half of the respondents in these two domains. Next is when communicating with family members (family domain). Among the 30 abbreviations examined, there are 10 abbreviations used by 30% or more of the respondents, but no abbreviations are used by more than half of the respondents in this domain. Overall, in the three informal domains of family, friendship, and entertainment, the usage rates of each abbreviation are roughly proportional. However, the proportion using swear words is significantly smaller in the family domain, with usage rates only between 2.3% and 12.1%.

As for the more formal scenarios of exams (education domain) and job interviews (work domain), over 80% and over 70% of respondents respectively indicated that they would never use these abbreviations in these situations. Among the abbreviations, only one - 綜援 *zung1 wun4* from the society category - is used by over 30% of respondents. Other slightly more commonly used abbreviations like 法援 *faat3 wun4* and 醉駕 *zeoi3 gaa3* are also from the society category, with the only exception being 網紅 *mong5 hung4* from the entertainment category, but this is also a kind of social phenomenon.

The following analyzes the main reasons for respondents' use or non-use of abbreviations in different domains.

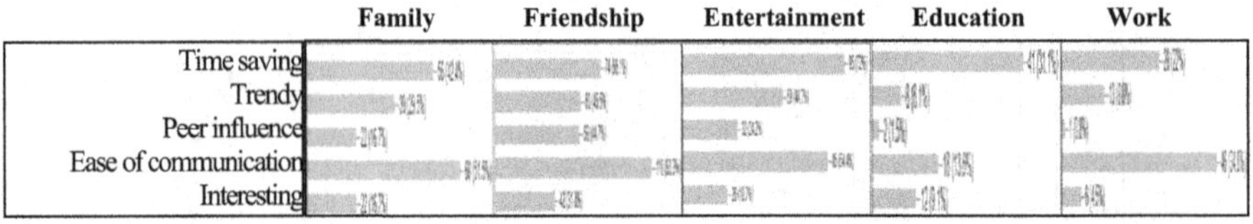

	Family	Friendship	Entertainment	Education	Work
Time saving					
Trendy					
Peer influence					
Ease of communication					
Interesting					

Fig. 3. Main reasons for using abbreviations (comparison across domains)

	Family	Friendship	Entertainment	Education	Work
The other doesn't understand					
Impolite					
Ungrammatical					
Informal					
Giving an impression of laziness					

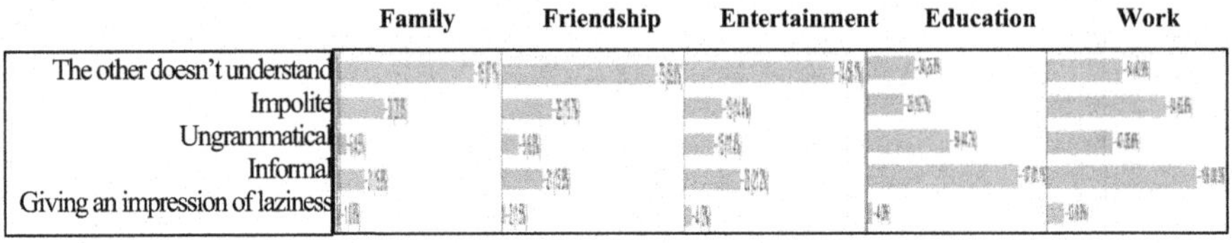

Fig. 4. Main reasons for not using abbreviations (comparison across domains)

Based on Fig. 3, the primary reason for using abbreviations fundamentally lies in pragmatic considerations (time-saving, ease of communication), these reasons being the most prevalent across all linguistic domains. As for the affective aspect, such as peer influence, being interesting or trendy, these are secondary considerations.

Figure 4 illustrates that the primary reason for not using abbreviations also stems from pragmatic considerations. In linguistic domains such as family, friendship and entertainment, the consideration of whether the other party understands the meaning is the top priority, accounting for between 56.1% and 87.1% of responses. However, in more formal linguistic domains such as education and work, whether or not a word is formally used is the primary consideration (accounting for 81.1% and 80.3% respectively). Abbreviations are considered to be informal, thus respondents tend to avoid using them.

An overview of these two figures reveals a seemingly contradictory phenomenon: while most respondents view abbreviations as "easy to communicate" (as illustrated in Fig. 3), they simultaneously fear that "others might not understand the meaning" (as shown in Fig. 4). In reality, this reflects that abbreviations serve as a form of "insider communication" or secret language, promoting communication internally while potentially excluding others.

3.3 Overall Evaluation

Section three of the questionnaire asked respondents about the overall impact of abbreviation usage on Cantonese. Here are some main responses (Fig. 5).

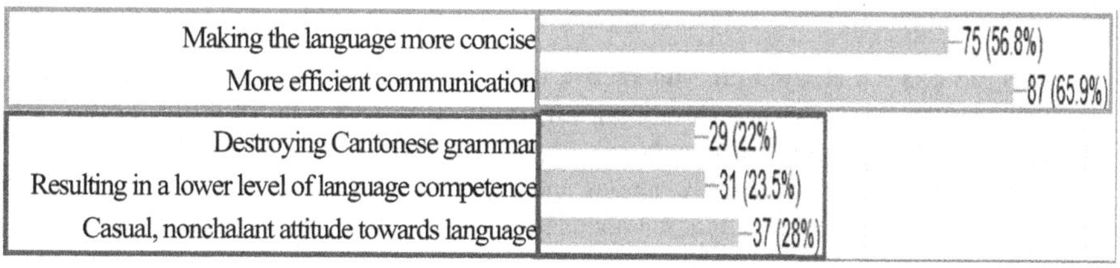

Making the language more concise	-75 (56.8%)
More efficient communication	-87 (65.9%)
Destroying Cantonese grammar	-29 (22%)
Resulting in a lower level of language competence	-31 (23.5%)
Casual, nonchalant attitude towards language	-37 (28%)

Fig. 5. Main impact of using abbreviations on Cantonese as perceived by the respondents

If these responses were categorized into positive, negative and neutral, "making the language more concise" and "more efficient communication" would be positive evaluations; "destroying Cantonese grammar", "resulting in a lower level of language competence", "casual, nonchalant attitude towards language" would be negative evaluations. The percentages reveal that positive evaluations (56.8%–65.9%) far exceed negative evaluations (22%–28%).

There were 22 individual remarks, each raised by a single respondent (accounting for 0.8% each). Among these, there were 13 positive comments (like "makes Cantonese more interesting", "makes the conversation lively and interesting", "having a common language makes it easy to bring up topics and resonate", "more contemporary features", "greater lexicon", "identifying, reinforcing generational identity" etc.), 8 neutral remarks ("no comment", "cannot generalize", "language evolves with cultural shifts, always developing" etc.), and merely one negative comment ("some abbreviations imported from other Chinese-speaking regions affect the tradition of Cantonese vocabulary and cause weird phonetic situations"). Therefore, the overall evaluation of abbreviations by respondents is positive.

4 Conclusions

This study finds that popular Cantonese abbreviations in Hong Kong originate from different languages and regions, with various abbreviation strategies adopted (including extracting Chinese characters, Cantonese romanization initials, homophonic numeric substitution, translating foreign words into Chinese characters). Some abbreviations involve a change in part of speech (from noun to verb). These abbreviations originate from different grammatical structures, but primarily from modifier-head and predicate-object structures. Some individual abbreviations present homophonic or avoiding taboos rhetorical effects. From a sociolinguistic perspective, the younger generation (30 years old or below) has better command over these abbreviations. Furthermore, abbreviations are prevalently used in informal linguistic domains like family, friendship, and entertainment, being less used in formal linguistic domains like education (exams) and work (job interviews). The main reason to use abbreviations is the pragmatic aspect, the affective aspect is secondary. Abbreviations also function as insider communication or secret language. Overall, the respondents' evaluation of Cantonese abbreviations is positive.

References

1. Chen, S., Luo, J.: A study on the interactive relationships between the formation of three-syllable abbreviations and the prosody. In: Lu, Q., Gao, H. (eds.) CLSW 2015. LNCS, vol. 9332, pp. 270–280. Springer, Cham (2015). https://doi.org/10.1007/978-3-319-27194-1_28
2. Chen, S.L.: A redefinition of abbreviations and acronyms in Chinese and a study of neologisms. In: The Seventh World Chinese Language Teaching Conference. Taipei: World Chinese Language Education Association, Taipei (2003)
3. Chin, C.O.: The Linguistics of Fandom. Echo, October 2021
4. Guo, G.Q.: A discussion on the definition of acronyms and related issues. J. Soc. Sci. Jiamusi Univ. **2009**(6), 63–65 (2009)
5. Hong Kong Internet Encyclopedia Website. https://evchk.fandom.com/zh/wiki/%E7%8B%97%E8%A1%9D. Accessed 31 Dec 2021
6. Jyutping: The Linguistic Society of Hong Kong Cantonese Romanization Scheme. https://jyutping.org/en/jyutping/. Accessed 15 Oct 2023
7. Lai, Q.Y.: A study on the word formation of trendy language in Hong Kong and Mainland China. In: The First Symposium of Four Hong Kong and Taiwan Universities on Undergraduate Papers. Hong Kong: Hong Kong Shue Yan University, Hong Kong (2017)
8. Wu, J.X.: A study on the lexical and grammatical features of new abbreviations. J. Huzhou Norm. Univ. **2013**(1), 94–98 (2013)
9. Yu, L.M.: The definition and interpretation of word abbreviation. J. Sichuan Univ. (Philos. Soc. Sci.) **2000**(2), 124–128 (2000)

The Semantic Features and Construal Mechanisms of the Expectational Negative Adverb *Kong* in Mandarin

Jinghan Zeng[1]([✉]) and Yulin Yuan[2,3]

[1] Beijing Normal University, Beijing 100875, China
jhzeng@bnu.edu.cn
[2] Peking University, Beijing 100871, China
[3] University of Macau, Macau 999078, China

Abstract. This paper examines the synchronic semantic features and pragmatic functions, as well as construal mechanisms of the adverb *kong* in Mandarin from multiple perspectives. First, it introduces the phenomenon of implicit negation in Mandarin and the main issues of this paper in the introduction part. Then, the synchronous semantic versatility of *kong* in Mandarin are summarized in the second part, revealing its implicit negative features that differ from dominant negation in the third part. Furthermore, the fourth part analyzes the expectational negative function brought about by the implicit negation of *kong* and extracts the speaker's intentions during speech communication from extensive natural language materials. This paper finds that the adverb *kong* carries implicit negative meaning, enabling it to negate the shared expectations of both conversational participants. These expectations represent the felicity condition, where both parties believe the proposition should have been met. The expectational negation reflects various subjective intentions of the speaker, such as the belief that the VP-event should not occur or that the VP-event should yield specific results. It also showcases ultimate humanistic care through empathy with the listener.

Keywords: The adverb *kong* · Expectational negation · Construal mechanisms

1 Introduction: Implicit Negation and the Adverb *Kong* in Mandarin

All languages employ mechanisms to convey negation, each exhibiting its unique nuances. In Mandarin, negation primarily employs an analytic form. This structure involves prefixing verbs or verbal phrases (VP) with negation markers such as *bu* (not) or *mei* (not/haven't), thereby creating a Neg.*Implicit*+VP construction to negate the intended VP. For instance, consider the following (1a–a'):

(1) a. 看 ~ 没看

kan mei kan

look Neg. look

Read ~ haven't read

a'. 我看过那本书。 ～ 我没看过那本书。

wo kan-guo na-ben shu. wo mei kan-guo na-ben shu.

I look-Perf. that book   I Neg. look-Perf. that book.[1]

I have read that book.   I haven't read that book.

However, Mandarin also features several adverbs that, while not overtly negative, carry implicit negative undertones. When affixed to a verb, they create an $Neg._{Implicit} + VP$ structure, conveying a subtle negative sentiment. The statements thus negated can entail a proposition with explicit negation markers. For instance, consider the following (2a–b):

(2) a. 我是真正为她心疼，为自己白吃白喝感到羞愧。

wo shi zhen-zheng wei ta xin-teng, wei zi-ji bai chi bai he gan-dao xiu-kui.

I genuinely feel compassion for her and am embarrassed by consuming without offering compensation.)

白吃白喝

Bai chi bai he → Consuming with **no** payment or consuming with **no** compensation.

Adv. Eat Adv. drink

bai: Getting something but do **not** pay any obligation or cost

b. 要调动科学和教育工作者的积极性，空讲不行，还要给他们创造条件。

yao diao-dong ke-xue he jiao-yu gong-zuo-zhe de ji-ji-xing, kong jiang bu-xing, hai yao gei ta-men chuang-zao tiao-jian.

To motivate scientists and educators, mere rhetoric falls short; it is imperative to provide them with the right conditions.

空讲

kong jiang → Advocating principles with **no** actual application.

Adv. talk

kong: Doing something but do **not** genuinely act

In Example (2), the adverbs *bai* and *kong* modify the verbal phrases, imbuing them with implicit negative sentiments, akin to a form of compound negation. Yuan, Y (2012) research on verbs with implicit negation termed this form *implicit negation*, which lacks clear negation markers [1]. Zeng, J & Yuan, Y (2018, 2021) extensively explored the inherent negation attributes and semantic trajectory of the adverb *bai* [2, 3]. While *kong* and *bai* share similarities in their inherent semantics, *kong* presents a more intricate semantic construal. For instance, the phrase *kong jiang dao-li* implies the endorsement of primary principles without subsequent action. However, some English machine translations misinterpret this as *empty preaching* (a literal translation of *kong*) or *speaking the truth in vain*, misconstruing the essence of *kong*. Such interpretation errors involving *kong*

---

[1] Neg.- Negation, Perf.- Perfective marker, Adv.- Adverb.

are widespread in both machine translations and Chinese teaching for non-native speakers. Examining the semantic structure, construal mechanisms, and functional attributes of *kong* provides a remedy for these challenges. Therefore, this paper delves into the semantic feature, the semantic structure and construal mechanisms associated with the adverb *kong*. We argue that a profound understanding of these elements can significantly benefit the fields of Chinese information processing and teaching Chinese as a foreign language.

2   The Implicit Negative Meanings of the Adverb *Kong* in Modern Mandarin

In Mandarin, when *kong* is used as an adverb, it conveys two meanings, as in ①–② [4]:

① Engaging in an activity ineffectually or without achieving the desired outcome, as seen in examples such as *kong mang* (busy in vain) and *kong pao* (run in vain).
② Engaging in actions without substantive content or real action, as seen in examples such as *kong han* (shout without meaning) and *kong tan* (talk without substance).

These two usages are common in Mandarin and have implicit negation features. When they modify verb structures, they often result in statements that entail explicit negation markers such as *bu* (not) and *mei* (haven't) [5]. For instance, consider the following:

(3) a. 业内人士分析，杭州前几家集散中心采取的是松散的市场式联合体，本身只提供场地，由进驻的景区开出专线车，一旦有点变故就取消专线，往往让市民<u>空</u>跑一趟。

Industry insiders analyzed that the initial consolidation centers in Hangzhou adopted a loose market consortium model. They merely provided venues, with individual scenic areas operating dedicated transportation routes. If there was any mishap, these routes were canceled, often leaving citizens to make a trip in vain.

→ b. 业内人士分析，杭州前几家集散中心采取的是松散的市场式联合体，本身只提供场地，由进驻的景区开出专线车，一旦有点变故就取消专线，往往让市民跑一趟却<u>坐不上</u>专线车。

Industry insiders analyze that the initial consolidation centers in Hangzhou adopted a loose market consortium model. They merely provided venues, with individual scenic areas operating dedicated transportation routes. If there is any mishap, these routes are canceled, often leaving citizens without access to the dedicated transportation buses.

(4) a. 要调动科学和教育工作者的积极性，空讲不行，还要给他们创造条件；切切实实地帮助他们解决一些具体问题。

To motivate scientists and educators, mere rhetoric falls short; it is imperative to provide them with the right conditions, such as genuinely assisting them in addressing specific problems.

→ b. 要调动科学和教育工作者的积极性，讲了道理却没有实际行动不行，还要给他们创造条件，切切实实地帮助他们解决一些具体问题。

To motivate scientists and educators, talking principles without actionable steps will not work; it is imperative to provide them with the right conditions, such as genuinely assisting them in addressing specific problems.

In Examples (3–4a), *kong* signifies either *Doing something ineffectually or without achieving the desired outcome* or *Acting without substantive content or real action*. When modifying verb structures, both can result in statements that incorporate explicit negation markers, as seen in Examples (3–4b). The compound form conveys that the proposition which VP represents lacks the expected outcome: the anticipated results following an action or subsequent steps after expressing an opinion. The implicit negation encapsulated by *kong* is integral to its monosyllabic form, representing synthetic negation that is distinctly different from Mandarin's explicit analytic negation, such as *bu* VP and *mei* VP (as shown in Examples 1–2). Thus, when both negation forms co-occur with negation markers, they present starkly different semantic expressions. For instance, consider the following:

(5) a. I will **not** go to Jimmy's school today. ~ a'. I will go to Jimmy's school today.

   b. **It's not that** I won't go to Jimmy's school today. ≈ b'. I would like to go to Jimmy's school today.

(6) a. Je **ne** prends **pas** de desserts. ~ a'. Je prends du desserts.

   I Neg. eat Neg. Def. dessert   I eat   Def.   Dessert.[2]

   I don't eat desserts.   I eat desserts.

   b. **Ce n'est pas que** je **ne** prends **pas** de desserts. ≈ b'. Je peux prendre du desserts.

   Pron. Neg.Pron.I Neg. eat   Def. dessert I Aux. eat Def. dessert

   It's not that I don't eat fish.   I (can) eat fish.

(7) a. 我空等一个月。 ≠ a'. ~我等了一个月。

   wo kong deng yi-ge yue.   wo deng-le yi ge yue.

   I waited in vain for a month. I waited for a month.

   b. 我没空等一个月。 ≠ b'. 我等了一个月。

   wo mei kong deng yi ge yue. wo deng-le yi-ge yue.

   I Neg. Adv. wait a month I wait a month

   I didn't wait in vain for a month. I waited for a month.

   c. 我没空等一个月，只等了半个月。

   wo mei kong deng yi-ge yue, zhi deng-le ban-ge yue.

   I Neg. Adv. wait a month only wait half month

   I didn't wait in vain for a month, I only waited for half a month.

---

[2] Pron.- pronoun, Def.- definite article, Aux.- auxiliary.

Examples (5a–6a) represent explicit negation in English, and French. They are constructed by adding negation markers such as *bu, not*, or inserting verbs into negation structures such as *ne...pas*. When these negation markers are removed, the result is the corresponding affirmative forms (Examples 5a–6a), which have meanings opposite to their negated versions. When further negation is applied to these explicit negations (Examples 5b–6b), the two negations effectively cancel each other out, making the meaning roughly equivalent to the affirmative VP (Examples 5b–6b). However, the adverb *kong*, which carries implicit negation, exhibits a significant distinction from this pattern, as illustrated in Examples (7a–c). When *kong* is removed, the resulting affirmative proposition (Example 7a) does not semantically oppose the structure with the implicit negative adverb (Example 7a). Moreover, when negation is applied to the implicit negation (as in Example 7b), the negations do not cancel each other out. The resulting meaning is significantly different from the affirmative VP. It may encompass only a portion of the VP's event meaning (Example 7c). For instance, *mei kong deng yi-ge yue* can mean *didn't wait for an entire month*, in which case the negation *mei* targets *yi-ge yue* (one month).

3   The Expectational Negative Function of the Adverb *Kong*

The transformative overlap between the adverb *kong* and negation markers illustrates a crucial distinction. The targets of implicit negation in *kong* differ from those of explicit negation. Explicit negation uses markers such as *bu, not*, and *ne...pas* to modify the VP structure, thereby negating the event described by the VP. The focus of this negation is on either the lexical truth value or the truth conditions of the sentence proposition. For instance, in *mei kong deng yi-ge yue* (didn't wait in vain for a month), what is negated is *kong deng yi-ge yue* (wait in vain for a month). The negation pertains to the veracity of the facts that words or sentences depict, a phenomenon termed semantic negation. Contrastingly, the implicit negation feature of *kong* diverges. Within the $Neg._{Implicit} + VP$ framework, *kong* negates certain supplemental conditions necessary for a proposition to materialize, such as underlying premises (as seen in *kong jiang*, or advocating principles without actual application) and outcomes (such as *kong deng*, or waiting in vain). This represents a distinct linguistic negation type, termed pragmatic negation. Classic pragmatic negation does not refute the truth value of a sentence's proposition. Instead, it challenges the felicity conditions, or the commonly accepted foundational circumstances for a proposition's realization. For instance, consider the following:

(8) a. *jin-tian tian-qi nuan-he.*
    today weather warm
    The weather is warm today.
b. *jin-tian tian-qi bu nuan-he.*
    today weather Neg. warm
    The weather isn't warm today. (Possibly, it's very cold)
c. *jin-tian tian-qi bu-shi nuan-he, shi yan-re.* [6]
    today weather Neg. warm   is hot
    The weather isn't warm today, it's sweltering.

In Example (8), we observe semantic negation. In (8b), *bu* is used to negate the proposition about warmth, signifying coldness. In contrast, Example (8c) employs pragmatic negation. *Warm* entails a sensation of warmth and comfort, and negating this perception yields *sweltering*. Evidently, semantic and pragmatic negations produce distinct results for the same proposition.

Thus, *kong,* with its pragmatic negative function, refutes the inherent prerequisites or outcomes of the event signified by the proposition, challenging the proposition's felicity conditions. But what are these conditions that *kong* negates? Zhang, Y (1996, 2000) and Cai, K (2013) postulate that *kong* acts as an adverb negating presupposition [7–9]. The refuted object *is not the proposition but the mutually understood context between the speaker and listener*, known as presupposition. While the *negating presupposition* perspective is illuminating, its ambiguity may foster confusion. In logic, a typical method for discerning presupposition is this: if a proposition *p*, in both its affirmative and negative forms, implies a proposition *q*, then *q* is the presupposition of *p*. Absence of such conditions means it is not a presupposition [10–12].

Based on the general definition of presupposition in logic, we extract the propositions represented by the adverb *kong* in natural language materials for testing:

(9) 什么事儿只有先
干、先做了, 才能取得发言权, 掌握主动权。否则, **空讲**一 通不着边际的道理, 怎能赢得人心?[3]

shen-me shi er zhi-you xian-gan, xian-zuo le, cai-neng qu-de fa-yan-quan, zhang-wo zhu-dong-quan. fou-ze, kong jiang yi-tong bu-zhao bian-ji de dao-li, zen-neng ying-de ren-xin?

For anything, you can only talk about it or take initiative with after you have has started or acted on it. Otherwise, if you just spout off irrelevant principles,   how   can   you   win   people over?

a1. 他空讲道理。   →   b. 他讲了道理。
ta kong jiang dao-li.   *ta jiang-le dao-li.*
he Adv. talk principle   he talk   principle
He spoke about the principles without taking action. (9a1)
He spoke about the principles. (9b)

a2. 他没空讲道理。   →   b.他讲了道理。
ta mei kong jiang dao-li.   *ta jiang-le dao-li.*
he Neg. Adv. talk principle   he talk   eprinciple
He didn't just speak about the principles without taking action. (9a2)
He spoke about the principles.(9b)

(10) 过去我们需要购买一些农机小零件或者修理机器的配件, 都要跑一百多里到县城, 有时候还空跑一场, 影响了农业生产。
Guo-qu wo-men xu-yao gou-mai yi-xie nong-ji xiao-ling-jian huo-ze xiu-li ji-qi de pei-jian, dou yao pao yi-bai duo li dao xian-cheng, you shi-hou hai kong pao yi-chang, ying-xiang le nong-ye sheng-chan. In the past, when we needed to purchase some minor agricultural machinery parts or repair parts, we had to travel over fifty

---

[3] The natural language examples in this article, which are not indicated with the source, are all from the CCL Corpus of the Center for Chinese Linguistics, Peking University.

kilometers to the county town. Sometimes, we'd end up making a futile trip, which affected agricultural production.)

a1. 他空跑了一场。   →   b. 他跑了一场。
ta kong pao-le yi-chang.   *ta pao-le yi-chang*
he Adv. run one time   he run one time
He made a futile trip.)   He made a trip.)

a2. 他没空跑一场。   →   b. 他跑了一场。
ta mei kong pao yi-chang.   *ta pao le yi-chang.*
he Neg.Adv. run one time   he run one time
He also got something done.)   He made a trip.

From Examples (9–10), we can infer that propositions formed by the implicit negative adverb *kong* modifying the verbal structure (Examples 9a–10a), imply propositions in Examples (9b–10b), both in the affirmative and negative forms. Therefore, they serve as the presuppositions of Examples 9a–10a. This indeed aligns with the concept of presupposition, which refers to the prerequisite conditions for the proposition *kong* VP to be established, as well as the shared knowledge between the speaker and the listener. However, it's crucial to clarify that this shared knowledge is not what *kong*, negates. For example, *kong jiang* (advocating principles without actual application) indicates actions without practical support, where *kong* negates the expected yet absent actions that should follow the initial action. Similarly, *kong pao* (make a trip in vain) suggests effort expended without the desired outcome, where *kong* negates the anticipated but missing result of an action.

Thus, the content negated by the implicit negative adverb is not the presupposition of the proposition in a strict sense, and the term *negating presupposition* can be misleading. Yuan, Y (2014) distinguishes between two different presuppositions: semantic presupposition and pragmatic presupposition [13]. Negation of the latter nullifies the felicity conditions that a proposition should possess to be established. We can summarize these conditions as involving a moral sense of balance in an event that both the speaker and the listener believe should exist – an ethical pre-judgment or expectation. This expectation includes a balance between cause and effect (as in *kong pao*, or making a trip in vain) and consistency between name and reality (as in *kong jiang*, or advocating principles without actual application). Thus, the implicit negation function of the adverb *kong* belongs to the category of pragmatic negation and can be further classified into the category of negation of expectation.

4 The Function of Evaluation and Subjectivity of the Adverb *Kong*

Based on our previous investigations, it is evident that the adverb *kong* embodies features of implicit negation and negation of expectation. This section explores the distinct functions that these types of negation impart to *kong*. Notably, the majority of adverbs serve an evaluative function, revealing the speaker's subjectivity. Consider the following examples:

(11) 河南 6 名少女被骗做洗头女,获救后还为骗子说情。[4]

he-nan liu ming shao-nv bei pian zuo xi-tou nv, huo-jiu hou hai wei pian-zi shuo-qing.

Six young girls from Henan were deceived into becoming shampoo girls, and even after their rescue, they still advocated for their deceiver.

(12) 我又不知道你说的是谁!

wo you bu zhi-dao ni shuo de shi shei!

I even have no idea whom you're referring to!

(13) 这可不能告诉别人。

zhe ke bu-neng gao-su bie-ren.

This certainly shouldn't be told to others.

In Example (11), *hai* suggests that the speaker perceives the event depicted by VP as unexpected and unreasonable, emanating a sense of surprise. In (12), *you* conveys the speaker's irritation and resistance. Meanwhile, in (13), *ke* serves as a reminder and emphasis.

Shen, J (2001) emphasizes that subjectivity correlates with a speaker's emotions and attitudes [14]. Observably, the adverb *kong* also encapsulates this capacity to convey the speaker's subjective position, emotions, and perspectives. To elaborate, this subjectivity reflects the speaker's ex-post contemplation and assessment, expressing regret for an unmet result (as in *kong pao yi-tang*, or making a trip in vain) or dissatisfaction over the absence of substantial content (as in *kong tan li-xiang*, or lofty talk of ambitions). Additionally, such retrospective evaluations synchronously align with *kong* VP, indicating an ex-post assessment, and thus can coexist with the perfective marker le_1. However, explicit negation markers bu and mei, representing unactualized events, cannot co-occur with le_1. For instance, consider the following:

(14) 不经意间, 你已经悄然离去。空留下了一段回忆。[5]

bu jing-yi jian, ni yi-jing qiao-ran li-qu. kong liu-xia-le yi-duan hui-yi.

Neg. carefully you already quietly leave Adv. leave a period of memory.

Unconsciously, you've silently departed, Only leaving behind a memory.

(15) 这个根本问题没有解决, 一切都是空谈, 空谈了五千年。

zhe-ge gen-ben wen-ti mei-you jie-jue, yi-qie dou shi kong-tan, kong tan-le wu-qian nian.

this prime problem Neg. solve all Qua. is empty talk Adv. talk 5000 year.[6]

The core issue remains unresolved. It's all been mere talk, spanning five thousand years.

---

[4] Example (11–13) and its accompanying analysis are drawn from the lecture notes utilized by Professor GUO Rui during the 2012 course on *Semantic Analysis* at the Department of Chinese Language and Literature of Peking University.

[5] Examples (14–15) are sourced from the BCC corpus of Beijing Language and Culture University.

[6] Qua.-universal quantifier.

The modal function conveyed by *kong* is intricately linked to its syntactic position. According to reference [15], sentence structures can be categorized into three distinct layers: the lexical, the inflectional, and the complementizer layers. The lexical layer represents the propositional content of a sentence, situated at the foundational level. The inflectional layer accounts for temporal and morphological variations in the sentence, positioned in the intermediate level. The complementizer layer, often at the uppermost level, predominantly conveys the modal significance of a sentence, mirroring the subject's cognitive realm. The verb structure VP, which the adverb *kong* modifies, is anchored in the lexical layer, while the associated temporal and morphological particles reside in the inflectional layer. On the other hand, *bai* is positioned at the complement position of the predicate verb, belonging to the complementizer layer. Although *kong* directly modifies the predicate verb, it occupies a more elevated position than the entire verb structure VP. Consequently, it can semantically influence the entire VP, signifying the speaker's tone, attitude, and worldview. In Examples (34–35), while *kong* directly modifies the verbs *liu-xia* (leave behind) and *tan* (talk), the entire clause's syntactic structure aligns as VP[COMP[kong V[liu-xia le]]yi-duan hui-yi]/VP[COMP[kong V[tan le]]wu-qian nian], as illustrated in Fig. 1:

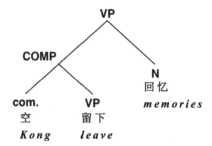

Fig. 1. The normal syntactic structure of the *Kong*-VP clause

However, *kong* denotes the speaker's subjective stance formed after the completion of the event that the entire VP encapsulates. Thus, from a functional perspective, the whole clause structure should be demarcated as COMP[kong VP[liu-xia le NP[yi-duan hui-yi]]]/COMP[kong VP[tan le NP[wu-qian nian]]]. *Kong* is situated within the complementizer layer, the perfective marker *le* within the inflectional layer, and the pivotal verb structures *liu-xia le yi-duan hui-yi* (leave behind a memory) and *tan wu-qian nian* (talk spanning five thousand years) are nestled within the lexical layer, as depicted in Fig. 2:

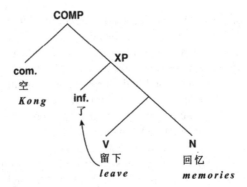

Fig. 2. The functional syntactic structure of the *Kong*-VP clause

5   Deciphering the Construal Strategies of *Kong*

Given that *kong* embodies implicit negation and conveys evaluative connotations, how should this attribute be discerned in speech communication? We have found that the adverb *kong,* characterized by negation of expectation, directly imparts counter-expectational effects, reflecting the speaker's emotive stance when reality deviates from their anticipated scenario. More precisely, the verbal phrase modified by *kong* results in or comprises content misaligned with the speaker's subjective anticipation. When *kong* conveys a *lack of effect*, the actual outcome of the VP diverges from the speaker's projection. Conversely, when *kong* denotes the *absence of concrete action or substance*, the essence of the VP veers from the speaker's anticipation. Yuan (2014) delves into the construal challenges of the adverb *bai* (white), asserting that the construal of *bai* entails a shared foundational knowledge: the principle of input-output equilibrium, accentuating the balance between efforts and gains [13]. *Kong* mirrors this notion but encompasses a broader scope. The communal understanding entails: first, a parity between efforts and results; second, a balance between form and essence. When endeavors yield no return, *kong* is perceived as *fruitlessly* or *ineffectively.* If an event merely possesses superficial attributes without genuine substance or tangible actions, *kong* resonates as *lacking tangible actions or content.*

However, solely elucidating the counter-expectational facet of *kong* is not our sole focus. The paramount goal of speech communication hinges on grasping the speaker's intent. Consequently, discerning the subjective motive the speaker aspires to convey via *kong* is quintessential. In our corpus analysis of the *kong* construct, we extrapolated the speaker's intent rooted in context, unraveled the construal mechanisms of negation of expectation, and charted the construal strategies. While the adverb *kong* in Mandarin is bifurcated in meaning, the gamut of speakers' or narrators' intents are multifaceted.

Initially, *kong* signifies an anticipatory effect from the VP. The speaker's subjective foresight dictates: having expended effort, one should accrue benefits from the event delineated by the VP. If the actual scenario fails to match the speaker's or subject's envisioned outcome, it deviates, with *kong* encapsulating the *ineffectively* sentiment, spawning a counter-expectational nuance. For instance, consider the following:

(16) 别有寄托的友谊, 不是真正的友谊, 而是撒入生活海洋里的网,
到头来空收无益。

*bie you ji-tuo de you-yi, bu shi zhen-zheng de you-yi, er shi sa ru sheng-huo hai-yang
li de wang, dao tou lai kong shou wu-yi.*

Attachments with ulterior motives aren't genuine friendships; they resemble nets
cast into life's vast ocean, only to retrieve emptiness and gain nothing in the end.

(17) 常见有些厂家

、商家一厢情愿地将一些库存积压物品拉下乡，结果往往鞍,
马劳顿空忙一场。

*chang-jian you-xie chang-jia, shang-jia yi-xiang-qing-yuan de jiang yi-xie ku-cun
ji-ya wu-pin la xia xiang, jie guo wang-wang an-ma-lao-dun kong mang yi chang.*

Often, certain manufacturers and merchants, driven by wishful thinking, transport surplus stock to the countryside. The outcome, more often than not, is
exhausting effort spent in vain.

In Examples (16–17), the speaker anticipates that following the events depicted by
the Verbal phrases, *casting the net* and *arduous endeavors*, and there would emerge
the results they had hoped for: either the formation of friendships or the realization
of profits from the sale of excess inventory. However, reality deviates, as they neither
acquire genuine friendships nor gain profits from sales. Such outcomes contrast starkly
with the initial expectations, leading to counter-expectations.

Second, *kong* often signifies an expectation that a certain event, represented by the
verbal phrase, should not transpire. In these contexts, the speaker's intent suggests that
the event described by VP should ideally not occur or is something the speaker would
rather avoid. If the event delineated by VP does manifest in reality, then the speaker's
anticipations are rendered ineffective, resulting in a deviation from these original expectations. In such instances, *kong* can still be construed as *ineffective* or *futile*. For instance,
consider the following:

(18) 律师辩论不必举与本案无关的事实做证据, 我国并无《案例法》, 举例也白举,
只能空费口舌，白耗时间。

*lü-shi bian-lun bu-bi ju yu ben-an wu-guan de shi-shi zuo zheng-ju, wo guo bing
wu an-li-fa, ju-li ye bai ju, zhi-neng kong fei kou-she, bai hao shi-jian.*

When lawyers present arguments, they shouldn't unnecessarily introduce facts
irrelevant to the current case as evidence. China does not have a *Case Law*, hence
such examples are moot, resulting only in pointless rhetoric and wasted time.

(19) 这些年, 我带孩子在家累心, 他一个人孤零零地在外受苦, 空耗了大好时光。

*zhe xie nian, wo dai hai-zi zai jia lei-xin, ta yi ge ren gu-ling-ling de zai wai shou-ku,
kong hao le da-hao shi-guang.*

Over the years, I've exhaustively cared for our child at home, while he endured
hardships alone outside, squandering precious years in the process.

In (18), the narrator's expectation is that lawyers should refrain from unnecessarily
expending energy on irrelevant facts, rather than needlessly consuming energy without
achieving the intended results. In (19), the speaker conveys that neither they nor *he*
should have squandered their golden years, instead of wastefully spending them without
attaining a significant outcome.

Third, in certain scenarios, the expectation implied by *kong* escalates to a loftier level. Here, the speaker's intent leans towards desiring an event superior in quality or scale to what is expressed by VP. This nuanced intention can be categorized as a more refined subcategory under the general expectation of achieving a result from VP. It implies the hope for an enhanced outcome or the event reaching an elevated magnitude. In these contexts, *kong* conveys the notion of *unfruitfully* and can also be perceived as *merely* or *solely*. If the tangible result disappointingly falls short, it diverges from the speaker's aspirations. For instance, consider the following:

(20) 悄悄地过去了，一年的光景。没有收获，<u>空</u>留一地破碎的诺言。
qiao-qiao de guo qu le, yi-nian de guang-jing. mei you shou-huo, kong liu yi di po-sui de nuo-yan.

A year has discreetly slipped by. With no tangible gains, all that remains are the fragments of broken promises.

(21) 人们只看到她们脸上的笑容，却没有意识到她们所作出的牺牲，
空剩下一片寂静和黑暗，   的小蟋蟀停止了吟唱，和美的阳光消逝而去，
直到炉边。
ren-men zhi kan dao ta-men lian shang de xiao-rong, que mei you yi-shi dao ta-men suo zuo-chu de xi-sheng, zhi-dao lu-bian de xiao xi-shuai ting-zhi le yin-chang, he-mei de yang-guang xiao-shi er qu, kong sheng xia yi-pian ji-jing he hei-an.

People only noticed their radiant smiles, remaining oblivious to the sacrifices they made. It wasn't until the gentle chirping of the hearth's cricket ceased and the alluring sunlight vanished that a pervasive silence and darkness prevailed.)

In (20), surrounding the phrase of *kong* VP, a hierarchy of events can be established, ascending from minimal to maximal:

a. Abandoning shattered promises that remain unfulfilled
    (minimal, lightweight order event)
b. Leaving behind vows that might see realization in the future
    (marginally superior, Medium-low weight order event)
c. Keeping promises with some gains, albeit at the expense of a year
    (moderate, middleweight order event)
d. Upholding promises with genuine rewards, justifying the year's commitment
    (optimal, high weight order event)

Among these tiers (a, b, c, and d) that progress from the minimal to the optimal, *a* signifies the least preferred outcome in the narrator's anticipations, whereas *d* epitomizes the zenith of hope. The reality, however, is marked by the emergence of only the lowest-tier outcome, deviating from the ideal aspirations and thereby reflecting the narrator's profound sense of regret.[7]

---

[7] It is essential to emphasize that the term *kong* serves as a sufficient means to express the speaker's intention, it is not a necessary one. In essence, while *kong* can manifest this intention, such intent is not exclusively expressed by the use of *kong*. There are alternative syntactical and lexical avenues, such as *que zhi-you...* (only), which can convey a similar sentiment. However, if a specific speaker's intention is absent from a sentence, it generally avoids the use of *kong*. Hence, a unidirectional implication exists between the *kong* VP structure and this distinct speaker intent.

Fourth, when *kong* implies that the VP possesses substantive content, it reveals the speaker's subjective expectation that the event portrayed by the VP should present substance congruent with its form. In this context, *kong* signifies *actions without genuine substance or execution*. Given this intention, reality often showcases the subject or the speaker exhibiting a disparity between word and deed, making proclamations without concrete action, or revealing a divergence between outward appearance and intrinsic substance. Such realities diverge from the expectations of the speaker or the narrator. For instance, consider the following:

(22) 不过, 他早已不是上海杂志公司的老板, 只能空说, 不能实行。

　　　bu-guo, ta zao yi bu shi shang-hai za-zhi gong-si de lao-ban, zhi neng kong shuo, bu neng shi-xing.

　　　However, he has long ceased to be the boss of the Shanghai Magazine Company. He can only offer empty talk without the ability to take action.

(23) 那么, 什么是现代企业制度？ 怎样逐步建立现代企业制度？ 这里面有什么值得注意的问题？ 对这些问题, 总觉得坐在屋里空论不行。

　　　na-me, shen-me shi xian-dai qi-ye zhi-du? zen-yang zhu-bu jian-li xian-dai qi-ye zhi-du? zhe-li mian you shen-me zhi-de zhu-yi de wen-ti? dui zhe-xie wen-ti, zong jue-de zuo zai wu-li kong lun bu-xing.

　　　So, what defines a modern corporate system? How can one systematically establish such a system? What are the noteworthy issues within? Addressing these questions, mere armchair theorizing seems insufficient.

In (22), *kong shuo* (empty talk) suggests presenting viewpoints without the capability for genuine execution. The narrator aspires for the subject *he* to maintain his position as the boss, ensuring actions accompany his words. However, in reality, *he* no longer holds that authority. The usage of *kong* underscores the contrast between reality and expectation.

6 Conclusion

This study primarily focuses on the implicit negative adverb *kong* in Mandarin, which can be used to negate expectations, shedding light on its unique semantic attributes and the nuances of its pragmatic functions and mechanisms. The analysis suggests that the negative semantics, counter-expectation functionality, and construal mechanisms of *kong* are progressively layered and sequentially realized.

First, the term *implicit negation* highlights the semantic features of the adverb *kong*. The semantic interpretation of *kong* implicitly includes a negation component. The $Neg._{Implicit} + VP$ structure, formed by modifying the predicate structure, can entail sentences with explicit negation markers such as *bu* (not) and *mei* (haven't). *Kong* serves as an adverb within a compound negation form. This form of implicit negation belongs to the pragmatic negation category. The object of negation is not the truth-value condition that makes the proposition true but the felicity condition that establishes the proposition. This markedly differs from the explicit analytic negations represented by *bu* VP and *mei* VP.

Second, the *felicity condition* negated by *kong* refers to the interlocutors' expectations of an event. Accordingly, *kong* can further be categorized as an adverb for negation of expectation. Such expectations are what interlocutors perceive in their cognitive world as the inherent balance or consistency an event should exhibit. This includes a balance between efforts and rewards, consistency in word and deed, and congruence between external appearances and internal realities. Discrepancies between reality and these expectations give rise to *kong's* functions for counter-expectation and negation of expectation. Based on this, negation of expectation showcases ex-post evaluations and consistently manifests itself in semantic, syntactic, and pragmatic interactions. The expectation negation adverb *kong*, with its inherent implicit negation semantics, negates the manner or results an event should have in expectation but does not. Pragmatically, it reveals the speaker's ex-post evaluation and reflection. Therefore, syntactically, it can co-occur with the perfective marker le_1. Meanwhile, the expectation negation adverb in syntactic structures is positioned just after the subject on the complementizer layer, denoting modality and aligning with the subjective modal meaning conveyed by ex-post evaluations.

Lastly, the ex-post evaluation conveyed by *kong* can express the *speaker's intention* and has been used to decipher the construal mechanisms of *kong* in speech communication. Due to the counter-expectation effect *kong* has pragmatically, this counter-expectation is often achieved through the interaction between listeners and speakers during communication, aiming to evoke empathy between the two. This process further expresses various subjective intentions of the speaker.

Acknowledgements. This article has received support from the National Social Science Fund's special project (19VXK06), the Ministry of Education's 2022 International Chinese Language Teaching Practical Innovation Project (YHJXCX22-076), and the Fundamental Research Funds for the Central Universities project (310422133). We sincerely thank these organizations for their support.

References

1. Yuan, Y.: On the semantic levels and overflow conditions of the implicit negative verbs in Chinese. Stud. Chin. Lang. **2**, 99–113 (2012). (in Chinese)
2. Zeng, J., Yuan, Y.: A Study on the counter-expectation and semantic construal. In: Wu, Y., Hong, J.F., Su, Q. (eds.) CLSW 2017. LNCS, vol. 10709, pp. 17–26. Springer, Cham (2018). https://doi.org/10.1007/978-3-319-73573-3_2
3. Zeng, J., Yuan, Y.: Functional diffusion and decategorization of *bai*: from a colour term to an implicit negative adverb. In: Liu, M., Kit, C., Su, Q. (eds.) CLSW 2020. LNCS, vol. 12278, pp. 206–214 (2021). Springer, Cham. https://doi.org/10.1007/978-3-030-81197-6_18
4. Lexicographical Editing Room, Institute of Linguistics, Chinese Academy of Social Sciences (Ed.): Modern Chinese Dictionary. The Commercial Press, Beijing (2012). (in Chinese)
5. Zeng, J., Yuan, Y.: The study on the implicit negative meaning of bai in Chinese. Macao J. Linguist. **46**(2), 4–14 (2015). (in Chinese)
6. Shen, J.: A study of pragmatic negation. Stud. Chin. Lang. **5**, 321–331 (1993). (in Chinese)
7. Zhang, Y.: The semantic features of seven adverbs of presupposition negation in modern Chinese. Chin. Teach. World **2**, 30–34 (1996). (in Chinese)

8. Zhang, Y.: Study of Adverbs in Mandarin. Xuelin Press, Beijing (2000)
9. Cai, K.: Difference analysis on the syntactic forms of kong and xu. Acad. J. LIYUN (Lang. Vol.) **2**, 251–267 (2013). (in Chinese)
10. Allwood, Andersson, Dahl.: Logic in linguistics. Cambridge University Press, Cambridge (1977)
11. Lyons, J.: Semantics. Cambridge University Press, Cambridge (1977)
12. Leech, G.: Semantics. Penguin Books (1981)
13. Yuan, Y.: Conception-driven and syntax-directed constructions and construal of sentences: a case study of the interpretation of sentences with the adverb bai (for free vs. in vain). Stud. Chin. Lang. (5), 402–417 (2014). (in Chinese)
14. Shen, J.: A survey of studies on subjectivity and subjectivisation. Foreign Lang. Teach. Res. **33**(4), 268–275 (2001). (in Chinese)
15. Rizzi, L.: The fine structure of the left periphery. In: Haegeman, L. (ed.) Elements of Grammar. Dordrecht Kluwer (1997)

The Formation Features and Structural Mechanism of Modern Chinese "V$_{cooking}$+N" Structure

Yuqi Shen[1] and Jiapan Li[2(✉)]

[1] School of International Chinese Language Education, Beijing Normal University, Beijing, China

[2] Teachers College, Beijing Language and Culture University, Beijing, China
lijiapan@blcu.edu.cn

Abstract. The monosyllabic verbs in modern Chinese should not be used as attributives directly, but the monosyllabic verbs that express the cooking meaning can be used as attributives directly, forming the ambiguous structure of "V$_{cooking}$+N". For example, kǎobáishǔ (roasted white potato) can express both the verb-object relationship and the attributive-head relationship. The reason for the formation of this ambiguous structure is the semantic transfer from verb-object phrase to attributive-head compound. The semantic attribute of "produce or change" of V$_{cooking}$ and the conventional production method in N's meaning are the main factors that affect its semantic reference. From the perspective of the structural mechanism of "V$_{cooking}$+N" structure, the semantic class attribute of N determines the anchoring of the semantic attribute of V$_{cooking}$, and the implication or presentation of "production method" affects the selection of structural properties.

Keywords: V+N · Cooking Verb · Semantic Feature

1 Introduction

Since Lv Shuxiang (1963) raised the issue of monosyllabic and bisyllabic collocations in Modern Chinese, the conditions for verbs to act as determiners have received sustained attention in the academic community, and the nature of monosyllabic verbs not suitable to act as determiners directly has become a consensus (Wang Guangquan 1993; Zhang Guoxian 1997; Zhang Min 1998: 313; Wang Hongjun 2001; Guo Rui 2002: 259; Shen Jiaxuan 2012; Deng Dun 2021; Li 2022, etc.). In the 21st century, with the deepening attention to V-N attributive-head structures, studies have found that there are many types of monosyllabic verbs that can act constituents directly in attributive-head structures, and the number of these verbs is quite large (Shi Tingxu 2003; Shen Jiaxuan 2016: 367–368, Zhao Qian 2020; Qin Zuxuan and Duanmusan 2021). Some monosyllabic verbs can act as attributives under certain conditions and constitute attributive-head compounds, among which monosyllabic verbs expressing the cooking meanings are productive, such as jiān (pan-fry), chǎo (stir-fry), zhá (deep-fry), kǎo (roast), zhǔ (boil), etc. For examples (All examples in this paper are from the BCC Corpus):

M. Dong et al. (Eds.): CLSW 2023, LNAI 14514, pp. 116–129, 2024.
https://doi.org/10.1007/978-981-97-0583-2_10

(1) a. Gānggāng líhūn de tā, lián zěnme chǎo jīdàn dōu búhuì. (He, newly divorced, doesn't even know how to fry an egg.)

b. Xià zhème dà yǔ, yīnggāi chī ge chǎo jīdàn. (With such heavy rain, one should have a fried egg.)

In (1a), "chǎojīdàn (frying an egg)" refers to the process of preparing a dish with eggs as the main ingredient, emphasizing the cooking process. In contrast, in (1b), it denotes the finished dish itself. It can be observed that the "$V_{cooking}+N$" structure formed by combining a cooking verb and food noun can represent both verb-object relationships and attributive-head relations, thus forming an ambiguous structure.

How then does monosyllabic cooking verbs break through the rule that "monosyllabic verbs are not suitable for direct attributive use", enabling them to appear in attributive positions within compound words? Furthermore, not all instances of "$V_{cooking}+N$" structures simultaneously represent verb-object and attributive-head relationships in actual language use. Some lexical examples show stronger nominal tendencies and hardly appear as verb-object phrases; such as "kǎochì (roasted wings)", "zhájī (fried chicken)", and "jiānjiǎo (pan-fried dumplings)".

On the other hand, some instances only appear as verb-object phrases without highlighting their nominal nature; like "áozhōu (boiling porridge)", "zhǔkāfēi (brewing coffee)", or "kǎodàn'gāo (baking cake)". This indicates an imbalance among members of "$V_{cooking}+N$" structures when they manifest as either attributive-head compounds or verb-object phrases.

It is evident that there are more implicit constraints involved during combination processes between monosyllabic cooking verbs and nouns which have yet to be thoroughly discussed - this warrants further research.

2 The Imbalance of Ambiguity of Modern Chinese "$V_{cooking}+N$" Structure

2.1 Quantitative Statistics of Modern Chinese "$V_{cooking}+N$" Structure

Language materials that mentioned in this article are collected from Literature Subcorpus of Beijing Language and Culture University Corpus Center (BCC Corpus). We chose 11 common monosyllabic cooking verbs in Modern Chinese: jiān (pan-fry), chǎo (stir-fry), kǎo (roast), zhá (deep-fry), zhǔ (boil), zhēng (steam), shāo (braise), dùn (stew), áo (simmer), mēn (simmer), pēng (poach), and made a complete retrieve of the collocations that constituted with these cooking verbs and food noun. The results were filtered to exclude following conditions:

(1) N is a non-food noun. For examples: shāotiě (burning iron), zháguō (fryer), zhēngqì (steam).
(2) "$V_{cooking}+N$" in Chinese dishes' name like "$N_1 + V_{cooking}+N_2$". For example: xiǎojī dùn mógu (chicken stewed with mushrooms).
(3) $V_{cooking}$ is a non-monosyllabic verb. For examples: qīngzhēng lúyú (flatfish steamed in broth), hóngshāo páigǔ (simmer-fried pork chop).

After searching and screening, this research analyzes the final 1038 examples of "V cooking + N" structure one by one, according to the linguistic context in which they appear, manually annotates and counts the number of lexical examples in terms of structural property, prosodic pattern, and semantic attribute.

The semantic features referred to herein are the two different ways in which the cooking action affects food: the food is produced by the cooking action (denoted as [+produce]), or the cooking action undergoing a qualitative change (denoted as [+change]). Fodor and Lepore (1998) proposed that the term "bake" in structures such as "bake a cake" and "bake a potato" carries two distinct meanings. The former implies "to create" and the latter means "to heat". A similar phenomenon of polysemy occurs with Chinese cooking verbs. For instance, in the case of "kǎodàn'gāo (baking a cake)" and "kǎotǔdòu (baking a potato)", the former means to bake a cake, so the cake is made through the action of "baking", and unbaked raw material cannot be called a cake. The latter suggests heating potatoes as ingredients, leading to changes from cold to hot, raw to cooked. That is to say, only qualitative changes occur in potatoes; an unheated raw potato remains a potato. The influence of cooking actions on food within "$V_{cooking}$+N" structure usually selects one of these two situations and stays optional before entering into this structure, which we term hereafter as "produce/change" semantic attribute of cooking verb. All collected statistical data can be found detailed out comprehensively within Table 1.

Table 1. "$V_{cooking}$+N" prosodic- semantic-structural statistical data

	Verb-object						Attributive-head						Both					
	Prosodic pattern			Semantic attribute			Prosodic pattern			Semantic attribute			Prosodic pattern			Semantic attribute		
	[1+2]	[1+3]	others	prod uce	change	total	[1+2]	[1+3]	others	produ ce	change	total	[1+2]	[1+3]	oth ers	prod uce	change	total
zhǔ(boil)+N	41	11	3	2	53	55	72	36	26	60	74	134	15	2	7	1	23	24
kǎo(roast)+N	75	25	16	8	108	116	19	12	9	17	23	40	27	2	5	3	31	34
zhá(deep-fry)+N	65	22	11	4	94	98	10	4	2	8	8	16	9	3	4	1	15	16
chǎo(stir-fry)+N	49	23	6	3	75	78	16	5	4	7	19	26	16	1	8	2	23	25
shāo(braise)+N	30	5	4	2	37	39	32	6	5	25	18	43	3	0	3	0	6	6
jiān(pan-fry)+N	30	15	4	8	41	49	6	3	5	3	11	14	9	2	7	7	11	18
dùn(stew)+N	27	8	3	1	37	38	14	7	3	10	14	24	9	0	4	1	12	13
zhēng(steam)+N	19	3	7	5	24	29	18	3	5	18	8	26	1	0	3	2	2	4
áo(simmer)+N	5	1	2	0	8	8	16	7	13	33	3	36	0	0	1	1	0	1
mèn(simmer)+N	12	0	3	2	13	15	3	0	0	0	3	3	2	0	0	1	1	2
pēng(poach)+N	1	0	0	0	1	1	0	0	5	0	5	5	0	0	2	1	1	2

As can be inferred from Table 1: In terms of prosodic patterns, the dominant rhythms for the "$V_{cooking}$+N" structure are [1+2] and [1+3], accounting for 857 instances or 82.56% of the total. Structurally, the "$V_{cooking}$+N" structure indicates three types: attributive-head compound, verb-object phrase, or an ambiguous combination of both with a significant disparity in quantity among these types. Semantically speaking, food that undergo a qualitative change through cooking actions are noticeably more numerous than those produced by cooking actions. Furthermore, the semantic attribute of "produce/change" inherent to cooking verbs have an impact on the structure of "$V_{cooking}+N$".

The subsequent discussion will delve into specific compositional characteristics of modern Chinese's use of the "$V_{cooking}+N$" structure based on these quantitative statistical results.

2.2 Disproportionate Ambiguity of Modern Chinese "$V_{cooking}+N$" Structure

The previous statistical findings indicate that not all members of "$V_{cooking}+N$" can concurrently manifest as attributive-head compounds and verb-object phrases. We selected a subset of lexical examples for retrieval, extracted all entries in BCC Corpus, annotated the structural types of "$V_{cooking}+N$", and calculated their respective percentage distributions. Detailed data is presented in Table 2.

Table 2. Differential Preferences in the Structure of "$V_{cooking}+N$"

$V_{cooking}+N$	Total frequency	Frequency of attributive-head	Frequency of verb-object	Percentage of attributive-head	Percentage of verb-object
shāoyā (Roasted Duck)	37	37	0	100%	0%
kǎochì (Grilled Wings)	10	10	0	100%	0%
jiānjiǎo (Pan-fried Dumplings)	9	9	0	100%	0%
zhájī (Fried Chicken)	226	224	2	99.11%	0.89%
zháyóutiáo (Deep-fried Dough Sticks)	148	11	137	7.44%	92.56%
zhǔkāfēi (Brewed Coffee)	142	2	140	1.41%	98.59%
kǎodàn'gāo (Baked Cake)	14	0	14	0%	100%
áo zhōu (Slow-cooked Porridge)	103	0	103	0%	100%

It is evident that there exists an imbalance among members of "$V_{cooking}+N$" when they are represented as attributive-head compounds or verb-object phrases. Some tend to form verb-object phrases more frequently, while others with high semantic solidity exhibit a pronounced tendency towards nominalization.

In order to quantitatively display this imbalance of ambiguity, an "ambiguity index", denoted by p (rounded to two decimal places), was established for "$V_{cooking}+N$". Herein, m and n respectively represent the frequencies at which the "$V_{cooking}+N$" structure appears as an attributive-head compound or a verb-object phrase in the corpus, so:

$$p = \frac{-m + n}{m + n} \qquad (1)$$

In this formula, the ambiguity index is calculated by the difference in quantity of the same "$V_{cooking}+N$" manifesting as attributive-head compounds and verb-object phrases ($-m + n$), divided by the total number of lexical examples ($m + n$). This setup allows for a clear demonstration of structural type preferences through positive/negative values and absolute value sizes. When the ambiguity index p is positive, "$V_{cooking}+N$" prefers to present as a verb-object phrase; conversely, when p is negative, it leans towards an attributive-head compound. The closer |p| approaches 1, the more extreme the preference becomes. For instance, "zhēngmántou (steaming buns) (-1)" in all retrieved contexts signifies the process of making steamed buns while "jiānjiǎo (frying dumpling) (1)" across all contexts indicates a name of food. As |p| nears 0, indicating that frequencies between verb-object phrases and attributive-head compounds are roughly equivalent, therefore exists stronger structural ambiguity. Examples include "dùntǔdòu (stewing potatoes/stewed potatoes) (0)" and "kǎomiànbāo (toasting bread/toasted bread) (0.02)", which can denote either action or object in native speaker intuition and without significant preference in actual usage.

By calculating this ambiguity index, we find that members of "$V_{cooking}+N$" structure reside on a continuum from attributive-head compound to verb-object phrase as depicted in Fig. 1 below. Lexical examples at different positions show varying tendencies towards one structure over another; those closer to either end exhibit strong preference for one form while rejecting another, whereas those located relatively centrally indicate similar frequency levels for both.

Attributive-Head ◄──► Verb-Object

jiān chǎo	jiān kǎo	jiān shāo	jiān zhá	kǎo	dùn	dùnkǎo	chǎo	kǎo	chǎo	zhǔ	zhǔ	chǎo jiān	zhǔ	zhēng
jiǎo zhǔ	dàn hóng	jī	yú	niú nián	lù	jī	tǔ miàn	dòu	yóu	ròu	ròu	guā	chá yào	zhōu	mán
gān	shǔ	dàn -0.5	juàn	pái	gāo	ròu	-0.08	dòubāo 0.11	yú	piàn	miàn	0.8 0.84	0.9	tou
-1	-0.95 -0.87 -0.78		-0.43	-0.33	-0.20		0 0.02		0.2	0.33 0.58	0.67			1
			-0.6											

Fig. 1. Continuum Statistics of Attributive-Head Compound and Verb-Object "$V_{cooking}+N$"

So, what factors contribute to the imbalance of ambiguity in the modern Chinese "$V_{cooking}+N$" structure? To further explore the causes of ambiguity, we will delve into prosody and semantics.

3 Form-Meaning Collocation in Modern Chinese "$V_{cooking}+N$" Structure

3.1 Formal Collocation Features of Modern Chinese "$V_{cooking}+N$" Structure

Given that our research object has a fixed V+N form type collocation pattern, we will focus on the features of its prosodic collocation pattern. As known from Sect. 2.1, the distribution of prosodic patterns in "$V_{cooking}+N$" is not uniform. To identify its dominant prosodic structure, we now examine how monosyllabic cooking verbs pair with multi-syllable food nouns; see Table 3 for statistics.

Based on these statistics, the prosody patterns can be classified into five categories: [1+1], [1+2], [1+3], [1+4] and [1+5]. Among them, three-syllable pattern [1+2] predominates across all subcategories of cooking verbs and makes up more than half in most

Table 3. Statistics on Prosodic Patterns in "$V_{cooking}$+N"

$V_{cooking}$+N	Prosodic pattern				
	1+1	1+2	1+3	1+4	1+5
zhǔ(boil)+N	12.68% (27)	60.09% (128)	23% (49)	2.82% (6)	1.41% (3)
kǎo(roast)+N	10.53% (20)	63.68% (121)	20.53% (39)	3.68% (7)	1.58% (3)
zhá(deep-fry)+N	10% (13)	64.62% (84)	22.31% (29)	2.31% (3)	0.77% (1)
chǎo(stir-fry)+N	11.63% (15)	62.79% (81)	22.48% (29)	3.10% (4)	0% (0)
shāo(braise)+N	11.36% (10)	73.86% (65)	12.50% (11)	2.27% (2)	0% (0)
jiān(pan-fry)+N	16.05% (13)	55.56% (45)	24.69% (20)	2.45% (2)	1.23% (1)
dùn(stew)+N	12% (9)	66.67% (50)	20% (15)	1.33% (1)	0% (0)
zhēng(steam)+N	22.03% (13)	64.41% (38)	10.17% (6)	3.39% (2)	0% (0)
áo(simmer)+N	17.78% (8)	46.67% (21)	17.78% (8)	11.11% (5)	6.67% (3)
mēn(simmer)+N	15% (3)	85% (17)	0% (0)	0% (0)	0% (0)
pēng(poach)+N	87.5% (7)	12.5% (1)	0% (0)	0% (0)	0% (0)
Total	13.29% (138)	62.72% (651)	19.85% (206)	3.08% (32)	1.06% (11)

subclasses. It is therefore considered as a dominant prosodic model for "$V_{cooking}$+N". On contrary, five syllables patterned [1+5] occurs least frequently and hence represents an edge case. The overall dominance order appears as follows: [1+2] > [1+3] > [1+1] > [1+4] > [1+5].

To further investigate whether or not this rhythmic model affects the structure of "$V_{cooking}$+N", Table 4 provides statistics about rhythmic distributions within each structural property. By observing frequency counts for each rhythm of different structural properties, it's possible to determine if they conform to rhythmic dominance order. If certain rhythms appear anomalously often, thus breaking general rule set by dominance, then it could be inferred that this particular rhythm might have influenced choice regarding structure property. See Table 4 for details.

Table 4. Rhythmic Distribution across Different Types within "$V_{cooking}$+N"

Prosodic pattern	Structural Property		
	Attributive-Head	Verb-Object	Both
1+1	47	47	44
1+2	354	206	91
1+3	113	83	10
1+4	9	23	0
1+5	3	8	0

Based on the statistical results, it is evident that under any structural type, the distribution of prosodic patterns generally conforms to the ordinal rule of [1+2] > [1+3] > [1+1] > [1+4] > [1+5]. No special circumstances breaking this prosodic pattern were found.

Additionally, there was no evidence that a particular prosodic pattern prefers a specific structural type, indicating that the prosodic pattern does not significantly influence the choice of "$V_{cooking}$+N" structure.

As mentioned earlier, many holds that for V-N attributive-head structures, [1+2] is exceptional rhythmic form. However, ironically enough, the least acceptable [1+2] rhythmic form appears most frequently and productively in "$V_{cooking}$+N". Out of 651 collected lexical examples of [1+2] "$V_{cooking}$+N", 445 are attributive-head compounds - accounting for an astonishing 68.36%. Feng Shengli (1996) pointed out that general rhythmic word formation does not allow monosyllabic notional words to modify disyllabic nouns unless absolutely necessary; if modification is unavoidable then monosyllabic words must undergo qualitative change and become affixes to escape from rhythmical governance. This suggests that a [1+2] rhythmical structure may force semantic ambiguity upon attributive elements appearing in position "1".

However, this hypothesis seems ill-fitted when applied to "$V_{cooking}$+N". When phrases like "zházhūpái (fried pork chop)", "chǎojīdàn (scrambled egg)", or "dùnniúròu (stewed beef)" appear as attributive-head compounds; $V_{cooking}$ do not lose their specific meaning nor should they be considered as having been transformed into affixes.

This raises questions about how such action-intensive cooking verbs manage to escape from rhythmic control and appear in an attributive position? Why would rhythm yield to certain syntactic or morphological concessions? To answer these queries we need further observation on semantic attributes of both constituents in "$V_{cooking}$+N".

3.2 Semantic Collocation Features of "$V_{cooking}$+N" Structure

Based on Sect. 2.1, $V_{cooking}$ possesses an undefined semantic attribute of "produce/change". This attribute becomes anchored and prominent only when it is combined with food nouns to form a "$V_{cooking}$+N" structure. From here, we start by examining the two distinct ways that $V_{cooking}$ affect food, analyzing how the anchoring of V's "produce/change" semantic attribute impacts the overall structure of "$V_{cooking}$+N".

According to Zhao Qian (2020), ambiguity arises in such structures due to an unmarked semantic transfer - initially, "$V_{cooking}$+N" was a verb-object phrase but later transferred towards an attributive-head compound. As both structures have certain usage frequency, this leads to an ambiguous structure. To highlight differences between these two structural properties, we can merge and observe both attributive compounds and ambiguous verb-object/attributive structures together as they are transferred examples that represent attributive relations; thus further exploring what motivates this semantic transfer and its influencing factors. The statistical results in Table 5.

Generally, when qualitative change occurs in food due to cooking action V, it is more likely for the "$V_{cooking}$+N" to transfer towards an attributive-head compound.

It should be noted that among the 1038 lexical examples collected, 800 $V_{cooking}$ in the structure possess [+change] semantic attribute, while 238 possess [+produce]. The former is more common attribute, thus the number of V[+change] examples surpasses V[+produce]. Interestingly, despite the generally higher proportion of V[+change], V[+change] is overwhelmingly dominant among attributive-head compounds, whereas show little difference in quantity with V[+produce] among verb-object phrases, even

Table 5. Statistics on Semantic Collocation for "$V_{cooking}+N$"

$V_{cooking}+N$	Attributive-Head Tendency		Verb-Object Tendency	
	V[+produce]	V[+change]	V[+produce]	V[+change]
zhǔ(boil)+N	3	76	60	74
kǎo(roast)+N	11	139	17	23
zhá(deep-fry)+N	5	109	8	8
chǎo(stir-fry)+N	5	98	7	19
shāo(braise)+N	2	43	25	18
jiān(pan-fry)+N	15	52	3	11
dùn(stew)+N	2	49	10	14
zhēng(steam)+N	7	26	18	8
áo(simmer)+N	3	8	33	3
mēn(simmer)+N	3	14	0	3
pēng(poach)+N	1	2	0	5

the number of V[+produce] surpasses occasionally. This implies that among these lexical examples undergoing a transfer from verb-object to attributive-head, there's an extremely high proportion of V[+change]. Further inference suggests if V[+change], then "$V_{cooking}+N$" are more likely to transition into attributive-head compounds.

In summary of the above analysis, it was found that the primary factor influencing whether "$V_{cooking}+N$" undergoes a semantic transfer from verb-object to attributive-head structure is its "produce/change" semantic attribute:

(I) When V[+change] and N has undergone qualitative changes as ingredient being cooked, then "$V_{cooking}+N$" undergoes semantic transfer and function both attributive-head compound and verb-object phrase. For instance:

(2) kǎoròu (roasting/roasted meat), zháxiā (frying/fried shrimp), kǎoyáng (roasting/roasted lamb), zhájīchì (frying/fried chicken wings), kǎoniúròu (grilling/grilled beef), zhēngpáigǔ (steaming/steamed ribs), jiānjīdàn (frying/fried eggs), chǎoqīngcài (stir-frying/stir-fried vegetables)

In example 2 above N are raw materials and ingredient of cooking actions. Cooking actions cause shape, color, temperature or other qualitative changes in N without creating new dishes. The entire structure can represent both process and result of cooking action. These lexical examples can be represented either as attributive-head compounds or verb-object phrases.

(II) When V[+produce], that is, the structure satisfies "N is a dish produced through V", in most cases there is no semantic transfer and it only indicates a verb-object relationship. For example:

(3) zhǔzhōu (cooking porridge), áotāng (boiling soup), kǎodàn'gāo (baking cakes), kǎobǐnggān (baking cookies), chǎoshūcài (stir-frying vegetables), zháyóutiáo (frying dough sticks), zhǔjiǎozi (boiling jiaozi)

In example (3), all N are created by the cooking action V. Only through the action of boiling can a mixture of ingredients and water be called "porridge" or "soup". Dough that hasn't been baked remains raw dough and cannot become a "cake" or "cookie". When the structure meets the condition that "N is made through V", the semantics of V contain an implicit information that "the result made through V way". The entire structure will not undergo semantic transfer in actual use and can basically only be verb-object phrase.

The two rules above apply to most "$V_{cooking}$+N". However, examples like "jiānjiǎo (fried jiaozi), kǎonáng (baked flatbread), kǎobāozi (baked buns), zhēngdàn'gāo (steamed cakes), zháshǔtiáo (fried fries)" seem to be exceptions. Above N are obviously created by cooking action, according to previous rules they should behave as verb-object phrases. Nevertheless, whether from language sense of Chinese native speakers or from actual usage results, they are dominantly interpreted as attributive-head compounds. How could this be explained? It seems not all structures satisfying V[+produce] can indicate verb-object only, whether semantic transfer happens or not also relates with conventional production method.

Conventional production method (hereinafter referred to as Vo) refers to what people perceive as most common way of making certain foods—for instance: dumplings are usually boiled; cakes are baked; buns need steaming; dough sticks require frying... If such conventional method indeed exists for certain foods, then native speakers from same cultural background could easily make judgement based on life experience. Also, some foods like "meat, tofu, eggs, etc." have no conventional preparation method. Natural food materials fit into many cooking methods and there is no default priority. Vo mainly exists in certain man-made foods. The relationship between Vo and semantic transfer goes like this:

(III) When V [+produce], but N lacks V0 or $V_{cooking} \neq$ V0 in the structure, then "$V_{cooking}$+N" can undergo semantic transfer as well. For instance:
(3) jiānjiǎo (fried jiaozi), zhēngjiǎo (steamed jiaozi), zhēngbǐng (steamed buns), zhǔbǐng (boiled buns), shāobǐng (baked buns), jiānròubāo (grilled meat buns), kǎobāozi (baked buns)

Jiaozi are usually boiled. When the cooking method $V_{cooking}$ = V0, no structural transfer occurs. Hence "zhǔjiǎozi (boiled jiaozi)" remains verb-object phrase – examples in (3) fall under this rule. However, for "jiānjiǎo (fried jiaozi)" and "zhēngjiǎo (steamed jiaozi)", which are not boiled or $V_{cooking} \neq$ V0, they transfer from their original verb-object structure to attributive-head compounds.

Based on the above analysis, "jiānjiǎo (fried jiaozi)" and "zhēngjiǎo (steamed jiaozi)" have undergone semantic transfer that allow them to represent both verb-object phrase and attributive-head compound simultaneously. Yet there are also "jiānjiǎo zi (frying jiaozi)" and "zhēngjiǎo zi (streaming jiaozi)", which can only appear as attributive-head compound. We believe this phenomenon aligns with the trend of bisyllabification in Chinese nouns on one hand; on the other hand, it serves as a means to differentiate ambiguous structures in practical language use.

In terms like "jiānjiǎo (fried jiaozi)" and "zhēngjiǎo (steamed jiaozi)", "jiaozi" loses its affixes becoming an unbound morpheme "jiao", retains its referent and gains stronger adhesion with cooking verbs, forming closer combinations. Since attributive structures have tighter internal component combination than verb-object phrases (Ke Hang 2012:48), hence "fried dumps" or "steam dumps" take up usage as compound words representing food names while "jiānjiǎo zi (frying jiaozi)" and "zhēngjiǎo zi (streaming jiaozi)" are more frequently used as verb-object phrases.

However, Chinese does not primarily rely on morphological marking for grammar; thus not all food nouns can lose their affixes making this differentiation quite limited due to imbalance of ambiguity.

We designed a process for how semantic transfer may occur based on aforementioned analyses - refer Fig. 2.

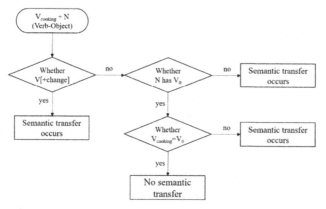

Fig. 2. The process by which semantic transfer occurs on "$V_{cooking}+N$"

[1+2] is predominant prosodic pattern of "$V_{cooking}+N$", yet rhythm does not significantly influence the choice of its structural property. Rather, "produce/change" semantic attribute within $V_{cooking}$ and the conventional method V0 for N are what truly exert an impact. When V [+change], an unmarked semantic transfer from verb-object to attributive-head occurs, enabling the structure to function as either. When V[+produce] and same as V0 for N, the structure only manifests as a verb-object phrase. In examples V[+produce] but $V_{cooking} \neq$ V0 or N lacks V0, semantic transfer still occurs.

Why do "produce/change" semantic attribute and the conventional methods of food become significant factors influencing whether or not transference occurs? And how does $V_{cooking}$ anchor the semantic attribute after combining with N? We will delve further into cognitive mechanisms.

4   Construction Mechanism of the Modern Chinese "$V_{cooking}+N$" Structure

4.1   Encyclopedic Knowledge Semantic View

The encyclopedic knowledge semantic view of cognitive linguistics posits that word meaning carries encyclopedic knowledge, and semantic concepts are directly derived from experiential perceptions formed by human interactions with surrounding environmental objects. Linguistic knowledge and encyclopedic knowledge are intertwined and inseparable, when necessary, introducing encyclopedic knowledge as an extension of semantic features can help open new perspectives for us to better understand the inherent characteristics of things themselves.

The two major elements that affect whether "$V_{cooking}+N$" undergoes semantic transfer - the "produce/change" semantic attribute featured in cooking verbs V and conventional methods used for food - rarely appear in dictionary definitions (with few exceptions, see 4.3). Instead, they originate from language users' practical life experiences. Without integrating encyclopedic knowledge for comprehensive analysis, it becomes difficult to differentiate among members of "$V_{cooking}+N$". Therefore, the differentiation ambiguity of the structure can be seen as one positive example supporting the validity of the encyclopedic knowledge semantic view.

4.2   The Semantic Class Attribute of N Determines the Anchoring of $V_{cooking}$'s Semantic Attribute

The formation of compound words or phrases necessitates taking into consideration the compatibility of semantic attribute when combining elements. For instance, the verb "róu (knead/rub)" must be directly paired with an object [+solid], as in "róumiàn (knead dough)" or "róuyǎnjīng (rub eye)", and we cannot knead coffee or oxygen. $V_{cooking}$ carries [+produce/change] semantic attribute that remains unselected until it enters a "$V_{cooking}+N$" structure. Only after being combined with food noun does this semantic attribute become anchored and highlighted. For example, in "kǎoyángròu (roasting/roasted lamb)," only a qualitative change occurs; hence, "kǎo" [+change] and the entire structure can represent both verb-object phrase and attributive-head compound; whereas in "kǎodàn'gāo (baking cake)," baking action produces a cake so here, "kǎo" [+produce] and the entire structure can only appear as verb-object phrase.

A single cooking verb paired with different nouns displays varying semantic attributes and structural types. It suggests that within the "$V_{cooking}+N$" structure, post-positioned food nouns serve to anchor $V_{cooking}$'s semantic attribute.

N reveals two types of arguments within "$V_{cooking}+N$": object or resultative argument. When N is a cooking material and natural object, it serves as object argument within the structure such as "niúròu (beef)" in "kǎoniúròu (grilled beef)", "jīdàn (egg)" in "jiānjīdàn (fry egg). These ingredients are obtained from nature rather than artificially made, thus remain themselves even after undergoing culinary processes. In this context $V_{cooking}$ opt for [+change] indicating only qualitative change occurs to N.

Conversely, when N is created by the cooking action and classified semantically as man-made object, it serves as resultative object in the structure denoting completed dishes, like "zhōu(porridge)" in "zhǔzhōu (boiling porridge)". These N are produced by culinary activities, therefore possess artificial attribute. When combining with verb, $V_{cooking}$ choose [+produce] signifying creating new items.

In conclusion within "$V_{cooking}$+N", the natural or man-made classification of N determines $V_{cooking}$'s semantic attribute. When N is natural object the verb manifests [+change], while for man-made the verb opts for [+produce].

4.3 Implied and Manifested Conventional Production Method

Food and cooking actions are inherently inseparable. Different production methods determining the fundamental differences between foods, marking their most significant and prominent distinguishing characteristics. Thus, production method is either implied or manifested in the name of food.

4.3.1 Implied Production Method: "V+N" Displays Verb-Object Relationship

If N paired with V [+prepare] and represents a dish, then the conceptual structure of N inherently includes the attribute "made in V's way". Sometimes this characteristic is also reflected in dictionary definitions, as seen for instance the definition for "cookie" in The Modern Chinese Dictionary: small thin pieces **baked** from flour mixed with sugar, eggs, milk etc. Similar instances like dòujiāng(soymilk), máhuā (twisted dough-strips), miànbāo (bread), húntún (dumplings), yóutiáo (deep-fried dough sticks) etc.

Upon seeing a food noun, language users can quickly associate it with its conventional method V0 by drawing upon their encyclopedic knowledge; therefore, $V_{cooking}$ doesn't need to serve distinguishing function anymore. If there is still a V0 appears before N, then what V0 undertakes are its own semantic meanings, and "V0+N" structure can be interpreted as a verb-object phrase itself without semantic transfer.

The previously mentioned phenomena: when V[+prepare], "$V_{cooking}$+N" rarely undergo semantic transfer - they now have reasonable explanations too.

Examples of this category: zhǔzhōu (boiling porridge), áotāng (simmering soup), kǎodàn'gāo (baking cakes), kǎobǐnggān (baking cookies), kǎopīsà (baking pizza), zhámáhuā (deep frying twisted dough-strips), zhǔjiǎozi (boiling jiaozi), zhǔkāfēi (brewing coffee), etc.

4.3.2 Manifested Production Method: The Structure "V+N" Displays Attributive-Head

When N paired with V[+change] and represents food material, various cooking methods naturally leads to dishes that necessitates differentiation from others. Hence $V_{cooking}$ has to bear the distinction and appear at attributive position, and "$V_{cooking}$+N" can undergo semantic transfer, shifting from action to food name. Examples of this category: chǎofàn (fried rice), kǎoròu (roasted meat), zháxiā (deep-fried shrimp), kǎoyáng (grilled lamb), zhēngpáigǔ (steamed pork ribs), jiānjīdàn (pan-fried eggs), etc.

If what precedes the food noun is not the conventional preparation method V0 but another $V_{cooking}$ instead, the structure represents a new dish which requires highlighting its unique in expression, thus $V_{cooking}$ takes on the distinguishing role and appears as an attribute. For instance: "zhēngdàngāo (steamed cake)" emphasizes its difference from typically baked ones and highlights its specific characteristics. In such cases semantic transfer can also occur within "$V_{cooking}+N$" - examples include: jiānjiǎo (fried jiaozi), zhēngjiǎo (steamed jiaozi), zhēngbǐng (steamed buns), zhǔbǐng (boiled puns), shāobing (baked buns), jiānròubāo (pan-fried meat buns), jiānxiànbǐng (fried stuffed pies), zháwánzi (deep-fried meatballs), kǎonáng (roasted naan breads), zháshǔtiáo (fried French fries), etc.

However, kǎonáng (roasted naan breads) and zháshǔtiáo (fried French fries) seem to be exceptions because according to native speakers naan is typically grilled and French fries are usually fried; why does structural transfer still occur?

Because naan and French fries are foreign foods introduced from ethnic minorities or other countries, local people unfamiliar with these newly appeared foods. So $V_{cooking}$ provides adequate information so that people could find out preparation methods from the cooking verb in their names: "this food called naan is grilled", "this snack known as French Fries is fried". Hence $V_{cooking}$ still undertakes distinguishing roles so essentially kǎonáng and zháshǔtiáo are not real exceptions. As these two kinds of foods gradually integrate into Chinese culture circle, the frequency of using "náng (naan)" and "shǔtiáo (French Fries)" to refer to foods increases, kǎonáng and zháshǔtiáo also used as verb-object phrases in BCC's dialogue sub-corpus. It can be predicted that, in future, kǎonáng and zháshǔtiáo may eventually only be understood as verb-object phrases without semantic transfer.

In summary, we have deduced one rule regarding whether or not semantic transfer occurs within "$V_{cooking}+N$": when $V_{cooking}$ needs to undertake distinguishing role semantic transfer occurs, the structure could represent attributive-head compound, but when $V_{cooking}$ doesn't need to undertake distinguishing role then "$V_{cooking}+N$" manifests as verb-object phrase.

5   Conclusion

In modern Chinese, monosyllabic verbs generally cannot directly serve as adjectival modifiers. However, an exception to this rule lies in monosyllabic cooking verbs. This study utilized a corpus-driven research methodology and exhaustively examined the collocation structures of 11 monosyllabic cooking verbs with nouns in the BCC Corpus. The findings revealed that the "produce/change" semantic attribute of cooking verbs and conventional food preparation methods significantly influence whether semantic transfer occurs:

When $V_{cooking}$[+change], semantic transfer occurs within "$V_{cooking}+N$" structure.
When $V_{cooking}$[+produce] and equals to the conventional preparation method of N ($V_{cooking} = V0$), no semantic transfer occurs.
When $V_{cooking}$[+produce] but N lacks conventional preparation method or "$V_{cooking} \neq V0$", then semantic transfer still occurs.

On this basis, constraints on construction are explained from two perspectives: semantic class attributes of N and implied/manifested conventional production method.

When N is natural material, $V_{cooking}$ opts for [+change], while when N is man-made material, $V_{cooking}$ displays [+produce]. When $V_{cooking}$ undertake distinguish role, semantic transfer occurs in "$V_{cooking}$+N" structure. Conversely, when $V_{cooking}$ does not need to undertake such distinguishing role, "$V_{cooking}$+N" only appears as original verb-object phrases.

Acknowledgments. This paper was supported by Major Project of Key Research Institute of Humanities and Social Sciences (22JJD740014); Humanities and Social Sciences Planning Fund of the Ministry of Education of China (23YJC740031); International Chinese Language Education Project of Center For Language Education and Cooperation (22YH65D); Science Foundation of Beijing Language and Culture University (supported by "the Fundamental Research Funds for the Central Universities") (YJT15).

References

Deng, D.: Can verbs serve as adjectives? Lang. Teach. Res. **5**, 78–89 (2021)

Feng, S.L.: The 'prosodic words' in Chinese. Chin. Soc. Sci. **1**, 161–176 (1996)

Guo, R.: Studies on Modern Chinese Word Classes. (Revised Edition). The Commercial Press, Beijing (2002)

Fodor, J.A., Lepore, E.: The emptiness of the lexicon: reflections on James Pustejovsky's the generative Lexicon. Linguist. Inq. **2**, 269–288 (1998)

Ke, H.: Study on the Collocation of Monosyllabic and Disyllabic in Modern Chinese. The Commercial Press, Beijing (2012)

Li, J.: The development trend and form-meaning features of contemporary Chinese lexical patterns. In: Dong, M., Gu, Y., Hong, J.F. (eds.) CLSW 2021. LNCS, vol. 13249, pp. 391–401. Springer, Cham (2022). https://doi.org/10.1007/978-3-031-06703-7_30

Lü, S.X.: Preliminary exploration of monosyllabic and disyllabic issues in modern Chinese. J. Chin. Lang. **1**, 10–22 (1963)

Qin, Z.X., Duanmu, S.: The length collocation of compound words with verbal-nominal predicative structure in mandarin: a quantitative study based on corpus. World Chin. Teach. **4**, 509–524 (2021)

Shen, J.X.: Nouns and Verbs. The Commercial Press, Beijing (2016)

Shen, J.X.: Reflections on "noun-verbs": problems and countermeasures. World Chin. Teach. **1**, 3–17 (2012)

Shi, D.X.: The predicative structure of verb-noun compound words in mandarin. J. Natl. Lang. **6**, 483–495 (2003)

Song, Z.Y.: Features of construction Grammar and its implications for lexical studies in mandarin — taking naming patterns in dish names as an example. Lang. Teach. Res. **2**, 88–102 (2022)

Wang, G.Q.: Several issues regarding verbs as adjectives. J. Beihua Univ. (Soc. Sci. Edn.) **2**, 24–26 (1993)

Wang, H.J.: Monosyllable and disyllable, tone range convergence and grammatical structure type and component order. Contemp. Linguist. **4**, 241–252 (2001)

Zhang, G.X.: Understanding factors of "V double + N double" phrases. J. Natl. Lang. **3**, 176–186 (1997)

Zhang, M.: Cognitive Linguistics and Mandarin Noun Phrases. Chinese Social Sciences Press, Beijing (1998)

Zhao, Q.: Semantic structure and word formation reasoning of V + N bias formal compounds in mandarin. World Chin. Teach. **2**, 201–214 (2020)

Classifiers of Mandarin Alphabetical Words with Character-Alphabet Structure

Xinlan Zhao[✉], Yu-Yin Hsu, and Chu-Ren Huang

Department of Chinese and Bilingual Studies, Hong Kong Polytechnic University, Hong Kong, People's Republic of China
xinlan.zhao@connect.polyu.hk

Abstract. Mandarin alphabetical words (MAWs) refer to the code-mixing of Romanized letters and characters such as X光 'X-ray' in the Mandarin lexicon. Previous studies have mainly focused on MAWs' formation but lacked empirical evidence regarding their morpho-syntactic behaviours. Classifiers have been used to infer nominals' semantic properties and characteristics. An intriguing yet less explored issue is the classifier-selection pattern of MAWs and MAWs' morpho-syntactic idiosyncrasies. We adopt a corpus-based approach to handle this issue. Assuming that a MAW's classifier is motivated by the head of that MAW, we hypothesize that when a MAW is integrated into the Mandarin lexicon, its dominant classifiers will be the semantically more specific ones and not the neutral classifier. We show that MAWs share a dominant compounding structure in Mandarin and that MAW's classifier is decided by that head even when the head is represented by alphabets.

Keywords: Mandarin Alphabetical Words · Classifiers · Code-mixing · Corpus-based approach

1 Introduction

In recent years, Chinese-English code-mixing has become increasingly common in Chinese society with frequent foreign exchanges. Code-mixing is the mixed usage of different languages, varieties, or orthographic systems, typically within the same sentence [1]. With frequent language contacts, people code switches/mixes to find proper expressions when there is no appropriate translation for the language being used or when communicators generate code-mixing language; social factors such as education, religion, gender, and age also have influences on the degree of this phenomenon [2, 3]. Mandarin Alphabetical Words (MAWs), as a result of language contact, mainly refer to the code-mixed words in Chinese, which usually consist of Chinese Characters and alphabetical letters (e.g., BB霜 'blemish balm', and 维C 'vitamin C') [4].

In the literature, MAWs are further divided into three major subcategories based on the positions of the alphabetic letters and characters: A-C (alphabet + character), C-A (character + alphabet), and C-A-C (alphabet in the middle) [4]. Typical MAWs follow

M. Dong et al. (Eds.): CLSW 2023, LNAI 14514, pp. 130–145, 2024.
https://doi.org/10.1007/978-981-97-0583-2_11

the Chinese modifier-modified (head)[1] Morphological rule. The morphological head of a MAW can be a Chinese character, as in BB霜 'blemish balm' with the character霜 'cream' as its head, and can also be alphabets, as in 气垫BB 'air cushion blemish balm', which has the alphabets 'BB' as its head.

MAWs have attracted much attention from scholars because of their wide use in natural settings and the complicated linguistic idiosyncrasies they demonstrate concerning the combined features of both Chinese and foreign languages [5]. The previous studies of MAWs have mainly focused on language policy issues [6, 7], action techniques [4, 5, 8, 9], and the evolutionary traits of MAWs [10, 11]. More recently, scholars have begun to investigate the language behaviours of MAWs on morpho-phono-orthographical levels via experimental approaches [12, 13] and corpus-based approaches [4, 5, 14, 15]. Despite significant work, scholars still need to answer whether or to what extent MAWs adapt to the Mandarin language system.

Among the linguistic issues, it is well known that Chinese is a classifier language [16]. The selection of the Chinese classifier (hereafter CL) for a noun is driven by the semantic properties of the head noun [17–19]. The CL-noun agreement and the CL choice are the two dominant topics in recent research on Chinese CL. Unfortunately, this vital reference has not been linked to the linguistic manifestations of MAWs, although it is intriguing to consider how the two lines of lexicons interact.

Therefore, this paper addresses the relationship between CLs and MAWs by studying the CL distribution of the C-A type of MAWs with alphabetic letters as the morphological heads. The reason for investigating this C-A structure of MAWs was that we were curious about how well the alphabetic letters were integrated into the Chinese lexicon at the syntactical level, mainly when they played an important role as head morphemes (the MAWs mentioned in the rest of the paper refer only to C-A MAWs).

In summary, our work aimed to answer the following research questions:

(1) Does the CL distribution of MAWs follow the semantically motivated rule the same as Mandarin nominals do (e.g., 一台车载GPS/一台车载导航, 'a vehicle navigator' vs 一台电脑 'a computer')?
(2) Are the MAW's dominant CLs the semantically more specific ones rather than being the neutral classifier 个(GE)?

Since MAWs share a typical modifier-head compounding structure, we hypothesized that the CLs of MAWs should be motivated by the semantic meaning of the head regardless of the orthography of the head; thus, their CLs would not be replaced by the neutral CL 个(GE) as well.

The rest of the paper is structured as follows: The criteria for the data selection are described in Sect. 2, the method is introduced in Sect. 3, the results of the data analysis are presented in Sect. 4, and the paper ends with a discussion and a conclusion in Sects. 5 and 6.

---

[1] Like many languages, Chinese compound nouns or nominal phrases often have the "modifier-head" structure; for example, 火车站 'train station' has the modifier 火车 'train' modifying the head 站 'stop, station', and the syntactic status of the word is classified by the head 站 'stop, station' instead of by the modifier 火车 'train'.

2 Selection of the MAWs and CLs

2.1 Criteria for MAW Selection

The selection of the MAW seed words for the present study was based on two corpus-based wordlists and one published dictionary. The first wordlist is built by [4] from both the Sinica Corpus [20] and the Chinese Gigaword Corpus [21]. The second one is the wordlist built by [5] from Sina Weibo, a predominant social media platform in China. These two wordlists are up-to-date and considerable in scale. However, the words were not manually checked, so we also consulted the *dictionary of Lettered-words* [22] to balance the bias of word source. The dictionary has over 2000 MAW entries covering all structures of A-C, C-A, C-A-C, and pure alphabetical words with different POS statuses.

However, to capture the essential properties of MAWs relevant to the research questions, the MAWs were shortlisted using the following criteria:

- the MAWs are nouns or compound nouns
- the form of the MAWs is C-A (character-alphabet) type
- the MAWs can co-occur with at least three CLs in the corpus
- the MAWs have over 200 hits in the corpus

During the selection process, it is noticed that there are subcategories of MAWs. Most MAWs have alphabetic letters as the heads (e.g., 蓝光DVD 'Blu-ray DVD' has DVD as the head), but few present structures differently. For example, 卡拉OK 'karaoke' is single morpheme word, where卡拉and OK phonetically transcribed the first two and the last syllables in *karaoke*, respectively; 维生素C 'vitamin C' in which 维生素 'vitamin' has properties more as the semantic head and C indicates the subtype of vitamin; 甲A 'First Division Group A-League', and甲B 'First Division Group B League', instead, having the alphabetic letters, A and B modifying the First Division Group to show its sub-levels.

Considering that the semantic head of a noun is a crucial factor that affects the selection of Chinese CLs, the MAWs are sorted into two groups. One group has alphabetic letters as the head; the other group contains other structures.

After careful selection, 30 focused MAWs are listed in Tables 1 and 2. The amount of seed words in this study is limited due to two facts. First, the MAWs are much less than the others by nature. For example, in *The Dictionary of Lettered-words,* there are only 38 MAWs out of the total over 2000 entries. Second, the candidates went through a strict filtering process to retain only those with high frequency and at least three co-occurring CLs in the corpus.

2.2 CL Selection Rules

In general, a CL tends to occur before a noun in Mandarin Chinese when it needs to be individualized for counting [17, 18], including the individual reading 一本书 'a book', the kind reading 一种希望 'a hope', and event reading 一次比赛 'a competition' [19]. It is generally agreed that CLs are distinguished from measure words [24, 25]. According to Tai [24], CLs "pick out the salient perceptual properties associated with the noun". On the other hand, measure words only "denote the quantity of nouns and are used to

Table 1. MAWs with the lettered-head.

MAWs	Hits in corpus[a]	English translations
阿SIR	358	policeman, the cop (Cantonese)
短T	516	short-sleeved T-shirt (short T)
长T	354	long-sleeved T-shirt (long T)
深V	8173	deep V-neck dress
气垫BB	1523	air cushion blemish balm
蓝光DVD	1134	blue ray digital video disk
车载GPS	5291	vehicle global position system
电台DJ	1040	radio disc jockey
人均GDP	34488	per capita GDP
硬盘DV	237	hard drive digital video
终极PK	1993	the ultimate player killing
真人CS	5949	cosplay of counter-strike
量贩式KTV	451	buffet-style KTV
螺旋CT	8829	spiral computed tomography
亲子DIY	591	parent-child Handmade (do it yourself)
企业HR	3144	Human Resource manager of an enterprise
职场OL	538	office lady in the workplace
高清MV	737	music TV of high-definition
白光LED	5841	white light LED (light-emitting diode)

[a]The Chinese Web 2017 Simplified corpus (zhTenTen17) [23]: https://www.sketchengine.eu/zht enten-chinese-corpus/

count or measure". Based on the CL & measure word dichotomy, Ahrens and Huang [18] proposed the Chinese CLs taxonomy shown in Fig. 1. Based on this categorization, only sortal CLs (individual CLs, kind CLs, and event CLs) are relevant in the current study, while measure words are not investigated. The detailed interpretations of each CL mentioned in the rest of the paper (including CLs in the tables) are listed in the Appendix.

Table 2. MAWs without lettered-head.

MAWs	Hits in corpus	English translations
甲A	5822	First Division Group A
甲B	2084	First Division Group B
傻B	1839	silly person
卡拉OK	25526	Karaoke
维生素A	53996	Vitamin A
维生素B	29566	Vitamin B
维生素C	105054	Vitamin C
维生素E	44331	Vitamin D
维生素D	45499	Vitamin E
维C	8994	short form of 'Vitamin C'
维E	1757	short form of 'Vitamin E'

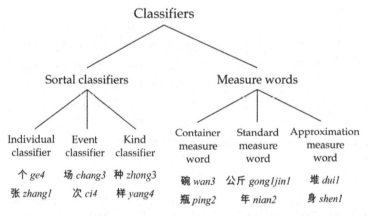

Fig. 1. Taxonomy of classifiers [18].

3   Data

The data of this study were generated from an up-to-date Chinese corpus: the Chinese Web 2017 Simplified corpus (zhTenTen17) [23], which can be accessed through the platform Sketch Engine [26]. This corpus has the advantages of considerable size (15 billion tokens), genre and style diversity, adequate functions, and linguistic annotations.

3.1   Data Extracting Process

Native Chinese speakers can name a few CLs of a specific noun easily by intuition but may not be able to retrieve all the possible CLs; however, a corpus-assisted extraction of CLs can help to provide a more comprehensive CL set. The Sketch Engine platform has a function to get a CL reference list for a specific noun to gain an ideal range of CLs. That is the "word sketch" function. For instance, a list of CLs (indicated as "measure") co-occurring with the noun 维C 'vitamin C' can be obtained together with the Mutual Information (MI) scores indicating the strength of the collocation. After getting the CL lists suggested by the corpus, the next step is to obtain qualified CL-MAW data.

The whole process of extracting data has three steps. The first step was to obtain the concordances of a target noun in the corpus. In the second step, we filter the concordance examples by each co-occurring CL. Then, each filtered data set was shortlisted by manual checking.

Noted that, in step three, if the data set was too large, such as containing over 1000 concordance lines, a random sample of 100 concordances was extracted automatically, and a rate of valid data was gained by counting the valid data out of the 100 examples. For example, suppose 3950 sentence examples contain both the noun 维生素A 'vitamin A' and the CL 种 'kind'; 100 random samples will be checked to see how many valid examples there are. If there are four valid examples out of 100, the valid data rate would be 0.04 and the total number of 维生素A 'vitamin A' and 种 'kind' combination will be 3950*0.02, that is 158. In our dataset, seven MAW-CL combinations underwent this random sample process; the others were checked based on the full concordance results.

3.2 Data Examples

Based on the primary semantic functions of CLs, which are to individuate and to identify the units for enumeration or reference [18], the common types of CL-MAWs are shown below with authentic examples taken from the corpus of zhTenTen:

(1) CLs with a numeral preceding the noun:

一	件	短T	就	够	了。
yi	jian	duanT	jiu	gou	le。
one	CL	short T	just	enough	LE

'One short T is enough.'

(2) CLs be used with a referential demonstrative without a numeral:

这	款	气垫BB	一共	有	两	个	色号。
zhe	kuan	qidian BB	yigong	you	liang	ge	sehao。
this	CL	air cushion BB	altogether	have	two	GE	colour type

'This air cushion BB has two colour types altogether.'

(3) CLs with ordinal numbers preceding the noun:

1994	年	研制	出	第一	颗	白光LED。
yi jiu jiu si	nian	yanzhi	chu	diyi	ke	baiguang LED。
1994	year	develop	out	first	CL	white light LED

'The first white LED was developed in 1994.'

(4) The numeral-CL combinations are placed after the noun:

卡拉OK	300元	一	场。
kala OK	san bai yuan	yi	chang。
Karaoke	300 Yuan	one	CL

'The Karaoke is 300 Yuan one time.'

(5) CLs and nouns are separated by other modifiers (e.g., a relative clause):

一	件	带	有	萌宠	图案	的	短T。
yi	jian	dai	you	mengchong	tu'an	de	duanT。
one	CL	take	have	cute pet	motif	DE	short T

'A short T-shirt with a cute pet motif.'

4 Results

The main results of MAWs' CL distributions are listed in Table 3 and 4. Table 3 focuses on the CLs of MAWs with alphabets as a head, while Table 4 is about the CL results of single morpheme MAWs or MAWs with characters as a head.

In Table 3, the results show us that first, MAWs can co-occur with multiple CLs covering all three types of sortal CLs. For example, the individual CLs个 (GE), 张 'to classify objects that are flat, two-dimensional, and horizontal or objects', 件 'to classify clothes'; the event CLs 场 'to classify scheduled events', 次 'a general classifier for events', 局 'to classify the occurrence of games'; and the kind CLs 种 'to classify the kinds of entities', 类 'to classify kinds of entities', 款 'to classify the categories of products'. Second, all three types of sortal CLs can be dominant CLs of a specific MAW. The most dominant CLs are individual CLs, followed by the kind and event CLs. Third, the dominant CL of each MAW is consistent with the semantic meaning of the head morpheme, which is also the alphabetical part of the word.

As examples to the third point, 阿SIR 'policeman' and 职场OL 'office lady' has the semantic meaning of certain kind of people. The semantic meaning is denoted by the head morphemes SIR and OL; according to the heads, the CLs selected are CLs for people, such as 个 (GE), 位 'to classify people with a polite sense', and 名 'to classify people when their social role refers to them'. Interestingly, for the two words of真人CS 'cosplay of counter strike' and 亲子DIY 'parent-child handmade', although the character parts indicate people, their collocating CLs 'to classify scheduled events', 次 'a general classifier for events', and 期 'to classify events that involve stages of completion' are consistent with the alphabetical head morphemes CS 'counter strike' and DIY 'do it yourself' which refer to specific activities.

Table 3. CL-distributions of MAWs with the lettered-head.

MAW	English	Frequency of CLs
阿SIR	Policeman, cop (Cantonese)	个9, 位6, 名2, 群1
短T	short-sleeved T-shirt (short T)	件55, 款15, 种3, 个3, 套1
长T	long-sleeved T-shirt (long T)	件27, 款20, 个2, 种2, 身1
深V	deep V-neck dress	件14, 个5, 款3, 种3, 袭1
气垫BB	air cushion blemish balm	款132, 个13, 种6, 套1, 波1, 批1
蓝光DVD	blue ray digital video disk	张13, 台3, 个2, 代2, 批2
车载GPS	vehicle global position system	款75, 台13, 个10, 种6, 部2
电台DJ	radio disc jockey	位37, 名34, 个33, 家5
人均GDP	per capita GDP	项5, 种2, 条1, 类1
硬盘DV	hard drive digital video	款20, 代2, 台1
终极PK	the ultimate player killing	场60, 轮25, 次22, 个5, 番2
真人CS	cosplay of counter-strike	场29, 次12, 个5, 局3, 种1, 款1
量贩式KTV	buffet-style KTV	家11, 个2, 种2
螺旋CT	spiral computed tomography	台167, 次31, 个9, 种4, 款2
亲子DIY	parent-child Handmade (do it yourself)	场5, 种3, 个1, 项1, 份1, 期1
企业HR	Human Resource manager of an enterprise	位44, 名27, 个24, 类1
职场OL	office lady in the workplace	个11, 位2, 名2
高清MV	music TV of high-definition	首9, 个5, 部2, 支1
白光LED	white light LED (light-emitting diode)	个110, 颗54, 种50, 只44, 类6, 组6, 支6, 款4, 粒2, 串1, 排1

The CLs of the second group (Table 4) are also diverse in type and plentiful in numbers. According to Table 4, the CLs of these MAWs are also semantically motivated by the head morphemes. For example, event CLs轮 'to classify sequences of events', 场 'to classify scheduled events', and 届 'to classify scheduled events' are classifying events of 甲A 'First Division Group A', and 甲B 'First Division Group B'; the individual CLs 群 'to classify a swarm of people', 帮 'to classify a group of people' and 名 'to classify people when their social role refers to them' are classifying the people of 傻B 'silly people'. In addition, the single-morpheme word卡拉OK 'Karaoke' is mainly classified by 家 'to classify institutions', indicating that it is often related to the venue. Meanwhile, it is also referred to as songs, singing events, or singing equipment because there are other CLs such as 首 'to classify songs or music', 场, and 代 'to classify people, technologies or products of an equal generation'.

The vitamin MAWs, the characterized维生素 'vitamin' or its short form 维 'V-' denotes the core physical meaning, whereas the letters indicate the categories of vitamins. We can see that the coverage of CLs to these vitamin words is similar, as all of them have the shape CLs such as 颗 'to classify round objects', 粒 'to classify small round objects', and 片 'classify objects that are flat and thin' classifying their common feature of small round physical shapes. Additionally, several kinds of vitamins select the kind CL 种 'to classify the kinds of entities as their dominant CL; this may be due to their common feature of being referred to as kinds of vitamins in most contexts.

Table 4. CL-distributions of MAWs without lettered-head.

MAW	English translations	Frequency of CLs
甲A	First Division Group A	轮57, 届23, 场7, 支1, 局1
甲B	First Division Group B	轮14, 场2, 届1
傻B	silly person	个177, 群27, 种11, 帮11, 名1
卡拉OK	Karaoke	家74, 个36, 次30, 首30, 场19, 曲7, 种6, 代1
维生素A	Vitamin A	种158, 粒11, 颗2, 个2
维生素C	Vitamin B	片238, 种149, 粒46, 颗12, 款9, 个2
维生素E	Vitamin C	粒85, 种67, 片45, 颗27, 个4
维生素D	Vitamin D	种53, 粒3, 款3, 类2, 片1
维生素B	Vitamin E	种154, 片104, 粒9, 颗6, 类2
维C	Vitamin C	片25, 粒7, 颗4, 个4, 种3, 枚1
维E	Vitamin E	颗7, 粒7, 片4, 种1, 款1

Generally, the data results above verify our first hypothesis that the CL selection rule of MAWs conforms to the Mandarin grammar rule, which is highly semantic motivated. Meanwhile, the CLs can demonstrate the lexical semantics of MAWs or coerce different semantic readings of MAWs.

5   Discussion

Based on the above results, we elicit further observations to compare the CL behaviours of MAWs with their traditional Chinese canonical forms.

First, for the group of MAWs with lettered-heads, we generated the CLs of some of the equivalent Chinse canonical forms in Table 5. Note that only some MAWs have canonical forms with good CL collocations. From Table 5, the MAWs and the Chinese canonical words behave similarly regarding CL selection in most cases. Both can select a group of CLs to emphasis different semantic facets in an authentic context. For example, 件 'to classify clothes' is preferred by clothes; 个 (GE), 位 'to classify people with a polite sense', and 名 'to classify people with social role' are preferred by people; 款 'to classify the categories of products' and 个 are selected by products, etc.

Nevertheless, within each pair, the preference difference of a dominant CL exists. For instance, 警察 'policemen' has a particular preference for the CL 位, while 阿SIR 'policemen (Cantonese)' mostly choose the neutral CL 个. In the sense that 位 is more polite than 个 when classifying a person, it may indicate that 警察 is more respectful than 阿SIR in most contexts. Most importantly, there is no evidence that the MAWs have a trend of using more 个 than the canonical forms.

Table 5. CL-distributions of letter-head MAWs and their canonical forms.

Keywords	English translations	Frequency of CLs
短T	short T-shirt	件55, 款15, 种3, 个3, 套1
短袖衫	short T-shirt	件159, 款21, 种10, 身2
长T	long T-shirt	件25, 款12, 个2, 种2, 身1
长袖衫	long T-shirt	件76, 款11, 条3, 种2
气垫BB	air cushion blemish balm	款132, 个13, 种6, 套1, 波1, 批1
气垫粉底	air cushion foundation	款72, 个10, 种6, 类1, 套1, 批1,件1
车载GPS	vehicle global position system	款75, 台13, 个10, 种6, 部2
车载导航	vehicle global position system	款43, 台3, 个10, 代7, 种3, 部3
终极PK	the ultimate player killing	场60, 轮25, 次22, 个5, 番2, 版1
终极对决	the ultimate player killing	场110, 次14, 轮7, 个2, 局1
企业HR	Human Resource manager	位44, 名27, 个24, 类1
企业人事	Human Resource manager	位3, 名3, 个3
白光LED	white light LED	个110, 颗54, 种50, 只44, 类6, 组6, 支5, 款4, 粒2, 串1, 批1, 排1, 条1
白光发光二极管	white light LED	个5, 种2, 只1, 代1, 层1
阿SIR	policeman (Cantonese)	个9, 位6, 名2, 群1
警察	policeman	名36219, 个18382, 位5697, 群1165, 帮452, 批391, 种207, 类44, 波16, 枚4
亲子DIY	parent-child Handmade DIY	场5, 种3, 个3, 项1, 份1, 期1
亲子手工	parent-child Handmade	次3, 个3, 场1, 份1, 种1, 款1

Second, to have a more general view of the two forms of words, the CLs are sorted into three types: the general 个 (GE), other individual CLs (IN), and kind CLs (KD), and each CL-type percentage is calculated in Table 6. Here, the reason that the general CL 个 is separated from individual CLs is that it is different from other individual CLs, which are decided explicitly by the salient semantic meaning of the noun; 个 is vague in semantic meaning and sometimes only used to fulfil the CL function; also, it can replace any other individual CLs grammatically. To some extent, the rich range of individual CLs of a noun is a good symbol of their identity as a typical Chinese word. It is also noticed that the event CLs are not being investigated here since most words are not event nouns.[2]

Table 6. Percentages of three-type CLs.

English	MAW	GE	IN	KD
short T-shirt	短T	3.90	72.73	23.38
long T-shirt	长T	3.85	53.85	42.31
air cushion BB	气垫BB	8.50	1.31	90.20
Vehicle GPS	车载GPS	9.43	14.15	76.42
The ultimate player killing	终极PK	83.33	16.67	0
Human Resource manager	企业HR	25.00	73.96	1.04
white light LED	白光LE	38.73	40.14	21.13
policeman	阿SIR	50.00	50.00	0.00
parent-child Handmade	亲子DIY	28.57	28.57	42.86
	Average	**27.92**	**39.04**	**33.04**
English	**Canonical**	**GE**	**IN**	**KD**
short T-shirt	短袖衫	4.95	79.7	15.35
long T-shirt	长袖衫	0.00	85.87	14.13
air cushion BB	气垫粉底	8.55	1.32	90.13
Vehicle GPS	车载导	11.24	37.08	51.69
The ultimate player killing	终极对决	100.0	0.00	0.00
Human Resource manager	企业人事	33.33	66.67	0.00
white light LED	白光发光二极管	55.56	22.22	22.22
policeman	警察	29.35	70.24	0.4
parent-child Handmade	亲子手工	50.00	16.67	33.33
	Average	**32.74**	**42.2**	**25.25**

From Table 6 above, it is highlighted that firstly, the average difference between the three kinds of CLs is minor between the MAW group and the canonical group, less than 10% each. Secondly, the MAW and canonical groups share that the individual CLs (IN) have the highest mean among all three CL types. That is to say, the similarities testify to our second hypothesis that there are no major differences between MAWs and the canonical forms regarding the CL selecting methods and the regular range of 个 (GE).

---

[2] Event nouns are a subtype of nouns that lexically encode process readings [19]. For example, 真人CS 'cosplay of counter strike'.

The other MAWs group can also enhance the generalization stated above. We consulted the CL distributions of 甲A联赛 'First Division Group A-League', 甲B联赛 'First Division Group B League', 傻子 'fool', and维生素 'vitamin' as the character-headed comparative items, to look at whether their CLs behave differently. Table 7 shows that the dominant CLs and the range of CLs between these MAWs and their counterparts are highly consistent. For instance, event CLs such as 轮 'to classify sequences of events', 场 'to classify scheduled events', 届 'to classify scheduled events' are shared by football games; individual CLs个 (GE), 群 'to classify a swarm of people', 种 'kind' is used to classify foolish people, and the CLs of 维生素 'vitamin' can mostly be shared with the words of sub vitamin categories. It is also noticeable that these character-headed words are taking more CLs than the MAWs, probably because, for these particular cases, the emergence of the MAWs is later than their counterparts, and they also have a broader and stronger application in the Chinese language. Still, it does not affect MAWs' tendency toward traditional Chinese lexicon, considering the same set of CLs is involved in syntax.

Table 7. CL-distributions of MAWs without lettered-head and their canonical forms.

Keyword	English	Frequency of CLs
甲 B	First Division Group B	轮14, 场2, 届1
甲 B 联赛	First Division Group B	轮22, 场5, 届3, 个1
甲A	First Division Group A	轮57, 届23, 场7, 支1, 局1
甲 A 联赛	First Division Group A	轮143, 届62, 场24, 个3, 次1
傻B	silly person	个177, 群27, 种11, 帮11, 名1
傻子	silly person	个7135, 群271, 种132, 帮79, 位26, 批15, 名8, 波2, 枚1, 类1
维生素A	Vitamin A	种158, 粒11, 颗2, 个2
维生素C	Vitamin B	片238, 种149, 粒46, 颗12, 款9, 个2
维生素E	Vitamin C	粒85, 种67, 片45, 颗27, 个4
维生素D	Vitamin D	种53, 粒3, 款3, 类2, 片1
维生素B	Vitamin E	种154, 片104, 粒9, 颗6, 类2
维C	short form of 'Vitamin C'	片25, 粒7, 颗4, 个4, 种3, 枚1
维E	short form of 'Vitamin E'	颗7, 粒7, 片4, 种1, 款1
维生素	Vitamin	种8499, 类555, 粒93, 款47, 片42, 颗39, 个28, 份8

The data results above may have pedagogical implications for L2 Chinese learning and teaching. While Chinese-English code-mixing is the inevitable result of the contact between Chinese and English [27], teachers should hold an open mind towards the code-mixed MAWs. From the learners' side, on the other hand, in the sense that the CLs are highly dependent on the semantic meaning of the head morpheme, the L2 learners should be aware that when coming across the situation of a MAW co-occurring with a CL, it is not always acceptable to attach the general GE to it; instead, the CL choice should obey the same rule of other typical Chinese words.

6 Conclusion

Mandarin Alphabetical Word (MAW) is a unique lexicon in the Chinese language complex system where the Chinese language code-mixes with another foreign language at the lexical level. It is certain that when two languages come into contact, words and even syntactic structures of the foreign language will appear in the dominant language. What is still being determined is the extent to which the dominant language formally accepts the foreign language units. The MAW entries documented by official dictionaries are one hint; the other evidence is their similar linguistic behaviours in Chinese grammar. Thus, this paper has utilized a corpus-based method to empirically explore the lexical semantic status and language usage of MAWs from the perspective of their classifier selection tendency, a characteristic feature of the Chinese grammar system.

The corpus evidence indicated that MAWs with character-alphabet structure follow the traditional Chinese modifier-modified (head) morphological rule, and the classifiers are semantically motivated by the semantic feature of the head without overusing the general classifier 个 (GE). This phenomenon confirms the essential role of alphabets that are loan into the Chinese lexicon; in other words, people may accept MAWs, especially the alphabets, as the Chinese lexicon in a unique way that the distribution of CL collocations is comprehensive, productive, and dynamic.

This work may present certain limitations as a preliminary investigation on the opaque issue of classifier selection in MAWs. For example, the MAW seed words are limited in number due to the strict selection criteria in semantics, which leads to occasional sparseness in the corpus. Second, only the C-A type of MAWs has been studied, while another essential direction would be to probe into the A-C type, for instance, characters as head of nouns, or to investigate the pure alphabetical words' CL selections. Third, the manual checking of data examples can ensure a higher quality of the data, yet it may introduce bias to the data selection. Hence, future studies on this topic shall consider employing automatic metrics or tools in finding more seed words and their CL collocation samples, and we are also interested in applying the current line of research to a broader scope of MAW structures based on more prosperous language facts in corpus and with more reliable data.

Appendix

CL	Category	Interpretation/ translation	CL	Category	Interpretation/ translation
个	General	A general individual classifier	群	individual	to classify a swarm of people or animals
位	individual	to classify people with politeness	帮	individual	to classify a group of people

(continued)

(continued)

CL	Category	Interpretation/ translation	CL	Category	Interpretation/ translation
批	individual	to classify a group of objects or people	名	individual	to classify different identities of people
枚	individual	to classify circular objects	粒	individual	to classify small granular objects
颗	individual	to classify granular objects	片	individual	to classify flake-shaped objects
项	individual	to classify distributed items in group	份	individual	to classify distributed items in group
支	individual	to classify long rod-shaped objects, also groups or teams	串	individual	to classify items in clusters
排	individual	to classify entities in the form of rows	条	individual	to classify long thin and soft objects
代	individual	to classify objects of a certain generation	层	individual	to classify layers of substance
版	individual	to classify the editions of a book or product	件	individual	to classify clothes, or general implements
套	individual	to classify a pack/set of artifacts	身	individual	to classify wearing clothes
家	individual	to classify families or institutions	首	individual	to classify poems, songs, or music
曲	individual	to classify songs or music	部	individual	to classify machines, automobiles, volumes of books or movies
台	individual	to classify machines or large appliances	袭	individual	to classify clothes especially long dresses
波	event	to classify series of actions	轮	event	to classify sequences of events
场	event	to classify scheduled events	届	event	to classify events held on a regular basis
局	event	to classify the occurrence of games	期	event	to classify events that involve stages of completion
番	event	to denote times of a repeated event	种	kind	to classify kinds of entities
类	kind	to classify entities in categories	款	kind	to classify categories of manufactured products

References

1. Muysken, P.: Two linguistic systems in contact: Grammar, phonology, and lexicon. The Handbook of Bilingualism and Multilingualism, pp. 193–216 (2013)
2. Grosjean, F.: Life With Two Languages: An Introduction to Bilingualism. Harvard University Press (1982)
3. Ritchie, W.C., Bhatia, T.K.: Social and psychological factors in language mixing. In: The Handbook of Bilingualism and Multilingualism, pp. 375–390 (2012)
4. Huang, C.R., Liu, H.: Jiyu Yuliaoku De Hanyu Zimuci Zidong Chouqu Yu Fenlei [Corpus-based Automatic Extraction and Analysis of Mandarin Alphabetic Words]. Yunnan Shifan Daxue Xuebao (Zhexue Shehui Kexue Ban) [Journal of Yunnan Normal University (Humanities and Social Sciences Edition)] (2017)
5. Xiang, R., Wan, M., Su, Q., Huang, C.R., Lu, Q.: Sina mandarin alphabetical words: a web-driven code-mixing lexical resource. In: Proceedings of the 1st Conference of the Asia-Pacific Chapter of the Association for Computational Linguistics and the 10th International Joint Conference on Natural Language Processing, pp. 833–842 (2020)
6. Su, X., Wu, X.: Zimucci De Shengmingli Yu Juxianxing Jianlun Xiandai Hanyu Cidian De Chuli Zimuci De Shenzhong Zuofa [Vitality and Limitation of Lettered Words -- the Discretion of lettered Words in Modern Chinese Dictionary]. Beihua Daxue Xuebao (Shehui Xueke Ban) [Journal of Beihua University (Social Sciences)] (2013)
7. Zhang, T.W.: Zimuci Shiyong Shi Yuyan Jiechu De Zhengchang Xianxiang [The Use of Chinese Lettered-words is a Normal Phenomenon of Language Contact]. Beihua Daxue Xuebao (Shehui Xueke Ban) [Journal of Beihua University (Social Sciences)] (2013)
8. Jiang, S., Dang, Y.: Zidong Tiqu Han Zimuciyu De Xinyu Xinshuyu Yanjiu [Research on Automatic Extraction of New Terms in the Field of Alphabetic Words]. Computer Engineering, pp. 47–49 (2007)
9. Zheng, Z.Z., Zhang, P., Yang, J.G.: Research on the automatic extraction of letter words based on corpus. J. Chinese Inf. Process. 78–85 (2005)
10. Kozha, K.: Chinese via English: a case study of "lettered-words" as a way of integration into global communication. In: Chinese Under Globalization: Emerging Trends in Language Use in China 105–125 (2012)
11. Miao, R.: Loanword adaptation in Mandarin Chinese: Perceptual, phonological and sociolinguistic factors (Doctoral dissertation) (2005)
12. Ding, H., Zhang, Y., Liu, H., Huang, C. R.: A preliminary phonetic investigation of alphabetic words in Mandarin Chinese. In Interspeech, pp. 3028–3032 (2017)
13. Li, X.H.: Zai Tang Zimuci De Duyin Wenti [Talk about the pronunciation of letter words]. Yuyan Wenzi Yingyong [Applied Linguistics] (2002)
14. Riha, H.: Lettered Words in Chinese: Roman Letters as Morpheme-Syllables, pp. 93–99. The Ohio State University, Columbus (2010)
15. Riha, H., Baker, K.: Lettered Words: Using Roman Letters to Create Words in Chinese (2010)
16. Allan K.: Classifiers. Language (1977)
17. Tai, J.H.Y.: Chinese classifier systems and human categorization. In: Honor of Wang, W.S.-Y.(ed.) Interdisciplinary Studies on Language and Language Change, pp. 479–494 (1994)
18. Ahrens, K., Huang, C.-R: Classifiers. In: Huang, C.-R., Shi, D.X. (eds.): A Reference Grammar of Chinese, pp. 169–198. United Kingdom: Cambridge University Press (2016)
19. Wang, S., Huang, C.R.: Towards an event-based classification system for non-natural kind nouns. In: Chinese Lexical Semantics: 13th Workshop, CLSW 2012, Wuhan, China, July 6–8, 2012, Revised Selected Papers 13, pp. 381–395. Springer, Heidelberg (2013). https://doi.org/10.1007/978-3-642-36337-5_39

20. Chen, K.J., Huang, C.R., Chang, L.P., Hsu, H.L.: Sinica corpus: design methodology for balanced corpora. In: Proceedings of the 11th Pacific Asia Conference on Language, Information and Computation, pp. 167–176 (1996)
21. Huang, C.R.: Tagged Chinese gigaword version 2.0, ldc2009t14. Linguistic Data Consortium (2009)
22. Liu, Y.Q.: Zimuci Cidian [The Dictionary of Lettered-words]. Shanghai Cishu Chubanshe [Shanghai Lexicographical Publishing House] (2001)
23. Jakubíček, M., Kilgarriff, A., Kovář, V.: The TenTen corpus family. In: 7th International Corpus Linguistics Conference CL. Lancaster University 125–127 (2013)
24. Tai, J.H.Y: Variation in classifier systems across Chinese dialects: towards a cognition-based semantic approach. Chinese Language and Linguistics 587–608 (1992)
25. Croft, W.: Semantic universals in classifier systems. Word 145–171 (1994)
26. Kunilovskaya, M., Koviazina, M.: Sketch engine: a toolbox for linguistic discovery. J. Linguistics 503–507 (2017)
27. Lu, D.H.: Hanyu Zhong De Zimuci Yinyici He Hunhe Yuma [Lettered and transliterated words and code-mixing in Chinese]. Waiguoyu [Journal of Foreign Languages] 59–65 (2010)

Feasibility of Direct Language Transfer of the Verb "to Eat" from Cantonese to Mandarin

Ka-Hang Leung[(✉)] and Jia-Fei Hong

National Taiwan Normal University, Taipei, Taiwan
{61184037i,jiafeihong}@ntnu.edu.tw

Abstract. The verb "to eat" is commonly used in both Cantonese and Mandarin. According to the analysis result, we can see that the most frequently occurring senses of the verb in both languages are "to ingest". Even though both Cantonese and Mandarin use the same set of Chinese characters, the verb "to eat" in both languages does not develop into the same set of senses. From the employed dictionaries and corpora, the number of senses of the verb in both languages are 11, while the developed pathways follow the ingestion process.

After comparing the similar senses, we found that even for the same senses, the verb "to eat" in a Mandarin sentence cannot be replaced by the Cantonese one directly, while the objects in the sentences of both languages are different due to the lexical difference between the languages. The above analysis provides an insight for designing the Mandarin teaching materials on the verb "to eat" to the native Cantonese students.

Keywords: Cantonese · Mandarin · Language transfer · "Eat" · Lexical semantics

1 Introduction

"Eating" is an indispensable part of human survival, and the verb "*chi1*" has become a frequent term in modern Mandarin used in everyday life. "*Chi1 fan4*" (to eat rice) in Mandarin corresponds to "*sik6 faan1*" in Cantonese, conversely, Cantonese "*sik6 jin1*" (to smoke) corresponds to Mandarin "*xi1 yan1*." From the examples, it shows that Cantonese "*sik6*" does not always directly correspond to Mandarin "*chi1*," and vice versa. While these two verbs may appear similar, they also exhibit differences, which can easily lead to confusion for native Cantonese speakers learning Mandarin.

Currently, research on the verb "*chi1*" is diverse. For instance, Zhuang et al. [1] studied the gestalt and the nominal collocation of "*chi1*". Yin [2] employed a semantic cognitive model to analyze the various senses of "*chi1*," categorizing metaphorical and metonymic senses into seven major categories. Jia and Wu [3] also explored the polysemy of "*chi1*" verbs and their semantic extensions. They proposed that from a cross-linguistic perspective, "*chi1*" can also mean "to inhale or smoke pleasantly," which corresponds to the aforementioned "*sik6 jin1*" in Cantonese.

M. Dong et al. (Eds.): CLSW 2023, LNAI 14514, pp. 146–159, 2024.
https://doi.org/10.1007/978-981-97-0583-2_12

However, there has been relatively limited analysis of the semantic senses of Cantonese "*sik6*" and a comprehensive comparison between the senses of Mandarin "*chi1*" and Cantonese "*sik6*." Therefore, this paper will follow the framework of Polysemy Sense Analysis mentioned in Ou's paper [4] and analyze the various senses of "*chi1*" and "*sik6*," comparing the two to explore their relationship. Finally, based on these results, it will discuss the differences between their senses and the feasibility of direct transference from Cantonese "*sik6*" to Mandarin "*chi1*."

2 Literature Review

This paper aims to explore the mechanism of bilingual transference between "*sik6*" and "*chi1*" by examining the differences in their semantic senses, utilizing Ou's [4] framework. This section will begin by providing a brief overview of the differences between Cantonese and Mandarin and the lexical selection mechanisms employed by learners when using Mandarin. Then, it will introduce Ou's [4] theoretical framework of polysemy sense analysis, serving as the theoretical foundation for the subsequent analysis of semantic sense and discussion part.

2.1 Vocabulary Differences Between Cantonese and Mandarin

Cantonese and Mandarin both utilize Chinese characters for writing and speaking, yet they possess distinct vocabulary systems. Mandarin follows the concept of "I write as I speak" while Cantonese does not. "I write as I speak" refers to the idea of writing down what is spoken, aligning spoken language with written language. Cantonese, however, does not support this concept.

The reasons behind the differences are highlighted in the works of scholars like Qian [5] and Zhou [6]. Qian [5] points out that Cantonese still preserves archaic words that are no longer in use in Mandarin. For instance, the term "*do1 ze6*" in Cantonese, originally denoting polite greeting, now corresponds to the Mandarin word "*xie4 xie5*", meaning "thank you." Zhou's [6] research on monosyllabic food-related verbs in Ancient Chinese proposes that the original sense of "*sik6*" had a food-related meaning, referring to the process of biting and swallowing food. Conversely, the original sense of "*chi1*" was related to speech difficulties or stuttering. These examples further illustrate that the Cantonese term "*sik6*" has a longer historical origin compared to the Mandarin "*chi1*" and emphasizes a closer connection between Cantonese and archaic Chinese vocabulary.

2.2 Language Transfer by Cantonese Native Speakers to Mandarin

"Language transfer" refers to the influence of one language has on the learning or use of another language, where learners might adopt the elements of their native language's vocabulary or cultural concepts on the second language [7]. Liu [8] analyzed the vocabulary errors made by Cantonese native speakers when using Mandarin and concluded that learners often use Cantonese as an auxiliary language. Students with weaker proficiency in Mandarin tend to directly use Cantonese words when they are unsure. For example, in the sentence "*wo3 men5 zhong1 wu3 qiu2 qi2 (sui2 bian4) chi1 dian3 shen2 me5 du1 xing2*" (We can eat anything for lunch), learners may not realize that they have used the Cantonese word "*qiu2 qi2*", but upon closer examination, they can identify the Cantonese element within the sentence. In addition to spoken language, learners may also use Cantonese words in their writing. However, it is suggested that for words with the same origin, Cantonese and Mandarin are treated as separate lemma models by users, rather than shared lemma models [9]. This means that Cantonese and Mandarin are perceived as distinct vocabulary modules, even when they share a common etymology.

2.3   Framework of Polysemy Sense Analysis

This paper relies on the theoretical framework of polysemy sense analysis proposed by Ou [4] as the basis for analyzing the distinct senses of the two words. Tyler and Evans [10] used the word "over" to present the idea that polysemous words typically have prototype senses, and this further extends to the differentiated senses. However, their theory did not involve a synchronic analysis of corpus data, making it unable to confirm its synchronic reality.

The relationships between word senses can also be explained through cognitive linguistics. Lakoff [11] stated that conceptual structures are fundamental to the human cognitive system, and human cognition is a process of conceptualizing oneself and the world. Cognitive linguistics asserts that the forms of language are the result of human conceptualization. The phenomenon of polysemy, involving metaphor and metonymy, exemplifies cognitive conceptualization, as it extends the central meaning of a word to different senses.

3   Research Method

This paper will primarily rely on the different sense entries provided by dictionaries for both languages, supplemented by corpus data to include senses and example sentences not found in dictionaries. For the corpus data, only the usage of verb will be considered. The main dictionaries used for researching Cantonese and Mandarin are "words.hk" and the "Revised Mandarin Chinese Dictionary" respectively.

For collecting primary data on Cantonese "*sik6*," the main corpus used is the "The Linguistics Corpus of Mid-20th Century Hong Kong Cantonese." This corpus consists of dialogues from 21 Hong Kong movies from the 1940s to the 1970s. "words.hk" is a Cantonese dictionary project focused on Hong Kong Cantonese. Which can help compensate for the lack of modern Cantonese usage in the mid-20th century corpus.

The data for Mandarin "*chi1*" is collected from the "Academia Sinica Balanced Corpus of Modern Chinese." The search conditions are set to "Audiovisual Media" and "Conversational Interviews" in order to align with the nature of the Cantonese "*sik6*" corpus, which is primarily spoken language.

This paper, referring to Ou's [4] analysis of the polysemous word "*kan4*" (to see), will first identify the independent senses of Cantonese "*sik6*" and Mandarin "chi1" through a thorough analysis. It will then employ the syntactic criteria mentioned in Evans' [10] principled polysemy theory to determine their prototype senses. The paper will also apply theories from cognitive linguistics [11] to explore the connections between these independent senses.

After analyzing the different senses of Cantonese "*sik6*" and Mandarin "*chi1*," this paper will compare them and explore the similarities and differences between them.

4 Analysis of the Senses of Cantonese "*sik6*"

In the annotations of the "Commentary on the *Shuo1 Wen2 Jie3 Zi4*", it is stated that character of "*sik6*" derived from the components "亼" (*hau2*) and "皀" (*gwai2*). It further mentions that "*sik6*" encompasses all characters related to food. The explanation also elaborates on the components "*hau2*" and "*gwai2*," where "*hau2*" represents "opening the mouth downward" and "*gwai2*" signifies "vessel for food," indicating that in ancient times, "*sik6*" had a primary sense related to eating.

4.1 Sense of "Eating"

This sense aligns with the explanation of "*sik6*" in the "Commentary on the *Shuo1 Wen2 Jie3 Zi4*." Examples that fit this definition in the corpus include:

(1) *ngo5 soeng2 **sik6** go3 ping4 gwo2 zaa1 maa3*. (I just want to eat an apple.)
(2) *hai2 dou6 **sik6** maan5 faan6 sin1 laa1*! (Let's have dinner here!)

In all the above sentences, "*sik6*" carries the sense of "eating." These sentences also include objects, which are typically nouns, but not necessarily an entity. "*sik6* + entity" (as in (1)) indicates the specific food the subject is consuming, such as an apple, rice, or bread. "*sik6* + meal" or "*sik6* + type of meal" (as in (2)) doesn't specify the exact food but refers to the meal itself, such as dinner or vegetarian meals.

Among the various senses of the Cantonese verb "*sik6*," the sense of "eating" is the most prevalent in the corpus data. This indicates that the sense of "eating" is the most commonly used meaning of "*sik6*" in Cantonese. Hence, it is believed that Cantonese "*sik6*" aligns with the annotations in the "Commentary on the *Shuo1 Wen2 Jie3 Zi4*."

4.2 Sense of "Tasting"

While analyzing the sense of "eating," it was found that "*sik1*" shares characteristics of "eating" but do not necessarily involve the process of consumption:

(3) *aai1 jaa1 go3 sei2 zai2 gam3 sik1 **sik6** aa1*. (That little brat is such a (food) connoisseur.)

In these sentences, the subjects must have engaged in the process of "eating" to be considered someone who understands or appreciates food. Unlike the "eating" sense, in this context, "*sik6*" doesn't solely refer to the act of chewing or swallowing but rather to distinguishing flavors. Since being a connoisseur of food doesn't necessarily require a specific type of food, the verb can be used without an object.

Furthermore, in the sentence, "*sik6*" is used in conjunction with "*sik1*", where "*sik1*" functions as an auxiliary verb with the meaning of "to know." Ye [12], in analyzing various scholars' research on auxiliary verbs, suggests that one of the functions of auxiliary verbs is to modulate the main verb's mood. In the structure *"sik1"* + *"sik6,"* the "eating" sense may be modified by the auxiliary verb *"sik1."*

4.3 Sense of "Taking Medicine"

The analysis also identified examples that involve swallowing but have a distinct semantic meaning. Example includes:

(4) **sik6** *gwo3 hou2 do1 joek6*. (Took a lot of medicine.)

In these sentences, the object of *"sik6"* is not food but rather medicine or nutritional supplements. Medicines do not provide a sense of satiety, while their absorption is more crucial. Unlike the previous senses, this sense focuses more on the moment of swallowing. This sense also does not require a specific object; for example, in sentence (4), *"joek6"* (medicine) means medicine in general.

This sense is believed to be derived from the "eating" sense, where the action involves placing something in the mouth and swallowing. However, given the difference in emphasis in the ingestion process, this paper does not consider this sense a sub-sense of the "eating" sense.

4.4 Sense of "Inhaling"

In the corpus data, this study identified a sense that is shorter in the ingestion process than the "taking medicine" sense, as shown in the following examples:

(5) *ngo5 m4 sik1* **sik6** *jin1 gaa2*. (I don't know how to smoke.)
(6) **sik6** *baak6 fan2*. (To shoot heroin.)

In these examples, the objects associated with *"sik6"* are drugs which are harmful to the body. Unlike the "eating" sense, in this sense, there is no chewing involved, and even the act of swallowing and subsequent processes is not part of the meaning. Additionally, this sense involves the trachea as a medium rather than the esophagus, indicating that the digestive system is not involved in this sense.

It is believed that there are two reasons for the emergence of this sense. First, in the process of *"sik6 jin1"* (smoking), the cigarette is held in the mouth, a motion that is roughly similar to the first step in the eating process. And since smoking is a harmful and addictive substance, it extended to *"baak6 fan2"* (heroin) even though it is inhaled through the nose. Second, in formal written Cantonese, *"kap1 sik6 duk6 ban2"* (inhaling drugs) is the formal term. Whilst *"sik6"* is a common verb, and its frequency of use in this daily life context is higher than *"kap1"* (to inhale). Therefore, *"sik6"* may have been extracted and used as colloquial terminology.

4.5 Sense of "Expressing a State"

The following examples *"sik6"* is even paired with adjectives but not food:

(7) *ji4 gaa1* **sik6** *mung2 nei5 aa4?* (Are you becoming ignorant now?)

(8) *dim2 gaai2 gam1 jat6 hou2 ci5* **sik6** *zo2 fo2 joek6 gam2 ze1*? (Why do you seem bad-tempered today?)

In all these examples, "*sik6*" in phrases like "*sik6 mung2*" (becoming muddled) and "*sik6 zo2 fo2 joek6*" (seem bad-tempered), does not carry the sense of "eating." The state described in these examples depends on the adjectives or objects that follow "*sik6.*"

In example (7), "*sik6 mung2*" refers to a state of ignorance. The context of this sentence does not necessarily need to be related to eating, and the focus is on the adjective "*mung2*", not "*sik6.*" Similarly, in example (8), "*sik6 zo2 fo2 jeok6*" rather refers to the metaphorical explosion of emotions, with "*fo2 jeok6*" (gunpowder) originally being a substance used to ignite explosives.

These examples illustrate that Cantonese "*sik6*" no longer necessarily implies the act of eating. Furthermore, "sik6" primarily conveys negative states.

4.6 Sense of "Winning"

The sense of "*sik6*" as "winning" is found only in the context of Hong Kong Mahjong terminology.

(9) *bin1 go3* **sik6** *wu2 aa1*? (Who won the Mahjong?)

In the sentence, "*sik6 wu2*" refers to winning a round of Mahjong. This sense is specific to the Mahjong culture and is considered a local term in Hong Kong's Chinese [13]. There is currently a lack of research on the use of "*sik6*" in "*sik6 wu2*," so the etymology of the use of "*sik6*" in this context have not been deeply explored.

4.7 Sense of "Taking Advantage"

The sense of "*sik6*" as "taking advantage" did not appear in the selected corpus but is included in "words.hk.*"

(10) **sik6** *zyu6 soeng5*. (To take advantage of a situation to further one's interests.)

From sentence (10), "*sik6*" is followed by "*zyu6*," which serves as a verb suffix. Regarding the meaning of "*zyu6*," Deng [14] introduced the concept of "homogeneous event," suggesting that the verbs modified by the suffix "*zyu6*" refer to "homogeneous events." In the context of "*sik6 zyu6 soeng5*," the "*zyu6*" appears to align with Deng's concept of "homogeneous event." Taking advantage of an opportunity could be a continuous action, as long as the opportunity exists.

4.8 Sense of "Controlling"

The sense of "*sik6*" as "controlling" also requires an object:

(11) *nei5 fong1 keoi5 wui3* **sik6** *zo2 nei5 me1*? (Don't be scared of him.)
(12) *bou2 him2 lou2* **sik6** *hou2 do1 jung2, siu2 sam1 bei2 keoi5 dei6 aak1.* (The insurance salesmen extract large commissions; beware of their sales tactics.)

In these example sentences, the object of "*sik6*" is not food; it can be a person or an item. After "*sik6*", the subject gains possession or control over the object, which is often beneficial, such as controlling someone to help oneself or gaining control over a commission from insurance sales. This sense of "*sik6*" likely extends from the process of "swallowing" during eating to the metaphorical sense of "to annex," ultimately leading to the sense of control. Eating is a process of obtaining nutrients from food, which aligns with the idea that the subject gains advantages from the object.

4.9 Sense of "Relying on for Livelihood".

In most cases, this sense of "*sik6*" requires an object, except for "*wan2 sik6*," which is a verb-verb compound.

(13) *naam4 jan4 daai6 zoeng6 fu1 dou1 hai6 zi6 gei2 wan2 **sik6** hou2 ge3*. (It is better for a man to work and gain money himself.)

(14) *m4 hou2 wan2 maai4 di1 cin2 gung1 go2 di1 **sik6** jyun5 mai5 ge3*! (Do not work so hard just to support those who sponge off one another.)

In example (13), "*wan2 sik6*" consists of two verbs, carrying the meanings of "seeking" and "making a living" respectively. "*wan2 sik6*" is a verb-verb compound, meaning to first seek employment and then earn a living through work. Whilst verb-verb compounds are not common in Cantonese idiomatic expressions [15].

Meanwhile, "*sik6 jyun5 mai5*" follows the "*sik6*" + object structure, where the object doesn't refer to food. "*sik6 jyun5 mai5*" refers to one partner in a romantic relationship relying on the other for financial support. This sense of "*sik6*" is related to the concept mentioned by Yin [2] that eating involves the intake of external elements to obtain "nourishment," such as money or life resources.

4.10 Sense of "Consuming"

This sense of "*sik6*" appears only once in the corpus (see example 20), so this paper also includes example sentence provided by "words.hk" for this synonymous sense.

(15) ***sik6** jau2 jau6 m4 do1*. (It does not consume a lot of oil.)

(16) *ni1 zek3 App hou2 **sik6** din6 aa1*. (This app consumes a lot of battery.)

The objects of "*sik6*" in this sense are things that can be consumed or wasted, such as oil and electricity. Just as the process of eating involves digestion, where food is absorbed, human activities invariably require energy and nutrients from food. Similarly, the "consumption" sense involves a similar process where the consumed object provides the required energy to the subject. For example, driving a car requires gasoline and running applications on a smartphone requires electricity.

4.11 Sense of "Enduring"

This sense of "*sik6*" also appears only once in the corpus, as shown below:

(17) *ngo5 dou1 **sik6** gwaan3 fu2 gaa2 laa1*. (I get used to suffering.)

While this sense of "*sik6*" shares the characteristic of needing an object like most other Cantonese "*sik6*" senses, the difference lies in the fact that the object is not directly connected to "*sik6*." There is a morpheme or word separating "*sik6*" and the object. Additionally, the objects typically have negative meaning, as the example sentences involve psychological and physical burdens. It seems that in this sense, "*sik6*" mainly extends to mean "to endure suffering."

5 Analysis of the senses of Mandarin "*chi1*"

In classical Chinese, "*chi1*" was associated with speech difficulties or stammering. This meaning, however, does not align with the primary sense of "*chi1*" in contemporary Mandarin, which mainly denotes the act of eating to satisfy physiological needs.

5.1 Sense of "Eating"

In the analysis of the semantic range of Mandarin "*chi1*," the most prevalent and primary sense observed in the corpus is the "eating." This frequent usage in modern Mandarin contradicts its historical interpretation. The following sentences from the corpus exemplify instances of this primary sense:

(18) *nan2 sheng1 hen3 xiang3 qu4 **chi1** lu3 rou4 fan4, zai4 sheng1 ri4 de5 shi2 hou5…* (The boy really wanted to eat Braised pork on rice, on his birthday…)

(19) *rang4 wo3 men5 de5 xia4 yi1 dai4 **chi1** bu2 dao4 mu3 ru3…* (Making our next generation not able to be breast-fed…)

(20) *zhe4 ge5 mu3 qin1 gang1 hao3 chu1 qu4 **chi1** xi3 jiu3…* (It so happened that this mother goes out to attend a wedding…)

These examples showcase the versatility of "*chi1*" in conveying the act of eating, with variations in the nature of the objects. Sentence (18) employs "*chi1*" with solid food items, which is the most common scenario in the corpus. In contrast, sentence (19) introduces a liquid as the object of "*chi1*," representing a less common usage.

Moreover, sentence (20) uses "*chi1*" in an unconventional way where the complement is not a food item but an event or occasion. Here, "*chi1*" represents the act of partaking in the food provided at the event.

5.2 Sense of "Taking Medicine"

The examples in the sense of "taking medicine" of the Mandarin Chinese character "*chi1*" shares similarities with the corresponding sense in Cantonese "*sik6*.":

(21) *zai4 wo3 de5 men2 zhen3 li3, bing4 bu2 jin4 bing4 ren2 **chi1** zhong1 yao4.* (In our clinic, we don't prohibit patients from taking Chinese medicine.)

In the example, "*chi1*" focuses on the act of swallowing, particularly the process of taking medications and the effects these substances have on the human body. This interpretation aligns with the sense of "Taking Medicine" of "*sik6*" in Cantonese, where the objects predominantly consist of medicinal items rather than regular food.

5.3 Sense of "Controlling"

The sense of "controlling" in the Mandarin *"chi1"* involves objects that are not food items but rather entities or systems. This usage implies the control of something, often for one's own benefit. The following sentences illustrate this sense:

(22) *shei2 **chi1** le5 gong1 yi1 zhi4?...* (Who controlled the public health system? ...)
(23) *wo3 de5 chu3 xu4 quan2 gei3 ta1 **chi1** le5!* ("He took all of my savings!")

    In sentences (22) and (23), the subjects acquire the objects through *"chi1,"* but this acquisition is often perceived negatively by one another, implying a sense of seizing or taking control of something that originally did not belong to them. This extension of meaning in this sense shares some similarities with the "Controlling" sense of *"sik6"* in Cantonese, both of which involve the concept of acquisition or control rather than the consumption of food.

5.4 Sense of "Taking Advantage"

The sense of "Taking Advantage" of Mandarin *"chi1"* shares similarities with the previous sense, as both involve *"chi1"* being used to obtain the advantages of something that does not originally belong to the subject, often resulting in personal benefits. However, unlike Cantonese in this sense of "Taking Advantage," the subject does not necessarily gain possession or control of the object but rather enjoys temporary advantages or benefits. Additionally, the objects in this context are often used metaphorically. Here is an example illustrating this sense:

(24) *gu4 shi4 zhong1 chang2 **chi1** nan2 sheng1 dou4 fu5, wan2 nong4 nan2 sheng1* (In the story, (pronoun) was always handsy to the boys and tricked them...)

    In the sentence, *"chi1"* does not necessarily gain possession or control of the objects. This usage of *"chi1"* metaphorically likens the subjects' actions to enjoying the benefits or pleasures of certain situations. For example, *"dou4 fu5"* (tofu) means the body of the boys but not tofu as the food.

5.5 Sense of "Consuming"

Similar to the sense of "Eating", the sense "Consuming" also involves both subjects and objects, as shown in the following sentences:

(25) *pao2 qi3 lai5 shi2 fen1 **chi1** li4.* (It takes a lot of effort to run.)
(26) *zui4 jin4 wo3 de5 che1 che1 **chi1** you2 **chi1** de5 hen3 xiong1 er2 qie3 wei4 su4 ye3 ti2 bu2 shang4 qu4 le5.* (Recently my car consumed so much gasoline, and the spin rate failed to speed up.)

    Similar to the same sense in Cantonese *"sik6,"* the object following *"chi1"* is being consumed. For example, *"chi1 li4"* in sentence (25) describes the subject's physical state as strenuous, *"chi1 you2"* in sentences (26) indicates the consumption of resources such as gasoline.

5.6 Sense of "Enduring"

Similar to Cantonese "*sik6*," Mandarin "*chi1*" also encompasses the "enduring" sense, including similar types of burdens.

(27) *zhe4 ge5 fa1 xian4 shi3 ta1 fei1 chang2 **chi1** jing1* (This discovery surprised him a lot.)

(28) *sui1 **chi1** le5 zhong4 zhong4 yi4 quan2, zi4 ye3 bu2 hui4 gen1 ta1 ji4 jiao4* (Even though if he got a strong punch, he would take it easy.)

In the examples above, "*chi1 jing1*" (surprised) and "*chi1 le5 yi4 quan2*" (took a punch) represent psychological and physiological burdens, which are conceptually similar to Cantonese "*sik6.*" However, in this context, these phrases may not necessarily require additional affixes or modifications.

5.7 Sense of "Accepting"

In this sense, the object paired with "*chi1*" is not food or physical objects but rather a method or approach. Examples include:

(29) *bie2 ba3 wo3 dang4 cheng2 ni3 de5 ge4 an4, wo3 cai2 bu4 **chi1** zhe4 yi1 tao4.* (Don't treat me as one of your cases; I won't buy this approach.)

In sentence (29), "*zhe4 yi1 tao4*" (this method) refers to methods or approaches in dealing with situations. Mandarin "*chi1*" has thus extended to include the sense of "accepting" certain methods. Just as during the process of eating, humans accept the nutrients from food. Furthermore, in both senses of "Eating" and "Accepting" of "*chi1*," the subject is typically a living entity, has the choice of whether or not to engage in the action.

5.8 Sense of "Estimating"

In this particular sense, "*chi1*" no longer follows the usual construction of "*chi1* + object". Instead, it takes the form "*chi1* + modal particle + adjective (zhun3, accurate)." Example includes:

(30) *shei2 neng2 **chi1** de2 zhun3!* (Who can be sure!)

In the example, "*chi1*" is predominantly paired with "*zhun3*" (accurate) and has evolved into a sense of "estimating." Regarding the extension of this sense, it can be seen as a metaphorical concept. Just as the body digests food, absorbs nutrients, and transforms them into energy, in this context, the mind processes and interprets events, leading the subject to make an educated guess or assessment. Since this cognitive process requires a subject similar to the previous senses discussed, it requires a living entity as the subject.

5.9 Sense of "Bearing"

Amongst the corpus data, it was observed that sentences illustrating this sense typically include the word "*bu2*" (not). For example, "*chi1 bu2 xiao1*" and "*chi1 bu2 zhu4*" are common expressions. Meanwhile, searching for "*chi1 xiao1*" or "*chi1 zhu4*" directly did not yield any results. Here is one of the examples:

(31) *wo3 dao4 shi5 dan1 xin1 zhe4 chang2 xue3 tai4 da4, wu1 ding3 **chi1** bu5 zhu4, ...*
(I am worried if the snow is too much that the rooftop can no longer bear it, ...)

This sense of "*chi1*" refers to bearing a burden that gradually accumulates over time. It differs from the sense of "Enduring" in both sentence structure and meaning where this sense emphasizes burdens that accumulate gradually. This article posits that the sense of "Bearing" is an extension of the sense of "Enduring."

5.10 Sense of "Sinking In"

The usage of "*chi1 shui3*" in the corpus mainly relates to sentences involving boats:

(32) *dui4 yu2 **chi1** shui3 jiao4 shen1 de5 chuan2 zhi1. Fei1 si4 man3 chao2 bu4 neng2 jin4 gang3.* (Ships with deeper drafts cannot enter the port until the tide is full.)

In this context, "*chi1 shui3*" refers to the depth at which a boat or ship sinks below the water's surface. It is used to indicate the boat's capacity to bear the water's weight. While it carries the idea of "bearing," it does not carry negative connotations.

5.11 Sense of "Absorbing"

The sense of "Absorbing" is relatively uncommon. The dictionary provides only two examples for this sense, namely "*chi1 yan1*" (absorbing opium) and "*chi1 mo4*" (absorbing ink). It's important to note that "*chi1 yan1*" refers to the outdated practice of opium smoking, not the modern concept of smoking tobacco. "*chi1 mo4*" refers to the absorption of ink.

The corpus from the Academia Sinica does not contain any sentences with "*chi1 mo4*." Therefore, it can be inferred that this sense of "*chi1*" is relatively not commonly used in modern language.

6 Discussion

6.1 The Senses Relationship Between "*sik6*" and "*chi1*"

The following figures show the semantic maps of the Cantonese "*sik6*" and Mandarin "*chi1*" respectively after the analysis.

By comparing Figs. 1 and 2 above, it's evident that both Cantonese "*sik6*" and Mandarin "*chi1*" share the primary sense of "eating," which is also the most frequent usage in both corpora. Both of them contain 11 individual senses.

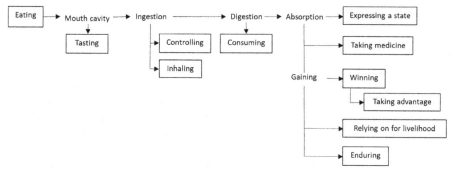

Fig.1. Semantic map of Cantonese "*sik6*"

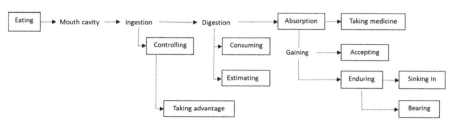

Fig.2. Semantic map of Mandarin "*chi1*"

Following this primary sense, they share five similar derived senses: "Controlling", "Taking advantage", "Consuming", "Taking medicine", and "Enduring." Notably, the Mandarin sense of "Taking advantage" is not explicitly mentioned in Cantonese "sik6."

When searching for "*sik6*" in the "words.hk," there is no direct mention of the "Taking advantage" sense of that in Mandarin. However, a direct search for "*sik6 dou6 fu6*" (eat tofu) does yield an explanation related to the sense, and it is labeled as "slang." This suggests that in Cantonese, the usage of "*sik6*" in the context of this specific sense is mainly associated with "*sik6 dou6 fu6*" (eat tofu), unlike in Mandarin "*chi1*," which can be paired with objects other than "*dou6 fu6*" (tofu).

Mandarin "*chi1*" has some senses that may only be idiomatic expressions in Cantonese and do not have equivalent usages. Apart from the primary sense of "eating" and the five derived senses shared by both languages, the remaining senses do not align between the two languages.

This disparity can be attributed to the fact that Cantonese and Mandarin are two distinct languages with their own unique linguistic features, which aligns with the findings that suggested Cantonese and Mandarin are separate lexical systems for users, rather than a shared one [9]. This discrepancy is also reflected in the absence of direct conversions between the shared senses.

6.2 The Feasibility of Direct Transference Between Cantonese "*sik6*" and Mandarin "*chi1*"

The sense of "eating" is the original sense in both languages, and it mainly involves solid food as the object. For example, "*chi1 ping2 guo3*" (eat apple) in Mandarin can be directly translated to "*sik6 ping4 gwo2*" in Cantonese. However, there are exceptions where the object is different. For instance, in Mandarin, "*chi1 mu2 ru3*" (to drink breast milk) involves a liquid, but in Cantonese, it is expressed as "*jam2 mou3 jyu5*." Similarly, "*chi1 xi2 jiu3*" (attend a wedding banquet) in Mandarin becomes "*jam2 hei2 zau2*" in Cantonese.

In terms of senses that can be directly transferred between the languages, there are "controlling" and "taking medicine." In the sense of "controlling," for example, in the Chinese sentence "*wo3 de5 chu3 xu4 quan2 gei3 ta1 chi1 le5!*" (He took all of my savings!), the Mandarin "*chi1*" can be directly translated to "*sik6*" in Cantonese, resulting in a similar meaning, such as "*bei2 jan4 sik6 saai3 sing4 fu3 san1 gaa1*" (He took all of someone's savings). Similarly, in the sense of "Taking medicine," since both languages typically involve medication as the object, the Mandarin "*chi1*" can be replaced with the Cantonese "*sik6*," for instance, "*chi1 zhong1 yao4*" (take Chinese medicine) becomes "*sik6 zung1 joek6*" in Cantonese.

On the other hand, even if both languages share the same sense, it doesn't mean that the Cantonese "*sik6*" can always replace the Mandarin "*chi1*" directly. For example, in the sense of "consuming," "*chi1 you2*" (consume oil) in Mandarin can indeed be translated to Cantonese as "*sik6 yau2*." However, the Mandarin phrase "*chi1 li4*" (take a lot of effort) cannot be replaced by "*sik6 lik6*" in Cantonese. Instead, "*hek3 lik6*" is used in Cantonese. Also, "*chi1 jing1*" (shocked) and "*chi1 kui1*" (suffer losses) in Mandarin do not have direct equivalents in Cantonese.

From these examples, it's clear that even if the sense is the same, Cantonese "*sik6*" cannot always be directly substituted for Mandarin "*chi1*." Additionally, word choices may differ between the two languages, as seen in the case of "*chu3 xu4*" (savings) in Mandarin, which becomes "*san1 gaa1*" in Cantonese.

7 Conclusion

This study extensively examines the semantic features of Cantonese "*sik6*" and Mandarin "*chi1*," as well as the similarities and differences between them. Furthermore, it highlights the potential language interference and learning challenges faced by Cantonese-speaking learners when dealing with Mandarin "*chi1*." This study underscores that even when the semantic senses align, direct transference between the two languages may not be a straightforward process. Additionally, it emphasizes the importance of understanding grammatical and lexical distinctions, as the differences in linguistic systems require Cantonese-speaking learners to adapt to Mandarin.

The paper has identified the potential hurdles for learners, offering a perspective on language transfer issues and learning strategies. Future research directions may involve investigating teaching methodologies tailored to Cantonese-speaking learners of Mandarin "*chi1*," taking into account the shared and divergent semantic categories as well as language interference challenges.

Acknowledgements. This study is supported by the National Science and Technology Council, Taiwan, R.O.C., under Grant no. MOST 110–2511-H-003 -034 -MY3. It is also supported by National Taiwan Normal University's Chinese Language and Technology Center. The center is funded by Taiwan's Ministry of Education (MOE), as part of the Featured Areas Research Center Program, under the Higher Education Sprout Project.

References

1. Zhuang, H., Zhang, Y., Li, X., Shen, S., Liu, Z.: On chi: its gestalt and collocations. In: Su, X., He, T. (eds.) CLSW 2014. LNCS (LNAI), vol. 8922, pp. 143–152. Springer, Cham (2014). https://doi.org/10.1007/978-3-319-14331-6_14
2. Yin, Y.M.: A Study of Semantic Generation Models for Vocabulary and Expression in Modern Chinese Ingestion Terminology. Shandong University, Jinan, China (2019). (In Chinese)
3. Jia, Y.Z., Wu, F.X.: A study of Chinese 'Eat' and 'Drink' type verbs from the perspective of lexical typology. Chin. Teach. World **31**(3), 361–381 (2017). (in Chinese)
4. Ou, T.F.: The distinction of senses of polysemy: a case study of perception verb "Kan." J. Chin. Lang. Teach. **10**(3), 1–39 (2013). (in Chinese)
5. Qian, W.: A comparative study of the differences between mandarin and Cantonese. J. Lang. Lit. Stud. **6**, 1–3 (2010). (In Chinese)
6. Zhou, W.H.: Examining the differences Between northern and southern ancient Chinese vocabulary in terms of food-related verbs. J. Chin. Dep., Natl. Chung Hsing Univ. **39**, 29–55 (2016). (In Chinese)
7. Lado, R.: Linguistics Across Cultures: Applied Linguistics for Language Teachers. University of Michigan Press ELT, Ann Arbor (1957)
8. Liu, J.L.: A Study of Learning Errors in Mandarin Chinese by Native Cantonese Speakers. Hunan Normal University, Hunan Normal University, Changsha (2010). (In Chinese)
9. Cai, Z.G., Pickering, M.J., Yan, H., Branigan, H.P.: Lexical and syntactic representations in closely related languages: evidence from Cantonese-Mandarin bilinguals. J. Mem. Lang. **65**(4), 431–445 (2011)
10. Tyler, A., Evans, V.: Reconsidering prepositional polysemy networks: the case of over. Language **77**(4), 724–765 (2001)
11. Lakoff, G.: Cognitive models and prototype theory. In: Neisser, U. (ed.) Concepts and conceptual development: Ecological and intellectual factors in categorization, pp. 63–100. Cambridge University Press, England (1987)
12. Yeh, H.: The categorization of auxiliary verbs in modern Chinese and its pedagogical applications. National Taiwan Normal University, Taiwan (2009). (in Chinese)
13. Tang, Z.: On region-specific vocabulary in Mandarin Chinese. Appl. Linguist. **2**, 40–48 (2005). (in Chinese)
14. Tang, S.-W.: Grammatical constraints on the Cantonese verb suffix "Zhu". Newsletter of OUHK Tin Ka Ping Centre Chin. Cult. **7**, 8–10 (2021). (in Chinese)
15. Zeng, Z.F.: A Study of Cantonese Idioms in Hong Kong. City University of Hong Kong Press, Hong Kong (2008). (in Chinese)

The Usage and Standardization of Function Words in Legislative Chinese Language Overseas: A Case Study of Auxiliary Words in the Civil Code of Macao

Linqian Bai[1], Lei Zhang[2], and Shanshan Yang[3(✉)]

[1] Primary Education College, Wuhan Polytechnic, Wuhan, China
[2] School of Chinese Language and Literature, Central China Normal University, Wuhan, China
[3] School of Foreign Languages, Central China Normal University, Wuhan, China
sunshineyang@ccnu.edu.cn

Abstract. This study presents a close investigation into the auxiliaries in legislative Chinese overseas focusing on the Civil Code of Macao. Research results showed that: 1) Structural auxiliaries are dominantly used in the legislative Chinese of Macao, with some cases of numeric auxiliaries and comparison auxiliaries. No tense auxiliaries or modal auxiliaries are found. 2) In addition to its regular usage, the "所"[suo] phrase has shown unconventional phrase combinations. Some cases of the "之"[zhi] phrase are found in too complicated structure, with lengthy syllables and multilayer inner nesting. Besides, the added components before "者"[zhe] are found diversified in nature, sometimes with lengthy syllables. 3) The readability of legislative Chinese overseas is to some extent compromised by the non-conventional combinations, lengthy syllables and multilayer inner nesting structures of the auxiliaries. 4) The standardization of auxiliaries in the Chinese language overseas may be attributable to multiple reasons. Therefore, standardizing the usage of the Chinese language overseas should resort to carefully designed strategies, "prioritizing the prominent issues", "referring to established principles", and "simplifying the standardization procedures".

Keywords: Chinese Language Overseas · Legislative Language · Auxiliaries · Standardization

1 Introduction

How to connect to the Chinese language overseas and maximize its communicative function has been a major research interest in the linguistics community. Concerning the standardization of Chinese language use in the new era, according to Li and Wang [1], several important relations should be highlighted, namely the relation between the "universality" and "domain-specificity", as well as the relation between "regionality" and "global nature" of language standardization. In this study, the focus of the investigation is the usage and standardization of legislative Chinese overseas, an issue of "regional" and "domain-specific" impact on Chinese language use and standardization.

M. Dong et al. (Eds.): CLSW 2023, LNAI 14514, pp. 160–172, 2024.
https://doi.org/10.1007/978-981-97-0583-2_13

As is known to all, the legislative language embodies the legislative spirit and conveys legislative intent. Compared with the daily language, legislative language distinguishes itself for its solemnness, accuracy and rigorousness. Chinese as a typical analytical language lacks morphological changes, and quite often relies on function words to convey its grammatical meaning, while in some Indo-European languages, this can be easily realized by verb inflexions. Therefore, Xing [2] called people's attention to auxiliaries which have a subtle position in the modern Chinese grammar system. Following Xing's [2] proposal, the Chinese research academia has conducted research on the usage of auxiliaries in the legislative Chinese language, focusing mainly on the structural auxiliary "的"[de] (see Zhou [3], Dong [4], Zhang [5], Jiang and Hu [6], etc.). Hu and Jiang [7] further investigated the similarities and differences concerning the usage of the "者/的"[zhe/de] structure in the legislative Chinese language in China's Mainland, China's Taiwan region and Hong Kong region.

Drawing inspiration from previous studies, this study investigated the Civil Code of Macao to look into the usage and standardization of auxiliaries in Legislative Chinese overseas. Macao boasts a unique language landscape of "three written languages and four spoken languages", featuring bilingual legislative language policies and Chinese legislative texts translated from Portuguese, making itself a distinctive case of legislative Chinese overseas. Against this backdrop, this study proposes the following research questions. What categories of auxiliaries are found in the legislative Chinese of Macao? How are these auxiliaries used in the legislative Chinese of Macao? What should be the proper strategies to improve the standard usage of the auxiliary words in the legislative Chinese of Macao? To shed some light on these questions, this study examined the language data of the Civil Code of Macao, with reference to the Civil Code of the People's Republic of China for comparison and analysis. The Civil Code of Macao has 286,964 characters in total and the Civil Code of the People's Republic of China has 111,304 characters in total.

2   The Usage of Auxiliaries in Legislative Chinese of Macao

Xing [8] classified auxiliaries into five major categories, including structural auxiliaries, tense auxiliaries, numerical auxiliaries, comparison auxiliaries, and modal auxiliaries. Previous studies have found that the auxiliaries used in the legislative Chinese of Macao are predominantly structural auxiliaries, with several cases of numerical and comparison auxiliaries, and no tense and modal auxiliaries. This absence of tense and modal auxiliaries probably can find its explanation in the fundamental function of laws, which is to enforce the rights and obligations of the action subjects. In other words, legal language in general does not involve event narration or emotional expressions. According to statistics, the representative numerical auxiliary and comparison auxiliary in the Civil Code of Macao are "第"[di] and "般"[ban] respectively, with 4476 and 18 appearances each. Due to the relatively simple nature of their usage, these two auxiliaries do not typically demonstrate standardization issues. Therefore, the focus of this study is put primarily on three structural auxiliaries, namely "所"[suo], "之"[zhi], and "者"[zhe].

2.1 The Auxiliary "所" [Suo] in Legislative Chinese of Macao

According to Lü [9], the auxiliary "所"[suo] is typically placed in front of transitive verbs in formal texts, constructing structures such as "所 + 动"[suo + verb], "有/无 + 所 +" [you/wu + suo + verb], "名 + 所 + 动"[noun + suo + verb], and "为 + 名 + 所 + 动"[wei + noun + suo + verb], etc. Besides these common usages, special collocations of "所"[suo] are also observed in the legislative Chinese of Macao, such as the "受 + 名 + 所 + 动"[shou + noun + suo + verb] structure, and the "由 + 名 + 所 + 动"[you + noun + suo + verb] structure, as is reflected in the following examples from the Civil Code of Macao.

A. 所 + 动**[suo + verb].**

Example 1: 基于不当得利而产生之返还义务之内容,包括因受损人之损失而取得之全部所得。(第473条).

The obligation to restitution based on unjust enrichment includes everything that has been obtained at the expense of the impoverished person or, if restitution in kind is not possible, the corresponding amount. (Article 473).

Example 2: 只要所涉及者非属各当事人不可处分之事宜或并未对时效之法定规则构成欺诈。(第322条).

as long as it is not a matter subtracted from the availability of the parties or fraud to the legal rules of prescription. (Article 322).

Example 3: 而所增加之数量系以有关种类物在调整日之价值予以确定。(第1001条) the amount of the update is convertible into an increase in kind, determined according to their value on the date of the update. (Article 1001).

Some other usages of "所"[suo] are also identified from the above examples. For example, the "所 + 动"[suo + verb] combination serving as a noun function is found in Example 1. In Example 2, "所"[suo] plus "者"[zhe] together serves as a noun function. And in Example 3, "所"[suo] plus "之"[zhi] is used to modify the noun.

B. 有 + 所 + 动**[you + suo + verb].**

Example 4: 如迟延作出某些行为会导致待禁治产人有所损失,则可在有关禁治产程序中之任何时刻指定一名临时监护人。(第125条).

At any time during the proceedings, a provisional guardian may be appointed... The acts the postponement of which could cause harm. (Article 125).

Example 5: 导致供公用之泉源或水库之水有所改变或减少者,须就所造成之损害向澳门地区承担责任。(第1296条).

The owner who, when exploiting groundwater, alters or diminishes the water of a source or reservoir intended for public use, is liable to the territory of Macao for the damage caused. (Article 1296).

In these two examples, the form of "动"[dong] includes both verbs (such as "损失"[sunshi] in Example 4 and verb phrases, such as "改变或减少"[gaibian huo jianshao] in Example 5.

C. 名 + 所 + 动**[noun + suo + verb].**

Example 6: 向受任人赔偿其因委任而遭受之损失, 即使<u>委任人所为</u>并无过错亦然。(第1093条).

Compensate him for the damage suffered as a result of the mandate, even if the <u>principal</u> acted without fault. (Article 1093).

Example 7: 如受寄人不推翻该推定, 即推定<u>寄托人所描述者</u>为真实。(第1117条) and, if this does not rebut the presumption, <u>the description made by the applicant</u> is presumed to be true. (Article 1117).

Example 8: 有效期维持<u>至b项规定所指期间</u>届满后五日止。(第220条).

If no deadline is set and the proposal is made to the absent person or, in writing, to the person present, it will remain until 5 days after <u>the deadline resulting from the provisions of paragraph b)</u>. (Article 220).

Example 9: 而预算所示之价额即为<u>出租人所负担之</u>最高限额。(第990条).

The beginning of the works must, however, be preceded by the elaboration of a budget of the respective cost, to be communicated to the lessor, in writing, and that represents the maximum value <u>for which he is responsible</u>. (Article 990).

In these examples, several varieties of the "名 + 所 + 动"[noun + suo + verb] structure is found, directly replacing noun form (Example 6), forming a combination with "者"[zhe] to replace a noun(Example 7), modifying noun (Example 8), and forming a combination with "之"[zhi] to modify a noun (Example 9).

D. 为 + 名 + 所 + 动[wei + noun + suo + verb].

Example 10: 只要行为人之行为不超越避免损失之必要限度, 则<u>为法律所容许</u>。(第328条).

It is <u>lawful</u> to resort to force in order to fulfill or ensure one's own right, provided that the agent do not exceed what is necessary to avoid injury. (Article 328).

Example 11: 或与该法律行为中任一<u>为冲突法所考虑</u>之要素有连结关系之法律。(第40条).

or is in connection with any of the elements of the legal transaction that can be <u>met in the field of conflict law</u>. (Article 40).

E. 受 + 名 + 所 + 动[shou + noun + suo + verb].

Example 12: 仍得请求返还有关之物,   而不受时效所影响。   (第297条) <u>notwithstanding the prescription</u>, demand the restitution of the thing when the price is not paid. (Article 297).

Example 13: 由法律行为所生之债以及法律行为本身之实质, <u>均受有关主体指定之法律或显示出为其意欲之法律所规范</u>。(第40条).

The obligations arising from a legal transaction, as well as its substance, <u>are governed by the law that the respective subjects have designated or have had in mind</u>. (Article 40).

F. 由 + 名 + 所 + 动[you + noun + suo + verb].

Example 14: 涉及<u>由第三人所提供</u>之担保时, 亦需要有该人作出之明确保留。(第852条).

If the guarantee <u>concerns a third party</u>, the express reservation of the third party is also required. (Article 852).

Example 15: 如合同未要求交付其它文件, 则出卖物之交付<u>由交付上述凭证及依习惯所要求之其它文件代替</u>。(第929条).

In the sale on documents, the delivery of the thing is replaced <u>by the delivery of its representative title and of the other documents required by the contract or, in the silence of this, by the uses.</u> (Article 929).

Table 1. "所"[suo] in the Civil Code of Macao and the Civil Code of the PRC

List of Items	the Civil Code of Macao	the Civil Code of the People's Republic of China
Corpus Size	286964 characters	106436 characters
Frequency	1718/6‰	80/0.8‰
Differences	"有/无 + 所 + 动"[you/wu + suo + verb]; "受 + 名 + 所 + 动"[shou + noun + suo + verb]; "由 + 名 + 所 + 动"[you + noun + suo + verb]	
Similarities	"所 + 动"[suo + verb]; "名 + 所 + 动"[noun + suo + verb]; "为 + 名 + 所 + 动"[wei + noun + suo + verb]	

The detailed descriptive statistics of the comparison are provided in Table 1. Comparing with the legislative texts of China's Mainland, the "所"[suo] in the legislative Chinese of Macao is used at a higher frequency and in more complicated forms, with a total appearance of 1718 cases in the Civil Code of Macao, accounting for 6‰ of its total word count. Statistics show that the frequency of "所"[suo] usage in the Macao Civil Code exceeds 7 times that of the Civil Code of the PRC.

2.2 The Auxiliary "之"[Zhi] in the Legislative Chinese of Macao

The auxiliary word "之"[zhi], as pointed out by Lü [9], is a structural auxiliary in the ancient Chinese legacy. The usage of "之"[zhi] more or less resembles "的"[de] in modern Chinese, mainly used "between the modifier and the headword", or "between the subject and the predicate". These two usages of "之"[zhi] are also observed in the legislative Chinese of Macao. The following examples are typical cases of "之"[zhi] used in these two structures.

A. Used between the modifier and the headword.

Example 16: <u>废止一法律之法律</u>被废止时, 不引致先前被该法律废止之法律再生效。(第6条).

<u>The repeal of the repealing law</u> does not matter the revival of the law that it repealed. (Article 6).

Example 17： 婚前协议之实质及效力, 以及法定或约定财产制之实质及效力, 均按缔结婚姻时结婚人之常居地法规定。(第51条).

The substance and effects of prenuptial agreements and the property regime, legal or conventional, are defined by the law of the habitual residence of the spouses at the time of the celebration of the marriage. (Article 51).

B. Used between the subject and the predicate.

Example 18： 法律人格之开始及终止, 亦由个人之属人法规定。(第25条).

The beginning and end of the legal personality are equally fixed by the personal law of each individual. (Article 25).

Example 19： 然而, 肖像之复制、展示或作交易之用, 按照第七十三条之规定可能侵犯肖像人之名誉权时, 即不得为之。(第80条).

The portrait cannot, however, be reproduced, exhibited or released for sale, if the fact could result in an offence against the right to honour, under the terms of Article 73. (Article 80).

Previous studies [10] argue that when "之"[zhi] is used between the modifier and the headword, "it is usually followed by monosyllabic characters". However, the use of "之"[zhi] in the legislative Chinese of Macao demonstrates a clearly more complicated pattern, as quite a number of the modifiers and headwords in the Civil Code of Macao are complicated phrases themselves, such as Example 17. The situation is further complicated when the modifier or the headword themselves are also in "之"[zhi] structure, which makes a complicated modifier-head construction with multilayer nesting of the "之"[zhi] structure, as is shown in the following examples.

Example 20： 对合伙适用为无限公司所定之制度, 但[[制度中与[[合伙]之非商业性质]之目的有抵触]之部分]或[[制度中以[商业企业主资格]之存在作为适用前提]之部分]除外。(第185条).

Civil companies are subject to [the regime established for [[companies in a collective name], except in what is [incompatible with the non-commercial nature of their object]] or [presupposes [the quality of commercial entrepreneur]]. (Article 185).

Example 21： [为进行任何救援或慈善活动计划, 或为促成[公共工程或纪念物]之施工、或为促成[喜庆节目、展览、庆典及类同行为]之进行而设立]之委员会。(第190条).

Commissions [set up [to carry out any aid or beneficence plan, or to promote the execution of [public works, monuments], [festivals, exhibitions, festivities and similar acts]]...(Article 190).

Example 20 shows a classic case of three-layer nesting of the "之"[zhi] structure. As is known, the complexity of the syntactic structure is negatively correlated with the text readability. It is easy to tell that excessive modifier-head structure nesting will to a large extent compromise the readability of the legal text.

2.3 The Auxiliary "者"[Zhe] in Legislative Chinese of Macao

The main function of the structural auxiliary "者"[zhe] is to turn verbs, verb phrases or sentences into noun phrases. He[11]argued that one of the main functions of the "者"[zhe] structure is to highlight certain features of the object of discussion as is necessary. The "者"[zhe] structure has strong vitality because of its robust expressive power. Statistics show a high frequency of "者"[zhe] usage in the Civil Code of Macao, totaling 1002 appearances. The elements before "者"[zhe] and the syntactic function of the "者"[zhe] structure both demonstrate diversity, as is shown in the following examples.

Example 22: 解释者仅得将在法律字面上有最起码文字对应之含义，视为立法思想。(第8条).

The interpreter cannot, however, consider legislative thought that does not have a minimum of verbal correspondence in the letter of the law, even if imperfectly expressed. (Article 8).

Example 23: 作成文书者之个人判断，仅作为供裁判者自由判断之要素。(第365条) the mere personal judgments of the documentator are only valid as elements subject to the judge's free appreciation. (Article 365).

Example 24: 债因失踪人死亡而消灭者，失踪人死亡时，债之可请求性亦视为已消灭。(第103条).

The enforceability of the obligations that would be extinguished by the death of the absentee is considered extinguished. (Article 103).

Example 25: 有益改善费用系指虽对物之保存非不可或缺，但可增加其价值者。(第208条).

Necessary improvements are those whose purpose is to avoid the loss, destruction or deterioration of the thing. (Article 208).

In the above examples, the elements before "者"[zhe] include both expressions (Example 22) and phrases (Example 23/24), and even more complicated compound sentence structures (Example 25). Syntactic analysis shows that the "者"[zhe] structure can serve as the sentence subject (Example 22) or the non-subject topic (see Gao and Lyu [12]), the object (Example 25), and attributes (Example 23/24).

Previous studies have identified multiple grammar standardization issues in the legislative Chinese of Macao. One direct observation is that, in the words of Ding [13], "Doctor of Philosophy in Criminal Law from China's Mainland may find it difficult to understand articles and items in the Criminal Code of Macao, while Professors teaching Private International Law find it certain stipulations concerning private international law in the Civil Code of Macao confusing." Compared with the legislative language in China's Mainland, the legislative Chinese of Macao normally use classical Chinese auxiliaries at an overwhelmingly higher frequency with more diversified usage, leaving the readability of the legislative Chinese of Macao at risk. Our primary investigation spotted similar issues in the legislative Chinese in China's Hong Kong and Taiwan region as well, which also calls for further research efforts.

3 Strategies for Standardizing Legislative Chinese Overseas

The fundamental nature of standardizing the legislative Chinese overseas is to standardize Chinese language use against the backdrop of language diversity. The inherent complexity of the situation calls for careful planning and corresponding strategies in the process. Based on the above analysis, this study proposes the following three strategies in the hope of unveiling more in-depth explorations in the future.

3.1 Pritorizing the Prominent Issues

Existing standardization issues have severely sabotaged the readability and authoritativeness of the legislative Chinese overseas. This study agrees with previous findings that the standardization of legislative Chinese overseas requires systematic work and meticulous efforts.

We propose the strategy of "prioritizing the prominent issues" and progressive measures for the purpose of standardizing the legislative language overseas. The "prominent issues" include both noticeable grammatical issues and critical standardization issues. For example, Due attention should be given to "之"[zhi] in the Civil Code of Macao, which has the top frequency (13825 appearances) and a high proportion of standardization issues. Two major usages concerning "之" [zhi] are observed in the legislative Chinese of Macao, namely working as a pronoun (such as in Example 26 "之$_3$") and working as a function word. When used as an auxiliary, it is used in two major scenarios, used between the modifier and the head(such as in Example 26 "之$_1$/之$_2$"), and used between the subject and the predicate(such as in Example 27 "之$_1$").

Example 26: 对于召集上之$_1$不当情事以及其它属程序上之$_2$不当情事，仅得由社员主张之$_3$。(第166条).

Irregularities in the summons$_1$ and, in general, procedural irregularities$_2$ cannot be invoked$_3$ except by the associates. (Article 166).

Example 27: 因债务人之$_1$欺诈导致债权人未有行使其权利者，适用上款之$_2$规定。(第313条).

If the holder$_1$ has not exercised his right as a result of the debtor's willful misconduct, the provisions of the previous number$_2$ shall apply. (Article 313).

Lü and Zhu [14] proposed clear principles on function words that "we should identify the usage of function words to avoid misuse and overuse. Misuse refers to using a wrong function word. Misusing the wrong function word also constitutes overuse of the wrongly used word." Our preliminary investigation revealed misuse and more prominently overuse of the character "之"[zhi] in the legislative languages of Macao. Besides, standardization issues are found disproportionately distributed in the cases investigated. Compared with pronouns, auxiliaries demonstrate a higher frequency of standardization issues. Among auxiliaries, standardization issues concerning the modifier and the head show a strikingly high frequency. Therefore, for standardizing the use of auxiliary words, priority should be given to the prominent issues.

3.2 Referring to Established Principles

Standardizing language usage is both socially and academically relevant [15]. Legislative text has its special language style, and the written Chinese in Macao has its distinctive features as well. How to ensure the proper practice of standardizing legislative Chinese usage overseas? How to conduct principles-guided standardization practices and avoid conflicts? We may draw inspiration from legal trials where "referring to previous cases" is a practiced tradition, which means following the judgments of previous cases of a similar nature, In this study the same strategy of "referring to established principles" is proposed in standardizing legislative Chinese overseas, namely learning from the existing fine standards or practices.

Two representative "established principles" may shed light on the standardization of legislative Chinese in Macao, namely the existing standards on legislative Chinese in China's mainland or Hong Kong, and similar stipulations concerning the legislative Chinese in Macao. A particularly instructive guidance, the Legislation Techniques Standards (Trial) was issued by the Commission of Legal Affairs of the National People's Congress in 2009 to pinpoint common issues in legislative techniques. For example, it is specifically stipulated that "when parallel relations of two levels exist in a sentence, the two parallel relations with inner connections should use the caesura sign, and the two parallel relations without inner connections comma". The legislative Chinese texts of Macao may also refer to the Legislation Techniques Standards (Trial) for language standardization concerning parallel relation expressions.

A further search shows that 62 cases of "从"[cong], a preposition introducing the source of location or place, did not appear together with expressions of location in the Civil Code of Macao. Interestingly in the same Civil Code 37 cases were used in conformity with the language standards. These standard usages could provide inspiration for handling the standardization issues.

Example 28: 遗嘱订立后, 受遗赠人以有偿或无偿方式自遗嘱人处取得遗赠之标的物时, 遗赠不产生效力。(第2087条).

If, after making the will, the legatee acquires from the testator, for consideration or free of charge, the thing that has been the object of the legacy, the legacy has no effect. (Article 2087).

Example 29: 对未成年人之替换及对类似未成年人之替换, 仅可包括被替换之人从遗嘱人处所取得之财产......(第2129条).

Pupillary and quasi-pupillary substitutions can only cover assets that the substituted person has acquired through the testator, albeit as legitimate. (Article 2129).

3.3 Simplifying the Standardization Procedures

As the carrier of overseas legal culture, overseas legislative Chinese language are in nature unique and precious language resources featuring special historical and cultural background and regional customs. Accurate and adequate standardization of the overseas legislative Chinese while maintaining its diversified multicultural legacy calls for the collective wisdom of the linguistics community and law community.

This study proposes the strategy of "simplifying the standardization procedures". For language standardization issues, it is strongly suggested to minimize the number and location of changes, with "minimal interference" to the original sentence structure as long as the standardization expectations are satisfactorily fulfilled.

For example, overusing "之"[zhi] in the legislative Chinese of Macao has led to overly complicated structure and semantic misinterpretation.

Example 30: 任何人均有权受保护, 以免被他人以指出某种事实或作出某种判断, 使其名誉、别人对其之观感、名声、声誉、个人信用及体面受侵犯。(第73条).

Everyone has the right to protection against accusations of facts or judgments offensive to his honor and consideration, good name and reputation, personal credit and decorum. (Article 73).

Example 31: [未经父母或监护人之许可、或未获得[法院之批准以取代上述之人之]许可而结婚之]未成年人, 在管理其带给夫妻双方之财产上, 或在管理其于结婚后至成年前以无偿方式获得之财产上, 继续视为未成年人。(第1521条).

A minor who marries without having obtained authorization from his parents or guardian, [or the respective judicial supply], continues to be considered a minor in terms of the administration of assets that he brings to the couple or that later come to him free of charge until he reaches the age of majority… (Article 1521).

According to Lü [16], "其"[qi] in Chinese works as address functions, similar to the use of "那"[na] or "他的"[tade]. When used as "他的"[tade], "其"[qi] equals a noun plus "之"[zhi] structure in function. In Example 30, "其"[qi] in "别人对其之观感" serves as "他的"[tade], constituting the semantic meaning of "别人对该人之之观感", with a duplication of "之"[zhi] in the sentence. It is clear that the "之"[zhi] in this example should be deleted. Example 31 presents a rather complicated modifier-head structure with a parallel structure serving as the modifier. Two nesting structures exist in the second parallel item, a modifier-head structure and a "subject-之-predicate" structure, the result of which is poor readability of the sentence with 5 "之"[zhi] in one structure. In fact, if the three "之"[zhi] words in the modifier are deleted, changing the sentence into "未经父母或监护人许可、或未获得法院批准以取代上述人之许可而结婚之未成年人", the structure and semantics integrity of the sentence is kept intact with readability improved.

In some cases, auxiliaries should be put in place to make the sentence right. As is previously argued, the main function of the structural auxiliary "者"[zhe] is to turn verbs, verb phrases or sentences into noun phrases "X者"[X zhe]. However, lengthy syllables and the complicated structure of "X者"[X zhe] may put the readability of the text at risk.

Example   32: 如有直接或透过他人将在争讼中之债权或其它权利让与法官或检察院司法官、司法人员或诉讼代理人 (者), 又或让与参与有关诉讼之鉴定人或其它司法协助人员者, 该让与无效。(第573条).

The assignment of claims or other litigious rights made, directly or through an intermediary, to judges or magistrates of the Public Prosecutor's Office, court officials or legal representatives, as well as the assignment of such claims or rights made to experts or other assistants of the justice that intervene in the respective process. (Article 573).

Example 33: 但因禁治产人配偶之过错而出现事实分居(者), 又或禁治产人之配偶因其它原因而在法律上无行为能力者除外。(第126条).

To the spouse of the interdicted person, unless he/she is de facto separated due to his/her own fault or if it is for another legally incapable cause; (Article 126).

Example 34: 而该等事实或情事系旨在否定被自认事实之效力 (者) 或旨在变更或消灭其效力者。(第353条).

If the confessional declaration, judicial or extrajudicial, is accompanied by the narration of other facts or circumstances tending to invalidate the effectiveness of the confessed fact or to modify or extinguish its effects…. (Article 353).

Example 35: 因故意或过失不法侵犯他人权利 (者) 或违反旨在保护他人利益之任何法律规定者, 有义务就其侵犯或违反所造成之损害向受害人作出损害赔偿。(第477条).

Anyone who, with intent or mere negligence, unlawfully violates the right of another or any legal provision intended to protect the interests of others is obliged to compensate the injured party for damages resulting from the violation. (Article 477).

The added components before "者"[zhe] in the above examples are all complicated parallel structures with lengthy syllables. In Example 32, the added components before "者"[zhe] have strikingly 64 syllables, connected by the conjunction "或"[huo] in a parallel structure. The two parallel structures both feature at least one nesting "或"[huo] phrase. The complicated sentence structure may negatively impact text understanding. Suggestions are made to add an auxiliary "者"[zhe] at the end of the first parallel structure (the added "者"[zhe] are highlighted in Example 32–35). Such changes will not influence the truth value of the semantics but will greatly enhance the text's readability. As a matter of fact, some similar cases in the Civil Code of Macao were properly handled and can serve as good references for standardization. Example 36a and 36b shows the comparison of changes.

Example 36a: 被指为公共当局、官员或公证员所认知而透过文书证明之任何事实, 而实际上并未发生者, 又或被指为负责之实体所作出而透过文书证明之任何行为, 而实际上并未作出者, 该文书即为虚假。(第366条, 原文).

The document is false when it attests as having been the object of the perception of the public authority, public official or notary any fact that in reality was not verified, or as having been practiced by the responsible entity any act that in reality was not. (original text, Article 366).

Example 36b: 被指为公共当局、官员或公证员所认知而透过文书证明之任何事实, 而实际上并未发生, 又或被指为负责之实体所作出而透过文书证明之任何行为, 而实际上并未作出者, 该文书即为虚假。(删除"者"后).

The document is false when it attests as having been the object of the perception of the public authority, public official or notary any fact that in reality was not verified, or as having been practiced by the responsible entity any act that in reality was not. (Article 366 with "者"[zhe]deleted).

To sum it up, standardization of legislative language should follow adequate principles and the natural law of language use. This study agrees with Li [17] that "language standardization is 'absolutely necessary' when language situation disorder is found. The self-organization mechanism of the language, with support and help of the society, should come into play to bring the language situation back to order."

4 Conclusion

The standardization of the Chinese Language overseas is an increasingly important area of research interest. By a focused analysis of the Civil Code of Macao, this study presents some preliminary attempts to investigate the usage and standardization of auxiliaries in legislative Chinese overseas. After looking into several key auxiliaries and their usage in the Civil Code of Macao, three strategies are proposed, "prioritizing the prominent issues", "referring to established principles", and "simplifying the standardization procedures" to cope with standardization issues identified in the legislative Chinese of Macao.

Legislative language requires clear-cut definitions of concepts and explicit expression of logical relations among concepts, which further requires the standardization of function words. Systematic planning and practice are called for to promote adequate standardization of legislative languages. It is hoped that this study may shed some light on more in-depth explorations among the academia into this issue in the future.

Acknowledgments. This work was supported by the Youth Project grant of the National Social Science Foundation of China [Project: Research on the interaction between generic references and stylistic varieties, Grant Number: 21CYY042], and by the research grant of the China Vocational Education Association, Hubei [Project: Development and Application of Children's Vocational Enlightenment Education Resources in the Context of High-Quality Development, Grant Number: HBZJ2023785].

References

1. Li, Y., Wang, M.: The necessity of language standardization in the new era and some important relationships. Lexicographical Stud. **5**, 1–10 (2020). (in Chinese)
2. Xing, F.: Chinese Grammar. Northeast Normal University Press, Changchun (1996). (in Chinese)
3. Zhou, X.: Case analysis on the language errors of administrative laws. Appl. Linguis. **3**, 64–67 (2002). (in Chinese)
4. Dong, X.: On the usage of "de" phrase as post-relative clauses-comments on the usage of "de" phrase in legal documents. Appl. Linguis. **4**, 120–126 (2003). (in Chinese)
5. Zhang, B.: Legal language should be the example of language standards. Contemp. Rhetoric **5**, 1–7 (2015). (in Chinese)
6. Jiang, C., Hu, D.: Self-desginationand transferred-desgination of de constructions in Chinese legal texts. J. Yunnan Normal Univ. Teach. Stud. Chinese Foreign Lang. Ed. **4**, 56–65 (2017). (in Chinese)
7. Hu, D., Jiang, C.: The linguistic expressions of conditions in legal sentences of mainland China, Taiwan district and Hong Kong. J. Huaqiao Univ. Philos. Soc. Sci. **5**, 147–156 (2017). (in Chinese)

8. Xing, F.: 300 Questions on Chinese Grammar. The Commercial Press, Beijing (2002). (in Chinese)
9. Lü, S. (ed.): 800 Words in Modern Chinese, the Revised and Extended Version. The Commercial Press, Beijing (2015). (in Chinese)
10. Bei, Y. eds.: Case Analysis on the Use of Function Words in Modern Chinese. The Commercial Press, Beijing (1982/2010) (in Chinese)
11. He, L.: On the Functions Words in the Chronicle of Zuo, revised The Commericial Press, Beijing (2004). (in Chinese)
12. Gao, Y., Lyu, G.: Functions of non-subject topics in mandarin conversations. In: Dong, M., Gu, Y., Hong, J.F. (eds.) Chinese Lexical Semantics, vol. 13250, pp. 325–338. LNCS. Springer International Publishing, Cham (2022)
13. Ding, W.: On law localization in Macao. Tribune of Pol. Sci. Law 5, 27–34 (1999). (in Chinese)
14. Lü S., Zhu, D.: Talks on Grammar and Rhetoric. Liaoning Education Press, Dalian (1952/2005) (in Chinese)
15. Wang, M.: Multiple perspectives of language standardization. J. Lang. Plan. 2, 19–23 (2017). (in Chinese)
16. Lü, S.: Grammar of Classical Chinese, in Collected Works of Lü Shuxiang, volume 9. Dalian: Liaoning Education Press, Dalian (1952/2005). (in Chinese)
17. Li, Y.: A tentative analysis on the language standards. Contemp. Rhet. 4, 1–6 (2015). (in Chinese)

The Licensing Contexts of Polarity-Sensitive Adverb *Sǐhuó* ('no matter what'): A Force-Dynamic Analysis

Yifa Xu[⊠]

Department of Chinese and Bilingual Studies, The Hong Kong Polytechnic University, Hong Kong, China
yifaxu@polyu.edu.hk

Abstract. The distribution of weak NPI adverbs such as *sǐhuó* ('desperately; no matter what') in Mandarin cannot be fully explained by the existing hypotheses about the general licensing conditions of NPIs such as downward entailment. This article attempts to provide a unifying explanation for the licensing contexts of the weak NPI adverbs *sǐhuó* by applying the force-dynamic model. I propose that the lexical meaning of *sǐhuó* carries a conceptual structure that involves a confrontation between two volitional forces at a physical or psychological/conceptual level. This analysis successfully explains why some verbs of implicit negation (such as *jùjué* 'refuse') can license *sǐhuó* while others cannot. It also explains why some affirmative predicates or apparently affirmative contexts can also license *sǐhuó*, because these predicates or contexts fulfill the semantic structure of force-confrontation. The force-dynamic analysis is also compatible with the historical development of the use of *sǐhuó*, which reflects a change from a physical interaction to a psychological or conceptual confrontation between two forces.

Keywords: Polarity sensitivity · Adverbs · Force dynamics · Verbs of implicit negation

1 Introduction

Some adverbs in Mandarin may carry implicitly negative meaning or may be sensitive to the polarity of the sentence [1]. Such kind of adverbs can be treated as weak NPIs [2, 3]. One example of this kind is the adverb *sǐhuó* ('desperately; no matter what'). *Sǐhuó* is a compound juxtaposed by *sǐ* ('die') and *huó* ('live'), whose literal meaning is 'to die and/or to live'; and it conveys a conventional meaning 'desperately; no matter what; anyway'. Previous studies have noted that *sǐhuó* prefers to occur in negative contexts [4 6]. For example, in Wang W.'s [5] corpus study, 187 sentences out of 213 examples of *sǐhuó* (87.8%) in her sample are negative sentences. *Sǐhuó* is treated as a 'weak' NPI because it can occur in affirmative sentences occasionally with some restrictions. Zheng [3] (pp.133) classifies the affirmative sentences which allow the occurrence of *sǐhuó* into three classes. The first class is a sentence where the main predicate is a modal verb denoting volition or ability, such as *yào* ('want'), *yuànyì* ('be willing to') or *gǎn* ('dare'), etc. The second class is when the main predicate denotes a certain kind of actions of the body, such as *sǐhuó zhuài zhe yìgēn shéngzi* ('hold on to a string firmly'). The third class is called 'other contexts', such as *sǐhuó tóng niáng zài yídào* ('stay with mother no matter what').

Some puzzles remain regarding the licensing contexts of *sǐhuó*. Firstly, *sǐhuó* can modify verbs that denote body actions, such as *zhuài* ('drag'), *lā* ('pull'), or *zhuā* ('grasp'), as in *sǐhuó lā-zhù wǒ* ('pull me back desperately'), which are apparently affirmative contexts. Zheng [3] (pp.133) argues that such use of *sǐhuó* should be treated separately from the NPI use of the word. However, we intuitively feel that there should be certain conceptual relatedness between the use of *sǐhuó* when it modifies a verb of body action and the use of this adverb in a negative context. How can we explain such a potentially conceptual connection?

Secondly, the existing theories cannot explain why some verbs of implicit negation (VINs) can guarantee the occurrence of *sǐhuó* while others cannot. For example, both *jùjué* ('refuse') and *lǎnde* ('do not feel like; not bother to') are verbs of implicit negation that can license some strict NPIs such as NPI-minimizers [7]. However, *jùjué* is fully compatible with *sǐhuó* while *lǎnde* is not:

(1) 張三死活{拒絕/??懶得}跟李四見面。

Zhāngsān sǐhuó {jùjué / ??lǎnde} gēn Lǐsì jiànmiàn.

Zhangsan dead-live refuse not feel like with Lisi meet.

('Zhangsan refused to meet Lisi no matter what.' / 'Zhangsan didn't feel like meeting Lisi no matter what.').

Meanwhile, it sounds odd when the verb of implicit negation *fàngqì* ('give up') co-occurs with *sǐhuó* while the apparent 'positive' counterpart, *jiānchí* ('persist'), is compatible with this adverb:

(2) 他死活{??放弃/坚持}参加比賽。

Tā sǐhuó {??fàngqì / jiānchí} cānjiā bǐsài.

3SG dead-live give up persist participate match.

('He gave up/persisted participating in the match no matter what.').

Several influential hypotheses on the licensing condition of NPIs such as downward entailment [8] or nonveridicality [9] seem not be able to explain the semantic property shared by all the contexts where *sǐhuó* occur. Wang. W [6] argues that *sǐhuó* is used in a context where the subject disobeys the volition of other participants in the context, or the subject's action is contrary to a certain fact, which the author generalizes as 'confrontation without condition'[1]. In other words, the context that licenses *sǐhuó* must fulfill the semantic requirement that there is a conflict between the agent's intention and the request or expectation of other people. Wang. W's [6] idea of 'confrontation' is inspiring in that it captures the characteristic of the force-dynamic relationship between the subject and the other participants in the context where *sǐhuó* can occur. However, the author did not develop such a concept to provide a unifying explanation for all the

---

[1] The original Chinese term is '無條件對抗義 *wútiáojiàn duìkàng yì* ('confrontation with no condition')'.

contexts that *sǐhuó* can appear. Also, the semantic content of such a 'confrontation' has not yet been elaborated in her study.

In the following section, I will show that the three uses of *sǐhuó* generalized by Zheng [3] can be explained by a unifying force-dynamic schema, which involves a force-confrontation between the subject and another participant in the context at a physical or mental level. The puzzles mentioned above will also be explained by the matching relationship of the force-dynamic schema between the predicates and the adverb *sǐhuó*.

2   A Force Dynamic Analysis of the Distribution of NPI-Adverb *sǐhuó*

2.1   The Force Dynamics Model

From the point of view of the collocational approach to polarity sensitivity, certain semantic features of the licensor and the licensee (NPIs) must match for the NPI to be licensed. Following this view, the (un)acceptability of the co-occurrence of a VIN and an NPI depends on whether the conceptual structures or semantic frames of both sides match. Such a claim is built upon an assumption that both a predicate and an NPI will evoke a certain conceptual structure or semantic frame in their lexical meanings. In this section, I attempt to apply the force dynamics model to analyze the conceptual structure of the adverbal NPI *sǐhuó*.

'Force dynamics' refers to 'how entities interact with respect to force' [10]. It is a generalization of the linguistic notion causality and analyzes causality by decomposing the causal event into finer primitives and elaborates how different participants interact with each other within a framework of force interaction. It applies diagrams to visualize the dynamic relations between different linguistic forces in a given setting. The purpose of force dynamics is to serve as "a fundamental notional system that structures conceptual material pertaining to force interaction in a common way across a linguistic range: the physical, psychological, social, inferential, discourse, and mental-model domains of reference and conception" [10] (pp.50). The force dynamics (FD) modal has been applied in many subfields in grammar and semantics including causality, modality, and verb aspects and causal structures [11], among others, to provide cognitive and functionally based representations of the conceptual structures of certain linguistic categories. Some basic components and their denotations are presented below, which are adapted from Talmy [10].

Table 1. Basic components and their meanings in the force dynamics model.

a. Force entities	$\bigcirc$ $\rbrack$ Agonist (Ago) Antagonist (Ant)
b. Intrinsic force tendency	Toward action: $>$ Toward rest: ●
c. Balance of strengths	The stronger entity: + The weaker entity: −
d. Resultant of the force interaction	Action: $\longrightarrow$ Rest: —————●—————

For example, the force dynamics of the English verbs 'stop/prevent' can be presented as Fig. 1 (as in the sentence *The plug stopped the gas from flowing out.*) The schema shown in Fig. 1 can be interpreted as follows by translating the information of each basic component: (a) **the Agonist:** a certain event or situation (denoted by VP, represented by entity 2 in the schema) is about to take place (in the status of towards-action); (b) **the Antagonist:** the entity '1' conducts a certain action to block the (potential) action of the entity 2; (c) the **interactions** between the two forces: the force of entity 1 is stronger than the force of entity 2, which results from a status of rest of entity 2.

Fig. 1. The force dynamics of stop/prevent [10] (pp.63).

Apart from the typical causal events involving physical movements of entities, the force dynamics analysis can also be applied to the 'inter-psychological' or 'social' force interaction, which Tamly calls 'sociodynamics'. More complex patterns of force dynamics, such as the force dynamics of lexical items like *try*, *refuse*, or *finally*, can be captured by the force dynamics model. In the following sections, I will apply the force dynamics model to explain the (in)compatibility between the weak NPI adverb *sĭhuó* and the predicates or contexts that may license it.

2.2 The Force Dynamics of *sǐhuó*

According to Talmy [10], adverbs such as *finally* project a force dynamic schema as a predicate does. This shows that certain information regarding force dynamics may be encoded in the lexical meaning of adverbs as well. Following this assumption, I propose the force dynamics of *sǐhuó* as Fig. 2:

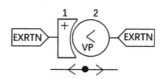

Fig. 2. The force dynamics of the context that licenses *sǐhuó*

The critical feature of this force dynamics script is that there are two forces from two opposite directions moving against each other (represented by the two arrows of opposite directions at the bottom). The resultant of the force interaction is towards 'rest' at the moment because of the continuity of the confrontation, as marked by the black dot on the line at the bottom. The resultant should be 'rest' rather than 'action' because *sǐhuó* is used to modify the state of confrontation, while the exact result of the confrontation is not yet clear to the speaker. The box of 'EXRTN' ('exertion') is added to indicate that it involves a great physical or mental effort from both sides, which can be marked as a feature [+exertion]. Below I would illustrate how this force dynamics schema explains various uses of *sǐhuó*, ranging from physical to conceptual force interactions.

2.3 Physical Force-Confrontation Denoted by Body Action Verbs

The force dynamic schema above explains the relatively 'concrete' sense of *sǐhuó* when it directly modifies verbs denoting body actions such as *zhuài* ('drag'), *lā* ('pull'), or *zhuā* ('grasp'). For example:

(3) 拿的時候他還不樂意, 覺得我搶他收藏了, 死活拽著一個紅頭繩就是不撒手,
跟我搞爭奪。(CCL\六六 温柔啊温柔 *liuliu Wenrou a wenrou*)
Ná de shíhòu tā hái bú lèyì, juéde wǒ qiǎng tā shōucáng le,
take DE when 3Sg even not happy think 1Sg rob 3Sg collection Perf.
sǐhuó zhuài zhe yí-gè hóngtóushéng jiùshì bù sā shǒu,
desperately pull Cont one-CL red-head-string be not let go.
gēn wǒ gǎo zhēngduó.

with 1Sg make contest.

'He was not happy when (I) took it. He thought that I was taking his collection. He pulled on a red string desperately and didn't let go, intending to struggle with me.'

(4) 我就要去拼命, 跟他一個對一個, 誰也別活算了。我爸爸死活拉住我。(CCL\馮
驥才作品 *Feng Jicai*'s work)

Wǒ jiù yào qù pīnmìng, gēn tā yí-gè duì yí-gè, shuí yě bié
1Sg then want go fight with 3sg one-CL versus one-CL who also don't
huó suàn le. Wǒ bàba **sǐhuó lā-zhù** wǒ
alive let it be Perf 1sg father desperately pull-ZHU 1sg
'I wanted to fight with him, one versus one, even if neither were to survive. My
father pulled me [back] desperately.'

In actions like 'drag' or 'pull', there are two forces from opposite directions acting
along a straight line. The strength of each force is roughly equal to the other so a balanced
state is maintained.

Such a physical relation between two forces matches perfectly with the force dynamic
modal of *sǐhuó* proposed above. This explains why verbs denoting body actions such as
'drag', which is apparently a non-negative context, can allow the occurrence of *sǐhuó*. If
we define the licensing environments of *sǐhuó* following the monotonicity thesis (such
as downward-entailment) or by purely formal criteria (such as the presence of negative
elements), we may have to exclude this collocation between *sǐhuó* and body-action verbs
from the normal NPI use of the adverb; Zheng [3], for example, defines such use of *sǐhuó*
as separate and different from the NPI use of the word. From the perspective of force
dynamics, however, the use of *sǐhuó* at the physical level and the mental level can be
explained uniformly.

2.4 Conceptual Force-Confrontation Denoted by Negative Words and Verbs of Implicit Negation

Negative Words. The force-confrontation encoded by *sǐhuó* also extends to the mental
or conceptual level. Since negative assertions are usually made against a certain (affirmative) assumption that has been established in the context [12], negation can be understood
as a blocking force which stops a pre-existing force from moving forward. In the example below, *sǐhuó* modifies a negative verbal phrase marked by the negative *bù* ('not'). In
this case, the *Agonist* ('2' in Fig. 2) represents the suggestion/request/assumption put
forth by other persons, and the *Antagonist* ('1' in Fig. 2) is foregrounded as the subject
who stands against this abstract force. The resultant state of a negative sentence should
be 'rest', which indicates the non-occurrence of the state of affairs. This explains why
negative *bù* ('not; do not intend to') can license *sǐhuó*.

(5) 他死活不去。
    Tā sǐhuó bù qù
    3SG no matter what not go
    'He doesn't want to go (there) no matter what.' (It implies that somebody asked
    the subject to go repeatedly but he kept refusing to do so.)

Volitional Modal Verb. The force-dynamic schema shown in Fig. 2. Also explains why
sǐhuó can be licensed by volitional modality such as *yào* ('want'). In the following
example, *sǐhuó* modifies an affirmative phrase which denotes the agent's intention to do
something. In this situation, the positions of '1' and '2' of the force-dynamic schema
in Fig. 2. Are reversed. Namely, the subject of the sentence now represents the *Agonist*
who intends to act against the *Antagonist* who tries to stop the subject from doing a
certain thing.

(6) 他死活要去。

> Tā sǐhuó yào qù.
>
> 3SG no matter what want go
>
> 'He wanted to go no matter what.'(It implies that the subject wanted to go but somebody else tried to stop him from going; and the subject insisted on going. Such a situation may repeat several times.)

This show that predicates denoting both positive and negative volition are compatible with the force dynamics schema of *sǐhuó*. The difference lies in which role of the force interaction (*Agonist/Antagonist*) is foregrounded as the subject.

It should be noted that the volitional modal verb *yào* ('want') alone is not sufficient to license *sǐhuó*. In the first example below, the pre-assumption that 'he should go' has been established in the context, and the intention of the agent ('he') is in accordance with the suggestion by other participants, which fails to fulfill the requirement of 'confrontation', leading to the unacceptability of the sentence. In the second example, however, the pre-assumption is that other participants in the context think that 'he should not go', while the intention of the agent ('he') went against the others' suggestions. In this context, the semantic requirement of confrontation between the subject and others' assumption is matched and the sentence is grammatical.

(7) a. #我們勸他去, 他死活要去。

> #wǒmen quàn tā qù, tā sǐhuó yào qù.
>
> 1PL advise 3Sg go 3SG no matter what want go
>
> (Lit: 'We advised him to go. He wanted to go no matter what.')

b. b.我們勸他別去, 他死活要去。

> wǒmen quàn tā bié qù, tā sǐhuó yào qù.
>
> 1PL advise 3Sg don't go 3SG no matter what want go
>
> 'We advised him not to go. He wanted to go no matter what.'

The above examples indicate that only when the agent's volition is against the expectation from others can *sǐhuó* be felicitous, which is captured by the encountering of two forces in the force-dynamic schema.

Verbs of Implicit Negation. In this section, I will explain why certain predicates may or may not license *sǐhuó*. First, I will explain why verb of 'refuse' can license *sǐhuó* while verb of 'accept' cannot; then I will explain why some verbs of implicit negation such as *lǎnde* ('not feel like doing; not bother') cannot license *sǐhuó*. Last but not least, I will explain the apparent 'flip-flop' phenomenon where *fàngqì* ('give up'), a verb with negative meaning, sounds odd with *sǐhuó* while the corresponding positive verb *jiānchí* ('persist') can co-occur with the adverb.

'Refuse/deny' versus 'promise/admit'. Apart from the negative word *bù* ('not; do not want to'), verbs of refusal such as *jùjué* ('refuse') and *fǒurèn* ('deny') can license *sǐhuó*. The positive counterparts such as *dāyìng* ('promise') and *chéngrèn* ('admit') seldom co-occur with *sǐhuó*. For example:

(8) 張三死活{拒絕/??同意/??答應}與李四見面。

> Zhāngsān sǐhuó {jùjué/??tóngyì/??dāyìng} yǔ Lǐsì jiànmiàn.
>
> Zhangsan no matter what refuse agree promise with Lisi meet.

('Zhangsan refused/agreed/promised to meet Lisi no matter what.')

(9) 張三死活{否認/*承認}自己與李四見過面。

Zhāngsān sǐhuó {fǒurèn/*chéngrèn} zìjǐ yǔ Lǐsì jiàn guò miàn.

Zhangsan no matter what deny admit self with Lisi see- Exp. -face.

'Zhangsan denied/admitted that he had met Lisi anyway. '

According to Talmy [10], the force dynamics of predicates such as *refuse* involve a complex structure of phases. He proposes two additional factors for this kind of complex pattern, namely, the 'phase' and the 'factivity'. The factor of 'phase' refers to 'the location along the temporal sequence at which focal attention is placed'. The factor 'factivity' refers to the 'occurrence or non-occurrence of portions of the sequence and the speaker's knowledge about this' [10]. In other words, 'factivity' is about the resultant of the force interaction implicated by the lexical meaning of the word. Based on Talmy [10], I propose a simplified version of the script of the force dynamics of *jùjué* ('refuse') in Mandarin as follows:

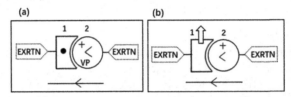

Fig. 3. The force dynamics of *dāyìng* ('promise')

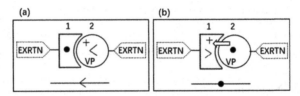

Fig. 4. The force dynamics of *jùjué* ('refuse')

The force dynamics schemas above reflect the fundamental difference between the REFUSE- type and the PROMISE- type predicates. While both of them express the agent's volition regarding a request or an invitation for conducting a certain action (which is reflected by the characteristic that the first phase (a) of the force dynamics of *dāyìng* and *jùjué* are the same), PROMISE **allows** the force of others' expectation to go through while REFUSE **blocks** the motion of such expectation. The verb-pair *fǒurèn* ('deny') and *chéngrèn* ('admit') shares a parallel asymmetrical relationship as 'refuse-accept/promise'. The difference lies in that it is an accusation of doing something rather than a request that is put towards the subject in the case of 'admit-deny'.

Jùjué ('refuse') versus lǎnde ('not feel like'). The second puzzle mentioned in the introduction is why some verbs of implicit negation like *lǎnde* ('not feel like; not bother') cannot license *sǐhuó*. In Fig. 4., I proposed an optional 'exertion' feature for the force dynamics of *jùjué*. This is motivated by the fact that refusal may or may not involve a great effort or determination from the subject. Unlike *jùjué*, there is no strong confrontation between the subject's volition and the others' expectation in the case of *lǎnde* ('do not feel like; not bother'). *Lǎnde* implies that the reason for someone's not feeling like doing something is merely due to some subjective reasons of the agent herself rather than some objective, external reasons (such as the lack of certain conditions). Conceptually speaking, we may say that the subject of *lǎndé* has an absolute advantage over the opponent in the force interaction, and as a result, there is no 'exertion' feature involved for the force dynamics of *lǎndé*. It sounds odd to modify *lǎndé* by an expression which denotes great effort or determination of the subject, while such an expression is compatible with *jùjué*:

(10) 他下了很大決心{拒絕/??懶得}參加比賽。

　　Tā xià le hěn dà juéxīn {jùjué /??lǎndé} cānjiā bǐsài.

　　3SG make Perf very big determination refuse not feel like participate match

　　'He made a firm decision to refuse to participate/?not to feel like participating in the match.'

This illustrates that the 'exertion' feature is incompatible with the force dynamics of *lǎndé* but should be compatible (optional) for *jùjué*. Since the context that license *sǐhuó* requires the feature of 'strong confrontation' between two forces, *lǎnde* is not compatible with *sǐhuó* as it does not match this semantic requirement.

Fàngqì ('give up') versus jiānchí ('persist'). Now let us turn to another pair of verbs: why the verb of implicit negation *fàngqì* ('give up') cannot license *sǐhuó* whereas the affirmative counterpart *jiānchí* ('persist') can? The first example below is repeated from Sect. 1 and the rest two examples are extracted from online articles:

(11) 他死活{??放弃/坚持}參加比賽。

　　Tā sǐhuó {??fàngqì / jiānchí} cānjiā bǐsài

　　3SG dead-live give up persist participate match

　　('He gave up/persisted participating in the match no matter what.').

(12) 談正確的戀愛，找對正確的人，遠比你死活堅持下去重要的多。(Souhu,2022–05-06[2])

　　Tán zhèngquè de liànài, zhǎo duì zhèngquè de rén, yuǎn bǐ nǐ.

　　talk right DE love find right right DE person far compare 2SG

　　sǐhuó jiānchí xiàqù zhòngyào de duō

　　desperately persist down important DE much.

　　'Starting the right relationship and finding the right person is much more important than persisting desperately (in the relationship).'

---

[2] The original text: https://www.sohu.com/a/544185766_120631996.

(13) 吳老師死活堅持該佚詩爲曹雪芹真作……(*Jinri Toutiao*,2022–03-20[3])
    Wú lǎoshī **sǐhuó jiānchí** gāi yìshī wéi Cáoxuěqín.
    Wu teacher desperately insist that anonymous poem is Cao Xueqin.
    zhēnzuò…
    real work

'Mr. Wu insisted desperately that the anonymous poem is a real work by Cao Xueqin.'

Similar to *jùjué* ('refuse'), the force dynamics of *fàngqì* ('give up') in Fig. 5. Contains both a presupposition stage (where the subject attempted to or was assumed to do something) and an entailment stage (where the subject stopped doing the thing in question). Unlike *jùjué* ('refuse'), however, the force dynamics of *fàngqì* ('give up') can be understood as that the subject intentionally withdraws the force of moving forward when he encounters the barrier and as a result; the resultant state is towards rest, which means the action/event intended by the subject does not happen at the end. In this case, there is no strong confrontation between the two forces involved because the subject has already withdrawn his force actively.

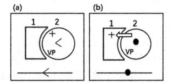

Fig. 5. The force dynamics of *fàngqì* ('give up')

Although compared to *fàngqì* ('give up'), *jiānchí* ('persist') seems to be a 'positive verb' in terms of the evaluative meaning, it is *jiānchí* instead of *fàngqì* that can license the weak NPI *sǐhuó*. This can be explained by the force dynamics of the verb *jiānchí* (Fig. 6). In the case of 'give up (doing something)', the subject withdraws the force of the intention of doing a certain thing; thus there is no strong confrontation between the subject and another force. In the case of *jiānchí* ('persist in doing something)', however, the subject moves forward against a barrier. In this case, a strong confrontation between the subject's intention and that other force arises (see Fig. 6.). This matches the semantic feature 'strong confrontation' of the force dynamics of *sǐhuó*, which explains the compatibility between the two.[4]

In fact, verbs like *persist/insist* are said to contain an implicitly negative meaning in their conceptual structures. Based on their corpus-based study, Pustejovsky et al. [13] (pp.349–50) argue that predicates like *insist* show sensitivity to 'discourse polarity'.

---

[3] The original text: https://www.toutiao.com/article/7077187025509712425/.

[4] Conceptually speaking, if it is the case that somebody 'gives up doing something' repeatedly and desperately, one may say that this person is actually **persisting** in 'giving-up'. This further supports the matching between the conceptual structure of NPI *sǐhuó* and that of 'persist' rather than that of 'give up'.

They found that *insist* usually co-occurs with discourse markers that denote negative affect, such as *although* and *but*, as well as explicit negatives such as *no* and *not*.

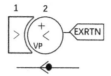

Fig. 6. The force dynamics of *jiānchí* ('persist')

In this section, I have showed that the (in)compatibility between *sǐhuó* and predicates can be explained by the force-dynamic model. The semantic property for a predicate to license the weak NPI adverb *sǐhuó* is not entailing a negative proposition or being downward-entailing in the complement. Instead, *sǐhuó* encodes an abstract conceptual schema which involves a confrontation between two forces. Predicates that encode such a force-confrontation may license *sǐhuó*, no matter whether the complement of the predicate is a downward-entailing environment or not.

2.5 Conceptual Force-Confrontation Indicated by the Context

On some occasions, the force confrontation between two subjects/entities is not indicated by negative words or verbs of implicit negation but by the context. The following example of *sǐhuó* is given in Zhao [14], which is drawn from CCL:

(14) 到了1980年, 我和兩名業務員去長春一家企業, 進了3次門都叫趕出來, 仨人一合計, 他們是用管大戶, 咱死活打進去。(CCL\1994年報刊精選\12)
    Dào le 1980 nián, wǒ hé liǎng míng yèwùyuán qù Chángchūn
    arrive Perf 1980 year 1SG with two CL salesman go Changchun
    yì-jiā qǐyè, jìn le sān-cì mén dōu jiào gǎn chūlái,
    one-CL company enter Perf three-CL door all PASS kick out
    sā rén yì héjì, tāmen shì yòngguǎn dàhù, zán **sǐhuó**
    three people one plan 2PL be use pipe big client 2PL no matter how
    dǎ jìnqù.
    hit enter.

> 'When it came to 1980, I went with two salesmen to a company in Changchun. We were kicked out from the building three times. We three agreed that since they were a big client, we would get into the company (and work with them) no matter what [it took].'

In this example, *sǐhuó* modifies the verb phrase *dǎjìnqù* ('fight one's way in'), which is clearly an affirmative expression with no implicitly negative feature in the lexical meaning. Also, the verb phrase 'fight one's way in' does not belong to the verbs of body action like *lā* ('pull') or *zhuā* ('grasp'). Zhao [14] suggests that the affirmative expression *dǎjìnqù* ('fight one's way in') can be analyzed as the opposite of the situation *jiào gǎnchūlái* ('to be kicked out'), and thus can be regarded as a kind of negation. I agree with the author's intuition about a sense of opposition implied in the context, but it was not made clear in [14] that how this can be treated as a kind of negation and how it is related to the felicity of *sǐhuó*. According to the force-dynamic analysis, the context of the above example involves a confrontation between two volitional forces. The previous sentence denotes that the speaker and his companions entered the company and got kicked out three times, but they still wanted to get into the company. This can be precepted as a back-and-forth process of the confrontation between the two forces in the context. Such a semantic structure provided by the context matches the force-dynamic schema of *sǐhuó* thus license the occurrence of the adverb.

3 Historical Development of *sǐhuó*

Apart from providing a unifying explanation for the synchronic distribution of *sǐhuó*, another merit of the force-dynamic analysis is that it also explains the diachronic change of the use of *sǐhuó* based on the conceptual similarity between the physical force interaction and the psychological or social ones. Historically, when *sǐhuó* developed the use of an adverb, it often modified verbs of body actions such as *chán* ('tangle') and *tuō* ('drag') at the early stage of grammaticalization. This suggests that the physical status of confrontation of two forces may be the prototypical meaning of *sǐhuó* and is the starting point of the development of other uses of the adverb. Let us look at some examples; the first two examples are cited from reference [4]:

(15) 如此沒用的老東西, 也來厭世, 死活纏人做甚麼? (《初刻拍案驚奇·卷二六》)

    Rúcǐ méiyòng de lǎodōngxi, yě lái yànshì, **sǐhuó chán**

    Such useless DE old thing also come make fool desperately tangle

    rén zuòshénme?

    people why

    'Such a useless old man—he came to make a fool of himself. Why did he tangle with me desperately?'

(16) 西門慶告他說: "韓夥計費心, 買禮來謝我, 我再三不受他, 他只顧死活央告, 只留了他鵝酒。(CCL\金瓶梅·崇禎本)

(17) 襲人又死活拉了香菱來。(CCL\紅樓夢 (中))

    Xírén yòu **sǐhuó lā** le Xiānglíng lái.

    Xiren then no matter how pull Perf Xiangling come

    'Xiren then dragged Xiangling [and begged her to come] desperately.'

    Xīménqìng yānggào tā shuō: "Hán huǒjì fèixīn, mǎi lǐ lái

    Ximen Qing beg 3SG say Han fellow concern buy present come

    xiè wǒ, wǒ zàisān bú shòu tā, tā zhǐ **sǐhuó yānggào**,

    thank 1SG 1SG repeatedly not accept 3SG 3SG only desperately beg

zhǐ liú le tā é jiǔ.
only keep Perf 3SG goose wine.

'Ximen Qing told him: "Han was very thoughtful and bought me presents to thank me. I refused his gifts again and again, but he just kept begging me desperately. I just kept the goose and the wine."'

The verbs *chán* ('tangle'), *lā* ('pull'), and *yānggào* ('beg') in the above examples do not denote pure body actions. They are all related to the meaning that the agent asks somebody to do something that this person is reluctant to do. It usually involves a back-and-forth process in which the agent asks or begs, while the person being asked rejects the request repeatedly. Such a dynamic process might serve as the bridging context where the physical confrontation extends to the mental confrontation between two agents.

4 Concluding Remarks

This article might be the first attempt to apply the force-dynamic model to the issue of the licensing conditions for adverbial NPIs in Mandarin. The distribution of the NPI adverbs *sǐhuó* ('no matter what') demonstrates that a strictly defined logical property based on monotonicity (such as 'downward entailment') or a hypothesized, covert negative operator (such as 'Op' or 'NOT') is not sufficient to explain the distribution of all adverbial NPIs in Mandarin. As Hoeksema [15] (pp.29) points out, "For a proper account [for the NPI-licensing condition], we will need a better understanding of each class of items, and we will need to see which set of semantic features they are sensitive to, so as to be able to predict, from these features, the set of contexts that make up their distribution." The 'semantic features' that an NPI is sensitive to may include a particular force-dynamic pattern carried by the lexical meaning of a predicate or by a context. This article shows that the licensing contexts of some adverbial NPIs in Mandarin such as *sǐhuó* can be properly described and explained from the perspective of force dynamics. Further studies can be conducted to testify whether the force-dynamic approach can be applied to the licensing contexts of other polarity-sensitive adverbs in Mandarin, such as the weak NPI-adverb *duànrán* ('flatly; categorically') and its positive counterpart *xīnrán* ('happily').

References

1. Zeng, J., Yuan, Y.: Functional diffusion and decategorization of *bai*: from a colour term to an implicit negative adverb. In: Liu, M., Kit, C., Su, Q. (eds.) Chinese Lexical Semantics. CLSW 2020. LNCS, vol. 12278. Springer, Cham (2021). https://doi.org/10.1007/978-3-030-81197-6_18
2. Zwarts, F.: Three types of polarity. In: Hamm, F., Hinrichs, E.W. (eds.) Plurality and Quantification, vol. 69, pp. 177–238. Springer, Heidelberg (1998)
3. Zheng, Y.G.: A Study of the negative polarity adverbs in modern Chinese, Ph.D. dissertation, Shanghai Normal University (2017). (in Chinese)
4. Wang, T.Y.: '*Sihuo*+VP' form and related questions. Journal of University of South China (Social Science Edition) 8(5), 81–84 (2007). (in Chinese)

5. Wang, W.Y.: A study on the '*Sihuo*+VP' construction in Mandarin. Modern Chinese **8**, 58–60 (2016). (in Chinese)
6. Wang, W.Y.: The study of construction '*sihuo* + VP' and the subjectivization of antonymous compound adverbs. Overseas Chin. Educ. **5**, 664–669 (2017). (in Chinese)
7. Xu, Y.F.: Verbs of Implicit Negation in Mandarin Chinese: An NPI-licensing Perspective, PhD. Dissertation, The Hong Kong University of Science and Technology (2022)
8. Ladusaw, W.: Polarity sensitivity as inherent scope relations, Ph.D. dissertation, University of Texas at Austin (1979). Also reproduced by Indiana University Linguistics Club (1980)
9. Giannakidou Anastasia. Negative and positive polarity items. In: Maienborn, C., von Heusinger, K., Portner, P. (eds.) Semantics: An International Handbook of Natural Language Meaning, vol. 2. Walter de Gruyter (2011)
10. Talmy, L.: Force dynamics in language and cognition. Cogn. Sci. **12**, 49–100 (1988)
11. Croft, W.: Verbs: Aspect and Causal Structure. OUP Oxford (2012)
12. Givón, T.: Negation in language: pragmatics, function, ontology. Pragmatics, Brill, pp. 69–112 (1978). Also in Givón, Talmy., On understanding grammar. Academic Press, pp. 91–142 (1979)
13. Pustejovsky, J., Bergler, S., Anick, P.: Lexical semantic techniques for corpus analysis. Comput. Linguist. **19**(2), 331–358 (1993)
14. Zhao, M.K.: A Study on modal adverb like *fanzheng* in Mandarin Chinese, M.A. thesis, Central China Normal University (2014). (in Chinese)
15. Hoeksema, J.: On the natural history of negative polarity items. Linguistic Analysis **38**(1), 3–33 (2008)

The Influence of Neologisms from Mainland China on Changes in the Lexical Semantics of Hong Kong Cantonese

Yike Yang[1(✉)] [iD] and Ho Kuen Ho[2]

[1] Hong Kong Shue Yan University, Braemar Hill, Hong Kong
yyang@hksyu.edu
[2] The Hong Kong Polytechnic University, Hung Hom, Hong Kong

Abstract. Numerous mainland Chinese neologisms have been introduced to Hong Kong due to the increased communication between Hong Kong and mainland China. The purpose of this paper is to examine the influence of neologisms from mainland China on Hong Kong Cantonese by observing the use of these neologisms in local newspapers in Hong Kong. It has been shown that the local newspapers began to use the mainland neologisms at an early stage, which has resulted in semantic changes in Cantonese lexical items. There are three ways in which lexical semantic change can occur: 1) redefining the Cantonese-Mandarin homographs to make the senses conveyed by the mainland neologisms the only interpretation; 2) replacing the Cantonese synonyms with mainland neologisms; and 3) providing new senses for the mainland neologisms to transform them into local neologisms.

Keywords: Mainland Neologisms · Hong Kong Cantonese · Lexical Semantic Change · Language Contact · Linguistic Communication

1 Introduction

Neologisms are a microcosm of society, and reflect the changes in the world [1]. In mainland China (henceforth 'mainland'), different agencies select neologisms every year. The mainland neologisms are not only used locally on the mainland, but may also spread to Hong Kong, Taiwan and even to overseas Chinese-speaking regions, thus affecting the language use of the local communities [2]. Although variations regarding the language use in the mainland and in Hong Kong have been reported (e.g. [3]), the increasingly frequent communication between the mainland and Hong Kong, coupled with various factors such as migration and online communication, results in constant contact of Mandarin and Cantonese, with each language having adopted lexical items from the other; this phenomenon has been called 'the northern language going south' and 'the southern language going north' [4]. The mainland neologisms are an obvious illustration of 'the northern language going south'. At present, mainland neologisms have taken root in Hong Kong and have entered all levels of society; as a result, local people may be using

M. Dong et al. (Eds.): CLSW 2023, LNAI 14514, pp. 187–195, 2024.
https://doi.org/10.1007/978-981-97-0583-2_15

these neologisms without knowing their origins. It is common for Hong Kong people to use mainland neologisms in their writing, and mainland neologisms are often found in online news reports and even in traditional newspapers. Frequent communication causes changes in languages [5]; thus, the aim of this study is to investigate the use of mainland neologisms in Hong Kong and to study their influence on the Cantonese that is spoken in Hong Kong.

1.1 Neologisms

Neologisms are terms that have contemporary and socio-cultural significance, and may be used by people of all ages. If neologisms are widely used, their scope is not limited to the internet, but encompasses the entire society. In the past decade, the popularisation of the internet and the public's recognition and acceptance of neologisms have broadened the coverage of neologisms, and neologisms are involved in every aspect of people's daily lives. At present, most of the academic discussions pertain to recognising the role and status of neologisms, and there is an optimistic attitude towards them. The scholarly discussions have also extended from the relationship between neologisms and Chinese grammar to other aspects, such as the significance of neologisms in sociolinguistic research [6].

It is worth noting that scholars, regardless of their stances on neologisms, share a similar viewpoint: Neologisms are inextricably linked to the social situation, and can express people's orientations towards and conceptions of current affairs. The composition of neologisms can take the form of the creation of new words or the evolution of old ones. In brief, the creation and existence of neologisms are based on people's concerns about social phenomena, while their wide dissemination depends on popularisation via the internet and the expansion of their scope of use.

1.2 Neologisms in Hong Kong

Few researchers have studied mainland and local neologisms in Hong Kong. In addition, few of the discussions are from a linguistic perspective; for example, some take the form of introducing Hong Kong's neologisms to the general public in a humorous manner. Some mainland neologisms, such as 坑爹 *kengdie* 'fraudulent' and 给力 *geili* 'powerful', are included in various collections, but with only a brief introduction to their origins and meanings. With regard to academic studies, most of them start from the perspective of morphology (for example, [7] has contributed significantly to verifying the word formation of mainland and local neologisms), but there is a lack of studies of mainland neologisms from the perspective of semantics. [8] discussed the online language ecology in Hong Kong, but he only focused on analysing the manifestations of online language and mainland neologisms in terms of the content of the neologisms without discussing how the neologisms have affected Cantonese. Therefore, this study attempts to fill this research gap by exploring the impact of mainland neologisms on Cantonese from a semantic perspective and to draw the attention of Hong Kong society to the mainland neologisms that have already entered Cantonese.

2 Data Collection

2.1 Data Collection

Neologisms from two representative selection activities called the *Top Ten Internet Words of the Year* (年度十大网络用语)[1] and the *Top Ten Neologisms of the Year* (年度十大流行语)[2] were selected for this study. The former operates under the direction of the National Language Resources Monitoring and Research Centre, an official organisation under the Ministry of Education of the People's Republic of China, while the latter is produced by the mainland's authoritative journal *Biting and Chewing Characters* (咬文嚼字); both sources are indicative and representative. The results of the most recent selections (from 2012 to 2021, totalling 200 neologisms) were collected first, and the duplicated neologisms were then deleted to produce a total of 166 neologisms (see Appendix I). In addition, to confirm the spread of mainland neologisms in Hong Kong, the researcher referred to the local Hong Kong website *Dictionary of Neologisms* (潮语字典)[3] to examine the results on the local website compared to those from the mainland selection activities.

Based on the verification and inspection, the *Dictionary of Neologisms* was found to contain 479 neologisms from 2010 to 2021, nineteen of which were mainland neologisms (see Appendix II). Of these nineteen neologisms, ten appear in Appendix I, and nine were additionally collected by the website (most of them are Chinese Pinyin acronyms for some vulgar terms). By combining the selection results from the mainland and the information from local websites, 175 mainland neologisms were finally identified as the data for this study.

2.2 Research Methods

In order to corroborate the popularity of the mainland neologisms in Hong Kong provided in Appendices I and II, these neologisms were searched via WiseNews (WiseNews electronic clippings)[4] to confirm whether they had spread to Hong Kong. The criterion adopted for this study was that the Hong Kong newspapers should incorporate the use of mainland neologisms in their texts rather than simply quoting them directly in their reports. The main reason for using the WiseNews database was that it is difficult to determine the time at which the neologisms were introduced to Hong Kong based on the thousands of or even millions of results on the internet. Thus, using the time at which the neologisms were adopted by Hong Kong newspapers is a relatively accurate method. Second, as newspapers are constantly updated on a daily basis, consulting them is often the fastest way to reflect the changes in the language habits of a society. Therefore, the news media is the best tool to study the usage of mainland neologisms in Hong Kong. Previous academics have also used WiseNews as a means of examining the usage of

---

[1] Data were accessed from: https://baike.baidu.hk/item/漢語盤點/12708641 on 20 December 2021.

[2] Data were accessed from: https://baike.baidu.hk/item/咬文嚼字/3416768 on 20 December 2021.

[3] Data were accessed from: https://hkdic.my-helper.com/ on 20 December 2021.

[4] Data were accessed from: http://libwisesearch.wisers.net/ 18 on 20 December 2021.

neologisms or mainland terms in Hong Kong newspapers and magazines (e.g. [9]). In this paper, the mainland neologisms will be considered to have entered the Hong Kong society if they have been used in local newspapers and magazines at least 100 times.

3   Findings

In total, 175 mainland neologisms have entered local newspapers, and the neologisms have various forms: simple words (such as 怼 *dui* 'blame' and 尬 *ga* 'embarrassing'), complex words (such as 佛系 *foxi* 'Buddha-like' and 洪荒之力 *honghuangzhili* 'primordial powers'), abbreviations (such as 脱单 *tuodan* 'stop flying solo' and 官宣 *guanxuan* 'officially announce') and phrases (such as 你有freestyle吗 *niyou* freestyle *ma* 'Do you have a freestyle?' and 厉害了我的X *lihaile wode* X 'awesome X'). While the majority of the neologisms have been used in local newspapers, a few (most of which are phrases) have not been accepted by Hong Kong people, including XX千万条, YY第一条 *XX qianwantiao YY diyi tiao* 'while there are millions of XX, YY comes first' and 你们城里人真会玩儿 *nimen chengliren zhen huiwaner* 'You people in the city really know how to play'. Moreover, the occurrences of certain neologisms (such as 高富帅 *gaofushuai* 'tall, rich and handsome', 女汉子 *nvhanzi* 'femme fatale' and 网红 *wanghong* 'internet celebrity') are much more frequent than others. For example, in 2015 alone (i.e. the year when the term was first introduced), the term 网红 *wanghong* 'internet celebrity' was used 1,311 times in Hong Kong newspapers; six years later (2021), 网红 *wanghong* 'internet celebrity' was used 3,007 times in Hong Kong newspapers in one year. This example suggests that the Hong Kong news media is willing to accept mainland neologisms, and that these accepted mainland neologisms have entered the local society. Furthermore, Appendix II also shows that the number of mainland neologisms included on the local website *Dictionary of Neologisms* has been increasing year on year and reached its peak in 2016, which is a trend that matches the anecdotal research [10] showing that the dissemination power of mainland neologisms has been increasing.

The above results show that the influence of mainland neologisms in Hong Kong is increasing in terms of usage and popularity; the impact of mainland neologisms on Cantonese will be discussed in the following section.

4   Influence of Mainland Neologisms on Hong Kong Cantonese

The most direct influence of mainland neologisms on Hong Kong Cantonese is undoubtedly the expansion of ways of enlarging the Cantonese lexicon and introducing new cultural traits into the Cantonese lexicon. At the same time, the arrival of mainland neologisms has resulted in changes to the lexical semantics of Hong Kong Cantonese, which will be discussed in this section.

4.1   Replacement of Cantonese Homonyms

First, there are several homonyms in Cantonese and Mandarin [11] due to the different cultures in Hong Kong and the mainland. If mainland neologisms enter Cantonese, they may replace the semantics of their corresponding Cantonese homonyms, and, eventually, the homonyms in both Mandarin and Cantonese will only contain the semantics of mainland neologisms. Take the word 光棍 *guanggun* 'bachelor', which is a synonym in Cantonese and Mandarin, as an example. In Cantonese, the word originally referred to a male swindler or a rogue, such as the Cantonese saying 光棍佬教仔—便宜莫贪 *guanggunlao jiaozai pianyi motan* 'A bachelor's lesson – Don't take advantage of a bargain'. The suffix 棍 *gun* 'stick' in Cantonese can also be used to form words such as 恶棍 *egun* 'scoundrel' and 神棍 *shengun* 'religious con men'; thus, words that have 棍 *gun* 'stick' as a suffix usually have a derogatory meaning, and are used to refer to a male liar or a scoundrel. In Mandarin, the word 光棍 *guanggun* 'bachelor' originally had two semantic meanings: 'rogue' and 'bachelor'. Since the emergence of the term 光棍节 *guanggunjie* 'Singles' Day' on the mainland, 光棍 *guanggun* 'bachelor' has become a neologism, which has eventually led to a change in the meaning of the word in Cantonese. The origin of 光棍节 *guanggunjie* 'Singles' Day' cannot be traced, but it is certain that it originated from the mainland internet culture, where the netizens used the numeral '1' to tease people who were single; therefore, they designated the 11th of November as 光棍节 *guanggunjie* 'Singles' Day' [12]. The public came to accept the semantic meaning of 光棍 *guanggun* 'bachelor' for single people due to large-scale sales events, and the semantic meaning of 'hooligan' has gradually been forgotten.

The change in the meaning of 光棍 *guanggun* 'bachelor' in Cantonese has mainly occurred due to the frequent exchanges between Hong Kong and the mainland. Hong Kong people are enthusiastic about online shopping on the mainland, and they subconsciously encounter the term 光棍 *guanggun* 'bachelor' when shopping. The increase in awareness and social circulation has led to the semantics of this mainland neologism gradually replacing the original semantics in Cantonese, and single people have become the only cognitive referents of the term 光棍 *guanggun* 'bachelor'. At present, Hong Kong society recognises 光棍 *guanggun* 'bachelor' as a general term for single people of both genders and no longer as an exclusive term for males. Moreover, 光棍 *guanggun* 'bachelor' is no longer a pejorative term with negative connotations, but has become neutral. Examples of mainland neologisms replacing Cantonese homonyms include 小鲜肉 *xiaoxianrou* (a semantic shift from 'fresh meat' to describe 'a young and handsome boy'), 老司机 *laosiji* (a semantic shift from 'an old driver' to 'an experienced or resourceful person'), 带货 *daihuo* (a semantic change from 'smuggling contraband' to 'selling products on live streaming') and so on [13]. Since the introduction of these mainland neologisms in Hong Kong, they have appeared rapidly at all levels of society, and the semantics of these neologisms have completely replaced those of the Cantonese homonyms.

4.2 Replacement of Cantonese Synonyms

However, some mainland neologisms have not only replaced Cantonese homonyms, but have even gradually replaced Cantonese synonyms. For example, there was originally a word 二奶 *ernai* 'mistress' in Cantonese to describe a mistress, which was later imported to the mainland and Taiwan, where it was absorbed by these regions and even included in the fifth edition of the *Dictionary of Modern Chinese* [14]. However, since the term 小三 *xiaosan* 'mistress' was introduced to Hong Kong from the mainland, the local people have switched to using the term 小三 *xiaosan* 'mistress' instead of 二奶 *ernai* 'mistress' in all contexts. According to our search results on WiseNews, there are interesting findings for the terms 二奶 *ernai* 'mistress' and 小三 *xiaosan* 'mistress' in the Hong Kong news media from 2012 to 2016 and from 2017 to 2021. During the first period, 小三 *xiaosan* 'mistress' appeared 15,559 times, while 二奶 *ernai* 'mistress' only appeared 3,462 times, at which time 小三 *xiaosan* 'mistress' had clearly surpassed 二奶 *ernai* 'mistress'. During the second period, 小三 *xiaosan* 'mistress' appeared 7,818 times, while 二奶 *ernai* 'mistress' only appeared 1,223 times, which is a six-fold difference between the two terms.

This example shows that mainland neologisms may cause the original Cantonese words to disappear, and that the neologisms will eventually replace the original Cantonese words. For this reason, some people are dissatisfied with the 'invasion' of mainland neologisms in Hong Kong and are concerned that mainland neologisms will fully penetrate Hong Kong and threaten the status of Cantonese in the region. In our opinion, while it is undeniable that the occurrences of mainland neologisms have increased in Hong Kong, Cantonese will evolve via exchanges amongst people over time. The frequent interactions between the mainland and Hong Kong, together with the catalytic effect of the mass media and the promotion of the internet, the absorption of mainland neologisms into Hong Kong Cantonese is an inevitable process of cultural diffusion and language exchange, and the change in the lexical semantics in Cantonese (and in any language) is also in line with general trends in language development.

4.3 Deriving New Senses

Furthermore, some mainland neologisms may undergo lexical changes in the course of their dissemination due to geographical influences, thus giving rise to newly derived senses. Specifically, Hong Kong people may impart a new sense to mainland neologisms by including some local features in the neologisms. The derivation of new senses from neologisms is not unique to Hong Kong. For example, after the English word 'skr' was introduced to the mainland network via a mainland show, it developed a new sense that is very different from its original meaning, and is used to express approval and appreciation in the mainland. Hong Kong people do not need to create new words when discussing issues related to the mainland; instead, they can adapt the neologisms that originated on the mainland slightly. The word 大妈 *dama* 'middle-aged women' is currently used to refer to middle-aged and elderly women or to new immigrants from the mainland. As one of the *Top 10 Internet Terms of the Year* in 2013, 大妈 *dama* 'middle-aged women' originally referred to middle-aged or elderly women who dressed in a rustic manner or were unsophisticated. As a neologism from the mainland, it is unlikely to be a term that intentionally targeted mainland women. However, the word 大妈 *dama* 'middle-aged women' in Hong Kong is mainly used to describe the immigration status of mainland residents instead of describing their characteristics, which is not in accordance with the original meaning of the term. According to the search results on WiseNews, the earliest time at which Hong Kong people used the term 大妈 *dama* 'middle-aged women' as a label for the identity of mainland people was in 2015 when the *Oriental Daily News* used the term 大妈 *dama* 'middle-aged women' in the headlines of three news stories, thus demonstrating that the term 大妈 *dama* 'middle-aged women' was already equated with the identity of mainland people in that year. At the same time, some people consider the word 大妈 *dama* 'middle-aged women' to have replaced the original Cantonese word 师奶 *shinai* 'housewife', which is why the word 大妈 *dama* 'middle-aged women' is widely used by the public. However, the term 师奶 *shinai* 'housewife' is still commonly used in the society as a whole and has not disappeared due to the arrival of 大妈 *dama* 'middle-aged women'. A WiseNews search comparing the use of the two terms in the local news media over the last five years revealed that 师奶 *shinai* 'housewife' was used 3,729 times, while 大妈 *dama* 'middle-aged women' was used 4,078 times, thus showing that neither of the two terms has fallen out of favour. Therefore, the argument that the term 大妈 *dama* 'middle-aged women' has replaced the term 师奶 *shinai* 'housewife' is not valid.

In summary, the spread of mainland neologisms to Hong Kong can lead to semantic variations in Cantonese in three ways: The first is redefining the synonyms for popular Cantonese words, the second is replacing the synonyms for Cantonese words, and the third is Hong Kong people giving the neologisms new senses by turning them into local neologisms. In addition, the semantic variation of neologisms is related to the public's perception of current affairs and identity. Therefore, regardless of whether mainland neologisms replace Cantonese words or Hong Kong people change the senses of mainland neologisms on their own, the semantics will have the greatest influence and will be widely used as long as the semantics are generally accepted by the public.

5   Conclusion

Neologisms are closely related to current social events, and the public can express their opinions about social phenomena via neologisms. At the same time, people are able to use neologisms to construct their own and others' identities. We believe that the spread of mainland neologisms to Hong Kong will continue in the future due to the increasing communication between the mainland and Hong Kong, and that the spread requires more research. In this paper, we analysed and discussed the lexical semantic variations in Cantonese resulting from mainland neologisms, including the redefinition of the original Cantonese vocabulary, the replacement of Cantonese synonyms, Hong Kong peoples' transformation of mainland neologisms and the derivation of new senses. Language is a combination of form, content and function [15], which complement each other. If one of them changes, the other two may be affected. It is worth conducting further studies to address the formal variations and pragmatic shifts in Cantonese that will be caused by mainland neologisms.

Appendix I: The 166 Mainland Neologisms from 2012 to 2021

Year	Neologisms
2012	中国好声音、元芳你怎么看、高富帅, 白富美、你幸福吗、江南Style、躺着也中枪、丝、逆袭、舌尖上的中国、最炫民族风、给跪了、正能量、中国式、压力山大、赞、最美、接地气

(continued)

(continued)

Year	Neologisms
2013	中国大妈、高端大气上档次、爸爸去哪儿、小伙伴们都惊呆了、待我长发及腰、喜大普奔、女汉子、土豪、摊上大事了、涨姿势、中国梦、光盘、点赞、奇葩、微XX、大V、倒逼、逆袭
2014	我也是醉了、有钱就是任性、蛮拼的、挖掘机技术哪家强、保证不打死你、萌萌哒、时间都去哪了、我读书少你别骗我、画面太美我不敢看、且行且珍惜、顶层设计、新常态、打虎拍蝇、断崖式、你懂的、断舍离、失联、神器、高大上
2015	重要的事情说三遍、世界那么大, 我想去看看、你们城里人真会玩儿、为国护盘、明明可以靠脸吃饭, 却偏偏要靠才华、我想静静、内心几乎是崩溃的、我妈是我妈、主要看气质、获得感、互联网＋、颜值、宝宝、创客、脑洞大开、任性、剁手党、网红
2016	洪荒之力、友谊的小船、吃瓜群众、葛优躺、辣眼睛、蓝瘦香菇、老司机、厉害了我的X、工匠精神、小目标、一言不合就XX、供给侧、套路
2017	打call、你的良心不会痛吗、惊不惊喜, 意不意外、皮皮虾, 我们走、扎心了, 老铁、还有这种操作、你有freestyle吗、不忘初心、砥砺奋进、共享、有温度、流量、可能XXX假XXX、油腻、尬、怼
2018	锦鲤、杠精、skr、佛系、确认过眼神、官宣、C位、土味情话、皮一下、燃烧我的卡路里、命运共同体、店小二、教科书式、退群、巨婴
2019	不忘初心、好嗨哟、是个狼人、雨女无瓜、14亿护旗手、断舍离、文明互鉴、区块链、硬核、融梗、XX千万条、XX第一条、柠檬精、996、我太难/南了、我不要你觉得, 我要我觉得、霸凌主义
2020	秋天的第一杯奶茶、带货、云监工、光盘行动、奥利给、好家伙、夺冠、不约而同、集美、人民至上, 生命至上、逆行者、飒、后浪、神兽、双循环、打工人、内卷、凡尔赛文学
2021	觉醒年代、YYDS、双减、破防、元宇宙、绝绝子、躺平、伤害性不高, 侮辱性极强、我看不懂, 但我大受震撼、强国有我、百年未有之大变局、小康、赶考、碳达峰, 碳中和、野性消费、鸡娃

Appendix II: The 19 Mainland Neologisms in Dictionary

Year	Neologisms
2010	装B
2011	(从缺)
2012	(从缺)
2013	(从缺)
2014	TMD、没女
2015	大妈、sb、小鲜肉、CNMD
2016	宝宝心里苦, 但宝宝不说、洪荒之力、老司机

(continued)

(continued)

Year	Neologisms
2017	网红
2018	光棍节、佛系
2019	666
2020	爷青回、NMSL
2021	YYDS、躺平、脱单

References

1. Liao, H.: The Inquiry of Mandarin Popular Language and the Application of Teaching. (Thesis). National Taiwan Normal University, Taiwan. (2019). (in Chinese). https://hdl.handle.net/11296/tu8k2m
2. Yuan, W., Yang, K.: Considering the evolutionary patterns and characteristics of neologisms in Taiwan in the past 10 years and its communication with neologisms in mainland. Modern Commun. (J. Commun. Univ. China) **6**, 55–62 (2019). (in Chinese)
3. Yang, Y.: Disagreement strategies on Chinese forums: comparing data from Hong Kong and Mainland China. SAGE Open **11**(3), 1–12 (2021). https://doi.org/10.1177/21582440211036879
4. Zhan, B.: The exchanged propagation between Putonghua and Cantonese dialect. Academic Research **4**, 67–72 (1993). (in Chinese)
5. Wang, S., Tang, L.: Comparison of changes between Mainland China and Taiwan. In: Liu, M., Kit, C., Su, Q. (eds.) Chinese Lexical Semantics. CLSW 2020. LNCS, vol. 12278, pp. 686–710. Springer, Cham (2021). https://doi.org/10.1007/978-3-030-81197-6_58
6. Su, J.: The sociolinguistic significance of internet language research. Chin. Char. Cult. **5**, 18–21 (2016). (in Chinese)
7. Tang, S.W.: Word formation of Hong Kong trendy expressions. Stud. Chin. Linguist. **28**(2), 11–21 (2009). (in Chinese)
8. Lai, S.M.: The preliminary study of Hong Kong internet language. Curr. Res. Chin. Linguist. **94**(1), 3–26 (2015). (in Chinese)
9. Yan, Y.: Language migration to the South in the early 21st century: the use of Putonghua words in Hong Kong texts. (thesis). University of Hong Kong, Hong Kong. (2011). Retrieved from: https://doi.org/10.5353/th_b4784992
10. Yuan, W., Gao, Y.: The pragmatic contrast and interactive propagation research between Hong Kong and Mainland from 2010 to 2019. Modern Publishing **2**, 59–64 (2021). (in Chinese)
11. Zhang, B., Yang, R.: Homograph: Contrasting Cantonese and Putonghua Vocabulary. Joint Publishing (Hong Kong) Company Limited, Hong Kong (2008). (in Chinese)
12. Yip, K.L.: A view of China from Popular Slang. Cosmos Books Ltd, Hong Kong (2011). (in Chinese)
13. Tsang, C.: A Study of Idiomatic Expressions in Hong Kong Cantonese. City University of Hong Kong Press, Hong Kong (2008). (in Chinese)
14. Li, K.S.: A glossary of new political terms of the People's Republic of China in the post-reform era. The Chinese University of Hong Kong Press, Hong Kong (2006). (in Chinese)
15. Bloom, L., Lahey, M.: Language Development and Language Disorders. Wiley, New York (1978)

Research on the Semantic Collocations of Mental Verbs and the Generative Mechanisms of Polysemy: The Generative Lexicon

Weili Wang[1,2]([⊠]), Jianshe Zhou[1,2], and Kai Zhang[1,2]

[1] Chinese Department, Capital Normal University, Beijing, China
wangweili100@cnu.edu.cn
[2] Research Center for Language Intelligence of China, Beijing, China

Abstract. In accordance with Pustejovsky's proposed Semantic Generation Mechanisms, this research aims to investigate the principles governing semantic collocations related to mental verbs and the generative mechanisms of polysemy. The research compiles lexical representations of select mental verbs and conducts a comprehensive analysis of the polysemy and categorizations associated with these verbs, with the intent of establishing guidelines for semantic generation from the collocations of mental verbs. When the argument structures of patient nouns partially align with those of these mental verbs, they can be effectively matched. In situations where different telic roles and agentive roles of the patient nouns are equally significant, polysemy may manifest within the collocations of these mental verbs.

Keywords: Generative Lexicon Theory · Semantic Collocation · Polysemy and Classification of Semantic Generation · Mental Verbs

1 Introduction

Mental verbs exhibit distinctive semantic characteristics, encompassing subjectivity, experiential nature, autonomy, and inherent ambiguity. These attributes also mirror key facets of semantic analysis within human language communication and natural language processing. Consequently, our research delves into the realm of mental verbs and their semantic counterparts, particularly those associated with the concept of 'love'. In the context of the collocational patterns of mental verbs, it becomes evident that different meanings are intricately intertwined with the context. Beyond contextual considerations, we also aspire to derive governing principles for semantic generation from the inherent collocational patterns of mental verbs themselves.

The Generative Lexicon Theory, as postulated by American scholar Pustejovsky, offers a framework for delineating word meanings with respect to argument structure, event structure, qualia structure, and lexical typing structure. This theory presents a perspective that delves into the examination of the semantic processing system, thereby shedding light on the potential and prospects of semantic features. Such an approach may

© The Author(s), under exclusive license to Springer Nature Singapore Pte Ltd. 2024
M. Dong et al. (Eds.): CLSW 2023, LNAI 14514, pp. 196–210, 2024.
https://doi.org/10.1007/978-981-97-0583-2_16

facilitate a more profound and systematic comprehension of the collocational patterns of mental verbs in conjunction with patient nouns.

Let's examine the collocations involving three categories of mental verbs with patient nouns:

① 喜欢面包	② 喜欢鱼	③ 喜欢猫
Xǐhuān miànbāo	Xǐhuān yú	Xǐhuān māo
'like bread'	'like fish'	'like cat'

In the case of ①喜欢面包Xǐhuān miànbāo 'like bread', the interpretation naturally leans towards 'an individual's fondness for consuming bread'. When examining ②喜欢鱼Xǐhuān yú 'like fish', we encounter the potential for dual interpretations, encompassing either 'an individual's preference for consuming fish' or 'an individual's fondness for fish as a species'. As for ③喜欢猫Xǐhuān māo 'like cat', the typical interpretation revolves around 'an individual's affection for cats as animal'.

Guided by the principles of the Generative Lexicon Theory, we endeavor to investigate the semantic patterns and generative factors underlying various collocational patterns associated with distinct categories of mental verbs, with a particular emphasis on the collocational structures involving mental verbs and patient nouns.

2   An Overview of Generative Lexicon Theory

The characteristics of Generative Lexicon Theory (GLT) lend themselves well to explaining the logical polysemy observed in nouns. Furthermore, they can be applied to elucidate the logical polysemy in verbs and the shifts in meaning that occur in the collocation of nouns with verbs. The formalization of GLT is marked by the publication of 'The Generative Lexicon' in 1995. [1] This theory delves into the signification of words and the mechanisms by which they reference the world. GLT seeks to enrich word meanings with encyclopedic knowledge and logical relationships, aiming to offer detailed descriptions of semantic word structures. It explores the operational mechanisms of semantics. To account for the contextual variations in word meanings, GLT categorizes word meanings into four distinct levels: argument structure, event structure, qualia structure, and lexical typing structure. [1, 2] Pustejovsky delineated three generative mechanisms in semantics: type coercion, selective binding, and semantic co-composition. Through an analysis of qualia structure, Pustejovsky devised a semantic type system encompassing natural types, artifactual types, and complex types. [1–5] Pustejovsky provided an update on the progress of Generative Lexicon Theory, including the compositional mechanisms of semantic types, the interplay between complex types and formal roles, and the collocations of adjectives with nouns from a Generative Lexicon Theory perspective, and more [3].

Drawing from the framework of Generative Lexicon Theory, this research aims to elucidate patterns within the varied collocations of mental verbs denoting affection, with the objective of establishing scientifically interpretable models for these collocations.

3   Researches on Mental Verbs Denoting Affection

This research will comprehensively define these mental verbs denoting affection by considering their meanings, grammatical usage, and pragmatic functions (Table 1).

Table 1. The criteria for defining

Word meaning	[+Mental State]; [+Subjective Attitude]; [+love]
Grammar Usage and Pragmatic Function	(S[person]) + (very) + V[P] + (O[N、V、S])

Table 2. Some symbols are explained as follows.

Some symbols	Explainations
S[person]	The subject is typically a personal pronoun or a noun that represents a person
V[P]	mental verbs
O[N、V、S]	object, substantive, predicate, or sentence

The mental verbs found within these corpora can be considered indicative of a specific mental state, allowing for the expression of subjective attitudes such as 'love'. In addition, personal pronouns or nouns representing individuals can function as the subject, while substantives, predicates, or entire sentences can serve as the object. On certain occasions, degree adverbs may also be incorporated (Table 2).

According to the criteria outlined above, the following mental verbs denoting affection have been extracted from《现代汉语词典》XiànDàiHànYǔCíDiǎn 'Modern Chinese Dictionary'[6]: 爱ài 'love', 爱好àihào 'hobby', 宠chǒng 'pamper', 宠爱chǒngài 'dote', 敬爱jìngài 'esteem', 酷爱kùài 'love passionately', 怜爱liánài 'love tenderly', 溺爱nìài 'spoil', 热爱rèài 'love ardently', 喜爱xǐài 'favor', 喜欢xǐhuān 'like', 心疼xīnténg 'love dearly', 钟爱zhōngài 'treasure'. Subsequent sections of this research will delve into the collocational patterns of these mental verbs denoting affection.

4   Researches on the Collocations of Mental Verbs Denoting Affection in Dictionaries

In our corpus, the objects following the mental verbs denoting affection can take various forms, including substantives, predicates, phrases, and even entire sentences. The most common collocations involving mental verbs denoting affection typically revolve around patient nouns, which constitute the predominant portion of the corpus. Consequently, we will utilize collocations of mental verbs denoting love and patient nouns as an illustrative example for our further research.

In order to ascertain the available collocations of mental verbs denoting affection, we consulted three dictionaries:《现代汉语词典》XiànDàiHànYǔCíDiǎn 'Modern Chinese

Dictionary'[6],《商务馆学汉语词典》ShāngWùGuǎnXuéHànYǔCíDiǎn 'Dictionary of Learning Chinese published by The Commercial Press'[7], and《当代汉语学习词典》DāngDàiHànYǔXuéXíCíDiǎn 'Contemporary Chinese Learner's Dictionary'[8]. We conducted a count of the patient nouns and nominal phrases associated with mental verbs denoting affection. The results of our analysis are as follows: (Table 3).

Table 3. The most characteristic collocations of mental verbs denoting affection

Mental Verbs	Modern Chinese Dictionary	Dictionary of Learning Chinese published by The Commercial Press	Contemporary Chinese Learner's Dictionary
爱ài 'love'	祖国zǔguó' motherland' 人民 rénmín 'people' 劳动láodòng 'labor' 姑娘gūniang 'girl' 公物gōngwù 'public property' 集体荣誉jítǐ róngyù 'collective honor'	妻子qīzi 'wife' (自己的家乡) (zìjǐ de jiāxiāng) '(own hometown)' (那个小伙子) (nàgè xiǎohuǒzi) '(that young man)'	妻子qīzǐ 'wife' 姑娘gūniang 'girl' 故乡gùxiāng 'hometown' 母亲mǔqīn 'mother' (她的孩子) (tā de háizi) '(her child)'
爱好àihào 'be keen on'	体育tǐyù 'Sports', 日用品rìyòngpǐn 'daily necessities'	运动yùndòng 'sports' 京剧 jīngjù 'Peking Opera'	运动yùndòng 'sports', 音乐yīnyuè 'music', 旅游lǚyóu 'travel'
宠chǒng 'pamper'	孩子háizi 'child'	孩子háizi 'children' 小孙子xiǎo sūnzi 'grandchildren'	-
宠爱chǒngài 'dote'	女儿nǚ'ér 'daughter'	孩子háizi 'children' 小动物xiǎo dòngwù 'small animals'	-
敬爱jìng'ài 'esteem'	父母fùmǔ 'parents'	老师lǎoshī 'teacher' 老人lǎorén 'old man' 祖父zǔfù 'grandfather' 市长hǎoshìzhǎng好 'good mayor'	总统zǒngtǒng 'president' 领袖lǐngxiù 'leader'
酷爱kù'ài 'love passionately'	书法shūfǎ 'calligraphy' 音乐yīnyuè 'music' 这孩子zhè háizi 'this kid'	音乐yīnyuè 'music' 书法shūfǎ 'calligraphy' 旅游lǚyóu 'travel'	-

(continued)

Table 3. (*continued*)

Mental Verbs	Modern Chinese Dictionary	Dictionary of Learning Chinese published by The Commercial Press	Contemporary Chinese Learner's Dictionary
怜爱lián'ài 'love tenderly'	-	小男孩儿xiǎonán hái'ér 'little boy' 女儿nǚ'ér 'daughter'	-
溺爱nì'ài 'spoil'	自己的孩子zìjǐ de háizi 'own child'	孩子háizi 'child'	-
热爱rèài 'love ardently'	工作gōngzuò 'work' 祖国zǔguó 'motherland'	祖国zǔguó 'motherland' 家乡jiāxiāng 'hometown' 自己的专业zìjǐ de zhuānyè 'own profession' 教师工作jiàoshī gōngzuò 'teacher's work' 学生xuéshēng 'students'	他自己的工作tā zìjǐ de gōngzuò 'his own work' 劳动láodòng 'labor' 和平hépíng 'peace' 土地tǔdì 'land' 专业zhuānyè 'profession' 祖国zǔguó 'motherland'
喜爱xǐài 'favor'	小孩xiǎohái 'kids' 游泳yóuyǒng 'swimming'	-	-
喜欢 xǐhuān 'like'	文学wénxué 'literature' 数学shùxué 'mathematics'	(北京的秋天) (Běijīng de qiūtiān) '(autumn in Beijing)' '	颜色yánsè 'colors' 运动yùndòng 'sports' 礼物lǐwù 'gifts'
心疼 xīnténg 'love dearly'	小孙子xiǎo sūnzi 'little grandson'	妻子qīzǐ 'wife' 孙子sūnzi 'grandson'	-
钟爱 zhōngài 'treasure'	小孙子xiǎo sūnzi 'little grandson'	大儿子dà érzi 'eldest son' 学生xuéshēng 'student'	-

The term 爱ài 'love' as defined in dictionaries exhibits the most extensive and diverse range of collocations with patient nouns. These patient nouns encompass abstract nouns, collective nouns, and nouns pertaining to relatives or specific individuals, and more. The term 热爱rèài 'Love ardently' in dictionary entries can be associated with numerous patient nouns, with a notable prevalence of collective nouns and work-related nouns in these collocations. On the other hand, terms like宠 chǒng 'pamper', 宠爱chǒng'ài 'dote', 怜爱 lián'ài 'love tenderly', 溺爱 nì'ài 'spoil', and 心疼xīnténg 'love dearly' are commonly employed in conjunction with relative nouns, primarily those representing close junior relatives. The term敬爱 jìng'ài 'esteem' is also frequently used with relative nouns, albeit typically involving elder relatives. Additionally, the term敬爱 jìng'ài 'esteem' can be extended to nouns denoting individuals with elevated social status, such as 总统zǒngtǒng 'president' or 领袖lǐngxiù 'leader'. The term 爱好àihào 'Hobby' and the term酷爱 kù'ài 'love passionately' are commonly linked with terms related to cultural and sports activities. The term喜爱 xǐ'ài 'favor' and the term 喜欢xǐhuān 'like' may both be used with nouns associated with cultural and sports activities, as well as with character nouns, particularly those referring to young individuals such as 孩子háizi 'children'. However, it is evident that 喜欢xǐhuān 'like' is the more prevalent choice. While the term 钟爱zhōng'ài 'treasure' is not frequently employed, it can be paired with character nouns, or nominal phrases like 田园风光tiányuánfēngguāng 'pastoral scenery'.

5 The Descriptions of the Mental Verbs Denoting Affection Within the Framework of Generative Lexicon Theory

Let us use the term 爱ài 'love' and the term热爱rèài 'love ardently' as examples to examine the collocations of mental verbs denoting affection and related issues concerning their lexical representations.

5.1 The Collocations of 爱ài 'Love' and 热爱rèài ' Love Ardently ' in the Corpora

(1) 爱ài 'Love'.

Within the CCL corpus, a total of 193,957 entries feature the term爱 ài 'love'. We have extracted 2,000 instances from this set in which 爱ài 'love' is employed independently as a standalone word. Among the total occurrences of爱 ài 'love', there were 123 instances where it was used independently. Additionally, there were 69 instances of collocational usage with patient nouns, accounting for 3.45% of these entries.

In the corpora, the term 爱ài 'love' exhibits a wide range of collocational patterns with various noun types, including character nouns, collective nouns, and abstract nouns, and more. Within the corpus, numerous instances are observed where爱 ài 'love' collocated with patient nouns, such as 爱国àiguó 'patriotism', 爱才àicái 'love talent',爱路àilù 'love road', 爱民àimín 'love people', and others collocated with 爱ài 'love'. Many of these usages have evolved over time, becoming established idiomatic expressions that persist from ancient times to the present. Examples of such enduring idioms include 君子爱财取之有道jūnzǐàicáiqǔzhīyǒudào 'A gentleman loves money in a good way' and 仁民爱物rénmínàiwù 'Benevolent people, love things'. Additionally, there exist numerous fixed expressions like 爱岗敬业àigǎngjìngyè 'Love and dedication to one's post' and尊老爱幼 zūnlǎoàiyòu 'Respect for the old and love the young', and more.

(2) 热爱rèài 'Love Ardently'.

In the CCL corpus, there are 8,358 instances featuring the phrase 'love ardently'. We have extracted 500 items from this corpus. Among these, 335 instances involve the usage of verbs, constituting a portion of the total usages of 'love ardently'. Out of these 500 items, 322 are found to collocate with nominal patient elements, accounting for 64.4% of the total. Numerous patient nouns exhibit grammatical collocations.

The term 热爱rèài 'love ardently' is among the few mental verbs that predominantly convey the emotion of love and are frequently collocated with abstract nouns and collective nouns. Furthermore, the term 热爱rèài 'love ardently' is commonly found in association with nouns such as characters, nature, arts, and sports, and more. Notably, our research reveals that when the term 热爱rèài 'love ardently' and 工作gōngzuò 'work' co-occur, such as in热爱工作 rèàigōngzuò 'love ardently work', the prevailing interpretation leans towards viewing it as the act of 'engaging in work', treating 工作gōngzuò 'work' as a verb. Conversely, when an attributive is added before 工作gōngzuò 'work', such as in the collocations 热爱本职工作rèàiběnzhígōngzuò 'love ardently your work', 热爱会计工作rèàikuàijìgōngzuò 'love ardently accounting work', or 热爱教学工作rèàijiàoxuégōngzuò 'love ardently teaching work', the inclination is to interpret 工作gōngzuò 'work' as a noun.

5.2 Lexical Representations of 爱ài 'Love' And热爱 rèài 'Love Ardently'

The lexical representations of 爱ài 'love' and热爱 rèài 'love ardently' are as follows:

$$
\begin{array}{l}
\textbf{Love} \\
爱\ \text{ài 'love'} \\[4pt]
\text{EVENTSTR}= \left[\ E1{=}c1{=}\ \text{state} \right. \\[6pt]
\text{ARGSTR}= \left\{
\begin{array}{l}
\text{ARG1}{=}\boxed{1}\ \text{animate\_ind} \\
\qquad \text{FORMAL=physobj} \\
\text{ARG2}{=}\boxed{2}\text{anthropic\_ind} \\
\qquad \text{FORMAL=physobj} \\
\text{ARG3}{=}\boxed{3}\ \text{abstract} \\
\text{ARG4}{=}\boxed{4}\ \text{collective} \\
\qquad \text{FORMAL=physobj}
\end{array}
\right. \\[28pt]
\text{QUALIA}= \left[
\begin{array}{l}
\text{FORMAL= loved\_state(e1,}\boxed{1}/\boxed{2}/\boxed{3}/\boxed{4}\text{)} \\
\text{AGENTIVE= love\_state(e1,}\boxed{1}/\boxed{2}\text{)}
\end{array}
\right.
\end{array}
$$

The event structure of 爱ài 'love' encompasses sub-events, including a state and concurrent events. The argument structure (ARGSTR) comprises four elements, namely the living physical entity 1 (ARG1), the individual physical entity 2 (ARG2), the abstract concept 3 (ARG3), and the physical collection 4 (ARG4). The 爱ài 'love' can be described as a conceptual amalgamation that primarily conveys a state. The formal role represents the state of the qualia entity or abstract concept that is the object of affection. The agent corresponds to the mental state of the living qualia entity 1, which is the experiencer of 爱ài 'love'.

Love Ardently

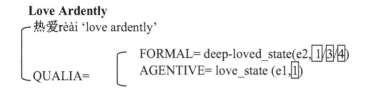

热爱rèài 'love ardently'

QUALIA=
FORMAL= deep-loved_state(e2, 1/3/4)
AGENTIVE= love_state (e1,1)

The event structure and argument structure of 热爱rèài 'love ardently' and 爱ài 'love' share a fundamental similarity. The formal roles associated with 热爱rèài 'love ardently' exhibit slight distinctions from those of 爱ài 'love'. Furthermore, 热爱rèài 'love ardently' conveys a deeper level of affection. Additionally, the formal role of 热爱rèài 'love ardently' differs from that of爱 ài 'love' in that it does not encompass human entities.

5.3 The Characteristics of Nouns in Collocations with Mental Verbs Denoting Affection

Upon summarizing the lexical representations of mental verbs denoting affection, it becomes evident that such verbs can encompass the meanings of 'having affection for a particular person', 'having affection for a specific object', or 'having affection for a particular activity'. The three collocations introduced at the outset of this paper, namely 喜欢面包xǐhuān miàn bāo 'like bread', 喜欢鱼xǐhuān yú 'like fish', and喜欢猫 xǐhuān māo 'like cat', can be interpreted in three distinct ways: expressing a fondness for a particular activity, an inclination towards a particular activity or object, or an affection for a particular object.

Based on noun collocations and distinct lexical representations, the 13 mental verbs denoting affection selected from the corpora can be broadly categorized into three groups:

(1) Mental verbs conveying affection towards a specific person, such as 宠chǒng 'pamper', 宠爱chǒngài 'dote', 怜爱liánài 'love tenderly', 溺爱nìài 'spoil', 心疼xīnténg 'love dearly', and钟爱 zhōngài 'treasure'. These verbs typically co-occur with character nouns. Their arguments are exclusively associated with human entities, with differences in meaning primarily arising from variances in qualia structures.

(2) Mental verbs indicating fondness for a particular object or activity, like 爱好àihào 'hobby' and 酷爱kùài 'love passionately'. These verbs are generally paired with nouns related to arts, sports, natural entities, and artifacts. Their arguments encompass both human entities and qualia entities.

(3) Mental verbs expressing affection for both specific objects or activities and particular individuals, including爱ài 'love', 热爱rèài 'love ardently', 钟爱zhōngài 'treasure', and 喜欢xǐhuān 'like'. These verbs exhibit a wider range of possible patient nouns, encompassing characters, arts, sports, nature, artifacts, collectives, abstract concepts, and more. Their arguments involve human entities, qualia entities, abstract concepts, and more. Polysemy is primarily linked to argument structure, with distinct meanings corresponding to different qualia structures.

The mental verbs denoting affection, such as 喜欢xǐhuān 'like' as discussed at the outset of this paper, belongs to the third category.

When the qualia structures of patient nouns align with those of mental verbs denoting affection, they can be collocated. In other words, when the argument structure of the nouns incorporates human entities, qualia entities, and abstract concepts, mental verbs denoting affection can be appropriately combined.

For instance, the lexical representation of 书shū 'book' is depicted as follows:

Book

书shū 'book'

$$
\begin{bmatrix}
\text{ARGSTR=} & \begin{bmatrix} \text{ARG1=}\boxed{1}\,\text{info} \\ \text{ARG2=}\boxed{2}\,\text{physobj} \end{bmatrix} \\
\text{QUALIA=} & \begin{bmatrix} \text{info·physobj\_1cp} \\ \text{FORMAL= hold (}\boxed{2},\boxed{1}) \\ \text{TELIC= read (}\boxed{1},\boxed{2}) \\ \text{AGENTIVE= write (}\boxed{1},\boxed{2}) \end{bmatrix}
\end{bmatrix}
$$

The term 书 shū 'book' encompasses two distinct components: argument information and qualia entities. It represents a complex noun. Its formal role (FORMAL) pertains to being a handheld qualia entity and an information carrier. Furthermore, its telic role (TELIC) is to function as both an information carrier and a qualia entity for reading purposes. Lastly, its agentive role (AGENTIVE) involves serving as both the qualia entity and the information carrier that have been compiled.

The argument of 书shū 'book' encompasses the argument of the 'qualia entity', aligning with the argument structure of the mental verb 爱ài 'love'. Consequently, 书shū 'book' can be aptly collocated with 爱ài 'love'. For instance, we might say, 我们喜欢在安静的环境中阅读经典书。Wǒmenxǐhuānzàiānjìngde huánjìngzhōngyuèdújīngdiǎnshū. 'We love reading classical books in a serene environment.' Within the category of nouns that can be collocated with various mental verbs denoting affection, character nouns and collective nouns typically incorporate human entity arguments, while abstract nouns involve abstract conceptual arguments. Natural and artificial nouns, on the other hand, incorporate qualia entity arguments. Additionally, arts and sports nouns may include either qualia entity arguments or abstract conceptual arguments.

When the argument structures of the patient nouns partially align with the argument structures of mental verbs denoting affection, these patient nouns can be associated with the aforementioned mental verbs. For instance, 面包miànbāo 'bread' which encompasses qualia entity arguments, can be collocated with 喜欢xǐhuān 'like', which also features qualia entity arguments. In situations where different telic roles and agentive roles hold equal importance within the qualia structures of these patient nouns, polysemous occurrences may arise. For instance, the argument structure of 鱼yú 'fish' involves a qualia entity. When the agentive role associated with 鱼yú 'fish' pertains to 'human', the telic role may involve aspects of edibility or ornamental value. Consequently, the phrase xǐhuān yú 喜欢鱼 'like fish' can be interpreted in two distinct ways: as an expression of enjoyment for eating fish or as an appreciation for fish as an animal. Moreover, polysemous phenomena are predominantly observed in nouns categorized as complex or indeterminate, which diverge from the natural and artifactual categories according to Generative Lexicon Theory.

5.4 Generative Mechanisms in Semantic Interpretation: Researches of Various Collocations of Mental Verbs Denoting Affection

(1) Generation Mechanism in Semantics

Generative Lexicon Theory posits that word meanings are relatively stable, yet they exhibit subtle variations contingent upon their contextual collocations. These slight alterations are facilitated by the generative mechanism within semantics, essentially the collocation mechanism. Pustejovsky introduced three generative mechanisms in semantics, encompassing type coercion, selective binding, and co-composition. [1] The Generative Lexicon Theory elucidates that logical metonymy arises from mismatches in semantic types, a phenomenon explicable through the generative mechanism of type coercion. When certain words are conjoined with others, type coercion compels these words to undergo semantic modifications to align with the demands of semantic collocations. Selective binding pertains to the nuanced associations formed when words are juxtaposed. Co-composition serves to resolve semantic groupings, primarily addressing issues related to verb logic ambiguity. In subsequent research endeavors, Pustejovsky integrated type coercion with argument selection. [4, 5] Depending on specific contextual factors, three generative mechanisms of argument selection emerge: pure selection, type accommodation, and type coercion.

When type coercion occurs, there are two scenarios in which semantic domains may remain unchanged and others where they may change. Several instances warrant consideration:

1) Entity Transformation into an Event: This represents the most prevalent alteration within the semantic domains when mental verbs denoting affection, such as 爱ài 'love', collocate with patient nouns. For example, the noun 书法shūfǎ 'calligraphy' primarily represents an abstract concept or a qualia entity. However, when the term 书法 shūfǎ 'calligraphy' is employed in conjunction with mental verbs denoting affection, such as喜欢 xǐhuān 'like', it undergoes a transformation from a static entity to a dynamic event. For instance, the sentence: 他请求他喜欢书法的哥哥写一些字在纸上。Tāqǐngqiútāxǐhuān shūfǎdegēge xiěyìxiēzìzàizhǐshàng. 'He asked his brother, who likes calligraphy, to write some characters on a piece of rice paper.' Here, 书法shūfǎ 'calligraphy' has transitioned from being an entity to an event of 'calligraphy creation'. A similar transformation is observed in cases mentioned earlier in this paper, such as 喜欢面包xǐhuān miànbāo 'like bread' and喜欢鱼 xǐhuān yú 'like fish', where the qualia entities of 面包miànbāo 'bread' and 鱼yú 'fish' evolve into events, i.e., 'like eating bread' and 'like eating fish'.

2) Event Transformation into a Time Interval: An example of this transformation can be observed when the event 'party starts' in the context of 'before the party starts' evolves into a time interval, i.e., 'before the time when the party starts'. These shifts in semantic domains are not as prominent in the collocations of mental verbs denoting affection, as found in the corpora.

3) Entity Conversion into a Proposition: Changes within semantic domains are infrequent in collocations involving mental verbs denoting affection. An illustration of this can be seen in the argument for 江山jiāngshān 'country,' encompassing substantive elements related to the earth, mountains, and rivers. When the term is used in the context of不爱江山爱美人 bùàijiāngshānàiměirén 'Don't love the country, love the beauty', 江山jiāngshān 'country' transforms into the proposition of 'national affairs'.The phrase 不爱江山爱美人bùàijiāngshānàiměirén 'Don't love the country, love the beauty' is often employed satirically to critique politicians who prioritize personal pursuits of beauty over national affairs.

In general, when mental verbs denoting affection are paired with patient nouns, three semantic generative mechanisms (pure selection, type accommodation, and type coercion) may come into play. Among these mechanisms, type coercion is particularly noteworthy. Type coercion can result in alterations within semantic domains, and it frequently gives rise to the transformation of entities into events.

The examples mentioned earlier primarily focus on the perspective of type coercion, where mental verbs denoting affection, such as 爱ài 'love', coerce the selection of patient nouns. However, in predicate-object structures, patient nouns serving as objects may also influence the choice of mental verbs with affectionate connotations in their collocations.

For the three aforementioned examples: ①喜欢面包Xǐhuān miàn bāo 'like bread', ② 喜欢鱼Xǐhuān yú 'like fish', ③喜欢猫 Xǐhuān māo 'like cat', the verb 喜欢xǐhuān 'like' can be collocated with two types of objects, either substantives or predicates. For instance, 李明喜欢面包。Lǐmíngxǐhuānmiànbāo. 'Li Ming likes bread' can be expressed as 'Li Ming likes eating bread'. And 李明喜欢鱼。Lǐmíngxǐhuān yú. 'Li Ming likes fish' can be equivalently stated as 'Li Ming likes eating fish.' While 'Like + V + NP' can serve as an explanation for the previous 'like + NP' pattern, the case of 'like cats' lacks a corresponding 'Like + V + NP' construction for explanation. This phenomenon is attributed to the characteristics of the nouns involved.

Bread

面包miàn bāo 'bread'

ARGSTR= (ARG1=[1] solid _ physobj

QUALIA= [CONST= farina etc（[1]）
TELIC = eat
AGENTIVE）= eat
= bake

The term面包 miànbāo 'bread' is an artifact noun, classifying it as a type of food. Its telic role (TELIC) is 'to eat', and its agentive roles (AGENTIVE) are also related to 'eating'. In the absence of specific context, the phrase 'like bread' typically conveys the meaning of 'enjoying the act of eating bread'.

Fish

鱼 yú 'fish'

ARGSTR=   (ARG1=[1] physobj

QUALIA=   1cp（animal·food）
TELIC = view
=eat
AGENTIVE= feed
= eat

The term鱼 yú 'fish' is a compound term that can be construed as referring to both an animal and a food item. It exhibits a duality in its telic role, encompassing the actions of 'watching' and 'eating', with corresponding agentive roles such as 'feeding' and 'eating'. Consequently, the phrase喜欢鱼 xǐhuān yú 'like fish' can be interpreted in two distinct ways: as an affection for fish as an animal, and as an affinity for the act of consuming fish.

In contrast, the term猫 māo 'cat' is a natural entity and does not conventionally pertain to food. It lacks a specific telic role. Consequently, 喜欢猫 xǐhuān māo 'like cat' can only be understood as an affection for cats as animals. From this perspective, the generation of semantics in the collocations of mental verbs denoting affection is not solely reliant on the verbs themselves but is also influenced by the nature of the patient nouns involved.

(2) Representations of Type Coercion

When we employ the construction 'Like + V + NP' to elucidate 'Like + NP', it can effectively be viewed as implying an implicit verb within 'Like + NP'.

Song Z.-Y. employed a series of transitional sentences to assess the presence of implicit verbs [9]:

(a) 我喜欢鱼，但我不喜欢吃鱼。
Wǒxǐhuānyú，dànwǒbùxǐhuānchīyú.
'I like fish, but I don't like eating fish.'

(b)？我喜欢饺子，但我不喜欢吃饺子。
Wǒxǐhuānjiǎozi, dànwǒbùxǐhuānchījiǎozi.
'I like dumplings, but I don't like eating dumplings.'

In the statement 我喜欢鱼wǒxǐhuānyú 'I like fish', the existence of the verb 'eat' is contingent. Transitional sentence (a) is deemed valid, while in the case of 我喜欢饺子 wǒxǐhuānjiǎozi'I like dumplings', the implication of the verb 'eat' is essential, making transitional sentence (b) invalid.

Let us now provide some examples of implicit verbs within the collocations of patient nouns or nominal phrases associated with mental verbs denoting affection.

Implicit verbs can indeed impact the meanings of certain sentences. For instance, the phrase 爱好古玩àihàogǔwán 'be keen on antiques' does not inherently signify 'a keen interest in collecting antiques', but rather denotes an enthusiasm for all aspects related to antiques. The implicit verbs in the collocation 爱好古玩àihàogǔwán 'be keen on antiques' exhibit uncertainty, and their meanings may encompass 'being enthusiastic about collecting antiques', 'having an enthusiasm for appreciating antiques', and more. In the given example, these implicit verbs within 爱好古玩àihàogǔwán 'be keen on antiques' are contextually determined.

The majority of implicit verbs in collocations with mental verbs denoting affection are intricately linked to the telic and agentive roles of the associated nouns. The implicit 'eat' in the expression 'like bread' represents both the telic and agentive roles of the noun 'bread.' There exists a conventional association between 'eat' and 'bread'. In the framework of Generative Lexicon Theory, this connection appears to be reflected in the telic and agentive roles of 'bread'. 'Like bread' typically constitutes the default collocation for 'like to eat bread.' If the combination of 'like' and 'bread' were no longer considered the default collocation for expressing this preference, an alternative verb would need to be introduced to the collocation, such as 'enjoy making bread'.

At times, the implicit verbs within the collocations of mental verbs denoting affection can be ambiguous and necessitate interpretation within the context. For instance, the phrase 酷爱文学kùaiwénxué 'love ardently literature' is open to multiple interpretations within its given context, encompassing both 'love writing literature' and 'love appreciating literature'. In the sentence, 小王子身受母教, 自幼酷爱读书, 酷爱文学和艺术。Xiǎowángzǐshēnshòumǔjiào, zìyòukùàidúshū, kùaiwénxuéhéyìshù. 'The little prince was taught by his mother and passionately loved reading, literature, and art since childhood', the context allows for the understanding of 'a fervent appreciation of literary works.'

In corpora analysis, the majority of instances of type coercion within the collocations of mental verbs denoting affection imply a relationship between humans and objects, encompassing actions such as 'consume', 'engage in', 'create' and 'appreciate', and more. Furthermore, artifactual nouns, when compared to natural nouns, typically involve telic and agentive roles. Notably, the patient nouns often found in the collocations of mental verbs denoting affection tend to be referential artifactual nouns, such as 'bread','fish','literature','book','lecture', and more.

6 Conclusions

When referring to the phrase喜欢面包 xǐhuān miàn bāo 'like bread', it is naturally interpreted as 'like to eat bread'. In the case of 喜欢鱼xǐhuān yú 'like fish', there are two potential interpretations: 'like to eat fish' and 'like fish as an animal'. Similarly, when referring to喜欢猫 xǐhuān māo 'like cat', it is generally understood as 'like cats as animals'. This research aims to discern patterns in the diverse meanings of mental verbs in collocations.

When 'like' conveys the 'meaning of love', the formal roles can represent the state or process of a qualia entity or an animate qualia entity, with its argument structure including animate qualia entities or other qualia entities. From a comprehensive analysis of semantic representations and corpora, if mental verbs collocated with patient nouns contain multiple arguments, particularly qualia entities and abstract concepts in their formal roles, it may result in polysemy. As such, qualia entities, animate qualia entities, states, processes, and other formal roles are presented in the three initial collocations of 喜欢面包 xǐhuān miàn bāo 'like bread', 喜欢鱼 xǐhuān yú 'like fish', and 喜欢猫 xǐhuān māo 'like cat', leading to potential ambiguity in 喜欢鱼 xǐhuān yú 'like fish'.

After summarizing the lexical representations of mental verbs denoting affection, it becomes evident that these verbs can signify 'loving people', 'loving certain things', or 'loving certain activities'. Based on noun collocations and variations in lexical representations, mental verbs denoting affection can be categorized into three main groups: those that mean 'loving people', those that mean 'loving certain things or activities', and those that encompass all three meanings of 'loving people', 'loving certain things', and 'loving certain activities'. The term 喜欢 xǐhuān 'like' falls into the third category, leading to multiple interpretations.

When the argument structures of patient nouns partially align with those of mental verbs denoting affection, they can be used in collocations with such verbs. For instance, 面包 miàn bāo 'bread', with a qualia entity argument, can be collocated with 喜欢 xǐhuān 'like' when it also contains the same qualia entity argument. When the qualia structure of these patient nouns holds equal importance in different telic roles and agentive roles, polysemous phenomena may arise. For instance, if the agentive role of 'fish' is 'human', the telic role can be 'eat' or 'watch'. When the argument structure of 'fish' is a qualia entity, 喜欢鱼 xǐhuān yú 'like fish' can be understood in two distinct ways: 'like to eat fish' and 'like fish as an animal'. Furthermore, polysemy typically occurs in nouns belonging to complex or indeterminate categories, which differ from the natural and artifactual categories as proposed by the Generative Lexicon Theory. More recently, a domain-based sentimental dictionary has been proposed to address the problem that the same words may have different meanings in various domains. [10, 11] This phenomenon poses a challenge to the computerized analysis of polysemy.

Acknowledgments. This paper has received support from various funding sources, including:The National Language Commission's key project: Research on the Construction of a Chinese Emotional Lexicon Corpus Based on Intelligent Computing (ZDI145–17); Beijing Municipal Social Science Foundation Key Project: Research on the Historical and Current Lexicon in Beijing Dialect Over the Past Century in the Context of Language Contact(22YYA002); Key Projects of Science and Technology Innovation 2030 - Research on Key Technologies of Recognition and Understanding of Handwritten Text and Text in Complex Layout (2020AAA0109700); National Language Commission Research Planning Project(YB145–56).We are grateful for the support provided by these funding sources, which has enabled us to carry out this research.

References

1. Pustejovsky, J.: The Generative Lexicon. MIT Press, MA (1995)
2. Pustejovsky, J.: Type construction and the logic of concept. In: Pierrette Bouillon and Fed erica Busa (Eds.) The Language of Word Meaning, pp. 91–123.Cambrideg University Press, London (2001)
3. Pustejovsky, J., Bouillon, P., Isahara, H., Kanzaki, K., Lee, C. (eds.): Advances in Genera-tive Lexicon Theory. Springer, Dordrecht (2013)

4. Nicholas, A., Pustejovsky, J.: Word meaning and commonsense metaphysics. Unpublished manuscrip. http://smanticsarchive.net/Archive/TgxMDNkM/asher-pustejovsky-wordmeaning.pdf (2005)
5. Pustejovsky, J.: Type theory and lexical decomposition. J. Cogn. Sci. **6**(1), 39–76 (2006)
6. Dictionary editing office, institute of linguistics, chinese academy of social sciences. : Modern chinese dictionary.7en edn. The commercial press, Beijing (2018)
7. Lu, J.-J., Lv, W.-H.: Dictionary of learning chinese by the commercial press. The Commercial Press, Beijing (2007)
8. Zhang, Z.-Y., et al.: Contemporary chinese learner's dictionary. The Commercial Press, Beijing (2020)
9. Song, Z.-Y.: Research on the generative lexicon theory and forced phenomenon of chinese incidents. Beijing University Press, Beijing (2015)
10. Naren, T., Xu, X.-Y.: Affective Semantics and Regulatory Modes of the Word "可 kě may" in Text-based sentiment analysis. In: Chinese lexical semantics, 21st Workshop, CLSW 2020, pp.288–302(2021)
11. Rosa, R.L., Schwartz, G.M., Ruggiero, W.V., Rodríguez, D.Z.: A knowledge-based recommendation system that includes sentiment analysis and deep learning. IEEE Trans. Industr. Inf. **15**(4), 2124–2135 (2018)

Profiling the Mandarin Physical Contact Verbs with *ná, wò, chí* and *zhuā* Using Collocational, Syntactic and Discourse Features

Qian Zhong[1] and Tianqi He[2(✉)]

[1] School of Foreign Languages, Wuhan Insititute of Technology, Wuhan, China
qzhong5-c@my.cityu.edu.hk
[2] School of Humanities, Central South University, Changsha, China
tianqihe5-c@my.cityu.edu.hk

Abstract. This study aims to provide a preliminary comparison of Mandarin Physical Contact verbs with *ná* 'carry', *wò* 'grasp', *chí* 'hold', and *zhuā* 'grab' by adopting a behavior profiling approach. Based on previous theoretical studies, the four verbs are intensively examined in terms of collocational, syntactic and discourse features in Sect. 2. Besides, the linguistic features are turned into categorical or binary features in Sect. 3 to generate the high dimensional vectors of the chosen verbs to allow multifactorial analysis to compare the subtle differences in meanings of the four verbs. The results support that *wò* 'grasp' and *zhuā* 'grab' share more semantic-syntactic similarities and *ná* 'carry' is more similar to *wò* 'grasp' and *zhuā* 'grab' cluster. Whereas *chí* 'hold' behaviors most differently from the remaining three. The study also finds out that *wò* 'grasp' and *zhuā* 'grab' cluster is differentiated from *chí* 'hold' and *ná* 'carry' cluster mostly in its syntactic features.

Keywords: Mandarin Physical Contact Verb · Behavior Profiling · Corpus-Driven Approach

1 Introduction

Physical Contact verbs have been generally viewed as an independent verbal class and intensively examined in terms of diathesis alternations [1], morpho-syntactic behaviors [2, 3], semantic features [4, 5] and syntactic-semantic interactions [6, 7]. Among them, *ná* 'carry', *wò* 'grasp', *chí* 'hold', and *zhuā* 'grab' were carefully examined under the frame-based constructional approach [8–10] as four representative *Mandarin Physical Contact* (MPC) verbs [11]. It was found that these verbs display both similar and distinctive patterns in corpus, thus can be considered as near synonymous verbs which should be further distinguished based on corpus data.

M. Dong et al. (Eds.): CLSW 2023, LNAI 14514, pp. 211–224, 2024.
https://doi.org/10.1007/978-981-97-0583-2_17

1.1 Previous Studies on Near-Synonymous Verbs

Numerous studies have investigated near-synonymous verbs in various approaches. For example, some scholars explored the grammatical function distributions and collocational features of near-synonymous verbs to reveal the subtle differences in their meanings. Major works include: i) Mandarin near-synonymous verbs: *gāoxìng* vs. *kuàilè* 'be happy' [12], *jiàn* vs. *zào* vs. *gài* 'build' [13], *tǎolùn* vs. *shāngliáng* 'discuss' [14] and *biànlì* vs. *fāngbiàn* 'to be convenient' [15]; ii) near-synonymous verbs with cross-linguistic evidences: verbs of *Contact by Impact* in English and Chinese [7], *Do* verbs in Taiwan and Mainland Mandarin [16], *Cut* verbs in English and Chinese [17].

Furthermore, the Module-Attribute Representation of Verbal Semantics (MARVS) theory was introduced to represent finer semantic properties of verbs by providing eventive information of the verb-related event structure, based on previous studies on more than 40 pairs of near synonyms and around 10 semantic fields [18–20]. Adopting this bottom-up approach, various studies have been conducted to further distinguish near-synonym pairs, such as [21] on verbs of *Throwing*, [22] on *Force-compulsion* verbs and [23] on verbs of *Closing*.

Following the same vein, the frame-based constructional approach was proposed as a top-down framework to classify near-synonymous verbs in terms of both semantic and syntactic features [8–10], on the basis of Frame Semantics [24, 25] and Construction Grammar [26–28]. Various works on verbal classifications have been completed under this approach, such as [29] on verbs of *Conversation*, [8] on verbs of *Statement*, [11] on verbs of *Physical Contact*.

1.2 Previous Studies on Mandarin Physical Contact Verbs

A detailed classification of *Mandarin Physical Contact* verbs was conducted by [11] under the frame-based constructional approach, which proposed three sub-categories of *MPC* verbs: verbs of *Contact by Impact* (*dǎ/qiāo/pāi/jī* 'hit/knock/pat/strike'), verbs of *Surface Contact* (*cā/shì* 'wipe') and verbs of *Holding* (*wò/zhuā* 'hold'). Among them, verbs of *Holding* were defined as '(intentional) prolong contact without motion' by collocating with stative or resultative markers. A former study focused on *ná* 'carry' and *wò* 'grasp' [30] proposed that although sharing similar semantic-syntactic features as verbs of *Holding*, *ná* 'carry' is more like a carry verb as it tends to collocate with directional markers while *wò* 'grasp' is a typical *Hold* verb.

On the other hand, previous studies held different opinions on the verbal classes of these four verbs. Basically, *ná* 'carry', *wò* 'grasp', *chí* 'hold', and *zhuā* 'grab' were generally accepted as physical or hand action verbs in traditional Mandarin verbal research [31, 32], as they are sharing hand-radical components in the characters [33]. Some scholars further distinguish *ná* 'carry' and *zhuā* 'grab' as *Take* verbs [34]. Whereas others viewed *ná* 'carry' as a *Carry* verb yet *wò* 'grasp', *chí* 'hold' and *zhuā* 'grab' as typical *Hold* verbs [30].

In sum, previous studies have analyzed MPC verbs along with the representative *ná* 'carry', *wò* 'grasp', *chí* 'hold', and *zhuā* 'grab' in terms of both syntactic and semantic features, but the conclusion can be further verified by corpus-driven approach.

1.3 Behavioral Profiles: A Corpus-Based Approach for Synonym Study

The present study uses behavior profiles to quantitatively study Mandarin physical contact verbs. The idea of behavior profiles (BP) originated from the research [35, 36] and has recently been used by various linguistic studies [37–39]. The method is advantageous in studying near synonyms, especially for the analysis of verb semantics since it offers a powerful representation of verbs that could possibly incorporate features from all linguistic levels, like the lexical level (e.g., collocational features), the syntactic level (e.g., agent, object or complement), and even the discourse level features. Obviously, this is an advantage that most previous theoretical linguistic studies could not rival given that they could not exhaust all these features of a given verb or a set of verbs all at once in one study. Given its power to present linguistic data in high dimensional space, the BP method is most appropriate in studying near synonyms overlapping in many senses but differ subtly in some. It makes it possible to offer a quantitative analysis towards the near synonym sets *ná* 'carry', *wò* 'grasp', *chí* 'hold', and *zhuā* 'grab' by identifying their similarities and differences, which helps us describe these similarities and differences in a corpus-driven way. Additionally, this study adopted a frame-based constructional approach [8, 9, 40] as the theoretical support of the behavior profiling method, which not only provides preliminary comparison of the four verbs in terms of their semantic-syntactic behaviors but also contributes to the descriptive features used for clustering.

2 Preliminary Comparison of *ná*, *wò*, *chí*, and *zhuā*

This section provides a preliminary comparison of the near synonym sets *ná* 'carry', *wò* 'grasp', *chí* 'hold', and *zhuā* 'grab' in terms of collocational, syntactic and discourse features. Adopting a corpus-driven approach, we randomly selected 300 sentences of each verb from BCC corpus as the initial data set. Then, the initial data set was manually checked. After deleting some wrong sentences, we acquire the pretreated data set. Finally, we randomly selected 100 sentences of each verb from the pretreated data set as our final corpus with 400 sentences in total. All sentences were manually tagged from the perspective of collocational, syntactic and discourse features, in order to reveal the subtle distinctions of these verbs.

2.1 Collocational Features

In this section, *ná* 'carry', *wò* 'grasp', *chí* 'hold', and *zhuā* 'grab' are preliminary compared in terms of collocational features such as aspectual markers, directional markers and time markers.

It is found that *ná* 'carry', *wò* 'grasp', *chí* 'hold', and *zhuā* 'grab' tend to collocate with aspectual markers (25%, 28%, 20% respectively) while only 7% of *chí* can co-occur with aspectual markers. More specifically, 28% of *ná* 'carry' collocate with stative aspectual marker *zhe* 'ZHE' and both *ná* 'carry' and *zhuā* 'grab' are used together with aspectual marker *le* 了 'LE' indicating change of state. Besides, *ná* 'carry', *chí* 'hold' and *zhuā* 'grab' may co-occur with directional markers (8%, 2%. 2% respectively) and thus connected with motion frame. It is also noticed that *ná* 'carry' and *zhuā* 'grab' are closely related to pre/post verb deictic markers, showing the dynamic character of its semantics.

Furthermore, both *ná* 'carry' and *zhuā* 'grab' tend to collocate with time markers (26% and 22% respectively) and temporal/frequency expressions (33% and 27% respectively), which means that these two verbs are more closely related to time and indicates 'change of state' rather than stative contact.

2.2 Syntactic Features

Distinctive syntactic features in this section mainly include four noun phrases: agent, object, complement and manner. Each feature is examined in terms of appearance and semantic types.

It is concluded that all verbs can omit the agent in sentences (31%, 24%, 17%, 40% respectively) and collocate with animate agents (39%, 61%, 55%, 55% respectively), which can be considered as the typical syntactic feature of MPC verbs. Except for *ná* 'carry', other verbs may co-occur with body-part agent, namely *shǒu* 'hand'. Besides, *wò* 'grasp' display as a pure *Hold* verb as it rejects inanimate agents. While *ná* 'carry', *chí* 'hold' and *zhuā* 'grab' experience semantic extension as they may have inanimate agents such as institutions (e.g., *gōngsī* 'company'), teams (e.g., *běijīng àoshén* 'the team of Beijing Aoshen') and places (e.g., *héběi* 'Hebei'). Correspondingly, *ná* 'carry', *chí* 'hold' and *zhuā* 'grab' tend to collocate with abstract objects (21%, 32%, 57% respectively) such as regulations (e.g., *zhāngfǎ* 'regulations and law'), opinions (e.g., *guāndiǎn* 'opinions') and opportunities (e.g., *jīyù* 'opportunities').

Moreover, four verbs display distinctive complement choices: i) only 7% of *chí* may collocate with complements and all of them are stative complements (e.g., *píng* 'flat'); ii) *wò* 'grasp' is more closely related to resultative (e.g., *zhù* 'ZHU', 22%) and impactive (e.g., *jǐn* 'tightly', 8%) complements, indicating intentional stative contact; iii) 64% of *zhuā* 'grab' are co-occurred with resultative (e.g., *zhù* 'ZHU') complements, implying 'change of state'; iv) *ná* 'carry' displays a more dispersive complement types as 18% of which are collocating with resultative complements (e.g., *xià* 'down') and 18% of which are co-occurring with directional complements (e.g., *chū* 'out' and *kāi* 'away'), underlining the connection with both change of state and motion event. In the same vein, *wò* 'grasp' and *zhuā* 'grab' may collocate with impactive manners such as *jǐnjǐn* 'very tightly', indicating the impactive feature in their verbal semantics.

2.3 Discourse Features

Discourse features in this section are mainly related to serial verb construction (SVC), a unique phenomenon in Mandarin which requires two semantically similar and syntactically equal verbs in one sentence. It is found that *ná* 'carry' and *zhuā* 'grab' tend to enter SVC construction together with emotion/judgement/perception verbs (18% and 29% respectively), indicating potential category transfers to these frames. Besides, four verbs are closely related to motion frame as all of them may co-occur with motion verbs in SVC construction. Furthermore, *ná* 'carry', *wò* 'grasp' and *zhuā* 'grab' may be used as social-interaction verbs as all of them may collocate with social-related verbs in SVC construction (8%, 8% and 5% respectively).

3 Data and Method: Profiling *ná*, *wò*, *chí*, and *zhuā*

3.1 Data Preparation

The present study chooses the BP approach to quantitatively profile the differences among the four Mandarin physical contact verbs ná 'carry', wò 'grasp', chí 'hold', and zhuā 'grab'. The BP approach is chosen because it is a multi-factorial method that could offer insight about characteristics of near synonyms by comparing different contextual features of words or constructions in a corpus [41]. Although the approach has been extensively used for revealing sets of near-synonyms in Indo-European languages such as Dutch [2], Russian [38], English [43], only few previous studies on Chinese have made such attempts in applying BP methods for near-synonym research. [44] is the first, to the author's knowledge, to use BP method to examine Chinese near synonym causative verbs ràng 'let', shǐ 'make' and lìng 'cause'. Following [44], the present study adopts the BP method to research four Chinese near synonyms ná 'carry', wò 'grasp', chí 'hold' and zhuā 'grab' through a comprehensive analysis of 34 contextual features (see Appendix 1) characterizing the near synonyms sets from collocational, syntactic, and discourse level. By using behavior profile approach, all contextual features of interest are well-represented by the high-dimensional data and made comparable, calculable and verifiable, offers a convincing, trackable, repeatable, and objective analysis for the similarities and the dissimilarities for various contextual features of the four holding verbs.

First, a dataset of 400 observations is randomly extracted from BCC [45]. Each of the four Mandarin physical contact verbs were represented by 100 observations. The dataset is then manually annotated for the 28 contextual features yielding 79 ID tags to determine the collocational, syntactic, and discourse environment of the underlying words. The features are both binary and categorical. Usually, the current study allows no more than 6 categories. However, in one special circumstance, a categorical feature termed as 'semantic_feature_of_the_other_VP' was annotated 16 categories given the linguistic observation. The contextual features annotated in the current study are all important linguistic features that were mentioned in previous linguistic studies on Mandarin physical contact verbs. The data-annotation was done by three expert annotators, double-blind validation, and majority voting to solve any discrepancy. Overall speaking, after annotation, we get 31,600 (400*79) data points.

The resultative table incorporating all the annotated data contains all the 400 instances of sentences with ná 'carry', wò 'grasp', chí 'hold', and zhuā 'grab' (rows) and 28 features (columns). We converted 28 features into 79 binary features and categorical features. The numeric BP vectors for the four verbs were then created. Then we computed the distance matrix between the BP vectors. And after the BP vector of the four Mandarin physical contact verbs are calculated, the study conducted a cluster analysis and identification of the optimal number of clusters for the four underlying verbs. Finally, the study interpreted the cluster solution and elaborates on some preliminary findings of the current study. The calculation was done in R and followed the approach adopted in [41].

3.2 Preliminary Findings: Hierarchical Cluster Analysis

Although many cluster analysis methods are available, the current study uses hierarchical agglomerative clustering (HAC). All objects are represented as leaves or branches of a clustering tree. This tree is called a dendrogram. One thing is particularly noteworthy is that this tree grows from the branches to the root. In the current study, each verb profile vector of ná 'carry', wò 'grasp', chí 'hold', and zhuā 'grab' represents its own cluster at the very beginning as 'leaf' and the statistics start to merge from there. Next, the ones yielding the smallest distances will be firstly merged since the algorithm considers the two most similar to each other. This procedure is repeated again and again until all leaves and branches are merged into one tree. The lower two elements emerge on the tree, the more similarities the two elements have. The higher two elements emerge on the tree, the more differences exist between the two elements. The lowest emerge in our case are wò 'grasp' and zhuā 'grab', which have the smallest distance. Then ná 'carry' emerges with wò 'grasp' and zhuā 'grab', showing that they yield smaller distance and closer to each other when compared with chí 'hold'. Finally, chí 'hold' forms the cluster with the remaining three. Therefore, according to our preliminary findings, zhuā 'grab' and wò 'grasp' are more similar to each other, as shown in Fig. 1. Secondly, ná 'carry' behaviors more similar to zhuā 'grab' and wò 'grasp' cluster in terms of the three levels of contextual features annotated in the present study. Finally, chí 'hold' yield the biggest difference from the remaining three. Therefore, the data will be divided into two clusters, zhuā 'grab' and wò 'grasp' and the remaining. This because zhuā 'grab' and wò 'grasp' form the smallest cluster and behavior differently from the remaining two verbs of ná 'carry' and chí 'hold'.

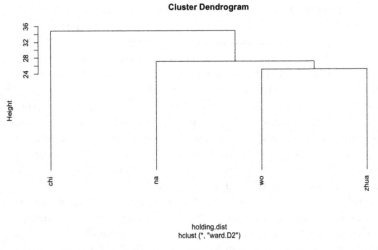

Fig. 1. Hierarchical cluster dendrogram of the four Mandarin physical contact verbs.

The current study then go a step further to study how theses contextual features make zhuā 'grab' and wò 'grasp' different from ná 'carry' and chí 'hold' cluster. To make such a comparison, the present study calculates the effect size of each of the 79 ID tags and draws a snake plot after computing the differences between the average values in both clusters. The factors are sorted in ascending order and the result is shown in Fig. 2.

nachi <...-> wozhua

Fig. 2. Overview of contextual features in na & chi cluster and wo & zhua cluster, ranked by effect size of each contextual feature.

The snake plot clearly shows the distinctive features distinguishing *zhuā* 'grab' and *wò* 'grasp' cluster and *ná* 'carry' and *chí* 'hold' cluster.

Moreover, the Table 1 lists the top 9 contextual features that distinguishes *ná* 'carry' and *chí* 'hold' cluster, measured by effect sizes.

Table 1. Overview of top 9 contextual features that distinguish the na & chi cluster from wo & zhua cluster; based on total effect size and Cramer's V test.

Contextual Feature Type	Contextual feature	Effective size rank (total)	Cramer's V
na & chi cluster			
complement semantic type	no complement	0.25 (1)	0.464
complement	no complement	0.25 (2)	0.264
quantitative	quantitative marker	0.22 (3)	0.293
object semantic type	animate	0.215 (4)	0.555
object semantic type	bodypart	0.165 (5)	0.555
order in SVC	first	0.12 (6)	0.166
for_to	yes	0.10 (7)	0.229
aspectual marker	zhe	0.095 (8)	0.178
semantic_type_of_the_other_VP	possession	0.090 (9)	0.273
complement semantic type	directional	0.090 (9)	0.464
manner_semantic_type	no manner	0.090 (9)	0.213
manner	no manner	0.090 (9)	0.121

Four contextual features ranked 9 have the same effect size. Therefore, there are a total of 13 features listed in the Table 1. Each feature in the list tends to occur with *ná* 'carry' and *chí* 'hold', but not with *zhuā* 'grab' and *wò* 'grasp'. That means the features listed in the table are where the two clusters of verbs behavior most differently. In our corpus, *ná* 'carry' and *chí* 'hold' attract these features while *zhuā* 'grab' and *wò* 'grasp' repel then.

The snake plot shows that only a few factors have the most distinctive power in differentiating the two clusters. The most distinctive feature, in the dataset, is the semantic type of the complement. Some of the factors listed have the same Cramer's V statistics since they are different tags for the same feature. It is shown that *ná* 'carry' and *chí* 'hold' cluster usually appears with no complement. Example (1) illustrates this pattern.

(1) a. 他 又 冲回 屋内 拿 了 碗 清水
    Tā yòu chōng huí wū nèi ná le wǎn qīng shuǐ
    He again rushed house inside take LE a bowl water
    'He rushed back to the house to take a bowl of water.'

  b. 雪峰 神尼 持 剑 环顾
    Xuěfēng shénní chí jiàn huán gù.
    Snow mountain magical nun holding sword looking around.
    'The nun in snow mountain holds sword and looks around.'

The third most prominent feature appearing with a quantitative marker in the context. The data indicate that in the context that *ná* 'carry' and *chí* 'hold' cluster usually appears with a quantitative marker. For example:

(2) a. 靓柔　　　　　拿出　一支　　口红
      Liàng róu　　*ná chū　yī zhī　kǒu hóng*
      Liangrou　　　take out　a　　lipstick
      'Liangrou takes out a lipstick.'

    b. 每人　　手　一块　　一汽大众　佛山　工厂　　的　　版面
      Měi rén　shǒu chí yīkuài　yīqìdàzhòng fóshān gōngchǎng de bǎn miàn
      Each person hand hold a piece of FAW-Volkswagen Foshan factory layout
      'Each holds in hand a piece of layout from the FAW-Volkswagen Foshan factory.'

Another prominent feature will be the semantic type of the object, it is shown that abstract object usually collocates with *ná* 'carry' and *chí* 'hold', as shown in example (3).

(3) a. 拿　　他　　的　　话　　讲
      Ná　tā　de　huà　jiǎng
      Take　his　　　words　speak
      'Use his word.'

    b. 虽然　现在　仍　有　一些　人　否定论　的　观点
      Suīrán　xiànzài réng yǒu yīxiē rén chí fǒudìnglùn de guān diǎn
      Although now still some people hold negativism DE point
      'Although there are still some people who hold a negative view.'

The dataset also annotated the order in SVC, which indicates that *ná* 'carry' and *chí* 'hold' usually appears in the first place if it is a serial verb construction. As illustrated below:

(4) a. 他 拿出　一片　消炎剂　　　和着　　　水 吞下
      Tā ná chū　yī piàn　xiāo yán jì　hé zhe　shuǐ tūn xià
      He take out a tablet anti-inflammatory together with water swallowed down
      'He takes out an anti-inflammatory tablet and swallows it with water.'

    b. 那 两个　道人　剑　追来，
      Nà liǎng gè dào rén chí jiàn　zhuī lái
      That two　Taoist　hold swords chase after
      'The two Taoists hold their swords and chased after them.'

The eighth feature the cluster occurs with for_to. It also noteworthy that the semantic type of the other VP tends to be possession when collocates with *ná* 'carry' and *chí* 'hold', which is mainly conveyed by the postverbal *yǒu* 'have'. Finally, *ná* 'carry' and *chí* 'hold' favors directional complement such as *lái* 'LAI' and *píng* 'flat' but has no preference for manner words. Among the 13 features, most of the features are syntactic whereas discourse features and collocational features are relatively less. Therefore, it could be inferred most of the difference of the two clusters of verbs occur at the syntactic level. Example (1) indicates the most prominent feature *ná* 'carry' and *chí* 'hold' cluster usually appears with no complement.

4 Conclusion

This study provides a quantitative perspective towards Chinese near-synonym study by comparing the four Mandarin physical contact verbs *ná* 'carry', *wò* 'grasp', *chí* 'hold', and *zhuā* 'grab'. Unlike most theoretical linguistic studies on verbs that only draw on one sub-senses of the meaning of *ná* 'carry', *wò* 'grasp', *chí* 'hold', and *zhuā* 'grab', this study uses the behavior profile approach and calculated the BP vectors of the four verbs in order to compare its similarities and differences from the collocational, syntactic, and discourse level. The hierarchical cluster analysis shows that by incorporating all the three levels of factors together, *wò* 'grasp' and *zhuā* are similar to each other, whereas *ná* 'carry' is more similar to *wò* 'grasp' and *zhuā* 'grab' cluster. Finally, *chí* 'hold' behaviors most differently from the remaining three. Their study also investigates how *wò* 'grasp' and *zhuā* cluster is differentiated from *chí* 'hold' and *ná* 'carry' cluster. The result shows that the two clusters behavior more differently in terms of the syntactic features, like the occurrence with a complement or not. The study adds some quantitative perspectives to the study of the four Mandarin physical contact verbs *ná* 'carry', *wò* 'grasp', *chí* 'hold', and *zhuā* 'grab'.

Appendix 1. Overview of Feature Types and Number of Categories of Each Feature

Feature level	Feature Type	Feature	Categories
Collocational	modifier	aspectual markers Le	2
	modifier	aspectual markers Zhe	2
	modifier	directional_marker	2
	modifier	locational marker	2
	modifier	DOU	2
	modifier	negation_marker	2
	modifier	deictic_ marker	2
	modifier	deictic_preverb_marker	2
	modifier	time_marker	2
	modifier	temporal/frequency	2
	modifier	quantitative marker	2
Syntactic	noun phrase	agent	2
	noun phrase	agent_semantic_type	4

(continued)

(*continued*)

Feature level	Feature Type	Feature	Categories
	noun phrase	object	2
	noun phrase	object_semantic_type	6
	noun phrase	complement	2
	noun phrase	complement_negation	2
	noun phrase	complement_semantic_type	5
	noun phrase	POS_verb	2
	noun phrase	manner	2
	noun phrase	manner_semantic_type	4
Discourse	sentence	with	2
	sentence	for_to	2
	clause	serial_verb_construction	2
	clause	order_in_SVC	3
	clause	semantic_relation_of_SVC	6
	clause	semantic_type_of_the_other_VP	7
	sentence	object_fronting	2
	sentence	syntactic function of VP	4
	sentence	FE_place	2

References

1. Levin, B.: English verb classes and alternations: A preliminary investigation. University of Chicago press, Chicago (1993)
2. Kemmerer, D.: Why can you hit someone on the arm but not break someone on the arm?—a neuropsychological investigation of the English body-part possessor ascension construction. J. Neuroling. **16**(1), 13–36 (2003)
3. Viberg, Å.: Physical contact verbs in English and Swedish from the perspective of crosslinguistic lexicology. In: Aijmer, K., Altenberg, B. (eds.) Advances in Corpus Linguistics: papers from the 23rd International Conference on English Language Research on Computerized Corpora (ICAME 23), Göteborg, Rodopi, pp. 327–352. (2004)
4. Wang, B.-H.: A lexical semantics approach: contact verbs of Chinese and the argument realization. Stud. Lang. Ling. [*Hàn-yǔ jiē-chù dòng-cí de yǔ-yì yǔ lùn-yuán biǎo-dá — cóng cí-huì yǔ-yì xué de jiǎo-dù tàn-tǎo*] **3**, 66–73 (2008). (in Chinese)
5. Zhao, M.: The valence study of Mandarin contact verbs. J. Hefei Normal Univ. [*Xiàn-dài hàn-yǔ jiē-chù dòng-cí de pèi-jià yán-jiū*] **26**, 107–110 (2008). (in Chinese)
6. Gao, H.: Notions of motion and contact for physical contact verbs. In: Svantesson, J.-O. (eds.) Proceedings of the 18th Scandinavian conference of linguistics, vol. 2, pp. 193–209. Lund University Press, Lund (2001)
7. Gao, H., Cheng, C.-C.: Verbs of contact by impact in English and their equivalents in Mandarin Chinese. Lang. Linguist. **4**(3), 485–508 (2003)

8. Liu, M.-C., Chiang, T.-Y.: The construction of Mandarin verbNet: a frame-based study of statement verbs. Lang. Linguist. **9**(2), 239–270 (2008)
9. Liu, M.: Emotion in lexicon and grammar: lexical-constructional interface of Mandarin emotional predicates. Lingua Sinica **2**(1), 1–47 (2016). https://doi.org/10.1186/s40655-016-0013-0
10. Liu, M.-C.: A frame-based morpho-constructional approach to verbal semantics. In: Kit, C.-Y., Liu, M.-C. (eds.) Empirical Corpus Linguist. Front., pp. 187–205. China Social Sciences Press, Beijing (2018)
11. Liu, M.-C., He, T.-Q., He, H.-F., Cao, Y.-F.: Mandarin physical contact verbs: a frame-based constructional approach. In: Liu, M.-C., Kit, C.-Y., Su, Q. (eds.) CLSW 2020, pp. 187–205. Springer, Hong Kong (2021). https://doi.org/10.1007/978-3-030-81197-6_17
12. Tsai, M.-C., Huang, C.-R., Chen, K.-J.: Corpus-based semantic information extraction and differentiation: a study of near synonyms. In: Proceedings of Rocling IX Computational Linguistics Conference IX, pp. 281–293. The Association for Computational Linguistics and Chinese Language Processing (ACLCLP), Taiwan (1996)
13. Liu, M.-C., Huang, C.-R., Lee, C.-Y.: Lexical information and beyond: Constructional inferences in semantic representation. In: Wang, J.-F., Wu, C.-H. (eds.) Proceedings of the 13th Pacific Asia Conference on Language, Information and Computation, pp. 27–37. National Cheng Kung University, Taiwan (1999)
14. Liu, M.-C.: From collocation to event information: the case of Mandarin verbs of discussion. Lang. Linguist. **4**(3), 563–585 (2003)
15. Tsai, M.-C.: Convenient during the process or as a result-event structure of synonymous stative verbs in TCSL. Journal of Chinese Language Teaching [*Guò-chéng fang-biàn, jiē-guǒ biàn-lì – zhuàng-tài dòng-cí shì-jiàn jié-gòu yǔ jìn-yì-cí jiāo-xué*] **8**(3), 1–22 (2011)
16. Jiang, M., Huang, C.-R.: A comparable corpus-based study of three DO verbs in varieties of Mandarin: gao. In: Chinese Lexical Semantics: 19th Workshop CLSW 2018, pp. 147–154. Springer, Taiwan (2018)
17. Neo, K.-H., Gao, H.-H.: Word learning by young bilinguals: understanding the denotation and connotation differences of 'cut' verbs in english and Chinese. In: Kwong, O. Y. (eds.) Proceedings of the 31st Pacific Asia Conference on Language, Information and Computation, pp. 241–248. City University of Hong Kong Press, Hong Kong (2017)
18. Huang, C.-R., Ahrens, K.: The function and category of gei in Mandarin ditransitive constructions. J. Chin. Linguist. **27**(2), 1–26 (1999)
19. Huang, C.-R., Ahrens, K., Chang, L.-L., Chen, K.-J., Liu, M.-C., Tsai, M.-C.: The module-attribute representation of verbal semantics: from semantic to argument structure. In: International Journal of Computational Linguistics & Chinese Language Processing: Special Issue on Chinese Verbal Semantics, pp. 19–46. IJCLCLP, Hong Kong (2000)
20. Chang, L.-L., Chen, K.-J., Huang, C.-R.: Alternation across semantic fields: A study on Mandarin verbs of emotion. Inter. J. Comput. Linguist. Chin. Lang. Process. Special Issue Chin. Verbal Semant. 61–80 (2000)
21. Liu, M.-C., Huang, C.-R., Lee, C.-C., Lee, C.-Y.: When endpoint meets endpoint: A corpus-based lexical semantic study of mandarin verbs of throwing. In: Inter. J. Comput. Linguist. Chin. Lang. Process. Special Issue Chin. Verbal Semantics, pp. 81–96. IJCLCLP, Hong Kong (2000)
22. Liao, X.-T.: A Corpus-Based Lexical Semantic Study of the Mandarin Force-Compulsion Verbs. Master's thesis of National Chiao Tung University, Hsinchu (2003)
23. Lin, M.-C., Chung. S.-F.: A corpus-based lexical semantic study of Mandarin verbs: Guān and Bì. In: Hong, J.-F., Su, Q., Wu, J.-S. (eds.) Chinese Lexical Semantics: 19th Workshop, CLSW 2018, pp. 358–371. Springer, Taiwan (2018). https://doi.org/10.1007/978-3-030-04015-4_30
24. Fillmore, C.-J.: Frame semantics. In: Linguistic Society of Korea, Linguistics in the Morning Calm, pp. 111–137. Hanshin Publishing Company, Seoul (1982)

25. Fillmore, C.-J., Atkins, B.-T.: Toward a frame-based lexicon: the semantics of 'Cut' and its neighbors. In: Lehrer, A., Kittay, E. (eds.) Frames, Fields, and Contrasts: New Essays in Semantic and Lexical Organization, pp. 75–102. Lawrence Erlbaum, Hillsdale (1992)

26. Goldberg, A.-E.: Constructions: A Construction Grammar Approach to Argument Structure. University of Chicago Press, Chicago (1995)

27. Goldberg, A.-E.: The relationships between verbs and constructions. In: Verspoor, M.H., Lee, K.-D., Sweetser, E. (eds.) Lexicon and grammar, pp. 383–398. John Benjamins Publishing, Amsterdam/Philadelphia (1997)

28. Goldberg, A.-E.: Verbs, constructions, and semantic frames. In: Hovav, M., Doron, E., Sichel, I. (eds.) Syntax, Lexical Semantics and Event Structure, pp. 39–58. Oxford University Press, Oxford (2010)

29. Liu, M.-C., Chang, C.-E.: From frame to subframe: collocational asymmetry in Mandarin verbs of conversation. Inter. J. Comput. Linguist, Chin. Lang. Process. **10**(4), 431–444 (2005)

30. He, T.-Q., Liu, M.-C., He, H.-F.: Lexical semantics of mandarin carry and hold verbs: a frame-based constructional analysis of ná and wò 握. In: Su, Q., Zhan, W.-D. (eds.) From Minimal Contrast to Meaning Construct: Corpus-based, Near Synonym Driven Approaches to Chinese Lexical Semantics, pp. 39–50. Springer, Hong Kong (2020). https://doi.org/10.1007/978-981-32-9240-6_3

31. Lin. Z.-T.: A study of the lexical meanings of the physical action verb 'Zhua' in Chinese [Hàn-yǔ shēn-tǐ dòng-zuò dòng-cí 'Zhua' de cí-yì tè-zhēng yán-jiū]. Doctoral dissertation of Nanyang Technological University, Singapore (2011). (in Chinese)

32. Chin. S.: A study of the use of the Mandarin Chinese taking verbs (NA verbs) by independent school students in Southern Malaysia [Mǎ-lái-xī-yà nán-bù dú-zhōng-shēng huá-yǔ 'NA'-lèi shǒu-bù dòng-zuò dòng-cí de yìng-yòng yán-jiū]. Doctoral dissertation of Nanyang Technological University, Singapore (2013). (in Chinese)

33. Lv, Y.: A corpus-based study of hand verbs in modern Chinese [Jī-yú yǔ liào-kù de xiàn-dài hàn-yǔ shǒu-bù dòng-cí yán-jiū]. Doctoral dissertation of Shandong University, Jinan (2008). (in Chinese)

34. Demidova, T., Solovyeva, T., Tavberidze, D.: How is the word "take" in Chinese? on the semantics and teaching of corresponding Chinese verbs. In: 11th Annual International Conference of Education, Research and Innovation (ICERI2018) Proceedings, pp. 1286–1292. IATED, Spain (2018)

35. Atkins, B.-T.-S.: Semantic ID tags: corpus evidence for dictionary senses. In: Proceedings of the Third Annual Conference of the UW Centre for the New Oxford English Dictionary, pp.17–36. University of Waterloo, Waterloo (1987)

36. Hanks, P.: Contextual dependency and lexical sets. Inter. J. Corpus Linguist. **1**(1), 75–98 (1996)

37. Divjak, D.: On trying in Russian: A tentative network model for near(er) synonyms. Slavica Gandensia **30**, 25–28 (2003)

38. Divjak, D., Gries, S.-T.: Ways of trying in Russian: Clustering behavioral profiles. Corpus Linguist. Theory **2**, 23–60 (2006)

39. Gries, S.-T., Stefanowitsch, A.: Corpus-based methods and cognitive semantics: the many senses of to run. In: Gries, S.-T., Stefanowitsch, A. (eds.) Corpora in Cognitive Linguistics, vol. 172, pp. 57–99. De Gruyter Inc., Berlin (2006)

40. Liu, M.-C.: A frame-based morpho-constructional approach to verbal semantics. In: Kit, C.-Y., & Liu, M.-C. (eds.), Empirical and Corpus Linguistic Frontiers. China Social Sciences Press, Beijing (2018)

41. Levshina, N.: How to do linguistics with R. Data exploration and statistical analysis. Benjamins, Amsterdam (2015)

42. Levshina, N., Geeraerts, D., Speelman, D.: Towards a 3D-grammar: Interaction of linguistic and extralinguistic factors in the use of Dutch causative constructions. J. Pragmat. **52**, 34–48 (2013)
43. Zakaria, M.: Behavioral Profile: Synonyms of 'Disagree. East West Journal of Humanities 6&7, 44–55 (2016–2017)
44. Liesenfeld, A., Liu, M.-C, & Huang, C.-R: Profiling the Chinese causative construction with rang, shi and ling using frame semantic features. Corpus Linguist. Theory **18**(2), 263–306 (2022)
45. Xun, E.-D., Rao, G.-Q., Xiao, X.-Y., Zang, J.-J.: The development of BCC corpus in big data. Corpus Linguistics [*Dà-shù-jù bèi-jǐng xià BCC yǔ-liào-kù de yán-zhì*] **3**(1), 93–118 (2016). (in Chinese)

Temporal *Hái* in Mandarin Chinese Revisited: A Presuppositional Account

Chih-Hsuan Chung and Jiun-Shiung Wu[⊠]

Institute of Linguistics, National Chung Cheng University, Minhsiung 621, Chiayi County, Taiwan
joanne109@alum.ccu.edu.tw, Lngwujs@ccu.edu.tw

Abstract. This paper re-examines temporal *hái* thoroughly. Two issues concerning *hái* cannot be taken care of by previous studies. The firs one is why *hái* always scopes over negation, syntactically and semantically. The second is related to the first one: why the continuation reading expressed by *hái* cannot be canceled. Temporal *hái* is argued, in this paper, to denote continuation of a situation and to presuppose modal necessity of a negated proposition, either weak epistemic necessity or deontic necessity. The two issues raised are explained in the following way: the reading which negation + *hái* could theoretically express is redundant with the presupposition, and redundancy is dispreferred. This paper also discusses other minor issues including how the underspecification between weak epistemic necessity and deontic necessity can be resolved and why it is weak epistemic necessity, instead of regular or even intensified epistemic necessity.

Keywords: Temporal *hai* · Presupposition · Semantics · Chinese

1 Introduction

Hái in Mandarin Chinese (henceforth, Chinese), often referred to as a scalar particle, has received much attention in Chinese linguistics, e.g. [1–10], etc.

[9] provides an exhaustive list of usages of *hái*: (i) repetition as in (1a), (ii) a connective marker as in (1b), (iii) an additive force as in (1c), (iv) temporal use as in (1d), (v) moderate use as in (1e), (vi) comparative use as in (1f), (vii) concessive in *háishì* 'still', as in (1g), and (viii) counter-expectation as in (1h). Let's see some examples.[1]

All correspondence regarding this paper is directed to the second author.

[1] The abbreviations used in this paper are: ASSO for an associative marker, CL for a classifier, MW for a measure word, DEON for a deontic modal, EPI for an epistemic modal, Pfv for a perfective aspect marker, Prc for a particle, Prg for a progressive aspect marker, Q for an interrogative particle.

M. Dong et al. (Eds.): CLSW 2023, LNAI 14514, pp. 225–238, 2024.
https://doi.org/10.1007/978-981-97-0583-2_18

(1) a. Tā   jīntiān lái   le,   míngtiān   hāi   huì   lái   bāngmáng.
       He   today   come   Prc   tomorrow   HAI   will come   help
       'He came today, and he will come to help again tomorrow.'

   b. Xiǎowáng   sòng   wǒ   yì-shù   huā,   hái   qǐng   wǒ
      Xiaowang   give   I   one-bouquet   flower HAI   treat I
      chī-le   yì-dùn   fàn.
      eat-Pfv   one-MW   meal
      'Xiaowang gave me a bouquet of flowers and also treated me to a meal.'

   c. Xiǎolǐ hái   qù-le   rìběn.
      Xiaoli HAI   go-Pfv   Japan
      'Xiaoli also went to Japan.'

   d. Lǎozhāng   hái   zài   shuìjiào.
      Laozhang   HAI   Prg   sleep
      'Laozhang is (was) still sleeping.

   e. Zhè-jiàn qúnzi   hái   piányí.
      this-CL   skirt   HAI   cheap
      'This skirt is moderately cheap (not too expensive or cheap).'

   f. Lǎozhāng bǐ   xiǎowáng   hāi   gāo.
      Laozhang compared.to   Xiaowang   HAI   tall
      'Laozhang is still taller than Xiaowang.'

   g. Wǒmen gāngcái   xià-le   yì-pán qí,   wǒ   háishì   shū le.
      We   just.now play-Pfv   one-MW chess   I   HAISHI   lose Pfv
      'We played chess just now. It is still the case that I lost.'

   h. Nǐ   hái   bù   qǐchuáng!
      You   HAI   not get.up
      'You are still not getting up!'
      'Lit. You should get up.'

                                                  = Ex. 1-8, pp. 237-238

Basically, those works which attempt to provide a unified semantics for all the usages of *hái* all rely on the concept of degree to a certain extent. [2] examines the gradable properties of *hāi*. [9] and [11] both utilize a scalar approach to account for the different interpretations of *hái*. [10] discuss the order-sensitivity of particles such as *hái*. [12] proposes a scale segment-based semantics for *hái*, which basically is a generalized form of degree as explicitly stated (p 569).

The temporal usage is often treated as the primary among the various usages of *hái*. [9] points out that the temporal interpretation of *hái* was developed from the *return* sense of *hái* around the 8th century. Both [11] and [12] discuss temporal *hái* first in their discussion of the possible readings of *hái*.

While it is generally agreed that temporal *hái* expresses a sense of continuation, as stated in [9, 11, 12], etc., or continuation is implied in the semantics of a proposition being true at a past time and at the reference time, e.g. [2, 8, 10], and so on, three issues are not discussed and are very difficult for those works to account for. The first one is that temporal *hái* always scopes over negation, syntactically and semantically, but not vice versa. The second is related to the first: the continuation sense expressed by *hái* cannot be canceled. Third, *yìzhí* 'always, continuously' also describes continuation of a situation. But, *yìzhí* apparently expresses continuation of different type than *hái* does, as shown by the English translations of the following two examples.

(2) a. Tā yìzhí zài shuìjià.
He continuously Prg sleep
'He has been sleeping.'
b. Tā hái zài shuìjiào.
He HAI Prg sleep
'He is still sleeping.'

Intuitively, *yìzhí* simply describes continuation of a situation, but *hái* denotes something more. So, exactly how are *yìzhí* and *hái* different? To put it another way, what does *hái* denote, which *yìzhí* does not?

In this paper, the focus is on temporal *hái*. A detailed re-examination is conducted so that the linguistic phenomena of temporal *hái* which cannot be answered by the previous studies can be accounted for. And, hopefully, this study can serve as a foundation for the quest for a new unified semantics for all the usages of *hái*.

This paper is organized as follows. Section Two is a literature review, where the analyses of *hái* are critically reviewed. The attention will be paid to temporal *hái* specifically. Section Three presents a presuppositional account for temporal *hái* and demonstrates how this prepositional account can explain what the previous accounts cannot. Section Four summarizes this paper.

2 Literature Review

[2, 9–12] all provide enlightening analyses for *hái*. Due to limited space, only [2, 9, 11] are critically reviewed here. Moreover, only the part on temporal *hái* is discussed in this section because this paper aims to conduct a thorough re-examination on temporal *hái*.

[9] approaches the semantics of *hái* from a historical perspective. *Hái*, originally pronounced as *huán*, means to return or to come/go back to somewhere around the 5th or 6th century. Then, the temporal usage, to indicate repetition, is developed around 6th-10th century. The other uses, such as exclamation, comparison, moderate sense, and *háishì*, are developed after the 10th century. Based on this historical development, [9] suggests that, among the current usages of *hái*, the temporal usage is the most basic and primary one.

Following [13, 14], [9] proposes a scalar analysis for *hái*, which induces a "scale of alternative phrases, *p* and *not-p*." The temporal usage of *hái* brings into existence a time scale corresponding to the alternative scale:

(3)

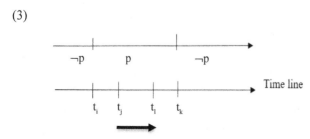

The first line in (3) is the alternative scale invoked by *hái*, which shows an alternation between *p* and ¬*p*. The second one is a timeline, where the future is on the right. Temporal *hái* draws attention to (part of) the interval where *p* is true, as shown by the bold arrow.

[9] also demonstrates how a scalar analysis such as (3) can be extended to the other uses of *hái*.[2] While [9]'s unified semantics for *hái* seems to work on the examples in her paper, there are three major problems with [9]'s proposal. The first two are pointed out in Sect. 1. First, *hái* always scopes over negation syntactically and semantically. It is not clear how [9]'s proposal explains this outscope relationship. Second, the continuation sense expressed by *hái* cannot be canceled. [9] has difficulties with this linguistic fact, as well.

The third problem with [9] is that the scalar proposal as in (3) overgeneralizes. It appears to me that a proposal such as (3) works for the temporal interpretation of perfective *le* as well. [15–17] and so on all state that perfective *le* denotes a relative anteriority reading, in addition to a perfective interpretation. To put it in a very simplified way, perfective *le* locates a situation, as a whole, before a reference time. So, basically, the alternative scale in (3) can also describe a situation presented by perfective *le*: a situation is not true before a certain time point, is true at a latter interval and is not true, again, after the interval. Perfective *le* brings attention to the interval when a situation starts, continues and terminates (or finishes). In (3), this is an interval between t_i and t_k. Obviously, this interval properly includes the interval [9] proposes to be the semantics of temporal *hái*. That is, [9]'s proposal for *hái* works for perfective *le* as well. Given this subset property, it is concluded that [9]'s scalar proposal overgeneralizes and needs further constraining to be specific for temporal *hái*.

[11] proposes another scalar analysis, based on [18]. [11], p56, summarizes her analysis as the following. First, *hái* is persistent, which means that *hái* indicates the continuation of a situation. Second, *hái* identifies an interaction between two propositions: one that can be derived from the background and the other uttered by the speaker, which contains *hái*. Third, the proposition denoted by the utterance with *hái* is stronger than the one from the background and provides more information. A proposition *p* being stronger and more informative than another proposition *q* means that *p* entails *q*, as stated on page 56. Let's see an example.

---

[2] [18] also proposes a scalar analysis for English *still*. [9] on page 267 explains how her analysis differs from [18]'s.

(4) a. **Lǎowáng** gāngcái   shìbùshì   zài   kàn   diànshì?
       Laowang just.now be.not.be Prg   watch   TV
       'Was Laowang watching TV just now?'

    b. Duì,tā xiànzài (yě)   hái   zài   kàn.
       yes, he now   (also)   HAI   Prg   watch
       'Yes, he is still watching now.'

    c. Duì,   kěshì,   tā xiànzài *hái   bù   zài   kàn.
       Yes   but   he now   HAI   not   Prg   watch
       'Yes, but he is *still not watching now.'

    d. Bù, kěshì   tā   xiànzài *hái zài kàn.
       no   but   he   now   HAI Prg watch
       'No, but he is (*still) watching now.'

[11] points out that *hái* is fine only in (4b) because the sentence entails the positive answer to the question in (4a). In (4b), *he is still watching TV now* entails *he was watching TV just now*, which is a positive answer to the question. (4c) does not entail *he was watching TV just now* and hence *hái* is not good. (4d) does not entail *he was not watching TV now* and as a result *hái* cannot be used.

While [11] shows that her scalar proposal can account for the various semantic functions of *hái*, this work still faces three major difficulties as well. Just like [9, 11]'s account cannot explain why *hái* always scope over negation syntactically and semantically and why the continuation reading expressed by *hái* cannot be canceled.

The third difficulty is specific to [11]'s proposal. What [11] refers to as an inference is, as a matter of fact, more like a presupposition. For example, [11] claims that *tā xiànzài hái zài kàn diànshì* 'he is still watching TV now' entails *tā gāngcái zài kàn diànshì* 'he was watching TV just now'. However, *tā gāngcái zài kàn diànshì* 'he was watching TV just now' must be true so that *tā xiànzài hái zài kàn diànshì* 'he is still watching TV now' can get an evaluation. If the former is not true, the latter does not make any sense, rather than be false. This is just like a standard example of a possessive's presupposition. *Tā jiějiě shì ge yīshēng* 'his sister is a doctor' presupposes that *tā yǒu ge jiějiě* 'he has a sister'. If *tā yǒu ge jiějiě* 'he has a sister' is not true, *tā jiějiě shì ge yīshēng* 'his sister is a doctor' cannot get an appropriate interpretation.

If what [11] refers to as an inference is actually a presupposition, as discussed above, then [11]'s definition of informativeness is not specific to *hái*. Instead, so-called informativeness is a property of all cases of presupposition. [22] suggests that a proposition p entails another proposition q if p presupposes q as well. That is, just like [9]'s scalar account, [11]'s proposal overgeneralizes as well, because it works for all examples of presupposition.

[2]'s proposal for temporal *hái* essentially relies on temporal precedence. She states the following (p. 600):

(5) *Temporal hái*

"Zhāngsān hái niánqīng' is true under a temporal interpretation if 'Zhangsan is young' is true at t and there is another point in time t', which precedes t, for which the proposition is also true.

[2] (ibid) further states that "[...] *hái* must be interpreted as an additive item, which contributes to the sentence of an ordered presupposition." That is, she recognizes a proposition presented by *hái* being true at a past time as a type of presupposition. Her account certainly captures the temporal reading of *hái*. However, she also faces the two problems presented in Sect. 1: why *hái* always scope over negation syntactically and semantically and why the continuation sense denoted by *hái* cannot be canceled. Moreover, her temporal account cannot distinguish *hái* from *yízhí* because the latter expresses something exactly the same as (5).

To sum up, most of the previous studies on *hái* adopt an account of degree or scale to explain its different uses and recognize its continuation/repetitive sense. However, these studies all share two major difficulties: why *hái* always outscopes negation, both syntactically and semantically, and why the continuation sense expressed by temporal *hái* cannot be canceled. Therefore, a further re-examination of the temporal use of *hái* is called for.

3   Presupposed Contradiction and Temporal *Hái*

It has been pointed out that temporal *hái* expresses continuation, such as [9, 11, 12] and so on. Moreover, it is suggested that temporal *hái* presents the continuation of a state, e.g. [2, 11], etc. Stativeness is not sufficient to characterize the aspectual property required by temporal *hái* because an activity can go with *hái* only under very restricted circumstances. Let's see some examples.

(6) a. Tā   hái   zài   shuìjiào.
        he   HAI   Prg   sleep
        'He is still sleeping.'
    b. *Tā hái   shuìjiào.
        he HAI   sleep
    c. Nǐ   hái   shuìjiào!
        you HAI   sleep
        'You are still sleeping! (You are not supposed to!)'
    d. Lǎoshī   hái   hěn   shēngqì.
        teacher   hai   very   angry
        'The teacher is still very angry.'

As shown in (6a) and (6b), *shuìjiào* 'sleep', which is an activity, needs to be in its progressive form to be compatible with *hái* under unmarked circumstances. Only functioning as a condemnation of an addressee can *hái* be used with a bare activity, just like (6c). (6d) shows that a state, such as *shēngqì* 'angry', is compatible with *hái*. All of the grammatical examples in (6), including (6c), express a continuation reading: *he sleep* continues up to a reference time.

In addition, temporal *hái* can present a negative situation and describe the continuation of a proposition being not true, that is, the proposition being false lasts for an interval. For example, (7a) states that *he not sleep* continues and (7b) says that *he cannot go to bed* continues.

(7) a. Tā hái méi shuì.
　　 he HAI not sleep
　　 'He has not slept yet.'
　　 'Lit. He is still not sleeping.'

　 b. Tā hái bù néng shuì.
　　 he HAI not can sleep
　　 'It is still the case that he can't go to bed.'

Even though it is almost a consensus that temporal *hái* expresses continuation, yet, is continuation the only meaning that *hái* can denote? The answer is negative. Let's compare *hái* to *yìzhí* 'always, continuously'. *Yìzhí* 'always, continuously' describes the continuation of a situation, just like *hái*. But, they are not always interchangeable. Let's see the examples below.

(8) a. Chuānghù yìzhí shì pùò de.
　　 window always be broken Prc
　　 'The window is always broken.'

　 b. Chuānghù hái shì pùò de.
　　 window hai be broken Prc
　　 'The window is still broken.'

(9) Q: Zhè-shàn chuānghù zěnme pùò le?
　　 this-CL window how.come broken Prc
　　 'How come this window is broken?'

　 A: Yìzhí (dōu) shì zhèyàng.
　　 always (all) be so
　　 'It's always like that.'

　 A': #Hái shì zhèyàng.
　　 HAI be so
　　 '#It is still so.'

As shown in (8), *hái* and *yìzhí* seems interchangeable. However, intuitively, these two sentences express something slightly different, even though they both describe a continuation of some sort. The question-answering pair in (9) confirms this intuition: while A tries to describe the continuation of the window being broken, only *yìzhí* is felicitous in this case, but the response with *hái* is not. The contrast in felicity between (9A) and (9A') suggests that *yìzhí* simply describes the continuation of the window being broken, nothing else, and this is why (9A) is a felicitous response to (9Q). On the other hand, while expressing the continuation of the window being broken, *hái* denotes something preventing (9A') being a felicitous response to the question (9Q). What is this something else denoted by *hái*? Let's look at another pair of examples:

(10) a. Zhème wǎn le,   nǐ   hái   bù   shuì?
        so   late Prc you   HAI   not   sleep?
        'It's been so late. Why haven't you gone to bed?'
        'Lit. It's been so late. Why is it still the case that you do not sleep?'
      b. Zhème wǎn le,   #nǐ   yìzhí bù   shuì?
        so   late Prc you   always not   sleep

(10), contrary to (9), are examples where *hái* is felicitous, but *yìzhí* is not. The difference between (10) and (9) lies in that, by uttering *zhème wǎn le* 'it's been so late', the speakers presupposes that it is already time for bed. *Yìzhí* simply describes a continuation and does not answer to this presupposition and therefore the sentence with *yìzhí* is infelicitous. Since the sentence with *hái* is a felicitous response to *zhème wǎn le* 'it's been so late', which has a presupposition as stated above, the semantics of temporal *hái* needs to address this presupposition one way or another.

I would like to argue that *hái* presupposes $\Box\neg p$, where $\Box$ is either epistemic or deontic, given *hái(p)*. That is, if we have *tā hái zài shuì* 'he HAI Prg sleep', $\Box\neg(zài(shuì(tā)))$[3] is presupposed. For *tā hái méi shuì* 'he HAI not sleep', it is presupposed that $\Box\neg(\neg shuì(tā))$, which turns out to be $\Box shuì(tā)$.

The reason why $\Box\neg p$ is treated as a presupposition is because it needs to hold so that *hái(p)* can get an interpretation. This is exactly the behavior of presupposition. *Zhāngsān-de mèimei shì yīshēng* 'Zhangsan's sister is a doctor' presupposes that *Zhangsan* has a sister. The proposition *Zhangsan has a sister* needs to hold so that the proposition *Zhāngsān-de mèimei shì yīshēng* 'Zhangsan's sister is a doctor' can get an interpretation.

The same applies to *hái*. If $\Box\neg p$ is not presupposed, to express continuation of a situation, *yìzhí* 'always, continuously', rather than *hái*, should be used. To state it slightly differently, if $\Box\neg p$ is not presupposed, *hái(p)* cannot get an appropriate interpretation. Therefore, *hái(p)* is argued to presuppose $\Box\neg p$.

One might wonder why $\Box\neg p$ is not considered as an inference. That p entails q means q is true if p is true, but the other way around does not necessary hold. Let's take a resultative verb compound (RVC) as an example. *Zhāngsān dǎpuò chuānghù* 'Zhangsan broke the window', represented as p, entails *chuānghù pò le* 'the window was broken', represented as q. That is, q is true if p is true. However, q does not have to hold first for p to get an interpretation. As a matter of fact, if q holds, it is redundant to utter p. This is why $\Box\neg p$ is not considered an inference from *hái(p)*.

(11) Presupposition of temporal *hái*.
        Suppose that p is a proposition. *hái(p)* presupposes $\Box\neg p$, where $\Box$ is either (weak) epistemic or deontic.[4]

The presuppositional account for *hái* proposed in (11) can explain the semantic difference between *hái* and *yìzhí* and the infelicity to substitute one for the other in

---

[3] Please note that formally a pronoun such as *tā* 'he/she' should be represented as a variable or an underspecified label, both of which require an antecedent, e.g. [19]. In this paper, because it does not affect our analysis of temporal *hái*, the pronoun *tā* 'he/she' is used in the formalism, as a simplification.

[4] [20] suggests that English modals such as *ought to* is weak epistemic necessity. The epistemic necessity presupposed by temporal *hái* is also weak in the same sense.

(9) and (10). In (9), the answer with *hái* is not felicitous can be explained as below. The question is about the reason of why the window is broken at the speech time. A response which states the continuation of the window being broken is a felicitous one. However, a response which describes the continuance of the window being broken with a presupposition that the window should not be broken is not felicitous because the presupposition is not part of the potential (or expected) answer to the question.

On the other hand, in (10), the response with *hái* is felicitous but the one with *yìzhí* is not. This can also be explained by the presuppositional account in the following way. One of the conversational implicatures of *zhème wǎn le* 'it's been so late' is that it is time for bed. The sentence with *yìzhí* is not felicitous because this conversational implicature is not responded to. The sentence with *hái* is felicitous because *hái*'s presupposition responds to this conversational implicature of *zhème wǎn le* 'it's been so late'.

The major advantages of the presuppositional account proposed here is that it can explain the two issues raised in Section One: why *hái* always outscopes negation syntactically and semantically, and why the continuation sense denoted by *hái* cannot be canceled. For the first one, see the examples below.

(12) a. Tā   hái   méi   shuìjiào.
         he   HAI   not   sleep
         'He has not slept (yet).'
      b. Tāi hái   bù   huì   zǒulù.
         he   HAI   not   can   walk
         'He has not been able to walk (yet).'
      c. *Tā méi   hái   shuìjiáo.
         He not   HAI   sleep
      d. *Tā bù   hái   huì   zǒulù.
         he not   HAI   can   walk

As shown in (12), negators such as *méi* and *bù* must follow *hái* in terms of syntax. In term of semantics, *hái* plus negation does not negate continuation of a situation. Instead, it expresses the continuation of a negated situation: in (12a), the continuation of *not sleep* and in (12b) the continuation of *not be able to walk*.

So, why does temporal *hái* always outscope negation syntactically and semantically? I would like to argue that the proposed presupposition of temporal *hái* plays an indispensable role in this outscoping relationship. It has been argued that *hái* presupposes $\Box\neg p$. Given a positive proposition, e.g., *tā hái zài shuìjiào* 'he HAI Prg sleep', it is presupposed that $\Box\neg sleep(he)$. For a negative proposition, such as *tā hái méi shuì* 'he HAI not sleep', its presupposition is $\Box\neg\,(\neg\, sleep(he))$, that is, $\Box sleep(he)$.

(12c) and (12d) are syntactically ill-formed because redundancy is detected between the presupposition of *hái* and what the sentences are intended to denote. The construction *neg hái VP* would denote the negation of continuation of the situation described by VP since negation syntactically precedes *hái* VP, based on the isomorphism principle proposed in [23]. As far as the construction *negation hái VP* is concerned, the presupposition of *hái* and its (intended) denotation are (almost) identical and therefore a redundancy arises. Redundancy is strongly dispreferred in language and, as a result, prevents negation from outscoping *hái*, both syntactically and semantically.

One question that immediately arises is that how Chinese expresses discontinuation of a situation, if *hái* cannot be negated. The answer is that sentential *le* plays this role. In reference grammars such as [24], sentential *le* is suggested to describe a change of state. To put it another way, sentential *le* describes discontinuation of a situation. See below.

(13)   a. Tā   hái   zài   shuì.
          He   HAI   Prg   sleep
          'He is still sleeping.'
       b. Tā   bù   shuì   le.
          he   not   sleep   Prc
          'Lit. He is not sleeping anymore.'
          'He has woken up.'

As shown in (13b), negation along with sentential *le*, together, describe discontinuation of a situation. In a sense, at least part of the semantics of sentential *le* is complementary to that of temporal *hái*.

There are some minor points about temporal *hái* raised in the literature that are discussed here. Counter-expectation and surprise are often suggested to be part of denotation of *hái*, e.g. [9–11], etc. However, On page 258, [9] points out that counter-expectation is not an inherent part of the semantics of *hái*, based on the example below:

(14)   Zhèng rú wǒ   suǒ   liào,   tā hái   zài   shuìjiào.
       just   as I   SUO   expect, he HAI Prg   sleep
       'Just as I expect, he is still sleeping.'

If *hái* expressed counter-expectation, (14) would be infelicitous. The presuppositional account argued in this paper does not contradict *zhèng rú wǒ suǒ liào* 'as I expect' and therefore has no problem here.

I agree with [9]'s proposal that counter-expectation is a conversational implicature. In fact, counter-expectation is a conversational implicature from the $\Box\neg p$. Since $\neg p$ is weak epistemic necessity or deontic necessity but p is the reality, contrast is detected. Contrast can further derive surprise and/or counter-expectation, although it is not a necessary derivation.

Yet, on page 258, [9] points out that for one of the uses of *hái* an implicature of counter-expectation is conventionalized, as shown below.

(15)   *Zhèng   rú   wǒ   suǒ   liào,   nǐ   hái   bù   kuài   bài.
        just   as   I   SUO   expect you HAI   not quickly greet

[9] suggests that the speaker expects the addressee to cease not greeting and to greet (someone) now, and hence an implicature of counter-expectation is conventionalized. However, it seems ad hoc to suggest that one of the usages of *hái* has a conventionalized implicature. I would like to argue that the incompatibility between *zhèng rú wǒ suǒ liào* 'just as I expect' and *nǐ hái bù kuài bài* 'Lit. You still do not greet (someone)! Intended: why don't you greet quickly!' comes from the incompatibility between an expectation and an imperative.

[25–27] propose that an imperative denotes a deontic ordering source. Since an imperative denotes a deontic ordering source, it cannot express possible worlds which are a subset of the worlds denoted by an expectation, which is epistemic.

The counter-expectation sense of the latter part of (15), containing *hái*, arises from the combination of the presupposition $\Box\neg p$ and an imperative. *Nǐ hái bù kuài bài* 'greet (somebody) quickly' is an order for an addressee to perform this action. The presupposition of *hái* in this case is $\Box\neg(\neg bài(nǐ, \_))$[5], which can be reduced to $\Box bài(nǐ, \_)$. Because in this example *p* is a deontic necessity but the reality is $\neg p$, $hái(\neg p)$ denoting an imperative helps the addressee infer that something which should have been carried out has not be carried out yet. Hence, counter-expectation is derived. There is no need to treat one of the uses of *hái* as a conventionalized implicature.

Moreover, on page 271, [9] states that $hái(p)$ presupposes that *p* is true at a time in the past of a reference time. This temporal semantics is shared in the literature, such as [2, 8, 10, 12], etc. But, I would like to suggest that this temporal semantics is not a presupposition of *hái*, but an inherent, indispensable part of the semantics of *hái*.

It has been pointed out that temporal *hái* expresses continuation in the literature. Since temporal *hái* expresses continuation of a situation, the proposition that describes the situation remains true for a period of time, up to a reference time, which is realized as the speech time under neural circumstances. That is, that *p* is true at a time in the past of a reference time is *not* a presupposition or inference, but is, in fact, an inherent part of the temporal semantics of *hái*.

The last issue is concerning the weak epistemic necessity or deontic necessity in the presupposition of *hái*. Essentially, whether the presupposition is weak epistemic necessity or deontic necessity is determined contextually, as shown in the following examples.

(16) a.Tā   hái   zài   shuìjiào?   Tā   fángjiān-de   dēng   bù   shì   liàng
      he   HAI   Prg   sleep   he   room-ASSO   light not be   on
      le   ma?
      Prc Q
      'He is still sleeping? Aren't the lights in his room already on?'
      → weak epistemic necessity presupposition

   b. Tā   hái   zài   shuìjiào?   Bù   shì   zǎo   gāi   xǐng   le!?
      he   HAI   Prg   sleep   not be   early DEON   wake.up   Prc
      'He is still sleeping? Shouldn't he have waked up already?'
      → deontic necessity presupposition

The weak epistemic-deontic necessity underspecified in the presupposition of *hái* in (16) is resolved contextually. Specifically, it is resolved by the sentence following *tā hái zài shuìjiào* 'he is still sleeping' in (16a) and (16b). In (16a), *the lights in his room being on already* helps the speaker make an educational guess regarding whether he is awake or not. This continuance resolves the underspecification to weak epistemic necessity. On

---

[5] *Bài* 'greet' is a transitive verb, which subcategorizes for both a subject and an object. In this example, the object is understood from the context. An underline is used to represent an understood object in the formula.

the other hand, in (16b) the deontic modal *gāi* 'should' resolves the underspecification to deontic necessity.

Many pragmatic factors can help with this underspecification resolution, including speaker's attitude toward a situation, the compatibility of a situation with an epistemic reading or a deontic reading, etc. Let's see two examples.

(17) a. Tā   hái   zài   nào.
        he   HAI   Prg   make.noise
        'He is still making noise.'
    b. Fàncài   hái   rè.   Gǎnkuài   chī.
       Food   HAI   warm   quickly   eat
       'The food is still warm. Hurry and eat.'

People's attitude to someone making noise is negative and the behavior is dispreferred or even not allowed. Therefore, the presupposition of (17a) is a deontic one. On the other hand, it is very difficult, if possible at all, get a deontic interpretation for food being warm. Moreover, (17b) is used when the food has been left on the table for a while and people would think that the food might not be warm anymore. As a result, the presupposition of (17b) is an epistemic one.

As for why it is *weak* epistemic necessity, instead of regular epistemic necessity, the answer is that the reality has been spelled out and regular epistemic necessity is too strong for such as case. Let's use (17b) as an example for illustration. The reality is that the food is warm at the speech time. If the speaker uses *huì*, regular epistemic necessity modal in Chinese, or *yídìng*, an intensified epistemic necessity modal, as argued in [28], the presupposition would seem like an overstatement or even a contradiction to the reality. Therefore, if the presupposition of *hái* expresses epistemic necessity, it is weak epistemic necessity.

To sum up, *hái*(*p*) is argued to denote continuation of *p* and to presuppose $\Box\neg p$, where $\Box$ is either weak epistemic necessity or deontic necessity. Two issues are addressed in this section, which cannot be explained by the previous studies. First, why does *hái* always outscope negation, both syntactically and semantically? Second, why can't the continuation sense expressed by *hái* be canceled? These two issues are explained in the following way. Based on the isomorphism principle proposed in [23], the construction negation + *hái* will express discontinuation of a situation. However, *hái* presupposes that $\Box\neg p$. This results in redundancy, which is not preferred. Other minor points raised in the literature are discussed: whether *hái* inherently expresses counter-expectation, whether counter-expectation is a conversational implicature, and whether a proposition being true at a past time is a presupposition, an inference or an inherent part of the semantics of *hái*. Finally, two issues concerning the weak epistemic necessity and deontic necessity are clarified: how the underspecification between weak epistemic necessity and deontic necessity are resolved and why it is *weak* epistemic necessity.

4 Conclusion

This paper focuses on temporal *hái* only. Two questions are raised, with which the previous studies all have difficulties. First, why does *hái* always outscope negation, both syntactically and semantically? Second, related to the first one, why can't the continuation sense denoted by *hái* be canceled? *hái(P)* is argued to present continuation of a situation and to presuppose $\Box \neg p$. The fact that *hái* must outscope negation syntactically and semantically and that the continuation sense denoted by *hái* cannot be canceled is because redundancy arises between the presupposition and what the negation + *hái* could theoretically denote. A few more issues are clarified: whether counter-expectation is part of the semantics of *hái*, whether counter-expectation is a conversational implicature, and whether *p* being true at a time in the past of a reference time is a presupposition, an inference or actually an inherent part of the semantics of *hái*, how the resolution of underspecification between weak epistemic necessity and deontic necessity is conducted and why it is weak epistemic necessity, rather than regular or even intensified epistemic necessity.

References

1. Alleton, V.: Les adverbs en chinois modern. Mouton, Hague (1972)
2. Donazzan, M.: Presupposition on Times and Degrees: The Semantics of Mandarin Hái. In Chan, M., Kang, H. (eds.): Proceedings of the 20th North American Conference on Chinese Linguistics, pp. 597–610. Ohio State University, Ohio (2008)
3. E, C.: Syntactic behaviors driven by lexical semantics: a study on *geng* (更) and *hai* (還) in Chinese comparatives. In Lu, Q., Gao, H. (eds): Chinese Lexical Semantics, CLSW 2015, LNAI 9332. Springer, Switzerland, pp. 408–417 (2015)
4. Jiang, Q., Jin, L.: Zai yu hai chongfuyi de bijiao yanjiu [on the repetitive use of *zai* and *hai*]. Zhonguo yuwen [Chinese Language], 187–191 (1997)
5. Lǚ, S. (ed.): Xiandai hanyu ba bai ci zengding ben [Eight hundred words in Modern Chinese: Extended Version]. Shangwuj, Bejing (2015)
6. Ma, Z.: Guanyu biaoshi chengduqian de fuci "hai" [on the adverb *hai* expressing a lower degree]. Zhongguo yuwen [Chinese Language], 166–172 (1984)
7. Paris, M.: Encore 'encore' en Mandarin: *hai* et *haishi*. In: Proceedings of the XXXth European Conference of Chinese Studies (Cina 21). Istituto Italiano per l'Africa e l'Oriente, Roma, pp. 265–279 (1988)
8. Yang, C.: On the syntax-semantics interface of focus particles: the additive particle 還 *hai* in Mandarin Chinese. Lingua Sinica **3**, 1–33 (2017)
9. Yeh, M.: On *hai* in Mandarin. J. Chin. Linguist. **26**, 236–280 (1988)
10. Zhang, L., Ling, J.: Additive particle with a built-in Gricean pragmatics: the Semantics of German *noch*, Chinese *hái* and Hungarian *még*. Proc. Linguist. Soc. Am. **1**, 1–15 (2016)
11. Liu, F.: 2000. The scalar particle *hai* in Chinese. Cahiers de linguistique – Asie Orientale **29**, 41–84 (2000)
12. Luo, Q.: A scale segment-based Semantics for Mandarin Chiense Adverb *hai*. Yuyan kexue [Language Science] **19**, 592–609 (2020)
13. König, E.: Temporal and non-temporal uses of noch and schon in German. Linguist. Philos. **1**, 173–198 (1977)
14. Löbner, S.: Schon-erst-noch: an integrated analysis. Linguist. Philos. **12**, 167–212 (1989)
15. Lin, J.: Temporal reference in Mandarin Chinese. J. East Asian Linguist. **12**, 259–311 (2003)

16. Lin, J.: Time in a language without tense: the case of Chinese. J. Semant. **23**, 1–53 (2006)
17. Wu, J.: The semantics of the perfective LE and its context-dependency: an SDRT approach. J. East Asian Linguis. **14**, 299–366 (2005)
18. Michaelis, L.: 'Continuity' within three scalar models: the polysemy of adverbial *still*. J. Semant. **10**, 193–237 (1993)
19. Asher, N., Lascarides, A.: Logics of Conversation. Cambridge University, Cambridge (2003)
20. von Fintel, K., Iatridou, S.: 2008. How to say ought in foreign: the composition of weak necessity modals. In: Guéron, J., Lecarem, J. (eds.) Time and modality, pp. 115–141. Springer, Berlin (2008)
21. Fillmore, C., Kay, P., O'Connor, C.: Regularity and idiomaticity in grammatical constructions: the last of *let alone*. Language **64**(1988), 501–538 (1988)
22. Kadmon, N.: Formal Pragmatics. Blackwell, Malden, Massachusetts (2001)
23. Huang, H.: On the scope phenomena of Chinese quantifiers. J. Chinese Linguist. **9**(1981), 226–243 (1981)
24. Tang, S.: Aspectual system. In: Huang, C., Shi, D. (eds.) A Reference Grammar of Chinse, pp. 116–142. Cambridge University, Cambridge (2016)
25. Portner, P.: The semantics of imperatives within a theory of clause types. In: Young, R. (ed.) SALT XIV, pp. 235–252. Cornel University, Ithaca (2004)
26. Portner, P.: Imperatives and modals. Nat. Lang. Seman. **15**, 351–383 (2007)
27. Portner, P.: Imperatives. In: Aloni, M., Dekker, P. (eds.) Cambridge Handbook of Formal Semantics, pp. 593–626. Cambridge University, Cambridge (2016)
28. Wu, J.: Intensification and Modal Necessity in Mandarin Chinese. Routledge, London (2019)

A Study on Semantic Shift of Uncivilized Words in Bullet-Screen Comments

Juanjuan Fan[1]([envelope]) [ORCID] and Jianguo Yang[2] [ORCID]

[1] Training Department, Beijing Chinese Language and Culture College, Beijing, China
fanjuanjuan@bjhwxy.com
[2] Beijing Philosophy and Social Science Research Center for Intercultural Studies, Beijing Language and Culture University, Beijing, China

Abstract. Based on the theory of sentiment analysis and semantic prosody, this paper investigates the semantic shift of uncivilized words in bullet-screen comments by analyzing the sentiment polarity of co-occurrence emotional words. According to the swear level and frequency of uncivilized words in the bullet-screen dataset, six kinds of words are selected for analysis. Within both the bullet-screen dataset and the BCC corpus, the semantic shifts of prototypes and their alternative forms are gauged using the sentiment lexicon and the PMI-IR algorithm. The paper offers a statistical analysis of the semantic shifts observed in these uncivilized terms and subsequently delves into the underlying motivations for these shifts.

Keywords: Bullet-Screen Comments · Uncivilized Words · Semantic Shift · Sentiment Lexicon · PMI-IR Algorithm

1 Introduction

The emergence and swift growth of the bullet-screen culture have transformed traditional methods of film and television consumption. The audience's perception structure has shifted from mere "watching" and "appreciating" to actively "intervening" and "participating" [1]. Bullet screens serve as a medium for users to instantly convey their emotions and reactions to video content. Given the constraints of time and the word count, bullet-screen comments are typically spontaneous, reflecting the audience's immediate impressions [2]. Most viewers post brief comments or phrases as they watch, encapsulating their personal feelings and reactions. As such, bullet-screen comments tend to be succinct and mirror everyday spoken language, where uncivilized terms are not uncommon.

The existing research on uncivilized words primarily focuses on static descriptions, categorizing their usage and other characteristics. The dynamic shifts in the usage of these words, however, have received limited attention. While static analyses are valuable, understanding the evolving nature of language usage is equally crucial. Based on a large number of the bullet-screen dataset and the co-occurrence relationship between uncivilized words and emotional words, this paper calculates the frequency of uncivilized words appearing in various contexts, and then pinpoints the positive semantic shift values associated with these terms.

© The Author(s), under exclusive license to Springer Nature Singapore Pte Ltd. 2024
M. Dong et al. (Eds.): CLSW 2023, LNAI 14514, pp. 239–253, 2024.
https://doi.org/10.1007/978-981-97-0583-2_19

2 Construction of a Semantic Shift Measurement Model for Bullet-Screen Comments

2.1 Acquisition of Bullet-Screen Comments

We employed Python to extract bullet-screen comments from Bilibili. The videos covered 17 themes on Bilibili, encompassing entertainment, life, science and technology, knowledge, fashion, cars, games, sports, drama, food, music, film and television, news, animation, dance, national innovation, and more. For each theme, we selected the top 100 videos based on popularity from October 1, 2021, to January 1, 2022. This amounted to a total of 1,700 videos and 4,373,359 bullet-screen comments.

In the word collocation studies, it was appropriate to define the span as -4/ + 4 or -5/ + 5 [3]. We analyzed the character length of the extracted bullet-screen comments, finding an average length of 10.5 characters. From the results, it can be seen that the character length of bullet-screen comments aligns well with the lexical span of -5/ + 5.

2.2 Selection of Uncivilized Words

Ruth Wajnryb [4] categorized uncivilized words into three concentric circles: the geo-center, the earth's surface, and the surrounding atmosphere. The uncivilized words in Chinese also have the core circle and non-core circle. Sexual behavior, sexual organ, gender and age are undoubtedly the "core circle" of uncivilized words in Chinese. These words have the highest level of swearing.

Sexual Behavior and Sexual Organ. Zhang [5] pointed out that the most representative uncivilized words were predominantly linked to sexual organ or sexual behavior. Among the typical Chinese uncivilized words, the words 屄*bī*'female genitalia', 屌*diǎo*'male genitalia', 尻*kāo*'buttocks', 肏*cào*'copulate', 入*rì*'copulate' are seldom employed in written form, with alternative versions being more common. Phonetic-based alternatives are particularly popular among netizens [6].

Gender and Age. Lu [7] identified 他妈的*tā mā de*'Damn it!' as one of the most emblematic swear words in China, given its widespread usage, high frequency, varied linguistic forms, and diverse contexts of application. Since Lu's mention of 他妈的*tā mā de*, several scholars [5, 8, 9] have successively conducted research on it. Previous studies have shown that the emotions expressed by words containing 妈*mā*'mother' have changed.

Considering the severity of swearing, frequency, and other criteria, we chose the following six types of words for our analysis (Table 1).

2.3 Analysis Steps of Bullet-Screen Comments

Based on the co-occurrence of emotional words and uncivilized words in semantic prosody, this study employed sentiment polarity analysis of co-occurring emotional words or the sentences they appeared in to detect the semantic shift of uncivilized words. The measurement model for this semantic shift encompassed the following steps:

Table 1. Frequency of using alternative forms of bullet-screen comments.

Prototypes	Alternative forms	Frequency
肏 cào 'copulate'	卧槽 wò cáo	13727
	握草 wò cǎo	1454
	woc/Woc/WOC	1194
	我擦 wǒ cā	1133
入 rì 'copulate'	rnm	573
	沃日 wò rì	128
尻 kāo 'buttocks'	我靠 wǒ kào	3752
	我考 wǒ kǎo	22
屄 bī 'female genitalia'	mb	58
屌 diǎo 'male genitalia'	沙雕 shā diāo	969
	碉堡 diāo bǎo	63
妈 mā 'mother'	tm	5707
	特么 tè me	2070
	他妈 tā mā	1509
	踏马 tà mǎ	723
	尼玛 ní mǎ	1528
	你妈 nǐ mā	151
	你妹 nǐ mèi	244

(1) Bullet-screen Crawling:

Extracted data from 1,700 videos across 17 themes on Bilibili.

(2) Text Preprocessing:

Filtered out noisy text, such as illegal characters, from the bullet-screen comments.

(3) Bullet-screen Dataset Construction:

Constructed a bullet-screen dataset.

(4) Construction of an Uncivilized Words Dictionary:

(1) Integrated existing dictionaries and consulted the works of relevant scholars to create a foundational uncivilized words dictionary.

(2) Selected 9 videos of popular game anchors labeled by "Zu'an culture" and processed 28,108 bullet-screen comments through word segmentation. Post-segmentation, part-of-speech tagging was performed. Uncivilized words from nouns, verbs, adjectives, and interjections were then added to expand the dictionary.

(5) Construction of Sentiment Lexicon and Rule Base:

(1) Sentiment Lexicon: Scholars from psychology, linguistics, and natural language processing have explored emotions and their classifications [10, 11]. On the basis of HowNet, TSING, NTUSD, DLUT-Emotionontology and CLIWC dictionary,

770 emotional words were incorporated. Words with inconsistent labels across dictionaries or those with both positive and negative connotations were excluded. The final lexicon comprised 33,813 emotional words, with 15,537 being positive and 18,276 negative.

(2) Emotional Rule Base: This included negative words, degree adverbs, association markers (labels for transitional, causal, and coordinate relationships), and sentence rules (end-of-sentence punctuation, rhetorical question).

(6) Statement Recognition:

(1) Identified bullet-screen comments containing uncivilized words, excluding those with only uncivilized words and no co-occurring emotional words.

(2) Extracted uncivilized words and used Jieba segmentation software for sentence breakdown.

(7) Sentiment Polarity Analysis:

Using the sentiment lexicon and rule base, the sentiment polarity of bullet-screen sentences containing uncivilized words was analyzed.

(8) Semantic Shift Analysis:

Following the sentiment polarity analysis, a statistical analysis was conducted to understand the semantic shift of uncivilized words.

3   Semantic Shift Measurement Based on Sentiment Lexicon

3.1   肏 *cào* 'copulate'

Table 2. Measurement results of semantic shift: 肏 cào 'copulate'.

Source of corpus	Written form	Positive usage frequency	Negative usage frequency
BCC Corpus	我肏 wǒ cào	11	54
	我操 wǒ cāo	435	991
Bullet-screen Dataset	卧槽 wò cáo	3219	1024
	握草 wò cǎo	254	116
	woc/Woc/WOC	205	98
	我擦 wǒ cā	155	92

Neither 我肏 *wǒ cào* nor 我操 *wǒ cāo* appeared in the bullet-screen dataset, prompting us to source these words from the BCC corpus. Within the BCC corpus, 我肏 *wǒ cào* was used positively 11 times and negatively 54 times. For 我操 *wǒ cāo*, there were 435 positive instances and 991 negative ones. This indicated that both 我肏 *wǒ cào* and 我操 *wǒ cāo* were still mainly used in negative semantic prosody.

From the analysis results of the bullet-screen dataset, it can be seen that the positive usage frequencies of 卧槽 *wò cáo*, 握草 *wò cǎo*, woc/Woc/WOC, and 我擦 *wǒ cā* were higher than the negative usage frequencies. This indicated that these terms had begun to be widely used in positive semantic context (Table 2).

3.2   入 *rì* 'copulate'

Table 3. Measurement results of semantic shift: 入 *rì* 'copulate'.

Source of corpus	Written form	Positive usage frequency	Negative usage frequency
BCC Corpus	我日 wǒ rì	387	900
	日你妈 rì nǐ mā	18	271
Bullet-screen Dataset	沃日 wò rì	29	27
	rnm	28	411

We conducted a search for the prototype 我日 *wǒ rì* within the BCC corpus and found that its usage frequency was notably high. Out of the first 1,500 instances we analyzed, 387 were positive and 900 were negative. From the data, it can be seen that 我日 *wǒ rì* mainly appeared in the negative semantic prosody. However, in the bullet-screen dataset, 沃日 *wǒ rì* underwent a positive semantic shift, appearing slightly more in positive contexts than negative ones (Table 3).

In the BCC corpus, the term 日你妈 *rì nǐ mā* 'fuck your mother' appeared 306 times. Out of these, 18 instances were positive, while 271 were negative. This indicated that 日你妈 *rì nǐ mā* was mainly used with a negative semantic prosody and had a minimal positive shift. The swearing level of the Pinyin abbreviation form "rnm" was still relatively high. Upon further analysis of example sentences, this high swearing level can be attributed to the frequent use of the internet slang "rnm, 退钱 *tuì qián* 'refund me money'".

3.3   尻 *kāo* 'buttocks'

Table 4. Measurement results of semantic shift: 尻 *kāo* 'buttocks'.

Source of corpus	Written form	Positive usage frequency	Negative usage frequency
BCC Corpus	我尻 wǒ kāo	0	7
	我靠 wǒ kào	683	382
Bullet-screen Dataset	我考 wǒ kǎo	10	3

Within the BCC corpus, 我尻 *wǒ kāo* was exclusively used in a negative context, with no instances of positive usage. However, in the bullet-screen dataset, 我靠 *wǒ kào* was predominantly used in a positive semantic prosody, far outweighing its negative usage. While the overall frequency of 我考 *wǒ kǎo* was not high, its usage was still primarily characterized by a positive semantic prosody (Table 4).

Table 5. Measurement results of semantic shift: 屄 *bī* 'female genitalia'.

Source of corpus	Written form	Positive usage frequency	Negative usage frequency
BCC Corpus	妈屄 mā bī	2	15
	妈逼 mā bī	376	889
	妈比 mā bǐ	165	277
Bullet-screen Dataset	mb	4	16
	逼 bī	25	25

3.4 屄 *bī* 'female Genitalia'

Within the BCC corpus, 妈屄 *mā bī*, 妈逼 *mā bī* and 妈比 *mā bǐ* were mainly used with a negative connotation, appearing more frequently in negative semantic prosody. Among these, 妈屄 *mā bī* exhibited the least positive shift, appearing in a positive context only twice. While 妈逼 *mā bī* and 妈比 *mā bǐ* had a higher frequency in positive semantic prosody, they were still primarily characterized by negative connotations (Table 5).

In the bullet-screen dataset, 16 cases of "mb" appeared in negative semantic prosody, and only 4 cases appeared in positive semantic prosody, indicating that "mb" was mainly used negatively. Further semantic shift analysis of 逼 *bī* when used as a noun revealed that its occurrence in both positive and negative prosody was evenly matched.

3.5 屌 *diǎo* 'male Genitalia'

Table 6. Measurement results of semantic shift: 屌 *diǎo* 'male genitalia'.

Source of corpus	Written form	Positive usage frequency	Negative usage frequency
BCC Corpus	傻屌 shǎ diǎo	10	68
	屌爆 diǎo bào	753	449
Bullet-screen Dataset	沙雕 shā diāo	241	66
	碉堡 diāo bǎo	14	1

The prototype 傻屌 *shǎ diǎo* 'dumbass' predominantly appeared with a negative semantic prosody. In contrast, its alternative form 沙雕 *shā diāo* had a noticeably milder swearing tone. The frequency of 沙雕 *shā diāo* in positive semantic prosody was significantly higher than in negative contexts, indicating a positive semantic shift (Table 6).

The prototype 屌爆 *diǎo bào* 'Damn cool!' appeared more frequently in positive semantic prosody than in negative semantic prosody. 碉堡 *diāo bǎo*, the primary online alternative form of 屌爆 *diǎo bào*, had a relatively low overall frequency in the bullet-screen dataset. However, its positive shift value was notably high, with only one instance of negative usage.

3.6 妈 *mā* 'mother'

Table 7. Measurement results of semantic shift: 妈 *mā* 'mother'.

Source of corpus	Written form	Positive usage frequency	Negative usage frequency
Bullet-screen Dataset	tm	1025	639
	特么 tè me	397	241
	他妈 tā mā	365	397
	踏马 tà mǎ	134	85
	尼玛 ní mǎ	104	214
	你妈 nǐ mā	10	14
	你妹 nǐ mèi	13	27

Lu [7] highlighted that the term 他妈的 *tā mā de* 'Damn it!' was occasionally used in unconventional manners: either to convey surprise or to express a sigh. As early as 1925, Lu had observed instances where 他妈的 *tā mā de* was used to denote positive emotions. Nearly a century later, how have these "exceptional uses" evolved?

The probability of 他妈 *tā mā* 'his mother' appearing in the positive semantic prosody was slightly lower than that in the negative semantic prosody. Contrasting with Lu's observation of its "occasional" positive use, 他妈 *tā mā* in bullet-screen comments was frequently associated with positive sentiments, indicating a gradual positive semantic shift. The alternative forms "tm", 特么 *tè me*, and 踏马 *tà mǎ* were more commonly found in positive semantic prosody than in negative, suggesting a positive semantic shift for these terms as well. On the other hand, terms like 尼玛 *ní mǎ* 'your mother', 你妈 *nǐ mā* 'your mother', and 你妹 *nǐ mèi* 'your sister' primarily exhibited a negative semantic shift, predominantly appearing in negative semantic prosody (Table 7).

4 Semantic Shift Measurement Based on PMI-IR Algorithm

The PMI-IR algorithm is a widely-used, corpus-based method that merges Point-wise Mutual Information with Information Retrieval. It gauges the association degree between words by examining the text co-occurrence rate of the target words and seed words. This, in turn, helps determine the semantic shift of the analyzed words. The calculation method of word sentiment polarity based on PMI generally includes the following steps: initially selecting positive and negative seed words, then computing the co-occurrence probability of the target words and seed words within the corpus, and finally ascertaining the sentiment tendency of the target words based on this co-occurrence probability [12]. Based on this algorithm, we assess the semantic of uncivilized words as detailed below:

4.1 Selection of Emotional Seed Words

High-Frequency Seed Words. We began by selecting seed words that appeared frequently. A statistical analysis was conducted on the co-occurrence probability of the target words and the seed words. Words with a higher co-occurrence probability were chosen as potential seed word candidates.

Seed Words with Clear Sentiment and High Emotional Intensity. Seed words should have distinct positive or negative connotations and exhibit high emotional intensity values. For determining these values, we primarily referred to the emotional intensity scores in the DLUT-Emotionontology and BOSON sentiment lexicons. We assessed the emotional intensity values of high-frequency candidate seed words and ultimately chose those with pronounced positive or negative sentiments that were commonly found in the bullet-screen dataset. This led to the selection of 20 positive and 20 negative seed words.

4.2 Calculate the Mutual Information Value with the Emotional Seed Word

Calculate the mutual information value of the analyzed word and positive emotional word:

$$\text{PMI(word, posword)} = \log_2\left(\frac{\text{p(word\&posword)}}{\text{p(word)} \times \text{p(posword)}}\right) = \log_2\left(\frac{\text{C(word\&posword)} \times N}{\text{C(word)} \times \text{C(posword)}}\right) \quad (1)$$

Calculate the mutual information value of the analyzed word and negative emotional word:

$$\text{PMI(word, negword)} = \log_2\left(\frac{\text{p(word\&negword)}}{\text{p(word)} \times \text{p(negword)}}\right) = \log_2\left(\frac{\text{C(word\&negword)} \times N}{\text{C(word)} \times \text{C(negword)}}\right) \quad (2)$$

4.3 Semantic Shift Calculation

The mutual information value of negative emotional words is subtracted from the mutual information value of positive emotional words, and then the value of semantic positive shift is determined according to the difference between them.

Calculation formula:

$$\text{SO} - \text{PMI(word)} = \sum_{\text{posword} \in \text{Poswords}} \text{PMI(word, posword)} - \sum_{\text{negword} \in \text{Negwords}} \text{PMI(word, negword)}$$

$$(3)$$

The larger the value of analysis results, the higher the mutual information value between the analyzed word and the positive emotional word. The smaller the value, the higher the mutual information value between the analyzed word and the negative emotional word.

4.4 Measurement Results and Analysis

From the measurement outcomes, several observations can be made:

Among the alternative forms of 肏 *cào* 'copulate', "woc" exhibited the highest positive shift value, followed by 我擦 *wǒ cā*, 握草 *wò cǎo*, and 卧槽 *wò cáo*. In the 入 *rì* 'copulate'

Table 8. Semantic shift measurement results based on PMI-IR algorithm.

Category	Written form	Mutual information value
肏 *cào* 'copulate'	卧槽 wò cáo	-15.45264
	握草 wò cǎo	-8.19745
	woc/Woc/WOC	-4.92130
	我擦 wǒ cā	-5.85490
入 *rì* 'copulate'	rnm	-13.42652
	沃日 wò rì	-8.36475
尻 *kāo* 'buttocks'	我靠 wǒ kào	-22.39395
	我考 wǒ kǎo	-18.70949
屄 *bī* 'female genitalia'	mb	-6.52591
屌 *diǎo* 'male genitalia'	沙雕 shā diāo	-9.04670
	碉堡 diāo bǎo	-1.89844
妈 *mā* 'mother'	tm	-15.75603
	特么 tè me	-25.96223
	他妈 tā mā	-29.67201
	踏马 tà mǎ	-20.98570
	尼玛 ní mǎ	-22.43752
	你妈 nǐ mā	2.49477
	你妹 nǐ mèi	-9.09301

word category, 沃日 *wò rì* had a higher positive shift value than "rnm". For the 尻 *kāo* 'buttocks' category, 我考 *wǒ kǎo* surpassed 我靠 *wǒ kào* in terms of positive shift. Regarding the 屄 *bī* 'female genitalia' words, only "mb" was analyzed for mutual information value. While "mb" leaned negative, its value wasn't particularly high. The word 逼 *bī* wasn't analyzed due to its rich semantic meanings, with five distinct interpretations, making it challenging for the algorithm to differentiate between them. In the 屌 *diǎo* 'male genitalia' category, 沙雕 *shā diāo* remained negative, whereas 碉堡 *diāo bǎo* leaned positive (Table 8).

Among the 妈 *mā* 'mother' words, the prototype 他妈 *tā mā* 'his mother' had the least positive shift, while "tm" had the most. The PMI calculation result of 你妈 *nǐ mā* 'your mother' was positive, which was contrary to our expectations. The alternative 尼玛 *ní mǎ* 'your mother' remained negative, but 你妹 *nǐ mèi* 'your sister' had a relatively high positive shift.

In the process of data analysis, the limitations of PMI-IR algorithm are exposed. First of all, this algorithm heavily relies on corpus. If the frequency of the occurrence of analyzed words and emotional words in the corpus is very low, the accuracy of mutual information value calculation cannot be guaranteed. Secondly, the algorithm does not distinguish multiple meanings of words. There are not many monosyllabic words in Chinese, which makes the applicability of the algorithm greatly reduced. For instance, the high frequency co-occurrence words of 我考*wǒ kǎo* include meanings related to "scholarship", "achievement", "full mark" and "pass", which are more related to "exam" than the uncivilized words under analysis. Despite these drawbacks, the PMI-IR algorithm can still serve as a supplementary tool for analyzing the general trend of word semantic evolution.

5   Analysis of Semantic Shift Measurement Results

Data analysis reveals that the lexical system of uncivilized words undergoes changes both within the system members and in the semantics of each member.

5.1   Evolution of Members

At present, primary approach to standardizing internet language involves filtering and blocking sensitive words. More and more words are added to the filtering and shielding system. As more words are added to this filtering system, netizens have innovatively employed homophonic and font changes to bypass these restrictions [13].

The alternative form refers to the replacement of older uncivilized words with new words or forms. For example, 我入*wǒ rì* and 我尻*wǒ kāo* have largely been replaced by 我日*wǒ rì* and 我靠*wǒ kào*. The coexistence form refers to the coexistence of different word forms in the same period. The different word forms are used by netizens. Both 屌爆了*diǎo bào le* and 碉堡了*diāo bǎo le* are popular among netizens. Various written forms such as 牛逼*niú bī*, 牛比*niú bǐ*, and 牛B*niú* B are prevalent across different online platforms.

The emergence of new words can be attributed to two primary reasons: new terms for novel concepts and new terms for existing concepts. While new words often arise to describe emerging phenomena or to cater to societal and communicative needs, they also adapt to shifts in people's perspectives and mindsets [14]. The proliferation of new uncivilized expressions on the internet is not solely due to these reasons but also stems from efforts to evade online filters, seek novelty, and garner attention. This has spurred the evolution of the uncivilized word system.

5.2   Semantic Evolution

The semantics of uncivilized words have diversified. While they were traditionally used to convey negative sentiments, they are now frequently employed to express positive emotions. We term this transition from a negative to positive semantic prosody as a "positive semantic shift".

To determine the positive semantic shift value of uncivilized word prototypes and their alternatives, we employ the sentiment lexicon and PMI-IR algorithm. Using the sentiment lexicon algorithm, the semantic shift of uncivilized words is gauged by the polarity of co-occurring emotional words. When uncivilized words appear alongside positive emotional words, their sentiment polarity is deemed positive, and vice versa.

The semantic positive shift value serves as an indicator of a word's degree of semantic shift. The calculation method for semantic positive shift value is as follows:

Semantic Positive Shift Value = Frequency of Positive Word Usage / (Frequency of Positive + Negative Word Usage).

Table 9. Statistics of Semantic Positive Shift Values.

Category	Written form	Sentiment lexicon	PMI-IR
肏 cào 'copulate'	我肏 wǒ cào	0.17	
	我操 wǒ cāo	0.31	
	woc/Woc/WOC	0.68	-4.92130
	握草 wò cǎo	0.69	-8.19745
	卧槽 wò cáo	0.76	-15.45264
	我擦 wǒ cā	0.76	-5.85490
	哇塞 wa sài	0.87	-4.67144
入 rì 'copulate'	我日 wǒ rì	0.30	
	沃日 wò rì	0.52	-8.36475
	日你妈 rì nǐ mā	0.06	
	rnm	0.06	-13.42652
尻 kāo 'buttocks'	我尻 wǒ kāo	0.00	
	我靠 wǒ kào	0.64	-22.39395
	我考 wǒ kǎo	0.77	-18.70949
屄 bī 'female genitalia'	妈屄 mā bī	0.12	
	妈逼 mā bī	0.30	
	妈比 mā bǐ	0.37	
	mb	0.20	-6.52591
屌 diǎo 'male genitalia'	傻屌 shǎ diǎo	0.13	
	沙雕 shā diāo	0.79	-9.04670
	屌爆 diǎo bào	0.63	
	碉堡 diāo bǎo	0.93	-1.89844
妈 mā 'mother'	他妈 tā mā	0.48	-29.67201
	踏马 tà mǎ	0.61	-20.98570
	特么 tè me	0.62	-25.96223
	tm	0.62	-15.75603
	你妈 nǐ mā	0.29	2.49477
	尼玛 ní mǎ	0.33	-22.43752
	你妹 nǐ mèi	0.33	-9.09301

From the semantic positive shift values of prototypes and alternative forms, it can be seen that, Table 9.

(1) The prototypes exhibit lower semantic positive shift values compared to their alternative forms.

The semantic positive shift value of the prototype 我肏 *wǒ cào* is lower than its alternative forms. 我肏 *wǒ cào* is used more often with negative emotional words, and less in positive prosody. Compared with the prototype, its alternative forms 我操 *wǒ cāo*, Woc/Woc/WOC, 握草 *wò cǎo*, 卧槽 *wò cáo* are used more often with positive emotional words and more often in positive prosody, resulting in a higher value of positive shift. The positive shift value of 哇塞 *wa sài* 'Wow' is the highest, followed by forms such as 我擦 *wǒ cā* and 卧槽 *wò cáo*. The PMI calculation results also show that different alternative forms have different positive shift values.

The prototype 我尻 *wǒ kāo* does not appear in the positive semantic prosody, and the alternative forms 我靠 *wǒ kào* and 我考 *wǒ kǎo* all have semantic positive shift, among which the positive shift value of 我考 *wǒ kǎo* is higher than 我靠 *wǒ kào*. The scmantic shift value of the prototype "妈屄" is lower than that of the alternative forms 妈比 *mā bǐ*, 妈逼 *mā bī* and "mb".

(2) The more distinct an alternative form is from its prototype, especially if it's more obscure, the higher its semantic positive shift value.

Compared to 卧槽 *wò cáo*, 握草 *wò cǎo*, and woc/Woc/WOC, the alternative form 我擦 *wǒ cā* has a greater difference from the prototype 我肏 *wǒ cào*. Their font shapes and phonetics are different. The greater the difference, the higher the positive shift value of the alternative form. The popular phrase 哇塞 *wa sài* is from Minnan dialect, which is equivalent to the northern dialect's 我操 *wǒ cāo*. However, when it is borrowed into Mandarin and network languages, it is regarded as a common exclamation expressing surprise [15]. Compared to other forms, 哇塞 *wa sài* is more obscure and differs greatly from the prototype, even being treated as semantically unrelated interjections, which also leads to the highest value of semantic positive shift.

(3) Words containing the character 妈 *mā* 'mother' generally have lower semantic positive shift values.

The prototype 日你妈 *rì nǐ mā* and the alternative form "rnm" are used negatively, mainly appearing in negative semantic prosody. The word 妈 *mā* 'mother' is omitted, the positive shift value of 我日 *wǒ rì* and 沃日 *wò rì* is higher.

The use of prototype 你妈 *nǐ mā* is negative, mainly appearing in negative semantic prosody. The positive shift value of the alternative forms 尼玛 *ní mǎ* and 你妹 *nǐ mèi* is relatively higher, but it is still mainly used in the negative semantic prosody. The probability of 他妈 *tā mā* appearing in the positive semantic prosody is slightly lower than that in the negative semantic prosody. The alternative forms "tm", 特么 *tè me* and 踏马 *tà mǎ* without the word 妈 *mā* have a higher value of semantic positive shift.

6 Analysis of the Motivation of Semantic Shift Evolution

6.1 High-Frequency Use of Vocabulary

Uncivilized words, when frequently used, become less taboo and lose their shock value [4]. When such words become buzzwords, they appear excessively in sentences, and their capacity to convey semantic information diminishes, often serving primarily for emotional release. For instance, with the frequent use of 他妈的*tā mā de*, its original meaning fades, leaving it to express strong emotions [16]. Frequent use of language has brought semantic wear and tear. When 神经病*shén jīn bìn* 'mental disorder', 猪*zhū*'pig', 白痴*bái chī*'idiot', 变态*biàn tài*'psycho', 垃圾*lā jī*'trash' and other abusive terms are used as buzzwords, their meanings become diluted, serving mainly as mood or referential markers or for emotional venting [17]. Zhang [5] noted that as these terms became more ambiguous, their derogatory connotations lessened. Over time, the original negative emotions associated with these words faded, evolving into symbols of identity or idiomatic expressions. Sexual behaviors and organs, as well as gender and age-related terms, are central to the category of uncivilized words. These terms exhibit the highest levels of abuse and frequency in the bullet-screen dataset. Such frequent usage suggests a diminishing derogatory connotation, leading to a positive semantic shift.

6.2 Suppression of Co-Occurrence Words

Semantic prosody is a combination of keywords that habitually attracts words with similar semantic tendencies. Due to the high frequency of co-occurrence of keywords with these words in the text, keywords are "infected" with similar semantic characteristics, forming a certain semantic diffusion atmosphere within a specific range [18, 19]. This specific semantic atmosphere permeates all the gaps within the context, whether it is the lexical items in the core collocation, the collocation words that are not closely related to the node words, or even some words beyond the limited span are more or less influenced by the semantic atmosphere [20]. If the co-occurring words in a sentence are mostly positive, the analyzed words are more likely to appear in a positive semantic prosody, and vice versa.

6.3 Development of Network Technology

With societal advancements and the rapid evolution of network technology, people's lives have transformed significantly. The network is actually the language network, the information running on the network is mostly language information, network construction and network information operation technology can be regarded as "language technology". Every advancement in language technology will have a huge impact on language ecology. The internet has amplified the function of language, altering its ecology [21]. While the internet provides a platform for free expression, it also implements measures to ensure the healthy evolution of online linguistic interactions. In order to promote the healthy development of network language life, the network language supervision technology and system is constantly improving. In order to avoid the network supervision, netizens begin to constantly create and use new words or forms of words to meet the needs of language expression and communication. New words or forms of words are constantly changing, and the distances from the prototype are also getting farther and farther.

6.4 Influence of Psychological Factors

Human beings have a mindset of pursuing elegance and avoiding vulgarity, avoiding ugly things and preferring beautiful things. For uncivilized words with high dirty values, people will also avoid it, unless it is "unavoidable". When having to use these uncivilized words with high dirty values, there may also be differences due to factors such as gender, education level, occupation, age, region, and field. For instance, individuals with higher education levels are less likely to use highly derogatory terms.

6.5 Constraints of Cultural Factors

The pursuit of interpersonal harmony is the manifestation of human rationality, while the use of uncivilized words will have a negative impact on interpersonal relationship. In speech communication, the use of uncivilized words will lead to collision between individuals and thus interrupt conversation. The use of uncivilized words will also damage the communicative relationship and lead to the breakdown of interpersonal relationship [22]. In order to reduce the direct negative impact of uncivilized words, new forms of uncivilized words have been introduced on online platforms, which not only meet the need for emotional expression but also slow down the destruction of harmonious interpersonal relationships.

7 Conclusion

Utilizing sentiment analysis and semantic prosody theories, this study delved into the positive semantic shift of uncivilized words within bullet-screen comments, achieved by analyzing the sentiment polarity of co-occurring emotional words. Our methodology began with the construction of a bullet-screen dataset encompassing 1700 videos. We then established a sentiment lexicon and rule base, drawing from five existing sentiment lexicons, and selected six categories of uncivilized words for analysis. By employing both the bullet-screen dataset and the BCC corpus, we measured the semantic positive shift of these words' prototypes and their alternative forms, using the sentiment lexicon and the PMI-IR algorithm. This allowed us to compare the semantic shifts and delve into the underlying motivations for these evolutions.

A pivotal component in sentiment analysis methods rooted in sentiment lexicons is the lexicon itself. The comprehensiveness of a sentiment lexicon directly impacts the accuracy of sentiment analysis outcomes. This is especially pertinent in our contemporary, internet-driven society where linguistic evolution is rapid, and new terms emerge continually. To ensure the continued relevance and high coverage rate of sentiment lexicons, it's imperative to perpetually update them with new emotional terms, warranting ongoing research in this domain.

References

1. Zeng, Y.G.: The emotional needs and value demands of young people behind the bullet screen. People's Forum **701**(10), 34–37 (2021). (in Chinese)
2. Yang, T.: The development and transformation of bullet screen culture in the 5G era. Young J. **35**, 16–17 (2020). (in Chinese)
3. Jones, S., Sinclair, J.: English lexical collocations: a study in computational linguistics. Cah. Lexicol. **2**, 15–61 (1974)
4. Ruth, W.: Language most foul. Wenhui Press, Shanghai (2019)
5. Zhang, Y.S.: The lexicalization, labeling, and structuring of abusive words. Contemp. Rhetoric **4**, 1–13 (2010). (in Chinese)
6. Zhang, Y.W.: Variations of meaning in cyber language. Appl. Linguis. **4**, 108–115 (2014). (in Chinese)
7. Lu, X.: Discuss "*tā mā de!*". In: Selected Collection of Lu Xun's Essays, Beijing United Publishing Co., LTD., Beijing (2015). (in Chinese)
8. Yin, J.Q.: Saying the phrase "*tā mā de*". Lang. Constr. **6**, 20–22 (1998). (in Chinese)
9. Liu, Y.S.: Usage characteristics and causes of "*tā mā de*". Chin. J. **22**, 14–16 (2011). (in Chinese)
10. Chengyu, D., Liu, P.: Linguistic knowledge based on attention neural network for targeted sentiment classification. In: Hong, J.-F., Zhang, Y., Liu, P. (eds.) CLSW 2019. LNCS (LNAI), vol. 11831, pp. 486–495. Springer, Cham (2020). https://doi.org/10.1007/978-3-030-38189-9_50
11. Huang, L., Li, S., Zhou, G.: Emotion corpus construction on Microblog Text. In: Lu, Q., Gao, H. (eds) Chinese Lexical Semantics. CLSW 2015. Lecture Notes in Computer Science, Vol. 9332, pp. 204-212. Springer, Cham (2015)
12. Wang, Z.Y., Wu, Z.H., Hu, F.T.: Words sentiment polarity calculation based on HowNet and PMI. Comput. Eng. **38**(15), 187–189 (2012). (in Chinese)
13. Xu, T.C., Fang, Y.Q., Xing, H.L., Li, J.L.: Cause analysis and purification countermeasures of network dirty words. Stand. in China **22**, 259–261 (2019). (in Chinese)
14. Cheng, J.: Comparative study on new words and new meanings of words. Chin. Teach. World **4**, 48–59 (2001). (in Chinese)
15. Liu, D.Q.: Interjectionization of content words and deinterjectionization of interjections. Chin. Lang. Learn. **3**, 3–13 (2012). (in Chinese)
16. Li, J.: Koutouchan: Form. Shanghai International Studies University, Formation and function (2013). (in Chinese)
17. Shen, Y.: Evaluation on newly emerging foul and abusive language in chinese from the perspective of language standardization. Chin. J. Lang. Policy Plann. **1**(3), 70–75 (2016). (in Chinese)
18. Sinclair, J.: Corpus, Concordance. Collocation. Oxford University Press, Oxford (1991)
19. Liu, J.P., Hong, M.: A language network-based approach to semantic prosody. J. Zhejiang Univ. (Humanit. Soc. Sci.) **48**(6), 69–82 (2018). (in Chinese)
20. Wei, N.X.: General approach to semantic prosody. Foreign Lang. Teach. Res. **4**, 300–307 (2002). (in Chinese)
21. Li, Y.M.: Language technology and language ecology. Foreign Lang. Edu. **41**(6), 1–5 (2020). (in Chinese)
22. Ran, Y.P.: The rapport management model in interpersonal relations and its violation. Foreign Lang. Edu. **33**(4), 1–5 (2012). (in Chinese)

A Multiple Correspondence Analysis on the Adverbial Uses of the Chinese Color Term *Bai* 'White'

Jinmeng Dou[✉] , Meichun Liu , and Zhuo Zhang

Department of Linguistics and Translation, City University of Hong Kong, Tat Chee Avenue, Kowloon, Hong Kong, China
jmdou2-c@my.cityu.edu.hk

Abstract. This paper conducts a corpus-based semantic analysis on the adverbial uses of the Chinese color term *bai* 'white' regarding its two metaphorical meanings – "In vain/For no reason" and "Free of charge". Based on distributional semantics, it is hypothesized that the semantic (dis)similarities of the two meanings can be captured by their usage features in real corpora. In the current study, the multiple correspondence analysis technique is employed to explore the distinctive usage patterns of the two metaphorical meanings based on a dataset that consists of 195 sentences randomly extracted from corpora. These sentences are manually annotated with 19 usage features, encompassing linguistic information from lexical-collocational, semantic, and discourse levels. By visualizing the general distributional patterns of the two meanings and their association strengths with the distinctive usage features, it is found that there are remarkable (dis)similarities between the two metaphorical senses regarding their usage variations, which can be used to explain the cognitive motivations of the two meanings in line with the Conceptual Metaphor theory.

Keywords: Chinese Color Term · Conceptual Metaphor · Multiple Correspondence Analysis · Polysemy

1 Introduction

Besides the literal meaning of natural color in physics concepts, many Chinese color terms (CTs) have more than one metaphorical meaning when interacting with other linguistic items, namely, metaphorical polysemy [1, 11]. Example (1) provides an initial illustration.

(1) 你白看了一场戏.
ni bai kan le yichang xi.
Meaning 1 – Free of charge: 'You watched a free play.'
Meaning 2 – In vain/For no reason: 'You watched a play in vain.'

In this sentence, the syntactic structure is quite clear - *bai* 'white' behaves as an adverb to modify the verb *kan* 'watch'. However, the exact meaning of *bai* 'white' is controversial since there are two possible explanations to interpret this sentence, as

M. Dong et al. (Eds.): CLSW 2023, LNAI 14514, pp. 254–265, 2024.
https://doi.org/10.1007/978-981-97-0583-2_20

shown in Example (1). It is proposed that there must be some underlying semantic relations between the two metaphorical meanings since both of them can provide a reasonable interpretation of this instance. The current study aims to investigate semantic (dis)similarities between the two metaphorical senses of the adverbial uses of *bai* 'white' via examining their prototypical usage patterns with a corpus-based approach. Methodologically, the Multiple Correspondence Analysis (MAC) technique is employed to visualize the association strengths between a set of manually annotated linguistic features and the two target meanings. The data processing and analysis are conducted with R language.

This paper is organized as follows. Section 2 reviews the previous studies. Section 3 introduces the research methodology. Section 4 demonstrates the empirical results. Section 5 concludes this study.

2   Literature Review

Among linguistic studies on colors, Berlin and Kay proposed that every language chooses its CTs from a set of eleven color categories, named Basic Color Terms [3: 4]. They argued that white is one of the earliest CTs in any language as long as there are words referring to color concepts in that language. Chinese is no exception. Wu diachronically demonstrated that *bai* 'white' is one of the earliest-acquired CTs in Chinese from Late Shang Dynasty to Modern China (1500 BC - present) [16]. Many previous studies have discussed the semantics of Chinese CTs from different perspectives, e.g., the semantic fuzziness of Chinese CTs [21], and the semantic duality of CTs' associative meanings [22]. Furthermore, many studies analyzed the semantic extensions of Chinese CTs from a perspective of cognitive linguistics, such as [13, 15, 17–19], and [20].

As a powerful tool in explaining polysemy, conceptual metaphor provides convincing explanations about how varied extended meanings of CTs are associated with their literal meanings of natural colors [14]. However, most previous studies only focused on describing the possible metaphorical extensions of Chinese CTs from a pure analytical ground in an example-based fashion without considering their usage variations and semantic (dis)similarities. In other words, there is no empirically validated evidence to support their semantic analysis. Hence, the present study conducts a corpus-based analysis of the prototypical usage patterns and semantic relations of the two metaphorical senses of *bai* 'white' regarding the theory of Distribution Semantics [6, 10]. The reasons are twofold: First, the two metaphorical meanings of *bai* 'white' are frequently used in the Chinese context. Identifying their prototypical usage patterns may shed new light on teaching Chinese as a foreign language and computational modeling of semantics. Second, the adverbial uses of CTs are rather unusual in Chinese since only *bai* 'white' can serve as an adverb to modify verbs among the Chinese basic CTs - *hei* 'black', *bai* 'white', *hong* 'red', *lv* 'green', *huang* 'yellow' [3, 16]. Exploring the semantic (dis)similarities of the two meanings of adverbial *bai* 'white' may reveal cognitive mechanisms motivating the sense extensions of Chinese CTs, which cannot be found in other usages of CTs. To our best knowledge, there is still no study focusing on the adverbial uses of Chinese CTs.

3 Data and Method

3.1 Introduction to MCA

Pertaining to correspondence analysis, MCA is designed to explore the associations manifested in the dataset, e.g., patterns in the combinations of linguistic features. This technique can simultaneously depict the correlations between multiple linguistic features that structure the behaviors of the datasets in relation to syntax, semantics, or pragmatics by showing their relative proximity in a biplot. This tool has been applied to analyzing the semantic relations of polysemy, or other lexical semantic issues, e.g., [7, 12].

Several steps are involved in this study. Firstly, a dataset was created by compiling a corpus of sampled target sentences that contains the lexical items under the study. In our study, the lexical item is the adverbial *bai* 'white' with the two target meanings. And then, a set of usage features that can characterize the local context of the target lexical item was defined from different levels, such as lexical, semantic, and discourse levels. After manually annotating the collected sentences with defined features, the general distributional patterns of the two target senses and their association strengths with the distinctive usage features were visualized by MCA factor maps.

3.2 Data Collection

To provide balanced coverage, we selected the Chinese Web Corpus (zhTenTen) 2017 and Chinese Gigaword Corpus as the source of our dataset as the former featured on the internet text, and the latter is news-wire text. In this study, 195 instances referring to the adverbial uses of *bai* 'white' were randomly collected from the two source corpora - 100 for "In vain/For no reason" and 95 for "Free of charge". The collected sentences were then annotated manually based on our proposed contextual features. It is noted that, for each instance, the exact meaning of *bai* 'white' was manually identified based on its contexts in the sentence. The following section provides an overview of these features.

3.3 Data Annotation

In line with previous studies [8], 19 usage features (Table 1) in 46 variable levels (ID tags: [2, 9]) were proposed from three linguistic categories, including lexical-collocational information (15), semantic information (2), and discourse information (2), to profile the linguistic behaviors of adverbial *bai* 'white' in the real corpora. In other words, the 195 sample sentences were manually annotated with these 19 variables, producing a data frame of 8,970 data points. Appendix 1 provides a detailed description for the proposed features.

Table 1. Overview of the 19 usage features

Feature Type	Contextual Feature	Variable Levels
1. Lexical-Collocational Information		
modifier	*le* 了	2: yes/no
modifier	Negation marker	2: yes/no
modifier	*shi* 是	2: yes/no
modifier	*ye* 也	2: yes/no
modifier	*jiu* 就	2: yes/no
modifier	*bei* 被	2: yes/no
modifier	*rang/ling/shi* 让/令/使	2: yes/no
modifier	Past time marker	2: yes/no
modifier	Future time marker	2: yes/no
modifier	Frequency/Duration marker	2: yes/no
modifier	Capability/Intention marker	2: yes/no
modifier	Doubt	2: yes/no
compound word	Phase marker	2: yes/no
bai 白	Reduplication of *bai*	2: yes/no
verb	Reduplication of verb modified by *bai*	2: yes/no
2. Semantic Information		
noun phrase	Semantic T: subject of verb modified by *bai*	6: see notes
noun phrase	Semantic T: object of verb modified by *bai*	6: see notes
3. Discourse Information		
sentence	Object fronting	2: yes/no
sentence	The omission of co-arguments with *bai*	2: yes/no

Notes: the semantic types consist of abstract entity, body part, animate, inanimate, organization, and null

4   MCA Results and Analysis

4.1   Identification of the Distinctive Usage Features

To analyze the usage patterns of the two meanings, the distinctive usage features that set them apart were identified first, since MCA is only suitable for representing a few features simultaneously due to the difficulty of visualization. Precisely, Cramér's V was calculated to measure the distinctiveness of the usage features in setting the two meanings apart. The Fisher exact test was used to test whether Cramér's V is statistically significant. Table 2 lists the distinctive usage features with Cramér's V exceeding 0.15 and p-value below 0.05.

It is shown that there are seven distinctive usage features in distinguishing the two metaphorical meanings of *bai* 'white'. In specific, four features pertain to the lexical-collocational patterns, which are the collocation with the aspect marker *le* and the frequency/duration marker, as well as the reduplication of *bai* 'white' and the verbs modified

Table 2. Distinctive usage features in distinguishing the two meanings

No	Feature	Abbreviation	Cramér's V	p-value
1	*le*	*le*	0.366	< 0.05
2	Semantic type of obj	STO	0.344	< 0.05
3	Reduplication of verb	RV	0.25	< 0.05
4	Semantic type of sub	STS	0.223	< 0.05
5	Reduplication of *bai*	RW	0.204	< 0.05
6	Frequency/Duration marker	FDM	0.194	< 0.05
7	Object Fronting	OF	0.158	< 0.01

by *bai* 'white'. The two semantic features are both identified as distinctive usage features. At the discourse level, object fronting is the one that plays a significant role in profiling the semantic distinctions of these two meanings of *bai* 'white'. Based on the seven distinctive features, the dataset was further refined as a data frame consisting of 4290 (195*22) data points for feature analysis.

4.2 Semantic Distribution

This section provides a general observation of the distributional patterns of the 195 annotated instances with the MCA method based on the distinctive features. MCA describes the obtained variations between the categorical variables through several dimensions and uses the so-called 'Inertia' to represent the proportion of variation retained by each dimension. The higher the inertia one obtains, the better the dimension is. Table 3 provides an overview of the inertia of our MCA result of the refined dataset. It is shown that the variance of the dataset is decomposed into 15 dimensions. Each occupies an inertia value and thus explains the percentage of the total variation in the data.

Table 3. Inertia of MCA result on the annotated dataset

Dim	Eigenvalue	Inertia	Cum. Inertia (%)
1	0.263	12.278	12.278
2	0.223	10.424	22.702
3	0.193	9.003	31.704
4	0.184	8.585	40.289
……			
15	0.047	2.181	100.000

In the current study, the inter-individual variability of the 195 instances is displayed based on the first two dimensions (22.702%), as in Fig. 1. The data points (instances) in this figure are colored according to their corresponding meanings and labeled with numbers 1–195 (1–100 for "In vain/For no reason" and 101–195 for "Free of charge"). The positions of the two target meanings are predicated with 95% confidence ellipses by regarding them as supplementary variables.

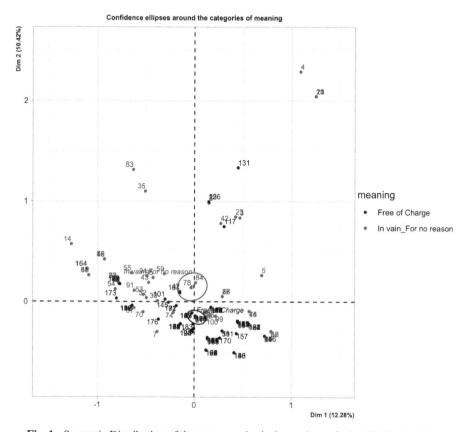

Fig. 1. Semantic Distribution of the two metaphorical meanings of adverbial *bai* 'white'.

In Fig. 1, the red data points demonstrate a broader distribution compared to the black ones, indicating that the usage variations of meaning "In vain/For no reason" (Red) may be more diverse than "Free of charge" (Black). Specifically, the black data points are mainly distributed in the two bottom quadrants, and the red points for "In vain/For no reason" are mainly in the top-left and bottom-right quadrants. Related to that, the confidence ellipses of these two meanings are distributed in the top-left and bottom-right quadrants, respectively, with a certain distance. The distributional patterns of these data points show that there may exist semantic distinctions between the two metaphorical senses of *bai* 'white' even though both of them pertain to the adverbial use. The next section focuses on identifying the prototypical usage patterns of the two meanings to provide empirical support for their semantic (dis)similarities.

4.3 Feature Analysis

Figure 2 depicts the association strengths among the two metaphorical meanings of *bai* 'white' and the distinctive usage features through visualizing their relative proximity. Data points with stronger associations tend to carry smaller proximity. It is noted that the usage features are colored in red, and the positions of the two metaphorical meanings are predicated in green. What follows is an analysis of the prototypical usage patterns of these two senses.

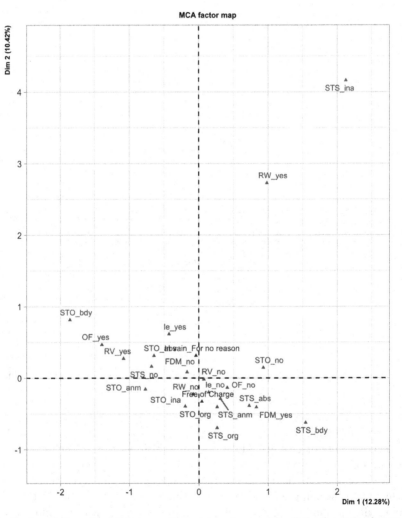

Fig. 2. Associations strength between the two meanings and the distinctive usage features

When referring to the meaning "In vain/For no reason", it is found that the adverbial *bai* 'white' tends to modify transitive verbs of which objects prototypically refer to an abstract entity, as indicated by feature "STO_abs". Furthermore, the locations of features "STS_no" and "OF_yes" provide more detailed semantic information on the core arguments of verbs collocating with the adverbial *bai* 'white'. Precisely, it is demonstrated that the subjects of these verbal predicates tend to be omitted, and their objects are more likely to be fronted. Example (2) illustrates this usage pattern.

(2) 我的MBA真的是白学了.

wo de MBA zhende shi bai xue le.

'My MBA is totally wasted.'

Given that the adverbial *bai* 'white' of "In vain/For no reason" mainly refers to an evaluation of the result of an event, it is expected that the verbs modified by *bai* 'white' frequently co-occur with the aspect marker *le*, as indicated by "le_yes". In other words, only a completed event with specific results can be evaluated. Besides, the feature "RV_yes" reveals a unique usage pattern of *bai* 'white' pertaining to "In vain/For no reason", as illustrated by Example (3).

(3) 咱知道说了也是白说.

zan zhidao shuo le yeshi bai shuo.

'We know that it is a waste of time.'

For the meaning "Free of charge", it is shown that the adverbial *bai* 'white' also tends to collocate with transitive verbs, of which objects mainly pertain to organization and inanimate things. It is mainly supported by positions of the features "STO_org" and "STO_ina". Besides, an animate subject (human in most cases) is observed to frequently collocate with the verbs modified by the adverbial *bai* 'white' as shown by "STS_anm". Example (4) illustrates this pattern.

(4) 他们不能躺在炕上白吃饭.

tamen buneng tang zai kang shang bai chi fan.

'They cannot just lie on the Kang and eat without paying.'

In addition, the feature "FDM" demonstrates that verbs modified by adverbial *bai* 'white' tend to collocate with a duration or frequency marker, as shown in Example (5). It is consistent with the semantic property of *bai* 'white' referring to "Free of charge" – the description of the manner of actions but no longer the evaluation of the event results.

(5) 你就可以每月白得3万元奖金.

ni jiu keyi meiyue bai de 3-wanyuan jiangjin.

'You'll get 30,000 yuan per month for free.'

In sum, the results showed that usage distinction does exist among the two metaphorical meanings of the adverbial *bai* 'white', "In vain/For no reason" and "Free of charge", especially regarding the co-arguments of the verbs modified by *bai* 'white' and the lexical-collocational patterns. Specifically, it is found that when referring to "In vain/For no reason", *bai* 'white' prototypically modifies transitive verbs with an abstract object and omitted subject with occurring with the aspect marker *le* to depict an evaluation of the result of an event; when referring to "Free of charge", *bai* 'white' is more likely to collocate with a transitive verb, which tends to take a human subject and an inanimate object, to denote the cost-free manner of actions.

5   Conclusion

The current study conducted a multiple correspondence analysis to investigate the semantic (dis)similarities in relation to metaphorical polysemy of the adverbial uses of the Chinese CT bai. Specifically, the meaning "In vain/For no reason" mainly describes the lack of incentives or outcomes in actions denoted by the collocated verbs with *bai* 'white', while "Free of charge" depicts the lack of cost in action. In other words, both two meanings refer to the mental evaluation (judgment) of speakers on whether some non-visual frame-based elements (i.e., effect or expense) are absent within an event regarding Frame Semantics [5]. Regarding the theory of three-dimensional color perception [4], a coherent picture can be drawn by the conceptual similarity between the key concept shared by two adverbial meanings - the absence of intended cost or result and one of the perceptual properties of white - the absence of hue. We argue that the semantic similarity of the two meanings can be summarized as both are conceptually associated with the source perceptual property of the white color - absence of hue - from the perspective of conceptual metaphor. On the other hand, the semantic dissimilarity among these two meanings can be analyzed regarding their target domains: "In vain/For no reason" describes the lack of outcomes in a completed action of which the patient is an abstract entity; "Free of charge" mainly depicts the lack of cost in a durative action with an animate agent and an inanimate patient.

In conclusion, the present study demonstrated the prototypical usage patterns and semantic (dis)similarities of the two meanings pertaining to the adverbial *bai* 'white' with the MCA technique. It may shed new light on dealing with metaphorical polysemy with a corpus-based empirical approach in the Chinese context.

Appendix 1

This section illustrates the contextual features focusing on collocational information.

1. Modifier: *le*

   - Whether *bai* collocated with *le* 了 'finish; realize; complete', e.g., 说白了 *shuo bai le* 'to be honest'.

2. Modifier: Negation Marker

   - Whether *bai* collocated with a negation marker: *bu* 不, *mei* 没, e.g., 汗没白流 *han mei bai liu* 'The sweater was not in vain'.

3. Modifier: *shi*

   - Whether *bai* collocated with *shi* 是, e.g., 这次算是白来了 *zheci suanshi bai lai le* 'This trip is for noting'.

4. Modifier: *ye*

- Whether *bai* collocated with *ye* 也 'also; as well; too', e.g., 也是白送 *ye shi bai song* 'also a free gift'.

5. Modifier: *jiu*

   - Whether *bai* collocated with *jiu* 就 'at once; already', e.g., 就怕白干 *jiu pa bai gan* 'be afraid of doing it for nothing'.

6. Modifier: *bei*

   - Whether *bai* with passive marker *bei* 被, e.g., 被白白扔掉 *bei baibai reng diao* 'be thrown away for nothing'.

7. Modifier: rang/ling/shi

   - Whether *bai* collocated with causative marker *rang* 让/ *ling* 令/ *shi* 使, e.g., 让你白赚钱 *rang ni bai zhuan qian* 'let you make free money'.

8. Modifier: Past Time Marker

   - Whether *bai* collocated with a past time modifier: *ceng* 曾, *yi* 已, *yijing* 已经, *zhiqian* 之前, *guoqu* 过去, e.g., 之前白白流失的雨水 *zhiqian baibai liushi de yushui* 'the rain that just ran off before'.

9. Modifier: Future Time Marker

   - Whether *bai* collocated with a future time modifier: *jiang*将, *jianghui* 将会, *hui* 会, e.g., 将不会白费 *jiang buhui bai fei* 'will not be in vain'.

10. Modifier: Frequency/Duration

    - Whether *bai* collocated with Frequency/Duration Marker: *yiyang* 一趟, *ci* 次,. e.g., 白跑一趟 *bai pao yitang* 'a wasted trip'.

11. Modifier: Capability/Intention

    - Whether *bai* collocated with a modifier of capability or intention marker: *neng* 能, *xiang* 想, e.g., 想白吃白喝 *xiang bai chi bai he* 'want to eat and drink for free'.

12. Modifier: Doubt

    - Whether *bai* collocated with a marker of doubt: *suan* 算, *keneng* 可能, e.g., 学区房可能白买了 *xuequfang keneng bai mai le* 'School district housing may be bought for nothing.'

13. Compound word: phase marker

    - Whether *bai* collocated with a phase marker: *cheng* 成 'become', *diao* 掉 'drop', e.g., 白白烂掉 *baibai landiao* 'rot away for nothing'.

14. Adverbial *bai*: Reduplication

    - Whether adverbial *bai* is reduplicated, e.g., *baibai xisheng* 白白牺牲 'sacrifice in vain'.

15. Verbs modified by adverbial *bai*: Reduplication

- Whether the verb modified by adverbial *bai* is reduplicated, e.g., 说了也是白说 *shuo le ye shi bai shuo* 'There is no difference in saying it or not.'

16. Noun phrase: Semantic type: dep-relation with *bai*: sub

   - Whether the semantic type of subject collocated with *bai* is of type:

Abstract entity: *zhenxiang* 真相 'truth'
Body part: *jenhuai* 襟怀 'mind'
Animate: *laoren* 老人 'elder'
Inanimate object: *xiaoshuo* 小说 'novel'
Organization: *guo'an dui* 国安队 'Guoan team'

17. Noun phrase: Semantic type: dep-relation with *bai*: obj

   - Whether the semantic type of direct object collocated with *bai* is of type:

Abstract entity: *yuanyin* 原因 'reason'
Body part: *xin* 心 'heart'
Animate: *ziji* 自己 'self'
Inanimate object: *shouji* 手机 'mobile phone'
Organization: *zuzhi* 组织 'organization'

18. Object fronting

   - Whether the object of *bai* is fronted, e.g., 今天的功算是白费了 *jintian de gong suanshi bai fei le* 'Today's work was in vain.'

19. Sentence: The omission of co-arguments

   - Whether the collocated arguments of *bai* is omitted, e.g., 这一下白耽误十几分钟 *zheyixia bai danwu shiji fenzhong* 'it wasted about ten minutes.'

References

1. Apresjan, J.D.: Regular polysemy. Linguistics **12**(142), 5–32 (1974)
2. Atkins, B. T. S.: Semantic ID tags: Corpus evidence for dictionary senses: the uses of large text databases. In: 3rd Annual Conference of the UW Centre for the New Oxford English Dictionary Proceedings, pp. 17–36. Waterloo, Canada (1987)
3. Berlin, B., Kay, P.: Basic color terms: their universality and evolution. University of California Press, Berkeley (1969)
4. Fairchild, M.D.: Color appearance models. Addison-Wesley, Boston (2005)
5. Fillmore, C.J.: Frames and the semantics of understanding. Quaderni di Semantica **6**(2), 222–254 (1985)
6. Firth, J. R.: Modes of Meaning. In: Palmer, F. R. (ed.) Reprinted in Papers in *Linguistics*. Oxford University Press, Oxford (1951)

7. Glynn, D.: Polysemy, syntax, and variation: a usage-based method for cognitive semantics. In: Evans, V., Pourcel, S. (eds.) New directions in cognitive linguistics, pp. 77–106. John Benjamins, Amsterdam (2009)

8. Gries, S.T., Divjak, D.: Behavioral Profiles: a corpus-based approach to cognitive semantic analysis. In: Evans, V., Pourcel, S. (eds.) New directions in cognitive linguistics, pp. 57–75. John Benjamins, Amsterdam (2009)

9. Hanks, P.: Contextual dependency and lexical sets. International Journal of Corpus Linguistics 1(1), 75–98 (1996)

10. Harris, Z.S.: Distributional structure. Word 10(2–3), 146–162 (1954)

11. Jurafsky, D.: Universal tendencies in the semantics of the diminutive. Language 72(3), 533–578 (1996)

12. Krawczak, K., Kokorniak, I.: Corpus-driven quantitative approach to the construal of Polish 'think.' Poznań Studies in Contemporary Linguistics 48, 439–472 (2012)

13. Lai, H.L., Chung, S.F.: Color polysemy: black and white in Taiwanese language. Taiwan Journal of Linguistics 16(1), 95–130 (2018)

14. Lakoff, G., Johnson, M.: Metaphors we live by. University of Chicago Press, Chicago (1980)

15. Li, Z.C., Bai, H.R.: Conceptual metaphors of black and white: a corpus-based comparative study between English and Chinese. Journal of Anhui Agricultural University (Social Science Edition) 22(4), 92–97 (2013)

16. Wu, J.S.: The evolution of basic color terms in Chinese. Journal of Chinese Linguistics 39(1), 76–12 (2011)

17. Xing, Z.Q.: Semantics and pragmatics of color terms in Chinese. In: Xing, Z.W. (ed.) Studies of Chinese linguistics: functional approaches, pp. 87–102. HKUP, Hong Kong (2008)

18. Chen, J.X., Qin, L.: Categorization and metaphorical cognition of basic colors in Chinese. Journal of Henan Normal University (Natural Science Edition) 30(2), 75–77 (2003)

19. Li, Y.: A Cognitive approach to the basic color terms in Chinese. Journal of Yunnan Normal University 2(2), 64–67 (2004)

20. Wang, S., Wu, L., Gong, Q. M.: The collocations of Chinese color words. The Collocations of Chinese Color Words. In: Dong, M., Gu, Y., Hong, JF. (eds) Chinese lexical semantics. CLSW 2021, vol 13249, pp. 121–143. Springer, Heidelberg (2021)

21. Wu, T.P.: Analysis on color terms and their fuzzy nature. Language Teaching and Linguistic Studies 2, 88–105 (1986). (in Chinese)

22. Zhang, W.X.: Analysis on the associative meanings of color terms. Language Teaching and Linguistic Studies 3, 112–121 (1988). (in Chinese)

The Semantic Interpretation of Implicit Negative Compound Nouns

Enxu Wang[✉] and Xiaoqing Lv

College of Chinese Language and Literature, University of Jinan, No. 336 Nanxinzhuang West Road, Shizhong District, Jinan 250022, China
wangbush000@126.com

Abstract. The problem of interpretation on implicit negation is a difficult problem in cross language translation, second language acquisition, and dictionary interpretation. This paper finds that expectations are the key to interpreting implicit negations. Unlike explicit negative expectations, implicit negative expectations are represented as conventionalized experiences, rules, etc., and syntactically expressed as "应该(should)…". Taking implicit negative compound nouns as an example, there are three kinds of conventionalized expectations implied in compound nouns, namely Gestalt expectations, criterion expectations, and ability expectations. Based on these expectations, this paper establishes three interpretation modes for implicit negative nouns. Such as "(应该有……实际上)没有 ((should have…but actually) doesn't have)…" and "(应该能……实际上)不能 ((should be able to… but actually) can't)…". Emphasizing and supplementing the expected meaning of implicit negation can not only improve the dictionary interpretations, but also reduce the difficulty of cross language translation and improve the efficiency of second language teaching.

Keywords: Implicit Negation · Conventionalized Expectations · Interpreting Modes

1 Introduction

According to whether it expresses asserted meaning or not, reference [1] divided the negation into two categories: one is explicit negation that expresses asserted meaning, with clear negation markers such as "no, not, never"; the other is implicit negation that does not express asserted meaning, without clear negative markers, and is usually expressed through words such as "forget, fail, doubt".

It is more difficult to understand or interpret implicit negation than explicit negation. Reference [2] finds by ERP experiments that it takes more time to understand implicit negation than explicit negation; reference [3] believes that implicit negation increases the difficulty of translating Arabic into English; reference [4] points out that translating English implicit negation into Chinese is not only slow but also inaccurate in general; implicit negation is a key and difficult point for international students to learn Chinese [5]. Then, why is the implicit negation difficult to understand or interpret? What is the difference between implicit and explicit negation? How is it constructed and how should it be interpreted? This paper will answer these questions.

© The Author(s), under exclusive license to Springer Nature Singapore Pte Ltd. 2024
M. Dong et al. (Eds.): CLSW 2023, LNAI 14514, pp. 266–277, 2024.
https://doi.org/10.1007/978-981-97-0583-2_21

2 Expectations and Explicit Negation, Implicit Negation

2.1 From the Perspective of the Relationship with Negation

The interpreting and understanding of explicit negation are related to human expectations [6: 419]. When the speaker utters a negative sentence, it actually denies a corresponding affirmative presupposition of the listener [cf. 7: 165]. When someone says "not-x", it usually means that "someone thought X" before that, e.g. "I didn't eat many of the chocolates" means before that "someone thought I ate many of the chocolates" [6: 419]. Without expectations, no negation can be understood or interpreted. For example:

(1) A: 厂里最近有什么事吗 (Is there anything new in the factory recently)?

B: a. 王师傅买彩票中奖了 (Master Wang won the lottery)。

b. 王师傅买彩票没有中奖 (Master Wang did not win the lottery)。[8: 43]

The answer of B(a) in the above dialog is natural, while B(b) is unnatural. The unnatural reason is that there is no clear expectation. "Only if B thought A was likely to think that Master Wang would win the lottery", B(b)'s answer is appropriate [8: 44].

Similar to explicit negation, the interpreting and understanding of implicit negation are also related to expectations. Taking "单身汉 (bachelor)" as an example, it is interpreted as "an unmarried adult man" based on social expectations for marriage and marriage age [9: 74–75]. According to this expectation, men should marry when they reach marriageable age. If they do not, they will be called "bachelors". But this expectation does not apply to men who grew up in the wild jungle, nor does it apply to men who deviate from social standards, such as long-term unmarried men who cohabit with the opposite sex, or John Paul II (1920–2005, the Catholic Emperor). For these men, society has no expectation of marriage, and even if they were not married, they would not be called "bachelors". This indicates that the use and understanding of implicit negation are also based on expectations. Without expectations, there is no implicit negation can be used and understood.

2.2 From the Perspective of the Extracting Difficulty

Explicit negation takes pre-assumed affirmative propositions as its expectations, usually with actual discourse forms. Sometimes the affirmative proposition does not appear, but it can be recovered from the context when needed [7, 10]. Reference [6: 419] points out the explicit negation contains two kinds of expectations: a canceled expectation, i.e., "the corresponding affirmative proposition of the negative sentence with the 'not' removed", and a factual expectation, i.e., "the remaining affirmative part of a proposition after removing the negative component". For example, in "I didn't eat many of the chocolates", the canceled expectation is "I eat many of the chocolates", and the factual expectation is "I eat some of the chocolates". When understanding or interpreting an explicitly negation, it is usually necessary to recover the former expectation first.

Unlike expectations of explicit negation, expectations of implicit negation "have no actual discourse forms", which usually exist "in the minds of the speakers" [10] and is less easy to identify. Please see the comparison below:

(2) a. Explicit negation

他没跑三趟 (He didn't run three times)。| **Expectation**: 他跑了三趟 (He run three times)

他没拿三个苹果 (He didn't take three apples)。| **Expectation**: 他拿了三个苹果 (He took three apples)

她没生孩子 (She didn't give birth to a child)。| **Expectation**: 她生孩子了 (She gave birth to a child)

  b. Implicit negation

他白跑了三趟 (He run three times in vain)。| **Expectation**: 跑三趟应有收获 (Running three times should be rewarded)

他白拿了三个苹果 (He took three apples in vain)。| **Expectation**: 拿三个应有付出 (Taking three apples should pay for them)

她白生孩子了 (She gave birth to a child in vain)。| **Expectation**: 生孩子应有收获 (Giving birth to a child should be rewarded)

Expectations of sentence (2a) can be identified directly from the context, that is, the remaining part after removing the negative word. Expectations of sentence (2b) cannot be identified directly from the context, but can be identified with the help of encyclopedic knowledge. Based on encyclopedic knowledge, it can be inferred that the expectation for "running three times in vain" is that "running three times should be rewarded".

Reference [11] classifies contexts into three categories: encyclopedic knowledge context, tangible communicative context, and discourse context, and believes that the convenient degree of extraction of linguistic knowledge varies from context to context. Among them, extracting encyclopedic knowledge is the least convenient and takes the longest time; extracting tangible contextual knowledge is second; and extracting discourse contextual knowledge is the most convenient and takes the shortest time. If the above analysis is correct, we can explain why implicit negation is more difficult to extract and understand than explicit negation. Because explicit negation expectations are discourse contextual knowledge stored in short-term memory, and are easy to activate and extract; while implicit negation expectations are encyclopedic knowledge stored in long-term memory, which require more time to activate and extract.

2.3 From the Form of Expression

The expectation of explicit negation is a logical-semantic expectation, which semantically denotes the propositional content expressed in the affirmative sentence corresponding to the negative sentence [12], and syntactically is expressed in the form of "有(there be, have, has, etc.)…" or "是(is, am, are)…". Negating this expectation will result in sentences such as "没有(there is not, don't have, doesn't have, etc.)…" or "不是(isn't, amn't, aren't)…". As shown in example (3a).

(3) a. Explicit Negation

他没孩子 (He doesn't have children)。 | **Expectation**: 他有孩子 (He has children)

他不是父亲，他还没结婚呢 (He's not a father, because he's not married)。 | **Expectation**: 他是父亲 (he is a father)

b. Implicit Negation

他是单身汉 (He is a bachelor)。 | **Expectation**: 到了结婚年龄应该结婚(He should be married at marriageable age)

他白跑了一趟 (He has run a race in vain)。 | **Expectation**: 跑一趟应该有收获 (Running a race should be rewarded)

Unlike the expectation of explicit negation, the expectation of implicit negation is a cognitive-pragmatic expectation, which semantically reflects people's expectation or belief about what should happen, and syntactically is expressed in the form of "应该(should) …" or "不应该(shouldn't) …". Negating this expectation will get sentences such as "something should happen but didn't happen" or "something shouldn't happen but did happen". As shown in example (3b).

In short, both the understanding or interpreting of explicit and implicit negation are related to expectations. However, these two expectations differ in terms of stability, extracting difficulty, and form of expression.

3 Expectations and Explicit Negation, Implicit Negation

The explicit negation is the denial or refutation of proposition that is pre-assumed in the discourse context [12]. Unlike the explicit negation, the implicit negation is the denial or refutation of pre-existing conventionalized expectations in the human mind, this is, "implicit negation = '不/没(no/not)' + conventionalized expectation". In that case, once we knows what the conventionalized expectation is, we can know roughly what the meaning of implicit negation is.

3.1 Conventionalized Expectations

The expectation of implicit negation is essentially a conventionalized implicature. The so-called conventionalized implicature, from previous studies, has the following characteristics: 1) it is subjective [13] and independent of the truth-value of the utterance; 2) it is an intrinsic part of the utterance that does not need to be inferred; 3) it is a conventional part of the language that does not change with the context, and therefore cannot be canceled [14–16]. So is the case with implicit negative compound nouns. Their expectations are implicit in the components of compound nouns, which cannot be canceled and does not need to be inferred. Such noun-components in Chinese include "死(dead)-, 瞎(blind)-, 谎(lie)-, 虚(false)-, 缺(lack)-, 谣(rumoured)-, 白(vain)-, 干(dry)-, 素(plain)-, 清(unmixed)-, 流(float)-, 空(empty)-, 软(soft)-, 光(bare)-, 处(virgin)-, 徒(futile)-, 哑(dumb)-, 盲(blind)-, 绝(exhausted)-, 幻(illusory)-, 浪(unrestrained)-", etc..

Most of the above components are conventionalized and usually imply only one expectation. For example, "清(unmixed/light)-" implies "应该添加或配有 (that should be added or equipped with)…", and "虚(false)-" implies "应该有实际内容 (that should have actual content". The same is true for "光(bare)-, 幻(illusory)-, 空(empty)-, 死(dead)-, 素(plain)-, 软(soft)-" and so on.

Of course, there are a few components that imply multiple expectations, but only one of them is commonly used and the rest are uncommon expectations. For example, " 白(vain)-" implies multiple expectations. Among them, only "应该有/添加 (that should have/add)…" is commonly used, and the rest are not. The same is true for "瞎(blind)-, 哑(dumb)-, 干(dry)-, 浪(unrestrained)-, 绝(exhausted)-" and so on.

> (4)a. Common expectations
>   白(vain)-: 应该有/添加(that should have/add)…
>   干(dry)-: 应该带有/含有 (that should have/contain)…
>   哑(dumb)-: 应该有(that should have)…
>   b. Non-common expectations
>   白(vain)-: 应该付出(that should pay for)…
>   干(dry)-: 应该付出(that should pay for)…
>   哑(dumb)-: 应该能(that should be able to)…

3.2 The Semantic Types of Implicit Negation

References [17–19] divided the conceptual meaning of a noun into 10 aspects: formal, constitutive, telic, agentive, handle, evaluation, material, unit, action, and orientation. Among these 10 aspects, the most highly conventionalized ones are constitutive, action, handle, and evaluation aspects, and it is often these aspects can become expectations of implicit negation nouns. Relatively, the aspects with lowly conventionalized ones (such as form and telic) rarely become expectations of implicit negation nouns.

Depending on the conceptual meaning reflected by expectations, this paper classifies implicit negative nouns into three types. The details are as follows:

3.2.1 Negating Expectations of Structural Gestalt

The so-called expectation of structural gestalt refers to an ideal thing that should be structurally complete without any missing parts, and its syntactic expression is "应该 有(there should be, should have, etc.)…". If some part is missing, it will be expressed in negative form, and its syntactic expression is "没有(there is not, don't have, without, etc.)…". Among compound nouns, the negating expectations of structural gestalt accounts for the majority, with a percentage of 87.1%[1]. Identifying and interpreting such compound nouns, there are the following modes.

Mode One: Pointing out that things "don't have or contain a certain part". The interpreting mode is: "(应该有/包含…但实际上) 没有/不包含某个部分 ((that should have or contain… but actually) don't have or contain a certain part)". For example:

---

[1] This paper collects a total of 241 implicit negative compound nouns. Among them, there are 210, accounting for 87.1%, that negate their structural gestalt expectations.

(5) [秃裙(bald skirt)] 没有贴边的裙子 (A skirt without attached edges)。(**Expectation**: that should have attached edges)

[虚职(void position)] 没有实际权力……的职位 (A position that... has no real power)。(**Expectation**: that should have real power)

[软水(soft water)] 不含或仅含少量钙、镁等的……水 (Water that does not contain mineral salts, such as calcium, magnesium, etc.)。(**Expectation**: that should contain mineral salts such as calcium, magnesium, etc.)

"应该有某个部分 (that should have a certain part)" is the general knowledge of human beings about gestalt things, e.g. the gestalt skirts should have attached edges. It is default, unmarked [8: 30], without special expression. Therefore, there is no such expression as "有贴边的裙子(skirts with attached edges)". On the contrary, markers are necessary only if the gestalt expectation is violated (missing a certain part). In addition to the above nouns, there are also similar nouns such as "清汤(light soup), 清漆(light lacquer), 哑剧(dumb opera), 空房(empty room), 单身汉(bachelor)" and so on.

Mode Two: Pointing out that things "don't have or don't contain a certain part" and give a reason: because they are not habitually handled. The interpreting mode is: "(应该有……但因没有处置而)没有某个部分 ((that should have or contain…… but due to a lack of necessary handling) does not have or contain a part)". For example:

(6) [白地(spare land)]① 没有种上农作物……的空地 (lands without crops planted on them)。(**Expectation**: that should be planted with crops)

[素描(literary sketch)]③ 文学上指……不加渲染的描写方法 (A method of depiction without any exaggeration)。(**Expectation**: that should be exaggerated)

[清茶(only tea)]② 没有其他糖果点心相配的茶水 (Tea served without sweets and treats)。(**Expectation**: that should provide sweets and treats)

People do not expect to handle every things, nor does every things need to be handled to achieve a gestalt state. Actually, people only have such expectations for things that are handled frequently and not for those that are rarely handled. This can explain why people have the expectation that "应该种上庄稼(should be planted with crops)" on spare land that is suitable for crops but not on spare land that is not suitable for crops (e.g. riverbanks, seashores, valleys). Because they have "planted with crops" frequently on the former but not on the latter. In addition to the nouns in example (6), there are similar interpreting modes for "白肉(plain boiled pork), 空额(vacancy), 死账(dormant account)" and so on. Due to space constraints, we will not repeat them.

Mode Three: Pointing out that utterances "do not have a certain part or are untrue". The interpreting mode is: "(应该真实/有……但实际上却)没有根据, 没有实际内容 或不真实 ((that should be true/have…… but in fact is) without actual content, or untrue)". For example:

(7) [流言(floating rumours)] 到处流传的没有根据的话 (Words without evidence that are spread around)。**(Expectation**: that should have evidence)

[谣言(rumor)] 凭空捏造的消息 (News that are fabricated out of thin air)。(**Expectation**: that should have evidence)

[虚言(false words] 不实在的话 (Words that are not true)。**(Expectation**: that should have actual content)

[谎言(lies)] 骗人的话 (Deceitful words)。**(Expectation**: that should be true)

The previous studies discussed the case of implicit negation in the physical world, without discussing the case in the language world. Expectations in the physical world are concrete, unambiguous, and relatively easy to judge and interpret, whereas expectations in the language world are abstract and difficult to perceive or grasp. Reference [14] states that in language communication, in order to ensure smooth communication, both parties will consciously or unconsciously abide by some principles, namely Quality, Quantity, Relation and Manner. Among these, the most relevant to communicative expectation is the Qualitative Principle: 1) Do not say what you believe to be false; and 2) do not say things that you lack adequate evidence. In other words, it is the Qualitative Principle that plays a decisive role in judging whether a communicative expression meets one's expectation. Only communicative expressions that violate the Qualitative Principle are negated and solidified into compound nouns, as shown in example (8). Apart from that, communicative expressions that violate other principles are hardly ever negated and do not form compound nouns.

Based on the qualitative principle, it is not only possible to determine whether the communicative expression meets expectations, but also whether opinions, ideas, evidence, etc. meet expectations. If they do not meet qualitative principles, they may be negated and solidified as compound nouns. Such as "空谈(burble), 幻想(fantasy), 妄想(delusion), 妄语(wild talk), 浪说(prate), 伪证(false testimony)" and so on.

3.2.2 Negating Expectations of Evaluative Criterion

The so-called evaluative criterion expectation refers to that the ideal things should meet some social statutes, professional rules, ethical regulations.

There are two differences between evaluative criterion expectations and structural gestalt expectations: 1) The latter belongs to the epistemic dimension, which focuses on the structural completeness of things. If it is incomplete, it will be described as "没有某个部分 (don't have a certain part)". The former belongs to the deontic dimension, and focuses on the appropriateness of things or behaviors. If it is not appropriate, it will be evaluated by "没有/不依照某标准 (that haven't follow a certain criterion)". For example, if a woman abides by the virtues of womanhood and keeps her duty, it is appropriate and will not be condemned; but if she violates the virtues of womanhood and does not keep her duty, it is inappropriate and will be criticized for "不守本分 (does not keep her duty)", "没守本分 (failing to keep her duty)", or she will be directly scolded as a "浪蹄子 (prodigal woman)" or "骚蹄子 (slutty woman)", as shown in example (8). 2) From the perspective of conceptual structure, the latter focuses on the constitutive meaning of things, negating this expectation means that things are structurally incomplete, and the basic interpreting mode is "(应该有某个部分, 但实际上却)没有 ((that should have a certain part but in fact) don't have)…"; the former focuses on the meaning of the speaker's evaluation of things, and violating this expectation means that the thing or the behavior is inappropriate, and the interpreting mode is "(应该依照某种标准…但实际上却)没有/不 ((that should be follow a certain criterion…but in fact) don't)…".

However, the criteria mentioned above are a broad concept with different definitions in different fields. As a result, people's expectations on criteria will also change accordingly. For example, in the field of behavior, it may be expected that "应该遵守某种道德标准 (that should follow some moral criteria)"; in the field of production, it may be expected that "应该符合劳酬均衡原理 (that should follow the principle of the equilibrium of payment and reward)" [cf. 20], this is, "获得收益应该付出相应的代价 (gains should be paid at a corresponding cost)" or "付出代价应该获得相应的收益 (paying a price should get a corresponding reward)". Therefore, negating different criteria expectations will produce different interpreting modes.

Mode One: Negating moral expectations and Pointing out that things do not follow some moral criteria, or do not constrain themselves according to moral criteria. The interpreting mode is: "(应该遵守/约束…实际上却)没有/不 ((that should follow/restrain…but in fact) don't)…". For example:

(8) [浪蹄子(prodigal woman)] 不守本分的女孩儿(A girl who doesn't keep her duty)。(**Expectation**: that should keep one's duty)
  [狂徒(fanatics)]胡作非为的人(A person who acts in an unruly manner)。(**Expectation**: that should restrain one's behavior)
  [浪子(prodigal son)] 不务正业…的年轻人(Young man who doesn't do his proper business)。(**Expectation**: that should engage in proper business)

Mode Two: Negating the expectation of equalization of payment and reward, and pointing out that gains are not paid at the corresponding cost. The interpreting mode is: "(获得收益应该付出…实际上却)没有/不付出 ((Getting benefits should be paid… but actually) don't)…". For example:

(9) [白食(free meal)] 不付代价而吃到的东西(Food and drinks one gets without paying for it)。(**Expectation**: that should pay at the corresponding cost)
  [干薪(salary drawn for a sinecure] 只挂名不做事而领取的工资(A salary received for doing nothing)。(**Expectation**: that should put in hard work)
  [干股(gratuitous share)] 无偿赠送的股份(Shares that are given for free)。(**Expectation**: that should pay a price)

Mode Three: Negating industrial quality expectations, and pointing out that the product doesn't meet the standards that it should. The interpreting mode is: "(应该达到…实际上却)没有/不 ((should meet…but in fact) don't)…".For example:

(10) [废品(waste product)] 不合出厂规格的产品(Product that does not meet fac-
    tory specifications)。(**Expectation**: that should meet factory specifica-
    tions)
    [次品(substandard goods)] 不符合质量标准的产品 (Product that does not meet
    quality standards)。(**Expectation**: that should meet quality standards)
    [副品(substandard goods)] 质量没有达到标准要求的产品(Product that does
    not meet the requirements of quality standards)。(**Expectation**: that
    should meet the requirements of quality standards)

Not all concepts that violate criterion expectations can be lexicalized. It is not clear
exactly what criterion expectations people have, and which ones can be lexicalized and
which ones cannot. But judging from the available compound nouns, it seems that people
are more concerned about the moral quality of people, the quality of the products, the
relationship between payment and reward, etc., and violating these expectations is easier
to be lexicalized and easier to form compound nouns.

3.2.3   Negating Expectations of Behavioral Ability

The so-called expectation of behavioral ability refers to the speaker's knowledge that
something has the ability to perform a certain habitual action or behavior, which is
expressed syntactically as "应该能 (should be able to)…". Compound nouns that negate
expectations of behavioral ability usually have only one interpretive mode, that is, "(应
该能…实际上却)不能 ((that should be able to…but actually) can't)…". As shown in
example (11).

(11) [谎花(fruitless flowers]不结果实的花(Flowers that do not bear fruit)。(**Ex-
    pectation**: that should be able to bear fruits)
    [瞎奶(blind nipple)] ①不突起的奶头 (A nipple that does not protrude)。(**Ex-
    pectation**: that should be able to protrude)
    [死水(dead water] 不流动的水(Water that does not flow)。(**Expectation**: that
    should be able to flow)

The "能 (ability)" mentioned above is people's conventionalized knowledge of
things. For example, in the case of "花 (flower)", people expect that it "should be able
to bear fruits" or "has the ability to bear fruits"; as for "水 (water)", people expect that
it "should be able to flow" or "has the ability to flow".

4   Conclusions and Related Discussions

The understanding or interpretation of implicit negation is an important challenge in
the fields of cross-linguistic translation, second language acquisition, and dictionary
interpretation. By studying the semantic constructions of implicit negative nouns and
their interpreting modes, this paper draws the following conclusions:

The key to interpreting implicit negation lies in expectations. By identifying what
the expectation is, one can roughly know the actual meaning of implicit negation. On

this basis, an interpreting mode of implicit negation can be established. For compound nouns, implicit negation highlights three aspects of noun's meanings, and forms three expectations. Negating these expectations, we can obtain the actual meanings of implicit negative nouns and establish their interpreting modes. As shown in Table 1.

Table 1. Internal structures and interpreting modes of implicit negative nouns.

	Expected meanings	Actual meanings	Interpreting modes
Gestalt expectation	应该有(should have)…	没有(don't have)…	（应该有…实际上却）没有((that should have or contain…but actually) does not have)…
Criterion expectation	应该按照 (should follow)…	没/不按照 (don't follow)…	（应该依照…实际上却）没有依照 ((that should follow a certain criterion…but actually) don't)…
Ability expectation	应该能(should be able to)…	不能(don't /can't)…	（应该能…实际上却）不能((that should be able to…but actually) can't)…

Previous studies on implicit negation have mostly focused on verbs and adverbs [21–24], with little attention paid to negative nouns and rarely used to solve problems such as dictionary interpretation, second language acquisition, and cross language translation. The research in this paper not only contributes to the identification and interpretation of implicit negative nouns, but also contributes to solve the problems of cross-language translation, second language teaching.

Taking cross language translation as an example, many implicit negations are difficult to translate because they ignore expectations. The *Collins COBUILD* (8th edition), that mistakenly translates "vainly" in example (12) as "没找到 (couldn't find it)" [4: 435], is a good example. Actually, "vainly" in English, like "白白 (in vain)" in Chinese, implies the same expectation that "paying a price should get a corresponding reward, but actually it doesn't". Based on this expectation, it is not difficult to identify that what the speaker is attempting to express is that "(paying a price should get a corresponding reward, but actually) there is no reward". Therefore, we can modify Collins' translation as follows:

(12) He hunted vainly through his pockets for a piece of paper.
Collins: 他翻遍口袋想找一张纸，结果没找到。(8th edition：2218)
This paper: 他翻遍口袋想找一张纸（期望有收获），结果一无所获。

Similarly, implicit negation is difficult to understand [2] and grasp by second language learners [5], which also ignores expectations. For example, The *Standard Dictionary of Contemporary Chinese* (3rd edition, abbr. SD) [24] usually interprets the literal meanings of implicit negative nouns (241 words), with little attention paid to expectations. Such interpretation is not helpful for interpreting implicit negations, nor is it helpful for teaching it to L2 learners. Therefore, supplementing the expectations is not only necessary to reduce the difficulty of translation and improve the efficiency of implicit negation acquisition, but also necessary to improve the dictionary interpretations.

(13) Supplementing expectation meanings for dictionaries

[白食(free meal)] **SD**: 不付代价而吃到的东西(Food and drinks one gets without paying for it)。**This paper**: (应该付出代价实际上却)不付代价而吃到的东西 (Food and drinks one gets should pay at the corresponding cost but actually without paying for it)。

[谎言(lies)] **SD**: 骗人的话 (Deceitful words)。**This paper:** (应该真实可实际上却是)骗人的话 (Words that should be true but actually are deceitful)。

[废品(waste product)] **SD**: 不合出厂规格的产品(Product that does not meet fac tory specifications)。**This paper:** (应该合格实际上却)不合出厂规格的产品 (Product that should meet factory specifications but actually does not)。

[死水(dead water] **SD**: 不流动的水(Water that does not flow)。**This paper**: (应该能流动实际上却)不流动的水 (Water that should be able to flow but actually docs not)。

In fact, some expectation meanings have already been incorporated into dictionary interpretations. Although the number is small, it can provide a reference for the improvement of dictionary interpretation. For example [24]:

(14) [缺(lack)]②应该有而没有或不够(There should be but in fact there is none or not enough)。

[瞎(blind)]③……没有收到预期效果(That does not get an expected reward)。

In summary, the key to interpreting implicit negations is expectations. Unlike explicit negative expectations, implicit negative expectations denote conventionalized rules, criteria, experiences, etc., and are syntactically expressed as "应该 (should)…". Exploring and supplementing the expectation meaning of implicit negation can not only improve the dictionary interpretations [25], but also reduce the difficulty of cross language translation and improve the efficiency of second language teaching.

Acknowledgments. This paper is supported by the National Social Science Fund (19BYY030) and Key Project of Shandong Province's 2022 Undergraduate Teaching Reform Research (Z2022332). The anonymous reviewers of CLSW2023 put forward many valuable comments. Here, we express our sincere thanks for them!

References

1. Clark, H.: Semantics and comprehension. In: Sebeok, T. (ed.) Current Trends in Linguistics, vol. 12, pp. 1291–1428. The Hague, Mouton (1976)
2. Xiang, M., Grove, J., Giannakidou, A.: Semantic and pragmatic processes in the comprehension of negation: an event related potential study of negative polarity sensitivity. J. Neurolinguist. **38**, 71–88 (2016)

3. Al-Ghazalli, M.: Translation assessment of Arabic implicit negation into English. Int. J. English Linguist. **3**, 129–144 (2013)
4. Hou, M., Lu, Z.: A research on the extraction of negative items in Chinese translation of English explicit negation and implicit negation. Foreign Lang. Teach. Res. **3**, 435–446 (2020). (in Chinese)
5. Li, B.G.: Pragmatic analysis of implicit negation. J. Liaoning Normal Univ. (Soc. Sci. Edn.) **1**, 86–88 (2002). (in Chinese)
6. Leech, G.: Semantics. Shanghai Foreign Language Education Press, Shanghai (1981/1987). (Translated by Li R. H. et al.)
7. Horn, L.R.: A Natural History of Negation. CSLI Publications, Stanford (2001)
8. Shen, J.X.: Asymmetry and Markedness Theory. Jiangxi Education Press, Nanchang (1999). (in Chinese)
9. Lakoff, G.: Woman, Fire and Dangerous Things: What Categories Reveal about the Mind. World Book Publishing Co., Beijing (1987/2017). (Translated by Li B. J. et al.)
10. Tottie, G.: Where do negative sentences come from? Studia Linguistica **36**, 88–105 (1982)
11. Ariel, M.: Referring and accessibility. J. Linguist. **24**, 65–87 (1988)
12. Givón, T.: Negation in language: pragmatics, function, ontology. In: Peter, C. (ed.) Syntax and Semantics: Pragmatics, vol. 9, pp. 69–112. Academic Press, New York (1978)
13. Feng, G.W.: On conventional implicature. Foreign Lang. Res. **3**, 1–6 (2008). (in Chinese)
14. Grice, H.P.: Logic and conversation. Stud. Syntax Semant. Speech Acts **1**, 101–136 (1967)
15. Horn, L.R.: Pragmatic theory. In: Newmeyer, F.J. (ed.) Linguistics: The Cambridge Survey, vol. 1, pp. 113–145. Cambridge University Press, Cambridge (1988)
16. Huang, H.X., Jin, L.: On the implication of stipulation of agreements. J. Huaiyin Teach. Coll. (Soc. Sci. Edn.) **5**, 648–652 (2003). (in Chinese)
17. Pustejovsky, J.: The Generative Lexicon. MIT Press, Cambridge (1995)
18. Yuan, Y.l.: On a descriptive system of qualia structure of Chinese nouns and its application in parsing complex Chinese grammatical phenomena. Contemp. Linguist. **1**, 31–48 (2014). (in Chinese)
19. Wang, E.X., Yuan, Y.L.: The qualia role distribution in word meaning and its influence on word interpretation——taking "Color (yán) + Noun (míng)" compound words as an example. J. Foreign Lang. **2**, 33–43 (2018). (in Chinese)
20. Yuan, Y.L.: On the factivity and NPI-licensing function of the implicit negative verbs in Mandarin Chinese. Linguist. Sci. **6**, 575–586 (2014). (in Chinese)
21. Yuan, Y.L.: On the semantic level and overflow condition of the implicit negation in verbs of Mandarin Chinese. Stud. Chin. Lang. **2**, 99–113 (2012). (in Chinese)
22. Zhang, Y.Sh.: An exploration of modern Chinese presuppositional negative adverbs. research in ancient Chinese language **1**, 27–35 (1999). (In Chinese)
23. Zeng, J.H.: Research on the semantic structure and conceptual basis of implicit negative adverbs. Peking University Doctoral Dissertation, Beijing (2018). (in Chinese)
24. Li, X.J. (ed.): Dictionary of Modern Standard Chinese, 3rd edn. Foreign Language Teaching and Research Press & Language and Culture Press, Beijing (2014). (in Chinese)
25. Wang, E.X., Zhang, Zh.: The pragmatic distribution and semantic explanation of evidential prepositions. In: Dong, M.H., et al. (eds.) Chinese Lexical Semantics 2021. LNAI, vol. 13249, pp. 219–229. Springer, Heidelberg (2022). https://doi.org/10.1007/978-3-031-06703-7_16

Semantic Preferences of *Biran* and *Yiding*: A Distinctive Collexeme Analysis of Chinese Near-Synonymous Constructions of "Mod + Verb"

Zhuo Zhang[✉] [ID], Meichun Liu[ID], and Jinmeng Dou[ID]

Department of Linguistics and Translation, City University of Hong Kong, Tat Chee Avenue, Kowloon, Hong Kong, China
jessy.zh@my.cityu.edu.hk

Abstract. The Chinese modals *biran* 'must be, definitely' and *yiding* 'must be, definitely' can both express the sense of epistemic necessity. "Modal + verb" is a representative construction that expresses modal judgment. The semantic types of verbs used in the pattern may serve as crucial indicators to differentiate the semantics of the two modals. We employed Distinctive Collexeme Analyses to compare the attracted verbal collexemes between the two near-synonym constructions *"biran/yiding + verb."* Data analysis was performed using a large-scale open-sourced corpus comprising approximately 2.5 billion Chinese words, collected from media articles spanning from 2014 to 2016. The results reveal that *yiding* is more likely to be associated with personal emotions, perspectives, and evaluations, whereas *biran* usually denotes impersonal causal consequences and trends. The proposed approach has the potential to differentiate the subtle semantic distinctions conveyed by diverse modal synonyms, which speakers may not even consciously recognize, and also offer methodological implications and empirical knowledge to the study of modals.

Keywords: Epistemic Necessity Modals · Distinctive Collexeme Analyses · Modal + Verb · Near-synonymous Constructions

1 Introduction

The Chinese modal *biran* 'must be, definitely, certainly' and *yiding* 'must be, definitely' are near-synonymous modal adverbs of necessity [1, 2]. The Chinese modals of necessity share several common features: 1) They are fixed in position, serving as adverbials before the Verb Phrase (VP), and cannot appear in front of subjects; 2) They usually precede the copular verb *shì* 'be'; 3) they often employ *bù* 'not' for negation; 4) The subjective comment is typically expressed in the outermost layer of propositional meaning; 5) They are frequently used at the beginning when co-occurring with other non-modal adverbs [2]. Based on these criteria, *biran* is considered typical, whereas *yiding* is marginal [3]. Among all modal uses, "Mod + verb" is one of the most frequent post-modal patterns,

M. Dong et al. (Eds.): CLSW 2023, LNAI 14514, pp. 278–287, 2024.
https://doi.org/10.1007/978-981-97-0583-2_22

and the verbs used in the structure may serve as crucial indicators to differentiate the two modals. According to the Distribution Hypothesis, a word is featured by the company it keeps [4]. The theory was later elaborated in various forms to facilitate distributional approaches to the explorations of semantic meaning. For example, Pantel [5] supported that words with the same contexts present a similar meaning." Echoing the distributional semantics, usage-based construction grammar also supported that differences in meaning come from variances in forms and that semantic compatibility is expected if a word occurs in a construction [6, 7]. Collocation divergence associated with near-synonyms can reflect their differentiated semantics [8]. Also, notably, Schütze & Pedersen [9] proposed that "words with similar meanings will occur with similar neighbors if enough text material is available." A large sample size can potentially ensure the accuracy of distributional properties associated with words and their companies. In the pattern of "Mod + verb," a verb can be utilized in a context only when an argument matches the construction semantically [6]. Apart from usage differences crucial in the teaching and learning of modals, the semantic preferences between the *biran* and *yiding* also offer essential clues to the nuanced semantic difference between the two modals. As a pilot study for quantitative modeling of two-character Chinese modals, this study aims to discover the subtle semantic variances of the two modals. Specifically, two research questions are proposed:

1) Between *biran* and *yiding*, how are verbs attracted (or repulsed) to each modal in the pattern "Mod + verb"?
2) How to explain such usage in terms of semantic variations?

Methodologically, we employed Distinctive collexeme analysis (DCA) to find the relative attractions of verbs between the two modals in the post-modal pattern. Collexemes are lexemes that are significantly attracted to particular slots in a pattern. In the case of "Mod + Verb" pattern, if a verb is attracted to this pattern, then it is referred to as a collexeme in the context of this approach. The purpose of DCA is to identify strong preferences of collocated words for one of two studied words as opposed to the other in a linear pattern [10]. In the usage-based study, frequency is being used too much and too simply with insufficient alternative methods [11]. However, DCA goes beyond the raw frequency and finds the attracted words between semantically related constructions through association measures [12]. The method also looks promising in studying near-synonymous modal patterns. For example, Lojanica [13] compared two constructions of present ability, namely, "Subject + *can* + verb" and "Subject + *be able to* + V." Moreover, *should*-constructions "*yinggai/yingdang* + verb" in Mandarin Chinese were also explored, and the results found that *yinggai* prefers self-motion and emotion verbs [14]. In contrast, *yingdang* takes a dominant proportion of verbs involving purposive efforts with a deontic sense [14]. These studies serve as the methodological foundation for our research on "biran/yiding + verb."

As for the organization of this paper, this section is followed by the method part in Sect. 2 with briefings of corpus and details of the method in concern. Section 3 presents the distinctive collexemes and discusses the results; the last section concludes this study.

2 Method

This section presents the corpus of this study, a brief introduction to Distinctive Collexeme Analyses, and the major procedures involved with the experiments.

2.1 Corpus

We built our corpus with an open-source large-scale natural language processing dataset shared by [15]. The dataset contains 2.95 billion characters from 2.5 million news articles in 2014 and 2016 crawled from thousands of media platforms. The dataset is quite suitable for this study because the data present good quality, a large size, diverse topics, and relative freshness. During the pre-processing, we deleted repetitive articles, garbled data, and articles containing sentences with abnormal lengths to further improve the data quality.

2.2 Distinctive Collexeme Analysis of *"biran/yiding* + verb"

This section presents an overview of DCA and major procedures guiding the experiment implementation.

Overview of Distinctive Collexeme Analysis. This approach belongs to collostructional analysis that evaluates the attractions between a word and functionally similar construction (or linear pattern) by calculating the collocation strengths (CLS) through association measures such as G^2 (the log-likelihood ratio), chi-square, Mutual Information (MI) [16–18]. In particular, DCA focuses on quantifying to what extent lexemes prefer to occur in slots of one pattern as opposed to the other [14] or finding the relative attractions between two near-synonymous patterns.

Major Procedures. The major steps are as follows:

First, the corpus was segmented and POS tagged via *Stanford Core Natural Language Processing Toolkit* [19].

Second, sentences containing the two constructions were extracted, and the number of each verb in each construction was calculated.

Third, we employed Distinctive Collexeme Analyses to compare the distinctive collexemes between the near-synonym constructions [6] and implemented via the R Package *Collostructions* [20]. We also set the threshold of observations as 100 to avoid including infrequent data and produce a manageable number of attracted collexemes.

Fourth, the seven semantic domains proposed by Biber et al. [21] were fine-tuned to categorize the semantic types of verbal collexemes. The chapter defines semantic domains of lexical verbs and provides the most frequent 100 words of each domain as examples. These materials were utilized as the guideline for analyzing the verbal collexemes.

3 Results and Preliminary Discussion

This section presents the verbal collexemes respectively distinctive to *biran* and *yiding*, and also categorizes them into different semantic types to explicate the semantic variations between the two modals.

3.1   Verbal Collexemes Distinctively Attracted to *Biran*

Some POS tags are not as expected from a linguistic standpoint, but these words should not be filtered. Two types of tags are marked as verbs: 1) modal auxiliaries like 会 *huì* 'will,' 能 *néng* 'can,' and 能够 *nénggòu* 'can,' 2) causative makers like 让 *ràng* 'let' and 使 *shǐ* 'enable,' and 3) existence or relationship verbs有 *yǒu* 'have,' 具有 *jùyǒu* 'possess,' and 是 *shì* 'be.' After DCA, 40 collexemes are found to be attracted to *biran*, see Table 1. A large majority of verbs are found to be causative verbs and occurrence verbs (See Example 1–6).

Causative verbs (domain)

1) 一次次的量变<u>必然</u>导致质变。

   *yīcìcì de liàngbiàn **bìrán** **dǎozhì** zhìbiàn.*
   Several times DE quantitative changes <u>inevitably</u> **lead to** qualitative changes
   'Quantitative changes will <u>inevitably</u> **lead to** qualitative changes.'

2) 同一个战争环境、同样严峻的斗争现实，以及共同的奋斗目标，<u>必然</u>使大家的选择趋向一致。

   *Tóng yīgè zhànzhēng huánjìng, tóngyàng yánjùn de dòuzhēng xiànshí, yǐjí gòngtóng de fèndòu mùbiāo, **bìrán shǐ** dàjiā de xuǎnzé qūxiàng yīzhì.*
   ....., <u>inevitably</u> **make** all DE choices tend to consistent
   'It is the same war environment, the same severe struggle reality, and the common goal of struggle that will <u>inevitably</u> **make** everyone's choices tend to be consistent.'

Occurrence verbs

3) AMC<u>必然</u>成为首选的外部实施机构

   *AMC **bìrán** **chéngwéi** shǒuxuǎn de wàibù shíshī jīgòu*
   AMC <u>must</u> **become** the top priority external implementation agency
   'AMC <u>must</u> **become** the top priority for external implementation agency.'

4) 然后再将供应链的价格压低当然质量<u>必然</u>下降

   *ránhòu zài jiāng gōngyìng liàn de jiàgé yādī dāngrán, zhìliàng **bìrán** **xiàjiàng**;*
   then also supply chain DE price lower of course quality <u>inevitably</u> **decline**
   'Then lower the price of the supply chain, of course, the quality will <u>inevitably</u> **decline**.'

Existence or relationship verbs

5) 所以, 百分之95的人<u>必然</u>是亏损的。

   *suǒyǐ, bǎi fēn zhī 95 de rén **bìrán shì** kuīsǔn de.*
   So 95% DE people <u>are bound to</u> **be** in a loss DE
   'So, 95% of people <u>are bound to</u> **be** in a loss.'

6) 因而, 即便艺术作品在形式上具有整一性, 也不<u>必然</u>具有真理性。

   *yīn'ér, jíbiàn yìshù zuòpǐn zài xíngshì shàng jùyǒu zhěng yī xìng, yě bù **bìrán jùyǒu** zhēnlǐ xìng.*
   ....., also not <u>inevitably</u> **have** truth

'Therefore, even if a work of art has unity in form, it does not <u>necessarily</u> **have** the truth.'

Table 1. Collexemes distinctive to of "*biran* + verb"

No.	Collexemes	OBS1	EXP1	OBS2	EXP2	STR
1	导致 *dǎozhì* 'lead to'	1290	121.3	32	1200.7	5906.9
2	会 *huì* 'will'	11461	5862.1	52412	58010.9	5865.3
3	带来 *dàilái* 'bring'	546	58.6	92	579.4	2106.4
4	成为 *chéngwéi* 'become'	422	45.9	78	454.1	1602.0
5	造成 *zàochéng* 'cause'	334	31.8	13	315.2	1489.7
6	伴随 *bànsuí* 'accompany'	272	29	44	287	1054.4
7	存在 *cúnzài* 'exist'	401	64.7	304	640.3	1013.4
8	影响 *yǐngxiǎng* 'influence'	263	29.2	55	288.8	975.6
9	胜利 *shènglì* 'win'	210	19.9	7	197.1	943.7
10	受到 *shòudào* 'suffer'	236	24.5	31	242.5	942.8
11	面临 *miànlín* 'face'	209	20.4	13	201.6	902.9
12	产生 *chǎnshēng* 'produce'	221	24.5	46	242.5	820.3
13	出现 *chūxiàn* 'appear'	263	34.9	117	345.1	811.1
14	使 *shǐ* 'enable'	186	19.4	25	191.6	740.5
15	有 *yǒu* 'have'	1803	943.6	8478	9337.4	719.9
16	涉及 *shèjí* 'involve'	170	16.9	14	167.1	716.4
17	要求 *yāoqiú* 'require'	307	55.7	300	551.3	684.7
18	选择 *xuǎnzé* 'choose'	236	35.9	155	355.1	633.2
19	引起 *yǐnqǐ* 'cause'	144	14	9	139	621.6
20	发生 *fāshēng* 'occur'	217	32.2	134	318.8	596.6
21	增加 *zēngjiā* 'increase'	145	15.7	26	155.3	552.3
22	引发 *yǐnfā* 'cause'	114	10.8	4	107.2	510.7
23	走向 *zǒuxiàng* 'go towards'	109	10.7	8	106.3	464.1
24	需要 *xūyào* 'need'	456	158.4	1270	1567.6	432.1
25	是 *shì* 'be'	5457	4359	42038	43136	324.0
26	等于 *děngyú* 'equal to'	82	12.7	56	125.3	216.2
27	失败 *shībài* 'fail'	73	10.2	38	100.8	213.5
28	下降 *xiàjiàng* 'decline'	72	11.6	54	114.4	182.3
29	提高 *tígāo* 'improve'	66	10.7	51	106.3	164.9
30	经历 *jīnglì* 'experience'	80	16.2	96	159.8	158.2

(continued)

Table 1. (*continued*)

No.	Collexemes	OBS1	EXP1	OBS2	EXP2	STR
31	离 *lí* 'be away from'	87	20	131	198	147.7
32	意味 *yìwèi* 'mean'	137	47.5	381	470.5	129.5
33	包含 *bāohán* 'include'	53	9.3	48	91.7	122.7
34	受 *shòu* 'suffer'	54	10.8	64	107.2	107.6
35	具有 *jùyǒu* 'possess'	70	18.4	130	181.6	100.5
36	有所 *yǒusuǒ* 'do'	63	15.3	104	151.7	99.7
37	遇到 *yùdào* 'meet'	44	11.5	81	113.5	63.6
38	上涨 *shàngzhǎng* 'rise'	37	12.9	104	128.1	34.5
39	让 *ràng* 'let'	157	106.4	1002	1052.6	23.5
40	成 *chéng* 'become'	32	14	120	138	19.5

* Note:
1. Abbreviations: OBS = Observed Construction Frequency; EXP = Expected Construction Frequency; STR = collocation strengths.
2. Parameters: Association measure = log likelihood (the default); Significance level = $p <$ .00001; threshold = 100 (Minimum number of observations to be included for the data analysis).

3.2 Verbal Collexemes Distinctively Attracted to *Yiding*

Although the total frequency of *yiding* in the corpus is almost ten times of *biran*, 32 collexemes are found to be distinctive to *yiding*, among which almost a half are single-character words (See Table 2). These collexemes belong to different semantic domains, such as modality, activity, mental, and communication, which seem to involve active subjects (See Example 1–4). Compared with *biran, yiding* is not only able to take causative and occurrence verbs but also welcomes other domains of verbs. As a usage consequence, *yiding* seems to involve more subjective speculation, whereas *biran* focuses more on the description of trends or relations.

Modal auxiliaries
5) 我们坚信<u>一定</u>能够打造出惊艳世界的产品。
*Wǒmen jiānxìn <u>yīdìng</u> **nénggòu** dǎzào chū jīngyàn shìjiè de chǎnpǐn.*
we firmly believe <u>must</u> **be able to** create surprise world DE products
'We firmly believe that we <u>must</u> **be able to** create products that will amaze the world.'

Activity verbs
6) 老师的初衷是让孩子参与和体验整个活动, 不是要求孩子<u>一定</u>做到什么。
lǎoshī de chūzhōng shì ràng háizi cānyù hé tǐyàn zhěnggè huódòng, bùshì yāoqiú háizi <u>yīdìng</u> zuò dào shénme.
…, not be require kids <u>must</u> **achieve** what
'The original intention of teachers is to let the children participate and experience the whole activity, not to ask the children to **accomplish** anything.'

Mental verbs

7) 看过很多次这张图的人, 一定知道两张图里的竖线是一样长的。

kànguò hěnduō cì zhè zhāng tú de rén, yīdìng zhīdào liǎng zhāng tú lǐ de shù xiàn shì yīyàng zhǎng de.

…, must **know** two pictures in DE vertical lines be the same length DE

Those who have seen this picture many times <u>must</u> **know** that the vertical lines in the two pictures have the same length.

Communication verbs

8) 当然, 国外其实没有中篇小说的概念, 所以你要一定说这两部小说是长篇小说也是对的。

dāngrán, guówài qíshí méiyǒu zhòng piān xiǎoshuō de gàiniàn, suǒyǐ nǐ yào yīdìng shuō zhè liǎng bù xiǎoshuō shì chángpiān xiǎoshuō yěshì duì de.

…, so you want must say this two novels be full-length novels also be correct DE.

Of course, there is no concept of novellas in foreign countries, so it is also right if you <u>must</u> **say** that these two novels are full-length novels.

Table 2. Collexemes distinctive to of "*yiding* + verb"

No.	Collexemes	OBS1	EXP1	OBS2	EXP2	STR
1	要 *yào* 'want'	2503	18990.2	204412	187924.8	37101.2
2	能 *néng* 'can'	228	1155.2	12359	11431.8	1213.2
3	盈利 *yínglì* 'profit'	1	132.4	1442	1310.6	266.4
4	可以 *kěyǐ* 'can'	80	289.8	3078	2868.2	230.0
5	得 *dě* 'have to'	53	207.1	2204	2049.9	175.8
6	记得 *jìdé* 'remember'	0	80.2	874	793.8	168.5
7	非 *fēi* 'is not'	11	103.7	1119	1026.3	144.4
8	注意 *zhùyì* 'note'	2	71	772	703	130.5
9	知道 *zhīdào* 'know'	22	119.6	1281	1183.4	128.8
10	适合 *shìhé* 'suit'	3	70.9	769	701.1	123.2
11	想 *xiǎng* 'think'	7	69.9	755	692.1	99.3
12	能够 *nénggòu* 'can'	195	347.3	3589	3436.7	86.8
13	听 *tīng* 'listen'	0	33.7	367	333.3	70.7
14	给 *gěi* 'give'	1	29.9	325	296.1	53.8
15	买 *mǎi* 'purchase'	0	24.6	268	243.4	51.6
16	行 *xíng* 'row'	5	38.3	412	378.7	49.1
17	去 *qù* 'go'	4	34.7	374	343.3	46.8
18	做 *zuò* 'do'	8	43.2	463	427.8	46.3
19	看 *kàn* 'look'	7	40.3	432	398.7	44.8

(continued)

Table 2. (*continued*)

No.	Collexemes	OBS1	EXP1	OBS2	EXP2	STR
20	听说 *tīngshuō* 'it is said …'	0	21.2	231	209.8	44.5
21	记住 *jìzhù* 'remember'	0	19.9	217	197.1	41.8
22	了解 *liǎojiě* 'understand'	2	24.3	263	240.7	36.7
23	觉得 *juédé* 'feel'	4	28.1	302	277.9	34.6
24	准确 *zhǔnquè* 'precise'	0	14.4	157	142.6	30.2
25	注明 *zhùmíng* 'indicate'	0	14.4	157	142.6	30.2
26	喜欢 *xǐhuān* 'like'	4	23.8	255	235.2	26.9
27	以为 *yǐwéi* 'think'	0	12.7	138	125.3	26.6
28	用 *yòng* 'use'	4	22.7	243	224.3	25.0
29	安全 *ānquán* 'safe'	0	11.3	123	111.7	23.7
30	吸取 *xīqǔ* 'draw'	0	11.1	121	109.9	23.3
31	请 *qǐng* 'please'	0	9.5	104	94.5	20.0
32	必须 *bìxū* 'must'	0	9.5	103	93.5	19.8

* Note:
Abbreviations and parameters are the same as.

4 Conclusion

In conclusion, the two constructions display critical preferences over verbs: *yiding* prefers modality verbs, activity verbs, mental verbs, and communication verbs, whereas *biran* tends to take verbs of facilitation or causation, verbs of existence or relationship, and verbs of simple occurrence. The strong inclination of the verbal collexemes also suggests *yiding* tends to take actions or events led by animated subjects, whereas *biran* enjoys collocating with causative results, existential states, and objective descriptions where the subjects are primarily inanimate entities.

The study reveals the semantic preferences of *biran* and *yiding* in the "modal + verb" construction and suggests that *yiding* is more likely to be associated with personal emotions, perspectives, and evaluations, whereas *biran* usually denotes impersonal causal consequences and trends. The usage preferences discovered through the proposed approach indicate the subtle semantic distinctions encoded with different modal synonyms that the speakers may not even realize, and such findings may be utilized in text understanding and language teaching education. It also demonstrates how corpus-based collexeme analysis can be applied to linguistic inquiries.

References

1. Wu, J.: Intensification and Modal Necessity in Mandarin Chinese. Routledge, London, United Kingdom (2018)
2. Zhang, K., Mu, L., Zan, H., Han, Y., Sui, Z.: Study on modality annotation framework of modern Chinese. In: Dong, M., Lin, J., Tang, X. (eds.) CLSW 2016. LNCS, vol. 10085, pp. 291–305. Springer, Cham (2016). https://doi.org/10.1007/978-3-319-49508-8_28
3. Han, W.: Modal adverbs of necessary in modern Chinese. Doctoral dissertation. Jilin University (2020). (in Chinese)
4. Firth, J.: A synopsis of linguistic theory, 1930–55. In: Palmer, F.R. (ed.) Selected Papers of J. R. Firth (1952–59), pp. 168–205. Longmans, London (1968)
5. Pantel, P.: Inducing ontological co-occurrence vectors. In: Proceedings of the 43rd Conference of the Association for Computational Linguistics, ACL'05, pp. 125–132. Association for Computational Linguistics, Morristown, NJ, USA (2005)
6. Goldberg, A.E.: Constructions. A Construction Grammar Approach to Argument Structure. Chicago University Press, Chicago, USA (1995)
7. Diessel, H.: The Grammar Network: How Linguistic Structure is Shaped by Language Use. Cambridge University Press, Cambridge, UK (2019)
8. Hilpert, M., Flach, S.: Disentangling modal meanings with distributional semantics. Digit. Scholarsh. Human. **36**(2), 307–321 (2021)
9. Schütze, H., Pedersen, J.: Information retrieval based on word senses. 17 In: Proceedings of the 4th Annual Symposium on Document Analysis and Information Retrieval, pp. 161–175. Las Vegas, Nevada (1995)
10. Gries, S.T., Stefanowitsch, A.: Extending collostructional analysis: a corpus-based perspectives on 'alternations.' Int. J. Corpus Linguist. **9**(1), 97–129 (2004)
11. Gries, S.T.: On, or against?, (just) frequency. In: Boas, H.C. (ed.) Directions for Pedagogical Construction Grammar: Learning and Teaching (with) Constructions, vol. 49, pp. 47–72. De Gruyter Mouton, Boston & Berlin (2022)
12. Flach, S.: Beyond modal idioms and modal harmony: a corpus-based analysis of gradient idiomaticity in mod + adv collocations. English Lang. Linguist. **25**(4), 743–765 (2021)
13. Lojanica, T.T.: Exploring present ability: a collostructional approach. Nasledje Kragujevac **18**(48), 105–115 (2021)
14. Zhang, Z., Liu, M.: A distinctive collexeme analysis of near-synonym constructions "ying-dang/ying-gai + verb. Paper presentation at the 36th Pacific Asia Conference on Language, Information and Computation, De La Salle University & National University, Manila, Philippines, 21 October 2022
15. Xu, B.: Sep. "NLP Chinese corpus: Largescale Chinese corpus for NLP." Corpus version 1.0 (2019). https://doi.org/10.5281/zenodo.3402023. ED: 10 March 2022
16. Stefanowitsch, A., Gries, S.T.: Collostructions: investigating the interaction of words and constructions. Int. J. Corpus Linguist. **8**(2), 209–243 (2003)
17. Gries, S.T.: More (old and new) misunderstandings of collostructional analysis: on Schmid and Küchenhoff (2013). Cogn. Linguist. **26**(3), 505–536 (2015)
18. Gries, S.T.: 15 years of collostructions: some long overdue additions/corrections (to/of actually all sorts of corpus-linguistics measures). Int. J. Corpus Linguist. **24**(3), 385–412 (2019)
19. Manning, C.D., Mihai, S., John, B., Jenny, F., Steven, J.B., David, M.: The Stanford CoreNLP natural language processing toolkit. In: Proceedings of the 52nd Annual Meeting of the Association for Computational Linguistics: System Demonstrations, pp. 55–60. Baltimore, Maryland (2014)

20. Flach, S.: Collostructions: an R implementation for the family of collostructional methods. Package version v.0.2.0 (2021). https://sfla.ch/collostructions/. ED: 3 March 2022
21. Biber, D., Stig, J., Geoffrey, L., Susan, C., Edward, F.: Longman Grammar of Spoken and Written English. Longman, Harlow, UK (1999)

Zero Anaphora Errors and the Restriction Rules of Zero Anaphora in Discourse for Middle and Senior International Students

Hao You[✉]

Department of Chinese Language and Literature, Peking University, Beijing 100871, China
Youhao0402@163.com

Abstract. Zero anaphora is an important form of textual cohesion in Chinese. However, there have been few previous studies on zero anaphora errors, and the analysis of the causes of zero anaphora errors has been too general, which is not suitable for teaching purposes. As a result, most international students are unsure about when to use zero anaphora. To help international students better understand and master zero anaphora, we selected 50 compositions written by international students from the HSK Dynamic Composition Corpus and annotated them. Based on the labeling results, zero anaphora errors are classified into two types: lack of zero anaphora and overuse of zero anaphora. Among these, the overuse of zero anaphora can be further categorized into two subtypes: topic missing due to overuse of zero anaphora and reference errors due to overuse of zero anaphora.In addition, we have also observed the limitations of zero anaphora in discourse by analyzing the errors made by international students, and fully explored its lexical and semantic features to provide more targeted guidance for their writing.

Keywords: Zero Anaphora · Zero Anaphora Error · Topic Missing · Reference Error

1 Introduction

Chinese discourse anaphora can be roughly divided into three types: noun anaphora, pronoun anaphora and zero anaphora. As a common anaphora type, zero anaphora can make the discourse more concise and cohesive if it can be used correctly. On the contrary, it will cause ambiguity. For example:

(1) ①爸爸那时三十岁, ②每天只要爸爸一上班, ③家里就只有我一个人, ④ 午餐时, ⑤爸爸 会叫公司的员工送饭给我, ⑥就这样一个人在家吃饭。(HSK动态作文语料库2.0)
① bà ba nà shí sān shí suì, ② měi tiān zhǐ yào bà ba yī shàng bān, ③ jiā lǐ jiù zhǐ yǒu wǒ yī gè rén, ④ wǔ cān shí, ⑤ bà ba huì jiào gōng sī de yuán gōng sòng fàn gěi wǒ, ⑥ jiù zhè yàng yī gè rén zài jiā chī fàn 。
① My father was thirty years old at that time. ② Every day as long as my father went to work, ③ I was the only person at home. ④ At lunch, ⑤ My father would ask the employees of the company to send me food.

M. Dong et al. (Eds.): CLSW 2023, LNAI 14514, pp. 288–301, 2024.
https://doi.org/10.1007/978-981-97-0583-2_23

In example (1), the sixth clause uses zero anaphora, and the fifth sentence contains multiple anaphora centers: "*bà bà* 爸爸 (dad)", "*gōng sī de yuán gōng* 公司的员工 (company employees)" and "*wǒ* 我 (I)". According to the Chinese principle of anaphora center ranking (topic > subject > object > others), "*bà bà* 爸爸 (Dad)" as the subject is more likely to become the anaphoric reference. However, based on the context, the actual anaphoric reference should be "*wǒ* 我 (I)" Therefore, to avoid ambiguity, the topic "*wǒ* 我 (I)" should be fully expressed. It can be seen from this that the incorrect use of zero anaphora can result in unclear expression of meaning.

Gao Shiyu pointed out that international students do not know when to use zero anaphora [1]. Gao Ninghui, Xu Hong and Zeng Lijuan summarized some tendency rules for using zero anaphora [2–4]. For example, within the same topic chain, there are very close semantic relationships between clauses, so zero anaphora tends to be used within the same topic chain. Xu Yulong's summary is more comprehensive, and he divides the factors that can affect the use of zero anaphora into five subcategories: discourse factors, semantic factors, pragmatic factors, stylistic factors, and salience of topics [5]. However, these rules are mostly not directly applicable to teaching international students writing. For example, although the topic chain can explain when to use zero anaphora, different scholars have different definitions of the topic chain [6, 7], which will inevitably cause difficulties when applied to teaching. Moreover, stylistic and pragmatic factors are relatively general and not suitable for use in teaching.

Therefore, this article aims to systematically observe some usage restrictions of zero anaphora in discourse and fully explore its lexical semantic features from the perspective of correcting international students' errors of zero anaphora in writing, so as to correct their errors more effectively.

2 Overview

Zero anaphora errors, as part of discourse errors, have been discussed in many studies, but there are relatively few studies specifically focusing on zero anaphora errors. Chen Si and Gao Shiyu conducted detailed analyses of zero anaphora errors in the narrative discourse of international students [1, 8]. In general, zero anaphora errors can be classified into two main categories: lack of zero anaphora and overuse of zero anaphora. Gao Shiyu further subdivides the errors into five subcategories: lack of zero anaphora, incorrect use of conjunctive adverbs, redundant attributive, topic change and semantic change between clauses [1]. Chen Si's classification is similar, but with slight differences [8]. Additionally, she adds the subcategories of lack of zero anaphora in continuous actions, lack of zero anaphora in non-obvious action topics, and lack of zero anaphora when the predicate has the same or opposite meanings. Zeng Lijuan, Chen Chen, Huang Yuhua, Yang Chun, Xiao Xiqiang, You Hao, and Lu Dawei also mentioned zero anaphora errors as part of discourse errors [5, 9–13]. For example, the omissions discussed by Chen Chen and the pronoun reference errors mentioned by Xiao Xiqiang, both fundamentally fall under the category of zero anaphora errors, which can be classified as either lack of zero anaphora or overuse of zero anaphora [9, 12].

Apart from the classification of types, scholars have also analyzed the causes of zero anaphora errors. From the characteristics of Mandarin itself, the distribution of zero anaphora in Chinese discourse is complex and it can occur in positions such as the topic, subject, object, and attributive. Furthermore, zero anaphora in Mandarin also exhibits the characteristics of multiple types and difficulty in identification, further increasing the difficulty for students to learn [8]. From the perspective of the native language of international students, negative transfer of the mother tongue is also an important influencing factor [1]. Scholars have also proposed some specific rules for the use of zero anaphora. Gao Ninghui has summarized many principles of when to use pronoun and zero anaphora in Chinese discourse [2]. For example, components in the same topic chain or parallel structures are tend to use zero anaphora, because the semantic relationship between the clauses is close. While if these components are between topic chain and topic chain or after conjunctions and time words, they are tend to use pronoun anaphora. Compared to abstract explanations like negative transfer of the mother tongue, the rules summarized by Gao Ninghui are more concrete, especially the rule that pronouns are preferred for anaphora after conjunctions and time words, which provides a formal marker and is more beneficial for international students to grasp the usage of zero anaphora [2].

The rules could go further. For example, between two topic chains, there is a tendency to use zero anaphora, but how to judge the boundary of the topic chain is still controversial between different scholars, and it will be more difficult for international students to understand. In addition, the concept of semantic distance, which refers to the closeness or remoteness of meaning between different clauses, is also relatively abstract. Therefore, it raises the question of whether there are any formal markers that exist to help us identify semantic distance. This is the issue we want to research.

3   Corpus Selection and Processing

3.1   Corpus Introduction

This article selected 50 narrative compositions titled "*wǒ de tóng nián* 我的童年 (My Childhood)" from the HSK Dynamic Composition Corpus (2.0), and the students who wrote these compositions are at an intermediate to advanced level. They come from Southeast Asian countries such as Malaysia, Thailand, and Indonesia.

3.2   Discourse Theory and Corpus Processing

Native speakers are not sensitive enough to discourse errors, and even annotated language materials may still contain many unrecognized errors [13]. To ensure a comprehensive observation of zero anaphora errors produced by international students, it is necessary to adopt a unified standard for annotation. In recent years, theories such as Centering Theory, Topic Chain, and The Clause Complex Theory have gradually been applied to discourse analysis. These theories are of significant importance for studying discourse anaphora. Centering Theory suggests that discourse entities can be coherently linked through anaphora, but different entities have different priority to be anaphora [14, 15]. Topic Chain Theory is similar and mainly explains how clauses are associated. However, both of these theories are suitable for explaining rather than observing discourse errors because they are analytical, not operable. Different from the previous two theories, The

Clause Complex Theory is a formal model of discourse with specific labeling methods. After labeling, the relationship between Naming and Telling is visually demonstrated. Another important finding of The Clause Complex Theory is that each clause with incomplete components can be turned into a Naming-Telling Clause[1] by simply adding topic to the beginning of a clause or Telling to the end of a clause through the context. By completing the components of the clause, we can clearly find out whether the clause is correct, or in other words, whether there is an error in the clause. After labeling in this way, the zero anaphora error generated by international students can be systematically analyzed.

Therefore, in this article, we have utilized The Clause Complex Theory to provide comprehensive annotations for the compositions of international students, leaving no omissions. Additionally, we have thoroughly examined zero anaphora errors in the compositions of international students, focusing on a complete topic structure. It is important to note that this article primarily focuses on zero anaphora errors made by international students, and thus, we have made unified corrections for other unrelated errors.

4   Zero Anaphora Error Analysis

From a broader perspective, zero anaphora errors can be divided into two categories: lack of zero anaphora and overuse of zero anaphora.

4.1   Lack of Zero Anaphora

Although Lack of zero anaphora will lead to lengthy text, it will not affect the interpretation of the sentence. This type of error can be easily identified after labeling. For example:

(2) 我特别高兴，一回到家就滔滔不绝地对父母讲了很多有趣的事情，我讲得很快，我认为父母都听懂了，也会和我一样感到有趣。

wǒ tè bié gāo xìng, yī huí dào jiā jiù tāo tāo bù jué de duì fù mǔ jiǎng le hěn duō yǒu qù de shì qíng, wǒ jiǎng de hěn kuài, wǒ rèn wéi fù mǔ dōu tīng dǒng le, yě huì hé wǒ yī yàng gǎn dào yǒu qù 。

I was very happy. As soon as I got home, I talked a lot of interesting things to my parents. I spoke so quickly that I thought my parents understood me and were as amused as I was.

Example (2) can be represented as follows according to The Clause Complex Theory:

(2a)我特别高兴，
　　一回到家就滔滔不绝地对父母讲了很多有趣地事情，
　　我讲得很快，
　　我认为父母都听懂了，
　　也会和我一样感到有趣。

---

[1] In topic-Telling Clause, he semantic components of the clauses need to be complete, the semantic relations between the components should be clear, and the syntactic order of the components should be customary, without unexplainable components.

After labeling, we can easily find that the clauses in (2a) all share the topic "*wǒ* 我(I)", "*tè bié gāo xìng* 特别高兴 (especially happy)", "*yī huí dào jiā jiù tāo tāo bù jué de duì fù mǔ jiǎng le hěn duō yǒu qù de shì qíng* 一回到家就滔滔不绝地对父母讲了很多有趣地事情(I talked a lot of interesting things to my parents when I got home)", "*jiǎng de hěn kuài* 讲得很快(I spoke very quickly)", "*rèn wéi fù mǔ dōu tīng dǒng le* 父母都听懂了(I think my parents understood)" are all Tellings of "*wǒ* 我(I)", so the last two "*wǒ* 我(I)" can be omitted. In this way, The sentences will be simpler and clearer.

After labeling, we can find that a fundamental principle of zero anaphora is the presence of shared constituents between the current clause and the preceding clause. These shared constituents can either be the topic of the preceding clause or other elements such as objects or modifiers. This only serves as a basic guideline for the use of zero anaphora, as the usage can be influenced by various factors.

4.2 Overuse of Zero Anaphora

Overuse of zero anaphora refers to the situation where pronouns or nouns should have been used for reference, but zero anaphora is mistakenly used instead. It includes two types: topic missing due to overuse of zero anaphora and reference errors due to overuse of zero anaphora.

Topic Missing due to Overuse of Zero Anaphora. Topic missing due to overuse of zero anaphora refers to the phenomenon where a clause without a topic cannot share the topic from the previous clause. The reason for this error may be that the topic of the missing clause does not appear in the previous clause or that the topic cannot be carried over from the previous clause due to other reasons. According to our annotations, the factors that affect the use of zero anaphora include time words, conjunctions, prepositional phrases, predicate phrases, and stylistic structure.

Time Words. After time words, there is a tendency to use pronoun anaphora instead of zero anaphora. However, international students often still use zero anaphora after time words. According to our statistics, this type of error frequently occurs when the preceding time words include "… + *hòu/shí* 后/时 (after/when)", "*xiǎo shí hòu* 小时候 (when I was young)", "*yǒu shí hòu* 有时候(sometimes)", and similar expressions.For example[2]:

(3) 妈妈听了, 也不明白我说什么, 只好挥手又摇头, 无可奈何。又到了上小学时, (妈妈)把我送到了康文小学。

mā mā tīng le, yě bù míng bái wǒ shuō shén me, zhǐ hǎo huī shǒu yòu yáo tóu, wú kě nài hé。yòu dào le shàng xiǎo xué shí, (mā mā) bǎ wǒ sòng dào le kāng wén xiǎo xué。

After listening, my mother did not understand what I said, so she waved and shook her head, helpless. When it was time for primary school again, (my mother) sent me to Kangwen Primary School.

(4) 我出生在泰国, 知道他们的困难, 就有很大的决心要把语言及念书方面一定达到大学的程度。小的时候(我)在一家学校念泰文及中文的小学。毕业再转到传达夜间部读中文。

---

[2] Complete topics are added in parentheses according to the context.

wǒ chū shēng zài tài guó, zhī dào tā men de kùn nán, jiù yǒu hěn dà de jué xīn yào bǎ yǔ yán jí niàn shū fāng miàn yī dìng dá dào dà xué de chéng dù。 xiǎo de shí hòu (wǒ) zài yī jiā xué xiào niàn tài wén jí zhōng wén de xiǎo xué。 bì yè zài zhuǎn dào chuán dá yè jiān bù dú zhōng wén。

I was born in Thailand, and knowing their difficulties, I have a great determination to study well and make the language and learning reach up to university level. When I was young, (I) studied Thai and Chinese in a primary school. After graduation, I transferred to the communication night department to learn Chinese.

According to Gao Ninghui [1], time words often indicate an upcoming change in semantics, which means the beginning of a new topic chain. Therefore, there is a tendency to use pronouns instead of zero anaphora. In example (3), the topic for both "bù míng bái wǒ shuō shén me, zhǐ hǎo huī shǒu yòu yáo tóu, wú kě nài hé 也不明白我说什么, 只好挥手又摇头, 无可奈何(did not understand what I said, so I had to wave and shake my head, and there was nothing to do)" and "bǎ wǒ sòng dào le kāng wén xiǎo xué 把我送到了康文小学(sent me to Kangwen Middle School)" is "mā mā 妈妈(mom)". However, the appearance of the time phrase "yòu dào le shàng xiǎo xué shí 又到了上小学时 (by the time I was in elementary school)" signifies a change in the topic chain, thus requiring the repetition of the topic "mā mā 妈妈(mom)". In example (4), the preceding topics are all "wǒ 我(I)", and the subsequent time words "xiǎo de shí hòu 小的时候 (when I was small)" and "bì yè 毕业(by the time I graduated)" indicate a change in time, therefore pronouns should be used for anaphora instead of zero anaphora.

Conjunctions. After conjunctions, there is a tendency to use pronoun anaphora instead of zero anaphora. However, international students sometimes use zero anaphora after conjunctions, resulting in a missing topic in the sentence. This type of error frequently occurs when conjunctions like "yīn cǐ 因此 (therefore)"and "rán ér 然而 (however)" are present.

(5) 我这做二姐的有时也会帮他们出头, 然而(我)也会遭到被打、被骂的命运。
wǒ zhè zuò èr jiě de yǒu shí yě huì bāng tā men chū tóu, rán ér(wǒ) yě huì zāo dào bèi dǎ, bèi mà de mìng yùn。
As the second elder sister, sometimes I will help them to fight back, but (I) will also be beaten and scolded.

(6) 我们家中的共同点就是有浓厚的旅游遗传因子, 因此(我们)从小就和家人到处旅行, 北上南下, 吃尽美食。
wǒ men jiā zhōng de gòng tóng diǎn jiù shì yǒu nóng hòu de lǚ yóu yí chuán yīn zǐ, yīn cǐ (wǒ men) cóng xiǎo jiù hé jiā rén dào chù lǚ xíng, běi shàng nán xià, chī jìn měi shí。
The common denominator in our families is a strong travel genetic factor, so (we) grew up traveling with our families, traveling from north to south, eating good food.

Gao Ninghui pointed out that there is a tendency to use pronoun anaphora, especially after adversative conjunctions, which indicates an upcoming semantic shift [1]. Therefore, it is unlikely to use zero anaphora. For example, in sentence (5), the topic of "yě huì zāo dào bèi dǎ, bèi mà de mìng yùn 也会遭到被打, 被骂的命运 (will also be beaten and scolded)" is "wǒ zhè zuò èr jiě de 我这做二姐的 (As the second elder siste)" (as mentioned in the previous clause). However, the presence of the adversative conjunction "*rán ér* 然而 (however)" suggests an impending change in the semantic meaning of the sentence, thus favoring the use of pronoun anaphora instead of zero anaphora.

Prepositional Phrases. When a prepositional phrase functions as an independent clause, its topic generally appears in the following clause. In other words, the topic of the clause that follows the prepositional phrase should be fully supplemented, and zero anaphora should not be used, as it may result in topic missing. According to our statistics, this type of error frequently occurs when prepositions such as "*chú le* 除了 (besides)" and "*yóu yú* 由于(due to)" are used. For example:

(7) 六岁是上小学的年纪, 当然我也不落人后地上了小学, 由于语言不通, (我)常常闹笑话。可是班主任却十分疼爱我, 一起帮我解决学业上的问题, 放了学还留下替我做课后指导, 我的功课也日趋进步。

liù suì shì shàng xiǎo xué de nián jì, dāng rán wǒ yě bù luò rén hòu dì shàng le xiǎo xué, yóu yú yǔ yán bù tōng , (wǒ) cháng cháng nào xiào huà 。 kě shì bān zhǔ rèn què shí fēn téng ài wǒ, yī qǐ bāng wǒ jiě jué xué yè shàng de wèn tí, fàng le xué hái liú xià tì wǒ zuò kè hòu zhǐ dǎo, wǒ de gōng kè yě rì qū jìn bù 。

I also went to primary school at the age of six, because the language we used is different, (I) often be laughed at. But the head teacher is very concerned about me, he always help me solve the academic problems, stay with me to do after-school guidance, my study is also improving day by day.

(8) 从我七岁开始, 除了上学以外, (我)回到家还要帮妈妈煮饭、洗衣服和照顾幼小的弟妹。

cóng wǒ qī suì kāi shǐ, chú le shàng xué yǐ wài, (wǒ) huí dào jiā hái yào bāng mā mā zhǔ fàn 、 xǐ yī fú hé zhào gù yòu xiǎo de dì mèi 。

Since I was seven years old, in addition to going to school, (I) have to help my mother cook, wash clothes and take care of my younger siblings after school.

(9) 我不但当了班上的主席, 还被选为学生会的学习部, 工作更忙了。除了要与各班主任联系, 了解各班的学习成绩外, (我)还要派人或亲自给别班学进行辅导、举行演讲比赛等等。

wǒ bù dàn dāng le bān shàng de zhǔ xí, hái bèi xuǎn wéi xué shēng huì de xué xí bù, gōng zuò gèng máng le 。 chú le yào yǔ gè bān zhǔ rèn lián xì, liǎo jiě gè bān de xué xí chéng jì wài, (wǒ) hái yào pài rén huò qīn zì gěi bié bān xué jìn xíng fǔ dǎo, jǔ xíng yǎn jiǎng bǐ sài děng děng 。

I not only became the chairman of the class, but also was elected to the study department of the student Union, which made my work even busier. In addition to contacting each class teacher to know the academic performance of each class, (I) have to send or personally give guidance to other classes, hold speech competitions and so on.

In Chinese, clauses without topics can appear in both the beginning and the end of a sentence. When a clause without topic appears at the beginning of a sentence, the function of such clauses is similar to that of non-finite verb clauses in inflectional languages. Specifically, the stronger the syntactic contrast between the clauses, the higher the possibility of the topic appearing in the following clause. When a prepositional phrase appears as an independent clause, it is generally adverbial in function and serves as background information, while the clause that follows is the main content. Therefore, when a prepositional phrase appears independently as a clause, it usually requires the topic to appear in the following clause. In Example (7), the topic of "*cháng cháng nào xiào huà* 常常闹笑话 (often make jokes)" is "*wǒ* 我(me)". Ideally, it should be able to be inferred from the preceding clause. However, the prepositional phrase "*yóu yú yǔ yán bù tōng* 由于语言不通(due to the language barrier)" functions as an adverbial expressing a cause, and it contrasts strongly with the result "*cháng cháng nào xiào huà* 常常闹笑话 (often make jokes)". Therefore, the topic "*wǒ* 我(me)" tends to be supplemented from the following clause.In Example (8), the entire clause "*chú le shàng xué yǐ wài* 除了上学以外(besides going to school)" expresses an excluding condition. To highlight the result that follows, the topic "*wǒ* 我(me)" also tends to be supplemented from the following clause.

What's more, prepositional phrases often appear together with time words to influence the use of zero anaphora. For example:

(10) 上了初中之后, 由于功课较繁重, (我)便减少了在店里帮忙。父亲便请了一个伙计来协助料理店里的工作。
shàng le chū zhōng zhī hòu, yóu yú gōng kè jiào fán zhòng, (wǒ) biàn jiǎn shǎo le zài diàn lǐ bāng máng。fù qīn biàn qǐng le yī gè huǒ jì lái xié zhù liào lǐ diàn lǐ de gōng zuò。

After entering junior high school, due to heavy homework,(I) reduced my help in the store. My father asked a man to help with the work in the restaurant.

(11) 当我放学回来, 吃过午饭后, 就丢下书包跟堂妹及附近的小孩出游去了。小时候, 由于少年不知愁滋味, (我)便天真烂漫地以为, 人生最大的乐趣莫过于有一班契合的朋友, 每天嘻嘻哈哈地过日子。
dāng wǒ fàng xué huí lái, chī guò wǔ fàn hòu, jiù diū xià shū bāo gēn táng mèi jí fù jìn de xiǎo hái chū yóu qù le。xiǎo shí hòu, yóu yú shào nián bù zhī chóu zī wèi, (wǒ) biàn tiān zhēn làn màn de yǐ wéi, rén shēng zuì dà de lè qù mò guò yú yǒu yī bān qì hé de péng yǒu, měi tiān xī xī hā hā de guò rì zi。

When I came back from school, after lunch, I left my bag and went out with my cousin and the children in the neighborhood. As a child, do not know the taste of sorrow, (I) innocently thought that the greatest pleasure in life is to have a group of good friends, and live happily every day.

Example (11) not only involves changes in time, but also has a prepositional phrase that appears as background information, and the subject tends to refer back. Therefore, even if the referring object "*wǒ* 我(me)" appears in the preceding clause, it is still necessary to supplement the complete topic of "*wǒ* 我(me)" in the following clause.

Predicate Phrases. Similar to prepositional phrases appearing as independent clauses, some predicate phrases also function as background information when used as independent clauses. Their purpose is to highlight the content expressed in the following sentence. After such clauses, pronouns or nouns should be used for referencing, and zero anaphora should not be used, otherwise it would result in topic missing. These types of predicate phrases are mainly composed of verbs such as "*kàn* 看(see)", "*tīng* 听(listen)", "*xiǎng* 想" (think), and so on.

(12) 我成年后感到很遗憾，因为小时候不努力学习，华语掌握得不好。而现在看教华语实在吃香, (我)才手忙脚乱学好汉语来教汉语。

wǒ chéng nián hòu gǎn dào hěn yí hàn, yīn wèi xiǎo shí hòu bù nǔ lì xué xí, huá yǔ zhǎng wò de bù hǎo。ér xiàn zài kàn jiāo huá yǔ shí zài chī xiāng, (wǒ) cái shǒu máng jiǎo luàn xué hǎo hàn yǔ lái jiāo hàn yǔ。

When I became an adult, I was sorry that I did not study hard enough as a child and did not master Chinese well. But now that teaching Chinese is really popular, (I) have been scrambling to learn Chinese well in order to teach Chinese.

(13) 年纪轻轻的我，却对狗的死感到挺伤心的。刚踏入小学一年级，看见身旁的同学每天都有父母接送, (我)真的有些埋怨父母的不是。

nián jì qīng qīng de wǒ, què duì gǒu de sǐ gǎn dào tǐng shāng xīn de。gāng tà rù xiǎo xué yī nián jí, kàn jiàn shēn páng de tóng xué měi tiān dōu yǒu fù mǔ jiē sòng, (wǒ) zhēn de yǒu xiē mán yuàn fù mǔ de bù shì。

At my young age, I felt sad about my dog's death. At the first grade of primary school, and saw the students around me have parents pick up every day, (I) really have some complaints about my parents.

In Example (12), the predicate "*xiàn zài kàn jiāo huá yǔ shí zài chī xiāng* 现在看教华语实在吃香 (Now it seems that teaching Mandarin is very popular)" functions as an independent clause. Its purpose is to highlight the content of the following sentence, and the topic tends to be supplemented from the following clause. The topic tends to be supplemented from the following clause, so it is necessary to complete the topic "*wǒ* 我(me)" before "*shǒu máng jiǎo luàn xué hǎo hàn yǔ lái jiāo hàn yǔ* 手忙脚乱地学好汉语来教汉语 (frantically learn Mandarin to teach Mandarin)".

Stylistic Structure. In the "Introduction-Body-Conclusion" style of writing, these three parts typically adopt different discourse structures. Therefore, different parts tend to use pronouns or nouns for reference, and zero anaphora should not be used. Such errors often contain evaluative elements indicating a summary or evaluation of the event.

(14) 我和同班的同学非偷向侧窗外的那家电视机看电视节目不可, (这)算是很有趣也很高兴。

wǒ hé tóng bān de tóng xué fēi tōu xiàng cè chuāng wài de nà jiā diàn shì jī kàn diàn shì jié mù bù kě, (zhè) suàn shì hěn yǒu qù yě hěn gāo xìng。

My classmates and I usually sneak to the TV set outside the side window to watch TV programs, (which) is very interesting and happy.

(15) 有一次我把一粒珠子塞入鼻孔内拿不出来，只有大声地哭，爸妈不知怎么办，最后妈妈用口吸出来, (这)真叫大家虚惊一场。

yǒu yī cì wǒ bǎ yī lì zhū zi sāi rù bí kǒng nèi ná bù chū lái, zhǐ yǒu dà shēng de kū, bà mā bù zhī zěn me bàn, zuì hòu mā mā yòng kǒu xī chū lái, (zhè) zhēn jiào dà jiā xū jīng yī chǎng。

Once I put a bead into the nostril can not get out, crying loudly, parents do not know what to do, and finally mother sucked it out with the mouth, (this thing) turned out to be a false alarm.

In example (14), the previous clause describes the entire event, while the latter clause provides an evaluative summary of the event. The conclusion and the body tend to use different discourse structures, so the topic "*zhè* 这 (this)" needs to be added before "*suàn shì hěn yǒu qù yě hěn gāo xìng* 算是很有趣也很高兴 (can be considered interesting and enjoyable)". The same applies to example (15), where the previous clauses describe the entire event, and the last clause provides an evaluative summary "*zhēn jiào dà jiā xū jīng yī chǎng* 真叫大家虚惊一场 (turned out to be a false alarm)". Therefore, the topic "*zhè* 这 (this)" also needs to be completed. In the "Introduction-Body-Conclusion" style of writing, there is a close semantic connection within each part, forming a whole, while the connection between different parts is relatively weaker. Therefore, pronouns are also commonly used for referencing between different parts.

From the observation of actual language data, it can be seen that the topic missing caused by overuse of zero anaphora can often be compensated for by the previous clause, but due to some special pragmatic habits or other factors in Chinese, the continuity of the topic is affected. International students may not be able to master these rules well, thus leading to such errors.

Reference Errors Due to Overuse of Zero Anaphora. The reference errors due to overuse of zero anaphora refer to the situation where a clause that employs zero anaphora tends to select a constituent from the preceding clause as the topic, but based on the context, it is not the intended referent by the author. For the sake of convenience in explanation, we define two concepts: the topic semantic requirement, which refers to the semantic requirement of a clause lacking a topic in relation to its topic, and the habitual matching topic, which refers to the shared constituent found in the context that is most likely to serve as the topic. The reference errors due to overuse of zero anaphora occur when there is a mismatch between the topic semantic requirement and the habitual matching topic. Based on statistical analysis of real corpora, such errors can be broadly categorized into two types: inconsistency between the habitual matching topic and the entity required by the topic semantic requirement, and inconsistency between the habitual matching topic and the scope required by the topic semantic requirement.

Inconsistency Between the Habitual Matching Topic and the Entity Required by the Topic Semantic Requirement. The inconsistency between the habitual matching topic and the entity required by the topic semantic requirement refers to the situation where a clause lacks a topic, and there are multiple constituents in the preceding clause that could possibly serve as the topic, but the entity referred to by the constituent serving as the habitual matching topic is inconsistent with the entity required by the topic semantic requirement, leading to a reference error in the clause. This type of error often occurs when the preceding clause is a ditransitive structure, which means a sentence containing two or more parallel verb predicates, each with an object that could potentially be selected as the topic. In this case, the presence of multiple candidate constituents may lead to inconsistent selection and subsequent reference errors.

(16) 爸爸会叫公司的员工送饭给我, (我)就这样一个人在家吃饭。
bà bà huì jiào gōng sī de yuán gōng sòng fàn gěi wǒ, (wǒ)jiù zhè yàng yī gè rén zài jiā chī fàn。

My father would ask the employees of the company to bring me food, (I) ate at home alone.

(17) 医生不让我读书。(我)在家里休养了差不多一年之久。

yī shēng bù ràng wǒ dú shū。(wǒ)zài jiā lǐ xiū yǎng le chà bù duō yī nián zhī jiǔ。

The doctor don't let me go to school. (I) convalesced at home for almost a year.

Wang Deliang pointed out that different grammatical constituents in Chinese have varying abilities to serve as the center of reference, roughly following the sequence of "theme > subject > object > others" [14]. For example, in sentence (16) "*jiù zhè yàng yī gè rén zài jiā chī fàn* 就这样一个人在家吃饭 (ate at home alone)", the topic is missing, and the constituents "*bà bà* 爸爸 (father)", "*gōng sī de yuán gōng* 公司的员工 (employee of the company)", and "*wǒ* 我 (me)" in the previous clause could all potentially serve as the topic. However, their abilities to serve as the topic differ. "*bà bà* 爸爸 (father)" is the habitual matching topic, so sentence (16) is likely to be understood as "*bà bà jiù zhè yàng yī gè rén zài jiā chī fàn* 爸爸就这样一个人在家吃饭 (fatherate at home alone)", but the topic required by the semantic requirement is "*wǒ* 我 (me)". To avoid misunderstanding, the topic "*wǒ* 我 (me)" should be explicitly stated. In sentence (17) "*zài jiā lǐ xiū yǎng le chà bù duō yī nián zhī jiǔ* 在家休养了差不多一年之久 (convalesced at home for almost a year)", the topic is missing. The habitual matching topic is "*yī shēng* 医生(doctor)", but the topic required by the semantic requirement is "*wǒ* 我 (me)", so "*wǒ* 我 (me)" should also be explicitly stated to avoid ambiguity.

Inconsistency Between the Habitual Matching Topic and the Scope Required by the Topic Semantic Requirement. The inconsistency between the habitual matching topic and the scope required by the topic semantic requirement refers to the situation where a clause lacks a topic, and the habitual matching topic is a part of the topic semantic requirement. That is, the habitual matching topic refers to a specific entity, while the topic semantic requirement requires a set or a group of entities. Therefore, the habitual matching topic and the topic semantic requirement are inconsistent in terms of their scope or range.

(18) 我总是带着弟妹到原野里游玩，到小溪边捕捉小鱼虾、小鸟，青蛙。(我们)有时候就跳进河里游泳，享受美好的欢乐时光。

wǒ zǒng shì dài zhe dì mèi dào yuán yě lǐ yóu wán, dào xiǎo xī biān bǔ zhuō xiǎo yú xiā, xiǎo niǎo, qīng wā。(wǒ men) yǒu shí hòu jiù tiào jìn hé lǐ yóu yǒng, xiǎng shòu měi hǎo de huān lè shí guāng。

I always take my brother and sister to the field to play, to the bank of stream to catch fish, shrimp, birds, frogs. Sometimes (we) just jump in the river and swim to have a good time.

(19) 我有一个姐姐比我大六岁, (我们)在父母的关怀中成长, 小学在泗水华侨小学读书。

wǒ yǒu yī gè jiě jiě bǐ wǒ dà liù suì, (wǒ men) zài fù mǔ de guān huái zhōng chéng zhǎng, xiǎo xué zài sì shuǐ huá qiáo xiǎo xué dú shū。

I have a sister that six years older than me, (we) grew up with the care of our parents and studied in the Overseas Chinese Primary School in Surabaya.

(20) 我在家庭之中, 倒数第二, 只有一个弟弟。其他兄姐, 都很关心弟妹, (我们)算是一个美满的家庭组织。

wǒ zài jiā tíng zhī zhōng, dào shǔ dì èr, zhǐ yǒu yī gè dì dì 。 *qí tā xiōng jiě, dōu hěn guān xīn dì mèi, (wǒ men) suàn shì yī gè měi mǎn de jiā tíng zǔ zhī* 。

I was the second youngest child in the family, with only one brother. The other brothers and sisters, they care about them, (we) are a happy family.

In example (18) "*yǒu shí hòu jiù tiào jìn hé lǐ yóu yǒng* 有时候就跳进河里游泳(Sometimes I jump into the river to swim)", the topic is missing. The habitual matching topic is "*wǒ* 我 (me)", but based on the context, the topic required by the semantic requirement is "*wǒ men* 我们 (we)". To avoid misunderstanding, the topic "*wǒ men* 我们 (we)" should be explicitly stated.In example (19), the sentence with the character "*yǒu* 有 (have)" has a strong function of introducing a topic. The following clause is more likely to describe the entity after the character "*yǒu* 有 (have)". Therefore, the object referred to by "*zài fù mǔ de guān huái zhōng chéng zhǎng* 在父母的关怀中成长(growing up under the care of parents)" is more likely to be "*jiě jiě* 姐姐 (sister)". However, the topic required by the topic semantic requirement is "*wǒ hé jiě jiě*我和姐姐 (me and my sister)". Therefore, the topic "*wǒ men* 我们 (we)" should also be explicitly stated to avoid ambiguity.

Zero anaphora errors resulting from overuse often occur when there are multiple referents in the previous clause. In such cases, the predicate in the previous clause often takes a ditransitive verb, such as "*dài* 带(take)", "*jiào* 叫(call)", "*péi* 陪(accompany)" and so on. The preferred referent sequence for zero anaphora in Chinese is "theme > subject > object > others", which means that when using zero anaphora, the referent priority is given to the topic or subject. Therefore, if an object other than the topic or subject needs to be referred to, a pronoun should be used instead of zero-form anaphora to avoid errors.

4.3   The Usage Restriction Rules and Lexical Features of Zero Anaphora

Based on the analysis in the previous context and the annotation of real textual corpus, we have found that a fundamental criterion for the use of zero anaphora is the presence of shared constituents between the previous and current clauses. However, the existence of shared constituents does not automatically lead to the use of zero anaphora. In discourse, the use of zero anaphora is influenced by various factors. For instance, time words, conjunctions, prepositional phrases function as independent clauses or appear in a "Introduction-Body-Conclusion" rhetorical structure, the topic generally does not continue from the previous clause but introduces a new topic or emerges in the next clause. Additionally, caution should be exercised when using zero anaphora when there are multiple potential topic candidates in the previous clause, as different syntactic constituents possess varying abilities to serve as the topic of the next clause. Generally speaking, the topic or subject of the previous clause is more likely to become the topic of the current clause, whereas other constituents as topics are generally not referred to using zero anaphora. We summarize these factors that influence the use of zero anaphora as follows (Table 1):

According to the annotated results, we have discovered that international students tend to make limited errors in zero anaphora. For example, after time words, international

Table 1. The usage restriction rules and lexical features of zero anaphora.

Factors	Lexical semantic feature
Components sharing	Continuous use of the same pronoun or noun
time words	"yǒu shí hòu 有时候(sometimes)"
conjunctions	"yīn cǐ 因此 (therefore)", "rán ér 然而 (however)"
Prepositional phrases	"chú le 除了 (besides)", "yóu yú 由于(due to)"
predicate phrases	"kàn 看(see)", "tīng 听(listen)", "xiǎng 想" (think)
stylistic structure	Evaluative components
ditransitive structure	"dài 带(take)", "jiào 叫(call)", "péi 陪(accompany)"

students often continue to use zero anaphora to refer back to the previous topic, rather than initiating a new topic chain. In ditransitive structures, there are multiple constituents that can be referred to, but different constituents have varying abilities to serve as the center of anaphora. Consequently, international students may erroneously use zero anaphora, leading to referential errors. By analyzing the lexical and semantic features associated with the occurrence of zero anaphora errors, we can further develop teaching strategies targeted at helping international students master the usage of zero anaphora.

5 Conclusion

International students often have difficulty mastering the usage of zero anaphora, which can lead to a lack of clarity in their writing. However, previous studies on zero anaphora errors have been relatively scarce, and analyses of the causes of such errors have been mostly broad and unable to effectively guide international students in their writing. Therefore, in this study, we selected 50 compositions written by international students from the HSK Dynamic Composition Corpus for annotation. Based on the annotation results, we classified zero anaphora errors into two types: lack of zero anaphora and overuse of zero anaphora. Lack of zero anaphora does not lead to misunderstandings, but can make the text lengthy and repetitive;overuse of zero anaphora, on the other hand, may cause misunderstandings. According to the results, overuse of zero anaphora can be further divided into topic missing and referential errors. Additionally, we summarized some restrictions on the use of zero anaphora that were observed in international students' writing. Topic missing caused by zero anaphora often occurs after time words, conjunctions, prepositional phrases, predicate phrases, and changes in writing style. Referential errors caused by zero anaphora mainly occur in ditransitive structures. By analyzing the lexical and semantic features associated with the occurrence of zero anaphora errors, teachers can develop further teaching strategies to help international students master the usage of zero anaphora.

References

1. Gao, S.Y.: Analysis of zero anaphora error in narrative texts of middle and senior British and American students. J. Mudanjiang Inst. Educ. **1**, 19–22 (2020). (in Chinese)

2. Gao, N.H.: The pronoun errors of international students and the principles of using pronoun in discourse. Chin. Teach. World **2**, 61–71 (1991). (in Chinese)

3. Xu, H.: Analysis on anaphora bias of Chinese discourse for Japanese students in middle and advanced level. Chin. Construct. **30**, 13–14 (2013). (in Chinese)

4. Zeng, L.J.: Analysis of anaphora bias in Chinese discourse for Intermediate level Korean Students. Overseas Chin. Educ. **4**, 67–377 (2012). (in Chinese)

5. Xu, Y.L.: Contrastive Linguistics. Shanghai Foreign Language Education Press (2010). (in Chinese)

6. Qu, C.X.: Chinese textual sentences and their flexibility – starting from topic chain. Contemp. Rhetoric **2**, 1–22 (2018). (in Chinese)

7. Yang, B.: The redefinition of "topic chain." Contemp. Rhetoric **1**, 72–78 (2016). (in Chinese)

8. Chen, S.: A study of zero anaphora error in Chinese discourse among French native speakers. Shanghai International Studies University (2021). (in Chinese)

9. Chen, C.: Common errors of coherence that made by English-speaking students in learning Chinese. J. Sichuan Univ. (Philos. Soc. Sci. Ed.) **3**, 6–83 (2005). (in Chinese)

10. Huang, Y.H.: Analysis of Korean students' textual error. J. Minzu Univ. China **5**, 100–106 (2005). (in Chinese)

11. Yang, C.: A survey on the textual reference bias of English speaking students in elementary Chinese. Chin. Learn. **3**, 62–66 (2004). (in Chinese)

12. Xiao, X.Q.: An analysis of the reference error of foreign students – the third part of a cluster of error analysis. Chin. Learn. **1**, 50–54 (2001). (in Chinese)

13. You, H., Lu, D.W.: A study on the errors of the naming-telling structure of the Chinese clause complex in the written language of international students. Lang. Teach. Res. **1**, 12–23 (2023). (in Chinese)

14. Wang, D.L.: Analysis of Chinese zero-shaped anaphora: a study based on centripetal theory. Mod. Foreign Lang. **4**, 350–359+436 (2004). (in Chinese)

15. Fu, S.: Topic and focus in the left periphery of Old Xiang: syntactic cartography and semantic constraints. In: Su, Q., Xu, G., Yang, X. (eds.) CLSW 2022. LNCS, vol. 13495, pp. 553–566. Springer, Cham (2023). https://doi.org/10.1007/978-3-031-28953-8_40

A Cognitive Semantic Analysis of the Spatial Dimension Adjective "Deep/Shallow" from the Perspective of Lexical Typology

Jia Yi and Bing Qiu[✉]

Department of Chinese Language and Literature, School of Humanities and Social Sciences, Tsinghua University, Beijing 100084, China
qiubing@mail.tsinghua.edu.cn

Abstract. Lexical typology research starts from concepts that commonly exist in human languages. In accordance with the cross-linguistic comparisons, both the shared characteristics and distinctions of these universal categories within the lexical systems of diverse languages are revealed. From a lexical typology perspective, this paper takes the spatial dimension adjectives "deep/shallow" as a case study, exploring the diachronic semantic evolution of "shen(深)/qian(浅)" in ancient Chinese. At the same time, the cross-linguistic comparisons of the lexicalization and semantic expansion patterns of "deep/shallow" in six languages are carried out at the synchronic level. The basic meanings and extended meanings of "deep/shallow" within these six languages are found to have a close-knit relationship. The spatial dimension adjectives "deep/shallow" exhibit the capacity to extend from the spatial domain to various other abstract domains, embodying the universality of human cognition. Being subject to the impact and constraint of national culture, the semantic expansion in these languages presents specific characteristics, shedding light on both the commonalities and distinctions in spatial perception and conceptual structures among different ethnic groups.

Keywords: Lexical Typology · Spatial Dimension Adjectives · Lexicalization · 'Deep/Shallow' Semantic Field · Semantic Expansion

1 Introduction

Space is a fundamental concept in relation to time, and its universality is reflected in the presence of specialized vocabulary people adopt to express spatial concepts and semantic relationships, known as spatial vocabularies. Space and dimension are intimately interconnected, in which spatial dimensions are used to measure and describe space. These dimensions are linguistically represented through the use of spatial dimension words in languages. Various languages may have words to express similar spatial categories, such as the use of "shen(深)/qian(浅)" and "deep/shallow" by Chinese and English respectively to convey spatial dimension concepts. Within the modern Chinese vocabulary system, spatial dimension words encompass terms such as "gao(高)/di(低);chang(长)/duan(短); shen(深)/qian(浅); kuan(宽)/zhai(窄)", etc. "Shen (深)/qian(浅)" among

M. Dong et al. (Eds.): CLSW 2023, LNAI 14514, pp. 302–316, 2024.
https://doi.org/10.1007/978-981-97-0583-2_24

these represents a prototypical set of spatial dimension adjectives. The terms "shen(深)/qian(浅)" can be used to describe both vertical dimensions (upper and lower) and horizontal dimensions (front and rear) within objects or spaces, possessing both dimensional and positional meanings. These can be verified in phrases such as "shenhai(深海), shenkeng(深坑), qianhai(浅海), qiantan(浅滩)", conveying dimensional meanings, and "shenchu(深处), qianceng(浅层)", presenting positional meanings.

In various languages, spatial concepts are conveyed by using expressions like "deep/shallow", yet word forms and collocations may find the existence of differences. Let's take "Deep" as an example, the Chinese word "shen(深)" can be paired with "shan(山)", whereas the English word "deep" cannot be paired with "mountain". Instead, it can be paired with "valley". The extension of spatial concepts into the domain of time is a common phenomenon, but this extension exhibits different specifics. For example, "shenqiu(深秋)" "shendong(深冬)"can be equivalent to "秋も深く(深秋)" in Chinese and Japanese. While "deep" is not commonly paired with seasonal words in English, but is more aptly matched with terms like "late autumn" or "late winter". The differences in the semantic extension of "Deep/Shallow" across different languages raise questions about whether these variations have some connections with national cognitive patterns. A worthwhile endeavor focuses on the further exploration on these questions.

Many studies in the past have explored the semantics of Chinese vocabulary from a typological perspective (such as Bian W. 2022 [1], etc.), Previous studies on the spatial adjectives "Deep/Shallow" have predominantly focused on the Chinese language itself. Some have given their attention to the analysis on the literal and metaphorical meanings of "shen(深)/qian(浅)" (such as Wu Y. 2013 [2], Dou Y. 2016 [3], etc.), while others have conducted comparative investigations of "shen(深)/qian(浅)" within the context of language comparisons between Chinese and foreign languages. It is notable that most of these comparisons have involved Han-Korean comparisons (e.g., Jin M.S. 2009 [4], Min Z. 2012 [5]). Despite these studies delving into the syntactic semantics of "shen(深)/qian(浅)", a comparative approach limited to two languages was predominantly adopted, failing to make the verification from a typological perspective.

Therefore, from the perspective of lexical typology, in addition to studying the diachronic semantic evolution of the term "shen(深)/qian(浅)" in Chinese, this paper also emphasizes cross-linguistic comparisons at the synchronic level. The analysis on the lexicalization methods and semantic expansion patterns of the "deep/shallow" concept in six different languages is conducted. With the intention of uncovering and analyzing both the cross-linguistic commonalities and individual differences in the semantic extension patterns of the "Deep/Shallow" concept across these languages, this research explores the shared features and differences at the cognitive level among these languages.

2 The Diachronic Semantic Evolution of "shen/qian" in Chinese

"Shen(深)" and "qian(浅)" are two commonly used words in the Chinese vocabulary. This section will begin by exploring the prototypical meanings of "shen(深)" and "qian(浅)", organize their semantic developmental processes, infer their semantic evolution, and elucidate the interplay between the various meanings of "shen(深)/qian(浅)" within the historical Chinese vocabulary system.

In accordance with the "Gucibian" (Wang F.Y. 2011 [6]), this paper investigates the prominent terms in Chinese that convey the concept of "Deep/Shallow" across both ancient and modern periods. These words primarily consist of "shen(深), sui(邃), you(幽)" for expressing the concept of "Deep", and "qian(浅), bao(薄)" for expressing "Shallow". When conveying the idea of spatial depth, "shen(深), sui(邃), and you(幽)" can all denote depth, albeit with different origins and characteristics. Compared to "shen(深)", "sui(邃)" signifies extreme depth, often suggesting a depth that is challenging to fathom; And "you(幽)" carries profound implications, frequently encompassing the idea of dim or faint light. Its extended usage is often related to notions of depth and secrecy. "shen(深)" and "qian(浅)" are antonyms, while the antonyms corresponding to "bao(薄)" are "hou(厚)". Consequently, in terms of visual perception, "qian(浅)" is frequently employed, while for describing things that accumulate over time or originate from the bottom and surface, "bao(薄)" is commonly used.

In contemporary Chinese, the predominant terms for expressing these concepts are "shen(深)/qian(浅)". "Sui(邃)" and "you(幽)" are no longer used independently in modern Chinese; instead, they have been reduced to morphemes. Additionally, the distinction between "qian(浅)" and "bao(薄)" has become more evident. By examining the evolution of the semantic meanings of "shen(深)/qian(浅)" in Chinese across different historical periods, we can further explore the cross-linguistic commonalities among spatial adjectives and the distinctive characteristics of diachronic vocabulary systems.

2.1 The Diachronic Semantic Evolution of "shen"

The original meaning of "shen(深)" is related to the name of water, although this meaning is rarely encountered in corpora. Instead, the "depth" associated with water has evolved into the prototype meaning at the central position. The prototype meaning of "water depth" encompasses two semantic origins: one involves "a large distance span", and the other relates to "a large quantity" due to the accumulation of water depth. The various meanings of "shen(深)" are derived from these two semantic origins.

(i) Prototype meaning
   As mentioned previously, "water depth" serves as the prototype meaning of "shen(深)", a usage that has persisted since the Western Zhou Dynasty and continues to be employed to this day. For example:

   (1)水泉深则鱼鳖归之······（吕氏春秋 • 仲春纪）
   Shui   quan   shen   ze   yu   bei   gui   zhi
   water   spring   deep   and   fish   turtle   return   3SG
   'If the spring is deep, the fish and turtles will return... (*Lv's Spring and Autumn Annals*) '

(ii) Extended meaning
   The semantic evolution of "shen(深)" can primarily be categorized into two forms: chain extension and radiative extension. Chain extension involves the progression from "water depth" to "a large distance from top to bottom", further extended to "a large distance from outside to inside", and subsequently extended to "long distance from the beginning".

The usage of "shen(深)" to indicate "a large distance from top to bottom" is the closest to the prototype meaning of "shen(深)", which has been used since ancient Chinese, as exemplified by:

(2)战战兢兢，如临深渊，如履薄冰。（《诗经·小雅·小旻》）

Zhanzhan-jingjing,	ru	lin	shen	yuan,	ru	lv	bao	bing
trembling with fear,	like	face	deep	abyss,	like	step	thin	ice

'I am trembling in the face of the political situation, like facing a deep abyss, like stepping on thin ice.*(The Book of Songs)* '

Similarly, in ancient Chinese, "shen(深)" expanded from its prototype meaning to signify "a large distance from the outside to the inside." This semantic evolution underwent a directional shift, further extending from the original vertical spatial to the horizontal space, which can be used to describe the depth of palaces, alleys, forests, courtyards, etc., such as:

(3)譬之富者，有高墙深宫……（《墨子·尚贤》）

Pi	zhi	fu	zhe,	you	gao	qiang	shen	gong
like	Stru	rich	people,	have	high	wall	deep	palace

'For example, the wealthy have high walls and deep palaces.*(Mozi)* '

The usage of the spatial domain term "shen(深)" to indicate significant distances both "from top to bottom" and "from outside to inside" emerged during ancient times, gradually stabilized and became widely used in the Middle Ages. In the Tang and Song dynasties, "shen(深)" further extended its meaning from the spatial domain to the temporal domain, indicating "a long time from the beginning", such as:

(4)夜深忽梦少年事，梦啼妆泪红阑干。（《琵琶行》）

Ye	shen	hu	meng	shao-nian	shi,
night	deep	suddenly	dream	young	day,
meng	ti	zhuang	lei	hong	lan-gan
dream	cry	makeup	tear	red	criss-cross

'Deep into the night I suddenly dreamed about my young days and wept in dream as tears streaked through my rouge.*(Pipa Xing)* '

The second semantic evolution path of "shen(深)" involves radiative extension, which extends from "deep water" to encompass "deep degree", "deep emotion", "deep color", and "deep reason". Due to the broad scope of the degree category, "shen(深)" finds various applications in extending to the domain of degree, such as:

(5)君之病在肌肤，不治将益深。（《韩非子·喻老》）

Jun	zhi	bing	zai	ji-fu,	bu	zhi	jiang	yi	shen
king	Stru	illness	in	skin,	Neg	treat	will	further	deep

'The illness within your body manifests on your skin; if left untreated, it will deteriorate. *(Hanfeizi)* ' "shen(深)"can be metaphorically extended from the spatial domain to the mental domain, indicating "deep emotions". This usage originates from the intensity of people's emotions or psychological states when they are particularly strong, such as:

(6)天犹有春秋冬夏旦暮之期，人者厚貌深情。（《庄子·杂篇》）

Tian	you	you	chun	xia	qiu	dong	dan	mu
nature	still	present	spring	summer	autumn	winter	sunrise	sunset

zhi	qi,	ren	zhe	hou	mao	shen	qing
Stru	period	people	Stru	funky-fresh	surface	deep	feeling

'In nature, there are spring, summer, autumn, winter, sunrise, and sunset. However, people may appear honest on the surface, yet they conceal a city within them.*(Zhuangzi)* '

"shen(深)" indicates "a large amount of aggregation". When abstract principles are regarded as concrete quantities, the more significant the accumulation, the deeper the principle, as illustrated by:

(7)古之善为道者，微妙玄通，深不可识。（《道德经》第十五章）

Gu	zhi	shan	wei	dao	zhe,	wei-miao-xuan-tong,
ancient	Stru	master	Prep	Tao	Stru	subtle-and-mysterious

shen	bu	ke	shi
deep	Neg	can	understand

'The skillful masters of the Tao in old times, with a subtle and exquisite penetration comprehended its mysteries, and were deep also so as to elude men's knowledge.*(TaoTeChing)* '

In addition, "shen(深)"can also be mapped to the sensory domain of color perception, indicating "deep color" its earliest instances can be traced back the Warring States period, but it didn't become widely used until the Tang Dynasty, such as:

(8)一丛深色花，十户中人赋。（《买花》）

Yi	cong	shen	se	hua,	shi	hu	zhong	ren	fu
One	Clf	deep	colour	flower	ten	Clf	medium	household	tax

'A cluster of deep red peonies, valued at the equivalent of the taxes paid by ten medium-sized households. *(Maihua)* '

By examining the semantics of "shen(深)", it can be understood that its meaning extended from the spatial domain to the temporal domain and various other abstract domains. Its prototype meaning is "water depth", which can be projected into different cognitive domains from two semantic origins.

2.2 The Diachronic Semantic Evolution of "qian"

The original meaning of "qian(浅)" is "not deep". "Qian(浅)", like "shen(深)", encompasses two semantic origins: one related to "a small distance span" due to shallow water, and the other associated with "small quantity" due to shallow water. The numerous meanings of "qian(浅)" are derived from these two semantic origins.

(i) Prototype meaning

As previously mentioned, the prototype meaning of "qian(浅)" is "not deep". Its earliest recorded use can be found in the Book of Songs and continues to be used to this day. For example:

(9)就其浅矣，泳之游之。（《诗经》）

Jiu	qi	qian yi,	yong	zhi	you	zhi
encounter	3Pl.gen	deep Crs	swim	3Gg	swim	3Gg

'When encountering shallow waters, I either dive or leisurely float through them. *(The Book of Songs)* '

(ii) Extended meaning

The semantic evolution path of "qian(浅)", similar to "shen(深)", can be primarily categorized into two forms: chain extension and radiative extension. Chain extension started with "shallow water" and extended to "a small distance from top to bottom", which further extended to "a small distance from outside to inside", and subsequently extended to "a short duration and shallow age from the beginning".

Compared to "shen(深)", "qian(浅)" can also be used to indicate the magnitude of vertical spatial distance, such as:

(10)根浅难固，茎弱易凋。（《赠刘琨》）

Gen	qian	nan	gu,	jing	ruo	yi	diao
root	shallow	difficult	stabilize	stem	weak	easy	fade

'Shallow roots are difficult to stabilize, and if the stem is weak, it is prone to withering.*(Zeng Liukun)* '

The spatial distance from the outside to the inside can also represent the object's size or width, as demonstrated in examples like:

(11)江南庄宅浅，所固唯疏篱。（《寄义兴小女子》）

Jiang-nan	zhuang	zhuai	qian,	suo	gu	wei	shu	li
Jiang-nan	manor	residence	shallow	Str	surround	only	sparse	fence

'The Jiangnan Manor is shallow, surrounded only by sparse fences.*(Ji Yixing xiao nvzi)* '

"Qian(浅)" is extended from the concept of a small distance in space to a short duration in time. This usage is more abundant in ancient Chinese than in modern Chinese, as seen in examples like:

(12)但以刘日薄西山，气息奄奄，人命危浅，朝不虑夕。（《陈情表》）

Dan	yi	Liu	ri-bao-xi-shan,		qi-xi-yan-yan,	
but	because	Liu	at one's last breath		at one's last gasp	
ren	ming	wei	qian,	zhao	bu	lv	xi
people	life	danger	shallow	morning	Neg	consider	night

'But my grandmother is at her last breath, and she is like the setting sun beyond the western hills. Her life is at stake and she may die at any moment. *(A Letter to His Majesty)* '

The temporal meaning of "qian(浅)" in modern Chinese is primarily inherited from ancient Chinese.

The second semantic evolution path of "qian(浅)" is a radiative extension, which extended from "shallow water" to "shallow degree", "shallow emotion", "light color", and "shallow reason". The usage of "shallow water" to indicate "shallow degree" has early origins and can be traced back to the Warring States period. This usage is still prevalent today.

The term "shallow water" can also be used to refer to shallow emotions, indicating that a friendship or emotional connection is not deep. This usage dates back to the Western Han Dynasty and continues to be used today, as seen in examples like:

(13)交浅而言深，是忠也。（《淮南子》）
Jiao	qian	er	yan	shen,	shi	zhong	ye
friendship	shallow	Conj	speak	deep	is	loyalty	Crs

'Speaking deeply despite a shallow relationship is a sign of loyalty.*(Huai Nanzi)* '

Compared to "shen(深)", "qian(浅)" was introduced later in the context of color descriptions. Its usage in this context was first observed during the Western Jin Dynasty, such as:

(14)桃花一簇开无主，可爱深红爱浅红。（《江畔独步寻花》）
Tao	hua	yi	cu	kai	wu	zhu,	
peach	flower	one	Clf	bloom	Neg	master	
ke	ai	shen	hong	ai	qian	hong	
can	love	deep	red	love	light	red	

'Should I love the deep red or the light red when a peach blossom blooms without a master?*(Jiangpan dubu xunhua)* '

The meaning of "shallow water" can also be extended to "obvious". On the one hand, it signifies "simple and clear", denoting straightforward and easily understandable writing or content. On the other hand, it implies "superficial", indicating a lack of knowledge or cultivation, such as:

(15)多闻曰博，少闻曰浅。（《荀子·修身》）
Duo	wen	yue	bo,	shao	wen	yue	qian
many	hear	is	extensive	few	hear	is	shallow

'One who knows much is called knowledgeable, while one who knows little is called shallow. *(Xunzi)* '

In summary, "shen(深)/qian(浅)" has evolved into important member of the spatial dimension in modern Chinese. This group of words has remained relatively stable throughout the development of the Chinese language. The semantic extensions of these two words are quite similar, as they can both be mapped to multiple abstract domains, although "shen(深)" has earlier extensions than "qian(浅)". By examining the diachronic evolution of their semantics, we can gain a more detailed understanding of the evolutionary process of spatial dimension adjectives and enrich the individual characteristics of the diachronic vocabulary system.

3   Cross-Linguistic Analysis of Adjective "Deep/Shallow"

The previous text analyzed the diachronic semantic evolution of "shen(深)/qian(浅)" in Chinese. Conducting cross-linguistic comparisons of "Deep/Shallow" from a synchronic perspective can help us understand the lexicalization and semantic expansion patterns in different languages.

3.1   Lexicalization

This paper selects six languages from the Database of Cross-Linguistic Colexifications (CLILS[3]), and uses dictionary surveys and interviews with native speakers to identify the dominant words representing the spatial dimension of "Deep/Shallow" in these languages at a synchronic level [7–12]. As shown in Table 1:

Table 1. Dominant words representing the concept of "Deep/Shallow" in Chinese and foreign languages

Modern Chinese	Korean	Japanese	English	French	Indonesian
深(shen)	깊다 (gipda)	深い（fukai）	deep	profond	dalam
浅(qian)	얕다 (yatda)	浅い（asai）	shallow	peu profond	dangkal

Lexicalization refers to the process of transforming various concepts into words within a language system. Jiang S.Y. (1999) [13] once pointed out that "the process of people's cognition of the objective world is not a mechanical or camera-like reflection, but an active understanding of the world". According to the preliminary investigation of dominant words representing the concept of "Deep/Shallow" in the spatial dimension, it has been found that: (1) In most of the mentioned languages, there exists a word representing the "Deep/Shallow" concept in the spatial dimension. Typically, there is only one dominant word for this purpose, with French being an exception. In French, the phrase "peu profond" is used exclusively to represent the concept of "shallow" in the spatial dimension, without a separate word. "Peu profond" in French is generally used to describe specific items like "plates, bowls, plates, water, graves", while "superficiel" can be used to describe abstract things such as "people, ideas, writing skills, novels, movies, conversations". This reflects the cognitive and conceptualization differences among languages when it comes to these concepts; (2) In terms of the form and pronunciation of dominant words, Japanese uses Chinese characters, which have the same form as Chinese but different pronunciations.

The diverse ways in which languages encode the same concept reveal variations in the hierarchical structures of their respective conceptual systems, shedding light on distinct cognitive styles that operate at a deeper level.

Table 2. Semantic extension category distribution of "Deep/Shallow" in six languages

category		Chinese 深	Chinese 浅	Korean 깊다 gipda	Korean 얕다 yatda	Japanese 深い fukai	Japanese 浅い asai	English deep	English shallow	French profond	Indonesian dalam	Indonesian dangkal
space		+	+	+	+	+	+	+	+	+	+	+
time		+	+	+		+	+	+				
perception	visual	+	+	+		+	+	+				
	hearing			+	+			+	+	+	+	
	taste			+								
	smell					+						
degree		+	+	+	+	+	+	+	+	+	+	
level evaluation		+	+	+	+	+	+	+	+	+	+	+
mind		+	+	+	+	+	+	+	+	+		
relationship		+	+	+		+	+	+				
total		7	7	9	5	8	7	8	5	5	4	2

3.2 Semantic Extension

In the preceding discussion, we explored how different languages lexicalize concepts. However, it's important to note that the semantic expansion of "Deep/Shallow" varies among languages. Through cross-linguistic comparisons, we can investigate common patterns of semantic expansion present in languages, including the development of both basic and non-basic meanings. Therefore, this paper utilizes the internet to select Chinese and foreign dictionaries [7–12] of similar scope and type as the basis for investigating the semantics of "Deep/Shallow". We examine the dictionary definitions and semantic divisions of dominant words in these dictionaries and confirm their understanding by learners from various countries. Different dictionaries provide varying interpretations of words, and the division of semantic categories is subject to a certain degree of subjectivity. Nevertheless, dictionary definitions remain a crucial means of comprehending the meanings of language vocabulary and serve as fundamental material for the study of world languages.

Metaphor is an important way of representing concepts, and extended meanings are derived and developed through metaphorical mechanisms [14, 15]. People are always accustomed to mapping spatial domains to time domains or other abstract domains, in order to grasp various non-spatial categories. The term "Deep/Shallow" was first applied to the spatial domain, and both words further extended to other abstract domains, with specific differences in metaphorical extension patterns. This article focuses on examining the semantic expansion patterns of the spatial adjective "Deep/Shallow" in six languages, as well as the differences in semantic expansion patterns between different languages. By analyzing the basic meaning of "Deep/Shallow" and studying the characteristics and laws of its metaphorical mapping, as well as comparing the different metaphorical mechanisms of the adjectives "Deep/Shallow" across various languages, we can further explore the factors that limit the expression of adjective meanings.

"Deep/Shallow" as a spatial dimension adjective, from a cross-linguistic perspective, its most prominent feature is downward orientation, and the extended meanings of "Deep/Shallow" are primarily rooted in this feature. Based on the analysis of the definition of "Deep/Shallow" in different language dictionaries, it can be observed that the primary semantic extensions of these terms manifest in the following categories: time domain, perception domain, degree domain, level evaluation domain, mental domain, and relationship domain.

(i) "Deep/Shallow" indicates the amount of time

In human thought, time and space have always been regarded as the two most fundamental and important philosophical categories. Mapping the spatial concept of "Deep/Shallow" to the time domain is a common cognitive approach. In the time domain, "Deep" means "a long time from the beginning" and "Shallow" means "a short time from the beginning". Except for French and Indonesian, all four other languages can use "Deep" to indicate time. The cognition and container schema projection of the combination of "Deep" with different types of time-related words vary across the four languages. In Chinese and Japanese, "Deep" can be paired with seasonal words. For example, in Chinese, "shen(深)" has a preference for pairing with "dong(冬)" "qiu(秋)", while in Japanese, "秋も深いくなった (late autumn)", and "浅い (asai)" has limited usage in describing seasons. The vast majority of the usage of "deep" mapped into the time domain is to describe night, which is reflected in all four languages. This extension is associated with visual brightness and the challenge of perceiving internal features. For example, English "deep" is often paired with "night", Chinese "shen(深)" is often paired with "yese(夜色)" "wan(晚)", and Korean " 깊은 밤(late at night)". The mapping of "shallow" to the time domain only appears in Chinese and Japanese, such as "知り合ってから日が浅い (haven't known each other for a long time)" in Japanese.

(ii) "Deep/Shallow" indicates perceived quantity

The five fundamental human senses operate collaboratively, shaping our perception and comprehension of the world. Vision, hearing, smell, taste, and touch serve as indispensable instruments for our interaction and communication with the external environment, and they are crucial avenues through which we experience life. The spatial dimension adjective that represents depth can be metaphorically extended from the spatial domain to the visual domain. "Deep color" is a visual metaphor, where darker colors are associated with greater intensity or richness. Except for French and Indonesian, the other four languages can use "Deep" to represent visual feelings. For example, in English "deep" is often paired with "color", while in Chinese "shen(深)" is commonly paired with "yanse(颜色)" or specific color names to describe particular color characteristics. Both Japanese and Chinese can use "Shallow" to convey visual perceptions, as seen in examples like "yanse qian(颜色浅, light color)" in Chinese and " だ浅い草木の緑(The green of the plants is still light)" in Japanese.

The spatial concept of "Deep/Shallow" also exhibits a phenomenon of mapping to the auditory domain. For instance, in English, "deep/shallow" is frequently combined with "voice, sound, noise" to indicate the depth or fineness of the sound. In Korean, "깊다(deep)" can also describe sound. Similarly, in French, "Une voix profounde(deep voice)" and in Indonesian, "dalam" can also be used to describe the sound, such as "La berbicara perlahan-lahan, suaranya dalam (he spoke slowly, with a deep voice)". There is no usage of "shen(深)" in Chinese for describing sound, and this difference in usage is primarily related to the phenomenon of Chinese polysyllablization. As the range of meanings of "shen (深)" expanded, in order to accurately convey certain meanings, "shen (深)" has undergone polysyllablization in various contexts, and the disyllabic term "shenchen (深沉)" is often employed to describe sound [16].

The spatial concept of "Deep" can also be mapped to the taste domain, which is observed specifically in Korean, as in " 맛이 깊다(rich flavor)". Additionally, the spatial concept of "Deep" can extend to the olfactory domain, found exclusively in Japanese, as in "深い香り (rich aroma)".

(iii) "Deep/Shallow" indicates degree

From the perspective of human cognition of the objective world, specific concepts typically precede abstract concepts, and the degree domain represents the most abstract domain projected by "Deep/Shallow". The similarity between the increase of spatial metrics and the accumulation of degree metrics is the basis for the projection of "Deep/Shallow" from the spatial domain to the degree domain. The mapping of "Deep/Shallow" to the degree domain indicates the stage or degree of development within a situation, where "Deep" signifies progressing toward a deeper stage, while "Shallow" signifies progressing toward an initial stage. In all six languages, this usage exists. For example, in Chinese, you can say "yanjiu henshen(研究很深)" or "shuijiao henqian(睡觉很浅)".In English, "deep/shallow" can be paired with "sleep" or "session". In Korean, it can be "깊은 잠(deep sleep state)", in Japanese, it can be "眠りが浅い(shallow sleep)", and in Indonesian, it can be said as "Perselihannya sudah dalam (their differences are already deep)".

(iv) "Deep/Shallow" indicates level evaluation

The spatial concept of "Deep/Shallow" can be extended from the degree domain to the level evaluation domain, representing evaluations related to various aspects such as level, ability, luck, or status. This metaphorical mapping exists in all six languages and is rooted in the transition from spatial measurement to subjective evaluation in the "Deep/Shallow" spatial domain. In English, "deep" can be paired with "life", while in Chinese, "shen(深)" is often paired with "gongdi(功底)", "zili(资历)", "yueli(阅历)", etc. In Korean, there are "조예가 깊다(deep attainments)", "学識が深い(profound knowledge)" in Japanese, and "mengandung makra yg dalam(has profound meaning)" in Indonesian.

(v) "Deep/Shallow" indicates the mind

"Deep/Shallow" as a metaphorical concept can also be used to describe the mind or mental states. This metaphor exists in various languages and is often related to the depth or complexity of one's thoughts or feelings. This usage is present in all five other languages, apart from Indonesian. For example, in English, "deep" and "shallow" are frequently paired with words like "thought", "knowledge", and "affection". In Chinese, "shen(深)" is commonly associated with phrases like "yingxiangshen(影响深)" "jianzhiqian(见识浅)". In Korean, expressions like "감정이 깊다(deep emotions)" are used, and in French, "Un esprit profonde(profound thoughts)" finds application.

(vi) "Deep/Shallow" indicates a relationship

The spatial concept of "Deep/Shallow" can also be metaphorically applied to the relational domain, much like the way tree roots extend underground. The deeper the extension, the more intricate the resulting relationships become. This usage is found in Chinese, Korean, Japanese, and English. For instance, in English, "deep" is often paired with "relationship", "roots", etc. In Chinese, it can be expressed as "yuanfen buqian(缘分不浅)". In Japanese, there are usages like"深い仲 (deep friendship)".

To sum up, the semantic expansion patterns of "Deep/Shallow" in the six languages can be summarized as Table 2:

Based on the above analysis, the semantic expansion of the adjective "Deep/Shallow" in six languages can be summarized as follows:

(i) From the perspective of semantic expansion, the spatial dimension adjectives "Deep/Shallow" in this article can be observed to transition from the spatial domain to the abstract domain in all six languages. In the field of cognitive linguistics, it is generally believed that spatial metaphors hold special and significant roles in the formation of human concepts, as many abstract notions are conveyed and comprehended through spatial conceptual metaphors. The mapping of "Deep/Shallow" in the expression of spatial dimensions from the spatial domain to the abstract domain reflects a universal principle in human cognition.

(ii) In various languages, the semantic expansion of "Deep/Shallow" is more extensive in categories related to time, degree, and level evaluation. These categories can be seen as reflecting common cognitive tendencies among humans. Conversely, categories with less semantic expansion may indicate individual or language-specific cognitive tendencies.

(iii) From the quantity statistics presented in the table above, it is evident that Korean exhibits the highest degree of semantic expansion for the spatial dimension adjectives "Deep/Shallow", mapping them from the spatial domain to the abstract domain. In contrast, Indonesian shows the weakest semantic expansion ability, with other languages fall in between these extremes.

(iv) From the above table, it can be seen that the asymmetry of adjectives exists in world languages, and asymmetry is not only reflected in the basic meaning, but also in the extended meaning.

In summary, the metaphorical degree of "Deep/Shallow" representing spatial dimension concepts varies among the six languages, with Korean having the highest degree of metaphoricality. The "Deep/Shallow" concept of table space in the six languages can be mapped to the degree domain and level evaluation domain, with the most distinct mappings occurring in the perception domain. The "Deep" concept in Chinese is only extended to the visual domain, while the "깊다(gipda)" in Korean is mapped to the three perception domains of visual, auditory, and taste. In addition, the "深い(fukai)" in Japanese can also be mapped to the olfactory domain.

4   Conclusion

By starting from concepts commonly present in human languages, the study of lexical typology reveals the commonalities and differences of universal categories in various language vocabulary systems through cross-linguistic comparison. As one of the most fundamental cognitive categories, the spatial category forms the foundation for the construction of other abstract concepts, playing an extremely significant role in the human cognitive processes of the world. The spatial category is reflected in spatial vocabularies through human cognitive processing, and different languages and ethnic groups have words that represent the same spatial categories.

"Deep/Shallow" is a complex pair of spatial dimensional adjectives. From the perspective of lexical typology, this paper examines the semantic evolution of "shen(

深)/qian(浅)" in Chinese at the diachronic level. In addition to analyzing the prototype and extended meanings of "shen(深)/qian(浅)" within the historical Chinese vocabulary system, it also compares the lexicalization and semantic expansion patterns of "Deep/Shallow" in six languages at the synchronic level across languages. In French, the concept opposite to "Deep", which is "Shallow", can only be expressed through phrases, highlighting differences in lexicalization and conceptualization methods among languages. The fundamental and extended meanings of "Deep/Shallow" in the six languages have close connections, as "Deep/Shallow" is metaphorically extended from the spatial domain to various abstract domains, presenting the universality of human cognition. Simultaneously, semantic expansion in certain languages displays specificity due to differences in national thinking patterns, language characteristics, and projection structures. For example, the prominent phenomenon of "Deep/Shallow" mapping to perceptual domains in Korean and Japanese reflects the distinct cognitive characteristics of these ethnic groups.

Acknowledgments. This work was supported by the Beijing Social Science Foundation Project (Grant No. 17YYC019), the Major Programs of the National Social Science Foundation of China (Grant No. 20&ZD304 and 21&ZD310) and The National Youth Talent Support Program.

References

1. Bian, W.: The relationship between the emphatic meaning and the adversative meaning from the perspective of linguistic typology: the cases of Chinese Kě and Jiùshì. In: Su, Q. et al. (eds.) CLSW 2022. LNAI, vol. 13495, pp. 169–185. Springer, Cham (2023). https://doi.org/10.1007/978-3-031-28953-8_14
2. Wu, Y.: A study on the semantic system of the spatial dimensional adjectives in Modern Chinese. Doctoral dissertation, Wuhan University (2011). (in Chinese)
3. Dou, Y.: Semantic expansion framework of spatial adjectives—taking 'shen' as an example. Bull. Chin. Lang. Teach. **6**, 48–50 (2016). (in Chinese)
4. Jin, M.S.: Studies on the spatial adjective "shēn"—the Chinese equivalent of the word meaning 'deep'. Doctoral dissertation, Beijing Language and Culture University (2009). (in Chinese)
5. Min, Z.: A contrastive study on the space dimension words of Korean and Chinese. Doctoral dissertation, Yanbian University (2012). (in Chinese)
6. Wang, F.Y.: Gucibian. Zhonghua Book Company, Beijing (2011). (in Chinese)
7. Hornby, A.S.: Oxford Advanced Learner's English-Chinese Dictionary, 9th edn. The Commercial Press, Beijing (2018). (in Chinese)
8. Song, C.M., Zuo, H.L.G., Yang, L.M.S., Shao, Y.F.: A New Century Dictionary of Japanese and Chinese Interpretations. Foreign Language Teaching and Research Press, Beijing (2009). (in Chinese)
9. Edited by the New Indonesian Chinese Dictionary Writing Group, Indonesian Language and Literature Teaching and Research Office, Department of Oriental Language and Literature, Peking University. New Indonesian Chinese Dictionary. The Commercial Press, Beijing (1997). (in Chinese)
10. Edited by the Dictionary Editing Office, Institute of Linguistics, Chinese Academy of Social Sciences. Modern Chinese Dictionary, 7th edn. The Commercial Press, Beijing (2016). (in Chinese)

11. Edited by the Compilation Committee of Chinese Dictionary: Chinese Dictionary. Shanghai Dictionary Publishing House, Shanghai (2011). (in Chinese)
12. Xue, J.C.: Larousse Dictionary. Foreign Language Teaching and Research Press, Beijing (1995). (in Chinese)
13. Jiang, S.Y.: Word meaning and conceptualization, lexicalization. Essays Linguist. **2**, 249–279 (2014). (in Chinese)
14. Lakoff, G., Johnson, M.: Metaphors We Live By. University of Chicago Press, Chicago (1980)
15. Dirven, R., Verspoor, M.: Cognitive Exploration of Language and Linguistics. John Benjamins Publishing Company, Amsterdam, Philadelphia (1998)
16. Qiu, B., Yi, J.: A corpus-based study on the syllablic form selection of ancient Chinese high-frequency nouns in the middle ages. In: Su, Q. et al. (eds.): CLSW 2022. LNAI, vol. 13495, pp. 14–24. Springer, Cham (2023). https://doi.org/10.1007/978-3-031-28953-8_2

A Study on the Restraining Factors and Its Acting Forces of Selected Components of Chinese Abbreviations

Yaolin Feng[✉]

Beijing Language and Culture University, Beijing 100083, China
gatimi@163.com

Abstract. Previous studies offer little quantitative analysis of the restraining factors in selected components of Chinese abbreviations, and the influence of each factor remains controversial. In order to solve these problems, this study firstly put forward an important concept - "internal segment", which attached importance to the hierarchical grammar structure of the original forms. Secondly, we sorted out, refined and tested the 10 restraining factors of selected components of Chinese abbreviations mentioned by predecessors; and based on their influence on the abbreviations as a whole, they can be categorized into three levels: strong, medium and weak. In addition, we found that the acting force of those restraining factors were overlapping and no single factor could operate independently. The findings could help to trigger a deeper consideration of theoretical and applied research on Chinese abbreviations.

Keywords: Restraining Factors · Components · Selected · Chinese Abbreviations

1 Introduction

In general, a long language unit that is commonly used will soon be selected to take out some components to form a shorter, consensus-based fixed expression. And, the creation of that consensus-fixed expression is not arbitrary, but is subject to a number of restraining factors. That is, the process of selecting components from the longer original form to form a fixed abbreviated form[1] is constrained. How is the process of selecting abbreviated components constrained? What are the factors that restrain the selection of components for Chinese abbreviations?

---

[1] The term "abbreviated form" in this paper refers to all forms that are abbreviated from the same original form, including the abbreviation and potential abbreviated forms. The term "abbreviation" refers exclusively to the abbreviated form which is already widely recognized by the public. Like "生化" (biochemistry) is one of the abbreviated forms and the only abbreviation of the original form "生物化学" (biochemistry), but "生学", "物化", "物学" are the potential abbreviated forms of the original form "生物化学".

Currently, several researchers have studied the restraining factors on components selection of Chinese abbreviations (e.g. [1, 2]), and they focused on different perspectives. Scholars such as Lv and Zhu [3], Yin [4], and Wang [5] believe that "taking the first character of the original form" is the main restraining factor of the selection of the components of abbreviations, while Zhang [6] believes that the type of grammatical structure of the original form determines the selection of the components of abbreviations, and some scholars have proposed their own restraining factors on the selection of the components of abbreviations from different perspectives such as phonology, semantics and pragmatics, and so on [7–10]. It can be seen that researchers have made different judgments on the magnitude of the acting force of these restraining factors on the selection of abbreviations components. This study is intended to categorize and refine the restraining factors, and quantitatively examine them one by one in a closed corpus, aiming at exploring the magnitude of acting force of these restraining factors. If there is a superimposed effect among them?

2   The Selecting of Corpus and the Description of Internal Segment

2.1   The Selecting of Corpus

Chinese abbreviation is strictly defined as: a word that is condensed from a longer unique fixed form, which must be formed with Chinese characters[2] of the original form, can't contain new components that the original form doesn't have, and the conceptual meaning is exactly the same as the original form. One abbreviation can only relate to one original form, and the abbreviation appears later than the original form.

Therefore, the following cases do not belong to Chinese abbreviations: (1) letter words, such as "RMB" (the acronym of "人民币" Pinyin), "GPS" (the acronym of "global positioning system"); (2) aliases, such as "赣" (Jiangxi province); (3) numerical summation, such as "三牲" (referring to pigs, cows, and goats); (4) later extended structures, such as "民间风俗" (folk customs) and "民间习俗" (folk customs) are in fact the structures that have been extended from the semantic meaning of "民俗"[3].

In order to ensure the recognition of corpus, this paper collected all non-monosyllabic entries from five abbreviations dictionaries [11–15], totaling 18,311 entries. By deleting the duplicates and those with incorrect original forms, a total of 537 entries were selected for detailed analysis. The reason for deleting monosyllabic entries is that it is not easy

---

[2] We use the term "Chinese characters" instead of "morpheme" because the original forms of some abbreviations don't necessarily correspond to one Chinese character per morpheme, which is often the case with phonetically transliterated words. For instance, the original form of "亚" is "亚细亚洲 (Asia)", which is an abbreviation of the single morpheme phonetic component "亚细亚". We don't use the term "syllable" because it is biased in favor of phonology. Since "form, sound, and meaning" are the three elements of Chinese characters ([10]), we use the term "Chinese characters" here.

[3] The term "民俗" existed as early as in the pre-Qin period (before 221 BC), while the "民间风俗" this expression appeared much later in the Song Dynasty (960–1279), the Ming (1368–1664) and Qing Dynasties (1616–1912) used it more frequently. "民间习俗" appeared even later in the Ming Dynasty (1368–1664). It is inappropriate to consider "民俗" as the abbreviation of original forms "民间风俗", "民间习俗".

to distinguish between the morphemic meaning of the entries and the meaning derived from the abbreviations.

This study doesn't cover new abbreviations for three reasons: firstly, the dictionary corpus is closed for statistical purposes; secondly, the entries have a certain degree of acceptance, making the results of the study more reliable; and thirdly, no new abbreviation dictionaries have been published in recent years. However, the age of the abbreviations (20 or 30 years) should not be a constraining factor affecting the selection of the components of the abbreviations.

We have classified abbreviations into three types based on the continuity of the selected components: abridged, contracted, and item in common. Abridged abbreviations remove the beginning or end of the original form and retain only an internal segment in the first level of the original form, such as "清华" (清华大学 Tsinghua University). Contracted abbreviations are produced by selecting discontinuous components of different internal segments of the first level of the original form and combining them, for example, "民调(民意调查 poll)". Item in common abbreviations refer to the original form being combined by several (usually two) isomorphic compound words, from which the selection can distinguish the meaning of the morphemes plus the common morphemes combined to form the abbreviation. For example, "上班 + 下班" → "上下班" (going to and get off work). The continuity of the item in common abbreviation is between the abridged abbreviations and the contracted abbreviations. Contracted abbreviations are the most prevalent type of abbreviations, accounting for more than 90% of all abbreviations. The other abridged and item in common types are less common.

2.2   The Definition and Delineation of Internal Segments

Original forms of abbreviations are not simple linear sequential combinations, but have distinct structural levels. Previous studies lacked a reasonable name for the units at different levels of the original forms of abbreviations. For example, in "外国货币 (foreign currency)" - the original form of abbreviation "外币 (foreign currency)" - "外国(foreign)" and "货币 (currency)" are used, and "断绝 (break off)", "外交关系 (diplomatic relation)", "外交 (diplomatic)", "关系 (relation)" are in "断绝外交关系 (break off diplomatic relation)"-the original form of "断交" (break off diplomatic relation). What is the appropriate term for those components like "货币", "断绝", "外交关系"? Scholars have named these components differently, such as "节" (part or segment) [3], "段 (part or segment)" [16], "直接成分" (component) or "直接组成成分" (direct component) [7], "意义段(meaning segment)" [5], etc.; however, they have barely paid attention to the hierarchical grammatical nature of the original forms.

In this paper, we call "internal segment" for the internal components in the original form at each level, and naming and dividing them are two basic tasks that must be done in this study, which is highly important to the study of constraining factors on abbreviations components selection. The internal segments are divided by the hierarchical analysis method, and they are generally the source units of abbreviations' components selection. The consecutive parts omitted from abridged abbreviations are also internal segments, e.g., "清华" (Tsinghua University) omits the internal segment[4] "大学 (university)". The

---

[4] See Sect. 2.2 on "internal segments" for details.

direct components of each level are internal segments regardless of their structure and the number of syllables. The detailed and precise division of internal segments can explain the problem of taking or leaving components of original forms and make the statistics of selecting components more reliable.

The reason for the name "internal segment" rather than "internal component", "direct component" or other terms is that the designation "internal segment" reflects the fact that it is part of the original form; the term "component" is more general, but it is not easy for the reader to specify the referring object, such as "外", "外交", "外交关系" can be regarded as "internal components" of the original form "断绝外交关系(break off diplomatic relation)"; "direct component" is an exclusive designation of "hierarchical analysis method". In this study, 1015 internal segments of 537 abbreviations original forms of all levels were finally obtained.

Labeling the grammatical structure relations among the original forms, internal segments, and abbreviations is not only feasible but also conducive to further analyzing the selection of abbreviated components. To ensure the correctness of the annotation of grammatical structure relations in the corpus, this research mainly refers to the annotation of grammatical structure types of entries in the "Dictionary of the Chinese Shuiping Kaoshi". [17]. Figure 1 shows an example of the internal segments and its hierarchy grammatical relations of "促红细胞生成素" (erythropoietin)-the original form of "促红素" (erythropoietin).

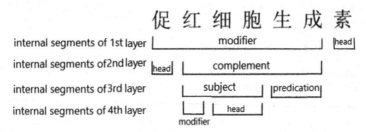

Fig. 1. Hierarchical grammar structure of internal segments of "促红细胞生成素 (Erythropoietin)".

3   Quantitative Tests of Constraining Factors on Abbreviation Components Selection

Previous scholars mentioned above have explored the constraining factors on the selection of Chinese abbreviations components from a multidimensional perspective, usually by proposing a certain constraining factor and then citing the relevant examples to illustrate it. This method of argumentation by examples lacks a comprehensive examination of the corpus, and its reliability is unconvincing. In the current research on the constraining factors of abbreviation components selection, only selecting the initial characters [5, 7, 18] and the meaning status of morphemes [6] have been analyzed with data, while other constraining factors, such as the number of syllables and grammatical structure, often have only a few words, resulting controversies in the current ranking of the importance of constraining factors on abbreviation components selection in the academic community. For example, Wang [5] argues that the length of syllable combinations in the original forms and the original forms' "meaning segments" play a greater role in the construction of abbreviations than the frequency of use of original forms and the degree of social acceptance of the original forms, but this view lacks strong data support. Zhang [6] argues that the meaning status of morphemes is the first and foremost constraining factor, followed by the category and position of the morphemes; the shortcoming is that her comparison is limited and she is not entirely sure that the meaning status of the morphemes is the most important factor.

This section sorts out 10 constraining factors on abbreviation components selection that have been proposed by previous authors, and examined each of them within a closed corpus.

3.1 Constraining Factor I: Selecting the First Character of the Internal Segment

From the 537 abbreviations selected in this paper, 37.2% of the abbreviations corresponding to a single layer of internal segments in the original form, which select the first characters of the internal segments of the first layer, e.g., "彩电" (color TV). In the total corpus, there are 489 abbreviations (91.1%) with the first word of an internal segment of the first layer of the original form, and 502 abbreviations (93.5%) with the first word of an internal segment of a certain layer. In other words, more than 90% of the abbreviations partially selected internal segment initials, which may have led previous researchers such as Yin [4] to believe that the selection of internal segment initials is the dominant constraining factor on the selection of abbreviation components, but in fact less than half (43.3%) of the abbreviations fully selected initials.

3.2 Constraining Factor II: The Grammatical Structure Remains Unchanged

Zhang [6] and Zhou [8] advocate that abbreviations are isomorphic with original forms. The statistics of this study found that 96.4% of the grammatical structure of the first level of the original form is the same as the corresponding abbreviation.

More than 80% of the original forms and abbreviations are the type of modifier-head. If the first structure of the original form is continuous actions, the structure of the abbreviation must also be continuous actions, and vice versa; for example, the structure of the original form "生产销售" (production and sales) and its abbreviation "产销" are both continuous actions. The original forms corresponding to verb-object abbreviations are also basically verb-object, except for "说文", whose original form "说文解字" (origin of Chinese Characters) is parallel.

3.3 Constraining Factor III: The Ordering of Selective Components Remains Unchanged

Gong and Nie [2] view the sequence of selective components as a crucial constraint in constructing abbreviations for four-character original forms. Barcelona [19] introduced the concept of "naturalness", referring to the extent a clipped segment mirrors the phonological or graphemic similarity to the original form's continuous sequence. However, this study doesn't fully apply to Chinese. We examined whether the component order in each abbreviation aligns with the original form.

In the 537 items of the corpus, the component order of each abbreviation is identical to that of the original form. For instance, the components of the abbreviation "全麻" and the original form "全身麻醉" (general anesthesia) are in the same order, despite being separated by "身". However, not all Chinese abbreviations follow the same component order as the original form. We discovered some abbreviations that differ from the original component order, such as "女附中" corresponding to "附属女子中学" (female secondary school) and "十一三中全会" corresponding to 中国共产党第十一届中央委员会第三次全体会议 (the Third Plenary Session of the Eleventh Central Committee of the Communist Party of China), etc. These abbreviations all denote a specific organization or meeting and can be classified into two categories: one emphasizes the property, such as "联邦德国" (德意志联邦共和国) (Federal Republic of Germany); the other highlights the order, such as "四次妇代会" (全国妇女联合大会第四次代表大会) (The Fourth National Women's Union Congress). This type of abbreviation is a tiny fraction of the vast number of abbreviations. As a result, the percentage of abbreviated phrases with the same component order as the original ones is almost 100%.

3.4 Constraining Factor IV: Selecting Components from as Many Internal Segments as Possible

Retaining components from all internal segments of the original form facilitates people to activate the complete meaning of its corresponding original form in their mind according to the abbreviated form, and researchers such as Wang [5] hold a similar view. According to our data, the abbreviations with retained components from all internal segments of the original form accounted for 65.4%. The first level of internal segments is the most important denotational level; 88.6% abbreviations retained the components from the first level. For example, "长春电影制片厂 (Changchun Film Studio)", the original form of "长影", components internal segments in the first level are retained, while only one component in the internal segment of the second level is retained at the end of the word "电影 (film)". It can be seen that the more complete the internal segments of the original form retained in the abbreviation, and the higher the level at which the internal segments are located (in particular, the first level), the more likely it is that the abbreviated form will be selected.

3.5 Constraining Factor V: Ability to Denote the Meaning of the Internal Segment

The meaning-expressing capacity of the selected component in an internal segment depends critically on its ability to represent the core meaning of that segment. The core meaning is represented by the core part, which is relatively better able to express the meaning of the whole segment. The judgment of the core part of a segment depends on the type of that segment. According to Zhang [6], if the grammatical structure between two morphemes is different, then the meaning status of the two morphemes in the compound word is also different. For example, the meaning status of "减" in the head-complementary compound word "减少 (reduce)" is higher than that of the complementary morpheme "少". Among the five types of compound words, namely, joint, modifier-head, predicate-object, object-complementary, and subject-predicate, only joint and modifier-head are really from the perspective of the meaning status of morphemes to determine the type of compound words, while the other three are not.

We improved on Zhang's method of determining morpheme meaning status based on the types of grammatical structural relations of compound words: in order to safeguard a consistent perspective of categorizing the meaning of internal segments' representations, they are classified into five categories: conjunctive, collocational, tandem, others, and monosyllable. The details are shown in Table 1:

Table 1. Classification of internal segment grammatical structure types.

Type of internal segment structure	Grammatical structures of internal segments
Conjunctive: equal meaning status of morphemes	Joint, continuous actions
Collocational: one morpheme is more important in terms of status of meaning	Modifier-head, head-complementary
Tandem: both morpheme meaning status are important	Subject-predicate, predicate-object
Others: the status of morpheme meaning is not easily distinguishable	Transliteration, geographical names, personal names
Monosyllable	Monosyllabic nouns, verbs, adjectives, prepositions and affixes

(1) Conjunctive (16.8%) is divided into three categories according to the semantic equality of the components of the internal segments. Class I: the meaning of several components is basically the same, and they can be explained to each other, and the semantic status of the two of them is relatively equal, e.g., "边疆 (border)", which accounts for 49.7% of the total number of the conjunctive. Class II: several components are in a semantic category and need to be used together in order to express a complete meaning, eg. "工农 (workers and peasants)", and the continuous actions also belongs to this category, accounting for 35.6% of the total number of conjunctives. Class III: two internal components are in the same semantic category, but the meaning of one of them has disappeared, reduced to an accompaniment, relying on the other component to express its meaning, such as "国家 (country)", there are only 25 of them, accounting for 14.7%. (2) The most common type of internal segment is the collocational type (60.7%), which is divided into the modifier-head, head-complementary types, in which the significance of one of the components is more important than the other. For example, "法" in the modifier-head compound "法院 (court yard)" is more likely to emphasize the trial function of "法院" than "院", and "集" in the head-complementary compound "集中 (gathering)" is more likely to express "gathering" than "中". (3) The two components of the tandem form (7.5%) are both important, including the subject-predicate form and the predicate-object

form, for example, "制片 (production)" and "自主 (autonomy)". (4) There are 67 other forms (6.6%), such as "印度 (India)" and "天津 (Tianjin)". (5) Monosyllabic (8.5%) are inconveniently grouped with other components in the division of internal segments, eg. " 铵(ammonium)" is taken from the original form, " 硫酸铵(ammonium sulfate)" which directly enters the abbreviation " 硫铵(ammonium sulfate)".

3.6 Constraining Factor VI: Unique Form

Abbreviations must be "semantically explicit" and "no ambiguity", and a clear way to measure this is that the abbreviation should not be identical to an existing word form, i.e., it should have formal uniqueness. Fu [20] points out that an arbitrary abbreviation may probably bring about difficulties in people's understanding, for example, if we abbreviating "军大衣 (military coat)" to "军大", it will easily be interpreted as "军政大学 (military political university)".

We searched all the abbreviations in Baidu search engine and BCC corpus, and about 97% of the abbreviations are not duplicated with existing word forms. Occasionally, a few abbreviations are chosen to increase their spreading ability by intentionally adopting already occupied word forms, such as "白骨精 (白领, 骨干, 精英 white-collar, core member, elite)". When choosing the components of an abbreviation, two ways are often used to avoid ambiguity: one is to try to avoid conflicts with homonymy, homophones, or near-sound words that already exist in the vocabulary system of modern Chinese, such as "帮教", the original form of which is "帮助教育 (help educate)", if "助教" was chosen, it would be the same as the word "助教 (assistant teacher)" that has already taken its place. The second is to minimize the use of basic morpheme as a constructive component, for example, "地(dì)" has 14 meanings in Contemporary Chinese Dictionary, and there are even 384 compound words composed of it; therefore, many abbreviations avoid using "地" and choose other morphemes, such as "方志" (local journal), "赛场" (playing field) and so on. The study of Lin and Hsieh [21] proves that latent semantic distance does exist between Chinese basic words and Non-basic Words.

3.7 Constraining Factor VII: Disyllable

Researchers such as Wang [5], Yu [1] and Yu [22] have pointed out that disyllables are a common number of syllables in abbreviations, and our statistics also prove that disyllabic syllables are the dominant number of syllables chosen for abbreviations (70.7%). The reason for this phenomenon is obvious, as disyllables are the standard natural foot in Chinese [23]. In addition, nearly half (46.7%) of the original forms are tetrasyllabic, which consist of exactly two foots. The two-foot original form itself is easy to be recognized and promoted among Chinese speakers, and it is easy to be entrenched as a commonly used fixed phrase, which is used with high frequency, is easy to be abbreviated. A study related to loan words in Chinese also found that people prefer to choose disyllable rather than tri-syllable or four syllable even if they express same meaning [24].

In addition, we also found that there is a certain correspondence between the number of syllables in the abbreviations and the number of internal segments in the first level of the original form, with 71.7% of them have the same number. For example, there are four internal segments in the first level of the original form "比先进, 学先进, 赶

先进, 帮后进 (Comparing the advanced, learning from the advanced, catching up with the advanced, helping the backward)", and the corresponding number of syllables in the abbreviation "比学赶帮 (Comparing, learning, catching up, helping)" is also four.

3.8 Constraining Factor VIII: Same Consonant or Vowel

We looked separately at whether the components of an abbreviations have the same consonant or vowel, with only about 3.9% of them having identical vowels or consonants. However, if an abbreviation's components have the same vowel or consonant, this is likely to be an important factor in making the abbreviation stand out. For example, when choosing one component from the conjunctive internal segment "调查 (investigation)", generally take "调" instead of "查", like "流调" (流行病学调查 epidemiological investigation)," "调研" (调查研究 investigate and search), but the abbreviation "查处" chose "查" instead of "调" from the original form "调查处理 (investigate and punish)", mainly because "查" and "处" have the same consonant.

3.9 Constraining Factor IX: Affected by Analogy

The phenomenon of analogy in abbreviation is the creation of new abbreviations by imitating the structure of existing abbreviations. To realize analogy in a language, there are three key steps: first, to have an initial, imitable model; second, to extract a imitate rule from that model; and third, to apply the extracted rule to create a form similar to the initial model.

Analogically constructed abbreviations can be viewed as new words constructed in a certain lexical pattern. Li [25] summarizes four features of a typical lexical pattern: 1) having fixed components of constructions; 2) indeterminate components belonging to the same semantic category; 3) fixed structural relations between components; and 4) fixed semantic relations between components. Where 1) is a formal requirement, while 2), 3), and 4) are meaning requirements. Li [25] argues that 3) is the core feature of the lexical pattern, and 4) only affects whether it is typical or not. A structure that satisfies both 1) 3) or 2) 3) can be regarded as a lexical pattern. As far as the analogy of abbreviations is concerned, it is also important to have formally the same components of the construction. A certain pattern of abbreviated constructions can be regarded as an analogous pattern of abbreviations as long as it complies with 1) 3) and more than 3 examples of abbreviations can be found in that pattern. The analogical patterns of abbreviations found in the corpus are as follows: [X + 代会], "代会" stands for "Representative Assembly": 文代会 (文学艺术工作者代表大会 Representative Assembly of Literature and Art Workers), 团代会 (共产主义青年团代表大会 Representative Assembly of the Communist Youth League), and 职代会 (职工代表大会 the congress of employees). About 22.9% of the abbreviations in the total corpus are found in some kind of analogical pattern.

3.10 Constraining Factor X: Different Social Usage

From a social usage perspective, the factors that affect the selection of abbreviation components are geographical and community differences. Firstly, the same original form can have different selection results in different regions. For instance, mainland China and Taiwan may choose different components for the same original form to form different abbreviations. For example, the original form "彩色电视 (color TV)" is commonly abbreviated as "彩电" in mainland China, while "彩视" is commonly used in Taiwan. The same abbreviated form may also have different priority to understand the meaning in different places. For instance, "山大" in Shanxi is often understood as "山西大学 (Shanxi University)", while in Shandong, it is generally understood as "山东大学 (Shandong University)". Secondly, the difference in people's usage habits for a certain collocation sometimes affects the selection of abbreviation components. "北京 (Beijing)" and "天津 (Tianjin)" use the monosyllables "京" and "津" to refer to cities, especially when used singly. If "Beijing" is combined with other components to denote an organization as a whole, the abbreviation will take the first character "北", such as "北大" (北京大学 Peking University), "北图" (北京图书馆 Beijing Library), "天汽" (天津汽车制造厂 Tianjin Automobile Works). Overall, the percentage of differences in abbreviation selection due to different social usage is very small, about 2%.

To summarize, the 10 constraining factors are related to position, grammatical structure, components ordering, semantics, prosodic, analogy and social usage, and the constraining factors vary in their degree of significance.

4 Acting Force of Constraining Factors and Their Overlapping Effects

In the past, scholars have not agreed on the strength of constraining factors. The above observation on the corpus from multiple perspectives has yielded more comprehensive statistics, clarifying in detail the 10 constraining factors in multiple aspects. The next question to consider is: what is the magnitude of acting force of these constraining factors? Is there an overlap between the constraining factors?

4.1 The Magnitude of the Acting Force of the Constraining Factors

The ratio of the number of abbreviations constrained by a certain factor reflects the strength of the factor's power. For ease of measurement, we divided the strength of the force of the constraining factor on all abbreviations into strong, medium, and weak levels by dividing 100% in thirds: the division interval of [0, 33.3%) is the weak level, [33.3%, 66.6%) is the medium level, and [66.6%, 100%] is the strong level. Tables 2, 3 and 4 show the constraining factors for the strong, medium and weak grades, respectively, and the factors are listed according to the force from smallest to largest.

According to the table above, there are five strong constraining factors, whose acting force varies from 70.7% to 100%. The factor of ability to denote the meaning of the internal segment is constrained by the type of internal segment, and if the internal segment is a head-complementary, conjunctive, others or predicative monosyllabic, then there is a clear tendency for selecting the core part of the internal segment, which ranges from 77% to 100%.

As can be seen from the table above, there are two constraining factors with medium strength, ranging from 50% to 65.4%. The constraining factor "ability to denote the

Table 2. Strong constraining factors on abbreviation component selection.

Type of constraining factors	Strength of acting force
The ordering of selective components remains unchanged	100%
Unique form	97%
The grammatical structure remains unchanged	96.4%
Selecting the first character on the first layer of internal segments	91.1%
Ability to denote the meaning of the internal segment	77%–100%
Disyllable	70.7%

Table 3. Medium constraining factors on abbreviation component selection.

Type of constraining factors	Strength of acting force
Selecting components from as many internal segments as possible	65.4%
Ability to denote the meaning of the internal segment	50%–65%

meaning of the internal segment" spans two magnitude grades, but it includes different types of internal segments-if the selective components is originated from a modifier-head, tandem, or nominal monosyllabic internal segment, then selecting its core components is a medium constraining factor with a force of 50–65%.

Table 4. Weak constraining factors on abbreviation component selection.

Type of constraining factors	Strength of acting force
Affected by analogy	22.9%
Same consonant or vowel	3.9%
Different social usage	2%

According to the above table, the constraining factors imposed by analogy, same consonant or vowel, and social usage on the selection of components for abbreviations are relatively small, with the most powerful analogical pattern constraining factors affecting only one-fifth of the abbreviations.

According to the three tables above, we can know: (1) There are more constraining factors on the strong and medium level of acting force, and they are mainly related to structural and semantic aspects. (2) Only by distinguishing the types of internal segments from which selective components originate can we judge the ability of components to denote the meaning of the internal segment. (3) On the whole, the sequence of the strength of the constraining factors on abbreviation components selection can be ranked as follows: {The ordering of selective components remains unchanged > Unique form

> The grammatical structure remains unchanged > Selecting the first character on the first layer of internal segments > Ability to denote the meaning of the internal segment: head-complementary, conjunctive, others or predicative monosyllabic > Disyllable} > [Selecting components from as many internal segments as possible > Ability to denote the meaning of the internal segment: modifier-head, tandem, or nominal monosyllabic] > [Affected by analogy > Same consonant or vowel > Different social usage]. The constraining factors within "{ }" are strong, those within "[]" are medium, and those within "[]" are weak.

4.2 Overlapping Effects of Constraining Factors

Although the constraining factors listed above have different magnitude, none of the constraining factors can act alone on the selection of the components of an abbreviation. Because of the complexity of abbreviations and the variety of internal segments corresponding to their original form, the selection of abbreviations has its own unique characteristics.

The factors governing the components selection of each abbreviation are different, this does not mean that the superposition of constraining factors on abbreviation components selection is random; it is still regular. We carefully analyzed all 537 abbreviations to examine the co-occurrence or mutual exclusion of different constraining factors. If the original form has multiple layers of internal abbreviations, the selection of the first layer of internal abbreviations prevails.

It was observed that: (1) the ordering factor and the grammatical structure factor often jointly contributed to the selection of components in more than 90% of the abbreviations. (2) For "Selecting components from as many internal segments as possible", "Ability to denote the meaning", and "Unique form", at least one of these three factors will be superimposed on the other constraining factors and work together as a constraining factor. (3) The factor of "selecting the first" seems to be common in abbreviations, but in fact there must be semantic constraining factors superimposed on it, especially the factor of "Unique form".

Some abbreviations seem to violate a strong constraining factor, but they are in fact subject to the combined force of other constraining factors, which is greater than the force of the strong constraining factors being violated. For example, "劳保" corresponds to two original forms – "劳动保护 (labor protection)" and "劳动保险 (labor insurance)" - which violates the "Unique form" factor. But the selection of "劳保" is subject to the factors - "Disyllable", "The ordering", "The grammatical structure", "Selecting the first character", "Ability to denote the meaning" - which are combined together that outweigh the "Unique form". Thus, the overlapping effect of constraining factors on the selection of abbreviated components can be used to explain examples that violate a strong constraining factor.

5   Conclusion

In this paper, we examine and evaluate the 10 constraining factors that previous researchers have identified regarding the component selection of modern Chinese abbreviations. We categorize these factors into strong, medium, and weak based on their impact on the abbreviations as a whole. The "Ability to denote the meaning of the internal segment" factor falls under both the strong and medium categories because the internal segment types affect this ability. Additionally, there is an overlapping effect between these constraining factors, and no single factor can determine abbreviation component selection alone. Some abbreviations that appear to violate the strong constraining factors are in fact subject to the combined effects of the other constraining factors.

This study bases on specific data, which can trigger in-depth thinking about the practical application of abbreviations.

The study of constraining factors can help standardize the selection of abbreviated forms. Different abbreviated forms used to be chosen from the same original form, leading to a great deal of controversy. For instance, the debate on "邮编" and "邮码" (post code) in newspapers and magazines lasted from 1991 to 1997. Experts opposed the use of "邮编" from the beginning but later sought rationality for its popularity. [1]. At the beginning of 2020, the abbreviation of "新型冠状病毒感染的肺炎" (Corona Virus Disease 2019, COVID-19) had not yet been standardized in news reports, and "新冠肺炎" eventually defeated forms like "新型肺炎", "新型冠状病毒" and "冠状病毒" [26]. The results of this study help to explain the conventionalization of abbreviated forms and to standardize the use of abbreviations.

Second, this study could help to solve the unknown abbreviations in Chinese language processing. Mistakes of abbreviation recognizing still remains in in some word segmentation software (e.g., Language Cloud, Sogou Segmentation, SCWS Chinese Segmentation, and NLPIR, etc.). If the computer can store the constraining factors of abbreviation construction, it may be able to better cope with the endless abbreviations, solve the problems of automatic word segmentation and word sense understanding, and promote machine learning.

Third, clarifying the constraining factors may also provide some new ideas and inspirations for Chinese second language teaching of vocabulary. Some learners lack the awareness of abbreviation and often use the original form in their expressions, which makes the utterances not concise and authentic, for example, students will use "营业运行成本" instead of "营运成本" (operating cost) which is customarily used by Chinese [27]; learners also have difficulties in understanding many commonly used abbreviations. Some learners, after learning the construction of certain Chinese abbreviations, wonder why the abbreviation of a certain original form is form A instead of form B. For example, why is the abbreviation of "国家政策" (national policy) is "国策" instead of "国政" [28]? Teachers can introduce the constraining factors of abbreviations in teaching, so that students can deduce most of the original forms of abbreviations. This is of great significance in helping learners understand and learn new words independently, and improve their Chinese expression level.

Acknowledgments. This paper is supported by the Fundamental Research Funds for the Central Universities, and the Research Funds of Beijing Language and Culture University (23YCX156). The anonymous reviewers of CLSW2023 put forward some valuable comments, and I express my sincere thanks to them!

References

1. Yu, L.-M.: Studies on Chinese Abbreviations: Abbreviation: The Re-signification of Linguistic Symbols. Bashu Books, Chengdu (2005). (in Chinese)
2. Gong, Q., Nie, Z.-P.: Constraining conditions on modern Chinese four-character abbreviations. Appl. Linguis. **1**, 64–70 (2006). (in Chinese)
3. Lv, S.-X., Zhu, D.-X.: Grammatical and Rhetorical Speech. The Commercial Press, Beijing (1952). (in Chinese)
4. Yin, Z.-P.: Methods and principles of constructing abbreviations. Lang. Teach. Res. **2**, 74–82 (1999). (in Chinese)
5. Wang, J.-H.: Modern Chinese Abbreviations. Tianjin People's Publishing House, Tianjin (2001). (in Chinese)
6. Zhang, M.-X.: The constraining factor mechanism of morpheme selection in modern Chinese bisyllabic condensed words. Master thesis, Beijing Language and Culture University (2003). (in Chinese)
7. Ma, Q.-Z.: Abbreviations and Their Composition. Linguistic Research Series, pp. 78–104. Nankai University Press, Tianjin (1988). (in Chinese)
8. Zhou, G.-G.: Introduction to Modern Chinese Lexicography. Guangdong Higher Education Press, Guangzhou (2004). (in Chinese)
9. Liu, S.-X.: Chinese Descriptive Vocabulary, 2nd edn. Commercial Press, Beijing (2005). (in Chinese)
10. Zhu, Z.-P.: Theories of Chinese character formation and the teaching of Chinese characters to Foreigners. Lang. Teach. Res. **4**, 35–41 (2002). (in Chinese)
11. Liu, Y.-L.: Dictionary of Contemporary Chinese Abbreviations. Sichuan People's Publishing House, Chengdu (1998). (in Chinese)
12. Wang, K.-J., Nasu, M.: Dictionary of Modern Chinese Abbreviations. Commercial Press, Beijing (1996). (in Chinese)
13. Zhong, J.-L.: Dictionary of Modern Chinese Abbreviations. Qilu Book Company, Jinan (1986). (in Chinese)
14. Y, K., X, Y.: Dictionary of Practical Abbreviations. New World Press, Beijing (1992). (in Chinese)
15. Shi, B.-Y., Xu, Y.-W.: Dictionary of Chinese Abbreviations. Foreign Language Teaching and Research Press, Beijing (1990). (in Chinese)
16. Chen, J.-M.: Abbreviations in modern Chinese. Chin. Lang. **4**, 44–49 (1963). (in Chinese)
17. Shao, J.-M.: Dictionary of the Chinese Proficiency Test. East China Normal University Press, Shanghai (2000). (in Chinese)
18. Jiang, X.-Y.: A Cognitive Study of Modern Chinese Abbreviations. Chinese Social Science Press, Beijing (2017). (in Chinese)
19. Barcelona, A.: Salience in metonymy-motivated constructional abbreviated form with particular attention to English clippings. Cogn. Semant. **2**, 30–58 (2016)
20. Fu, H.-Q.: Modern Chinese Vocabulary, Updated Peking University Press, Beijing (2004). (in Chinese)
21. Lin, Y.-H., Hsieh, S-K.: Latent semantic distance between Chinese basic words and non-basic words. In: Su, X., He, T.-T. (eds.) CLSW 2014. LNAI, vol. 8922, pp. 270–277. Springer, Heidelberg (2014). https://doi.org/10.1007/978-3-319-14331-6_27
22. Yu, C.-M.: A Comparative Study of Abbreviations in Modern Chinese Dictionary (7th edn.) and Modern Chinese Standardized Dictionary (3rd edn.). Master thesis, Hebei University (2017). (in Chinese)
23. Feng, S.-L.: On "Rhyming Words" in Chinese. Chin. Soc. Sci. **1**, 161–176 (1996). (in Chinese)

24. Chen, W.-Q., Gan, J.-M., Gu, X.-L., Li, J., Wang, R.-Z.: A study on the selection mechanism of the Chinese loan words of the same signified with different signifiers. In: Su, Q., Xu, G., Yang, X.-Y. (eds.) CLSW 2022. LNAI, vol. 13495, pp. 350–367. Springer, Cham (2023). https://doi.org/10.1007/978-3-031-28953-8_27
25. Li, J.-P.: A study of lexical patterns in contemporary Chinese based on the theory of constructions. Doctoral dissertation, Beijing Language and Culture University (2018). (in Chinese)
26. Liu, D.-Q., Feiyan, X.-G.: (COVID-19)-an emerging Chinese abbreviation. Chin. J. Lang. Policy Planning **5**(02), 5–7 (2020). (in Chinese)
27. Shao, X.-Q.: Research on Chinese abbreviations for teaching Chinese as a Foreign language. Master thesis, Heilongjiang University (2019). (in Chinese)
28. Xiang, Y.-H.: Research on teaching abbreviations in newspaper reading class. Master thesis, Liaoning Normal University (2019). (in Chinese)

On the Verb *Huaiyi* with Passive Voice in Hong Kong-Style Chinese

Hantao Xu[1,2](✉)

[1] School of Chinese Language and Literature, Beijing Normal University, Beijing, China
xuhantao0728@foxmail.com
[2] School of Humanities, Nanyang Technological University, Singapore, Singapore

Abstract. Different from Putonghua, the verb *"huaiyi"* 'suspect' in Hong Kong-style Chinese, can be used in the passive voice without a passive marker. It generally acts as an attributive or a predicate. A comparison of the Chinese and English versions of the Hong Kong government gazettes shows that *"huaiyi"* in Hong Kong-style Chinese has multiple correspondences with the English word "suspect". The usage of is influenced by the linguistic and pragmatic factors of English, as well as the phenomenon of the implicit experiencer of Chinese grammar.

Keywords: *Huaiyi* · Passive voice · Hong Kong-style Chinese

1 Introduction

Hong Kong-style Chinese is "written Chinese predominantly based on Standard Chinese, with some Classical Chinese influence, and deeply influenced by Cantonese and English. It differs from Standard Chinese in terms of lexical system, semantic understanding, structural combinations, sentence patterns, and language usage. It is primarily used in the written Chinese language commonly in Hong Kong" [1] 6. The term "Standard Chinese" refers to the written form of Putonghua used in the Mainland. Compared to Putonghua, Hong Kong-style Chinese is more influenced by English, hence it has adopted numerous vocabulary and grammatical structures from English. This is mainly evident in loanword, word class shifting, and coordinate relation [2–4].

There are differences between Hong Kong Chinese and Mandarin in the usage of the common verb *"huaiyi"* 'supect'. In the *Modern Chinese Dictionary* (7th Edition, 2017), the definition of the verb is "*dong ①yihuo; bu hen xiangxin: ta de hua jiao ren huaiyi|duiyu zhege jielun shui ye meiyou huaiyi. ②caice: wo huaiyi ta jintian laibuliao*". 'verb ①doubt; not very convinced: His words make people doubt|No one has any doubts about this conclusion. ②suspect: I suspect that he won't be able to come today.'

In Putonghua, *"huaiyi"* with the second meaning is usually used in the active voice. It always acts as a predicate in the sentence, where the subject represents the person who holds the suspicion, and the object (usually a clause) is the thing being suspected [5], and as shown in example (1a).

M. Dong et al. (Eds.): CLSW 2023, LNAI 14514, pp. 332–342, 2024.
https://doi.org/10.1007/978-981-97-0583-2_26

(1) a. Pu jingfang huaiyi gaichuan touyun dupin. (CCL Yuliaoku)[1]
'The Portuguese police suspect that the ship is trafficking drugs.'(CCL Corpus)
b. Gaichuan bei pujingfang huaiyi touyun dupin./Gaichuan bei huaiyi touyun dupin.
'The ship is suspected of trafficking drugs by the Portuguese police./The ship is suspected of trafficking drugs.'
c. Bei pujingfang huaiyi touyun dupin de chuan/bei huaiyi touyun dupin de chuan/bei huaiyi de chuan
'The ship suspected of trafficking drugs by the Portuguese police/The ship suspected of drug trafficking/The suspected ship'

When used in passive voice, it is necessary to add a passive marker to "*huaiyi*", which mostly is "*bei*". In example (1b), the original object clause is split into two parts. The subject of the subordinate clause is promoted to the subject in front of "*bei*", while the predicate remains after the verb. The passive structure formed by *bei* can be fronted as the attributive, as seen in example (1c) "*Bei pujingfang huaiyi touyun dupin de chuan*". In the context, certain words in the attributive can be omitted as needed, resulting in forms such as "*bei huaiyi touyun dupin de chuan*" and "*bei huaiyi de chuan*" in example (1c). Howerver, when expressing a similar meaning of example (1c), it is more common to use synonyms of huaiyi like "*shexian*" 'be suspected to do', "*yisi*" 'be suspected to do, or "*keyi*" 'suspicious'. For example, "*Gaichuan shexian touyun dupin*" 'the ship is suspected of being involved in drug trafficking', "*yisi touyun dupin de chuan*" 'the ship that is suspected of drug trafficking', or "*keyi de chuan*" 'the suspicious ship' are more frequently.

In Hong Kong-style Chinese, the "*huaiyi*" 'suspect' can be used in the passive voice without a passive marker. Previous studies have indicated that *huaiyi* with the passive meaning (hereinafter written as "*huaiyi passive*") in Hong Kong-style Chinese is commonly used as an attributive and a predicate. While Shi et al. provided examples of the "*huaiyi passive*"used as an attributive, they did not investigate the origin of this usage [1] 267–268. Tian discussed the expression and origin of *huaiyi passive* used as a predicate, suggesting that its emergence was influenced by the corresponding English word "suspect", which is often used in the structure of "NP be V-ed infinitive VP" [6] 268–270. This led to the formation of the pattern "NP + *huaiyi* + VP", which is referred to as the "*xingzhu yibei beidongju*" 'sentences that using an active form to express a passive meaning' [6] 268. To our knowledge, there has been no comprehensive study on the overall performance of the "*huaiyi passive*" and the English-Chinese correspondence pattern represented by this word has not been thoroughly demonstrated. Additionally, little discussion has been conducted on the impact of factors other than English on the "*huaiyi passive*". This article examines the "*huaiyi passive*" in Hong Kong-style Chinese and focuses on the following two issues:

Firstly, how is the usage of "*huaiyi passive*"? to what extent does it correspond to the English word "suspect"?

Secondly, apart from English, is the "*huaiyi passive*" construction influenced by other factors?

---

[1] The website is: http://ccl.pku.edu.cn:8080/ccl_corpus/.

2   The Usage of *"huaiyi passive"*

The Hong Kong government gazettes are issued by the Hong Kong Government Information Services to the public. The majority of the reports are presented in bilingual versions, with both Chinese and English translations. Because both Chinese and English are official languages in Hong Kong. Depending on the circumstances and needs, one of the official languages is initially used to write the gazettes, followed by the translation into another official language.

We collected all the bilingual news articles from the Hong Kong government gazettes between August 15, 2022, and September 30, 2022. Upon searching, *"huaiyi"* appeared 462 times, with *"huaiyi passive"* accounting for 308 occurrences, making up 66.67% of the total. It is evident that in Hong Kong-style Chinese, the *"huaiyi passive"* has become the main usage. When comparing the Chinese and English texts, we discovered that among these 308 instances, 299 cases corresponded to forms or structures of the word "suspect", which means that the usage of *"huaiyi passive"* is closely related to "suspect". In the following discussion, we will focus on these 299 examples of *"huaiyi passive"*.

2.1   Acting as an Attributive

The *"huaiyi passive"* used as an attributive appeared 252 times, accounting for a high percentage of 84.28%. The *"huaiyi passive* + NP" structure formed by it mostly expresses the meaning of "the person or thing being suspected as NP". In other words, NP is not the patient of suspicion but rather a preliminary guess or judgment about the nature of the entity being suspected. Here are some examples. The Chinese news in the gazettes is presented first, followed by the corresponding English news, with a equal sign " =" in between, and an underline "_"indicates *"huaiyi passive* + NP".

(2) Dangzhong huaiyi siyan de guji shizhi gong yue sishier wan yuan, ying ke shuizhi yue ershijiu wan yuan.
= 'The estimated market value of the suspected illicit cigarettes was about $420,000 with a duty potential of about $290,000.'
(3) Shimin ke zhidian haiguan ershi si xiaoshi rexian 2545 6182, huo touguo jubao zuian zhuanyong dianyou zhanghu (crimereport@customs.gov.hk) jubao huaiyi siyan huodong.
= 'Members of the public may report any suspected illicit cigarette activities to Customs' 24-h hotline 2545 6182 or its dedicated crime-reporting email account (crimereport@customs.gov.hk).'

In the above three examples, *"huaiyi siyan"* 'suspected illicit cigarettes' means "the item suspected to be illicit cigarettes", and *"huaiyi siyan huodong"* 'suspected illicit cigarette activities' denotes "the event suspected to be illicit cigarette activities". These examples demonstrate that the *"huaiyi passive"* used as an attributive corresponds to derived forms of "suspect", which is the adjective "suspected".

In English, the meaning of "suspected" is "being suspected", and it typically acts directly as an attributive, forming the "suspected + NP" structure, which means "the person or thing suspected to be NP". For example, the Oxford Advanced Learner's Dictionary (8th edition) lists phrases such as "a suspected broken arm", "suspected tax evasion" and "suspected terrorists". Hong Kong-style Chinese directly uses *huaiyi* to transplant the meaning and usage of "suspected", resulting in the structure of "*huaiyi passive* + NP". However, in Putonghua, the "suspected" before a noun phrase is usually translated as the adjective "*keyi*" and the verbs "*yisi*", "*shexian*". For example, in Baidu Translate[2] for mainland Chinese, "suspected terrorists" is translated as "*yisi kongbu fenzi*", and "the suspected illicit cigarettes" is "*keyi de feifa xiangyan*", and "any suspected illicit cigarette activities" is "*renhe shexian feifa xiyan de huodong*".

In English, the noun phrases modified by "suspected" can sometimes be complex, resulting in corresponding complexity in the "*huaiyi passive* + NP" structure. For example, the "NP" in "suspected NP" can also be a compound noun phrase, and so does the structure of "*huaiyi passive* + NP".

(4) Shimin ke zhidian haiguan ershisi xiaoshi rexian 2545 6182, huo touguo jubao zuian zhuanyong dianyou zhanghu (crimereport@customs.gov.hk) jubao <u>huaiyi weifan</u> <u>"shangpin shuoming tiaoli" de shiyi he qingxi heiqian de huodong</u>.
= 'Members of the public may report any <u>suspected violation of the TDO and money</u> <u>laundering activities</u> to Customs' 24-h hotline 2545 6182 or its dedicated crime-reporting email account (crimereport@customs.gov.hk).'

In the English version of the news, when the head of a noun phrase is "case", there can be other modifiers inserted between it and "suspected", resulting in a significantly longer noun phrase. The corresponding structure in Hong Kong-style Chinese also exhibits similar characteristics. For example:

(5) Weishengshu weisheng fanghu zhongxin jinri (jiuyue wuri) zheng diaocha yizong <u>huaiyi jinshi yesheng gulei hou yinzhi shiwu zhongdu de ge'an</u>.
= 'The Centre for Health Protection (CHP) of the Department of Health is today (September 5) investigating <u>a suspected case of food poisoning related to the consumption of</u> <u>wild mushrooms</u>.'

In this example, the content introduced by "of" provides additional information about the "case". The corresponding Chinese version put the content after "of", which is "*jinshi yesheng gulei hou yinzhi shiwu zhongdu*" 'food poisoning related to the consumption of wild mushrooms', forward and uses it as the modifier of the noun "*ge'an*" 'case'.

When the meaning is clear, the modifiers before the head noun "case/*ge'an*" may be omitted. Therefore, in gazettes, there are numerous "suspected cases/*huaiyi ge'an*", for example:

(6) Ruo yu <u>huaiyi weifa ge'an</u> hui genjin diaocha......shuiwushu hui miqie liuyi youguan danwei shouqu shuifei de qingkuang, yu <u>huaiyi ge'an</u> hui genjin diaocha.
= 'If there are <u>suspected offence cases</u>, follow-up investigations will be conducted......the WSD will closely monitor the water charges collected by the landlord from the relevant unit, and carry out a follow-up investigation of any <u>suspected cases</u>.'

In addition to the government gazettes, in other materials of Hong Kong-style Chinese, "*huaiyi passive* + NP" can express the meaning of "NP which is suspected", which is consistent with the expression in Putonghua. For example:

---

[2] The website is: https://fanyi.baidu.com/.

(7) Ciwai, youyu xianggang shuhuan yanzhong, erqie jing shiyan zhengshi N501Y bianzhong bingdu ke chuanran laoshu, yinci laoshu ye chengle <u>huaiyi duixiang</u>.("Xianggang zhongguo tongxunshe"2021.6.16)
'Moreover, due to the serious rat problem in Hong Kong, it has been proven that the N501Y variant virus can be transmitted to rats, so rats have also become the <u>suspected objects</u>.'(Hong Kong China News Agency 2021.6.16)

In "*huaiyi duixiang*" 'the suspected objects', the noun "*duixiang*" 'object' is the patient of "*huaiyi*".

To sum up, "*huaiyi passive* + NP" in Hong Kong-style Chinese has two semantic interpretations: one is "the person or thing being suspected to be NP", and the other is "NP which is suspected", and the former is extremely more commonly used.

2.2 Acting as a Predicate

The predicate "*huaiyi passive*" appears in 47 cases, accounting for 15.72%. For example:

(8) Youguan chanpin yi huaiyi shu weijing zhuce yaoji zhipin.
= 'The products are also suspected to be unregistered pharmaceutical products.'
(9) Yiming liushiliu sui nüzi huaiyi xiru nongyan bing daowo yu shifa danwei nei, ta hunmi bei songwang guanghua yiyuan zhili.
= 'After the fire was put out, a 66-year-old woman, who was suspected of smoke inhalation, was found lying unconscious inside the unit……'

As illustrated by the two previous examples, verbs in Chinese, when in the passive voice, don't undergo the same inflectional changes as they do in English. There's no distinction between finite and non-finite forms in Chinese. Hence, Hong Kong-style Chinese use *huaiyi passive* to correspond the passive infinitive structures of "suspect" in English, which are "be suspected to do" and "be suspected of sth".

In English, "be suspected to do" and "be suspected of sth" frequently appear in postposed relative clauses, serving to modify the preceding nouns. As a result, in Hong Kong-style Chinese, the construction "*huaiyi passive* + X" can also serve as an attributive phrase. However, according to Chinese grammar, the attributive phrase must be positioned before the noun it modifies. In the following examples, we use an underline "_" to indicate the construction "*huaiyi passive* + X" and "=" to highlight "X".

(10) Jubu sanming nianling jiehu ershier sui zhi ershiliu sui de <u>huaiyi she'an</u> nannü.
= 'two men and a woman, aged between 22 and 26 years old, <u>suspected to be connected with the case</u> were arrested.'

In the English version of example (10), "suspected to be connected with the case" is a postposed attributive clause. In the Chinese version, the descriptive-object structure "*huaiyi she'an*" 'suspected to be connected with the case' is moved before the head noun "*nannü*" 'man and women' to function as an attributive.

It is worth noting that in English, the relative clauses are typically placed after the head noun, forming a left-branching structure that allows for greater expansion and the inclusion of more modifiers. In Hong Kong-style Chinese, however, the originally postponed relative clauses are fronted, leading to their elongation due to the presence of multiple modifiers.

(11) Shiwu huanjing weisheng shu (shihuanshu) yizhi zhili daji yi bingxian huo lengcan-grou maochong xinxianrou chushou de qingkuang, jinri (jiuyue sanshiri) yu shatianqu he kuiqingqu xiang huaiyi yi lengcangrou chongdang xinxianrou chushou de chipai xinxian liangshidian caiqu xingdong.

= 'The Food and Environmental Hygiene Department (FEHD) has all along been com-mitted to combating the sale of chilled or frozen meat disguised as fresh meat, and raided licensed fresh provision shops (FPS) in Sha Tin and Kwai Tsing Districts suspected of selling frozen meat as fresh meat today (September 30).'

(12) Jing shenru diaocha he zijin liuxiang fenxi hou, haiguan zai suoding liangming huaiyi liyong touzhu hukou, geren yinhang hukou, chuzhi zhifu gongju hukou ji zhaohuandian shouqu he chuli huaiyi fanzui deyi, jinxing qingxi heiqian huodong   de bendi nanzi。

= 'Subsequent to an in-depth investigation and fund-flow analysis, two more local men, who were suspected of using betting accounts, personal bank accounts, stored value facility accounts and a money changer in dealing with crime proceeds and participating in money laundering activities, were targeted.'

Sometimes, the construction "*huaiyi passive* + X" can also remain after the noun. For example:

(13) Jingfang jianhuo wukuai guanggaoban, huaiyi yu an youguan.
= 'Police seized five advertisement panels which were suspected in connection with the case.'

In this example, according to the Chinese grammar, "*huaiyi yu an youguan*" 'suspected in connection with the case' should be considered as the second clause. As a result, *huaiyi* can be understood as an active verb, with the omitted subject *jingcha* 'the police' from the previous context. However, compared with the English text, it can be observed that "*huaiyi yu an youguan*" is actually a postponed attributive clause modifying the noun "*guanggaoban*" 'advertisement panels'.

In addition to corresponding to infinitive structures, the *huaiyi passive* as a predicate can also correspond to the adverb "suspectedly" derived from "suspect". For example:

(14) Yiliang yan lianxiangdao nanxing de xiaoba huaiyishouche buji, zhuangxiang gailiang zhongxing huoche chewei.
= 'A school bus traveling along Lin Cheung Road southbound suspectedly failed to brake in time and bumped into the rear of the HGV.'

In conclusion, based on the analysis of the Chinese-English version, the majority of instances show that "*huaiyi passive*" corresponds to words or structures related to "suspect". There are three main performances:

Firstly, Chinese does not exhibit the morphological changes present in English. As a result, "*huaiyi passive*" correspond to the inflected forms of "suspect", such as the passive form "suspected", and derived forms like the adjective "suspected" and the adverb "suspectedly".

Second, due to the absence of finite and non-finite structures in Chinese, "*huaiyi passive*" correspond not only to single words but also to the infinitive structures "be suspected to" and "be suspected of".

Third, given the difference in word order between Chinese and English, *"huaiyi passive"* often needs to be fronted in a pre-nominal position. In some cases where the word order is consistent, *"huaiyi passive"* generally remains in its original position.

3 The Motivation of *"huaiyi passive"*

The emergence and evolution of the *"huaiyi passive"* in Hong Kong-style Chinese are primarily influenced by the dominant language - English in Hong Kong, which encompasses both linguistic forms and pragmatic factors. The usage of *huaiyi passive* also is constrained by the principle of the implicit experiencer of Chinese grammar.

3.1 The Dual Influence of English: Linguistical and Psychological

In the Sect. 2, we discussed in detail the distribution and usage of *"huaiyi passive"* in Hong Kong-style Chinese. The majority of instances can be traced back to corresponding words and structures related to the English word "suspect", demonstrating that the former originated under the influence of the latter. Putonghua does not have the *"huaiyi passive"*, as mainland Chinese uses words such as *"shexian"*, *"yisi"* and *"keyi"* to correspond to relevant English words and structures. Apart from the direct borrowing of linguistic forms, the influence of English on Hong Kong-style Chinese is also evident in terms of pragmatic psychology.

Since the Magna Carta, the protection of human rights has been emphasized in the United Kingdom, and the rights of suspects are enshrined in law. One manifestation of this is the principle of "presumption of innocence". This means that before being formally convicted in a legal trial, a person should not be treated as a criminal, and their rights should be protected. As a result, when media outlets report on cases, they cannot directly identify the perpetrators to avoid legal liability. This "blame avoided" of pragmatic psychology influences the usage of discourse [7]. Therefore, in British news, words and phrases such as "suspected" and "be suspected of" are frequently used to indicate the media's neutral stance toward suspects and related objects. The legal system in Hong Kong shares a common lineage with that of the United Kingdom, and the media in Hong Kong are equally cautious when reporting on suspects and related objects. They exhibit the same "blame avoided" pragmatic psychology as British society. For example, in Hong Kong-style Chinese, the neutral marker *youren* 'someone' is often used to avoid using any statements that explicitly identify the person responsible for the crime [6] 322–334, and the *"huaiyi passive"* serves the same purpose.

Firstly, when using the *"huaiyi passive"* the experiencer of suspicion (usually government agencies and news media) is hidden, which can prevent them from unnecessary trouble.

(15) Jingfang zuo zai jubu 2nan 1nü tongzhu zuke, she zuzhi hefa maizang shiti, juxi 3 ren huaiyi zhidao yifan xingxiong er wei baojing. ("Mingbao" 2022.5.1)
'Yesterday, the police arrested two male and one female tenants living together again, involved in preventing legal burial of bodies. It is reported that three people were suspected to know the suspect had committed the crime but did not report it to the police.'(*Ming Pao* 2022.5.1)

In the above example, it is not difficult to infer that it was "Jingfang" 'police' who suspected the tenant, but the former did not appear in the clause where the "huaiyi passive" located. That is to say, when reporting the speculation and opinions of the three men and women, the experiencer were intentionally concealed, thereby reducing the responsibility of the "police" for this speculation.

Secondly, when it comes to individuals or objects involved, the *huaiyi passive* indicates that the subsequent content is only preliminary speculation, highlighting an objective and neutral attitude and leaving room for further investigation. For example:

(16) Wei jing diaocha hou xiangxin huaiyi zhadan zhishi dipan lingjian, zhengshi xujingyichang. ("Xianggang 01 wang" 2022.7.18)
'After investigation, it is believed that the suspected bomb is just a construction site component, confirming that it was a false alarm.' ("Hong Kong 01 website" 2022.7.18)

In this example, the *"huaiyi passive"* modifies *"zhadan"* 'bomb', indicating "an object suspected to be a bomb", which was later confirmed by the police to be a component found at a construction site. The initial report did not directly state that the object was a bomb, leaving room for interpretation and aligning with the facts.

3.2 The Implicit Experiencer of Chinese Grammar

In Modern Chinese, when perception verbs act as the predicate, the subject experiencing the perception can be absent. Wang discusses the phenomenon of implicit experiencer in Putonghua [8], providing examples such as:

(17) Fanzheng zhe yiqunren ganjue shiqu toudu de.
'I think this group of people is going to smuggle.'

In example (17), the subject before the predicate *"ganjue"* 'think' is *"zhe yiqunren"* 'this group of people', which is not the experiencer or perceiver. The experiencer *"wo"* 'I' referring to the speaker, is absent.

Li and Zhang pointed out that in Malaysian Chinese, Singaporean Chinese, and Hong Kong-style Chinese, when the perception verb *"xiangxin"* 'believe' is the predicate, the experiencer can also be absent [9]. Here are examples provided in the article:

(18) Ta renwei, guaitong shijian xiangxin shi you muhou jituan caokong, liyong gezhong fangfa xiyin xiaohai duoru xianjing.
'He think, the child trafficking incident is believed to be orchestrated by a behind-the-scenes group, using various methods to lure children into traps.'

In this example, the subject of *"xiangxin"* 'believe'" is *"guaitong shijian"* 'child trafficking incident', which is the patient of suspicion. And the experiencer can be recognized as *"ta"* 'he' in the previous context.

When the *"huaiyi"* passive is used as the predicate, it exhibits semantic, functional, and usage similarities to the aforementioned *"xiangxin"*, and *"huaiyi passive"* is also involved in the phenomenon of the implicit experiencer.

In classical Chinese, the perception verb *"yi"* 'suspect' was already used in the passive voice, where the experiencer can be absent and the preceding subject is the patient of the suspicion. For example:

(19) Baigu yi xiang, wufu lei yu, ci jie si zhi er fei zhe ye. (Xihan "Zhanguoce")
'Bones are suspected to be the skeleton of elephants, and wǔfū seem to be like jade. All these are only similar but not the same thing.')(Western Han Dynasty *Strategies of the Warring States*)
(20) Shi you dao guanwu zhe, yi wunanshi shiming. (Xijin "Sanguozhi")
'At times, the theft of official belongings was suspected to be Shi Ming, who serves as wúnánsh'. (Western Jin Dynasty *Records of the Three Kingdoms*)

In Mandarin Chinese, the subject before "*yi*" is also involved in the phenomenon of implicit experiencer. However, "yi" needs to form a disyllabic rhythmic word with passive marker "*bei*" "*shou*""*zao*" and word like "*yin*" 'because of', "*shi*" 'be'. For example:

(21) 2018nian 3yue, mou shejiao pingtai you chaoguo 5000wan ming yonghu geren ziliao yi zao xielu ...... ("Renmin Ribao" 2019.9.16)
'In March 2018, over 50 million users' personal information on a certain social platform was suspected to have been leaked'. (*People's Daily* 2019.9.16)
(22) Youde zuke yi yin wenti fangwu shengbing. ("Renmin Ribao" 2018.9.20)
'Some tenants are suspected to have fallen ill due to problematic housing'. (*People's Daily* 2018.9.20)

As seen above, in both ancient and modern Chinese, the experiencer of "*yi*" can be hidden. Although "*huaiyi*" can not be used in the passive voice in Putonghua, the usage of "*huaiyi passive*" in Hong Kong-style Chinese follows the rules of the implicit experiencer of Chinese grammar.

It is worth noting that the absence of the experiencer of "*huaiyi passive*" weakens its action meaning and further develops modal meaning of might. For example:

(22) Ling yiming zhiyuan huaiyi ceng buqiadang duidai yiming you'er.
= 'another staff member might have treated a child inappropriately'.

This example is taken from the Hong Kong government gazettes, and based on the parallel Chinese-English version, we can see that "*huaiyi passive*" directly corresponds to "might", which is an English modal verb typically translated as "*keneng*". However, we have only found this one example, indicating that the use of "*huaiyi passive*" to express the meaning of "might" is still in the process of development and is not yet stable.

4   Conclusion

In Hong Kong-style Chinese and its researches, the importance of English is self-evident, and many studies have focused on the contact between English and Chinese in Hong Kong. For example, Zhao and Shi analyzed the usage characteristics of the "*youxinxin*" 'have confidence' construction and the use of "*jing*" 'through' [10, 11]. However, researches in this area are still in early stages, and discussions on related phenomena are relatively limited.

Based on this, this article focuses on a micro-level examination of "*huaiyi passive*" from a synchronic perspective. By using the parallel Chinese-English version of the

Hong Kong government gazettes, it examines the corresponding ways of *"huaiyi passive"* with related words and structures of "suspect". It also further analyzes the causes and development of *"huaiyi passive"* in conjunction with other internal and external linguistic factors.

The research in this article shows that the language contact represented by typical words, such as *"huaiyi passive"*, is also worthy of in-depth investigation. Through case studies and analysis of these feature words at a micro-level [12], we can explore the specific sources, usage, and development of language contact, which can enrich our understanding of the overall manifestation and patterns of it.

Based on the content of this article, we propose two suggestions for the study of language contact in typical words: firstly, to thoroughly discuss the input and influence of foreign languages while fully exploring the restrictions and transformations imposed by the rules of Chinese itself on related phenomena; secondly, to consciously and purposefully select directly comparable Chinese-English materials as the basis for comprehensive, in-depth, and detailed research.

Acknowledgments. This study was supported by the National Language Commission Research of China (Grant No. ZDI145-39).This article was written under the guidance of Professor Diao Yanbin, and with the assistance of Associate Professor Lin Jingxia, Assistant Professor Dong Sicong, and Zhang Yiyun. All errors remain my own.

References

1. Shi, D.-X., Shao, J.-M., Zhu, Z.-Y.: Comparison of Hong Kong-Style Chinese with Standard Chinese. Hong Kong Educational Publishing Company, Hong Kong (2006). (in Chinese)
2. Shi, D.-X., Zhu, Z.-Y.: The influence of English on syntax of Hong Kong written Chinese: language changes caused by language contact. J. Foreign Lang. **22**(4), 2–11 (1999). (in Chinese)
3. Shi, D.-X., Zhu, Z.-Y.: English influence on Hong Kong written Chinese: the case of homographs. J. Foreign Lang. **28**(5), 2–9 (2005). (in Chinese)
4. Feng, W.-H., Guo, H.-F., Cao, D.-X., Ren, H.: A comparative study on the coordinate relation of Chinese official documents in Mainland, Hong Kong and Macau. In: Hong, J.-F., Su, Q., Wu, J.-S. (eds.) Chinese Lexical Semantics. CLSW 2018. LNCS, vol. 11173, pp.758–771. Springer, Cham (2018)
5. Yuan, Y.-L.: On the sense extension mechanism and semantic construal strategy of the Chinese verb "huaiyi." Stud. Lang. Linguist. **34**(3), 1–12 (2014). (in Chinese)
6. Tian, X.-L.: Global Chinese Grammar Hong Kong Volume. The Commercial Press, Beijing (2021). (in Chinese)
7. Hansson, S.: Discursive strategies of blame avoidance in government: a framework for analysis. Discourse Soc. **26**(3), 297–322 (2015)
8. Wan, Q.: Speaking subject and inexplicit performative topic. Chinese Teach. World **30**(4), 470–483 (2016). (in Chinese)
9. Li, J.-W., Zhang, M.-F.: On the modal function of "xiangxin" (believe) and its origin in oversea varieties. Global Chinese **3**(2), 231–242 (2017). (in Chinese)
10. Zhao, C.-L., Shi, D.-X.: Synactic difference of "youxinxin" between mainland Chinese and Hong Kong, Macau and Taiwan Chinese. Chinese Linguistics **11**(2), 27–36 (2014). (in Chinese)

11. Zhao, C.-L., Shi, D.-X.: A comparative study of "Jing"-constructions in Hong Kong-Macau Chinese and in standard Chinese. J. Yunnan Norm. Univ. (Human. Soc. Sci. Edn.) **58**(1), 25–33 (2015). (in Chinese)
12. Diao, Y.-B.: On the foreign transplant meaning in Chinese vocabulary: a case study of Malaysian Mandarin. Appl. Linguis. **30**(1), 65–77 (2021). (in Chinese)

The Semantic Characteristics of the Counter-Expectation Adverbs "Fǎn'ér" and "Ohiryo" in Chinese and Korean from the Perspective of Comparison

Qingcong Shan[✉]

Shanghai International Studies University, Shanghai 201620, China
shanqingcong@163.com

Abstract. The adverbs "Fǎn'ér" in Chinese and "Ohiryo" in Korean are typical expressions of counter-expectation. Previous studies have given relatively less attention to the semantic comparison between these two expressions. This paper mainly conducts a preliminary analysis of their internal semantic features using the magnitude model theory. It is observed that although the two expressions directly correspond, their internal semantics differ. Through comparison, we hierarchy in semantic relations: 'inversion relation > anti-recursion relation > opposition(juxtaposition) relation', 'inversion relation > opposition(juxtaposition) relation > anti-recursion relation'. Moreover, there is a difference in sensitivity; Chinese "Fǎn'ér" tends to be more sensitive to the magnitude, whereas Korean "Ohiryo" exhibits lower sensitivity. The different typicality of the two expressions is closely related to the synchronic level of use, interuse characteristic and subjective emphasis, as well as the diachronic level of grammaticalization and internal semantic transfer.

Keywords: Counter-Expectation Adverbs · Fǎn'ér · Ohiryo · Inversion Relation · Anti-Recursion Relation · Opposition(juxtaposition) Relation · Magnitude Model

1 Introduction

The adverbs "Fǎn'ér" in Chinese and "Ohiryo" in Korean are typical expressions of counter-expectation. However, previous studies have shown an imbalance in the semantic analysis and characterization of the two. While the Chinese academic community has conducted rich and diverse research on "Fǎn'ér", relatively little attention has been paid to "Ohiryo" within the Korean academic context. Therefore, a comparative analysis between these two expressions must be further developed. This paper mainly focuses on the following three questions:

This paper was sponsored by the China Scholarship Council Fund Project (Grant No. 202206900045), and the 2022–2023 Korea Foundation (KF) Doctoral Scholarship

(1) The semantic comparison between the Chinese and Korean counter-expectation adverbs "Fǎn'ér" and "Ohiryo".

(2) The semantic similarities and differences between the Chinese and Korean counter-expectation adverbs "Fǎn'ér" and "Ohiryo".

(3) The reasons for the similarities and differences between the Chinese and Korean counter-expectation adverbs "Fǎn'ér" and "Ohiryo".

Through analysis, we seek to gain a preliminary understanding of the cognitive differences between Korean and Chinese in counter-expectation expressions based on the similarities, differences and related motivations of the adverbs "Fǎn'ér" in Chinese and "Ohiryo" in Korean and provide a preliminary understanding of the cognitive differences between Korean and Chinese people in counter-expectation expressions. Additionally, this study offers some reference for foreign language learners in terms of language ontology.

2 Literature Review

Much research has been conducted on "Fǎn'ér", with detailed analyisis of the semantics of "Fǎn'ér" made by scholars such as Ma [1, 2], Wang [3], Xing [4], Wu [5], Yuan [6], Lv [7], Gao [8]. Ma [1, 2] believes that the grammatical meaning of "Fǎn'ér" is 'to show the opposition of the actual situation or phenomenon to what should occur according to normal circumstances or unexpected under certain premises.' Wang [3] believes that 'when a certain phenomenon or situation deviates from the anticipated outcome, 'fǎnér' elicits the opposite result.' Xing [4] pointed out that the recursive sentence pattern 'not only does not p, but q' has both progressive and inversion relations. Wu [5] analyzed the semantic logic of "Fǎn'ér" sentences, asserting that they generally appear in a logical field that includes expectations in the preceding part followed by a result in the subsequent part. This semantic logical relation can be formatted as 'Expectation A + Result B'. The syntactic structure of the "Fǎn'ér" sentence can take two forms: 'not only not(expectation) A, fǎn'ér B' and implicitly '(expectation A) fǎn'ér B'. Yuan [6] compared "Shènzhì" and "Fǎn'ér" in terms of counter-expectation, progressive relation and pragmatic scale. He pointed out that both can use focus theory to explain the function of the focus operator and its semantic expression in related sentences. While both convey the counter-expectation relation through focus contrast, the nature of the focus domain is different. "Fǎn'ér" requires a counter-expectation progressive relation between the elements in the focus domain. The counter-expectation performance should align with common sense. P was not realized, but the opposite R (the element represented by the focus) was unexpectedly realized. Lv [7] explained that the opposite of 'P and Q' in the interpretation of "Fǎn'ér" refers to 'the relation between two situations that develop in positive and negative directions with a certain situation r as the point of origin,' which should be denoted as "Fǎn'ér2". She pointed out that the subjects of the two clauses before and after 'not only not P, fǎn'ér Q' should be consistent. Gao [8] contended that "Fǎn'ér" serves to emphasize developments contrary to expectations or conventions. At the sentence level, it can establish three major types of semantic relations: inversion relation, anti-recursion relation, and opposition(juxtaposition) relation. The semantics of these relations are characterized by factivity, opposite and subjective.

In comparison, Korean linguistic scholars have shown limited attention to 'Ohiryo'. Cho [9] mainly analyzed the semantic characteristics of "Mushiro" and "Ohiryo" from the perspective of contrast between Japanese and Korean. He emphasized that "Ohiryo" can function as a focus operator to form a 'comparative selection' relation between the sentence components before and after and expresses mirativity semantics and exclusive properties. He analyzed seven kinds of sentences with comparative properties in "Ohiryo", yet provided limited analysis and explanation of the differences in similar expressions in Japanese and Korean. Ma [10] conducted a diachronic investigation through the translation of "You" and "Ohiryo" in Gugyeol, Idu, and the Korean alphabet. It was noted that "Ohiryo" not only included [heterogeneity] but also [homogeneity]. This established a synonymous relation between "Ohiryo" and "Yojonhi", which express [homogeneity], with the possibility of interchange. Kim [11] analyzed the context and semantics regarding the emergence of "Ohiryo" in the 15th century from a diachronic analytical and comparative perspective. He analyzed it with synonymous expressions in the 15th century. He pointed out that "Ohiryo" has experienced a large semantic migration from medieval Korean to modern Korean. Preliminarily, the Korean linguistic community has some interest in "Ohiryo", but it remains relatively scattered, with few related studies from a comparative language perspective. There is room for further expansion and clarification of the existing comparative studies on the similarities and differences. Based on previous research, this paper takes advantage of the magnitude model and related theories to conduct a preliminary comparative analysis of the semantic characteristics of the adverbs "Fǎn'ér" in Chinese and "Ohiryo" in Korean, and provide a preliminary explanation for the differences between these two expressions.

3   Research Method

According to the semantic connotation of "Fǎn'ér", Gao [8] pointed out that the clause in which "Fǎn'ér" is used can form a reversal, retrogression and opposition(juxtaposition) relation with other clauses. Specifically, Q and R form a reversal relation, -Q and R form a progressive relation, and P'Q and PR form an opposition(juxtaposition) relation. These three main semantic associations are not confined to Chinese "Fǎn'ér"; they also apply to related expressions in Korean "Ohiryo". Based on this insight, we conducted a comparative analysis of the distribution of these three relation categories in Chinese and Korean corpora. We mainly extracted 300 examples from the Chinese BCC corpus and the Korean Sejong corpus and labeled and classified the relevant corpora. It can be found that the three main semantic types have different distributions in these two languages. The specific type distributions are as follows (Table 1):

The statistical results indicate that although the Chinese adverb "Fǎn'ér" and Korean adverb "Ohiryo" both convey counter-expectation semantics, in a more specific context, the related semantic types exhibit varying distribution characteristics. This reflects that while the two are synonymous, their semantics still show heterogeneity. Specifically, the three semantic types of "Fǎn'ér" in Chinese follow a hierarchical sequence of 'inversion > anti-recursion > opposition(juxtaposition)'. The 'reversal' semantics, that is, the semantic type in which the objectively occurring event does not match the expectations of the action subject or the speaker is the more typical semantic type of "Fǎn'ér"; the

Table 1. Semantic type distribution of "Fǎn'ér" and "Ohiryo" in Chinese and Korean

Heading level	Chinese "Fǎn'ér"		Korean "Ohiryo"	
	Frequency	Proportion	Frequency	Proportion
Type 1	185	61.67%	130	43.33%
Type 2	92	30.67%	66	22%
Type 3	23	7.67%	104	34.67%
Total	300	100%	300	100%

type that represents the semantics of 'anti-recursion' comes next, followed by the type that represents the semantics of 'opposition (juxtaposition)'. On the other hand, the three semantic types of the Korean adverb "Ohiryo" follow a hierarchical sequence of 'inversion > opposition(juxtaposition) > anti-recursion'. "Ohiryo" has many semantic types representing 'inversion' and 'opposition(juxtaposition)'. While the frequency and proportion of the two are roughly equivalent, the semantic type of 'inversion' is not typical enough in comparison, showing a certain gap compared with the Chinese "Fǎn'ér". Through the preliminary statistical analysis, it can be found that although the semantics of "Fǎn'ér" and "Ohiryo" share similarities, there are still differences in their internal semantics and even large heterogeneity characteristics. Understanding the internal differentiation of their respective semantics can provide a certain reference to distinguish between the two semantics. With this initial understanding of the possible differences in the internal semantics, a specific comparative analysis of the characteristics of "Fǎn'ér" and "Ohiryo" in expressing the expectation semantics should be conducted based on the theory of the magnitude model.

4   Semantic Comparison of the Counter-Expectation Adverbs "Fǎnér" and "Ohiryo" in Chinese and Korean

4.1   Inversion Relation

In the corpus related to "Fǎn'ér" and "Ohiryo" in Chinese and Korean, the expressions representing the reversal relation appear most frequently and account for the largest proportion. In other words, "Fǎn'ér" and "Ohiryo" denote the actual situation or phenomenon opposite to what should occur according to common sense or under certain conditions. The two expressions are the main semantic types, but the inversion relation expressed by the Chinese "Fǎn'ér" exhibit a more typical tendency than the Korean "Ohiryo".

（1）近几年却出现了一个独特的现象：高学历逐渐成为部分海归的"紧箍咒"，海外留学背景<u>反而</u>"绑架"了海归。"找男朋友难，找结婚的对象更难。"

In recent years, a unique phenomenon has emerged: high education has gradually become a 'curse' for some returnes, and overseas study background has instead 'kidnapped' returnes. 'It''s hard to find a boyfriend, but it's even harder to find a marriage partner.'

（2）这次没见到山羊，却见了几回羊汤。主人介绍了羊汤的许多优点之后，我<u>反而</u>一口也喝不下了，我在怀念山上壁挂着的山羊，那是真实的有生命的东西。

We didn't see goats this time, but we saw mutton soup several times. After the host introduced the many advantages of goat soup, I couldn't take a sip. I missed the goat hanging on the wall on the mountain. It was a real living thing.

（3）그 중에서도 청남대의 경우에는 지역 주민의 원성이 크고, 국회의 조사과정을 보더라도 쉬쉬하는 품이 국민의 의혹과 반감을 <u>오히려</u> 부채질하고 있는 듯한 인상이다.

Among them, in the case of Cheongnamdae, local residents' complaints are loud, and looking at the National Assembly's investigation process, it seems that the quiet attitude is actually fueling the public's suspicion and antipathy.

（4）그러나 교육의 다양성을 무시한 집단주의적 훈련, 또는 획일화된 프로그램이 <u>오히려</u> 청소년들의 창의력과 개성을 무디게 하는 역기능으로 작용할 가능성도 있음을 정책 당국이 얼마나 생각하고 있는지도 걱정스럽다.

However, it is also worrisome how much the policy authorities think that collectivist training that ignores diversity in education or uniform programs may rather serve as a dysfunction that blunts youth creativity and individuality.

In the above examples, a typical inversion relation is formed between the clauses before and after "Fǎn'ér". For instance, in example (1), according to common sense, 'highly educated returnees' have relatively better conditions and an easier time finding a 'boyfriend' or 'marriage partner'. However, the reality is quite the opposite. 'Highly educated overseas returnees' have become a restriction. Not only is it difficult to find a 'boyfriend', but it is even more so to find a 'marriage partner'. This example sentence exhibits an inverse magnitude relation. Generally, the further to the right in the hierarchical sequence of {low education without a study abroad background, low education with a study abroad background, middle education without a study abroad background, middle education with a study abroad background, high education without a study abroad background, high education with a study abroad background......}, the greater the likelihood of marriage. However, 'high education' and 'study abroad background', originally favorable conditions, not only fail to improve the marriage situation but have become 'minus points'. This signifies a reversal in the sequence to a certain extent. Although 'highly educated and with a background of studying abroad' may not be at the bottom of this magnitude sequence, it may cause a major change in the internal ranking of items. In example (2), it is common sense that 'after the host introduced the advantages of mutton soup,' the listener should prefer to drink it. However, the actual situation is quite the opposite - 'cannot drink a sip'. Similarly, this example sentence demonstrates an inverse magnitude relation. The host's introduction of the advantages of mutton soup should appear {drink more mutton soup, drink a lot of mutton soup, drink a normal amount of mutton soup, drink a small amount of mutton soup, don't drink even a mouthful of mutton soup}, that is, 'introducing the advantages of mutton soup' should match 'drink more mutton soup'. However, it matches 'not drinking a mouthful of mutton soup' at the bottom of the magnitude sequence, indicating an inversion of magnitude, alignment with the item containing the most negative magnitude. The above example sentences indicate a typical inversion relation between the clauses before and after "Fǎn'ér" in Chinese. The reality of the latter clause is contrary to the general expectation, showing a typical counter-expectation attribute.

Korean "Ohiryo" shares similarities with the Chinese "Fǎn'ér" in that it also expresses an inversion relation between the preceding and following clauses. As in example (3), the government may impose restrictions on some people for certain reasons, such as social stability. The matter was concealed, but the actual situation aroused confusion and disgust among the people, establishing a contradictory relation between the implicit expectations in the sentence and the actual situation. Nevertheless, from a magnitude perspective, the magnitude sequence in the example sentence is as obvious as in Chinese. The results of 'concealing and not reporting' can lead to many possibilities without grade characteristics. 'National doubts and disgust' and other possible results, such as 'maintaining social stability', 'causing social unrest', etc., lack a magnitude sequence similar to the relative dominance of "Fǎn'ér". In example (4), 'collectivist training and unified projects' failed to have an idealizing effect and instead had the counter-effect of 'blunting creativity and individuality'. Despite counter-effects similar to those in Chinese between the preceding and following clauses, the objective reality and the possible expected items cannot form a relatively explicit magnitude sequence. By comparing the reversal semantics of "Fǎn'ér" and "Ohiryo", it can be statistically found that the Chinese "Fǎn'ér" with its reversal semantics has a relatively more typical tendency, while "Ohiryo" expressing reversal semantics demonstrates a relatively less typical tendency. The typicality of this reverse semantics is closely related to the counter-expectation semantics, indicating that the counter-expectation typicality of "Ohiryo" may be weaker than "Fǎn'ér" in Chinese. In addition, in our analysis from the perspective of magnitude sequence, it can be found that the Chinese "Fǎn'ér" is more sensitive to magnitude, with a relatively implicit causal matching relation between the clauses before and after "Fǎn'ér". Due to the existence of "Fǎn'ér", this kind of matching is a reverse matching. In contrast, the example sentence where the Korean "Ohiryo" is located is not as sensitive to this magnitude relation, and there may not necessarily be an obvious sequence of magnitudes between objective reality and possible expectations.

4.2 Anti-recursion Relation

The anti-recursion relation is an important semantic type of "Fǎn'ér" and "Ohiryo". Compared with the other two semantics, anti-recursion semantics, in addition to 'reverse', also has typical 'progressive' semantics. This anti-recursion semantics is realized through syntactic means. Xing Fuyi(2001) summarized four kinds of Chinese anti-recursion sentence patterns: (1) advance words like "Bùdàn", (2) inversion words like "Fǎn'ér", (3) negation words like "Bù", "Méi", (4) opposite concepts 'P' and 'Q'. The retrogressive semantics of "Ohiryo" in Korean is similarly realized through more distinctive syntactic expressions. For example, in Korean anti-recursion expressions, '-neunkonyong(는커녕)', '-giboda(기보다)'and other contrastive expressions. Such expressions often bear implicit negative semantics. While implicitly negating the content of the previous clause, it affirms the semantics of the latter clause. The semantics of the latter clause involve anti-recursion from the previous clause. Specific examples are as follows:

（5）尽管（小西瓜）价位比大西瓜高出四五倍，小西瓜非但不压仓，**反而**一举占领了市场绝对份额。

Although the price (of small watermelons) is four or five times higher than that of large watermelons, instead of being ballast, small watermelons have occupied an absolute share of the market in one fell swoop.

（6）然而，时隔 20 年，这一宏大的发展计划不仅没有收到明显的效益，村民们的生活**反而**一年不如一年。

However, after 20 years, this ambitious development plan has not only failed to achieve obvious benefits, but the lives of the villagers have become worse year by year.

（7）보수적 양반가에서 태어났지만 일찍이 남녀평등의 신사고를 받아들여 차별은 커녕 **오히려** 딸을 편애하셨던 친정아버지 덕택으로 성차별이란 말만 들어왔던 나에게 시댁의 모습은 문맹과 야만 그 자체로 느껴졌다.

Although I was born into a conservative aristocratic family, I had only heard of gender discrimination thanks to my father, who accepted the new idea of gender equality early on and instead of discriminating against me, he favored his daughter. To me, the way my in-laws looked like illiteracy and barbarism itself.

（8）또 세계화는 국가들간의 '빈익빈, 부익부'를 조장하며 지구촌을 남북대립과 갈등으로 유도한다. 동시에 국내적으로는 소득불평등이 해소되기보다 **오히려** 심화되는 결과를 낳기도 한다.

In addition, globalization promotes 'the poor get poorer and the rich get richer' between countries and leads the world into North-South confrontation and conflict. At the same time, domestically, income inequality may worsen rather than be resolved.

When "Fǎn'ér" conveys anti-recursion semantics, it not only negates the previous clause or the negation of commonsense expectations, but the latter clause further deepens the negation of the previous clause. In example (5), under normal circumstances, small watermelons are expensive and scarce, making them relatively unaffordable. It is highly probable that consumers will not find them popular and will close their positions. However, the reality is that 'not only will they not be ballast, but they will also very popular'. The clause where "Fǎn'ér" is located negates the expectation of 'being ballast' implied in the previous clause. However, there may also be a situation where 'little watermelon' is neither popular nor left out, but reality exerts minimal influence on this possible situation. There is a magnitude sequence of {unpopular, neither popular nor neglected, popular} between the following sentence containing "Fǎn'ér" and the preceding sentence affected by it. The further the magnitudes, the more they negate the preceding ones. In example (6), under normal circumstances, a grand development plan should obtain obvious benefits, but in reality, it does not. In the clause before and after "Bùjǐnméiyǒu......Fǎn'ér", there are {no obvious benefits, benefits, certain benefits, no benefits but no losses, more losses, one year is worse than one year}, this magnitude exhibits a deviation and contradictory relation with expectations. At the top of the magnitude, 'one year is not as good as one year' is not only contrary to the implicit expectation of 'obtaining obvious benefits', but it is also the strongest expression.

Korean "Ohiryo" can also convey anti-recursion semantics, but its frequency of occurrence is lower than that of Chinese "Fǎn'ér", which expresses anti-recursion semantics, and it is not more prominent than other types among the three main types expressed by "Ohiryo". Here, we first briefly analyze its characteristics when expressing anti-recursion semantics. In example (7), in the case of 'born in a conservative yangban family', common sense might lead to the expectation that 'conservative yangban families have a preference for sons over daughters'. However, because the father from the natal family 'accepted the idea of equality between men and women very early', my father believed in 'equality between men and women'. Yet, reality surpasses this expectation and follows a progressive sequence of magnitudes: {son preference, no difference between men and women, preference for girls}. The further to the right on this scale, the greater the deviation from common sense. In example (8), general common sense would go like this: 'globalization' usually plays a positive role, that is, it may have the effect of 'promoting income equality'. However, objective reality deviates from general social expectations. There is a magnitude sequence of {eliminate income inequality, neither eliminates nor aggravates nor aggravates income inequality, exacerbating income inequality}. The further to the right on the scale, the greater the possibility of deviation from common sense.

Through the analysis of the retrogressive semantics of "Fǎn'ér" and "Ohiryo", it can be found that the anti-recursion semantics are the more distinctive expressions. Both involve clauses where "Fǎn'ér" or "Ohiryo" run contrary to implicit expectations. The semantics of the relevant clauses rank at a high level in the corresponding magnitude, and in many cases, the high magnitudes negate the low magnitudes. From a different point of view, the co-occurrences with the Chinese "Fǎn'ér" typically involve explicit negative expressions like "Fēidànbù", and "Bùjǐnméiyǒu", while the co-occurrences with "Ohiryo" tend to involve implicit negations. In other words, they are expressions with a comparative nature, such as '-neunkonyong(는커녕)', '-giboda(기보다)', etc. The related expressions also serve to negate part of the expression through comparison.

4.3 Opposition(Juxtapostion) Relation

The opposition(juxtaposition) relation is also an important semantic type for "Fǎn'ér" and "Ohiryo". However, the specific distribution is quite different between Chinese and Korean. In the Chinese corpus, "Fǎn'ér" occurs the least frequently and accounts for the smallest proportion among the three semantic types. Conversely, in the Korean corpus, "Ohiryo" appears more frequently among the three semantic types and accounts for a relatively large proportion. This difference in relative proportion indicates an obvious semantic differentiation within the relevant semantic expressions. Specific examples are as follows:

（9）比如伦敦政治经济学院虽然排名靠前、知名度高，但每年学生满意度的排名却不靠前，因为学生几乎很少能见到教授，很多课都由博士生来上。<u>反而</u>一些年轻的大学，教授很注重和学生在一起探讨。

For example, although the London School of Economics and Political Science ranks high and is well-known, it does not rank high in student satisfaction every year because students rarely see professors and many classes are taught by doctoral students. On the contrary, in some young universities, professors attach great importance to discussions with students.

（10）垄断资本集团强迫那些仆从国家，对苏联、中国和各人民民主国家实施禁运和经济封锁，企图来窒杀我们。结果怎样呢？非但"窒杀"不了我们，<u>反而</u>"自杀"了他们。

The monopoly capital groups forced those slave countries to impose embargoes and economic blockades on the Soviet Union, China and various people's democratic countries in an attempt to suffocate us. What was the result? Instead of "suffocating" us, it actually "suicides" them.

（11）서울에서는 전셋값 상승을 주도해오던 강남-서초-송파구보다 **오히려** 성북-노원-종로구 등의 오름세가 더 두드러졌다.

In Seoul, the increase in rent prices was more noticeable in Seongbuk-Nowon-Jongno-gu than in Gangnam-Seocho-Songpa-gu, which had been leading the rise in rental prices.

（12）온 나라 사람들은 모두 미쳐 있었기로 **오히려** 미치지 않은 국왕을 미친 사람으로 여기게 됐다.

Since everyone in the country was crazy, they came to regard the king, who was not crazy, as a crazy person.

In the above sentences, the related examples of the Chinese "Fǎn'ér" and Korean "Ohiryo" mainly express the opposition(juxtaposition) relation, that is, the comparison of the characteristics of similar entities. In example (9), the clauses before and after "Fǎn'ér" indicate that 'London School of Economics and Political Science', as a long-established and highly ranked school, has few opportunities for students to communicate with professors, while students at 'young universities' have more opportunities such interactions. The preceding and following clauses involve a comparison of the teaching conditions of similar entities such as 'universities. This sentence can be analyzed as a three-layer counter-expectation structure: 'prestigious university-many opportunities to communicate with professors (expectation)-not many communication opportunities (reality)', 'young university-few opportunities to communicate with professors (expectation)-many communication opportunities (reality)', 'prestigious university has more opportunities with professors/young university has few opportunities to communicate with professors; the prestigious university has few opportunities to communicate with professors/young university has more opportunities to communicate with professors'. In particular, the sentence containing "Fǎn'ér" emphasizes the comparison with the subject of the previous clause. In example (10), 'choking us' and 'killing them' mainly express an opposition(juxtaposition) relation in addition to counter-expectation semantics. There is also a sequence of magnitudes within the expressions of opposition(juxtaposition) in Chinese "Fǎn'ér", but the comparative relation of relative juxtaposition in the entire expression is more prominent than the internally implied semantics with progressive magnitude. Similarly, in the expression "Ohiryo" in Korean, 'Gangnam-Seocho-Songpa', as a traditional wealthy area, has seen an increase in the price of all-rental housing. Therefore, the increase in non-rich areas may not be as prominent. However, the reality is that the increase in the non-rich areas of 'Seongbuk-Nowon-Jonggno' is more obvious than that in affluent areas. Compared with the implicit counter-expectation semantics, this sentence emphasizes the juxtaposition and contrast between two regions. In example (12), the sentence containing "Ohiryo" contrasts 'crazy citizens' with 'not crazy king'. The juxtaposition nature of the comparison 'covers' the internal implicit reaction to a certain extent. In other words, it is insensitive to the internal implicit magnitude sequence. There are many similarities between the "Fǎn'ér" and "Ohiryo" when expressing opposition(juxtaposition) relation. They mostly compare certain characteristics of similar things. Although they contain counter-expectation semantics, the contrast and juxtaposition characteristics of the entire sentence are more prominent, and the sensitivity to magnitude is weaker than the first two semantic categories. However, there are some differences in the specific expression of these two expressions. The clauses before and after "Fǎn'ér" in Chinese often take the form of antithesis. In addition to the clauses before and after "Ohiryo" in Korean, which also have certain antithesis characteristics, "Ohiryo" is often preceded by '-boda(보다)', '-got anira(것 아니라)', '-neunde(는데)' and other contrastive expressions.

5   The Semantic Similarities and Differences Between the Counter-Expectation Adverbs "Fǎnér" and "Ohiryo" in Chinese and Korean

Above, we conducted a comparative analysis of the three main semantic categories of the Chinese counter-expectation adverb "Fǎn'ér" and the Korean counter-expectation adverb "Ohiryo" based on the measurement criteria of inversion, anti-recursion, opposition(juxtaposition) proposed by Gao [8]. The following characteristics can be obtained (Table 2).

First, regarding reversal semantics, both "Fǎn'ér" and "Ohiryo" exhibit the highest proportion among the three main semantic categories. They represent more typical counter-expectation semantics and are more sensitive to magnitude sequences. However, quantitatively, the Chinese "Fǎn'ér" tends to express reversal semantics than "Ohiryo", suggesting that the former's counter-expectation semantics may be stronger. From the perspective of magnitude sequence, "Fǎn'ér" is relatively more sensitive to magnitude, with a reverse matching relation. The example sentences containing "Ohiryo" are less sensitive to the magnitude relation. There is not necessarily an obvious sequence of magnitudes between objective reality and possible expectations.

Second, when expressing anti-recursion semantics, although it does not dominate the semantic types of "Fǎn'ér" and "Ohiryo", it is highly sensitive to the magnitude and can be considered a very typical one among the three main semantic types. That is to say, the clauses containing "Fǎn'ér" or "Ohiryo" generally contradict implicit expectations. The semantics of the relevant clauses are at a high level in the corresponding magnitude, with high magnitudes often negating the low magnitudes. Quantitatively, although there is no significant difference in the frequency of occurrence between the two in the retrieval corpus, the order they occupy in their respective semantic types is different. The anti-recursion semantics of "Fǎn'ér" occupies the second place among the three types, while "Ohiryo" is far different from the other two types. From the perspective of the magnitude sequence, the co-occurrence expressions differ when expressing anti-recursion semantics. Chinese "Fǎn'ér" often co-occurs with the explicit negative expressions "Fēidànbù", and "Bùjǐnméiyǒu", while Korean "Ohiryo" often co-occurs with the comparative expression '-neun keonyeong(-는 커녕)', '-gibod(-기보다)'with certain implicit negative characteristics.

Third, when expressing opposition(juxtaposition) semantics, both are comparing certain characteristics of similar things. Although the counter-expectation semantics are implicitly embedded, the opposition and juxtaposition characteristics of the entire sentence are more prominent, or the sensitivity to magnitude sequence is weaker than the first two types. Quantitatively, there is a significant gap between the two. The typicality of the Korean "Ohiryo" in expressing the opposition(juxtaposition) semantics is obviously higher than that of Chinese "Fǎn'ér". From the perspective of magnitude sequence, the two expressions are less sensitive to magnitude than the first two types, but they exhibit certain characteristics in the co-occurrence expression of specific sentences. The clause before and after "Fǎn'ér" mostly takes the form of antithesis. In addition to the antithesis characteristics, the clauses before and after 'ohiryo' often co-occur with the contrasting expressions '-boda(보다)', '-got anira(것 아니라)', '-neunde(는데)'.

Table 2. The semantic similarities and differences between the Chinese and Korean words "Fǎn'ér" and "Ohiryo"

Semantic Type	Similarities and Differences		Chinese "Fǎnér"	Korean "Ohiryo"
Type 1	Similarities		It accounts for the highest propotion amony the three main semantic types. They all represent typical coutner-expectation semantics and are sensitive to magnitude sequences	
	Differences	Quantity	More, relatively strong typicality	Less, relatively weak typicality
		Magnitude	More sensitive to magnitude, there is a reverse matching relation	Not very senstive to magnitude and may noot necessarily present an explicit magnitude sequence
Type 2	Similarities		It is the more distinctive type among the three semantic types	
	Differences	Quantity	It occupies the second place among the three semantic types	It occupies the third place among the three semantic types
		Magnitude	It often co-occurs with "Fēidànbù" and "Bùjǐnméiyǒu" with explicit negative expressions	It often co-occurs with the comparative expressions '-neunkeonyeong(-는커녕)"-giboda(-기)보다)"(with invisible negative characteristics)
Type 3	Similarities		When comparing certain characteristics of similar things, the contrasting and juxtaposing characteristics of the entire sentence are more prominent, 'covering' the implicit counter-expectation semantics to a certain extent, and the sensitivity to magnitude is less than the first two types; there are many parallels in the preceding and following clauses	
	Differences	Quantity	More	Less
		Magnitude	Insensitive to magnitude, the preceding and following clauses are repeated but there is no special marking form	Insensitive to magnitude, the preceding and following clauses are contrasting but have a special marking form (contrastive nature)

6 The Motivation Behind the Similarities and Differences Between the Chinese and Korean Counter-Expectation Adverbs "Fănér" and "Ohiryo"

In the preceding section, we conducted a comparative analysis of the semantic characteristics of the Chinese counter-expectation adverb "Făn'ér" and the Korean counter-expectation adverb "Ohiryo" based on the relatively objective classifications of predecessors. Additionally, we performed a preliminary analysis of the characteristics of the two expressions in different semantic types. It can be found that, overall, the boundaries among the three main semantics of 'faner' are relatively clear, with its reversal semantics and anti-recursion semantics particularly typical. However, the semantic boundaries among "Ohiryo" appear less clear, with its reversal semantics being quite distinctive. Why do these two expressions show such typical differences? We will now embark on a preliminary analysis of the reasons for the differences from a diachronic perspective.

Chinese "Făn'ér" emerged during the Warring States Period and the Western Han Dynasty. At that time, "Făn'ér" existed as a cross-structured phrase of "Făn" and "ér" with relatively concrete meanings. "Făn" itself means 'betrayal', 'opposition' and 'turn around' in ancient Chinese, often co-occurring "ér". Afterwards, during the transitional period of the Eastern Han Dynasty, it gradually transitioned from a phrase with some substantial meaning to an independent adverb, acquiring a semantic meaning indicating transition. Over time, with the frequent use of "Făn'ér", its status as an independent word gradually solidified. Meanwhile, conjunctions appeared, and when "Făn'ér", which denotes reversal, was combined with words such as "Búdàn", "Bùwéi", which means progression, "Făn'ér" truly underwent the virtual transformation from adverb into conjunction. It can be seen that the diachronic development of "Făn'ér" represents a continuum from real to virtual, from separation to solidification. Throughout this process, the semantic meaning of "Făn'ér" initially means 'opposite' as an important semantic throughout its grammaticalization. Relatively speaking, "Făn'ér" diachronically maintained a more typical reversion semantics. On the contrary, the diachronic development process of Korean "Ohiryo" is quite different from that of "Făn'ér". During the development process of "Ohiryo", there have been heteromorphic forms such as "Wehiryo" and "Ohilryo", but on the whole, its morphological changes were relatively modest. Instead, its changes were mainly presented in the alternation and transition of internal semantics. According to the research by Kim [11], "Ohilryo" in the 15th century and "Ohilryo" in modern Korean "Ohiryo" have undergone internal semantic alternation and migration. For instance, in the 15th century, "Ohiryo" bore semantic connotations such as 'even', 'still', and 'opposition', while "Ohiryo" in modern Korean carries meanings such as 'opposition' and 'simply' among other semantics (Fig. 1).

In other words, although "Ohiryo" in modern Korean mainly expresses counter-expectation semantics in contradiction to expectation, in specific contexts, "Ohiryo" still retains remnants of the semantics of 'even' and 'still', illustrating a phenomenon of semantic retention. This can also explain that the reversion semantics of "Ohiryo" may not be as prototypical, and its internal semantic differentiation may not be as clearly defined, with certain semantics internally displaying a continuum of transitions.

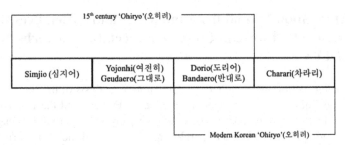

Fig. 1. The semantic migration between "Ohiryo" and modern Korean "Ohiryo" before the 15th century (Kim 2022:259)

7 Conclusion

This paper conducts a preliminary analysis of the internal semantics of the Chinese and Korean counter-expectation adverbs, "Fǎn'ér" and "Ohiryo", based on a certain magnitude model theory. The following preliminary summary can be obtained:

First, the three main semantic types of "Fǎn'ér" and "Ohiryo" exhibit different hierarchical sequences. Chinese "Fǎn'ér" follows a hierarchical sequence of 'inversion relation > anti-recursion relation > opposition(juxtaposition) relation', whereas Korean "Ohiryo" adheres to a hierarchical sequence of 'inversion relation > opposition(juxtaposition) relation > anti-recursion relation'.

Second, "Fǎn'ér" and "Ohiryo" are different in their sensitivity to magnitude. On the whole, "Fǎn'ér" displays greater sensitivity to magnitude, often showing a relatively dominant reverse matching relation. In contrast, "Ohiryo" is relatively less sensitive to magnitude. In addition, in terms of co-occurrence expressions of magnitude, especially in the anti-recursion relation, "Fǎn'ér" is mainly used with explicit negative expressions, while "Ohiryo" is mainly associated with comparative expressions.

Third, we analyzed the reasons for the differences between "Fǎn'ér" and "Ohiryo" from the diachronic perspective. At the diachronic level, although Chinese "Fǎn'ér" gradually solidified and developed through re-analysis of its cross-layer structure, the semantic meaning of "Fǎn", indicating opposite and turning, remained consistent. Conversely, Korean "Ohiryo" underwent internal semantic migration such as 'even', 'still', and 'opposition' during the development of Medieval Korean. During the development process, it may be affected by factors like semantic retention, showing transitional continuum characteristics.

Through comparative analysis, we seek to gain a preliminary understanding of the cognitive characteristics of Korean and Chinese speakers in counter-expectation expressions based on understanding the similarities and differences between these two expressions and provide some reference of language ontology for foreign language learners.

References

1. Ma, Z.: About the grammatical meaning of "Fǎn'ér." Chin. Teach. World **24**(1), 25 (1994). (in Chinese)
2. Ma, Z.: The adverbs "Bìng" and 'Yòu' that strengthen the negative tone-also analysing the semantic background of the use of words. Chin. Teach. World **61**(3), 12–18 (2001). (in Chinese)
3. Wang, H.: Teaching Chinese as a foreign language: a touchstone of the internal laws of Chinese—taking "Fǎn'ér" as an example. Chin. Teach. World **24**(1), (1994). (in Chinese)
4. Xing, F.Y.: A Comprehensive Study of Chinese Complex Sentences. The Commercial Press, Beijing (2001). (in Chinese)
5. Wu, C.X.: An analysis of the semantic logic relation of "Fǎn'ér" sentence. Lang. Teach. Linguist. Stud. **92**(4), 69–74 (2001). (in Chinese)
6. Yuan, Y.L.: Counter expectation, additive relation and the types of pragmatics scale: the comparative analyses of the semantic function of "Shènzhì"and "Fǎn'ér". Contemp. Linguist. **142**(2), 109–121+189 (2008). (in Chinese)
7. Lv, H.Y.: A supplement explanation of "Fǎn'ér." J. Leshan Norm. Univ. **32**(11), 52–56 (2017). (in Chinese)
8. Gao, Z.X.: Analyses of the semantic and syntactic functions of "Fǎn'ér." J. Taishan Univ. **41**(5), 131–138 (2019). (in Chinese)
9. Cho, A.S.: A study on the meaning and usage of the Korean-Japanese adverbs "mushiro" and "ohiryo." J. Jpn. Stud. **48**(2), 263–281 (2011). (in Korean)
10. Ma, Y.J.: About the explanation of the adverb ' 猶-focused on the homogeneity of 'ohiryo.' Kugyol Stud. **44**(1), 213–257 (2020). (in Korean)
11. Kim, J.O.: The meaning and morphological analysis of 'Ohiryŏ(Rather)' in the 15th century. J. Korean Historic. Linguist. **34**(1), 243–273 (2022). (in Korean)
12. Shan, Q.: A grammatical study of chinese counter-expectation marker "Jìngrán" -in comparison with Korean counter-expectation marker "-tani." In: Qi, S., Ge, X., Yang, X. (eds.) Chinese Lexical Semantics: 23rd Workshop, CLSW 2022, Virtual Event, May 14–15, 2022, Revised Selected Papers, Part I, pp. 295–311. Springer, Cham (2023). https://doi.org/10.1007/978-3-031-28953-8_23

A Cognitive Approach to the Semantic Change of the Polysemy *gàng* 'Wooden Bar'

Hongzhu Wang[1(✉)] and Yin Zhong[2]

[1] School of Humanities and Social Science, The Hong Kong University of Science and Technology, Clear Water Bay, Kowloon, Hong Kong SAR
hwangfi@connect.ust.hk
[2] Center for Language Education, The Hong Kong University of Science and Technology, Clear Water Bay, Kowloon, Hong Kong SAR
lcyinzhong@ust.hk

Abstract. The semantic meaning of the Chinese word 杠 *gàng* 'wooden bar at the front of bed,' has experienced a long derivational process driven by cognitive mechanisms such as metaphor and metonymy. In this study, we elaborated on the extended meanings of 杠 *gàng* based on the dictionaries and the corpus data. We have found a tendency of grammaticalization, denominalization, and deterioration of affective connotations for 杠 *gàng*. Further, we summarized five representative meanings of 杠 *gàng* and created image schemas respectively to discuss how the new meanings are generated and associated through the cognitive mechanism. With a radial framework of the semantic change of 杠 *gàng* presented in the end, we reiterate a continuum of metaphor and metonymy through realizations of image schemas and further highlight the interrelations between the cognitive mechanisms.

Keywords: Semantic Change · Metaphor · Metonymy · Image Schema · Cognitive Linguistics

1 Introduction

杠精 *gàngjīng* 'the person who loves to dispute with others' is rated as one of the buzzwords in 2018 in a Chinese magazine 咬文嚼字 *Yǎowén Jiáozì* that releases the most popular new (Internet) words every year [1]. This word is considered an Internet meme, sharing a similar meaning with the English word "troller," which labels people who pretend to be involved in the online discussion but whose real intentions are to cause disruption and/or to trigger or exacerbate conflict for their amusement [2, 3]. Although 杠精 *gàngjīng* is a newly coined word in the Internet age, it makes use of the original meanings and cultural connotations of 杠 *gàng* 'to get into a dispute with' and 精 *jīng* 'demon' in Chinese, and further gives rise to this neologism which is widely used in online interactions and is carried with multiple communicative functions in online communication [1].

The word 杠 *gàng* is a polysemy (i.e., using one word form to represent multiple related senses [4]). 杠 *gàng* in 说文解字 *Shuōwén Jiězì* is interpreted as "杠, 床前横

© The Author(s), under exclusive license to Springer Nature Singapore Pte Ltd. 2024
M. Dong et al. (Eds.): CLSW 2023, LNAI 14514, pp. 358–369, 2024.
https://doi.org/10.1007/978-981-97-0583-2_28

木也。从木, 工声" [5].[1] It indicates that the original meaning of 杠 *gàng* is "wooden bar at the front of bed" with a first tone and functions as a noun. However, diverse contextual and communicative purposes have complicated both the conceptual meanings and grammatical functions of 杠 *gàng* throughout history. In contemporary Chinese, this word has developed other meanings, including 旗杆 'flagpole' [N], 抬重物的粗棍 'stout poles used to carry heavy objects' [N], 体操器械 '(sports) bar' [N], 机床上的棍状零件 'rod-like spare part used for machine tools' [N], 粗的直线 'thick line (in a text)' [N], 用直线划去或标出 'to cross out' [V], 专横自是, 好与人争 'to get into a dispute with' [V], among others.

In this paper, we would like to dive into the word 杠 *gàng* 'wooden bar.' We aim to present a comprehensive list of semantic meanings for this word using the dictionaries and corpus data, to discuss its meaning changes through the lens of cognitive mechanisms (i.e., metaphors and metonymies), and to develop a semantic network illustrating how the original meaning and extended meanings are interrelated with each other.

2 Past Studies on Semantic Change and Polysemy

Semantic change is not simply a common language phenomenon but reflects a way of thinking that may be shared by different language communities. Metaphor and metonymy are the two widely recognized cognitive mechanisms that motivate the evolution of lexical meanings [e.g., 6, 7]. From the cognitive perspective, metaphor is not only a rhetoric device but is the "transfer" or the "mapping" of knowledge from one concept (the source domain) to another (the target domain) [8, 9]. That is, a metaphorical sense of a word may be derived from its literal sense via a "mapping" between the two domains based on their structural similarities, and usually, the source concepts are more embodied and concrete while the target concepts are more abstract and conceptual [8, 9]. Under this view, the extended senses derived from the basic meanings of polysemous words can be explained by conceptual metaphors, especially the transformations of image schemas [10–12]. Generally, an image schema is "a condensed redescription of perceptual experience for the purpose of mapping spatial structure onto conceptual structure" [13], which systematically structures our mental representations abstracted from our sensorimotor experiences via recurring and dynamic "schemas" [for a review of the image schema theory, see, e.g., 13, 14]. For instance, in the sentence "he has *gone through* a lot in life," a person (e.g., he) is depicted as a "traveler," and all this person has experienced in LIFE[2] (the target domain) can be understood as if this person is traveling on a JOURNEY (the source domain). In addition, the preposition *through* in the above sentence reflects the PATH schema, which highlights the recurrent behavior of physical travel in the conceptual metaphor of life is a journey. This explanation indicates the significance of image schema for excavating the associations between the original meaning and extended meanings

---

[1] The translation of this sentence is: the word 杠 *gàng* refers to the wooden bar at the front of bed. The left part of the character indicates that its property is wood, and the right part represents its pronunciation, which reads 工 *gōng*.

[2] We follow the convention in the cognitive linguistics literature to present conceptual metaphorical domains as well as image schemas in small capitals.

of a word, especially for the words that can be mentally visualized, such as 杠 *gàng* 'wooden bar.'

Another important device that drives semantic change is metonymy. Jakobson [15] differentiated metonymy from metaphor and stated that metonymy is based on contiguity. Lakoff and Turner [16] also emphasized that metonymy happens in one frame, claiming that metonymy is the mapping between two concepts that are in the same domain and conceptual structure. Aligning with these works, Shen [17] believed that being in the same cognitive frame is one of the prerequisites to activate metonymy, and the salience of a new concept is another. Further, Shen [17] argued that the cognitive frame is the mental gestalt, which is easier to recognize, store and retrieve than its components. This idea presents some similarities with the theory of topological mapping [18]. That is, they all indicate that people comprehend an extended concept within a complete frame that they imagine. The concept is static, while the process of cognition is dynamic. However, such a similarity seems to blur the boundary between metaphor and metonymy. In other words, from the perspective of metonymy, "journey", which represents life, can be the whole frame, and "a traveler" representing "a person" can be its part (or component). Consequently, to analyze the mechanism that results in the semantic change of 杠 *gàng* 'wooden bar,' the binary distinction of metaphor and metonymy seems to neglect the interaction between these two.

In fact, the intertwined relationship between metaphor and metonymy is still debated within the cognitive linguistics framework [e.g., 19, 20]. Early scholars tend to believe they are separate and independent cognitive phenomena [15, 21]. However, some semantic changes cannot be explained explicitly through only one of these mechanisms. Radden [22, 23] proposed that there is a continuum between the notions of metaphor and metonymy, and the interaction happens in the middle of this continuum. However, it assumes that all the derivations of semantic meanings are in one direction and measures how far they go from the original concept, omitting the differences between the domains. In contrast, Lu [24] claimed that the realization of metaphor and metonymy is based on "activation" instead of "mapping." The activation can be a chain reaction with both metaphor and metonymy playing a role successively. This view enables us to create a radial structure of the semantic change of 杠 *gàng* 'wooden bar' and avoid the ambiguities of the two mechanisms.

There are some studies investigating polysemous words in Chinese from a cognitive approach. Zhu [25] summarized a polysemous network of the spatial motion verb "穿 *chuān*" based on image schemas and discussed the ways (i.e., metonymy and specification) that the distinct senses are associated. Using an image-schema-based approach, Yin [26] illustrated the sense branches of the verb "推 *tuī*" and analyzed the linking mechanisms among them, that is, co-hyponymy analog, specification, and metonymy. By constructing the image schema of 杠 *gàng* 'wooden bar,' Ma and Xia [27] discovered the implicit control and balance of forces from its structure, explaining the emergence of the extended meaning 'to dispute.' The image schemas are embodied interactions with dynamic, structural, and qualitative features instead of skeletons that are simply abstracted from the images [28]. However, one of the limitations in the study of Ma and Xia [27] is that they treated metaphor and metonymy as two independent mechanisms, overlooking the joint role they play in the chain-like derivational process. Previous theories on cognitive semantics have built a bridge among image schemas, metaphors, and metonymy. For example, Lakoff and Johnson [9] and Lakoff [11] suggested that image schemas can transfer from the physical domain to a more abstract conceptual domain and extend concepts through metaphor and metonymy. Via metaphor, some high-level image schemas (e.g., MORE, QUANTITY) that are not directly perceptual in reality are derived preliminarily from the basic schemas based on sensory experience [28].

Taken together, in this paper, we will note the interrelation between metaphor and metonymy and visualize the structures of each conceptual meaning of 杠 *gàng* 'wooden bar' via image schemas to explore the underlying mechanisms of its semantic changes.

3 Method

We attempt to collect the conceptual meanings of 杠 *gàng* 'wooden bar' from dictionaries, including 说文解字 *Shuōwén Jiězì* 'Analytical Dictionary of Chinese Characters', 古汉语常用字字典 *Gǔhànyǔ Chángyòngzì Zìdiǎn* 'Common Use Character Dictionary of Ancient Chinese,' and 现代汉语词典 *Xiàndài Hànyǔ Cídiǎn* 'The Contemporary Chinese Dictionary.' The example sentences from the BLCU Chinese Corpus (BCC Corpus; http://bcc.blcu.edu.cn/) [29][3] will be provided to illustrate the contexts to which each meaning applies. By analyzing the semantic features and creating image schemas of the derived meanings of 杠 'wooden bar,' we will present the distinctions and associations among these meanings and demonstrate the process of semantic change in the end.

4 Findings

4.1 Semantic Analysis of 杠 *gàng* 'Wooden bar'

Based on dictionaries and the BCC corpus, we collected and classified the word senses of 杠 *gàng* 'wooden bar' and analyzed its grammatical functions as well as the affective connotations.

The senses in the dictionaries are shown in the table below (Table 1).

It can be noticed that the extensions of meaning accompany the changes in tone and parts-of-speech. The noun 杠 *gàng* 'wooden bar' has shifted to a verb, with the fourth tone consolidating the denominalization in its grammatical functions. Comparing the example sentences in the BCC corpus, it is found that the original meaning of 杠*gàng* 'wooden bar' is almost extinct in modern contexts, while the meanings with the fourth tone are still active in use. Besides, the extension of meanings makes 杠 *gàng* 'wooden bar' more productive when combined with other morphemes. For example:

(1) 大家用手摇车, 摇一阵子, 就得趴在保险杠上喘一阵粗气。(《人民日报》)

'Everyone cranked the car by hand, and after shaking it for a while, they have to lie on the **bumper** and pant for a while.' (The People's Daily)

---

[3] Beijing Language and Culture University Corpus Center (BLCU Corpus Center, BCC) is an online corpus with a size of around ten billion words including Chinese and other languages.

Table 1. Word senses of 杠 *gàng* in dictionaries.

Dictionaries	Tone	Word Senses
《说文解字》 Analytical Dictionary of Chinese Characters	First Tone	床前横木 'wooden bar'
《古汉语常用字字典》 Common Use Character Dictionary of Ancient Chinese	First Tone	①床前横木 'wooden bar' ②竹木杆子 'bamboo pole' ③独木桥, 小桥 'small bridge' ④通"扛", 抬 'to carry'
《现代汉语词典》 The Contemporary Chinese Dictionary	First Tone	①小桥 'small bridge' ②旗杆 'flagpole'
	Fourth Tone	①抬重物的粗棍 'stout poles used to carry heavy objects' ②体操器械, 单双杠、高低杠 等'(sports) bar' ③机床上的棍状零件 'rod-like spare part used for machine tools' ④出殡时抬送灵柩的工具 'tool for carrying a coffin during a funeral' ⑤粗的直线 'thick line (in a text)' ⑥一定的标准 'certain criteria' ⑦把不通的文字或错字用直线划去或标出 'to cross out or mark out words or typos with a straight line' ⑧在布或石头上摩擦使锋利些 'rub against a cloth or stone to sharpen something' ⑨专横自是, 好与人争 'to get into a dispute with'

(2) 作为一个'斜杠青年', 每一个'斜杠', 都是通过自身努力突破行业界限的勋章。(《人民日报》)

(3) 'As a **slash** youth, every **slash** is a medal for breaking through the boundaries of the industry through one's own efforts.' (The People's Daily)

(4) 青年一代似乎在关涉两岸经济的所有议题上跟当局杠上了。(《人民日报》)
'The younger generation seems **to be at odds** with the authorities on all issues related to the cross-strait economy.' (The People's Daily).

It is noted that 杠 *gàng* 'wooden bar' is frequently used in the context of the game of Mahjong to describe a situation where a player has the 'upper hand' and can deploy a strategic maneuver.[4] This term, originally, refers to a traditional activity of trapping

---

[4] We thank an anonymous reviewer for mentioning this point.

bird in ancient China that utilized a wooden stick as the main component of the bird-catching apparatus (cage). Apart from the verb usage of 杠 *gàng* in the Mahjong game, 杠 *gàng* is also lexicalized in an idiom 杠上开花 *gàngshàngkāihuā* 'hand completion with supplemental tile when melding a quad'. Despite its high frequency shown in the BCC corpus, this idiom has limited collocational and contextual diversity compared to other prevalent senses of 杠 *gàng* 'wooden bar,' thus suggesting a decline in its productivity.

When distinguishing between polysemy and homonymy, another noticeable fact is that, the verbal meaning of 杠 *gàng* 'to carry' is a loan concept with the action deriving from the prototype 扛 *gāng* 'to carry by hands'.[5] In other words, the verbal 杠 *gàng* 'to carry' is a Tongjia word exhibiting homonymy than polysemy, and should therefore be excluded from the present study. The absence of this specific sense in *The Contemporary Chinese Dictionary*, along with its limited representations in the BCC corpus, further substantiates its rare occurrence and diminished significance in terms of usage. As such, the following analysis of 杠 *gàng* in this study focuses on its more prevalent and presentative meanings.

Integrating the findings from the dictionaries and the BCC corpus, we summarized five representative meanings of 杠 *gàng* that are derived from its original meaning (see Table 2).

Table 2. The representative meanings of 杠 *gàng*.

Representative Meanings	Senses
①表横木状事物 [N] 'bar-shaped objects'	桥 'bridge,' 体操器械 'gymnastic equipment'
②表棍状事物 [N] 'stick-shaped objects'	竹木杆子 'bamboo pole,' 旗杆 'flagpole,' 粗棍 'thick pole,' 棍状零件 'rod-like spare part,' 抬灵柩的工具 'tool for carrying a coffin,' Mahjong term
③表横线 [N] 'lines'	粗的直线 'thick line,' 一定的标准 'certain criteria'
④表线性动势 [V] 'to move linearly'	用直线划去或标出 'to cross out or mark out,' 摩擦使锋利 'to sharpen'
⑤表冲突争辩 [V] 'to dispute'	好与人争 'to dispute'

The change in the parts-of-speech of 杠 *gàng* 'wooden bar' implies the development of grammatical functions. In addition, the extended concepts accelerate the grammaticalization of both the nominal and verbal meanings of 杠 *gàng* 'wooden bar' [30].

When 杠 *gàng* refers to ①表横木状事物 'bar-shaped objects,' ②表棍状事物 'stick-shaped objects,' and ③表横线 'lines,' it is used as a noun or in a nominal phrase. For instance:

---

[5] This point is suggested by an anonymous reviewer.

(5) 是什么样的工具、<u>杠杆</u>、机器、工人，建成了这么一座壮丽恢宏的建筑? (《蒙田随笔》)
'What kind of tools, **levers**, machines, and workers built such a magnificent building?' (Montaigne's Essay)

(6) 聪明才智是拨动社会的<u>杠杆</u>。(《幻灭》)
'Intelligence is the **lever that moves society**.' (Disillusionment).

(7) 帮助别人是好事，但应该是无偿的，不应该敲别人的<u>竹杠</u>。(《圣地》)
'Helping others is good, but it should be free of charge and should not be **ripped off**.' (Holy Land)

(8) 公益岗位工资水平的标准，也有<u>硬杠杠</u>——必须高于当地最低工资。(《人民日报》)
'The standard salary level for public welfare jobs also has **fixed criteria**—it must be higher than the local minimum wage.' (The People's Daily)

It is worth noting that the words 杠杆 *gànggǎn* 'lever' in sentences (4) and (5) have different referents. The former refers to a concrete and substantial instrument, while the latter is abstract and intangible, representing something that regulates and balances the force or matter. Similarly, the 杠 *gàng* 'bar' in the sentence (6) is not physically perceptible, and the compound word 竹杠 *zhúgàng* 'bamboo bar' refers to 'money' in this case. It is also quite common to compare 杠 *gàng* 'lines' to fundamental and unbreakable criteria (e.g., in the sentence 7). The nominal morpheme 杠 *gàng* in these sentences is grammaticalized.

When it refers to ④表线性动势 'to move linearly,' or ⑤表冲突争辩 'to dispute,' it functions as a verb or in a verbal phrase. For example:

(9) 他把已经写完的一页誊清，然后又一行行地<u>杠掉</u>。(《如果在冬夜，一个旅人》)
'He transcribed the page he had already written, and then **crossed it out** line by line.' (If on A Winter Night, A Traveler)

(10) 若是明早起来胭脂发现水盆不在原地，她可能又要跟他<u>杠上</u>了。(《绿痕》)
'If Yanzhi wakes up tomorrow morning and finds that the water basin is not in place, she may have to **fight with** him again.' (Green Mark)

What should be noticed is that the 杠 *gàng* 'to dispute' in the sentence (9) is not an actual action compared with that in the sentence (8). It contains the implicit meaning of conflict and debate, which indicates that grammaticalization also happens in the verbal meanings of 杠 *gàng*. Besides, compared with the nominal 杠 *gàng* 'bars/lines,' the verbal 杠 *gàng* 'to dispute/to cross out' are more likely to be solely used as words instead of morphemes. For example, resultative complements (e.g., 上*shàng* 'up' and 掉*diào* 'drop') can be attached to these verbs, grammatically representing the "start" or "end" of the actions.

With respect to the change of affective connotations, 杠 *gàng* gradually bears derogatory affection. Especially on the internet, the word 杠 *gàng* 'to dispute' appears with a high frequency to describe that someone stirs up trouble unreasonably (e.g., sentence 10). Consequently, 杠 *gàng* nowadays normally conveys negative sentiment.

(11) 我有好多好多缺点，比如懒惰，情绪化，缺乏耐心，爱<u>抬杠</u>。(微博)
'I have many shortcomings, such as lazy, emotional, impatient, and love to **argue**.' (WeiBo)

4.2 Metaphor and Metonymy in the Semantic Change of 杠 *gàng* 'Wooden Bar'

Metaphor and metonymy are two main ways to generate new meanings for polysemies. Based on these two ways, we can track the process of the semantic change of 杠 *gàng* 'wooden bar.' The original meaning of 杠 *gàng* 'wooden bar at the front of bed,' or the prototype of 杠 *gàng*, is marked as [+木 'wooden'][+长 'long'][+横着 'horizontal'][+床前 'at the font of bed']. The image schema is shown in Fig. 1.

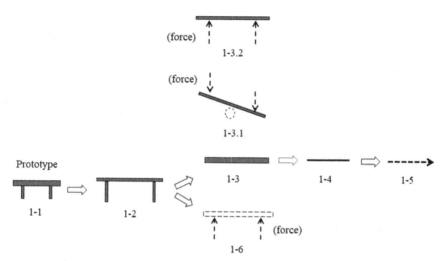

Fig. 1. The image schemas of each representative meaning and the derivational process of 杠 *gàng*.

The meaning of 杠①表横木状事物 'bar-shaped objects' is metaphorically derived from the original meaning. For instance, we can define the semantic features of 桥 *qiáo* 'bridge' (one of the sub-meanings of 杠①) as: [+木 'wooden'][+长 'long'][+横着 'horizontal'][−床前 'at the front of bed']. After comparing the image schema (see Fig. 1-2), it can be noticed that the shape and structure of 桥*qiáo* 'bridge' is quite similar to the prototype (Fig. 1-1). Besides, the earliest bridges in ancient China are made of wood or bamboo, which indicates that the property of the original meaning is preserved after derivation (only the domain has been transferred from furniture to architecture). As for another sub-meaning 体操器械 'gymnastic equipment' (e.g., parallel bars), the semantic feature is [−木 'wooden'][+长 'long'][+横着 'horizontal'][−床前 'at the front of bed']. The constraints on the property and location of the original meaning have been weakened, while the frame of the image, which is characterized as 'horizontal bar,' has been retained.

The meaning of 杠②表棍状事物 'stick-shaped objects' is a metonymy from 杠①. Generally, within the same cognitive domain, the whole is more prominent than the part [17]. Consequently, the complete structure commonly refers to its components. For instance, the thick sticks and some machine tools like screws contain the semantic feature of [±木 'wooden'][+长 'long'][±横着 'horizontal'][−床前 'at the front of bed']. With the visualized image in Fig. 1-3, only the top part of the prototype of 杠 *gàng*, which is also the most functional component, is retained, while the bottom, which supports the structure, is omitted. What should be noted is that although the entity of 杠② is physically not complete, the forces that support the remaining part still exist so as to create a mental gestalt of 杠 *gàng*. Specifically, when using the lever, there are separate forces that exert on the two sides of the tool to attain an equilibrium state (see Fig. 1-3.1). In this case, the substantial and abstract components jointly construct a structure that resembles the prototype of 杠 *gàng* 'wooden bar.' Additionally, the carrying tool is kept stable with (two) people supporting its two sides by their shoulders, during which the actual referent of 杠 *gàng* 'stick-shaped object' and the two people thus create a gestalt (see Fig. 1-3.2). Therefore, it can be inferred that the derived meanings of 杠 *gàng* inherit not only the property, shape, or structure of the prototype, but also the interaction forces that function in balancing.

The meaning of 杠③表横线 'lines' is derived metaphorically from the meaning of 杠②表棍状事物 'stick-shaped objects.' The similarity between the thick stick and thick line can be found by comparing the image schemas (see Fig. 1-4), while there are some significant differences in semantic features. 'Lines' are characterized by [−长 'long'][+ 平面 'plane'], which implies that the original tridimensional object changes to be a two-dimensional hallmark. Through verbal inflection, the new meaning of 杠④表线性动势 'to move linearly' is generated based on the nominal meaning of 'lines.' Simulating the motion of 杠④, we can find that this abstract concept hides a mental image similar to the 'lines' (see Fig. 1-5). In fact, the metaphorical verbs generally can activate the original image (nominal meaning), and the derivational process (N → V) reflects the loss of referential function in the source domain and the gain of descriptive function in the target domain [31]. In other words, when people draw a line or sharpen tools, they will track the motion mentally and recognize the image. Therefore, specific and transparent concepts (images) will be adopted to describe and refer to the action per se.

Based on 杠①, the meaning of 杠⑤表冲突争辩 'to dispute' is a metaphor (see Fig. 1-6), with the main concept visualized as the forces controlling and balancing the target to make it stable. More specifically, 杠⑤ focuses on the position of the forces. It is highlighted that the two supporting points are contrary and relative, and the forces are from two camps which potentially brew the discrepancy and paradox. However, the conflicts have been transferred from the physical domain to the domain of emotions. Moreover, balancing the strength is not a result but a dynamic and continuous state in this case, since the imbalance between the two forces activates the conflict endlessly.

5   Discussion and Conclusion

After summarizing and analyzing all the representative meanings of 杠 *gàng* 'wooden bar,' we can come up with a radial framework of the semantic change of 杠 *gàng* 'wooden bar' from the perspective of metaphor and metonymy (see Fig. 2).

Figure 2 demonstrates a chain-like developing process. The metaphorical derivation depends on the similarity between the neighboring concepts, and metonymy works in the frames of PART- WHOLE. The further the new meanings disperse from the original concept, the more abstract and distinct they are. Moreover, the extension of the meanings shows certain tendencies. In terms of the images, it seems that the top part of the prototype of 杠 *gàng* 'wooden bar' is the focus with more new concepts derived from it. Yet,

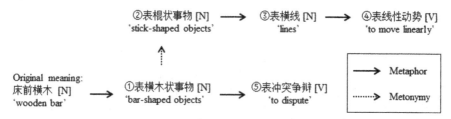

Fig. 2. The process of semantic change of 杠 *gàng* 'wooden bar' through metaphor and metonymy.

this prominent sub-structure becomes vague and insubstantial with the development of denominalization. As for the grammatical functions, denominalization and grammaticalization are the two significant tendencies. The expansion of the parts-of-speech equips 杠 *gàng* 'wooden bar' with more diverse collocations, and the abstract concepts break the restriction on image-likeness. Besides, new meanings enable 杠 *gàng* 'wooden bar' to be more productive as a content morpheme in the word-formation process, which further accelerates the semantic change. With respect to affective connotations, the implicit balance between the forces in the original meaning is highlighted and derives to be mutually exclusive, leading to deterioration.

Although we elaborated on the changing mechanisms explicitly in this study, there are still some debatable findings that should be noted. The first concern is the ambiguous judgment between metaphor and metonymy. We define the extension from 'lines' to 'to cross out' as a metaphor. However, some researchers argue that it is a metonymical process within the cognitive frame of ECM (EVENT = Action + Being) [32], and therefore, 杠 'lines' (Being) is the tool referring to the whole event 'to cross out' [27]. Another concern is the order of these two mechanisms. It is reasonable that 杠②表棍 状事物 'stick-shaped objects' is derived straightly from the prototype instead of the metaphorical meaning of 杠①, since metonymy is generally the basis of metaphor [22, 23]. However, we still believe that starting from the metaphor is more convincing in explaining the transfer between domains. Moreover, there exists a debate regarding the order of changes among derived meanings sharing the same developmental trajectory. For example, the prototype or 杠① is considered the starting point for the metaphorical process of 杠⑤表示冲突争辩 'to dispute.' Considering the conceptual distance between these domains, this study posits that 杠① is a more plausible starting point, as it has already transcended the constraints on location and property inherent in the prototype. This progression allows for a more flexible and abstract understanding of 杠⑤, thereby facilitating its metaphorical extension towards the concept of dispute or conflict.

"Survival of the fittest" is a common pattern for a semantic change. The use of 杠⑤表冲突争辩 'to dispute' is dominant nowadays due to the ever-expanding social network. It seems that the words in the language and emotion domains are more active for the needs of communication. Despite the deterioration of affective connotation, this new meaning reactivates the word 杠 *gàng* 'wooden bar' and generates new language forms and functions, thus contributing to communicating efficiency.

References

1. Xia, J., Wang, P.: Am I trolling?: A CA-informed approach to Gangjing in a Chinese online forum. Discourse Context Media **47**, 100609 (2022)
2. Hardaker, C.: Trolling in asynchronous computer-mediated communication: from user discussions to academic definitions. J. Politeness Res. Lang. Behav. Cult. **6**, 215–242 (2010)
3. Jenks, C.J.: Talking trolls into existence: on the floor management of trolling in online forums. J. Pragmat. **143**, 54–64 (2019)
4. Zipf, G.K.: The meaning-frequency relationship of words. J. Gen. Psychol. **33**, 251–256 (1945)
5. Xu, S.: Shuowenjiezi [Explaining Graphs and Analyzing Characters]. Zhonghua Book Company, Beijing (1963)
6. Lopukhina, A., Laurinavichyute, A., Lopukhin, K., Dragoy, O.: The mental representation of polysemy across word classes. Front. Psychol. **9**, 192 (2018)
7. Xu, Y., Malt, B.C., Srinivasan, M.: Evolution of word meanings through metaphorical mapping: systematicity over the past millennium. Cogn. Psychol. **96**, 41–53 (2017)
8. Lakoff, G., Johnson, M.: Philosophy in the Flesh: The Embodied Mind and Its Challenge to Western Thought. Basic Books, New York (1999)
9. Lakoff, G., Johnson, M.: Metaphors We Live by. University of Chicago Press, Chicago (1980)
10. Johnson, M.: The Body in the Mind: The Bodily Basis of Meaning, Imagination, and Reason. University of Chicago Press, Chicago (1987)
11. Lakoff, G.: Women, Fire, and Dangerous Things: What Categories Reveal About the Mind. University of Chicago Press, Chicago (1987)
12. Gibbs, R.W., Colston, H.L.: The cognitive psychological reality of image schemas and their transformations. Cogn. Linguist. **6**, 347–378 (1995)
13. Oakley, T.: Image schemas. In: Geeraerts, D., Cuyckens, H. (eds.) The Oxford Handbook of Cognitive Linguistics, pp. 214–235. Oxford University Press, New York (2007)
14. Tay, D.: Image schemas. In: Xu, W., Taylor, J.R. (eds.) The Routledge Handbook of Cognitive Linguistics, pp. 161–172. Taylor & Francis Group, Milton (2021)
15. Jakobson, R.: Two aspects of language and two types of aphasic disturbances. Fundam. Lang. 69–96 (1956)
16. Lakoff, G., Turner, M.: More Than Cool Reason: A Field Guide to Poetic Metaphor. University of Chicago Press, Chicago (1989)
17. Shen, J.: Zhuanzhi he Zhuanyu [A metonymic model of transferred designation of de-constructions in Mandarin Chinese]. DangdaiYuyanxue [Contemporary Linguistics] 3–15 (1999)
18. Brugman, C., Lakoff, G.: Cognitive topology and lexical networks (Chapter 3 Radial network). In: Dirk, G. (ed.) Cognitive Linguistics: Basic Readings, pp. 109–139. De Gruyter Mouton, New York (2006)
19. Barcelona, A.: Metaphor and Metonymy at the Crossroads: A Cognitive Perspective. De Gruyter Mouton, Boston (2000)
20. Littlemore, J.: Metonymy: Hidden Shortcuts in Language, Thought and Communication. Cambridge University Press, Cambridge (2015)
21. Croft, W.: The role of domains in the interpretation of metaphors and metonymies. Cogn. Linguist. **4**, 335–370 (1993)
22. Radden, G.: How metonymic are metaphors? In: Barcelona, A. (ed.) Metaphor and Metonymy at the Crossroads: A Cognitive Approach, pp. 93–108. De Gruyter Mouton, Boston (2000)
23. Radden, G.: How metonymic are metaphors? In: René, D., Ralf, P. (eds.) Metaphor and Metonymy in Comparison and Contrast. De Gruyter Mouton, New York (2002)

24. Lu, J.: Yinyu, zhuanyu sanyi [On metaphor and metonymy]. Waiguoyu [J. Foreign Lang.] 44–50 (2009)
25. Zhu, Y.: Ji yu yixiang tushi de dongci "chuan" de duoyi tixi ji yiyi lianjie jizhi [Polysemy of verb "chuan" and the linking mechanisms among senses: an image-schema-based approach]. Yuyan Kexue [Linguist. Sci.] 9, 287–300 (2010)
26. Yin, C.: Polysemy of tuī (推): an image-schema-based approach. In: Liu, M., Kit, C., Su, Q. (eds.) CLSW 2020. LNCS (LNAI), vol. 12278, pp. 87–99. Springer, Cham (2021). https://doi.org/10.1007/978-3-030-81197-6_8
27. Ma, J., Xia, Z.: Guanyu "gang" ciyi ji qi yanbian wenti de sikao [Thoughts on the meaning of "gàng" and its semantic change]. J. Liaoning Univ. Technol. (Soc. Sci. Ed.) 21, 75–78 (2019)
28. Hampe, B., Grady, J.E. (eds.): From Perception to Meaning: Image Schemas in Cognitive Linguistics. De Gruyter Mouton, New York (2005)
29. Xun, E., Rao, G., Xiao, X., Zang, J.: Dashuju Beijing xia BCC yuliaoku de yanzhi [The construction of the BCC corpus in the age of big data]. Yuliaoku Yuyanxue [Corpus Linguist.] 3, 93–118 (2016)
30. Li, Y., Wen, X.: Cong "tou" renzhi: zhuanyu, yinyu yu yi ci duo yi xianxiang yanjiu [Knowing from "head": a study of metonymy, metaphor and the phenomenon of polysemy]. Waiyu Jiaoxue [Foreign Lang. Educ.] 27, 1–5 (2006)
31. Liu, Z.: Mingci dongyong guocheng zhong de yinyu siwei [Metaphorical process in denominalization]. Waiyu Jiaoxue Yu Yanjiu [Foreign Lang. Teach. Res.] 32, 335–339 (2000)
32. Wang, Y.: Shijianyu renzhi moxing ji qi jieshili [The event-domain cognitive model]. Xiandai Waiyu [Mod. Foreign Lang.] 28, 17–26 (2005)

An Analysis of One-Dimensional Adjectives from the Perspective of Lexical Semantic Typology

Chaeri Kim[✉]

Department of Chinese Language and Literature, School of Humanities and Social Sciences,
Shanghai Normal University, Shanghai, China
cherry3880@163.com

Abstract. This paper examines the meanings and usages of one-dimensional spatial dimension adjectives in 13 languages using the theoretical framework and research methods of MLexT. Past studies have shown that 'HIGH/LOW', 'DEEP/SHALLOW', 'FAR/NEAR', and are different from 'LONG/SHORT', and they are not linear adjectives. Furthermore, 'FAR/NEAR' cannot be used to describe the shape of objects. Consequently, scholars rarely explore the associations between 'HIGH/LOW', 'DEEP/SHALLOW', 'FAR/NEAR', and 'LONGSHORT' in more detail. However, in specific use cases, they may intersect when describing one-dimensional point-to-point distances. Therefore, the author examines how 'LONG/SHORT', 'HIGH/LOW', 'DEEP/SHALLOW', and 'FAR/NEAR' are used, with a focus on the differences between those spatial dimension adjectives for one-dimensional space in basic meanings, which are highlighted in this paper. The objective of this study is to assist second language acquisition learners in accurately understanding the distinctions between spatial dimension adjectives as used and their native languages, thereby facilitating cross-linguistic language acquisition.

Keywords: Lexical Typology · Spatial Dimension Adjectives · Basic Meanings · Semantic Maps

1 Introduction

People are constantly situated within a particular space in their daily lives, and the concept of space has a significant impact on human cognition. Hence, the study of spatial dimension adjectives in various languages has been conducted extensively by linguists from various countries since the last century. Multiple languages have been studied in cross-linguistic research on spatial dimension adjectives, including Chinese (Ren 2000, Wu 2013) [1, 2], Korean (Min 2009, Feng 2016) [3, 4], English (Lyons 1977, Vandeloise 1988) [5, 6], French (Greimas 1996) [7], German (Bierwisch 1967) [8], Swedish (Vogel 2004) [9], and others.

In recent years, linguists from different countries have made remarkable advances in the study of spatial dimension adjectives. In most cases, however, most studies focus on

© The Author(s), under exclusive license to Springer Nature Singapore Pte Ltd. 2024
M. Dong et al. (Eds.): CLSW 2023, LNAI 14514, pp. 370–385, 2024.
https://doi.org/10.1007/978-981-97-0583-2_29

a specific language or fail to compare two languages adequately. In contrast to Wienold (1997) [10], Lang (2001) [11], and Kim (2021, 2022) [12, 13], who studied the semantic features of spatial dimension adjectives using a typological approach, no other scholars have explored typological research or examined and explained the basic meanings of spatial dimension adjectives from a cross-linguistic perspective. Prior studies on the semantics of spatial dimension adjectives have not addressed this aspect sufficiently. A new perspective and approach for examining cross-linguistic spatial dimension adjectives is presented in this study.

Ren (2000) conducted an early study on seven groups of spatial dimension adjectives in Chinese, such as 'LONG/SHORT', 'WIDE/NARROW', 'HIGH/LOW', 'DEEP/SHALLOW', 'COARSE/FINE', 'THICK/THIN', 'BIG/SMALL' [1]. In his research paper, he did not include the adjective pair 'FAR/NEAR' in his study. Reason being, he believed that 'FAR/NEAR' does not describe the shape of objects but rather their distance, a viewpoint that Chinese language scholars have tended to agree with in subsequent years. Additionally, Ren proposed classifying the shapes of spatial dimension adjectives according to the direction of extension in different dimensions. In his classification, 'LONG/SHORT', 'WIDE/NARROW' and 'THICK/THIN' were all included in the linear category, meaning they extended along the basis of the dimension from one point to two opposite ends. The terms 'HIGH/LOW' and 'DEEP/SHALLOW' were both included in the redial category, meaning the directions of their indicated dimensional extensions are all ray-type. It has been observed, however, that they overlap with 'LONG/SHORT' in some cases when describing one-dimensional point-to-point distances. Ultimately, this study examines the usage of spatial dimension adjectives such as 'HIGH/LOW', 'DEEP/SHALLOW', and 'FAR/NEAR', with a focus on the comparison of their basic meanings on a fundamental level.[1]

For this study, we selected four sets of spatial dimension words from the Database of Cross-Linguistic Colexifications(CLICS)[2] as our subject of research in 13 languages. The sample languages include Chinese, Thai, Vietnamese, Indonesian, Mongolian, Korean, Japanese, English, German, Latin, French, Spanish, and Russian. The data were collected using three methods: dictionaries, corpora, and surveys with native speakers. The author selected meanings based on the modern usage of the words, excluding ancient and dialectical usages.[3]

2   Introduction

Using the 13 languages listed above, the author checked the meanings of 'LONG/SHORT', 'HIGH/LOW', 'DEEP/SHALLOW', and 'FAR/NEAR' in their respective dictionary or corpus definitions, retaining the meanings that occur in at least

---

[1] The paper uses uppercase English letters to represent cross-linguistic concepts in accordance with the standard typological representation method. For example, 'LONG/SHORT' represents 'chang/duan' in Chinese and 'long/short' in English while 'HIGH/LOW' represents 'gao/di, ai' in Chinese and 'high,tall/low' in English.

[2] Database of Cross-Linguistic Colexifications can be accessed at https://clics.clld.org/.

[3] For instance, in ancient Chinese, the word 'chang' can be used to describe a person's height. As a measure of height, you may use 'shenchang(height)' in modern Chinese, but it is not a disyllabic word or a fixed collocation.

two languages. The corresponding word lists of Spatial Dimension Adjectives in 13 Languages are as follows. (Table 1).

Table 1. Reference Table for Corresponding Words of Three Sets of Spatial Dimension Adjectives in 13 Languages.

Language family	Language	Spatial Adjectives			
		LONG/SHORT	HIGH/LOW	DEEP/SHALLOW	FAR/NEAR
Sino-Tibetan languages	Chinese	chang/duan	gao/di,ai	shen/qian	yuan/jin
Tai–Kadai languages	Thai	yaaw/san	sung/tem	luk/thuun	klay/klai
Austro-Asiatic Languages	Vietnamese	dai/ngan	cao/thap	sau/nong	xa/gan
Austronesian Languages	Indonesian	panjang/pendek	tinggi/rendah	dalam/dangkal	jauh/dangkal
Altaic languages	Mongolian	urt/bogino	ondor/namkhan	gun/guyekhen	khol/oir
Language isolate	Korean	gilda/jjalda	nopda/najda	gipda/yatda	meolda/ gakkabda
	Japanese	nagai/mijikai	takai/hikui	fukai/asai	toi/chikai
Indo-European languages	English	long/short	high,tall/low	deep/shallow	far,distant/ near,close
	German	lang/kurz	hoch/niedrig	tief/flach	weit/nah
	French	long/court	haut/bas	profond/peu profond	lointain,distant/ proche
	Spanish	largo/corto	alto/bajo	profundo/poco profundo	lejos/cerca
	Latin	longus/brevis	altus/humilis	altus/humilis[4]	longinquus/ propinquus
	Russian	dlinnyj/korotkij	vysokij/nizkij	glubokij/neglubokiy	dalokij/blizkij

Since the dictionaries lack explicit explanations and examples of their basic meaning framework in this chapter, the author extracted content from corpora in each of the 13 languages corresponding to the basic meanings framework before compiling the nouns associated with 'LONG/SHORT', 'HIGH/LOW', 'DEEP/SHALLOW', and 'FAR/NEAR' and verifying their basic meanings. The author subsequently identified the typical characteristics of the referents of nouns in these combinations, which were then used to construct the framework presented in this paper. In this paper, semantic definitions describing spatial concepts are referred to as 'basic meanings', while those describing semantic meanings without any apparent spatial connection are referred to as 'extended meanings'.

---

[4] In Latin, 'altus/humilis' is polysemous and can be used to denote the meanings of 'DEEP/SHALLOW' or 'HIGH/LOW'.

2.1 Parameters and Semantic Framework for the Basic Meanings of 'LONG/SHORT'[5]

In MLexT, 'parameters' refer to semantic features that can be used to distinguish different members in specific semantic domains, whereas 'frames' refer to scenarios formed by combining parameters, often represented by individual words in different languages [14]. The basic meanings of 'LONG/SHORT' are related to the size of the distance between any two points in space. The parameters are primarily related to the spatial characteristics of the objects and can be described using the following two parameters of the two frames:

1. Orientation of dimension in space: This parameter reflects the orientation of the 'LONG/SHORT' dimension in a three-dimensional coordinate system. Through categorizing the objects described by 'LONG/SHORT' in 13 languages, this study finds that when 'LONG/SHORT' is used to describe one-dimensional linear and two-dimensional planar objects, they do not have a clear orientation in the three-dimensional coordinate system.
2. Whether or not an object is a living thing: This parameter indicates whether the described object is a living being. For example, 'neck', 'leg', 'nose', etc., are things associated with living things, while 'table', 'board', 'thread', etc., are non-human beings.

Combining these two parameters leads to two frames related to 'LONG/SHORT':

a. String-shaped objects: In the 13 languages, 'LONG/SHORT' is often used to describe string-shaped objects, such as one-dimensional lines like 'hair', 'wire', 'rope', etc.; regular or irregular two-dimensional surfaces like 'wooden board', 'belt', 'line', etc.; and three-dimensional solid objects with prominent features like 'table', 'crack', 'passage', etc.
b. Continuous vertical upward distance of living entities: In some languages, 'LONG/SHORT' can describe the vertical and continuous distance in living beings, such as a person's height.

2.2 Parameters and Semantic Framework of Basic Meanings of 'HIGH/LOW'

Most scholars believe that the basic meanings of 'HIGH/LOW' can be categorized into "dimensional" and 'positional' meanings. (Lyons 1977, Vogel 2004, Ren 2000, etc.) [1, 5, 9] 'Dimensional meaning' means that 'HIGH/LOW' describes the dimension of the object itself, i.e., it characterizes the distance from the ground to the top of the object placed on the ground, such as a high tower or a high wall. 'Positional meaning' means that 'HIGH/LOW' describes the distance between two positions in a vertical orientation, i.e. the distance from the ground to the bottom of an object or things that is not on the ground, such as a high sky. The basic meanings of 'HIGH/LOW' in 13 languages are the distances from the bottom upwards, and the individual parameters are mainly related to the spatial properties of the object. There can be three kinds of frames described by the following two parameters.

---

[5] Please refer to Kim (2021) for more information regarding the research on the basic meanings of 'LONG' and 'SHORT'. [12]

1. Whether it is continuous or not: Vogel (2004: 53–55) suggests that the lexical meaning of 'HIGH/LOW' is either dimensional or positional depending on the reference plane. When the points on the reference plane are outside the object of description, the lexical meaning of 'HIGH/LOW' will be positional. When the points on the reference plane are within the object of description, the lexical meaning of 'HIGH/LOW' will be dimensional [9]. This paper agrees with Vogel's point of view. Based on her view, the dimensions of objects in three-dimensional space are usually continuous and uninterrupted, so when 'HIGH/LOW' has a dimensional meaning, this means that 'HIGH/LOW' describes the distance from the reference plane to the top of the object itself, and describes spatial dimensions that are all continuous. Things in space do not exist in isolation, and observers usually seek out a reference plane when looking at objects. 'HIGH/LOW' can also describe the distance from the reference plane to the object of observation when the word 'HIGH/LOW' is positional. The lexical meaning of 'HIGH/LOW' when it is positional focuses solely on the distance between a point in the reference object and the object of description without regard to whether the intermediate distances are consecutive. 'HIGH/LOW', on the other hand, describes the distance between a point in the reference object and the object of description, regardless of whether the intermediate distances are consecutive. In such instances, 'HIGH/LOW' describes an object that is not continuous. As an example, people only pay attention to the distance from the ground to the cloud when they observe the height of the cloud, whereas the existence of a partition between the two does not affect the measurement of distance. In Fig. 1, this paper presents the object described by 'HIGH/LOW' in the three-dimensional coordinate system.

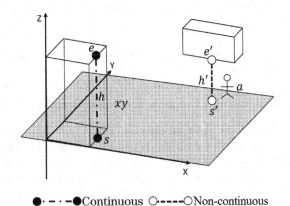

●– – ·–●Continuous ○-----○Non-continuous

Fig. 1. In a three-dimensional coordinate system, 'HIGH/LOW' indicates continuity and discontinuity of an object

In Fig. 1, '*s*' represents the bottom of the described object, '*e*' represents the top, and the distance '*h*' from '*s*' to '*e*' represents the dimension described by 'HIGH/LOW', which corresponds to the object's dimension as well. In three-dimensional spaces, '*h*' is continuous and uninterrupted. It is understood that 'The building is very high/low' refers to the distance between the bottom to the top of the building, and that this measurement has to be continuous, without interruption. In Fig. 1, the observer's position is indicated by the letter 'a'. 'HIGH/LOW' describes the distance 'h'' from point 's'' on the observer's plane 'xy' to point 'e'' in the observed object. In this measurement, only the observer's plane and the observed object are taken into account, not the path in between. For instance, the phrase 'The cloud is very high/low' can be comprehended as an observer measuring the distance between the ground and the cloud from his or her location.

2. Whether it's a living being: This parameter indicates whether the described object is a living being. Objects like 'people, animals', or 'body parts' are considered living things, while objects like 'buildings, the sky, clouds, skyscrapers' are not. This parameter is used to establish three frames related to the basic meanings of 'HIGH/LOW' as follows:

    a. Continuous distance from the bottom to the top: When an object has prominent features in vertical direction, 'HIGH/LOW' can describe the continuous distance from the bottom to the top of the object itself. Vertically upright bamboo poles, for example, have their most prominent dimensions from bottom to top. Therefore, 'HIGH/LOW' can be used to describe the continuous distance from the bottom to the top of the bamboo pole. If 'HIGH/LOW' is used without considering external factors to describe an object, then it signifies the object's dimensional meaning. When describing the dimensional meaning of objects in the 13 languages, 'HIGH/LOW' is often used with words such as 'building', 'tower', 'mountain', 'tree', 'wall, 'shoe sole', 'table', 'chair', 'water level'.

    b. Non-continuous distance from the object to the observer's plane: The term 'HIGH/LOW' can describe the distance between an object and the observer's plane when the observer's plane is above the observed object. A 'cloud', for instance, is typically above an observer, and in this case, the term 'HIGH/LOW' can be used to indicate the distance from the observer's ground to the cloud. The height of the object is not represented by the distance described by 'HIGH/LOW'; rather, it refers to the distance between the observer's plane and the object. 'HIGH/LOW' is therefore represented by this framework in terms of its positional meaning.

    c. Continuous vertical upward distance of living entities: In most of the 13 languages, 'HIGH/LOW' can be used to describe the height of people or animals and plants. However, in Korean, the terms 'HIGH' 'nopda' and 'LOW' 'najda' are not appropriate for this purpose. In English, only 'tall' is used, and 'low' cannot be used to describe the height of people or animals and plants. The height of a person or animal and plant is determined by the distance between the bottom and the top of the object itself. Therefore, this framework represents the positional meaning of 'HIGH/LOW'.

2.3 Parameters and Semantic Framework of Basic Meanings of 'DEEP/SHALLOW'

The term 'DEEP/SHALLOW' is used to describe a vertical downward dimension or a horizontal forward-backward dimension. The basic meanings of 'DEEP/SHALLOW' are 'distance from the top to the bottom or distance from the outside to the inside'. One framework can be described using the following one parameter: whether or not it is an entry type. This parameter relates to the idea that people have a fixed perception of the three-dimensional space they are currently in. However, people tend to perceive themselves as entering a new space when the spatial environment changes. When people transition from one fixed spatial perception to a new spatial perception, they are described as 'entry type adjectives' in this paper. 'DEEP/SHALLOW' describes the transition from an open space to a closed space or a narrow space, making it an 'entry type adjective'. For example, 'DEEP/SHALLOW' can be used to describe the depth of a pit. When people view the pit from outside, their perception of space is open. However, when they shift their gaze to the inside of the pit, their perception of space becomes closed. In this sense, 'DEEP/SHALLOW' describes the distance between the outside and the inside of the pit. Similarly, 'DEEP/SHALLOW' can be used to describe long alleys. A person's perception of space is open when his or her vision is outside the alley. However, when they shift their sight inside the alley, the perceived space becomes narrower. In an alley, 'DEEP/SHALLOW' refers to the distance between the outside and the inside. In the context of these basic meanings, 'DEEP/SHALLOW' can refer to 'vertical downward distances as well as horizontal front-back continuous distances' across all 13 languages. When used with words like 'earth', 'lake', 'sea', 'wound', 'wrinkle', it describes vertical downward distances, and when used with words like 'drawer', 'alley', it describes horizontal front-back continuous distances.

2.4　Parameters and Semantic Framework for Basic Meanings of 'FAR/NEAR'

The basic meaning of 'FAR/NEAR' is 'the size of the distance between any two points in space', and the parameter is mainly related to the spatial characteristics of things, which can be described by one of the following parameters to describe two kinds of frameworks. Precision of Measurement: Liu (2017: 40–43) pointed out that 'distant' for the concept of 'FAR' in English and 'far' for the concept of 'FAR' in Chinese are similar as they can both describe the precision of measurements [15]. This paper is in agreement with Liu Guiling's point of view, and through the search of 13 language corpora and the survey of native speakers, it is discovered that 'FAR/NEAR' can be used to describe distance in two ways. One is to describe a precise distance, e.g., '5 km from the current position to a certain point', where 'far' refers to a precise distance. Conversely, 'FAR/NEAR' can also be used to describe vague or approximate distances. For example, one might say, 'It's very far from the current location', with 'far' expressing an approximate or vague distance. In majority of the 13 languages, 'FAR/NEAR' can describe these two ways of expressing distance by using one single word separately. While in other languages, 'FAR/NEAR' can be described by two distinct words with one word for precise measurements and another for vague ones, for example, English and French. The following two frames are related to the basic meanings of 'FAR/NEAR':

1. Imprecise spacing distance: 'FAR/NEAR' can describe vague, approximate distances between two points in space in all 13 languages. For instance, English and French words like 'far', 'distant', and 'lointain' correspond to 'FAR', while words like 'near', 'close', and 'proche' correspond to 'NEAR'.
2. Precise spacing distance: 'FAR/NEAR' can be used to describe precise spacing distance in most of the 13 languages. However, in Chinese, 'NEAR' 'jin' is an exception and cannot be used to describe precise spacing distance.

3 Cross-linguistic Comparison of Basic Meanings of One-Dimensional Spatial Dimension Adjectives

3.1 Interrelation of Basic Meanings of One-Dimensional Spatial Dimension Adjectives

Based on the previous research, 'LONG/SHORT' typically refers to distances between one-dimensional points. In addition to spatial dimension adjectives, there are a number of adjectives that describe distances between one-dimensional points, including 'HIGH/LOW', 'DEEP/SHALLOW', and 'FAR/NEAR'. A summary of five fundamental parameters is presented in this paper, based on the analysis of basic meanings described in Sects. 2.1 to 2.4: the direction of the dimension in space, whether it refers to a living entity, whether it is continuous, whether it refers to an entry type, and precision of measurement. The parameters indicate that 'LONG/SHORT', 'HIGH/LOW', 'DEEP/SHALLOW', and 'FAR/NEAR' are spatial dimension adjectives that describe one-dimensional distances, but with varying areas of emphasis.

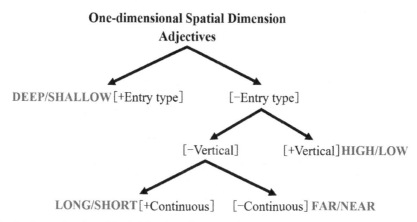

Fig. 2. Semantic Map of Basic Meanings for One-Dimensional Spatial Dimension Adjectives

As depicted in Fig. 2, among these one-dimensional spatial dimension adjectives, 'DEEP/SHALLOW' are characterized as entry type adjectives, while the other three are not. Among those non-entry spatial dimension adjectives, such as 'HIGH/LOW', describe the dimension's orientation in space as vertical, whereas 'LONG/SHORT' and 'FAR/NEAR' describe dimensions that are in any direction. Typically, "LONG/SHORT" is used to represent continuous distances, while 'FAR/NEAR' is used for non-continuous distances. Taking into account the analysis presented in Sects. 2.1 through Sect. 2.4, this paper that 'LONG/SHORT' encompasses two frameworks: 'string-shaped objects' and 'continuous vertical upward distance of living entities'. As for 'HIGH/LOW', it encompasses three frameworks, namely 'continuous vertical upward distance of living entities', 'continuous distance from the bottom to the top', and 'non-continuous distance from the object to the observer's plane'. Meanwhile, 'DEEP/SHALLOW' encompasses the framework of 'vertical downward distances as well as horizontal front-back continuous distances'. Last but not least, 'FAR/NEAR' encompasses two frameworks: 'imprecise spacing distance' and 'precise spacing distance'.

3.1.1 Interrelation of Basic Meanings of One-Dimensional Spatial Dimension Adjectives

Bierwisch (1967: 32–34) proposed that spatial dimension adjectives exhibit positive and negative semantic characteristics, with 'LONG, HIGH, WIDE, FAR' categorized as positive, and 'SHORT, LOW, NARROW, NEAR' as negative [8]. Using Bierwisch's perspective as a guide, this paper categorizes one-dimensional spatial dimension adjectives 'LONG/SHORT', 'HIGH/LOW', 'DEEP/SHALLOW', and 'FAR/NEAR' into two groups and addresses their positive and negative meanings. As illustrated in Figs. 3, 4, 5 and 6, using the frameworks discussed above for 'LONG/SHORT', 'HIGH/LOW', 'DEEP/SHALLOW', and 'FAR/NEAR' there are four groups of adjectives categorizing spatial dimensions on a one-dimensional scale.[6] This section first examines the positive meanings of spatial dimension adjectives describing one-dimensional distances, namely 'LONG, HIGH, DEEP, FAR'. Subsequently, it analyzes the negative meanings represented by 'SHORT, LOW, SHALLOW, NEAR'.

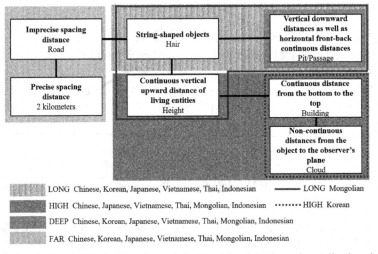

Fig. 3. Semantic Map of Basic Meanings of 'Positive' Spatial Dimension Adjectives in Asian Languages

As depicted in Fig. 3, 'LONG' can be used to describe 'string-shaped objects' as well as 'vertical downward distances as well as horizontal front-back continuous distances'

---

[6] According to Kim (2021, 2022) study on the base meanings of spatial dimension adjectives, the examination found that spatial dimension adjectives show obvious geographical differences in their usage, so this paper focuses on presenting the semantic maps of the base meanings of one-dimensional spatial dimension adjectives of the investigated languages in the following two maps of the Asian languages and the European languages. [12,13]

in 7 Asian languages among the 13 languages. Among the Asian languages, Mongolian stands out from its counterparts as it additionally describes 'continuous vertical upward distance of living entities' Meanwhile, in six Asian languages: Chinese, Japanese, Vietnamese, Thai, Mongolian, and Indonesian 'HIGH' means 'continuous vertical upward distance of living entities', 'continuous distances from the bottom to the top', and 'non-continuous distances from the object to the observer's plane'. Another exception within Asian languages is 'HIGH' in Korean, which does not describe 'continuous vertical upward distance of living entities', but rather conveys 'continuous distances from bottom to top' and 'non-continuous distances from the object to the observer's plane'. Across Asian languages, 'DEEP' universally refers to 'vertical downward distances as well as horizontal front-back continuous distances', while 'FAR' is a universal adjective for 'imprecise spacing distance' and 'precise spacing distance'.

In a nutshell, both 'LONG' and 'DEEP' are used in Asian languages when describing horizontal front-back continuous distances, as demonstrated by Chinese, which uses both to describe the length of a vertical alley. Notably, in Mongolian, 'LONG' and 'HIGH' are both used to describe 'continuous vertical upward distance of living entities', setting it apart from other Asian languages.

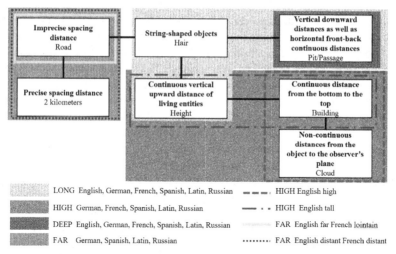

Fig. 4. Semantic Map of Basic Meanings of 'Positive' Spatial Dimension Adjectives in European Languages

As depicted in Fig. 4, among the 13 languages examined 'LONG' can be used to describe 'string-shaped objects' and 'continuous vertical upward distance of living entities' in 6 European languages. For five European languages: German, French, Spanish, Latin, and Russian, 'HIGH' can be used to describe 'continuous distance from the bottom to the top', 'non-continuous distance from the object to the observer's plane', and 'continuous vertical upward distance of living entities'. However, in English, the concepts corresponding to 'HIGH' are represented by the words 'high' and 'tall'. In English, 'high' describes 'continuous distance from the bottom to the top' and 'non-continuous distance from the object to the observer's plane' while 'tall' in English conveys 'continuous distance from the bottom to the top' and 'continuous vertical upward distance of living entities'. The term 'DEEP' is universally used to describe a 'vertical downward distances as well as horizontal front-back continuous distances" across European languages. Meanwhile, German, Spanish, Latin, and Russian refer to 'FAR' as a single concept encompassing both 'imprecise spacing distance' and 'precise spacing distance'. In contrast, English and French use two terms to refer to 'FAR'. In English, 'far' and 'distant' correspond to 'FAR'. In French, 'lointain' and 'distant' correspond to 'FAR'. Both 'distant' in English and 'distant' in French describe 'imprecise spacing distance' and 'precise spacing distance' while "far" in English and 'lointain' in French are limited to 'imprecise spacing distance'.

Based on the analysis presented above, this study shows that the semantic map of 'FAR' is generally similar in Asian and European languages. In all 13 languages, 'FAR' encompasses both 'imprecise spacing distance' and 'precise spacing distance'. The basic meanings of 'HIGH' are similar in European languages, such as German, French, Spanish, Latin, and Russian, as well as in Asian languages, such as Chinese, Japanese, Vietnamese, Thai, Mongolian, and Indonesian. In both groups, 'HIGH' can be used to describe 'continuous distance from the bottom to the top', 'non-continuous distance from the object to the observer's plane', and 'continuous vertical upward distance of living entities'. English, however, differs from other European languages in that it uses two distinct words to refer to the concept of 'HIGH'. 'high' in English can be used to refer to a 'continuous distance from the bottom to the top' as well as a 'non-continuous distance from the object to the observer's plane'. However, it cannot convey the idea of 'continuous vertical upward distance of living entities', which is why 'tall' is must use to describe 'continuous vertical upward distance of living entities' in English. In comparison with other European languages, this phenomenon is unique to English. The word 'LONG' refers to 'horizontal front-back continuous distances' in both Asian and European languages, and it overlaps with 'DEEP'. This convergence of concepts illustrates a common understanding of 'LONG'. However, notable differences exist between European and Asian languages with regard to 'LONG'. 'LONG' is used in European languages not only to describe 'string-shaped objects' but also to describe 'continuous vertical upward distance of living entities'. Although this is only applicable to Mongolian among Asian languages, 'LONG' in European overlaps with the word 'HIGH' when used to represent 'continuous vertical upward distance of living entities'. In other Asian languages, the word 'LONG' cannot describe 'continuous vertical upward distance of living entities'. These distinctions highlight the cross-linguistic and cross-regional differences in spatial dimension adjectives for describing one-dimensional distances. On the other hand, English and French differ from other European languages in the usage of the word 'FAR'. 'far' in English and 'lointain' in French can only be used to describe 'imprecise spacing distance', which is differ from the meaning of 'FAR' in other European languages. The disparity in interpretations of 'FAR' within the same region or language family illustrates the possibility of subtle differences even within the same region or language family.

3.1.2 Negative Meanings of One-Dimensional Spatial Dimension Adjectives

As depicted in Fig. 5, among the 13 languages investigated, 'SHORT' is used in seven Asian languages to describe 'string-shaped objects'. Moreover, 'SHORT' can also be used in Mongolian and Indonesian to describe the 'continuous vertical upward distance of living entities'. Five Asian languages, namely Japanese, Vietnamese, Thai, Mongolian, and Indonesian, use 'LOW' to express 'continuous distance from the bottom to the top', 'non-continuous distance from the object to the observer's plane', and 'continuous vertical upward distance of living entities'. The Chinese language employs two terms, 'di' and 'ai', to convey the concept of 'LOW'. 'di' can adequately describe the 'continuous distance from the bottom to the top' and 'non-continuous distance from the object to the observer's plane' but it cannot convey the idea of a 'continuous vertical upward distance of living entities'.

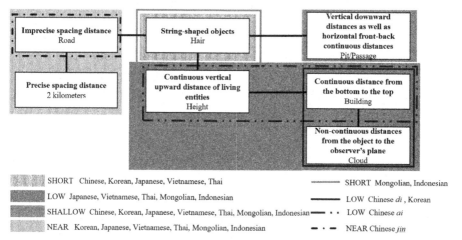

Fig. 5. Semantic Map of Basic Meanings of 'Negative' One-Dimensional Spatial Dimension Adjectives in Asian Languages

On the other hand, 'ai' can describe 'continuous vertical upward distance of living entities' and 'continuous distance from the bottom to the top' but cannot represent 'non-continuous distance from the object to the observer's plane'. The word 'LOW' can describe "continuous distance from the bottom to the top' and 'non-continuous distance from the object to the observer's plane' but does not convey 'continuous vertical upward distance of living entities'. All Asian languages use 'SHALLOW' to depict 'vertical distance downward or continuous distance in the horizontal front and back direction'. Meanwhile, 'NEAR' in most Asian languages can describe 'imprecise spacing distance' and 'precise spacing distance', except for 'jin' in Chinese, which can only express the idea of 'imprecise spacing distance' and not 'precise spacing distance'.

It can be seen from the above that 'SHORT' does not intersect with 'LOW' lexically in five Asian languages, namely, Chinese, Japanese, Vietnamese, Thai, and Korean, while 'SHORT' in only Mongolian and Indonesian do not overlap with 'LOW' when describing a living being's 'continuous vertical upward distance'. 'SHORT' in Mongolian and

Indonesian does not intersect with 'LOW' in the description of the 'continuous vertical upward distance of living entities' whereas 'SHORT' in all Asian languages cannot describe 'continuous vertical upward distance of living entities', but only 'SHALLOW' can. This reflects the cognitive difference between 'SHORT' and 'LONG' in Asian languages. Korean is the only Asian language that cannot describe 'continuous vertical upward distance of living entities', while all the others can.

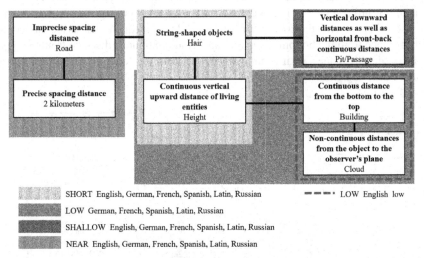

Fig. 6. Semantic Map of Basic Meanings of 'Negative' One-Dimensional Spatial Dimension Adjectives in European Languages

As depicted in Fig. 6, among the 13 languages studied, six European languages utilize the term 'SHORT' to describe both 'string-shaped objects' and 'continuous vertical upward distance of living entities'. Five European languages, namely German, French, Spanish, Latin, and Russian, utilize 'LOW' to convey the ideas of 'continuous distance from the bottom to the top', 'non-continuous distance from the object to the observer's plane', and 'continuous vertical upward distance of living entities'. In English, 'LOW' is only used to describe horizontal distances or non-continuous distances between objects and the observer's plane. It cannot refer to the 'continuous vertical upward distance of living entities'. In six European languages, the word 'SHALLOW' can denote 'vertical downward distances as well as horizontal front-back continuous distances'. On the other hand, 'NEAR' can be used to describe both vague and precise spacing distance.

Based on the above analysis, this paper observes that 'SHALLOW' and 'NEAR' have similar basic meanings in European and Asian languages. In general, 'SHALLOW' typically describes 'vertical downward distances as well as horizontal front-back continuous distances' across all 13 languages. Moreover, in most languages, 'NEAR' can refer to both 'imprecise spacing distance' and 'precise spacing distance'. However, in Chinese, 'NEAR' 'jin' cannot mean 'precise spacing distance'. Among European and Asian languages, the basic meanings of 'LOW' in German, French, Spanish, Latin, and Russian align quite closely with those in Japanese, Vietnamese, Thai, Mongolian, and Indonesian. In all of these languages, it is possible to describe 'continuous distance from the bottom to the top', 'non-continuous distance from the object to the observer's', and 'continuous vertical upward distance of living entities' with the same word. In spite of this, English stands out among European languages because 'low' in English is the same as 'najda' in Korean, denoting the idea of 'continuous distance from the bottom to the top' and 'non-continuous distance from the object to the observer's plane', but fails to convey the connotation of 'continuous vertical upward distance of living entities'. A comparison of 'SHORT' in European and Asian languages reveals significant differences between the two. 'SHORT' is not limited to describing 'string-shaped objects' in Europe; it also encompasses 'continuous vertical upward distance of living entities'. In German, French, Spanish, Latin, and Russian, 'SHORT' have the overlapping basic meaning with the word 'LOW' in the description of 'continuous vertical upward distance of living entities'. However, except Mongolian and Indonesian having the same meaning, the word 'SHORT' in other Asian languages cannot be used to describe 'continuous vertical upward distance of living entities'. These distinctions in European and Asian languages emphasize the differences across regions and languages in the way one-dimensional spatial dimension adjectives are used.

4 Conclusion

After thorough research on the use of 'LONG/SHORT', 'HIGH/LOW', 'DEEP/SHALLOW' and 'FAR/NEAR' in 13 languages, the following conclusions have been drawn and reflected in this paper.

To begin with, in the context of 'horizontal front-back continuous distances', the word 'DEEP' can describe meanings consistent with 'LONG' in both Asian and European languages, but 'SHALLOW' and 'SHORT' do not overlap in meanings. This reflects the shared characteristic between different languages in different regions when describing 'horizontal front-back continuous distances'.

Secondly, Asian and European languages differ significantly when it comes to the concept of 'continuous vertical upward distance of living entities'. It is generally not possible to use 'LONG/SHORT' as an adjective to describe this framework in Asian languages, which can only be described with 'HIGH/LOW'. Among Asian languages, only Mongolian and Indonesian can describe 'continuous vertical upward distance of living entities' alongside the 'LONG/SHORT' and 'HIGH/LOW' of European languages, which overlap in this framework. There are differences in expressions of 'continuous vertical upward distance of living entities' among the 13 languages, mostly due to regional variations rather than differences in language families.

Thirdly, the intersections of 'LONG' and 'DEEP' and of 'LONG/SHORT' and 'HIGH/LOW' are also related to the intrinsic characteristics of spatial dimension adjectives. 'LONG' typically describes continuous distances, while 'DEEP' is used to describe a confined or narrow space. In describing spatial characteristics, these two aspects are not contradictory. 'LONG' focuses on the distance from one point to another within an object whereas 'DEEP' focuses on the distance from outside a confined or narrow space to the inside. It is aligned with what 'DEEP' needs to describe: the distance from a point outside to a point inside a confined or narrow space. For "LONG", the degree of measurement begins at the beginning of entering a confined space and ends at the end of the space to describe the length of the entire space. Therefore, both 'LONG' and 'DEEP' can be used to describe confined or narrow spaces. For instance, in Chinese, 'LONG' 'chang' and 'DEEP' 'shen' may be used to describe the length of a corridor. When there is no obvious exit from a confined space, only 'DEEP' can be used, not 'LONG'. For example, 'DEEP' may be used to describe a deep pit, but 'LONG' cannot be used in the same context as it is a confined space that has no visible exits. On the other hand, 'HIGH/LOW' typically describes vertical distances, while the direction does not really matter when 'LONG/SHORT' is used for describing objects. Therefore, 'LONG/SHORT' can also be used to describe distances in spanning vertically. Considering that 'LONG/SHORT' normally describes continuous distances, it may only be applicable to continuous vertical distances. Nevertheless, 'HIGH/LOW' can refer to both continuous and non-continuous vertical distances since 'HIGH/LOW' deals primarily with vertical direction, while 'LONG/SHORT' is typically used for continuous distances.

In this paper, we examine the basic meanings of one-dimensional spatial dimension adjectives in 13 languages to demonstrate that they share cross-linguistic semantics, as well as validate the feasibility and adaptability of MLexT theory as a tool for lexical typology. To ensure the reliability of the conceptual space, we would like to obtain further validation in more languages to better aid language acquisition learners in their understanding and accurate mastery of the intended context of the researched vocabulary in specific contexts.

References

1. Ren, Y.J.: Study on The Semantics of the Spatial Dimensional Words in Modern Chinese. Master Degree Thesis in Yanbian University (2000). (in Chinese)
2. Wu, Y.: Research on the semantic features of dimensional adjective Gao 'high/tall' and di/ai 'low/short' in Chinese. In: Liu, P., Su, Q. (eds.) CLSW 2013. LNCS (LNAI), vol. 8229, pp. 153–162. Springer, Heidelberg (2013). https://doi.org/10.1007/978-3-642-45185-0_17
3. Min, Y.L.: A comparative analysis on the multivocal structure of keuda/jaktta and {da/xiao}. Korean Lang. Lit. **1**, 35–81 (2009)
4. Feng, J.J.: A comparative study on the meaning of the spatial terms of dimensions 'gilda/jjalbda' in Korean and 'chang/duan' in Chinese. J. Korean Culture. **8**, 7–35 (2016)
5. Lyons, J.: Semantics 2 vols, p. 739. Cambridge University Press, Cambridge (1977)
6. Vandeloise, C.: Length, width and potential passing. In: Rudzka-Ostyn (12), 403–428 (1988)
7. Greimas, A.: Sémantique structurale, pp. 43–47. Librarie Larousse, Paris (1966)
8. Bierwisch, M.: Some semantic universals of German adjectival. Found. Lang. **3**, 1–36 (1967)
9. Vogel, A.: Swedish dimensional adjectives. Doctor's Degree thesis in Stockholm University (2004)
10. Wienold, G., Rohmer, U.: On implications in lexicalizations for dimensional expressions. In: Yamanaka, K., Ohiro, T. (eds.) The Locus of Meaning, pp. 143–185. Kurosho, Tokyo (1997)
11. Lang, E.: Spatial dimension terms. In: Haspelmath, M.E., et al. (eds.). Language Typology and Language Universals. An International Handbook, vol. 2, pp. 1251–1275. Mouton de Gruyter, Berlin & New York (2001)
12. Kim, C.L: An analysis of 'LONG/SHORT' from the perspective of lexical semantic typology. Korean J. Chin. Lang. Lit. **3**, 223–248 (2021)

13. Kim, C.L.: An analysis of 'THICK/THIN' from the perspective of lexical semantic typology. J. Chin. Linguist. Korea **1**, 417–44 (2022)
14. Rakhilina, E., Reznikova, T.: A frame-based methodology for lexical typology. In: Juvonen, P., Koptjevskaja-Tamm, M. (eds.) The Lexical Typology of Semantic Shifts. De Gruyter Mouton, Berlin/Boston (2016)
15. Liu, G.L.: A contrastive study of English and chinese spatial dimensional adjectives from a cognitive semantic perspective, pp. 37–63. Doctor Degree thesis in Northeast Normal University (2017). (in Chinese)

Semantic Analysis of the Tool-Meaning Quasi-Affixes "*Jī, Qì, Yí and Jì*"

Ao Sun[✉]

Department of Chinese Language and Literature, Peking University, Beijing 100871, China
sunsaul@163.com

Abstract. Based on the examination of ancient Chinese language materials, this article further compares the semantic features of the tool-meaning quasi-affixes *jī* 机, *qì* 器, *yí* 仪, *jì* 计 in Chinese. The research reveals that compared to X *qì* 器, tools referred to by X *jī* 机 often have a more complex internal structure involving energy conversion. X *qì* 器, on the other hand, is commonly used to refer to higher-level concepts, expressing the overall meaning of "tool", with a simpler internal structure compared to X *jī* 机. X *jì* 计, due to the verb meaning of "*jì* 计", refers to tools with quantitative measurement, forming relatively limited tool names. The most prominent feature of X *yí* 仪 is "imaging", often requiring precision and accuracy, giving a sense of sophistication, scientificity, and professionalism. It was also observed that in Chinese, naming some tools using the "function + *jī/ qì* 机/器" word formation pattern can lead to unclear references. Therefore, other characteristic suffixes indicating form are chosen for word formation.

Keywords: *jī* 机 · *qì* 器 · *yí* 仪 · *jì* 计 · Quasi-affix · Semantics

1 Introduction: Differentiation of Semantically Similar Affixes

With the continuous development of modern society, an increasing number of new technologies and facilities have become part of our daily lives. Simultaneously, the language has adapted to these new phenomena by creating corresponding neologisms. To facilitate recording and usage, linguistic changes follow the principle of economy. The narrow sense of "Linguistic Economy" was proposed by the renowned French linguist Andre Martinet. This principle suggests that, while ensuring language meets communicative needs, people often make economical arrangements in linguistic activities [1]. The principle of Linguistic Economy plays a significant role in naming these new facilities: Naming often follows the pattern of "function + category name", utilizing existing vocabulary directly to name new things. In this process, some category names are used frequently, gradually becoming stable and acquiring relatively fixed meanings. These category names are continuously selected and used in naming new things, forming new words. Lv Shuxiang [2] proposed the term "quasi-affixes" to describe phenomena where "genuine affixes are not numerous in Mandarin Chinese". According to him, elements like "*yà*- 亚- (sub-), *lèi*- 类- (type-), *-jiā* -家 (-ist), *-rén* -人 (-er)" and so on fall into this category. Zhu Yajun [3] mentioned that quasi-affixes occupy a position between

M. Dong et al. (Eds.): CLSW 2023, LNAI 14514, pp. 386–399, 2024.
https://doi.org/10.1007/978-981-97-0583-2_30

morphemes and affixes. Unlike typical affixes, they retain some original vocabulary meanings and do not have a very rigid bond with the connected elements, sometimes they can even standing alone. However, on the other hand, their meanings have more or less changed, and they can derive more new words. Zeng Liying [4] found through the analysis of more than 80,000 words in the "Grammar Information Dictionary" that these quasi-affixes have characteristics such as productivity, positional specificity, and semantic generalization. With the emergence of new objects, language users use these quasi-affixes with productive capabilities for naming.

In this word-formation process, Mandarin Chinese has a group of quasi-affixes that are functionally and semantically similar but exhibit differences in specific usage. Dong Xiufang [5] pointed out that it is sometimes challenging to distinguish usage restrictions among lexically similar elements with the same function. For example, in Mandarin Chinese, the noun suffixes "*jiā* 家(ist), *zhě* 者 (er), *shǒu* 手 (er), *rén* 人 (er), *yuán* 员 (er), *gōng* 工 (er), *shī* 师 (ist), *jiàng* 匠 (ist)" that can form agents all refer to a certain type of person, but there are differences in the information about the individuals they refer to. For instance, *yuán* 员 involves a broad range of professions, but the general characteristic is either light physical or mental labor; *shī* 师 refers to professionals who are not simple manual laborers, often engaging in higher-status occupations. These generalizations are consistent with the characteristics of the compounds formed by these suffixes and can predict the naming patterns of new professions in society. For example, in March 2021, China's Ministry of Human Resources and Social Security announced new professions such as "*qìchē jiùyuányuán* 汽车救援员 (car rescue worker), *fúwùjīqìrén yìngyòng jìshùyuán* 服务机器人应用技术员 (service robot application technician), *guǎnláng yùnwéiyuán* 管廊运维员 (tunnel operation and maintenance worker), *tànpáifàng guǎnlǐyuán* 碳排放管理员 (carbon emission administrator)" and "*tiáoyǐn shī* 调饮师 (beverage maker), *jiànzhú mùqiáng shèjìshī* 建筑幕墙设计师 (building curtain wall designer), *jiǔtǐ shèjìshī* 酒体设计师 (wine flavor designer)" and so on [6]. The professional characteristics of these new professions generally correspond to Dong Xiufang's [5] generalizations about these two quasi-affixes. For quasi-affixes with similar functions like these, a comparative study is necessary to analyze their semantic and functional features and differences, thus providing a detailed description of different quasi-affixes and enabling the rational naming of new things.

In addition to the series of suffixes that can form "a certain type of person", Mandarin Chinese also has a series of quasi-affixes used in naming new facilities and tools, such as *jī* 机, *qì* 器, *yí* 仪, *jì* 计, etc. Wang Wenyin [7] compared the highly productive *jī* 机, *qì* 器, *yí* 仪 and found that these three affixes have strong word-forming abilities. x *qì* 器 is commonly used for relatively small household devices or tools; X *jī* 机 is usually larger than X *qì* 器, mainly referring to electric devices; X *yí* 仪 usually denotes specialized instruments in fields such as biology, medicine, and beauty, and it is constructed with precision. Song Zuoyan [8] examined the quasi-affixes *jī* 机, *qì* 器, *jì* 计 from the perspective of word meanings and found that X *jì* 计 often has an NP structure, implying the verb "measure". This implied verb is provided by the quasi-affix *jì* 计; the X in X *jī* 机 and X *qì* 器 is often VP. When X is a noun phrase denoting a concrete object, the implied verb often involves manufacturing, provided by the NP. Kong Deran [9] compared the semantic features, word structure, productivity, and morphological patterns of the quasi-affixes *jī* 机, *qì* 器, *yí* 仪, *jì* 计 and concluded that X *jī* 机 emphasizes the mechanical nature of objects; X *qì* 器 emphasizes the utility of objects; X *yí* 仪 highlights the professionalism and precision of tools; X *jì* 计 often refers to tools that can measure with clear units. These descriptions generally correspond to the tools referred to by the vocabulary formed by these quasi-affixes, but they lack explanatory power for individual vocabulary items. For example, Kong Deran [9] mentioned that "*dǎhuǒjī* 打火机 (lighter)" seems to be an exception: words with similar functions and structures like "*mièhuǒqì* 灭火器 (fire extinguisher)" comply with the "utility" rule, but "*dǎhuǒjī* 打火机" does not emphasize its mechanical nature. Existing studies have also observed words like *diànfànguō* 电饭锅 (electric rice cooker), *línyùtóu* 淋浴头 (shower head) and *diànbīngxiāng* 电冰箱 (refrigerator), which could have been formed using the pattern of "function + *jī/qì* 机/器" but did not follow this rule [9]. This indicates that the selection of quasi-affixes in the word formation process is influenced by other factors.

Currently, the examination of quasi-affixes denoting tools mainly relies on synchronic comparative analysis. However, there are still challenges in fully summarizing the semantic nuances of these quasi-affixes and distinguishing their usage. We believe that understanding the meanings of these affixes not only requires horizontal comparison but also an exploration of the sources of these quasi-affixes' meanings. Studying semantic changes in vocabulary helps us better understand the current semantic characteristics of these quasi-affixes [10]. This approach can help us better determine word meanings and elucidate the differences between various quasi-affixes. Additionally, when constructing new words, it is crucial to examine and explain other factors that influence the selection of quasi-affixes. Research and discussions on these issues are not only vital for differentiating and explaining the semantics of these vocabulary items but also provide guidance for naming new things.

Therefore, this paper will first examine the performance of the quasi-affixes "机 *jī*, 器 *qì*, 仪 *yí*, 计 *jì*" denoting tools in ancient Chinese language materials. This examination will clarify the semantic features of tools referred to by different quasi-affixes and distinguish the differences between these quasi-affixes. Secondly, it will investigate tool names formed using other lexical patterns, elucidating factors beyond semantic information that influence the selection of quasi-affixes.

2 Semantic Features and Internal Differences of Tool-Meaning Quasi-Affixes

In modern Mandarin, *qì* 器 serves as a superordinate concept for the other three quasi-affixes. The *XiànDài HànYǔ CíDiǎn* (7th edition) includes the words "*jīqì* 机器 (machine)" and "*yíqì* 仪器 (apparatus)":

[*jīqì* 机器]: 由零部件组装成, 能运转、能变换热量或生产有用功的装置。如发电机、起重机、计算机等。

Yóu língbùjiàn zǔzhuāng chéng, néng yùnzhuǎn, néng biànhuàn rèliàng huò shēngchǎn yǒuyònggōng de zhuāngzhì. Rú fādiànjī, fādiànjī, jìsuànjī děng.

An assembly of components capable of operation, heat conversion, or useful work. Examples include generators, cranes, and computers.

[*yíqì* 仪器]: 用于实验、计量、观测、检验、绘图等的比较精密的器具或装置
。

Yòngyú shíyàn, jìliàng, guāncè, jiǎnyàn、huìtú děng de bǐjiào jīngmì de qìjù huò zhuāngzhì.
Precision instruments or devices used for experiments, measurements, observations, inspections, drawings, etc.

"*jìqì* 计器" is not listed in the dictionary but can be found in corpora, for instance:

(1) 这装置上有显示高度的计器, 预先把高度设定好, 则当被拉到这高度时, 铃声会响。

zhè zhuāngzhì shàng yǒu xiǎnshì gāodù de jìqì, yùxiān bǎ gāodù shèdìng hǎo, zé dāng bèi lā dào zhè gāodù shí, língshēng huì xiǎng.
This device has a height indicator; when the height is preset and reached, a bell will ring.

Kong Deran [9] mentioned that X *jì* 计 often refers to tools used for measuring things that can be precisely measured in specific units. In example (1), *jìqì* 计器 refers to a tool used for measuring an exact unit of height.

Consider *shèyǐng qìcái* 摄影器材 (photographic equipment). It refers to a collection of items including cameras, lenses, and related accessories. It also encompasses tools like enlargers, timers, color printers, etc., related to photographic activities. Here, *qìcái* 器材 becomes a collective term for various *jī* 机, *qì* 器 and tools, including various "machines" and materials like films, tripods, reflectors, etc.

Therefore, within these four quasi-affixes, *qì* 器 can form compound words with the other three, indicating a superordinate concept of "tools" or "apparatus". Meanwhile, *jī* 机, *qì* 器, *yí* 仪, and *jì* 计 specify the particular category and represent the main features of the tool, forming subcategories of tools. As a result, the four affixes do not belong to the same hierarchical concept.

However, in modern Mandarin vocabulary related to tools, these four affixes exhibit a parallel relationship, each forming specific tool names without hierarchical distinctions. *Dǎdànqì* 打蛋器 (egg beater) and *dǎdànjī* 打蛋机 (egg beater), *ànmóqì* 按摩器 (massager) and *ànmóyí* 按摩仪 (massager) are different tools, not a superordinate concept and its subordinate members. Therefore, we first observe the semantic changes of *qì* 器 to understand its semantic evolution. Then, we employ the same method to examine the semantics of the other quasi-affixes, defining their scope of use and reference objects, and differentiating the subtle semantic differences among these quasi-affixes.

2.1 Semantic Features of Tool-Meaning Quasi-Affixes

The interpretation of *qì* 器 in the *ShuōWénJiěZì*《说文解字》[11] is: "A utensil. Resembles the mouth of a utensil, guarded by a dog (皿也。象器之口, 犬所以守之)." Duan Yucai further explained: "Utensil. Classified under the 'utensil' category. Utensil specifically refers to eating utensils. *qì* 器 is a general term for all utensils. When *qì* 器 is mentioned with *mǐn* 皿, in prose, they are not distinguished. Classified under the 'wood' category. Something used for containment is called *qì* 器. If it does not contain anything, it is called *xiè* 械...(皿也。皿部曰。皿, 饭食之器用也。然则皿专谓食器。器乃凡器统称。器下云皿也者, 散文则不别也。木部曰。有所盛曰器。无所盛曰械……)." This shows that "*mǐn* 皿" specifically refers to tools used for eating, while "*qì* 器" actually encompasses all tools used for containing items. The term "*shèng* 盛" refers to the grains placed in utensils for sacrificial purposes: "*shǔ* and *jì* are offered in the vessel。From *mǐn* 皿 it forms the sound (黍稷在器中以祀者也。从皿成聲。)."

In ancient Chinese texts, the modifier for *qì* 器 often indicates its material or function:

(2) 流漆墨其上, 输之于宫, 以为食器……舜禅天下而传之于禹, 禹作为祭器。

Líu qī mò qí shàng, shū zhī yú gōng, yǐ wéi shíqì… Shùn shàn tiānxià ér chuán zhī yú yǔ, yǔ zuò wéi jìqì.

Ink flows on lacquerware, delivered to the palace, used as tableware… After Emperor Shun ruled the world, he passed it on to Yu, who transformed it into sacrificial vessels.

(3) 诸贵人舍所有金器银器内外庄严具若在箱箧中。

Zhū guìrén shě suǒyǒu jīnqì yínqì nèiwài zhuāngyán jù ruò zài xiāngqiè zhōng.

All the noblewomen abandoned all their gold and silver utensils, both inside and outside, making the interior and exterior as splendid as if stored in boxes and chests.

In these instances, *qì* 器 does not necessarily refer to objective tools. The term is also used in abstract contexts:

(4) 国之利器不可以示人。

Guó zhī lìqì bù kěyǐ shì rén.

The country's political tactics should not be shown to others.

(5) 管仲者, 贤人也, 天下之大器也。

Guǎn Zhòng zhě, xián rén yě, tiānxià zhī dàqì yě.

Guǎn Zhòng was a wise man, a great talent in the world.

On the other hand, the meaning of *jī* 机 differs from *qì* 器. The interpretation of *jī* 机 in *ShuōWénJiěZì*《说文解字》emphasizes its connection with *fā* 发, meaning "shoot". It is evident that *jī* 机 emphasizes its relationship with "shoot", signifying the mechanisms used for shooting arrows or for weaving, highlighting the concept of mechanism. In early texts, *jī* 机 mainly referred to the critical elements of things:

(6) 言行, 君子之枢机。枢机之发, 荣辱之主也。

Yánxíng, jūnzǐ zhī shūjī. Shūjī zhī fā, róngrǔ zhī zhǔ yě.

Words and actions are the pivot of a gentleman. The pivot's movement determines honor and disgrace.

(7) 若皋之所观, 天机也。

Ruò Gāo zhī suǒ guān, tiānjī yě.

What Gao observes is the heavenly mechanism

In Qing dynasty literature, compounds with *jī* 机 continued to emphasize the concept of "mechanism":

(8) 被门槛绊足, 跪跌以致振动手指, 碰落火机, 凑燃火门药线, 枪内药砂发出, 中伤刘氏。

Bèi ménkǎn bàn zú, guì diē yǐ zhì zhèndòng shǒuzhǐ, pèng luò huǒjī, còu rán huǒ mén yào xiàn, qiāng nèi yào shā fā chū, zhòng shāng Liúshì.

Tripped over the doorstep, fell to the knees, causing fingers to shake, accidentally touched the lighter, igniting the fuse on the door, injuring LiuShi.

By examining the collocations and compound words involving *qì* 器 and *jī* 机 in ancient Chinese texts, we can observe their differences. *qì* 器 forms words like "*lìqì* 利

器 (edge tool)" or "*shíqì* 食器 (tableware)", emphasizing the overall tool's function. "机," on the other hand, forms words like "*huǒjī* 火机 (lighter)" or "*nǔjī* 弩机 (crossbow mechanism)", indicating the emphasis on mechanism. Unlike *qì* 器, *jī* 机 rarely directly represents specific machines; instead, it emphasizes the concept of mechanism.

Compared to X *jī* 机 and X *qì* 器, X *yí* 仪 and X *jì* 计 seem to have more justifiable semantic and lexical grounds. X *jì* 计 did not specifically denote concrete tools in ancient Chinese but gradually found applications in modern Chinese. According to Kong Deran [9], tools named with X *jì* 计 are often used to measure things that can be precisely quantified. This aligns with the research findings of Song Zuoyan [12], who discovered that the X in X *jì* 计 often represents NP and implies the verb "measure". This implicit verb is provided by the quasi-affix *jì* 计.

Jì 计 is also a verb, and its interpretation in *ShuōWénJiěZi*《说文解字》 is addition and calculation (會也。筭也。) Therefore, tools named with X *jì* 计 are closely related to quantity and calculation. Due to their role in measuring precise units, tools named with X *jì* 计 are relatively limited in number. According to Kong Deran's survey [9], X *jì* 计 appeared only 11 times in an 80,000-word lexicon, significantly fewer than X *jī* 机 (136 occurrences) and X *qì* 器 (90 occurrences). Under semantic constraints, X *jì* 计 has relatively low productivity in terms of quantity.

Compared to X *jì* 计, X *yí* 仪 has been used to refer to specific tools in ancient Chinese, forming polysyllabic compounds. For instance:

(9) 张平子既作铜浑天仪。

   Zhāng Píngzi jì zuò tóng húntiānyí.
   Zhang Pingzi made a bronze armillary sphere.

(10) 由是迁太史令衡作地动仪。

   Following this, Tai Shi Ling Heng created the seismometer…

   Yóushì qiān tàishǐlìng Héng zuò dìdòngyí.

"*Húntiānyí* 浑天仪 (armillary sphere)" was used to observe celestial phenomena, while "*dìdòngyí* 地动仪 (seismometer)" was used to detect earthquakes, directions. These X *yí* 仪 tools were designed to visualize complex and hard-to-observe information systematically, indicating a relatively sophisticated and intricate structure to ensure accurate observations.

2.2   The Semantic Difference Between "X *jī* 机" and "X *qì* 器"

As we've mentioned above, Wang Wenyin [7] pointed out that the term X *qì* 器 is commonly used for smaller daily devices or tools, whereas X *jī* 机 usually refers to larger devices, primarily powered by electricity. Kong Deran [9] suggested that X *jī* 机 emphasizes the mechanical nature of an object, while X *qì* 器 emphasizes its utilitarian function. This aligns with our observations to some extent, but there are also differences. According to Wang Wenyin [7], X *jī* 机 typically refers to larger devices, possibly because X *jī* 机 often contains various mechanisms and is structurally more complex than X *qì* 器. X *jī* 机 usually involves energy activation, such as electrical or thermal energy, to power its mechanisms, resulting in stronger transmission and mechanical characteristics. On the other hand, X *qì* 器 originates from tools used for carrying or storing items and generally lacks complex mechanical parts. As a result, X *qì* 器 tends to be smaller and doesn't require additional energy for transmission.

Analyzing the examples of "*xiāopíjī* 削皮机 (electric peeler)" and "*xiāopíqì* 削皮器 (manual peeler)", the former refers to an electric device capable of automatically peeling fruits or vegetables, while the latter is a manual tool used for peeling, which doesn't contain complex mechanisms inside. Similar distinctions can be observed with "*dǎdànjī* 打蛋机 (electric egg beater)" and "*dǎdànqì* 打蛋器 (manual egg beater)". The former is an electric tool, whereas the latter is operated manually. These distinctions align with the semantic extensions of X *jī* 机 and X *qì* 器. The term "*jī* 机" emphasizes the presence of "mechanisms" and often involves electrical components, while "*qì* 器" mainly conveys the general meaning of "tool" without complex internal mechanisms.

We can also examine the comparison between "*dǎhuǒjī* 打火机 (lighter)" and "*mièhuǒqì* 灭火器 (fire extinguisher)" from this perspective mentioned by Kong Deran [9]. In fact, we cannot assume that the components before the quasi-affix have opposite meanings just because there are also "*dǎhuǒqì* 打火器" and "*mièhuǒjī* 灭火机" as tools in daily life. To illustrate the commonalities and differences in the characteristics of these tools, it is more appropriate to compare corresponding X *jī* 机 and X *qì* 器. The "*dǎhuǒqì* 打火器" is actually a component inside the "*dǎhuǒjī* 打火机" responsible for generating sparks and igniting the gas sprayed out, which complements the function of "*huǒjī* 火机" described in example (8). The "*dǎhuǒjī* 打火机" is a familiar ignition tool that activates the internal "*dǎhuǒqì* 打火器" by pressing the button during use to complete the ignition work. In fact, the difference between these two still conforms to the characteristics summarized in the previous text. *jī* 机 emphasizes the existence of mechanism in the tool, while *qì* 器 is a more fundamental tool that focuses on the internal structure and function of the lighter.

From the definition of "*dǎhuǒjī* 打火机" in the *XiànDài HànYǔ CíDiǎn* (7th edition), we can also see the semantic difference between *jī* 机 and *qì* 器 as quasi-affixes:

[*dǎhuǒjī* 打火机]: 一种小巧的取火器, 主要用于点燃香烟等。

Yīzhǒng xiǎoqiǎo de qǔhuǒqì, zhǔyào yòngyú diǎnrán xiāngyān děng.

A small ignition device, mainly used for lighting cigarettes, etc.

According to the definition, *dǎhuǒjī* 打火机 is actually a type of ignition device. X *qì* 器 here represents the superordinate concept, which is the general term for all tools used for ignition. X *jī* 机 refers to specific members within this category.

There is a similar difference between "*mièhuǒjī* 灭火机" and "*mièhuǒqì* 灭火器". *mièhuǒqì* 灭火器 is a common firefighting tool. The steel barrel of the fire extinguisher is filled with chemicals that can be used to extinguish fires. It extinguishes fires by manually pulling down the safety pin and pressing the switch to spray gas. Compared to the *mièhuǒqì* 灭火器, the *mièhuǒjī* 灭火机 is often larger in size and higher in power. It is frequently used in large-scale fires such as forests and factories. *mièhuǒjī* 灭火机 can be backpack-mounted or vehicle-mounted and are more professional firefighting equipment. During use, they often require energy supply through electricity or fuel to generate tremendous airflow for firefighting. In comparison to the *mièhuǒqì* 灭火器, they are not only larger in size but also involve energy conversion through internal mechanisms. Therefore, the *mièhuǒjī* 灭火机 actually emphasizes the mechanical nature of the tool, with internal mechanisms and energy conversion involved. Based on the above comparison, the differences between these X *jī* 机 and X *qì* 器 mainly lie in the complexity of their internal structures, the presence of mechanisms, and whether they involve energy conversion. Compared to X *jī* 机, the construction of X *qì* 器 is relatively simple, with smaller size and little involvement in energy conversion.

There are also differences in the hierarchical relationships between some X *jī* 机 and X *qì* 器. For example, "*jiànshēnqì* 健身器 (fitness equipment)" refers to various fitness equipment collectively, and there is no corresponding "*jiànshēnjī* 健身机". In contrast, specific fitness equipment such as "*pǎobùjī* 跑步机 (treadmills), *tuǒyuánjī* 椭圆机 (elliptical machines)" often require electricity, fitting the word formation pattern of X *jī* 机.

(11) 不仅健身意识的强的南方人购买健身器的很多, 在北方, 在沿海城市, 甚至在一些中小城市和乡村, 健身器也很多人所认识和喜爱。

Bùjǐn jiànshēn yìshi de qiáng de nánfāng rén gòumǎi jiànshēnqì de hěnduō, zài běifāng, zài yánhǎi chéngshì, shènzhì zài yīxiē zhōngxiǎo chéngshì hé xiāngcūn, jiànshēn qì yě hěnduō rén suǒ rènshi hé xǐ'ài.

Not only do people in the south, where fitness awareness is strong, buy a lot of fitness equipment, but also in the north, in coastal cities, and even in some small and medium-sized cities and villages, many people recognize and love fitness equipment.

(12) 这两个泳池虽然长度只有4米, 但其原理就像跑步机一样, 有可调节的逆向水流阻挡游泳的人, 让他们永远游不到对岸。

Zhè liǎng gè yǒngchí suīrán chángdù zhǐyǒu 4 mǐ, dàn qí yuánlǐ jiù xiàng pǎobùjī yīyàng, yǒu kětiáojié de nìxiàng shuǐliú zǔdǎng yóuyǒng de rén, ràng tāmen yǒngyuǎn yóu bù dào duì'àn.

Although these two pools are only 4 m long, their principle is similar to that of a treadmill, with adjustable reverse water flow to prevent swimmers from reaching the other side.

This shows that when referring to superordinate concepts, we often use the word formation pattern of X *qì* 器. The choice of specific quasi-affixes depends on the specific features of the items, and the corresponding quasi-affixes are selected accordingly.

Of course, not all X *qì* 器 and X *jī* 机 fit this word formation rationale. Sometimes we need to explain the consistency of their word formation rationale through comparisons with related words. "*Jiāshīqì* 加湿器 (Humidifier)" is a commonly used device in households nowadays. It needs electricity and further utilizes ultrasound or high temperature to generate water vapor, playing a corresponding humidification role. From the working principle of the *jiāshīqì* 加湿器, it actually conforms more to the word formation rationale of X *jī* 机, involving mechanism and energy conversion. However, the corresponding "*Jiāshījī* 加湿机" is a large humidifying equipment used in industrial workshops, agricultural production, and fresh-keeping of fruits and vegetables. Compared to the *jiāshīqì* 加湿器, it is larger in size, higher in power, and more complex in internal structure, fitting the characteristics of X *jī* 机. These two humidifying tools have similarities and differences. To distinguish the names of these two devices, they are differentiated based on the differences in their forms and structures. The household device is smaller and relatively simple in structure, hence being named as X *qì* 器.

There are also some device names for which we find it difficult to identify their word formation rationale. For example, as mentioned earlier, a *pǎobùjī* 跑步机 (treadmills) refers to a motorized running fitness equipment that requires electricity to operate. In contrast, the corresponding *pǎobùqì* 跑步器 as described in example (13) does not require electricity. The *pǎobùqì* 跑步器 is often composed of multiple parallel rollers. Exercisers run on the rollers, maintaining their exercise on the *pǎobùqì* 跑步器 by the rollers' rotation. However, in daily language use, we do not strictly adhere to such semantic differences. Sometimes, as in example (14), we use *pǎobùqì* 跑步器 to refer to motorized fitness equipment commonly found in gyms and homes. Of course, in terms of usage frequency and scope, *pǎobùjī* 跑步机 mostly refers to electric fitness equipment. However, it cannot be denied that there are still some ambiguous areas between X *jī* 机 and X *qì* 器.

(13) 广场的左侧，健骑机、扭腰器、吊环、单杠、跑步器等健身器材，满满地摆放了三大排。一大早，每个器材上都已有了健身者。

> *Guǎngchǎng de zuǒcè, jiànqímǎchē, niǔyāoqì, diàohuán, dāngàn, pǎobùqì děng jiànshēn qìcái, mǎnmǎn de bǎifàng le sān dà pái. Yī dàzǎo, měi ge qìcái shàng dū yǐ yǒule jiànshēnzhě.*

On the left side of the square, there are three rows of fitness equipment, including spinning bikes, waist twisters, gymnastics rings, parallel bars, and treadmills. Early in the morning, each piece of equipment already had fitness enthusiasts on it.

(14) 这次有奖征名活动展示出瑞典、美国、德国等生产的名牌健身车、综合训练器材、电子跑步器等设备，已在我国16个城市为健身运动爱好者服务。

> *Zhècì yǒu jiǎng zhēng míng huódòng zhǎnshì chū Ruìdiǎn, Měiguó, Déguó děng shēngchǎn de míngpái jiànshēn chē, zōnghé xùnliàn qìcái, diànzǐ pǎobùqì děng shèbèi, yǐ zài wǒguó 16 gè chéngshì wèi jiànshēn yùndòng àihàozhě fúwù.*

This prize-naming event showcased branded fitness bikes, comprehensive training equipment, electronic treadmills, and other equipment produced in Sweden, the United States, Germany, and other countries, serving fitness enthusiasts in 16 cities in our country.

Similar tool names also include *Jiǎobànjī* 搅拌机 (mixer) and *Jiǎobànqì* 搅拌器 (stirrer). It is actually difficult to determine the difference between the tools referred to by these two names. Sometimes on shopping websites, the same product is listed under both names simultaneously to facilitate buyers' searches. In this pair of vocabulary, the semantic difference between X *jī* 机 and X *qì* 器 has become increasingly indistinguishable.

The emergence of this phenomenon is partly related to changes in the objective world. With the advancement of technology, more and more new tools and equipment often have complex internal structures, making it difficult for us to discern how these devices operate internally. Therefore, in naming these devices, the use of "X" is employed to indicate the specific function of the equipment. As for whether they should be classified as "*jī* 机" or "*qì* 器", further differentiation is often not made, leading to the gradual blurring of the relationship between the two. On the other hand, the ambiguity between X *jī* 机 and X *qì* 器 is also related to the widespread use of "*jīqì* 机器 (machine)" as a disyllabic compound word. The term "*jīqì* 机器" as a compound word was first used in novels during the Qing

Dynasty, often referring to mechanical tools used in factories to produce products or the power core of transportation vehicles:

(15) 把书局里头几个朋友的执事, 都分派得清清楚楚: 管批发的管批发, 管机器的 管机器, 管出入的管出入。

> *Bǎ shūjú lǐtou jǐ gè péngyǒu de zhíshì, dōu fēnpài dé qīngqīngchu chu: Guǎn pīfā de guǎn pīfā, guǎn jīqì de guǎn jīqì, guǎn chūrù de guǎn chūrù.*

The duties of several friends in the bookstore were clearly assigned: those in charge of wholesale managed wholesale, those handling machines managed machines, and those responsible for entries managed entries.

(16) 大车听了号铃, 便把机器开足, 那船便飞也似的向上水驶去。

> *Dàchē tīngle hào líng, biàn bǎ jīqì kāi zú, nà chuán biàn fēi yě shì de xiàng shàng shuǐ shǐ qù.*

When the large vehicle heard the bell, it accelerated the machine, and the ship flew up like it was going upstream.

These tools are often referred to as X *jī* 机 today, such as *fādòngjī* 发动机 (engines) and *yìnshuājī* 印刷机 (printing machines). The definition of *jīqì* 机器 in the *XiànDài HànYǔ CíDiǎn* (7th edition) mentioned earlier is actually an explanation of X *jī* 机, involving energy conversion and complex mechanisms. In reality, X *jī* 机 and X *qì* 器 are in a modifier-head relationship. However, due to the widespread use of this disyllabic compound word, the relationship between *jī* 机 and *qì* 器 has gradually become blurred, and people no longer pay attention to the differences between the two. Therefore, in language usage, the situation arises where X *jī* 机 and X *qì* 器 are used interchangeably, and the word formation rationale cannot be distinguished.

2.3 Semantic Features of "X *yí* 仪"

The gradual spread of X *yí* 仪 is closely related to the emergence of new types of products nowadays. Wang Wenyin [7] found that X *yí* 仪 are usually professional instruments used in fields such as biology, medicine, and beauty. Studies suggest that "X instruments" often exhibit characteristics of precision and professionalism [7, 9].

X *yí* 仪 seems to be able to demonstrate precision. For example, *wēndùjì* 温度 计(thermometer) and *cèwēnyí* 测温仪 (temperature measuring instrument). Both are used to measure the temperature of objects or the environment. *wēndùjì* 温度计 come into various types, including traditional mercury thermometers, pressure thermometers, optical high-temperature thermometers, and liquid crystal thermometers, etc., *cèwēnyí* 测温仪 mainly refer to infrared thermometers, which use infrared thermal imaging to sense the surface temperature of objects. In fact, *cèwēnyí* 测温仪 is a type of *wēndùjì* 温度计.

However, we believe that the most prominent feature of X *yí* 仪 is "imaging", or presenting data, images, or signals through these instruments. To accurately present information, X *yí* 仪 often require precision and professionalism. As mentioned earlier (9, 10), instruments like armillary sphere and seismometer visualize complex and subtle information such as celestial movements and earthquake directions. Naturally, such X *yí* 仪 demand precision and professionalism. Modern X *yí* 仪 such as *cèwēnyí* 测温 仪 (temperature measuring instruments), *cèjùyí* 测距仪 (rangefinders), *fēnzǐguāngpǔyí*

分子光谱仪(molecular spectrometers), *yǎndòngyí* 眼动仪 (eye trackers), *yǔtúyí* 语图仪 (speech analyzers), *diànyǒngyí* 电泳仪 (electrophoresis instruments), *dǎohángyí* 导航仪 (navigators), etc., also visualize information that is difficult to capture manually. Other X *yí* 仪 such as *tóuyǐngyí* 投影仪 (projectors), *sǎomiáoyí* 扫描仪 (scanners), *dìqiúyí* 地球仪 (globes) directly present visual information.

Wang Wenyin [7] observed that X *yí* 仪 are usually professional instruments used in fields such as biology, medicine, and beauty, such as *měiróngyí* 美容仪 (beauty instruments), *tuōmáoyí* 脱毛仪 (hair removal instruments), *ànmóyí* 按摩仪 (massage instruments), etc. These X *yí* 仪 have further departed from the original meaning of visualizing information and have retained the sense of precision and professionalis derived from the early X *yí* 仪. In fact, terms like *měiróngjī* 美容机, *tuōmáojī* 脱毛机, *ànmójī* 按摩机 are also used in language, but they have not competed with the term X *yí* 仪. This indicates that in pragmatics, X *yí* 仪 give people a sense of high-end, scientific, and professional feeling, making it more suitable for use on the human body. In the corpus, it can be found that *tuōmáojī* 脱毛机 is not used for removing body hair but rather for processing feathers of poultry:

(17) 店主接过鸡, 利索地在鸡脖子上抹了一刀, 随即把鸡扔进了脱毛机。

　　　Diànzhǔ jiēguò jī, lìsuǒ de zài jībózi shàng mǒ le yī dāo, suíjí bǎ jī rēng jìn le tuōmáojī.

　　　The shop owner took the chicken, skillfully made a cut on its neck, and then threw the chicken into the feather removal machine.

(18) 这时, 店主关掉了脱毛机, 把10多只鸡一一分发给等候的顾客, 随即又将另外一批鸡放了进去。

　　　Zhèshí, diànzhǔ guāndiào le tuōmáojī, bǎ 10 duō zhī jī yī yī fēnfā gěi děnghòu de gùkè, suíjí yòu jiāng lìngwài yī pī jī fàng le jìnqù.

At this point, the shop owner turned off the feather removal machine, distributed more than ten chickens to the waiting customers one by one, and then put another batch of chickens inside.

This shows that between X *yí* 仪 and X *jī* 机 which have same "X", the X *yí* 仪 are often more sophisticated, and have a closer relationship with the human body.

3 Other Morphological Patterns in Tool Naming

Kong Deran [9] pointed out that, in addition to the word formation pattern of "function + *jī*/ *qì* 机/器" mentioned above, there are also some words in Chinese that could have used this pattern but chose other morphological patterns for construction. For example, words like *diànfànguō* 电饭锅 (electric rice cooker), *línyùtóu* 淋浴头 (shower head) and *diànbīngxiāng* 电冰箱 (refrigerator) could have been named as *chuīfànqì* 炊饭器 (rice cooking machine), *línyùqì* 淋浴器 (shower machine), and *bǎoxiānqì* 保鲜器 (fresh-keeping machine), but they adopted different naming patterns.

We believe the reason for using other morphological patterns lies in the fact that X *qì* 器 cannot clearly specify these tools, making it difficult to distinguish them from similar tools. As analyzed earlier regarding X *qì* 器, the tools referred to by X *qì* 器 often have relatively simple internal structures and are commonly used to refer to higher-level concepts. Therefore, if we name these tools as "*chuīfànqì* 炊饭器, línyùqì 淋浴器, and *bǎoxiānqì* 保鲜器", it would lead to ambiguity about the primary purpose of the tools and confusion with other functionally similar tools. *Chuīfànqì* 炊饭器 seems to refer to a machine that can make rice, with *diànfànguō* 电饭锅 being just one type. Besides, there are larger tools like *zhēngfànjī* 蒸饭机 (steaming rice machine), *zhēngfànguì* 蒸饭柜 (steaming rice cabinet), and *zhǔfànjī* 煮饭机 (boiling rice machine), all of which can be used to make rice and fall under the category of *chuīfànqì* 炊饭器. Using this name to refer to *diànfànguō* 电饭锅 would lead to unclear semantics. X *qì* 器 tends to express superordinate concepts and does not specifically refer to the sub-tools such as *diànfànguō* 电饭锅.

The difference between *línyùqì* 淋浴器 (shower machine) and *línyùtóu* 淋浴头 (shower head) lies in the whole and part relationship. *línyùqì* 淋浴器 often refers to shower facilities in places like schools and public baths, such as *shuākǎlínyùqì* 刷卡淋浴器 (card-swiping shower machine), *diànrèlínyùqì* 电热淋浴器 (electric heated shower machine), *gǎnyìnglínyùqì* 感应淋浴器 (sensor shower machine), etc. The shower machine includes components like card-swiping device, pipes, valves, and the shower head. Showering is the function of this compound entity *línyùqì* 淋浴器, and *línyùtóu* 淋浴头 is just a part of it responsible for water outflow. Therefore, the name of the part cannot be the same as that of the whole.

The issue with using *bǎoxiānqì* 保鲜器 (fresh-keeping machine) to replace *diànbīngxiāng* 电冰箱 (refrigerator) lies in the fact that the functionality of *bǎoxiānqì* 保鲜器 cannot fully cover that of *diànbīngxiāng* 电冰箱. *bǎoxiānqì* 保鲜器 refers to tools that can maintain the quality of perishable items such as fruits, vegetables, and wine. These tools are frequently used in the catering and food sales industry, are relatively large-scale, and have a single function. This function aligns with the function of the refrigeration compartment in a modern refrigerator. However, a refrigerator also has a freezer compartment, which serves more than just keeping items fresh; it is used for freezing liquids, chilling ingredients, etc. The word formation pattern of X *qì* 器 confines the semantic expression of *diànbīngxiāng* 电冰箱.

From the comparison of these three pairs of words, we can see that when replacing tools named with the "function + *jī/ qì* 机/器" pattern with X *qì* 器, various issues arise: either the concepts are not at the same level, forming a superior-subordinate or whole-part relationship, or the tool's full functionality cannot be entirely represented. These situations lead to misunderstandings about the tool's function and characteristics when people hear the name X *qì* 器. In such cases, incorporating other features based on functionality and utilizing form or appearance characteristics for naming can highlight the tool's distinct features and serve the purpose of differentiation.

These naming conventions are also influenced by the names of other items and their related relationships. In fact, "X *xiāng* 箱 (box), X *guō* 锅 (pot), and X *tóu* 头 (head)" can be regarded as limited generative quasi-affixes. Some X *xiāng* 箱 is named based on materials, such as "*mùxiāng* 木箱 (wooden box), *zhǐxiāng* 纸箱 (paper box), *tiěxiāng* 铁箱 (iron box)", while others are named based on function, like "*shuǐxiāng* 水箱 (water tank), *fēngxiāng* 风箱 (wind box), *shōunàxiāng* 收纳箱 (storage box), *chǔwùxiāng* 储物箱 (storage box)." The *bīngxiāng* 冰箱 and *shuǐxiāng* 水箱, *fēngxiāng* 风箱 and other X *xiāng* 箱 indicating functionality use the same naming pattern. "X *jī/ qì* 机/器" often refers to a whole tool. For tools like "*shuǐlóngtóu* 水龙头 (faucet), *línyùtóu* 淋浴头 (shower head), *pēntóu* 喷头 (shower nozzle)", they cannot function independently; they require larger and complete machines to carry out the corresponding functions such as water flow, showering, etc. Therefore, X *jī/ qì* 机/器 cannot specify the parts within the whole tool. In such cases, other characteristics need to be found to describe the components of the tool. Thus, additional features like form are utilized for tool naming. Therefore, when X *jī/qì* 机/器 cannot differentiate tools with similar functions or tools with whole-part relationships, other quasi-affixes are employed for naming, serving the purpose of differentiation.

4 Conclusion

This article analyzes and discusses the semantic features of the four affixes in ancient Chinese, namely *jī* 机, *qì* 器, *yí* 仪, *jì* 计. It was found that compared to X *qì* 器 the tools referred to by X *jī* 机 often have more complex internal structures, higher power, and involve energy conversion. X *qì* 器, on the other hand, is commonly used to refer to superordinate concepts, expressing the overall meaning of "tools", with relatively simpler internal structures compared to X *jī* 机. X *jì* 计, due to the verb meaning of *jì* 计, refers to tools with the meaning of measuring quantities, forming a relatively limited range of tool names.

The most prominent feature of X *yí* 仪 is "imaging", often requiring precision and accuracy. Therefore, it gives people a more high-end, scientific, and professional feeling. Newly emerging tools in fields such as biology, medicine, and beauty also use this meaning, naming them as X *yí* 仪.

In addition, the article discusses some tools in Chinese that are named using other patterns. For these tools, using the "function + *jī/qì* 机/器" pattern for naming would lead to unclear semantic expressions. This is because sometimes there is more than one tool with a specific function; sometimes a tool may have more than one function, or it might only be a component of a tool with a specific function. In such cases, other features need to be identified for description, and different naming patterns are used to distinguish them from other related tools. Therefore, other affixes are adopted to name tools.

In summary, the semantic analysis of affixes requires not only the analysis of synchronic linguistic facts but also the use of diachronic data to find the sources of affix meaning features. Regarding different naming strategies, a comparative approach is necessary to analyze the reasons for choosing different affixes for naming. This article mainly focuses on the semantic features of these affixes. Further research on the semantics and derivational abilities of these affixes requires a combination of statistical analysis and corpus inspection.

References

1. Li, W.: A study of martinet's functional linguistics. Doctor's degree thesis of Nanjing University (2015). (in Chinese)
2. Lv, S.-X.: The Issues in Chinese Grammar Analysis. The Commercial Press, Beijing (1979). (in Chinese)
3. Zhu, Y.-J.: Study on the affixation characteristics and its classifications of modern Chinese. Chin. Lang. Learn. **2**, 24–28 (2001). (in Chinese)
4. Zeng, L.-Y.: A quantitative and qualitative study on the semi-affixes of modern Chinese. Chin. Teach. World **4**, 75–87+3 (2008). (in Chinese)
5. Dong, X.-F.: Chinese Lexicon and Morphology. Peking University Press, Beijing (2004). (in Chinese)
6. Revision Working Committee of Occupational Classification Code: Occupational Classification Code of the People's Republic of China (2021). China Human Resources & Society Publishing Group, Beijing (2022). (in Chinese)
7. Wang, W.-Y.: The formation of appliance compound words. Essays Linguist. **2**, 202–225 (2017). (in Chinese)
8. Song, Z.-Y.: On the affixoid which can trigger off event coercion. Chin. Teach. World **24**(04), 446–458 (2010). (in Chinese)
9. Kong, D.-R.: The comparison and lexical pattern of "X Jī" "X Qì" "X Yí" and "X Jì". In: The Proceedings of the 2018 Chinese as a Foreign Language Doctoral Student Forum and the 11th Academic Forum for Graduate Students of Teaching Chinese as a Foreign Language (2018). (in Chinese)
10. Liu, M.-C., Liang, Y.-Y., Wan, Y.-W.: Novel lexical semantic change and interactivization. In: Su, Q., Xu, G., Yang, X.-Y. (eds.) Chinese Lexical Semantics. CLSW 2022. LNCS (LNAI), vol. 13495, pp.125–138. Springer, Cham (2023). https://doi.org/10.1007/978-3-031-28953-8_11
11. Duan, Y.-C.: The Annotations to the Shuowen Jiezi. ZhongHua Book Company, Beijing (2013). (in Chinese)
12. Song, Z.-Y.: Construction coercion in modifier-head compound nouns. Chin. Teach. World **28**(04), 508–518 (2014). (in Chinese)

A Study of Adding Psychological Feeling into the Model of Synaesthesia at the Morpheme Level in Modern Chinese

Han Wen[1] and Shuwen Zheng[2(⊠)]

[1] Zhejiang International Studies University, No. 299 Liuhe Road, Xihu District, Hangzhou 310023, China
[2] Beijing Language and Culture University, No. 15 Xueyuan Road, Haidian District, Beijing 100083, China
zirenesw@126.com

Abstract. The synaesthetic mapping pattern of modern Chinese lexicon have long been a focal point in both national and international linguistic studies. However, issues at the morpheme level are scarce, and there is rarely incorporating psychological sensations into mapping models. This paper meticulously analyzes 279 synaesthetic cases, derived from 190 adjectival sensory words in the *Modern Chinese Dictionary (7th Edition)*. Through this analysis, 27 synaesthesia patterns are identified. It is discovered that the phenomenon of synaesthesia in modern Chinese significantly differs at the morpheme level and lexicon level. Notably, psychological feeling in Chinese synaesthesia is frequently mapped as destination, becoming a distinctive feature of these metaphors. This finding provides new perspectives and methods for research in lexicology, etymology, and machine translation. Studying sensory metaphors within words in the Chinese lexicon and comparing them with those within phrases revealed the characteristics of sensory word formation in modern Chinese, offering fresh insights and examples for research in etymology and semantic evolution.

Keywords: Synaesthesia · Morpheme · Mapping Patterns · Psychological Feeling

1 Introduction

Metaphor has been a core focus in the field of lexical semantics both nationally and internationally. Traditionally perceived as a rhetorical device, the study of metaphor has expanded to cognition, semantics, grammar, and various other dimensions following the proposition of "the universality of metaphor" and "the theory of conceptual metaphor" by Lakoff and Johnson [1]. Lakoff and Turner proposed that one of the central claims of the theory of conceptual metaphor is that there is no essentially different phenomenon between metaphors in poetry and those in everyday language, which means that their cognitive mechanisms are essentially the same [2]. But poetry can extend and recombine these mechanisms in ways that go beyond the norm. Within the realm of metaphor

© The Author(s), under exclusive license to Springer Nature Singapore Pte Ltd. 2024
M. Dong et al. (Eds.): CLSW 2023, LNAI 14514, pp. 400–414, 2024.
https://doi.org/10.1007/978-981-97-0583-2_31

research, the topic of "synaesthesia" has gained considerable attention in recent years. Ullmann proposed that synaesthesia refers to the phenomenon where one sensation in language can be described through another sensation [3]. Scholars have attempted to construct related models to simulate synaesthesia mappings in different languages, aiming to establish universal projection models. However, due to the nationality of languages and the existence of differences in intelligibility between languages, scholars, like Ullmann; Williams; Yu, N.; Wang, S.; Zhao, Q., and Huang, C.-R., have proposed numerous views and opinions on the differences in synaesthesia phenomena across different languages based on their respective corpora [3–7].

Based on the theory of conceptual metaphor, this paper studies an one-of-a-kind metaphor, synaesthetic metaphor. Our data is drawn from *Modern Chinese Dictionary (7th Edition)*. The paper delineates the unique characteristics of synaesthesia in the Chinese, distinct from other languages. Additionally, we attempts to propose a particular mapping model specific to synaesthesia in Chinese. In Sect. 2, we review previous studies on synaesthesia that show relevance to the present study, and argue some questions and shortages from them. In Sect. 3 and Sect. 4, we look closely at the Chinese data to show the differences of synaesthesia between the morpheme level and the lexical level in modern Chinese, and the importance of psychological feeling at the level of morpheme in Chinese synaesthesia. Section 5 is the conclusion.

2 Research Questions and Hypotheses

The mapping patterns of synaesthetic metaphor have been a central issue of research. Ullmann, using English, French, and Hungarian poetry as data, was the first to discuss the "panchronistic" nature of synaesthetic transfers and identified three tendencies. The first tendency is called as "hierarchical distribution", which is that synaesthesia tend to transfer from the "lower" to the "higher" sensory modes(touch → taste → smell → sound → sight). Secondly, touch, as the lowest level of sensation, serves as the predominant source of transfers. Thirdly, sound is the predominant destination of transfers [3]. Subsequently, Williams combining thalposis with touch and breaking sight into two subcategories, dimension and color, summarized the pattern of English synaesthetic metaphor based on over 100 adjectival sensory words [4]. In this linear-hierarchical model, only color and sound are mutually mapped, while the others exhibit unidirectional mapping, aligning with Ullmann [3] accessibility ordering. Yu examined 150 sensory adjectives in Chinese and found that the general patterns of synaesthesia mapping in Chinese align with Williams [4]. The main difference is that in Chinese, sound cannot be mutually mapped with color, which means that only the projection of color onto sound exists. There does not exhibit bidirectional mapping pattern in Chinese [5]. Wang, S. argued that in synaesthetic metaphor, sensory characteristics typically move from lower sensory forms to higher sensory forms, and the mapping direction is irreversible. This situation shows unidirectionality in Chinese synaesthesia [6]. Yu [8], from Chinese literary data, acknowledged first two tendencies in Ullmann [3] and Williams [4]. However, he disagreed with the third tendency in Ullmann [3]. Yu pointed out that although Chinese dimensional words systematically move not only to color and sound but also to taste and smell, the general tendencies in Chinese synaesthetic metaphors are consistent with the patterns observed in English and other languages [8]. Yet, Strik Lievers, based on corpus data, found the bidirectionality of synaesthetic metaphor in English and Italian [9]. Subsequently, based on Chinese corpus, Zhao, Q., and Huang, C.-R. constructed a modern Chinese synaesthesia mapping model. Its main features are recognizing bidirectionality in Chinese synaesthetic metaphor mapping, and revealing various mapping patterns between sensations, such as touch to smell and sight to smell [7] (Fig. 1).

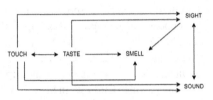

Fig. 1. Figure showing model of Chinese syneasthesia (Zhao, Q. and Huang, C.-R. 2018)

Zhao, Q., Huang, C.-R., Ahrens, K., extracted the Mandarin sensory adjectives from two comprehensive electronic Chinese lexical thesauri, HIT-CIR Tongyici Cilin (Extended) and HowNet, and pointed out the directionalities of linguistic synaesthesia in Mandarin: unidirectionality, biased-directionality, and bidirectionality [10]. However, previous studies primarily focused on lexical level and extended their research to phrases. The mapping patterns at the morpheme level remain unknown. In modern Chinese, compound words constitute a significant proportion of word formation, making the exploration of synaesthetic mappings at the morpheme level a vital and worthy linguistic phenomenon that requires investigation.

Furthermore, the following phenomena are observed in Chinese:

(1) 她的声音清亮 (林语堂《京华烟云》)。
     tāde shēngyīn qīngliang
     Her voice is clear and bright (Lin Yutang, *Moment in Peking*).

(2) 饭菜热乎乎的, 十分美味, 比德里寡淡无味的伙食强太多了 (维卡斯·斯瓦鲁普《贫民窟的百万富翁》)。
     fàncài rèhūhū de, shífēnměiwèi, bǐ délǐ guǎdàn wúwèi de huǒshí qiáng tàiduōle
     The food is piping hot, incredibly delicious, far superior to the bland fare in Delhi (Vikas Swarup, *Slumdog Millionaire*).

(3) 冬妮娅皮肤凉爽 (莫言《会唱歌的墙》)。
     dōngnīyà pífū liángshuǎng
     Donya's skin is cool (Mo Yan, *Big Breasts and Wide Hips*).

In (1), "清*qīng*"(bright) in the "说文解字*Shuōwén Jiězì*"Explaining Graphs and Analyzing Characters is defined as "朖*lǎng*"(bright). Similarly, "亮*liàng*"(bright) in the "说文解字注*Shuōwén Jiězì Zhù*"Annotation on Shuowen Jiezi is explained as "明*míng*"(shining). Both morphemes denote sight. However, in Mandarin, the word which is combined by these two morphemes is used to describe sound, which can be seen as a typical synaesthetic metaphor. In (2)–(3), visual sensations are metaphorically mapped onto taste and touch, respectively. These types of mapping patterns have rarely been mentioned in previous literature but are widely distributed and frequently used in actual language. Such phenomena are prevalent and unique to Mandarin, warranting in-depth research and incorporation into the Chinese synaesthesia system.

Therefore, based on these situations, this paper attempts to explore synaesthetic metaphors in modern Chinese at the morpheme level. Using *Modern Chinese Dictionary (7th Edition)* as the data source, it aims to identify compound words in modern Chinese that exhibit synaesthetic metaphors and statistically analyze mapping directions. This research aims to demonstrate the distinctive and crucial characteristics of synaesthetic mappings in Chinese compared to other languages. Additionally, it attempts to establish the role and position of psychological feeling within the Chinese synaesthetic metaphor system.

3 Selection of Data and Definition of Sensations

This study delves into compound words in modern Chinese at the morpheme level to explore the ways in which synaesthesia mappings occur. To classify sensations regarding morphemes used in word formation, this study adheres to the original meaning of morphemes as defined in the "说文解字*Shuōwén Jiězì*"Explaining Graphs and Analyzing Characters; if a morpheme is not included in the "说文解字*Shuōwén Jiězì*"Explaining Graphs and Analyzing Characters, its classification is determined based on relevant meanings found in the "康熙字典*Kāng Xī Zì Diǎn*"A 42-volume Chinese Dictionary Compiled during the Reign of Kangxi in the Qing Dynasty. Classification of sensations of compound words primarily relies on example sentences in *Modern Chinese Dictionary (7th Edition)*. If no examples are available, relevant sentences are searched for in the Beijing Language and Culture University BCC corpus. Ultimately, the classification is determined based on the sentence's complete context, placing it within the corresponding sensory category. If sensations beyond the five basic senses are encountered, they are temporarily categorized as SENSE$_6$.

TOUCH :   1. 这个摸起来很～。
           zhège mōqǐlái hěn ～
           This feels very [adjective] by touching.

SOUND :   2. 这个听起来很～。
           zhège tīngqǐlái hěn ～
           This sounds very [adjective].

TASTE :   3. 这个尝起来很～。
           zhège chángqǐlái hěn ～
           This tastes very [adjective]

SIGHT :   4. 这个看起来很～。
           zhège kànqǐlái hěn ～
           This looks very [adjective].

SMELL :   5. 这个闻起来很～。
           zhège wénqǐlái hěn ～
           This smells very [adjective].

$SENSE_6$:   6. 这个感觉很～。
           zhège gǎnjué hěn ～
           This feels very [adjective].

According to the definition of synesthesia in Qian, Z. [11], morphemes and compound words expressing sensations are drawn from *Modern Chinese Dictionary (7th Edition)*. The selection criteria were as follows:

1. The overall meaning of the word formed must represent one or two sensations.
2. The original meaning of the morphemes forming the word must express a particular sensation.

Table 1. Table showing examples of data selection.

Example	Sensation(s) of word	Sensation(s) of morphemes	Received as a data
白菜*báicài* white vegetable (cabbage)	−		×
高挑*gāotiǎo* tall and slender (tall and slender)	−	−	×
柔润*róurùn* soft and moist (soft and moist)	+	−	√

In Table 1, the word "白菜*báicài* (cabbage)" does not represent a sensation but a visual object, not matching criterion 1, so it is excluded. "高挑*gāotiǎo*(tall and slender)" represents a visual sensation, but the morpheme "挑*tiǎo*"does not convey any sensation. Although "高挑*gāotiǎo*"satisfies criterion 1, it does not meet criterion 2, which requires that both morphemes in a compound word convey sensations. Therefore, it is not selected. "柔润*róurùn* (soft and moist)"on the other hand, has an example sentence in Modern Chinese Dictionary ("柔润的嗓音*róurùn de sǎngyīn*"meaning "soft voice"), demonstrating sound. Additionally, each morpheme, "柔*róu*(soft)"and "润*rùn*(moist)" is related to touch. Therefore, this word is included in the analysis data.

Following the definitions in Peng, D. for various sensations, each morpheme in the selected synaesthetic lexicon is examined and tallied [12]. Broadly defined, touch includes haptic perception, pallesthesia, and thalposis. Totally, there are 23 morphemes expressing touch, 75 morphemes expressing sight, which refers to the sensation generated by the image of an object on the retina and includes dimension and color, 8 morphemes expressing taste, 6 morphemes expressing sound, while those expressing smell total 2. At the same time, there are 27 morphemes expressing SENSE6 (The classification of morphemes appears in Appendix 1).

4 Synaesthesia Mapping Phenomena in Lexicon

4.1 Methods for Determining Synaesthesia in Corpus

In the synaesthesia of lexicon, the directionality of synaesthesia mappings refers to when a morpheme representing a specific sensation in a word does not align with the overall sensation represented by the entire word. In such cases, the sensation represented by the morpheme is mapped onto the overall sensation of the word. These mappings demonstrate a relative directionality, meaning that certain sensations tend to map more frequently onto other sensations than in the opposite direction (Zhao, Q., Huang, C.-R., [7]). In the context of this study, the sensation represented by the morpheme in the lexicon is termed the source, while the overall sensation represented by the lexicon is termed the destination. In the collected 190 synaesthetic words, the mappings between sensations fall into three categories:

$$MORPHEME_{A\ sensation} + MORPHEME_{A\ sensation} \rightarrow WORD_{B\ sensation} \qquad (1)$$

$$MORPHEME_{A\ sensation} + MORPHEME_{B\ sensation} \rightarrow WORD_{A/B\ sensation} \qquad (2)$$

$$MORPHEME_{A\ sensation} + MORPHEME_{B\ sensation} \rightarrow WORD_{C\ sensation} \qquad (3)$$

In (1) falls into the first category: "清亮 *qīngliàng*(clear and bright)".. Both "清*qīng*(clear)"and "亮*liàng*(bright)"represent sight, but the overall meaning of the word pertains to sound. This case counts as two synaesthetic mappings cases of sight to sound.

The second category is exemplified by "响亮 *xiǎngliàng*(loud)". Here, "响 *xiǎng*(loud)"represents sound, and "亮 *liàng*(bright)"represents sight. The overall meaning of the word is sound, making sight as the source and sound as the destination. In this case, it is counted as one synaesthetic mapping case of sight to sound.

In the third category, using the example "美满 *měimǎn*(happy)", an appropriate sentence from the BCC corpus is found: "在家里，萨姆和莉莲的婚姻美满 *Zàijiālǐ,, sàmǔ hé lìlián de hūnyīn měimǎn*(In their home, Sam and Lilian's marriage is happy)". Here, "美满 *měimǎn*(happy)"represents SENSE$_6$, a sensation beyond the basic five senses. "美 *měi*(beautiful)"and "满 *mǎn*(full)", their original meanings represent taste and sight in Chinese, respectively. Thus, this case is counted as the synaesthetic mappings case of taste to SENSE6 andthe synaesthetic mappings case of touch to SENSE$_6$.

4.2 Mapping Statistics

According to analyzing 190 synaesthetic words, 27 mapping patterns comprising 279 synaesthetic mapping cases are identified. The following sections categorize and summarize these phenomena and patterns for different sensations (The detailed data appear in Appendix 2).

Touch Tends to be the Source and Allows Unidirectional and Bidirectional Synaesthetic Mappings. Lower level headings remain unnumbered; they are formatted as run-in headings. This study found that touch can map to taste, SENSE$_6$, smell, sight, and sound. In the selected corpus, touch as the source occurs in 65 cases. Among these, touch maps to taste in 2 cases, accounting for 3.08% (2/65); to sight in 9 cases, accounting for 13.85% (9/65); to sound in 8 cases, accounting for 12.31% (8/65); to SENSE$_6$ in 45 cases, accounting for 69.23% (45/65); and to smell in 1 case, accounting for 1.54% (1/65). Additionally, touch can combine with sight, taste, and SENSE$_6$, then mapping to other sensations. Touch as the destination occurs in 7 cases.

Examples of touch mapping to other sensations are shown in (4)–(7), sourced from BCC corpus:

(4) 萝卜糕外酥内嫩，味道清香而不甜腻（触觉→味觉）。

    luóbogāo wài sū nèi nèn, wèidào qīngxiāng érbù tiánnì

        The turnip cake is crispy outside, tender inside, and tastes fresh without being overly sweet(Touch → Taste).

(5) 她的面颊很丰满，皮肤白润（触觉→视觉）。

    tāde miànjiá hěn fēngmǎn, pífū báirùn

        Her cheeks are full, and her skin is white and tender (Touch → Sight).

(6) 百业兴旺，九流汇集，十分闹热（触觉→听觉）。

    bǎiyè xīngwàng, jiǔliúhuìjí, shífēn nàorè

        All trades prosper, all talents gather, and it is bustling (Touch → Sound).

(7) 心里无限悲凉（触觉→感觉$_6$）。

    xīnli wúxiàn bēiliáng

        Infinite sorrow in the heart. (Touch → SENSE$_6$).

Taste Tends to be the Source and Allows Unidirectional and Bidirectional Synaesthetic Mappings. Taste can map to touch, sound, sight, smell, and SENSE$_6$. In the corpus, taste as the source appears in 34 cases. Among these, taste maps to SENSE$_6$ in 23 cases, accounting for 67.65% (23/34); to sight in 4 cases, accounting for 11.76% (4/34); to touch in 2 cases, accounting for 5.88% (2/34); to smell in 1 case, accounting for 2.94% (1/34); and to sound in 4 cases, accounting for 11.76% (4/34). Additionally, taste can combine with touch, sight, SENSE$_6$, and smell, mapping to other sensations. Taste as the destination occurs in 6 instances.

Examples of taste mapping to other sensations are provided in (8)–(11):

(8) 浑身酸软 (味觉→触觉)。
  húnshēn suānruǎn
  The whole body sore and soft (Taste → Touch).

(9) 声线甜美 (味觉→听觉)。
  shēngyīn tiánměi
  The voice is sweet (Taste → Sound).

(10) 她果然很甜美 (味觉→感觉$_6$)。
  tā guǒrán hěn tiánměi
  She is indeed sweet (Taste → SENSE$_6$).

(11) 天边的浮云已经渐渐暗淡 (味觉→视觉)。
  tiānbiān de fúyún yǐjīng jiànjiàn àndàn
  Clouds on the horizon gradually fading (Taste → Sight).

Sight Tends to be the Source and Allows Unidirectional and Bidirectional Synaesthetic Mappings. Sight can map to touch, sound, smell, taste, and SENSE$_6$. In the selected lexicon, sight as the source appears in 170 instances. Among these, sight maps to SENSE$_6$ in 147 cases, accounting for 86.47% (147/170); to sound in 11 cases, accounting for 6.47% (11/170); to taste in 4 cases, accounting for 2.35% (4/170); to touch in 5 cases, accounting for 2.94% (5/170); and to smell in 3 cases, accounting for 1.76% (3/170). Additionally, sight can combine with touch, taste, SENSE$_6$, and sound, mapping to other sensations. Sight as the destination occurs in 18 instances.

Examples of vision mapping to other sensations are provided in (12)–(13):

(12) 鸡肉寡淡无味 (视觉→味觉)。
  jīròu guǎdàn wúwèi
  Chicken is tasteless (Sight → Taste).

(13) 响起了一阵粗重、有如要把心吐出来的声音 (视觉→听觉)。
  xiǎngqǐle yízhèn cūzhòng, yǒu rúyào bǎxīn tǔ chūlái de shēngyīn
  A heavy and crude sound occurs as if wanting to vomit the heart out (Sight → Sound).

Smell Tends to be the Destination. Smell can only map to SENSE$_6$. Smell as the source exists in 2 instances, and as the destination, there are 5 instances.

Example of smell mapping to SENSE$_6$ is as follows:

(14) 今晚的团会过得很开心很感动很温馨 (嗅觉+触觉→感觉$_6$)。
  jīnwǎn de tuánhuì guòdé hěnkāixīn hěn gǎndòng hěn wēnxīn
  Tonight, the party was happy, touching, and <u>warm</u> (Smell + Touch→ SENSE$_6$).

Sound Tends to be the Destination. Sound as the source exists in 5 instances, only mapping to sight and SENSE6. In the word "渾厚 húnhòu(deep and profound)",, "厚hòu(deep)"represents the sight, and "渾hún(deep)"represents the sound. The word as a whole represents sight, indicating that in this word, sound maps to sight via synaesthetic mapping. As per the statistics, there are 22 instances where sound acts as the destination.

Examples of sound mapping to sight are provided in Examples (34)–(35):

(15) 创造出一幅粗犷渾厚、古朴抽象的作品（听觉→视觉）。
   chuàng zàochū yìfúfú cū kuàng húnhòu, gǔpǔ chōuxiàng de zuòpǐn
   It creates rough and profound, ancient, and abstract works (Sound→ Sight).

(16) 祈福平安（视觉+听觉→感觉₆）。
   qífú píngān
   Pray for peace (Sight+ Sound→ SENSE6).

Chinese Synaesthetic Mapping Model Based on the Traditional Synaesthesia System which Only Includes Five Senses. In summary, touch acts as the source in 65 instances and as the destination in 7 instances; taste acts as the source in 34 instances and as the destination in 6 instances; sight acts as the source in 170 instances and as the destination in 18 instances; sound acts as the source in 5 instances and as the destination in 22 instances; smell acts as the source in 2 instances and as the destination in 5 instances (as shown in Fig. 2).

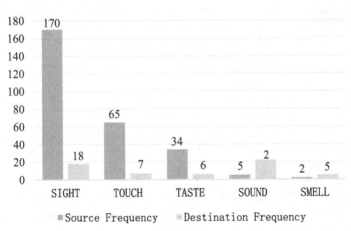

Fig. 2. Figure showing the frequencies of being source and destination among five senses

Through the analysis above, it is evident that there are differences in synaesthesia mapping among the five senses in modern Chinese. Sight, touch, and taste are more inclined to be source, and they can mutually map to each other. On the other hand, sound and smell are more inclined to be destination and cannot mutually map to each other.

4.3 Psychological Feeling as an Important Characteristic of Synaesthesia Mapping in Chinese

Research on synaesthetic metaphors in Chinese has primarily been based on the linguistic definition of "synaesthesia" provided by Qian, Z., which focused on the five basic senses [11]. Scholars like Wu, T. [13], Wang, B. [14], and Hou, B. [15, 16] expanded the scope of synaesthesia to include "psychological feeling" or "mental sensations." Wu, T. pointed out that synaesthesia in linguistics refers to the transfer of sensations from one sense to another, including various psychological sensations [13]. While Wu, T. introduced the concept of "psychological feeling", it was not extensively explored [13]. Wang, B. classified synaesthesia into three categories: synaesthesia between external senses, synaesthesia between external and internal senses, and synaesthesia within the same sense category. He argued for a balance between internal and external senses, emphasizing that internal senses should not be neglected [14]. Wang, S. highlighted the phenomenon where a sensory domain in perception is metaphorically mapped onto a psychological feeling domain in Chinese. She also pointed out that this phenomenon is common in Chinese but significantly different from Indo-European languages [17]. Hou, B. proposed the concepts of broad and narrow synaesthesia. Broad synaesthesia refers to the mapping between internal senses and external senses, including psychological feeling [15, 16]. Hou, B. emphasized that the omission of psychological feeling in previous studies was a research gap and advocated for the inclusion of psychological feeling [15, 16]. Building upon Hou, B. [16], Wang, L. [18] argued that the inner self acts as a bridge connecting external senses, making internal sensations a part of sensory experiences. This study investigates modern Chinese lexical-level synaesthetic metaphors, considering synaesthesia to include both the five basic senses and psychological feeling.

Through the analysis of the data and the presentation of (1)–(35), it is found that besides the basic five senses, there are instances where $SENSE_6$ participates in lexical-level synaesthetic metaphors in modern Chinese. After exhaustively listing and analyzing relevant compound words (The details can be found in Appendix 1 and Appendix 2), it is concluded that $SENSE_6$ corresponds to psychological feeling. Among these, psychological feeling acts as the source in 2 instances, both mapping to sight. In the word "饱满 bǎomǎn"(full), "满 mǎn"(full) represents sight, while "饱 bǎo"(full) represents psychological feeling. The word "饱满 bǎomǎn"(full) as a whole is an expression of sight, indicating a synaesthetic mapping from psychological feeling to sight.

Examples of synaesthetic mapping from psychological feeling to sight is shown in the following (17):

(17) 晶莹剔透，籽粒饱满（心理感觉→视觉）。
    jīngyíngtītòu, zǐlì bǎomǎn
    Crystal clear, grains plump and full (Psychological Feeling→ Sight).

However, psychological feeling acts as the destination in 220 cases, and the mapping from the five senses to psychological feeling accounted for the majority of synaesthesia. Among them, the ratio of synaesthesia mappings from sound to psychological feeling is 60%, the lowest among the five senses, in synaesthesia mappings of sound. The ratio of synaesthesia mappings from smell to psychological feeling is 100%, the highest among the five senses. The average ratio of synaesthesia mappings from the five senses to psychological feeling is 77%. Based on the corpus above and (1)–(35), and in line with the studies of Wang, S. [18], Hou, B. [16], and Wang, L. [18], this paper believes that psychological feeling occupies a significant position in the synaesthesia mappings at the morpheme level of Mandarin. Therefore, psychological feeling should be included in the synaesthetic mapping system of Modern Chinese at the morpheme level. Combining the previous data, the statistical frequencies of mapping and being mapped sensations at the morpheme level of the synaesthetic mapping system in Modern Chinese are shown in Fig. 3.

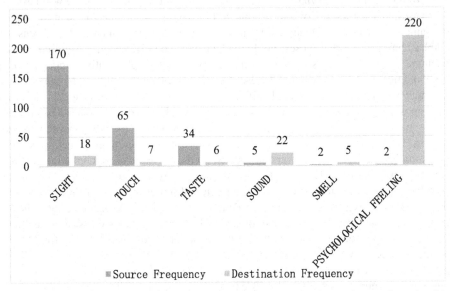

Fig. 3. Figure showing the frequencies of being source and destination at the morpheme level in modern Chinese synaesthetic metaphor mapping system

At the same time, as a part of cognition, synaesthetic metaphor exhibits specific cognitive differences among different languages. This means that the differences in nationality and culture-specific cognition manifest in distinct ways across various languages. Wen, H. found that different languages, due to the influence of linguistic nationality, exhibit certain language distance and relatively low intelligibility [19]. This implies that languages, due to the nationality and culture of cognition, show significant differences and diversity in the same aspects.

Therefore, this paper examines typical examples of synaesthetic metaphors in Chinese and their English counterparts, as follows:

(18) a.杜强调，每个城市都将营造热烈的接力氛围。
    Dù qiángdiào, měigè chéngshì dōujiāng yíngzào rèliè de jiēlì fēnwéi
    b.Du emphasized that each city will foster a warm atmosphere for the relay.

(19) a.年轻人将优质、稳定和幸福的婚姻作为首要任务。
    niánqīngrén jiāng yōuzhì, wěndìng hé xìngfúde hūnyīn zuòwéi shǒuyàorènwu
    b.The young are making quality, stable and happy marriage a priority.

(20) a.资本市场生意冷清。
    zīběnshìchǎng shēngyì lěngqīng
    b.Activities in the capital market have languished pathetically.

(21) a.不过，要想起诉高明的黑客格外困难。
    búguò, yàoxiǎng qǐsù gāomíng de hēikè géwài kùnnan
    b.But it is incredibly difficult to bring cases against sophisticated hackers.

(22) a.向外籍人士展示由深奥村大师制作的精美剪纸作品。
    xiàng wàijí rénshì zhǎnshì yóu shēn ào cūn dàshī zhìzuò de jīngměi jiǎnzhǐ zuòpǐn
    b.Exquisite paper-cutting works crafted by a local master in Shen'ao village are shown for expats.

In (18)–(22), words in Chinese denoting psychological feeling are all compound words formed through synaesthesia metaphors involving the five senses. In contrast, English equivalents utilize words with similar meanings, i.e., 18b and 19b, add affixes, i.e., 20b and 21b, and create new lexicon, i.e., 22b. This highlights significant disparities in synaesthesia metaphors at the morpheme level between different languages. In Chinese, there are internal synaesthesia metaphors within words, and psychological feeling is integrated into the synaesthetic metaphor system. However, in English, there are no internal synaesthetic metaphors within words, and psychological feeling are not part of the English synaesthetic metaphor system. Therefore, there are numerous compound words in Chinese representing psychological feeling, leading to a diverse and multi-faceted description of these sensations in Chinese. This difference can also be considered one of the influencing factors in the non-equivalence of words in Chinese-English translation.

5 Conclusion

This study represents the first exploration of synaesthesia metaphors within compound words at the morpheme level in modern Chinese. Through a meticulous screening of examples from the *Modern Chinese Dictionary (7th edition)*, this research revealed significant differences in synaesthesia metaphors at the morpheme and lexicon levels in modern Chinese. Firstly, at the morpheme level, it is evident that the five senses serving as the source and destination in synaesthetic metaphors differ significantly in quantity and mapping patterns compared to the lexical level. Touch, sight, and taste morphemes tend to be as the source, whereas smell and sound morphemes tend to be destination. Secondly, the overwhelming majority of synaesthetic metaphors involve mapping from the five senses to psychological feeling, emphasizing the crucial role of psychological feeling morphemes in these metaphors. Consequently, this study suggests incorporating psychological feeling morphemes into the synaesthesia metaphor system of modern Chinese. Comparative analysis with English reveals that the mapping of psychological feeling is a vital feature within the synaesthetic metaphor model of Chinese. Researching synaesthetic metaphors within word formation studies on synaesthetic metaphors within phrases. Understanding the characteristics of synaesthesia word formation in modern Chinese provides new interpretive perspectives and examples for etymology, semantic evolution, and related fields of research.

Acknowledgments. We would like to thank The National Social Science Fund of China for financial support from project (No. 19CYY006).

Appendix 1

See Table 2.

Table 2. The Classification of Sensation of Morphemes in Modern Chinese

Sensation	Example											Total
TOUCH	润	热	爆	腻	硬	涩	柔	脆	痛	温	软	23
	鲁	凉	尖	锐	僵	冷	紧	泰	寒	恻	滑	
	轻											
TASTE	甜	苦	淡	酸	美	酷	辣	辛				8
SIGHT	白	朗	枯	爽	清	细	圆	粗	重	壮	红	75
	亮	幽	空	亮	烈	浓	寡	静	薄	婉	贤	
	艳	暖	昧	暗	满	隐	明	隆	旺	炽	眇	
	充	盈	实	疏	高	妙	凶	涨	乖	张	畅	
	荒	乱	低	短	厚	繁	秀	促	密	迫	廉	
	俏	缺	近	便	精	博	粹	微	湛	准	浅	
	宽	大	旷	阔	老	峭	偏	狭	平			
SOUND	闹	寂	响	浑	安	定						6
SMELL	香	馨										2
PSYCHOLOGICAL FEELING	惨	康	贫	诚	良	严	哀	悲	急	危	巧	27
	昌	快	贵	难	劣	敦	富	悍	饱	恶	闷	
	险	优	欢	惊	慌	丑						

Appendix 2

See Table 3.

Table 3. Examples of Synaesthetic Metaphor in Modern Chinese

SOURCE	DESTINATION	EXAMPLE							QUANTITY	TOTAL
TOUCH	SIGHT	白润	热爆	热闹	甜腻	硬明	红润	枯涩	7	57
	SOUND	闹热	柔美	柔润	柔细	甜腻	脆亮		6	
	SMELL	甜腻							1	
	TASTE	甜腻	苦涩						2	
	FEELING	惨痛	恻隐	炽热	粗鲁	脆快	荒凉	尖锐	41	
		僵硬	紧足	紧密	紧迫	紧俏	紧快	康泰		
		冷酷	冷静	冷峭	冷清	冷艳	贫寒	冷淡		
		轻薄	轻淡	轻巧	轻贱	清寒	热爆	热诚		
		温厚	温良	温润	温馨	严紧	硬明	哀痛		
		悲凉	寒苦	寒酸	尖酸	紧急	苦涩			
SIGHT	TOUCH	滑爽	凉爽	清凉	细腻	圆润			5	121
	SOUND	粗重	粗壮	脆亮	清亮	柔细	幽静	空寂	8	
		响亮								
	SMELL	酸烈	浓烈						2	
	TASTE	寡淡	清静	淡薄					3	
	FEELING	哀婉	哀艳	暧昧	暗昧	饱满	恻隐	昌明	103	
		昌隆	爽快	畅旺	炽热	炽烈	充盈	充实		
		充裕	充畅	粗鲁	粗疏	惨重	高贵	高妙		
		高明	高难	高涨	乖张	荒凉	慌乱	低劣		
		短足	敦厚	敦实	繁难	繁重	富实	紧足		
		紧密	紧俏	紧迫	紧快	近硬	精博	精粹		
		精悍	精良	精美	精密	精妙	精明	精微		
		精巧	精细	精湛	精准	宽大	宽厚	宽广		
		宽阔	老辣	冷静	冷峭	冷清	冷艳	明朗		
		明亮	偏狭	平安	平白	平淡	平定	浅白		
		浅薄	浅近	浅明	巧妙	轻薄	清白	清高		
		清寒	清苦	清廉	清明	清贫	清爽	危重		
		微薄	温厚	鲜明	凶险	严明	严重	硬明		
		优厚	优秀	幽寂	幽妙	幽远	淡薄	殷实		
		怅艳	酸烈	宽畅	美满	圆满				
SOUND	TOUCH									5
	SIGHT	热闹	浑厚						2	
	SMELL									
	TASTE									
	FEELING	平安	平定	幽寂					3	
SMELL	TOUCH									2
	SIGHT									
	SOUND									
	TASTE									
	FEELING	温馨	香甜						2	
TASTE	TOUCH	酸软	酸痛						2	32
	SIGHT	甜腻	秀美	暗淡	淡薄				4	
	SOUND	柔美	甜美	甜腻					3	
	SMELL	酸烈							1	
	FEELING	惨淡	苦闷	老辣	冷酷	平淡	轻淡	清苦	22	
		甜美	香甜	优美	哀苦	悲苦	悲酸	悲辛		
		愁苦	淡薄	寒酸	尖酸	苦涩	酸烈	冷淡		
		美满	贫苦							

(continued)

Table 3. (*continued*)

PSYC HOLO GICAL FEELI NG	TOUCH									2
	SIGHT	饱满	丑恶						2	
	SOUND									
	SMELL									
	TASTE									

References

1. Lakoff, G., Johnson, M.: Metaphors We Live By. University of Chicago Press, Chicago (1980)
2. Lakoff, G., Turner, M.: More Than Cool Reason: A Field Guide to Poetic Metaphor. The University of Chicago Press, Chicago (1989)
3. Ullmann, S.: The Principles of Semantics. Basil Blackwell, Oxford (1959)
4. William, J.M.: Synaesthetic adjectives: a possible law of semantic change. Language **52**(2), 41–78 (1976)
5. Yu, N.: Synaesthetic metaphors: a cognitive perspective. J. Lit. Semant. **32**(1), 19–34 (2003). (in Chinese)
6. Wang, S.: Synaesthesia. Associations and cognition **25**(2), 187–194 (2002). (in Chinese)
7. Zhao, Q., Huang, C.-R.: Mapping models and underlying mechanisms of synaesthetic metaphors in Mandarin. Lang. Teach. Linguist. Stud. **189**(01), 44–55 (2018). (in Chinese)
8. Yu, N.: A possible semantic law in synaesthetic transfer: evidence from Chinese. SECOL Rev. **16**(1), 20–40 (1992)
9. Strik Lievers, F.: Synaesthesia: a corpus-based study of cross-modal directionality. Funct. Lang. **22**(1), 69–95 (2015)
10. Zhao, Q., Huang, C.-R., Ahrens, K.: Directionality of linguistic synesthesia in Mandarin: a corpus-based study. Lingua **232**(C), 102744 (2019)
11. Qian, Z.: Synaesthesia. Literary Rev. **19**(1), 13–17 (1962). (in Chinese)
12. Peng, D.: General Psychology. Beijing Normal University Press, Beijing (2008)
13. Wu, T.: The sound of weaving is sharp like a needle - a casual discussion on synaesthesia. J. PLA Univ. Foreign Lang. **23**(1), 61–63 (1984). (in Chinese)
14. Wang, B.: Synesthesia classification method. J. Hubei Eng. Univ. **18**(3), 29–32 (1998). (in Chinese)
15. Hou, B.: The semantic grammar study of Chinese sensory word. Nanjing Normal University, Master Degree dissertation (2008). (in Chinese)
16. Hou, B.: Several important issues on synaesthesia research. J. Heilongjiang College Educ. **31**(2), 126–128 (2012). (in Chinese)
17. Wang, S.: Synaesthetic metaphor of chinese modifier-noun phrase. Acad. Exchange **193**, 145–148 (2010). (in Chinese)
18. Wang, L.: Modern Chinese Synaesthesia Word Study. Zhejiang Normal University, Master Degree dissertation (2016). (in Chinese)
19. Wen, H.: Significance and application of time parameters in intelligibility test. In: Chinese Lexical Semantics: 21st Workshop, CLSW 2020, Hong Kong, 28–30 May 2020, Revised Selected Papers 21, pp. 785–795. Springer, Cham (2021). https://doi.org/10.1007/978-3-030-81197-6_65

Analysis of the Form and Meaning in Collocation of Chinese "V + Color" Verb-Object Compounds

Junping Zhang[1], Qi Zhu[1], and Ting Zhu[2(✉)]

[1] Beijing Language and Culture University, Beijing 10083, China
[2] Shenyang Normal University, Shenyang 110034, China
784576920@qq.com

Abstract. In modern Chinese, some color compounds appear in the form of "V + color", but they do not specifically refer to a particular color. They express metaphorical meanings related to that color. Based on data from Beijing Language and Culture University's BCC Corpus and Communication University of China's New Word Research Resources, this article focuses on the collocation of eight colors: green, black, red, cyan, yellow, white, blue, and purple. We compile and organize the number and proportion of these eight types of "V + color" verb-object compounds. Quantitative analysis of their form and meaning in collocation is also conducted. We find that "imparting meaning through color" is the cognitive principle behind these compounds. The mechanism of semantic transferred designation is achieved through metonymy. By examining the number of such compounds included in the *Modern Chinese Dictionary* (7th edition), these "V + color" verb-object compounds are classified into productive and non-productive types to assess their lexicalization degree.

Keywords: "V + color" compounds · Verb-object Pattern · Metonymy · Lexicalization Degree

1 Introduction

Colors play an indispensable role in human cognition and perception of the world, and categorizing the world by colors is one of the important cognitive pathways for humans. During the cognitive process involving metaphor and metonymy, the semantic connotations carried by color words have gradually expanded. They can be used to describe the surface level of things and refer to objects with specific color features. They can also express people's psychological associations and emotions, and convey specific emotional nuances related to that color. Due to their large quantity and rich semantics, color words have always held a significant position in the modern Chinese vocabulary system.

Currently, the academic community has conducted systematic research on color words. In the early stages, color words are mostly simple monosyllabic words, specifically referring to certain colors. People can make color descriptions more specific and diverse by adding adjectives in front of color words, such as "deep purple" "light blue" "bright red" and so on, or by adding nouns or noun-like modifiers, like "peach pink" "grass green" "parrot red" and so forth. Scholars generally classify the latter into object-color words and color-object words. They have conducted mature discussions on their conceptual boundaries, cognitive mechanisms, evolutionary trajectories, and morphological patterns, etc. (Ye Jun, 2002; Li Yao and Li Baojia, 2010; Ni Zhijia, 2017). These color words are closely related to the metonymic cognitive habit of using objects to express colors.

However, there is a special type of color words formed by combining a verb morpheme with a monosyllabic color adjective morpheme. Zhang Qingchang(1991) first mentions that some phrases belong to this category, such as *piǎobái* 'bleach', *kǎolán* 'blueing', and *shāohuáng* 'burnt yellow'. With the development of society, these "V + color" compounds have gradually moved away from the category of color words to objects or results of actions, such as *tàqīng* 'spring outing', *sǎohuáng* 'crack down on pornography', *dǎhēi* 'crack down on organized crime', *xǐbái* 'whitewash', *mǒhēi* 'smear someone's reputation'. The semantic center of these "V + color" compounds has shifted from color words to verbs, and the meanings of color words have correspondingly changed from specific color references. This reflects the cognitive process where people have transitioned from "using objects to express colors" to metaphorical cognition of "imparting meaning through colors".

Based on previous researches (Huo Jingjing, 2010; Huang Dan, 2020), "V + color" compounds can be divided into two forms: verb-object structure, such as *sǎohuáng* 'crack down on pornography', *dǎhēi* 'crack down on organized crime', where color words function as the objects of actions; verb resultative structure, such as *xǐbái* 'whitewash', *mǒhēi* 'smear someone's reputation', where color words represent the results of actions. Compared to the latter, verb-object structure has a larger number of examples, higher levels of lexicalization, and productivity, which is the focus of this paper.

From the perspective of the cognitive mechanism of metaphor and metonymy, this paper intends to examine the semantics of "V + color" verb-object compounds and analyze the rules of their form and meaning collocation based on collected corpus. We aim to deeply explore the cognitive basis of Chinese people's "imparting meaning through color". We hope to reveal the cognitive patterns of semantic metonymy in Chinese color words, and provide theoretical basis for Chinese language teaching practices. Additionally, we hope to serve as a reference for dictionary compilation, word definitions, and the processing of such words in the field of natural language processing.

2   Quantitative Analysis of "V + Color" Verb-Object Compounds in Chinese

After preliminary study, "V + color" compound words primarily consist of basic color words. According to Berlin & Kay (1969), they have identified 11 basic color terms in human languages, including black, white, red, green, yellow, blue, brown, purple, pink, orange, and gray. Among these basic color words, the earlier they are in the sequence, the easier they are to be included in "V + color" compounds structure, i.e., those that have been recognized by humans in their general cognitive systems of colors earlier are more likely to be included in "V + color" compounds structure and are more prone to metaphor and metonymy (Huang Dan, 2020). Based on corpus, we select 8 colors: green, black, red, cyan, yellow, white, blue, and purple as objects of analysis for "V + color" verb-object compounds.

A thorough search for double-syllable"V + color" verb-object compounds is conducted in BCC Corpus, Communication University of China's New Word Research Resources Data, and the *Modern Chinese Dictionary*(7th edition). During the selection process, color terms whose meanings have significant semantic differences from colors or with lower association of metonymy with colors are excluded. Examples include *biǎobái* 'express one's love' and *páhuī* 'scrape off dust'. Exclusion also include words with lower lexicalization levels and are generally considered phrases rather than compounds. Words with the same meaning but different wordings are grouped together, such as *fǎnqīng/huíqīng* 'regreening' and *fālán/kǎolán* 'blueing'. After retrieval and screening, a total of 87 "V + color" verb-object compounds are ultimately selected as objects of this study. As shown in Table 1:

Table 1. Quantity and Ratio of Double-syllable Compounds

Color	*lǜ* 'green'	*hēi* 'black'	*hóng* 'red'	*qīng* 'cyan'	*huáng* 'yellow'	*bái* 'white'	*lán* 'blue'	*zǐ* 'purple'
Quantity	18	16	15	14	12	6	4	2
Examples	zēng lǜ 'increase greenery'	dǎ hēi 'crack down on organized crime'	guà hóng 'hang red lan terns'	tà qīng 'go for a spring outing'	fàn huáng 'prostitution'	liú bái 'leave a blank'	shāo lán 'blueing'	fā zǐ 'turning purple'
	hù lǜ 'protect greenery'	mō hēi 'fumbling in the dark'	miáo hóng 'outline in red'	chōu qīng 'sprout and become green'	zhì huáng 'produce pornographic products'	bǔ bái 'fill a blank'	diǎnlán 'enamel filling'	chuí zǐ 'value greatly'
	tǔ lǜ 'greenery showing up'	lā hēi 'blocking someone'	fēn hóng 'distribute dividends'	shā qīng 'tea fixation'	dǎ huáng 'combat prostitution'	lòu bái 'reveal wealth'	hù lán 'protect blue sky'	
Ratio	20.69%	18.39%	17.24%	16.09%	13.79%	6.90%	4.60%	2.30%

2.1 "V + *lǜ* 'Green'" Verb-Object Compounds

Among the data sources mentioned above, the most abundant category consists of words formed with *lǜ* 'green', totaling 18 examples, among which the meanings of *lǜ* can be included as the following five types:

1. Referring to the color green itself, as in *tǔlǜ* 'green showing up' and *fālǜ* 'turn green', totaling 2 examples.

2. Referring to a type of green lacquer in traditional Chinese lacquerware, as in *tīlǜ* 'green lacquer', with only 1 example.
3. Referring to "greenery" as in *zēnglǜ* 'add greenery', *zhílǜ* 'plant greenery', *hùlǜ* 'protect greenery', *àilǜ* 'love greenery', *huǐlǜ* 'destroy greenery', *yǎnglǜ* 'nurture greenery', *jiànlǜ* 'build greenery', *zhànlǜ* 'occupy greenery', *shìlǜ* 'watch greenery', totaling 9 examples.
4. Referring to matters related to environmental protection, as in *zhùlǜ* 'live green', *piǎolǜ* 'green washing', *xǐlǜ* 'green washing', totaling 3 examples.
5. Used metaphorically in stock or securities trading market, where *lǜ* 'green' is associated with price declines, as in *piǎolǜ* 'stocks falling', *shōulǜ* 'closing in the red', and *fānlǜ* 'keep falling', totaling 3 examples.

Initially, the meaning of *lǜ* 'green' is within the category of its original color sense and it is used to indicate the color itself, as in *tùlǜ* meaning "green color start to appear." When *lǜ* starts to be used to refer to something with green characteristics, meanings gradually extend. Since green is closely associated with plants and is commonly encountered in people's daily lives, the usage of *lǜ* to describe actions related to plants becomes prevalent, resulting in most examples. The most frequent usage is related to green plants, and it is the most understandable, such as *zhílǜ* referring to planting green vegetation, *àilǜ* indicating the love for green plants, and *jiànlǜ* suggesting the construction of public green spaces, among others. People also like to use *lǜ* to describe actions or behaviors related to environmental protection, such as *zhùlǜ* for living in eco-friendly buildings. *Xǐlǜ* and *piǎolǜ* refer to unscrupulous businesses deceiving consumers by falsely presenting their products or services as environmentally friendly. Lastly, in the context of stock and securities trading market, where red represents price increase and green denotes price decline, people begin using *lǜ* 'green' and *hóng* 'red' to describe the fall and rise of security prices, such as *piǎolǜ* indicating stock prices falling generally, *shōulǜ* meaning the stock at that day ends in the red, and *fānlǜ* denoting the price today is lower than the closing price yesterday.

2.2 "V + *hēi* 'Black'" Verb-Object Compounds

The V + *hēi* 'black' compounds consist of 16 examples, coming second in quantity after V + *lǜ* 'green'. *Hēi* has the following semantic categories:

Firstly, it refers to specific entities characterized by the color black or situations related to darkness, totaling 5 examples. It can represent dark night, as in *rùhēi* 'entering darkness' and *mōhēi* 'fumbling in the dark', or it can refer to "black-colored food" as in *chīhēi* 'eating black food'. Additionally, *hēi* is used to describe black lacquer in traditional lacquerware, as in *tīhēi* 'engraved black', or to indicate the black coating formed during steel processing, as in *fāhēi/zhǔhēi* 'blackening'.

Secondly, it is employed metaphorically to denote abstract concepts related to illegality, such as *dǎhēi* 'crack down on organized crime', *bànghēi* 'associate with the organized gangdom', *sǎohēi* 'sweep away criminal forces', *chúhēi* 'eliminate illegal activities', *fǎnhēi* 'oppose criminal activities', *qiānhēi* ' unregistered vehicle', totaling 6 examples. Generally, *hēi* tends to evoke associations with gloomy or unlawful matters, invoking feelings of unease, which makes it suitable for expressions like *hēi shèhuì* 'criminal underworld', *hēi shìlì* 'criminal forces', and *hēihù* 'unregistered residents'.

With the rapid development of internet slang, *hēi* has taken on extended meanings. This paper collects 5 such examples. For instance, *zhāohēi* 'attracting negativity' and *zāohēi* 'being targeted for criticism' refer to actions that invite criticism or verbal attacks from others, with *hēi* denoting the act of making negative comments or critiques. *Lāhēi* 'blocking someone' refers to the act of adding someone to a blacklist, with *hēi* signifying the blacklist itself. *Shàihēi* 'expose darkness' refers to the act of exposing dark or negative incidents on the internet, with *hēi* referring to these dark incidents. *Kāihēi* 'assemble for gaming' is a term used in online gaming, mainly by young people, signifying the formation of a team to play games with real-time communication for better coordination. Under this scenario, *hēi* stands for *hēidiàn* 'a shady place' or *hēifáng* 'a covert strategy room', indicating a group of people gathering discreetly to plan their strategies against the opponent.

2.3 "V + *hóng* 'Red'" Verb-Object Compounds

There are 15 examples of V + *hóng* 'red' compounds. *Hóng* carries the following meanings:

Firstly, it refers to the color red itself or specific entities characterized by the color red, including *fāhóng* 'turn red', *yìnghóng* 'reflect red color', *guàhóng* 'hang red lanterns', *pīhóng* 'drape red national flag around shoulder', *jiànhóng* 'see red', *miáohóng* 'outline in red', *tàohóng* 'wrapping in red', and *tīhóng* 'engraved red', totaling 8 examples.

Secondly, it is related to money, signifying profits, dividends, or rewards, as seen in *fēnhóng* 'distribute dividends', *jiāohóng* 'pay dividends', and *xuánhóng* 'offer a reward', totaling 3 examples.

Thirdly, in the context of stock and securities trading, *hóng* is associated with price increases, as in *shōuhóng* 'closing with an increase', *piāo hóng* 'stocks rising', *biāo hóng* 'stocks rising rapidly' totaling 3 examples.

Fourthly, China's national flag and CPC flag are both red in color, so *hóng* can also be related to CPC, such as *mǒhóng* 'a touch of Chinese red'.

2.4 "V + *qīng* 'Cyan'" Verb-Object Compounds

There are a total of 14 examples of V + *qīng* 'cyan' compounds, and most of them are relatively old, with no recent creations. In V + *qīng* compounds, *qīng* is often used to describe cyan or green color, as seen in *fāqīng* 'turn cyan', *chōuqīng* 'sprout and become green', and *qùqīng* 'remove the outer green of bamboo'. It can also refer to green grass, tender shoots, tea leaves, crops, or anything with a greenish character, as seen in *tàqīng* 'spring outing', *cìqīng* 'tattoo', *chǎoqīng* 'fried tea', *shāqīng* 'tea fixation', *kěnqīng* 'eat unripe grain', *fǎnqīng/huíqīng* 'return to green, used in agriculture', *tānqīng* 'covet the greens', etc. However, in the case of *chuíqīng* 'value greatly', *qīng* is used to refer to "eyes" because in ancient times the term *qīngyǎn* 'cyan eyes' is used to describe one's eye balls.

2.5 "V + *huáng* 'Yellow'" Verb-Object Compounds

There are a total of 12 examples of V + *huáng* 'yellow' compounds. Among them, some use *huáng* to refer to entities characterized by the color yellow, totaling 2 examples, as seen in *shāohuáng* 'burnt yellow' and *tíhuáng* 'engraved yellow', referring to yellow jade and yellow lacquer, respectively. Some words indicate symptoms or illnesses characterized by yellow color such as jaundice, which is often found in medical terminology. There are 2 examples in this category, as seen in *fāhuáng* 'turn yellow' and *tuìhuáng* 'recede yellow'. The most common usage of *huáng* in these compounds is to indicate content related to obscenity or pornography, totaling 8 examples, as seen in *sǎohuáng* 'crack down on pornography', *dǎhuáng* 'combat pornography', *fànhuáng* 'prostitution', *zhìhuáng* 'produce pornographic products', *xiāohuáng* 'sell pornographic products', *jùhuáng* 'reject pornography', and *yìnhuáng* 'print pornographic products' *and biànhuáng* 'identify pornography', etc.

2.6 "V + *bái* 'White'" Verb-Object Compounds

There are 6 examples of V + *bái* 'white' compounds. In these words, some use *bái* to refer to the color white, as seen in *fànbái/fābái* 'turn white', totaling 2 examples. Others extend the meaning of *bái* to imply "blank", indicating filling or leaving a blank space, as seen in *liúbái* 'leave a blank' and *bǔbái* 'fill a blank', totaling 2 examples. *Bái* can also signify money or wealth, as seen in *lòubái* 'reveal wealth'. This usage starts from ancient China, because the silver coin used back then is close to white color, but it is less common in modern Chinese. With the widespread use of WeChat, *kāibái* 'open white list' which refers to "adding someone to a white list on a WeChat official account" come into being, where bái refers to the white list.

2.7 "V + *lán* 'Blue'" Verb-Object Compounds

There are only 4 examples of V + *lán* compounds, which is a relatively small number. *Lán* is used to represent the color blue in its original sense, such as *fàlán/kǎolán* 'appear blue' in the context of mechanical fields like iron production and rust prevention. *Shāolán* 'blueing' and *diǎnlán* 'enamels filling' are two steps in the production of cloisonne, during which enamels need to be applied to cloisonne and fired in the kiln. Every enamel applying means a firing process, where *lán* refers to the specific blue color or a type of blue glaze. *Hùlán* refers to the act of protecting the blue sky, with *lán* indicating blue sky.

2.8 "V + *zǐ* 'Purple'" Verb-Object Compounds

There are only 2 examples of V + *zǐ* compounds, which is the smallest number among the categories. *fāzǐ* means "turning purple", and it can be combined with *hóng* 'red' as in *hóngde fāzǐ* 'enjoy great popularity'. *Zǐ* also has the symbolic meaning of nobility, and *chuízǐ* 'value greatly' indicates a person's high social status.

3 Semantic Conversion Mechanism in Chinese Verb-Object Compounds "Verb + Color"

In principle, the object of a verb-object structure in Chinese is typically a noun. However, in "V + color" verb-object compounds, the morphemes in the object position are adjective in nature. This situation calls for an exploration of the semantic conversion mechanism involved in this shift from adjectives to nouns. Tan Jingchun (1998) suggests that the transformation from an adjective to a noun occurs through a referential process that causes a semantic change, wherein an adjective's property is used to refer to nouns possessing that property. This notion of "referential process" involves the concept of metonymy. Shen Jiaxuan (1999) proposes a cognitive model of metonymy: when using concept A to metaphorically refer to concept B, the two concepts must exist within the same "cognitive framework". This means there must be relatively fixed associations between concepts based on human experience, and concept A should have higher cognitive salience and the ability to activate concept B. According to this theory, we can analyze the cognitive metonymy mechanism in "Verb + Color" compounds.

Firstly, in these verb-object compounds, there exists a stable association between the color word and the metonymic object, meeting the criteria of being within the same cognitive framework. Generally, a certain object needs to possess the characteristics of a particular color for people to use that color word. Additionally, the metonymic object must have higher cognitive salience compared to the prototype for the possibility of semantic metonymy, such as the whole being more salient than the parts, visibility than invisibility. Salience can also change according to subjective factors (Shen Jiaxuan, 1999). Since people often rely on visual cues to understand objects, it is customary and easy to perceive and comprehend objects by referring to their most salient color. Therefore, the metonymy mechanism in "V + color" verb-object compounds can be summarized as follows: the color word is associated with an object based on semantic or characteristic features, and this color feature is salient in the object, making the color word's salience higher than that of the object. These conditions enable the color word to undergo semantic metonymy.

For instance, in words like *zhílǜ* 'planting greenery', *hùlǜ* 'protecting greenery', and *zēnglǜ* 'increasing greenery', people use *lǜ* 'green' to refer to "green plants". From the perspective of cognitive framework, the color *lǜ* is associated with the green color that plants inherently possess. When plants are considered as a whole, their most salient feature is their "green" color, which leads to the occurrence of semantic conversion. Similarly, in the word *tàqīng* 'spring outing', *qīng* 'cyan' is associated with "lush green grass", and the color *qīng* is the salient feature of "grass". In the case of *lòubái* 'reveal wealth', the color word *bái* 'white' is associated with the white color of silver, and the salient feature of "silver" is also its "white" color. In *pīhóng* 'drape red national flag around shoulder', the color word *hóng* 'red' is associated with the red color on the national flag, and the salient feature of our national flag is its "red" color. Examples like these demonstrate that "verb + color" compounds generally can meet the metonymic cognitive model.

4   Analysis of Productivity and Lexicalization of "V + color" Verb-Object Compounds

Inclusion of 87 Compounds in *Modern Chinese Dictionary* (7th edition) is shown in Table 2:

Table 2. Inclusion Number and Ratio of "V + color" Verb-object Compounds in *Modern Chinese Dictionary* (7th edition)

Color	Inclusion number	Inclusion ratio	Non-inclusion Number	Non-inclusion ratio	Sum
qīng 'cyan'	10	71.43%	4	28.57%	14
hóng 'red'	8	53.33%	7	46.67%	15
hēi 'black'	3	18.75%	13	81.25%	16
huáng 'yellow'	3	25%	9	75%	12
lǜ 'green'	2	11.11%	16	88.89%	18
bái 'white'	2	33.33%	4	66.67%	6
lán 'blue'	1	25%	3	75%	4
zǐ 'purple'	0	0	2	100%	2

Combining Tables 1 and 2, due to the limited number of examples for the words *bái* 'white', *lán* 'blue', and *zǐ* 'purple', they are insufficient for rule analysis. Therefore, this section will only discuss *qīng* 'cyan', *hóng* 'red', *hēi* 'black', *huáng* 'yellow', and *lǜ* 'green'.

Dong Xiufang (2004) points out that if a lexical pattern generates words that are widely included in *Modern Chinese Dictionary*, it indicates a higher degree of lexicalization for this type of word and a weaker productivity for the lexical pattern. Conversely, if such words are less included, it suggests a lower degree of lexicalization, making the lexical pattern more transparent and its productivity stronger. Based on this criterion, this paper categorizes the "verb + color" compounds as productive and non-productive.

4.1   Productive "Verb + Color" Verb-Object Compounds

Based on corpus collection and statistics, examples of "V + *lǜ*" 'green', "V + *huáng*" 'yellow', "V + *hēi*" 'black', etc. are relatively high in number, but few of them are included in *Modern Chinese Dictionary*, indicating a lower degree of lexicalization and a higher level of productivity. The metonymy of these color words are also relatively stable and clear, and the semantic types of verbs are relatively clustered, facilitating the creation of new words.

For the "V + *lǜ*" lexical pattern, *Modern Chinese Dictionary* currently includes only two examples *piāolǜ* 'stock prices falling' *shōulǜ* 'closing in the red'. *Lǜ* in these examples represents the decline in stock market prices, indicating a higher degree of lexicalization and lower productivity. However, when *lǜ* refers to "green plants", there are many examples such as *hùlǜ* 'protect greenery', *àilǜ* 'love greenery', and *zēnglǜ* 'increase greenery', where the verbs are mostly related to "protect, cherish, and plant". These words often originate from news headlines or promotional slogans, and the media and propagandists prefer to use concise double-syllabic words to summarize and promote activities. These words are catchy and concise, quickly capturing the key points of the topic. When *lǜ* represents "green plants", "V + *lǜ*" still has strong productive potential, but whether it can stabilize as words and be included in dictionaries need examination by time.

For V + *hēi* 'black' lexical pattern, *Modern Chinese Dictionary* includes three examples: *mōhēi* 'fumbling in the dark', *dǎhēi* 'crack down on organized crime', and *zāohēi* 'being attacked or smeared'. Based on the meaning of *hēi* in *dǎhēi* meaning "organized crime" and "evil forces", new phrases can be created like *chúhēi* 'eliminate evil forces', *fǎnhēi* 'against evil forces', *jùhēi* 'fear evil forces', *tōnghēi* 'associated with evil forces', and *hùhēi* 'protect evil forces'. Currently, this pattern still has strong productive potential.

For V + *huáng* 'yellow' pattern, *Modern Chinese Dictionary* includes three examples: *fànhuáng* 'engage in pornography', *zhìhuáng* 'produce pornographic products', and *sǎohuáng* 'crack down on pornography'. Based on the meaning of *huáng* being obscene and pornographic contents, new words like *dǎhuáng* 'fight against pornography', *biànhuáng* 'identify pornography', *jùhuáng* 'reject pornography' can be generated. From the perspective of criminal behavior, new words like *yìnhuáng* 'print pornographic products', *xiāohuáng* 'sell pornographic products' can also be created, which shows its productive potential.

4.2 Non-productive "Verb + Color" Verb-Object Compounds

Examples like *tàqīng* 'spring outing' have been in use for a long time and they are included in dictionaries for a while. They have very tightly connected internal semantic relationships, indicating a higher degree of lexicalization. People usually perceive them as a whole, imbuing the entire word with emotional or special meanings. We believe that words of this kind exist as a whole and have fixed and commonly used meanings. They do not have strong productive potential.

Modern Chinese Dictionary (7th edition) includes a total of 10 V + *qīng* 'cyan' compounds, making it the most included compound in this type of lexical patterns, which indicates a high degree of lexicalization. Additionally, there have been almost no recent new examples, suggesting extremely low productive potential. For example, *tàqīng* 'spring outing' refers to springtime excursions or walks, and we can consider that in this case, *qīng* refers to "greenery". However, the relationship between *qīng* and the verb is extremely close, and they are generally perceived as a whole, without being separated for interpretation. *Qīng* is also commonly used to refer to common plants such as crops, tea leaves, branches and buds, as seen in words like *kěnqīng* 'gnawing greens', *chīqīng* 'eating greens', *kànqīng* 'looking at greens', *tānqīng* 'coveting greens', *chǎoqīng* 'stir-frying greens', and *qùqīng* 'removing greens'. They are often used to reflect and describe activities related to life and production. Because these words have been in use for a long time, their overall meanings are stable and unique, resulting in low productive potential.

In V + *hóng*'red' pattern, there are already many examples included in *Modern Chinese Dictionary*(7th edition) such as *miáohóng*'outline in red', *tàohóng*'wrapping in red', *pīhóng*'drape red national flag around shoulder', *tīhóng*'engraved red', *fēnhóng* 'distributing dividends', *xuánhóng* 'hanging in red', *shōuhóng* 'receiving profits', and *piāohóng*'stocks rising'. In these words, the connection between the color words and the preceding verbs is very tight, and the verbs are irreplaceable. Each word can only be understood as a whole, indicating a high degree of lexicalization and relatively low productive potential.

5 Conclusion

In verb + color compounds, color words typically function as the object of an action and are often used to metaphorically refer to a specific color or something with color characteristics. This transformation involves a shift from an adjective to a noun, which is achieved through the cognitive mechanism of human metonymy. Among the eight verb + color compounds discussed in this paper, V + *lù*'green' has the highest number of examples, followed by *hēi* 'black', *hóng* 'red', *qīng* 'cyan', and *huáng* 'yellow', with *bái* 'white', *lán* 'blue', and *zǐ* 'purple' having the lowest number. The quantity of objects with the specific color characteristics or the symbolic meanings associated with color words can influence the number of verb + color compounds in this category. Through an examination of the number of inclusions in *Modern Chinese Dictionary*(7th edition), we find that V + *lù* 'green', V + *hēi* 'black', and V + *huáng* 'yellow' have strong productive potential, while V + *qīng* 'cyan' and V + *hóng*'red' have a higher degree of lexicalization and lower productive potential.

Acknowledgments. This research project is supported by Science Foundation of Beijing Language and Culture University (supported by "the Fundamental Research Funds for the Central Universities") (20YJ010105), the National Social Science Late-stage Fund Project Research on Multilingual Translation of Big Data Nouns (21FYYA003).Thanks to the anonymous reviewers for their valuable revisions. The authors are responsible for anything inappropriate. Ting Zhu is the corresponding author of this article.

References

Berlin, B.: Basic Color Terms: Their Universality and Evolution. University of California Press, Berkeley (1969)

Dong, X.: Lexicon and Morphology of Chinese [hànyǔ de cíkù yǔ cífǎ]. Peking University Press, Beijing (2004). (in Chinese)

Huang, D.: A cognitive construction analysis on "V+Adj$_{color}$" in the case of "XIb AI". J. Harbin Univ. 104–107 (2020). (in Chinese)

Huo, J.: Take "Sing red songs" and "Crack down on evil forces" for examples to remarks on "v.+color(adj.)". J. Lanzhou Vocat. Tech. College 52–54, (2010). (in Chinese)

Zhang, J.: Analysis of the collocation of AA-type adjectives based on MLC corpus. In: Chinese Lexical Semantics (CLSW 2019), pp. 690–700. Springer (2020)

Li, H.: A study of the characteristics of lexicalization of dissyllablic phrases in contemporary Chinese. Lang. Teach. Linguist. Stud. 50–55 (2007). (in Chinese)

Li, R.: The evolution track and cognitive mechanism of words denoting the natural color of objects [wùsècí de yǎnhuà guǐjì jíqí rènzhī jīzhì]. J. Southwest Minzu Univ. (Human. Soc. Sci. Edn.) 170–174 (2010). (in Chinese)

Ni, Z.: Lexical patterns of object-color words and color-object words in modern Chinese. Chinese Linguist. 9–16 (2017). (in Chinese)

Shen, J.: A metonymic model of transferred designation of de-constructions in Mandarin Chinese. Contemp. Linguist. 3–15 (1999). (in Chinese)

Song, R.: Study on the order of double-syllable double attributives and selection restrictions—take the structures of a1 + a2 + De + n and a1' + De + a2' + n' as examples. In: Chinese Lexical Semantics (CLSW 2022), pp. 56–71. Springer (2022)

Tan, J.: Semantic basis and related problems of the transformation of nouns and adjectives [míngxíng cílèi zhuǎnbiàn de yǔyì jīchǔ jí xiāngguān wèntí]. Stud. Chin. Lang. 368–377 (1998). (in Chinese)

Ye, J: Words denoting the natural color of objects, a special sub-group of color lexemes. J. Inner Mongolia Norm. Univ. (Philos. Soc. Sci. Edn.) 26–29 (2002). (in Chinese)

Zhang, Q.: Color words in Chinese (outline). Lang. Teach. Linguist. Stud. 63–80 (1991). (in Chinese)

The Effect of Working Memory Capacity on the Figurative Language Processing of Chinese Second Language Learners

Xun Duan and Xingsan Chai[✉]

Institute on Educational Policy and Evaluation of International Students, Beijing Language and Culture University, Xueyuan Road No. 15, Beijing 100083, China
cxs66@blcu.edu.cn

Abstract. This study used a 3 (working memory capacity (WMC): high, medium, low) × 3 (sentence type: metaphor, simile, metonymy) mixed design to investigate the impact of WMC on the comprehension of Figurative sentences by Chinese L2 (Second language) learners, as well as the cognitive representation and differences in processing metaphor, simile, and metonymy. The results of the study revealed the following: 1) Chinese L2 learners exhibited faster reaction time (RT) for metaphor sentences compared to simile and metonymy, and faster RT for simile compared to metonymy. The comprehension accuracy (ACC) for metaphor sentences was higher than that for simile and metonymy, and the comprehension ACC for simile was higher than that for metonymy. 2) The RT and ACC of metaphor, simile, and metonymy sentences were influenced by individual WMC, with higher WMC associated with faster processing speed and higher ACC. This study revealed that metaphor, simile, and metonymy processing require different cognitive resources. The comprehension of these sentences involves the comparison, interaction, and matching of semantic features between the source and target domains, which necessitates WMC for storage and integration, ultimately completing the cognitive mapping process.

Keywords: Chinese Second Language Processing · Metaphor · Simile · Metonymy · Working memory capacity

1 Introduction

Figurative language is generally understood as a form of language expression where the literal meaning does not convey the true intention of the speaker; figurative meaning and literal meaning are conceptually opposed [1].

In the study of figurative language, metaphor research has the earliest starting point, the longest duration, and has yielded abundant research outcomes. Prior to the 1930s, the traditional metaphor view proposed by Aristotle had been dominant, and metaphor was regarded as a language technique. In the 1930s, Richards and Black introduced a new theory of metaphor called "interaction theory". In 1980, American cognitive linguist Lakoff and British philosopher Turner shifted the focus of metaphor research from

M. Dong et al. (Eds.): CLSW 2023, LNAI 14514, pp. 426–439, 2024.
https://doi.org/10.1007/978-981-97-0583-2_33

"expression" to "concept", transforming it from a linguistic level to a cognitive level that revealed the principles of human thinking. During this period, western scholars proposed various theories of metaphor cognition. For example, the "Salience-imbalance Theory" [2, 3], the "Structure-Mapping Theory" [4–6], the "Class-Inclusion Theory" [7–11], the "Conceptual Metaphor Theory" [12–14], and the "Conceptual Blending/Integration Theory" [15–17]. In comparison, there is less research on cognitive theories and models of simile. The "Comparison Model" [2, 6] views metaphor as a condensed simile and argues that there is no essential difference between metaphor and simile comprehension, as both can be achieved through analogy or property matching: matching the features of the vehicle with the tenor and projecting them onto the latter. The "Categorization Model" [10] posits that there is an essential distinction between the two, suggesting that metaphor expresses categorical statements while simile conveys comparison assertions. The cognitive theories of metonymy mainly include the mapping view, cognitive reference point view, and salience view. The mapping view proposes that metonymy involves conceptual mapping within the same cognitive domain, including cross-domain mapping [13, 18, 19]; the cognitive reference point view suggests that metonymy is a cognitive process in which the source concept serves as a cognitive reference point for the target concept [20–23]; the salience view argues that metonymy is a cognitive process of "domain salience" [24] or "target concept salience" [25].

From the perspective of psycholinguistics, the emergence of the aforementioned cognitive theories and models indicated that the comprehension of metaphor, simile, and metonymy requires the storage and integration of different types of information, which is closely related to WMC [26]. WMC is derived from the central executive of working memory. North American psychologists, such as Daneman, Carpenter, and Cowan have pointed out that WMC is primarily involved in information storage, updating, and switching, playing an important role in language comprehension processing [27, 28]. In recent years, the impact of WMC on metaphor processing has attracted great interest among scholars, but the influence of WMC on simile and metonymy processing has yet to be investigated.

Currently, a substantial body of empirical research has shown a close relationship between working memory and second language reading, lexicon, and grammar [29–31]. However, research on the role of WMC in second language acquisition and processing is relatively scarce [32]. More studies are needed to investigate whether WMC and its individual differences affect language comprehension and the underlying mechanisms in second language learners. In light of this, the present study attempts to explore the impact of WMC on figuration comprehension in L2 learners and the underlying mechanisms.

1.1 The Studies of Figurative Language and WMC

[33] theoretically examined the relationship between working memory and language. The results showed that working memory involves temporary storage and manipulation of information, which is necessary for complex cognitive activities. Working memory can be divided into four subsystems. The first one involves language and acoustic information, and the phonological loop; The second one, the visuospatial sketchpad, provides its visual equivalent; Both of these depend on the third system, the central executive, which controls attentional limitations. The fourth subsystem, the episodic buffer, is a

multidimensional information storage system. Based on the relationship between working memory and language, scholars have studied the differences in working memory between monolingual and bilingual individuals. [28] investigated the impact of bilingualism on cognitive mechanisms and conceptual issues in executive control structures. The results showed that bilingual individuals consistently outperformed monolingual individuals in tasks involving executive control. [34] conducted a review on the existence of the "bilingual advantage in cognitive control" and concluded that there is an advantage in cognitive control among bilingual individuals.

[35] conducted a behavioral experiment to investigate individual differences in WMC and how these differences affect performance in the retrieval of primary and secondary memory. The results indicated that differences in WMC only appeared in the retrieval of primary memory. This suggested that WMC is indispensable for controlled retrieval but can be disregarded for retrieval based on automatic activation. Additionally, the authors found that individual differences in attentional resources may lead to differences in the ability to inhibit irrelevant information. [36] examined the contribution of WMC to Stroop interference through a behavioral experiment. The results showed that working memory was related to RT but not ACC. Stroop interference was determined by two mechanisms, target maintenance and conflict resolution, with the dominance of each mechanism depending on WMC. The aforementioned studies focused on the relationship between working memory and individual differences, while the relationship between working memory and language acquisition is also a topic of interest among scholars. [37] conducted a behavioral experiment to investigate the role of working memory in metaphor production and comprehension among bilingual individuals. The results revealed that bilingual individuals with high WMC exhibited faster RT to metaphors and required less inhibitory control. [38] explored the components of working memory in Spanish-speaking elementary school students' English reading and language acquisition through a behavioral experiment. The results indicated that the phonological storage system is a part of working memory. [30] conducted behavioral experiments to examine the relationship between verbal short-term memory (VSTM), verbal working memory (VWM), and lexicon and grammar acquisition in both first language (L1) and L2 children. The results showed significant associations between verbal short-term memory, verbal working memory, and mastery of morphology and syntax. Verbal short-term memory and verbal working memory had different relationships with language learning. L1 children and L2 children who acquired the language naturally employed the same memory mechanisms in lexicon and grammar learning.

[39] explored the interaction between the characteristics of metaphors and the WMC of comprehenders in metaphor comprehension, based on the metaphor standard pragmatic model. The results revealed that individual differences in WMC can influence metaphor comprehension. [40] conducted an empirical study comparing the class-inclusion theory, structure-mapping theory, and career theory of metaphor, to investigate the impact of WMC on metaphor and simile. The results indicated that WMC predicted the quality and form of both simile and metaphorical expressions. [41] investigated the role of working memory in metaphor interference effects through a behavioral experiment. The results showed that participants took longer to judge metaphorical sentences

compared to non-metaphorical sentences, suggesting that metaphor processing is automatic. They also found that WMC predicted the magnitude of metaphor interference effects, with higher WMC associated with smaller interference effects. This suggested that while metaphor comprehension is automatic, the early processing of metaphors is controlled by executive mechanisms. They proposed that working memory influences metaphor processing by affecting the effectiveness of the construction-integration process and the speed of identifying literal or figurative meanings. [42] investigated the role of working memory and attention in metaphor interpretation through a behavioral experiment. The study found that working memory contributed more to metaphor interpretation than attention. [43] conducted a behavioral experiment to explore metaphorical meaning retrieval, literal meaning retrieval, and the influence of working memory load and mental schemas on metaphor comprehension. The results showed that WMC facilitated the initial access to the literal meaning of metaphor, and metaphor that is difficult to form schemas required more WMC for comprehension.

Overall, the research on the relationship between WMC and metaphor processing has provided rich insights into the impact of WMC on metaphor comprehension. However, the influence of WMC on figurative expressions remains unclear. Additionally, most of the studies have focused on native language speakers, and further research is needed to understand how WMC affects metaphor processing in second language learners.

1.2   The Present Study

WMC refers to the ability to maintain, update, and manipulate information during task performance. In the context of language processing, WMC is considered crucial as it enables individuals to retain and manipulate a large amount of linguistic information, facilitating language processing and comprehension.

Existing research suggested a close relationship between WMC and second language learning and processing. Higher WMC is typically associated with better language learning and processing abilities. The role of WMC in second language acquisition and processing has therefore attracted considerable attention among researchers.

Regarding metaphor comprehension, studies have shown a correlation between WMC and the ability of L2 learners to understand metaphors. Higher WMC can aid L2 learners in better comprehending metaphors, as metaphors require the processing and integration of multiple types of information, including semantic, pragmatic, and sociocultural factors. Higher WMC facilitates the processing of these information, leading to improved metaphor comprehension.

In traditional rhetoric studies in Chinese, the distinction between metaphor, simile, and metonymy is primarily analyzed within the realm of grammatical morphology. Metaphor, simile, and metonymy are essentially the same, with the only difference being their grammatical forms: metaphor and simile involve the presence of a subject, vehicle, and tenor, explicitly expressed with words such as "ike" or "as", while metonymy involves only the vehicle without the subject and the words "is" as a copula. The basic types of these three figuration in Chinese have their own specific characteristics in terms of grammatical form, but it is unclear whether there are differences in processing. Further research is needed.

The study of the processing mechanisms of metaphor has been a hot topic in figurative language processing research. However, there has been limited research on other types of figuration, such as simile and metonymy. Are the processing mechanisms for simile and metonymy consistent with that of metaphor? What are the differences in the mental representations of metaphor, simile and metonymy? How does WMC influence the processing of these three types of figuration? These problems are worth exploring. Therefore, this study aims to investigate the following issues: 1) the mental representations and differences in processing simile, metaphor, and metonymy in Chinese L2 learners; 2) the impact of WMC on the processing of simile, metaphor, and metonymy. Based on aforementioned studies, theories and our experiment design, we have some expectations in the following:

RT: metaphor < simile < metonymy; ACC: metonymy < simile < metaphor; the influence of WMC on RT and ACC: the WMC is negatively correlated with RT and positively correlated with ACC.

2   Methods

2.1   Experimental Design

This experiment used a 3 × 3 two factors mixed design. The independent variable 1, as a between-subjects factor, was WMC, with three levels: high capacity, medium capacity, and low capacity. The independent variable 2, as a within-subjects factor, was sentence type, with three levels: simile sentences, metaphor sentences, and metonymy sentences. The dependent variables were RT and ACC.

2.2   Participants

The participants in this study were 33 college students who are learning Chinese as a second language, with a proficiency level of HSK[1]−4 or above. All participants had normal or corrected-to-normal vision. There was no history of reading difficulties or neurological disorders among the participants. Remuneration was provided to participants after the experiment. The participants were divided into three groups based on their WMC test scores (out of a maximum score of 70): low capacity (11 participants, score range: 32–42), medium capacity (11 participants, score range: 45–54), and high capacity (11 participants, score range: 56–70). A significant difference was found between the groups, $F(2, 30) = 113.519, p < .001$.

2.3   Materials

The stimuli materials in this study consisted of simile sentences, metaphor sentences, and metonymy sentences. With these three types of sentences as a factor, namely sentence type, each type of sentence consisted of 50 sentences, totaling 150 sentences, with

---

[1] Chinese Proficiency Test (HSK) is a standardized international Chinese Proficiency Test for individuals who are not Chinese native speakers (including foreigners, overseas Chinese, Chinese Americans and Chinese ethnic minorities).

each sentence referred to as a trial. The structure of simile sentences in the experiment was "tenor + 像(xiang) + vehicle"; the structure of metaphor sentences was "tenor + 是(shi) + vehicle"; and the structure of metonymy sentences was "context + vehicle". In addition, there are 150 filler sentences mixed in with stimuli materials. To ensure that each participant encounters all types of sentences without generating memory strategies, apart from the filler materials, the remaining sentences needed to undergo Latin square design and pseudo-randomization. Table 1 provided specific examples of the four types of sentences.

Table 1. Examples of the materials used in the experiment

Sentence type	Examples
Simile sentence	月亮　　像　　银盘 yueliang　xiang　yinpan moon　like　silver plate The moon is like a silver plate.
Metaphor sentence	月亮　是　银盘 yueliang　shi　yinpan moon　is　silver plate The moon is a silver plate.
Metonymy sentence	星空　有　银盘 xingkong　you　yinpan starry sky　have　silver plate There is a silver plate in the starry sky.

The three categories of sentences within the group had the same length, with $F(2, 296) = 1.56, p > 0.05$. There was no significant difference in familiarity among the three categories of sentences, with $F(2, 296) = 1.83, p > 0.05$.

2.4 Procedure

First, the participants underwent measurement of WMC. The WMC test followed the testing procedure of [44] and was divided into four sets, with each set consisting of five sections, for a total of twenty sections. Initially, a mathematical equation was presented on the computer screen, for example, $(3 \times 4) + 1 = 16$?, and the participants were required to judge its correctness. Then, a Chinese word (a two-character word) appeared on the computer screen, and the participants needed to remember it. The first set included two equations and two words, the second set included three equations and three words, and so on. Each Chinese word was presented for one second. At the end of each section, the participants were asked to report all the words they remembered to the experimenter, followed by the behavioral experiment.

In the behavioral experiment, each sentence was displayed in the center of the computer screen. To reduce eye strain caused by the computer screen, the experimental materials were presented with a gray background and white text. At the beginning of each trial, a red fixation "+" appeared for 800 ms to remind the participants to focus their attention. Then, a gray screen appeared for 500 ms, followed by the presentation of the sentence in the center of the computer screen. Below the sentence, there were two prompts – "correct" and "incorrect". The participants read the sentence at their own pace and pressed the "F" key if they believed the sentence had a semantic error, or the "J" key if they believed the sentence was semantically correct. Before the formal experiment began, there was a practice session. Once the participants were familiar with the experimental procedure, they could click the corresponding button to enter the formal experiment. If they had any questions, they could click the corresponding button to continue practicing. The experiment was divided into 3 blocks, with each block consisting of 100 sentences. There was a rest period after completing each block.

2.5 Data Analysis

In the WMC test, one point was awarded for correctly judging an equation and correctly recalling a word (maximum score of 60). Participants with equation ACC below 50% were excluded. In the sentence semantic judgment task, deleted fillers' data and ACC below 80% were removed. Additionally, RT outliers were removed based on boxplots, excluding values below 150 ms or above mean $\pm$ 2SD.

Traditional random effects modeling methods have several limitations, but these limitations can be overcome by using mixed effects linear models [45]. Therefore, this study used R language (Rstudio Version 2022) for statistical modeling using mixed effects models.

Inference statistical analysis of RT and ACC data was conducted using mixed effects models in R language. RT was a continuous variable, so the "lmer" function from the lme4 package was used for fitting. ACC, on the other hand, was a binary variable, so the "glmer" function from the lme4 package was used for fitting. The optimal models were selected based on the results of the function "anova" (choosing the model with the lowest AIC value).

All fixed factors of interest were analyzed for main effects and interaction effects using the function "Anova (model, type = "III")" function, and the χ^2 (Chisq value), Df, and Pr ($>$ Chisq) were reported. Post-hoc comparisons were conducted using the function "emmeans" and the function "contrast", and β (Estimate), SE (Std. Error), z-values, and p-values were reported.

3   Results

3.1   Descriptive Statistics

All the test formulas had a calculation ACC of over 50%, but 2 participants had a semantic judgment ACC of less than 80%, so they were excluded. The remaining participants' data were qualified. Descriptive statistical data were shown in Table 2.

Table 2. Descriptive statistical results

Sentence type	WMC	RT (ms)		ACC	
		Mean	SD	Mean	SD
Metaphor	high	2145	1062	93.72%	0.43
	medium	2186	1073	91.22%	0.37
	low	2445	1095	87.64%	0.55
Simile	high	2308	997	88.12%	0.56
	medium	2403	1021	87.79%	0.49
	low	2530	872	84.96%	0.72
Metonymy	high	2517	936	85.44%	0.66
	medium	2632	1155	84.83%	0.59
	low	2826	1297	81.35%	0.64

3.2 Analysis of Mixed Effect Model

RT

The main effect of WMC was not significant ($\chi^2(2) = 2.486, p = .289$). The main effect of sentence type was significant ($\chi^2(2) = 24.151, p < .001$); post hoc comparisons revealed that RT for processing metaphor sentences was significantly faster than simile sentences ($\beta = -139.000, SE = 63.200, z = -2.193, p = .028$); RT for processing metaphor sentences was significantly faster than metonymy sentences ($\beta = -307.000, SE = 63.200, z = -4.863, p < .001$); RT for processing simile sentences was significantly faster than metonymy sentences ($\beta = 169.000, SE = 63.300, z = 2.669, p = .008$).

There was a significant interaction between WMC and sentence type ($\chi^2(4) = 19.917, p < .001$); post hoc comparisons revealed that for processing metaphor sentences, RT for the high capacity group was significantly faster than the low capacity group ($\beta = -326.3, SE = 74.600, z = -4.375, p < .001$), and RT for the medium capacity group was significantly faster than the low capacity group ($\beta = 213.2, SE = 74.700, z = 2.852, p = .004$); for processing simile sentences, RT for the high capacity group was significantly faster than the low capacity group ($\beta = -444.1, SE = 75.200, z = -5.907, p < .001$), and RT for the medium capacity group was significantly faster than the low capacity group ($\beta = 272.8, SE = 75.300, z = 3.623, p < .001$); RT for the high capacity group was significantly faster than the medium capacity group ($\beta = -171.3, SE = 75.100, z = -2.281, p = .023$); for processing metonymy sentences, RT for the high capacity group was significantly faster than the low capacity group ($\beta = -152.9, SE = 76.200, z = -2.008, p = .045$). The high capacity group had significantly faster RT for processing metaphor sentences compared to processing metonymy sentences ($\beta = -306.4, SE = 73.000, z = -4.197, p < .001$); the high capacity group had significantly faster RT for processing simile sentences compared to processing metonymy sentences ($\beta = 243.3, SE = 73.000, z = 3.332, p < .001$); the medium capacity group had significantly faster RT for processing metaphor sentences compared to processing metonymy sentences ($\beta = -370.9, SE = 73.000, z = -5.097, p < .001$); the medium capacity group had significantly faster RT for processing simile sentences compared to processing metonymy sentences ($\beta = 253.3$, $SE = 73.000$, $z = 3.470$, $p < .001$). All other effects were not significant ($ps > 0.05$).

ACC

The main effect of WMC was not significant ($\chi^2(2) = 3.981$, $p = .137$). The main effect of sentence type was significant ($\chi^2(2) = 21.470$, $p = .021$); post hoc comparisons revealed that the ACC for processing metaphor sentences was significantly higher than simile sentences ($\beta = 1.689$, $SE = .120$, $z = 2.313$, $p = .017$); the ACC for processing metaphor sentences was significantly higher than metonymy sentences ($\beta = 1.365$, $SE = .120$, $z = 2.462$, $p < .001$); the ACC for processing simile sentences was significantly higher than metonymy sentences ($\beta = 1.839$, $SE = .120$, $z = 2.132$, $p = .005$).

There was a significant interaction between WMC and sentence type ($\chi^2(4) = 75.593$, $p < .001$); post hoc comparisons revealed that for processing metaphor sentences, the ACC for the high capacity group was significantly higher than the low capacity group ($\beta = .226$, $SE = .077$, $z = 3.442$, $p < .001$), and the ACC for the medium capacity group was significantly higher than the low capacity group ($\beta - .242$, $SE = .077$, $z = 3.148$, $p = .002$); the ACC for the high capacity group was significantly higher than the medium capacity group ($\beta = .231$, $SE = .077$, $z = 3.006$, $p = .003$); for processing simile sentences, the ACC for the high capacity group was significantly higher than the low capacity group ($\beta = .185$, $SE = .077$, $z = 2.415$, $p = .016$); for processing metonymy sentences, the ACC for the high capacity group was significantly higher than the low capacity group ($\beta = .384$, $SE = .077$, $z = 3.089$, $p = .028$). The high capacity group had significantly higher ACC for processing metaphor sentences compared to processing metonymy sentences ($\beta = .206$, $SE = .034$, $z = 3.749$, $p < .001$); the high capacity group had significantly higher ACC for processing simile sentences compared to processing metonymy sentences ($\beta = -0.167$, $SE = .034$, $z = -4.980$, $p < .001$); the medium capacity group had significantly higher ACC for processing metaphor sentences compared to processing metonymy sentences ($\beta = -0.126$, $SE = .034$, $z = -3.693$, $p < .001$); the medium capacity group had significantly higher ACC for processing simile sentences compared to processing metonymy sentences ($\beta = -0.146$, $SE = .034$, $z = -4.282$, $p < .001$). All other effects were not significant ($ps > 0.05$).

3.3 Regression Analysis

RT

The regression analysis model is "M.01 <- lm (RT~WMC, data = Gjc)." Regression analyses were performed separately on metaphor, simile, and metonymy. Results of the regression analyses indicated that WMC significantly affected RT for processing metaphor sentences ($\beta = -1.067$, $SE = .399$, $z = -2.673$, $p = .008$); WMC also significantly affected RT for processing simile sentences ($\beta = -8.052$, $SE = 1.544$, $z = -5.215$, $p < .001$); and WMC significantly affected RT for processing metonymy sentences ($\beta = -1.150$, $SE = .555$, $z = -2.072$, $p = .038$). The overall trend of the regression analysis was illustrated in Fig. 1. (with A is high capacity, B is medium capacity, and C is low capacity).

ACC

The regression analysis model is "M.01 <- glm (ACC~WMC, data = Gjc)." Regression analyses were performed separately on metaphor, simile, and metonymy. WMC significantly affected the ACC of metaphor sentences comprehension (β = .002, SE = .001, z = 2.515, p = .012); WMC also significantly affected the ACC of simile sentences comprehension (β = −0.006, SE = .001, z = −1.748, p = .025); and WMC significantly affected the ACC of metonymy sentences comprehension (β = −0.003, SE = .001, z = −2.343, p = .033). The overall trend of the regression analysis was illustrated in Fig. 2 (with A is high capacity, B is medium capacity, and C is low capacity).

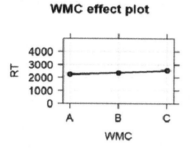

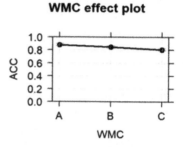

Fig. 1. Chart of WMC and RT

Fig. 2. Chart of WMC and ACC

4 Discussion

Based on the statistical analysis results, the influence of WMC on figurative sentences comprehension in second language learners can be inferred. The main effect of sentence type was found to be significant, with metaphor sentences being processed the fastest in terms of semantic understanding, followed by simile sentences, and metonymy sentences having the longest RT for semantic understanding, which aligned with our expectations. The interaction effect between WMC and sentence type was significant, with the high capacity group processing all three types of sentences faster than the low capacity group. The high capacity and medium capacity groups also processed metaphor and simile sentences significantly faster than metonymy sentences. This pattern was also observed in terms of ACC. The differences in RT and ACC clearly indicated the influence of WMC and reflected the different cognitive resources required for processing the three types of sentences, with metonymy sentences requiring more cognitive resources than metaphor and simile sentences.

Furthermore, multiple theoretical frameworks for understanding metaphor, simile, and metonymy comprehension can explain these results, such as the "Comparison Model" [2, 6], the "Interaction Model" [46], the "Feature Attribution Model" [9], the "Conceptual Metaphor Model" [13], the "Predicate Model" [47], the "Graded Salience Hypothesis" [48], the "Conceptual Blending Theory" [15, 16], the "Category Inclusion Theory" [11], the "Mapping View" [19], the "Cognitive Reference Point View" [23], and the "Prominence View" [24, 25]. These theories all posit that figurative language comprehension is a cognitive process in natural language processing, and individuals can find commonalities between the constituent features of different conceptual domains in the source and target domains through comparison, interaction, integration, and mapping.

Comprehending figurative language requires the application of semantic features from the "source domain" to the "target domain". This semantic transfer necessitates the integration and maintenance of information from both the source and target domains for a sufficient duration to establish connections with relevant cognitive networks. WMC plays a crucial role in storing and integrating this information, thereby impacting the efficiency of language structure integration. According to "Predicate Model" [46], comprehension of figurative sentences involves the activation of broader semantic regions compared to literal meaning.

When comprehending literal meaning, the semantic features related to the topic are usually the immediate neighbors of the predicate and are combined in a familiar way with familiar words, thus requiring relatively small memory storage space, and matching and integration are relatively easy and fast. However, when comprehending figurative sentences, the semantic features of the topic and predicate are often far apart, so integrating the commonalities between them may require the activation of larger semantic networks. However, figurative sentences have the word "is" as the metaphor, which directly compares the tenor with the vehicle, reflecting the formal similarity between the tenor and the vehicle, and mapping between them requires relatively less attentional resources and cognitive effort. Simile sentences have the word "like", which makes the vehicle clearly comparable to the tenor, reflecting the formal similarity between the tenor and the vehicle, and mapping between them requires relatively less attentional resources and cognitive effort as well. According to the experimental expectations and results from previous studies, the faster RT and higher ACC of metaphor sentences than simile sentences may be because Chinese is a language with valuing meaning association, and to some extent, metaphor is easier to understand than similes, so the cognitive resources required for processing metaphor may be less than those for processing simile. Metonymy sentences do not have a tenor and a figurative word, and it is difficult to establish a direct mapping relationship between the tenor and the vehicle, so the attentional resources and cognitive effort required for integration or mapping are relatively highest. When an individual's WMC is low, they have fewer attentional resources to allocate, so processing speed and ACC in comprehending figurative sentences are usually weaker than those of individuals with higher WMC. In summary, WMC significantly contributes to the comprehension of figurative language.

In conclusion, the processing of figurative sentences in second language learners involves the activation of semantic features related to the source domain and the target domain, as well as the interaction, comparison, and integration of these semantic features, which requires the involvement of WMC.

5   Conclusion

This study investigated the psychological representation and differences in processing metaphor, simile, and metonymy in Chinese L2 learners, as well as the impact of WMC on the comprehension of figurative sentences. The results showed that: 1) Chinese L2 learners comprehend metaphor sentences faster than simile and metonymy, and comprehend simile faster than metonymy; the ACC of comprehension for metaphor sentences is higher than simile and metonymy, and the ACC for simile is higher than metonymy; 2) the speed and ACC of comprehension for metaphor, simile, and metonymy sentences are influenced by individual WMC. The study revealed that the processing of metaphor, simile, and metonymy requires different cognitive resources, and their comprehension involves the comparison, interaction, and matching of semantic features between the source and target domains, which requires WMC for storage and integration, ultimately completing the cognitive process of mapping. Although this study explored the processing mechanism of figuration comprehension in L2 learners, there are still some obvious limitations. Future research on the cognitive mechanism of metaphor comprehension in L2 learners should consider the important role of language proficiency. In addition to investigating the role of cognitive abilities such as WMC, the language proficiency should also be considered as an important factor to further reveal the cognitive mechanism of figuration comprehension in L2 learners.

Acknowledgments. This study was supported by Beijing Language and Culture University Graduate Innovation Fund (Special Fund for Fundamental Scientific Research of Central Universities) (Grant No. 23YCX052). We thank all the participants, and we also thank the anonymous reviewers for their constructive remarks and suggestions.

References

1. Yang, B., Pang, C.W.: A review on the time course of metaphoric language processing based on three major patterns. Foreign Lang. Res. **32**(6), 28–33 (2015). (in Chinese)
2. Ortony, A.: Metaphor: A Multidimensional Problem. Cambridge University Press, Cambridge (1979)
3. Ortony, A.: Metaphor, Language, and Thought. Cambridge University Press, Cambridge (1993)
4. Gentner, D.: Structure-mapping: a theoretical framework of analogy. Cognit. Sci. **7**(1), 155–170 (1983)
5. Gentner, D., Markman, A.: Structure mapping in analogy and similarity. Am. Psychol. **52**(1), 45–56 (1997)
6. Gentner, D., Wolff, P.: Alignment in the processing of metaphor. J. Mem. Lang. **37**, 331–355 (1997)
7. Glucksberg, S., Keysar, B.: Understand metaphorical comparisons: beyond similarity. Psychol. Rev. **97**, 3–18 (1990)
8. Glucksberg, S., Keysar, B., McGlone, M.S.: Metaphor understanding and accessing conceptual schema: reply to Gibbs. J. Psychol. Rev. **99**(3), 578–581 (1992)
9. Glucksberg, S., McGlone, M.S., Manfredi, D.: Property attribution in metaphor comprehension. J. Mem. Lang. **36**(1), 50–67 (1997)
10. Glucksberg, S., McGlone, M.S.: When love is not a journey: what metaphors mean. J. Pragmat. **31**(12), 1541–1558 (1999)
11. Glucksberg, S.: The psycholinguistics of metaphor. Trends Cognit. Sci. **7**(2), 92–96 (2003)
12. Lakoff, G., Johnson, M.: Metaphors We Live By. The University of Chicago Press, Chicago (1980)
13. Lakoff, G.: Women, Fire, and Dangerous Things: What Categories Reveal About the Mind. The University Of Chicago Press, Chicago (1987)

14. Lakoff, G.: The Contemporary Theory of Metaphor. Cambridge University Press, Cambridge (1993)
15. Fauconnier, G., Turner, M.: Conceptual integration networks. Cognit. Sci. **22**(2), 133–187 (1998)
16. Fauconnier, G., Turner, M.: Rethinking Metaphor. Cambridge University Press, London (2006)
17. Fauconnier, G.: Compression and emergent structure. Lang. Linguist. **6**(4), 523–538 (2005)
18. Taylor, J.: Linguistic Categorization: Prototypes in Linguistic Theory. Clarendon Press, Oxford (1995)
19. Barcelona, A.: Metonymy. In: Dabrowska, E., Divjak, D. (eds.) The Handbook of Cognitive Linguistics, pp. 143–166. Mouton de Gruyter, Berlin (2015)
20. Langacker, R.W.: Reference-point constructions. Cognit. Linguist. **1**, 1–38 (1993)
21. Langacker, R.W.: Cognitive Grammar: A Basic Introduction. Oxford University Press, Oxford (2008)
22. Radden, G., Kövecses, Z.: Toward a theory of metonymy. In: Panther, K., Radden, G. (eds.) Metonymy in Language and Thought, pp. 17–60. John Benjamins Publishing Company, Amsterdam, Philadelphia (1999)
23. Littlemore, J.: Metonymy. Hidden Shortcuts in Language. Thought and Communication. Cambridge University Press, Cambridge (2015)
24. Croft, W.: The role of domain in the interpretation of metaphors and metonymies. In: Panther, K.U., Thornburg, L., Driven, R., Porings, R. (eds.)) Metaphor and Metonymy in Comparison and Contrast, pp. 161–206. Mouton de Gruyter, Berlin (2003)
25. Panther, K.U., Thornburg, L.: The role of conceptual metonymy in meaning construction. Metaphorik De **6**, 91–113 (2004)
26. Yi, B.S., Ni, C.B.: The role of executive working memory in second language metaphorical sentence comprehension and processing. Foreign Lang. **43**(3), 67–79 (2020). (in Chinese)
27. Daneman, M., Carpenter, P.A.: Individual differences in working memory and reading. J. Verbal Learn. Verbal Behav. **19**(4), 450–466 (1980)
28. Bialystok, E.: Reshaping the mind: the benefits of bilingualism. Can. J. Exp. Psychol. **65**(4), 229–235 (2011)
29. Denhovska, N., Serratrice, L., Payne, J.: Acquisition of second language grammar under incidental learning conditions: the role of frequency and working memory. Lang. Learn. **66**(1), 159–190 (2019)
30. Verhagen, J., Leseman, P.: How do verbal short-term memory and working memory relate to the acquisition of vocabulary and grammar? A comparison between first and second language learners. J. Exp. Child Psychol. **141**, 65–82 (2016)
31. Yang, J.: The Impact of Phonetic Working Memory on the Development of Reading Ability in Chinese People: Evidence from Behavioral and Brain Imaging Studies. People's Publishing House, Beijing (2015)
32. Wen, Z., Mota, M.B., McNeill, A.: Working Memory in Second Language Acquisition and Processing. Multilingual Matters, Bristol (2015)
33. Baddeley, A.: Working memory and language: an overview. J. Commun. Disor. **36**(3), 189–208 (2003)
34. Noort, V.D.M., Esli, S., et al.: Does the bilingual advantage in cognitive control exist and if so, what are its modulating factors? Syst. Rev. Behav. Sci. **9**(3), 27 (2019)
35. Conway, A.R.A., et al.: Working memory and retrieval: a resource-dependent inhibition model. J. Exp. Psychol. **123**(4), 354–373 (1994)
36. Kane, M.J., Engle, R.W.: Working memory capacity and the control of attention: the contributions of goal neglect, response competition, and task set to Stroop interference. J. Exp. Psychol. Gen. **132**(1), 47–70 (2003)

37. Chiappe, D.L., Chiappe, P.: The role of working memory in metaphor production and comprehension. J. Mem. Lang. **56**(2), 172–188 (2017)

38. Swanson, H.L., Orosco, M.J., Lussier, C.M.: Growth in literacy, cognition, and working memory in English language learners. J. Exp. Child Psychol. **132**, 155–188 (2015)

39. Blasko, D.: Only the tip of the iceberg: who understands what about metaphor? J. Pragmat. **31**, 1675–1683 (1999)

40. Pierce, R.S., Dan, L.C.: The roles of aptness, conventionality, and working memory in the production of metaphors and similes. Metaphor. Symb. **24**(1), 1–19 (2009)

41. Pierce, R.S., Maclaren, R., Dan, L.C.: The role of working memory in the metaphor interference effect. Psychon. Bull. Rev. **17**(3), 400–404 (2010)

42. Iskandar, S., Baird, A.D.: The role of working memory and divided attention in metaphor interpretation. J. Psycholinguist. Res. **43**(5), 555–568 (2013)

43. Sun, X., Liu, Y., Fu, X.: The effects of working memory load and mental imagery on metaphoric meaning access in metaphor comprehension. In: Kurosu, M. (ed.) HCI 2014. LNCS, vol. 8511, pp. 502–510. Springer, Cham (2014). https://doi.org/10.1007/978-3-319-07230-2_48

44. Unsworth, N., Heitz, R.P., Schrock, J.C., Engle, R.W.: An automated version of the operation span task. Behav. Res. Methods **37**, 498–505 (2005)

45. Baayen, R.H., Davidson, D.J., Bates, D.M.: Mixed-effects modeling with crossed random effects for subjects and items. J. Mem. Lang. **59**(4), 390–412 (2008)

46. Black, M.: Models and Metaphors. Cornell University Press, Ithaca (1962)

47. Kintsch, W.: Metaphor comprehension: a computational theory. Psychon. Bull. Rev. **7**, 257–266 (2000)

48. Giora, R.: Understanding figurative and literal language: the graded salience hypothesis. Cognit. Linguist. **8**, 183–206 (1997)

A Study on the Use and Integration
of the Network Buzzword 'Rùn'

Quan Li(✉)

College of Chinese Language and Culture, Jinan University, Guangzhou, China
854923058@qq.com

Abstract. In 2022, the network buzzword *Rùn*(润) was widely used on the online platform in Puatonghua circles. Its phonetic form is derived from the pinyinisation of the English word 'run', and its meaning is mainly transplanted from the meaning of 'run', most of the time with the additional meaning of displacement from [-comfortable] to [+comfortable], and in use there are two main variants of the meaning 'to escape' and 'to move abroad'. At the same time, the term quickly spread to other Chinese communities through online media, but its integration performance has significant community differences. The use and development of *Rùn* has the characteristics of explosive and no time difference, which is a vivid portrayal of social life and the psychology of netizens. The fact that it radiates and spreads outward reflects the language ecology of global Chinese language integration and coordination from one side.

Keywords: *Rùn* · Network Buzzwords · Chinese integration

1 Introduction

China is currently in an important period of transformation, with rapid social iteration and changes. The lives and psychology of the people have also been influenced by society, and network buzzwords are an important manifestation. Related studies such as 'Pan' [1], 'XX Zi' [2], 'Foxi' [3], etc. In early 2022, a feeling to escape spread among the people, prompting the emergence and development of the new word *Rùn*(润). This paper first traces the emergence and development of *Rùn* in the Putonghua circle, and then, based on the perspective of global Chinese, examines its spread and diffusion to the Taiwan, Hong Kong, and Macao Mandarin circles and overseas Chinese circles. Finally, we also explains the use and changes of this word from sociolinguistic perspective.

M. Dong et al. (Eds.): CLSW 2023, LNAI 14514, pp. 440–453, 2024.
https://doi.org/10.1007/978-981-97-0583-2_34

2 The Emergence and Development of 'Run' in Mandarin Circles

2.1 Basic Information of 'Run'

In the website of jikipedia.com that collects online languages, there are a total of 6[1] definitions of *Rùn*. Representative definitions are selected and listed as follows:

① The Chinese pinyin of *Rùn* is run, which is also the English word for 'run'. *Rùn* is a response to social social internalization, that is, running into other environments.

② *Rùn* has two meanings: one is to run away, the other is to emigrate abroad.

From the above interpretation, it can be seen that the basic meaning of the new word *Rùn* is equivalent to the verb 'run'. In the current online environment, it mainly means escape. Since foreign countries are ideal destinations for some young people, *Rùn* can also mean immigrate to other countries.

Different from other buzzwords, the origin of *Rùn* is relatively complex. Its pronunciation and meaning mainly derived from the English word 'run', but its formation process is also constrained by the laws of Chinese. The phonetic form of *Rùn* originates from Chinese Pinyin, which means using Chinese Pinyin to pronounce the English word 'run'. This can be seen as a coincidence in phonetics between the two languages. The meaning of *Rùn* also comes from 'run'. In the *Oxford Dictionary*, most of the example sentences of 'run' point to the physical movements, and the emotional colour is neutral, all of which are reflected in the *Rùn*. However, in the subsequent development process, *Rùn* still has a relatively obvious tendency to move from an uncomfortable place to a comfortable place, which is closer to 'escape', a near-synonym of 'run'. The example sentence for 'escape' in the *Oxford Dictionary* is 'She was lucky to escape punishment'. Escape and Lucky have a clear subjective intention when compared. From this, we can see that *Rùn* is a combination of 'run' and 'escape'. From this, it can be seen that *Rùn* first takes the signifier of 'run' and determines its pronunciation in pinyin form. The initial meaning corresponds to 'run', and later gradually approaches 'escape', with an additional meaning of shifting from [−comfortable] to [+comfortable].

According to Chinese spelling rules, *Rùn* can be pronounced as different words, and the *XIANDAI HANYU CIDIAN* includes forms such as *Rùn* (膶,闰,润). The reason for choosing *Rùn*(润) as the final form is mainly due to two factors: firstly, the frequency of use. *Rùn* is more familiar and used by the public, and it takes on new meanings, making it easier to have a refreshing effect; The second is the degree of semantic fit. The adjective *Rùn*(润) in *XIANDAI HANYU CIDIAN* means 'delicate, smooth, and moist', and 'smooth' has the meaning of 'comfortable'. Therefore, the original meaning of adjective *Rùn*(润) is exactly in line with the internal logic of its new network meaning, which is the transition from [-comfortable] to [+comfortable]. In summary, the emergence of buzzword *Rùn* is a recombination of its signifier and signified under the dual effects of English and Chinese, which extends the new meaning of 'run' in its original meaning.

The above process and its results can be simply illustrated as follows:

Signified, Correspondence between English and Chinese meaning.

---

[1] Jikipedia.com is a dictionary website used to collect and explain Internet buzzwords. As an open online dictionary, it supports users to write their own entries. The content includes the latest trendy buzzwords on the Internet, classic buzzwords from the early Internet, and Dialects and slang from all over the world.

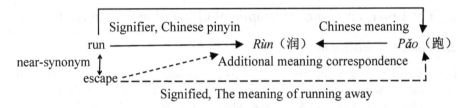

2.2 Development and Changes of *Rùn*

Rùn has been active in the network since its creation, so this paper mainly analyzes its development through the internet, and outlines the changes of the word by conducting phased searches on major online social platforms.

Changes in the Meaning of *Rùn*. As mentioned above, the buzzword *Rùn* mainly represents the meaning of escape and immigration, and is recorded as *Rùn₁* and *Rùn₂* respectively.

Both *Rùn₁* and *Rùn₂* emerged almost simultaneously, and their earliest cases on Sina Weibo appeared in early January 2022. For example:

(1) 本来我还想小熊真的好可爱, 我可以容忍一下她的个人污点, 算了, 我润了, 连夜退款。(2022.1.3)[2]

Běnlái wǒ hái xiǎng xiǎoxióng zhēnde hǎo kěài, wǒ kěyǐ róngrěn yīxià tā de gèrén wūdiǎn, suànle, wǒ rùn le, liányè tuìkuǎn.

Originally I thought little bear was really cute. I could tolerate her personal stains. Forget it, I ran away and got a refund overnight.

(2) 感觉社会越来越退步了, 我以后在这里会生活得更好吗?恐怕不会吧……所以只有润。(1.6)

Gǎnjué shèhuì yuè lái yuè tuìbù le, wǒ yǐhòu zài zhèlǐ huì shēnghuó de gèng hǎo ma? Kǒngpà búhuì ba……Suǒyǐ zhǐyǒu rùn.

It feels like society is getting worse and worse. Will I live better here in the future? I'm afraid not... so only immigrate.

The Weibo user of example (1) is dissatisfied with the brokerage company's purchase restriction behavior and changes his shopping attitude. She uses *Rùn* to mean 'run and leave', which refers to the behavior of not buying goods, and there is no specific direction and destination, and the meaning is relatively abstract. Example (2) with obvious negative and complaining emotions, the blogger hopes to escape the current society and pursue a relaxed life, but it requires context to infer the destination, indicating that the semantic meaning of *Rùn₂* is unstable in this period, and there is a cross with *Rùn₁*. In addition to Sina Weibo, in January 2022, the new word *Rùn* also began to appear on other online platforms.

In the complex network environment, the meaning of *Rùn* has gradually undergone significant changes. The following takes time as the axis to sort out and explain its development and changes.

---

[2] The use cases below are from 2022, so omit the year and only indicate the specific month and day.

In January 2022, the new word *Rùn* has a total of 20 cases, except for the above cited example (2), the remaining 19 were *Rùn₁*, indicating that it has an overwhelming dominant position at this stage, and the semantic prosody is neutral, which could be replaced with *Pǎo*(跑, run). For example:

(3) 我算是知道了, 在新年饭桌上要么吃饱了马上润, 要么从半饱就开始装吃饱了, 因为你的妈妈会一直给你夹菜。(1.31)

Wǒ suànshì zhīdào le, zài xīnnián fànzhuō shàng yàome chī bǎo le mǎshàng rùn, yàome cóng bàn bǎo jiù kāishǐ zhuāng chī bǎo le, yīnwéi nǐ de māmā huì yīzhí gěi nǐ jiá cài.

I know, in the New Year dinner table either run immediately when you're full, or start pretending to be full when you're half full, because your mother will always give you food.

(4) 润去洗头了, 等会儿润回来看忆江南, 明一早润去玩儿了。(1.31)

Rùn qù xǐ tóu le, děng huìer rùn huílái kàn Yìjiāngnán, míng yīzǎo rùn qù wáner le.

I went to wash my hair, and then ran back to see *Yìjiāngnán*. I will go to play tomorrow morning.

In March 2022, there were 97 cases of *Rùn* on Sina Weibo, of which *Rùn₂* accounted for 8 cases, and the frequency has increased, but *Rùn₁* was still in a dominant position. At the same time, the meanings of *Rùn₁* and *Rùn₂* also have obvious changes, which are manifested in the following two aspects respectively: First, *Rùn₁* began to show negative semantic prosody, showing a willingness to change from [-wishful] to [-wishful]. For example:

(5) 宿舍网又寄了, 我要润回家, 放我回家。(3.15)

Sùshè wǎng yòu jì le, wǒ yào rùn huí jiā, fàng wǒ huíjiā.

The dormitory network is broken again. I need to go home and let me go home.

The above sentence said that there was a problem with the school network, while the home network is smooth, and the two are compared to produce a desire to go home, showing the willingness to change from [-wishful] to [-wishful].

Second, the meaning of 'emigrate' in *Rùn₂* is further highlighted, such as in (6).

(6) 又去研究了一圈各国最新的政策, 现在哪哪儿都不好润。(3.15)

Yòu qù yánjiū le yī quān gè guó zuì xīn de zhèngcè, xiànzài nǎ nǎer dōu bú hǎo rùn.

I have studied the latest policies of various countries, and now it is difficult to emigrate anywhere.

Compared with example (2), *Rùn₂* at this time clearly indicates that the destination is abroad, and the meaning of 'emigrate' is more obvious, but there are still similarities between *Rùn₂* and *Rùn₁* in this period, such as "润出去读个第二硕士(*rùn chūqù dú gè dì èr shuòshì*, run out to study for a second master's degree)" is not a typical emigration behavior, only an indication of studying abroad, and after graduation, she may still choose to return to China to live and work. In the transition stage of *Rùn₁* to *Rùn₂*, sometimes returning home from abroad can also be called *Rùn*, such as "看前面那个润回来的(*kàn qiánmiàn nà gè rùn huí lái de*, look at the one who returned)" (returning from New Zealand). It can be seen that the meaning of *Rùn₂* referring to immigrating abroad is not yet stable, the connotation is not clear enough, and it is in the process of development and change.

In April 2022, due to the tightening of the epidemic prevention and control policy for the COVID-19 in Shanghai at the end of March, emigrating abroad gradually became a hot topic on the network platform, which also boosted the significant increase in the frequency of *Rùn*. The number in April was 5–6 times that in March, and its meaning also changed significantly. We investigated the meaning of *Rùn* on Sina Weibo on April 1, April 15 and April 30 respectively, and the results is presented in Table 1.

Table 1. Frequency Statistics of *Rùn*1 and *Rùn*2 in April

Time	Synonym		
	Rùn$_1$		*Rùn*$_2$
	Neutral	Negative	
April 1st	2	2	3
April 15th	2	6	8
April 30th	1	8	17

In Table 1, the frequency of *Rùn*$_2$ gradually increased, exceeding *Rùn*$_1$ at the end of April, and becoming the main meaning of *Rùn* in just one month. At the same time, the neutral color of *Rùn*$_1$ gradually took a disadvantageous position, and the negative color came behind and became its main semantic prosody. As for *Rùn*$_2$, its semantics have been further clarified, and basically used to indicate immigration abroad, highlighting the contrast between foreign and domestic situations, and showing the urgency of the speaker. Such as:

(7) 这辈子一定要去一次科切拉, 现在去不了等我以后润出去了就一定要去一次, 我的ma…… (4.18)

Zhè bèizi yīdìng yào qù yī cì Kēqiēlā, xiànzài qù bú liǎo děng wǒ yǐhòu rùn chūqù le jiù yīdìng yào qù yī cì, wǒ de mā……

I must go to Kochella once in my life. If I can't go now, I'll definitely go once when I run out. Oh, my God……

In addition to being widely used in social software such as Weibo and Little Red Book as popular buzzword for personal emotional release, some we-media videos also use *Rùn* as the title to analyze the advantages and disadvantages of emigrating abroad, such as "普通国人究竟值不值得润去日本(*pǔtōng guórén jiūjìng zhí bú zhídé rùn qù Rìběn*, Whether ordinary Chinese people are worth emigrating to Japan)" and "想润?先听听我留学宿舍楼里的枪击案吧?(*xiǎng rùn? xiān tīng tīng wǒ liúxué sùshě lóu lǐ de qiāngjī àn ba?* Want to emigrate? Let's hear about the shooting in my dorm building?)".[3] *Rùn*$_2$ has also been used in news reports. In a report on Guancha Syndicate on April 6, it analyzed the current migration boom with the topic of "润?润到美国有用吗?(*rùn? rùn dào Měiguó yǒuyòng ma?* Migrate? Is it useful to go to America?)" The article pointed out that the main reason of current immigration boom is the pursuit of better material conditions. The entry of *Rùn* from the network style into the news style shows

---

[3] These two video titles are from Bilibili (https://www.bilibili.com/), On April 2 and April 20.

that its use is no longer just a spontaneous word or rhetoric behavior of netizens, but a language practice that all social classes participate in. The social phenomenon and mass psychology it embodies have attracted extensive attention.

Since then, *Rùn* has maintained the momentum of rapid growth. We took Sina Weibo from May to December as the research object, and counted the frequency of *Rùn* on 5th, 15th and 25th of these months, as shown in the Fig. 1 below.

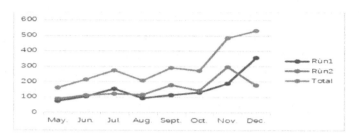

Fig. 1. Frequency of *Rùn₁* and *Rùn₂* from May to December

The two meanings were basically in a sustained growth trend from May to December. Except for a slight decline in August of *Rùn₁*, the other months were flat or increased. However, the two meanings were also slightly different, *Rùn₁* in July and December increased obviously, and *Rùn₂* in May to September continued to grow, peaking in November, and declining in October and December. Overall, the acceptance of *Rùn* is increasing. The ups and downs in use were closely related to social changes, which will be explained in detail in Sect. 4 of this paper.

Changes in the Usage of *Rùn*. While the meaning has changed, the usage of *Rùn* has also changed, mainly in the following four ways.

First, transitivity.

Since *Rùn* is mainly derived from the English intransitive verbs 'run' and 'escape', the word is also used as an intransitive verb in most cases, that is, the action or change expressed by the verb usually does not dominate or point to other people or things [4]. In the examples above, *Rùn* can be followed by a specific place to indicate a destination or direction, usually in the form of '*Rùn* + 到(*Dào*, to)/去(*Qù*, to)', such as "润去美国(*rùn qù měiguó*, emigrate to the United States)" "润到国外(*rùn dào guówài*, emigrate to foreign countries)". In the later development process, *Rùn* can be directly added to the place object, and its degree of transitivity was increased. For example:

(8) Love and peace, 五月顺利去工作然后润德国。(4.30)
Love and peace, wǔyuè shùnlì qù gōngzuò ránhòu rùn Déguó.
Love and peace, go to work smoothly in May and emigrate too Germany.

Besides the example above, the common place objects after *Rùn* such as 'the United States, Australia, Japan', etc., are all common destinations for immigrants.

In addition to the place object, *Rùn* can also carry a noun indicating the starting point, as the following example illustrates:

(9) 中秋要润学校了，见到不想见到的人，经历不可避免的魔幻的事情，烦啊。(9.5)

Zhōngqiū yào rùn xuéxiào le, jiàn dào bú xiǎng jiàn dào de rén, jīnglì bú kě bìmiǎn de móhuàn de shìqíng, fán a.

I'm going to leave school during the Mid Autumn Festival. It's annoying to see people I don't want to see and experience inevitable magical things.

In the above example, the meaning of *Rùn* is equivalent to 'leave' and "润学校(*Rùn xuéxiào*, leave school)" refers to 'leave school', which is sometimes introduced using 'from' in English. This type of situation appears much less frequently in the corpus than the previous type.

Second, reference.

Due to the semantic origin of *Rùn* from the English verb 'run', it is mostly used declaratively, and the above example all belong to this category. In use, *Rùn* is mostly combined with the dynamic auxiliary word "了(le)" to form a prosodic word, and can also be used alone or with directional verbs such as "去(qù)" and "回(huí)" to form a prosodic word. Short length and relatively simple form of complements can also be added later.

As the frequency of use increases, *Rùn* begins to appear in referential usage, serving as a subject, object, and attributive in sentences. For example:

(10) 润是少部分人才有的机会, 无论在时间还是金钱上, 润比卷和躺都需要更高的成本。(5.26)

Rùn shì shǎo bùfèn rén cái yǒu de jīhuì, wúlùn zài shíjiān háishì jīnqián shàng, rùn bǐ juǎn hé tǎng dōu xūyào gèng gāo de chéngběn.

Rùn is an opportunity for a small number of talents, both in time and money, and requires higher costs than *Juǎn* and *Tǎng*.

(11) 为什么学校那么好笑。非得让润与不润的人难堪才罢。前者用期末考牵着, 后者听你的话了, 但能给大家一些选择权?(12.5)

Wéishénme xuéxiào nàme hǎo xiào. Fēi dé ràng rùn yǔ bú rùn de rén nánkān cái bà. Qián zhě yòng qīmò kǎo qiān zhe, hòu zhě tīng nǐ de huà le, dàn néng gěi dàjiā yīxiē xuǎnzé quán?

Why is school so funny. You have to embarrass those who are both *Rùn* and not *Rùn*. The former is led by the final exam, while the latter follows your advice, but can you give everyone some choice?

Third, the ability to form words continues to strengthen.

Since its emergence, *Rùn* has mostly served as a separate syntactic component as a word. However, with increasing frequency of use, *Rùn* has gradually been used for word formation. Generally, it is used as a declarative morpheme combined with a nominal morpheme to form a attribute-head compound word, which is used to represent related people and things. Take the following two examples:

(12) 加了几个润群, 群友们来自各个地方, 本身条件也各不相同, 但是无一例外都目标明确。(6.25)

Jiā le jǐ gè rùnqún, qúnyǒu men láizì gègè dìfāng, běnshēn tiáojiàn yě gè bú xiàngtóng, dànshì wú yī lìwài dōu mùbiāo míngquè.

We have added several *Rùnqún* members, who come from various places and have different conditions, but without exception, they have clear goals.

(13) 润学真正流行是今年年初以来。美国、加拿大、澳大利亚, 还有欧洲列国, 都是润学的选择。(6.23)

Rùnxué zhēnzhèng liúxíng shì jīnnián niánchū yǐlái, Měiguó, Jiānádà, Aodàlìyà, háiyǒu Ouzhōu liè guó, dōushì rùnxué de xuǎnzé.

Rùnxué is really popular since the beginning of this year. The United States, Canada, Australia, as well as European countries, are the choice of *Rùnxué*.

The *Rùn* in the above example can be seen as a morpheme, forming words with relatively fixed meanings. Such as '润学(*Rùnxué*)' refers to the common theory of leaving the domestic environment in order to enjoy some high welfare in other countries, initially introduced by immigration and overseas study institutions. There are many words composed of *Rùn* as morphemes, such as "润人(*rùnrén*)" "润党(*rùndǎng*)" "润文化 (*rùnwénhuà*)" "润论 (*rùnlùn*)". It is worth noting that the morpheme *Rùn* can also form a group of synonyms, such as the references to"润党(*rùndǎng*)" and "润人党(*rùnréndǎng*)" have the same meaning. The semi-affix '党(*dǎng*)' indicates a certain type of person, and the '人(*rén*)' and '党(*dǎng*)' in '润人党(*rùnréndǎng*)' are synonymous with the text and semantic repetition, which reflects the general characteristics of confusion in the early use in the early use of the network language.

Although the current word formation pattern of *Rùn* still follows '*Rùn* + X' mainly, we predict that the future may further develop 'X + *Rùn*' type words. The referential *Rùn* can refer to the actions or events of 'escape' and 'immigration', and it may further refer to the person who completed these actions or events. When combined with morphemes representing place names, it can indicate the person who immigrated to these areas. This phenomenon has been manifested in the past, such as "吹(*chuī*)" means 'boast', indicating that there is no reliable source of information, relying solely on words or even completely fictional facts, infinitely exaggerating the strength of a country or region, such as "日吹(*rì chuī*)" "美吹(*měi chuī*)" and so on.

Fourth, idiomization.

As a kind of fixed and short phrases which are widely spread and have specific meaning, idioms are an integral part of language [5]. Idioms refer to a wide range, usually including colloquial sayings, aphorisms, allegorical sayings, proverbs, slang, jargon, etc., and also include irregular idioms, such as "好你个(*hǎo nǐ gè*) + X" "整个一个(*zhěnggè yīgè*) + X" and so on [6]. Idioms are the essence of language and the carrier of culture, with a high degree of generalization and expression ability. *Rùn* is very common in the irregular idiom construction, which reflects the strong characteristics of the times. For example:

(14) 虽然我们开玩笑说"应润尽润", 支持二鬼子润走, 留下的人真心实意建设祖国。(10.31)

Suīrán wǒmen kāiwánxiào shuō "yīng rùn jìn rùn", zhīchí èr guǐzi rùn zǒu, liú xià de rén zhēnxīnshíyì jiànshè zǔguó.

Although we joked that all people with immigration intentions be satisfied and supported the traitors to run away, the people left behind sincerely built our country.

The buzzword *Rùn* was formed and developed in the context of the COVID-19 epidemic, so it has also entered the idioms related to the epidemic. In addition to example (14), there are "能润尽润(*néng rùn jìn rùn*)" "愿润尽润(*yuàn rùn jìn rùn*)" "非必要不润(*fēi bìyào bú rùn*)", respectively from "应检尽检"(*yīng jiǎn jìn jiǎn*)"能检尽检(*néng jiǎn jìn jiǎn*)" "愿检尽检(yuàn jiǎn jìn jiǎn)" "非必要不返乡(*fēi bìyào bú fǎnxiāng*)". In addition, there are several idioms that are more traditional, such as "当润则润(*dāng rùn*) *zé rùn)*" "润了后悔一时, 不润后悔一辈子*(rùn le hòuhuǐ yīshí, bú rùn hòuhuǐ yībèizi)*", respectively, from "当断不断*(dāng duàn bú duàn)*" "当兵后悔两年, 不当兵后悔一辈子*(dāngbīng hòuhuǐ liǎng nián, bú dāngbīng hòuhuǐ yībèizi)*". It can be seen that the acceptance of *Rùn* has been improving, and the scope of use has gradually expanded.

Idiom is an important rhetorical device in language, such as "非必要不返乡*(fēi bìyào bú fǎnxiāng)*" is a language innovation made by students to ridicule the 'one-size-fits-all' management model of universities, in order to satirize the school's overly broad and inflexible interpretation of "非必要*(fēi bìyào)*".

In summary, the meaning and usage of *Rùn* have undergone significant changes in just one year. An [7] summarized the characteristics of online language into four aspects: heterogeneity, speed, anonymity, and openness. Among them, 'speed' refers to 'internet makes the release of information and communication between users very fast'. As the most direct reflection of social life and reality, network buzzwords can spread in a very short period of time, and their meaning and usage also undergo certain changes. The development of *Rùn* reflects this trend.

3 The Spread and Integration of Rùn from a Global Chinese Perspective

The world today is in an era of great development, great integration and great changes in the global Chinese [8], and the Chinese of different regions are showing remarkable convergence [9]. Many scholars call for actively promoting the integration of Chinese in communication [10], and in their research, they also should fully consider the convergence and differences of Chinese in different regions, as well as the issue of two-way interaction [11]. In the process of the integration of global Chinese, network buzzwords are the most direct and active symbol system reflecting the society, and play an important role in the communication of language and culture [12]. In this regard, there have been some preliminary investigations, such as Diao [13] examined the use of the top ten network languages in the *Chinese Inventory 2016* in Chinese newspapers in Taiwan, Singapore, Malaysia, the United States and Canada. Like most buzzwords, *Rùn* has rapidly spread to other Chinese communities, with a more obvious trend of integration.

Tang [8] divided the overseas Chinese words absorbed by Mainland Chinese subjects into three levels: beginning to enter, already entered and integrated; On the other hand, Diao [14, 15] summarized the fusion process into three stages: borrowing, self use, and variant, and investigated the integration between Chinese mainland and Taiwan, Hong Kong, and Macao regions. 'Borrowing' is the introduction of original words with context, which can be called direct use; 'self-use' refers to the independent use of the other party's context; 'variant' is the development of changing usage, including meaning and usage, which is an advanced stage of integration, indicating that the word has been integrated into the other party's vocabulary. Below, we will analyze the dissemination and use of *Rùn* in the Taiwan, Hong Kong, and Macao Chinese circles as well as overseas Chinese circles.

3.1 The Dissemination and Use of *Rùn* in Taiwan, Hong Kong, and Macao Chinese Circle

As far as we can see, there have been cases of *Rùn* in Taiwan, Hong Kong and Macao Chinese circle, mainly *Rùn*₂, but they are in different stages. First look at the situation of the Taiwan community, *Rùn* first appeared in Taiwan at the end of April 2022, such as "以英文run的中文谐音字"润"字来表达想法(*yǐ yīngwén* run *de zhōngwén xiéyīn zì rùn zì lái biǎodá xiǎngfǎ*)". This example mainly introduces the *Rùn* of mainland internet platforms, which has a clear mainland background, where *Rùn* mainly refers to immigration. Afterwards, the popularity of *Rùn* in Taiwan gradually increased, and self-use examples began to appear. Such as:

(15) 台湾最有名的"润者"当属谐星李立群。(11.6)

Táiwān zuì yǒumíng de "rùnzhě"dāng shǔ xiéxīng Lǐ Lìqún.

Taiwan's most famous *rùnzhě* is the comedian Li Liqun.

In this case, Li Liqun is a Taiwanese actor, therefore this case has been basically out of the context of Chinese mainland and belongs to a self-use case. In addition, the variable use of *Rùn* in Taiwan differs from that in Chinese mainland, mainly manifested in two aspects: firstly, the morpheme *Rùn* forms a new word, such as "大润潮(dà rù cháo)", which refers to a wave of immigrants from Chinese mainland, is a new word created by Taiwanese netizens using the morpheme *Rùn* and is not found on mainland websites. Secondly, the application of *Rùn* has expanded from humans to inanimate objects, resulting in a new meaning. For example, in "润了近八百亿美元(rùn le jìn bā bǎi yì měiyuán)", the subject of *Rùn* is money, and this usage is not found in Chinese mainland, indicating that *Rùn* has entered a stage of variant in Taiwan.

Let's look at the Hong Kong community. As far as we can see, Hong Kong's *Rùn* first appeared on April 23, 2022, slightly later than Taiwan, such as "网民以英文run 的谐音字"润"字来表达想法(*wǎngmín yǐ yīngwén* run *de xiéyīn zì rùn zì lái biǎodá xiǎngfǎ*)". This example is the explanation of the origin of *Rùn*, the main content comes from the mainland, belongs to the situation of quoting. Although *Rùn* is used slightly less frequently in Hong Kong than in Taiwan, it has also entered the stage of self-use. As shown in example (16).

(16) 毕竟在"一国两制"下, 香港对于内地不少"润友"仍具一定吸引力。(12.13)

Bìjìng zài Yīguóliǎngzhì xià, Xiānggǎng duì yú nèidì búshǎo rùnyǒu réng jù yīdìng xīyǐnlì.

After all, under the 'one country, two systems' policy, Hong Kong still has a certain attraction for many *rùnyǒu* in the mainland.

The term *rùnyǒu* in example (16) refers to people from mainland who come to work and live in Hong Kong. This example describes the relevant situation of mainland talents migrating to Hong Kong.

The frequency in the Macau community is the lowest, as of December 22, 2022, only one case of *rùnxué* was found in the Wise News, which is also an explanation of *Rùn* in mainland, indicating that Macau is still in the stage of introduction and popularization, that is, the borrowing stage.

In summary, the *Rùn* of the three language communities in Taiwan, Hong Kong, and Macao is in different stages of integration. The Taiwan has achieved full coverage of borrowing, self-use, and variant, while the Hong Kong community has both borrowing and self-use, and the Macau community is in the initial stage of borrowing.

3.2   The Dissemination and Use of *Rùn* in Overseas Chinese Circles

The survey of *Rùn* in the overseas Chinese circles mainly focuses on the situation in Southeast Asia, North America, and Australia. In the Southeast Asian Chinese community, Singapore introduced the *Rùn* earlier, with a situation similar to Taiwan, Hong Kong, and Macao, mainly introducing the source of *Rùn*. In addition, Chinese media in Malaysia, Indonesia, and Thailand have also followed up on the Putonghua circle to explain *Rùn*, including the causes and consequences of its occurrence. However, its use in Southeast Asian remains at the borrowing stage, and there have been no examples of self-use and variant.

North America takes the United States as an example, and its development situation is similar to that of Australia. Therefore, the two will be combined for discussion. The earliest cases in both regions appeared in April 2022, similar to other countries and regions, and were also used to illustrate the origin and reasons of *Rùn*

In addition to borrowing, there have also been cases of self-use in the United States and Australia, as shown in examples (17) and (18) below.

(17) 布林肯的说法是配合拜登政府，早点从台湾撤离台积电润(run、跑)到美国, 媒体不就报导美方兵推炸毁台积电、撤走晶片工程师?(10.21)

Bùlínkěn de shuōfǎ shì pèihé Bàidēng zhèngfǔ, zǎodiǎn cóng Táiwān chèí Táijīdiàn rùn (run, pǎo) dào Měiguó, méitǐ bú jiù bàodǎo měi fāng bīng tuī zhàhuǐ Táijīdiàn, chè zǒu jīngpiàn gōngchéngshī?

Blinken's statement is to cooperate with the Biden administration and evacuate TSMC from Taiwan to the United States early, and the media would not just report that the US troops pushed to blow up TSMC and remove chip engineers?

(18) 为了更高的工资，更好的就业机会，更多的阳光，越来越多的新西兰人跨越塔斯曼海峡, "润"(Run)到隔壁澳大利亚去了。(6.19)

Wèile gèng gāo de gōngzī, gèng hǎo de jiùyè jīhuì, gèng duō de yángguāng, yuè lái yuè duō de Xīnxīlán rén kuàyuè Tǎsīmàn hǎixiá, rùn(Run)dào gébì Aodàlìyà qù le.

To get higher wages, better job opportunities, and more sunshine, more and more New Zealanders are running across the Tasman Strait to Australia next door.

The above two case respectively reflect the local social reality, with obvious localization characteristics, indicating that *Rùn* has been integrated into the North American and Australian Chinese. Based on the usage of *Rùn* in the Taiwan, Hong Kong, and Macao Chinese circles and overseas Chinese circles, it is found that the dissemination and diffusion of *Rùn* has begun to take shape, but there are significant community differences.

To sum up, the spread of *Rùn* from the Putonghua circle to other Chinese communities began at the end of April 2022, which is closely related to the immigration problem caused by the Internet in mainland China, so it is mainly focused on the use of *Rùn₂*. Of course, due to the influence of political systems in different countries and regions, *Rùn₂* can also express the meaning of 'emigrating' to some regions, such as "润回台湾"(*rùn huí Táiwān*, run to Taiwan) and "润香港" (*rùn Xiānggǎng*, run to Xianggang). From the above survey, it can be seen that there have been many examples of *Rùn* for self-use in in many countries and regions, and the Taiwan community has had a change in form and meaning. Therefore, we have reason to believe that the degree of integration and interaction of *Rùn* in the global Chinese will be further deepened, the frequency will continue to increase, and the usage will be gradually enriched, which is very likely to appear more abundant variant usage.

4 Sociolinguistic Interpretation of *Rùn*

Sociolinguistics holds that language and society are not independent of each other, and there are complex relationships between them [16]. Language is the most important means of communication on which social life depends. Therefore, any change in social life, even the smallest change, will be more or less reflected in language, mainly in vocabulary [17].

As a kind of social dialect, network language obviously embodies the characteristics of covariation between language and society. Since 2012, the annual *Chinese Inventory* will release the 'Top ten Internet terms' of that year, and these internet terms all reflect the inextricable links with the society, such as "你幸福吗 (*nǐ xìngfú ma*, are you happy)" in 2012, "打call (*dǎ call*, applaud)" in 2017, "硬核 (*yìnghé*, hardcore)" in 2019, and "躺平 (*tǎngpíng*, lying flat)" in 2021. They were widely popular on the Internet first, and then enter social life in a very short time, and with the development of social reality, new changes have taken place. The buzzword *Rùn* is the same, which reflects the impact of social reality on public psychology and cognition. From the perspective of sociolinguistics, the use and development of *Rùn* have at least the following three characteristics.

Firstly, it embodies the social psychology of seeking novelty, diversity, and interest. In fact, there are already words in Chinese that have the same meaning as '跑(*pǎo*, run)', '逃(*táo*, escape)', '移民(*yímín*,immigration)', etc., but the new word *Rùn* still spreads rapidly on the internet, and its meaning and usage have undergone significant variations. This means that the online community, mainly composed of young people, has a strong desire for novelty, diversity, and interest in language use, innovating and transforming language forms to pursue trendy and fashionable trends.

Secondly, it reflects the profound impact of social reality. If the emergence of *Rùn* stems from the language psychology of netizens who pursue novelty, then the rapid development and changes in the later stage were driven by social reality. From the overall low frequency, mainly neutral color $Rùn_1$, to the sharp increase of negative color $Rùn_1$ and $Rùn_2$, which is closely related to the COVID-19 epidemic and the inconvenience of people's life, resulting in a wave of immigration spreading in the society. It is worth noting that $Rùn_1$ showed a significant growth trend in July and November, which is related to the concentration of college students leaving school in winter and summer vacation. College students, as an important part of the Internet users, frequently use $Rùn_1$ to express their intention to leave school in these two months, resulting in a significant increase in the use of $Rùn_1$.

Thirdly, it contains profound social and cultural motivations. Chinese netizens, who are at a major point of change in the times, exhibit a contradictory mentality when facing challenging social realities. On the one hand, they are in a severe and competitive reality, trapped in the spiritual anxiety of irrational competition; on the other hand, they hope to find an outlet for life. Therefore, the emergence and development of buzzwords like *Rùn* have a certain inevitability. However, when hope is difficult to turn into reality, the network buzzwords as a barometer of social emotions will also produce new changes. Taking *Rùn₂* as an example, when the drawbacks of immigrant life are exposed, the additional meaning of [−comfort] to [+comfort] no longer exists. For example:

(19) 一大堆说追求"人权"与"自由", 那么想要自由怎么不自己润去自由的国度, 确实是挺自由的, 吸毒自由, 持枪自由。(12.3)

Yī dà duī shuō zhuīqiú rénquán yǔ zìyóu, nàme xiǎng yào zìyóu zěnme bú zìjǐ rùn qù zìyóu de guódù, quèshí shì tǐng zìyóu de, xīdú zìyóu, chí qiāng zìyóu.

A lot of people say they pursue human rights and freedom, so why not immigrate to a free country if you want freedom. It is indeed quite free, with freedom to take drugs and hold guns.

In addition, netizens have also created the word "润物(rùnwù)" with a clear derogatory and critical color, referring to immigrants who maliciously smear the country. They express their fervent admiration for all the cultures, characteristics, and even physiological characteristics of other races, and blindly reject the traditional culture and customs of their own nation.

From this, it can be seen that the development of *Rùn₂* is closely related to the opposing debates of social culture, fully reflecting the language's reflection on social reality and psychology. With the development of network technology and the increase in the number of netizens, network language has an increasingly obvious impact on language use. From the perspective of sociolinguistics, expanding the examination of the social reality and psychological state behind language facts has profound significance.

5   Conclusion

This paper takes the network buzzword *Rùn* as an example to examine the process of its emergence and development, sorts out its dissemination and integration from the Putonghua circle, and finally analyzes its social significance from the perspective of sociolinguistics.

Compared to network language, the variation and change of the past language is usually relatively slow, taking years, decades, or even hundreds of years, while the change of network language is short and rapid, whether in terms of meaning, usage, or the social reality and psychology reflected behind it. If language variation and changes in the past were silent, then the changes and development of network language were explosive and spread without time difference through the internet. Due to these characteristics, many online language have achieved cross-community or even pan-community use through their vivid characteristics. Some buzzwords are still active in various Chinese community, with high adaptability and influence.

Finally, we should also pay attention to the study of new words. In fact, not only in Chinese mainland, but also in Taiwan, Singapore, Malaysia, Japan, South Korea and other countries and regions, they also attach great importance to new words, using language to record living conditions and social changes, reflecting the language ecology. It can be seen that new words are not only the main means to track the forefront of the times and grasp social dynamics, but also a powerful evidence to record social life and restore historical development. They are also the link to connect the world and have linguistic and transcending linguistic significance and value.

Acknowledgements. This paper is a partial outcome of the program 'A Study on the Applicability of Southeast Asian Chinese Textbooks', supported by State Language Commission Global Chinese Learning Alliance Research projects (YB145-29).

References

1. Li, C.: An analysis of the grammaticalization, coercion mechanisms and formation motivation of the new construction 'XX Zi' from the cognitive perspective. In: Dong, M., Gu, Y., Hong, F. (eds.) CLSW 2021. LNCS (LNAI), vol. 13249, pp.172–186. Springer, Cham (2021). https://doi.org/10.1007/978-3-031-06703-7_13
2. Yang, H., Yue, H.: A study on the construction features of "Pan X." In: Liu, M., Kit, C., Su, Q. (eds.) Chinese Lexical Semantics. LNCS (LNAI), vol. 12278, pp. 161–172. Springer, Cham (2021). https://doi.org/10.1007/978-3-030-81197-6_15
3. Zhang, M.: A study on the network buzzword 'Foxi' in the subcultural genealogy. China Youth Study **8**, 32–37+63 (2018). (in Chinese)
4. Li, Z.F.: Pre-Qin intransitive and transitive verbs. Zhongguo Yuwen **4**, 287–296 (1994). (in Chinese)
5. Wang, L., Sun, J.Y., Zhang, J.G.: Characteristics of Chinese idioms and their English translation. J. Lanzhou Univ. (Soc. Sci. Edn.) **37**(S1), 147–149 (2009). (in Chinese)
6. Shi, C.H.: Constructional view on syntactical structures and the relevant theories. Hanyu Xuebao **2**, 23–38+95 (2013). (in Chinese)
7. An, Z.W.: On the Social Influence of Contemporary Network Language. Theory J. **4**, 114–116 (2010). (in Chinese)
8. Tang, Z.X.: An examination of the hierarchies, categories and their proportions of overseas Chinese words bbsorbed by mainland subject Chinese. In: Li, X.X., Tian, X.L., Xu, Z.B. (eds.) Cross-Strait Modern Chinese Studies, pp. 111–142. Publishing House of Culture and Education (HK), Hong Kong (2009). (in Chinese)
9. You, R.J.: Global trend of Chinese language integration is becoming more and more obvious. Soc. Sci. Daily **05**, (2012). (in Chinese)
10. Zhou, Q.H.: On the study and trend of "Greater Chinese". Hanyu Xuebao **1**, 13–19+95 (2016). (in Chinese)
11. Guo, X.: On the research of Huayu. Appl. Linguis.Linguis. **2**, 22–28 (2006). (in Chinese)
12. Shao, J.M., Liu, Z.B.: The typicality and identification criteria of Chinese community words. Linguistic Res **3**, 1–7 (2011). (in Chinese)
13. Diao, Y.B.: Theoretical construction and empirical research on global Chinese language. Sinolingua, Beijing (2018). (in Chinese)
14. Diao, Y.B.: Mainland words in Taiwan: from entry to integration. Guangming Daily **07** (2016). (in Chinese)
15. Diao, Y.B.: A Study on the Difference and Integration of Modern Chinese Across the Strait and in Hong Kong and Macao. The Commercial Press, Beijing (2015). (in Chinese)
16. Guo, X.: Chinese Sociolinguistics. Zhejiang University Press, Hangzhou (2004). (in Chinese)
17. Chen, Y.: Sociolinguistics. The Commercial Press, Beijing (2000). (in Chinese)

A Semantic Analysis of *Suffocate* Verbs

Shaoming Wang[1] and Shan Wang[1,2(✉)]

[1] Department of Chinese Language and Literature, Faculty of Arts and Humanities,
University of Macau, Macao, Special Administrative Region, People's Republic of China
shanwang@um.edu.mo
[2] Institute of Collaborative Innovation, University of Macau, Macao,
Special Administrative Region, People's Republic of China

Abstract. The information of semantic roles can reflect important characteristics of verbs. Among verbs related to animals actions, *suffocate* verbs have received limited attention in the fields of linguistics and language teaching. This study has selected five *suffocate* verbs and analyzed 305 single sentences containing them from corpora. The results show that the verb 窒息 *zhìxī* 'suffocate' has both agent-like semantic roles and patient-like semantic roles, whereas the other 4 verbs only have agent-like semantic roles according to the analyzed sentences. Additionally, only 窒息 *zhìxī* 'suffocate' appears in the causative alternation. The common situational roles of *suffocate* verbs include Manner, Time, and Location. This paper is conducive to the enriching the research on *suffocate* verbs and provides an important reference for lexicography.

Keywords: Verbs · Semantics · *Suffocate* Verbs · Dependency Grammar

1 Introduction

Understanding sentences unfolds from syntactic and semantic relations between verbs and their governing constituents in sentences [1]. As breathing is the fundamental behavior of living organisms, verbs describing breathing can be found across various human languages. These verbs are also commonly included in the scope of second language teaching. For example, 呼吸 *hūxī* 'breathe' is classified as a fourth-level word in *The Syllabus of Graded Words and Characters for Chinese Proficiency* (revised) [2]. In contrast, less attention has been paid to verbs that express the disruption of breathing. [3] classified English verbs in the book titled *English Verb Classes and Alternations*. *Suffocate* verbs is a subtype of Verbs Involving the Body. [3] pointed out that these verbs are related to the disruption of breathing and have the characteristics of the causative alternation. Example (1a) shows the intransitive use of the verb *drown*, which simply means the sailor is in a state of death, while (1b) shows the transitive use.

(1) a. The sailor drowned.
  b. The pirates drowned the sailor.

Research on Chinese *suffocate* verbs is limited, with [4] conducting a detailed investigation of English and Chinese causative alternation. He found that the Causative Alternation Strength (CAS) of Chinese and English *suffocate* verbs differs. The CAS of monosyllabic verbs in Chinese is generally lower than that in English, whereas the CAS of disyllable verbs in Chinese is higher than that in English. He pointed out that the CAS of *suffocate* verbs is related to cognitive conception. Verbs concerning exterior organs of the respiratory system (namely neck), such as *throttle* and *strangle*, tend to have the lowest CAS, while verbs involving the inner part of the body (namely throat and trachea), such as *suffocate* and *choke*, tend to have the highest value. [4] divided subject arguments in the causative sentences containing 窒息 *zhìxī* 'suffocate' into five categories, namely the agentive force (你 *nǐ* 'you', 我 *wǒ* 'I', 人 *rén* 'people'), psychological forces (恐怖 *kǒngbù* 'terror', 孤独 *gūdú* 'loneliness'), natural forces (乌云 *wūyún* 'dark cloud', 刺骨的寒风 *cìgǔ de hánfēng* 'bitter wind'), instrumental forces (专制制度 *zhuānzhì zhìdù* 'autocratic system', 毒气 *dúqì* 'poisonous gas'), and social forces (填鸭式的教学 *tiányā shì de jiàoxué* 'spoon feeding education', 封建礼教 *fēngjiàn lǐjiào* 'feudal ethics'). The quantity of the agentive force is small. In terms of objects, English mainly allows living objects (such as *baby* and *children*), while Chinese also includes abstract nouns (爱 *ài* 'love' and 精神 *jīngshén* 'spirit'). Besides 窒息 *zhìxī* 'suffocate', [4] found that subjects and objects of other *suffocate* verbs in causative sentences also have their respective characteristics. For example, agent-like arguments of 掐 *qiā* 'pinch' can only be people, while agent-like arguments of 噎 *yē* 'choke' can only be 饭粒 *fànlì* 'rice' and 馒头 *mántou* 'steamed bread', etc.

Compared to [4]'s research, this paper focuses on verbs associated with the interruption of breathing. The research questions raised in this paper are: (1) Do *suffocate* verbs differ in terms of semantic roles and event relations? (2) Do they all exhibit causative alternation? To address the questions, this paper focuses on semantic roles of Chinese *suffocate* verbs. Semantic roles provide a way to classify the meaning relations between relevant structural components in a sentence [5], and semantic role labeling is a key aspect of current semantic analysis [6, 7]. Building a verb-centered semantic role knowledge base holds great significance for language research, language teaching, and natural language processing [1]. With labeling semantic roles, syntactic and semantic knowledge are made explicit [8]. Various annotation systems for semantic roles have been proposed by researchers [9–11]. Among these methods, this paper ultimately opts for dependency grammar [12, 13], which is suitable for languages with flexible word order like Chinese [14].

VerbNet [15] has six *suffocate* verbs, including *asphyxiate, choke, stifle, suffocate, drown, starve*. This study has selected five Chinese *suffocate* verbs (窒息 *zhìxī* 'suffocate', 断气 *duànqì* 'stop breathing', 屏息 *bǐngxī* 'hold one's breath', 屏气 *bǐngqì* 'hold one's breath', and 咽气 *yànqì* 'stop breathing'). In accordance with [16, 17], this study sampled 305 single sentences containing these verbs. A syntactic and semantic annotation tool based on dependency grammar was employed to manually correct the wrong automatic annotation, utilizing LTP of Harbin Institute of Technology [18, 19]. The semantic features of these verbs were then summarized according to the annotation results.

Table 1. The number of single sentences of *suffocate* verbs

Verbs	Single sentences after sampling
窒息 *zhìxī* 'suffocate'	134
断气 *duànqì* 'stop breathing'	42
屏息 *bǐngxī* 'hold one's breath'	71
屏气 *bǐngqì* 'hold one's breath'	28
咽气 *yànqì* 'stop breathing'	30
Total	305

2 Semantic Roles and Event Relations of *Suffocate* Verbs

This section focuses on agent-like semantic roles (主体角色 *zhǔtǐ juésè*), patient-like semantic roles (客体角色 *kètǐ juésè*), situational roles, and event relations of *suffocate* verbs. The semantic roles this paper discussed are the words that the verbs collocate with. Agent-like arguments and patient-like arguments are the core arguments [20]. Situational roles describe various scene factors such as where, how, and scope of an event. Event relations show the semantic relations formed between different events.

Different annotation rules can differ in judging semantic roles. For *suffocate* verbs, the difference is mainly reflected in the roles of the Agent and the Experiencer. LTP regards subjects who perform can actions deliberately, move continuously, or express mental activities as the Agent. 战士 *zhànshì* 'warrior' in Table 2 is a conscious subject, so the LTP considers it as the Agent. However, *The Knowledge Base of Content Words* [21] treats the Agent as the performers with an proactive action; it treats the person who undergoes some kind of change as the Experiencer. For example, in the sentence 爷爷去世了。*Yéye qùshì le.* 'Grandpa passed away', 去世 *qùshì* 'pass away' is not an action performed by grandpa deliberately, but a kind of change, so 爷爷 *yéye* 'grandpa' is the Experiencer. According to the definition of *The Contemporary Chinese Dictionary (7th Edition)* [22], 窒息 *zhìxī* 'suffocate', 咽气 *yànqì* 'stop breathing', 断气 *duànqì* 'stop breathing' are not proactive actions. For these words, this study used the criteria of *The Knowledge Base of Content Words*. Examples are shown in Table 2. First, 窒息 *zhìxī* 'suffocate' can have both agent-like roles and patient-like roles, whereas the other four verbs only involve agent-like roles. 窒息 *zhìxī* 'suffocate' involves the patient whose breathing is suffocated, such as 人民 *rénmín* 'people'. It also has metaphorical use, such as 工业 *gōngyè* 'industry'. In the case of 屏息 *bǐngxī* 'hold one's breath' and 屏气 *bǐngqì* 'hold one's breath', the person performing these actions is considered the Agent, such as 菊仙 *Júxiān* 'a woman's name' and 病人 *bìngrén* 'patient'.

The verb 窒息 *zhìxī* 'suffocate' is found in the causative alternation, as in (2a) and (2b). Using the semantic system of *A Thesaurus of Modern Chinese* [23], we summarized some common types of 窒息 *zhìxī* 'suffocate', as shown in Table 3.

(2) a. 我快窒息了。(BCC Corpus)
      Wǒ kuài zhìxī le.
      I_soon_suffocate_ASP

Table 2. Agent-like and patient-like semantic roles of *suffocate* verbs

Semantic roles		Examples
窒息 *zhìxī* 'suffocate'		
Agent-like Semantic role	Experiencer	两个战士已经窒息了！ Liǎng gè zhànshì yǐjīng *zhìxī* le! two_Classifier_fighter_already_suffocate_ASP 'Two fighters have suffocated!'
Patient-like Semantic role	Patient	德国人民被窒息在法西斯血腥的恐怖统治中。 Déguó **rénmín** bèi *zhìxī* zài Fǎxīsī xuèxīng de kǒngbù tǒngzhì zhōng. Germany_people_Passive Marker_suffocate_at_fascism_bloody_DE_ terrifying_ rule_inside 'The German people were suffocated by the bloody and terrifying rule of fascism.'
	Content	美国商品的大量倾销窒息了菲律宾的民族工业。 Měiguó shāngpǐn de dàliàng qīngxiāo *zhìxī* le Fēilǜbīn de mínzú **gōngyè**. America_goods_DE_mass_dumping_suffocate_ASP_the Philippines_DE_nation_industry 'The massive dumping of American goods suffocated the national industry of the Philippines.'
屏息 *bǐngxī* 'hold one's breath'		
Agent-like Semantic role	Agent	菊仙屏息。 **Júxiān** *bǐngxī*. Júxiān_hold one's breath 'Juxian held her breath.'
咽气 *yànqì* 'stop breathing'		
Agent-like Semantic role	Experiencer	他是星期一咽气的。 Tā shì xīngqīyī *yànqì* de. he_be_Monday_stop breathing_DE 'He stopped breathing on Monday.'
断气 *duànqì* 'stop breathing'		
Agent-like Semantic role	Experiencer	他是在那里断气的。 Tā shì zài nàlǐ *duànqì* de. he_be_at_there_stop breathing_DE 'There he stopped breathing.'
屏气 *bǐngqì* 'hold one's breath'		

(*continued*)

Table 2. (*continued*)

Agent-like Semantic roles	Agent	病人只须屏气一会儿就完成整个过程。 Bìngrén zhǐ xū *bìngqì* yīhuǐ'er jiù wánchéng zhěnggè guòchéng. patient_only_need_hold one's breath_a while_then_complete_whole_procedure 'The patient only needs to hold their breath for a while to complete the procedure.'

'I'm almost suffocating.'

b. 狐皮的臊气和樟脑刺鼻的臭气几乎窒息了我。(BCC Corpus).

Húpí de sāoqì hé zhāngnǎo cìbí de chòuqì jīhū zhìxī le wǒ.

Fox   fur_DE_   musky   odor _and_camphor_pungent_DE_stench_almost_suffocate_ASP_I

'The musky odor of fox-fur and the pungent stench of camphor almost suffocated me.'

Table 3. Semantic types related to 窒息 *zhìxī* 'suffocate'

Types	Examples
Natural substances	即使泥沙窒息了生命 Jíshǐ **níshā** *zhìxī* le shēngmìng. even if_sand_suffocate_ASP_life 'Even if the sand suffocated the life'
Society: Political and legal activities	监狱和镇压不能窒息人民拥护和平与民主的愿望。 Jiānyù hé **zhènyā** bùnéng *zhìxī* rénmín yōnghù hépíng yǔ mínzhǔ de yuànwàng. prison_and_repression_can not_suffocate_people_support_peace_and_democracy_DE_desire 'Prisons and repression cannot suffocate people's desire to support peace and democracy.'
Society: Economic and Trade Activities	但是现行的财务管理制度窒息了金融企业的活力。 Dànshì xiànxíng de **cáiwù guǎnlǐ zhìdù** *zhìxī* le jīnróng qǐyè de huólì. but_current_DE_financial_management_system_suffocate_ASP_finance_enterprise_DE_vitality 'But the current financial management system suffocated the vitality of financial enterprises.'
Mental activities	苦闷与困惑窒息着每一个人。 Kǔmèn yǔ **kùnhuò** *zhìxī* zhe měi yī gè rén. depression_and_confusion_suffocate_ASP_every_one_Classifier_people 'Depression and confusion are suffocating everyone.'

The common semantic collocations of 窒息 *zhìxī* 'suffocate' are summarized in Table 4. "Experiencer + 窒息 *zhìxī* 'suffocate'" expresses that someone or something feels suffocated. Both "Experiencer + 窒息 *zhìxī* 'suffocate' + Content" and "Experiencer + 使 *shǐ* 'make'/让 *ràng* 'make'/令 *lìng* 'make' + Content + 窒息 *zhìxī* 'suffocate'" express that someone or something makes others feel suffocated.

Table 4. Common semantic collocations of 窒息 *zhìxī* 'suffocate'

Collocation	Examples
Experiencer + 窒 息 *zhìxī* 'suffocate'	我快窒息了。 Wǒ kuài *zhìxī* le. I_soon_suffocate_ASP 'I'm suffocating.'
Experiencer + 窒 息 *zhìxī* 'suffocate' + Content	监狱和**镇压**不能窒息人民拥护和平与民主的**愿望**。 Jiānyù hé **zhènyā** bùnéng *zhìxī* rénmín yōnghù hépíng yǔ mínzhǔ de **yuànwàng**. prison_and_repression_can not_suffocate_people_support_peace_and_democracy_DE_desire 'Prisons and repression cannot stifle people's desire to support peace and democracy.'
Experiencer + 使 *shǐ* 'make'/ 让 *ràng* 'make'/令 *lìng* 'make' + Content + 窒息 *zhìxī* 'suffocate'	沉闷的**空气**让人窒息。 Chénmèn de **kōngqì** ràng rén *zhìxī*. dull_air_make_people_suffocate 'The dull air makes people suffocate.'

Regarding situational roles, *suffocate* verbs can collocate with Manner, Time, Location, Measure, State, Scope, and Reason as shown in Table 5. Overall, frequently used situational roles are Manner, Time, and Location. Manner describes how the suffocating action occurs, such as 严重 *yánzhòng* 'seriously'. Time indicates when the action happens, such as 分钟 *fēnzhōng* 'minute'. Location is where the action happens, such as 草丛 *cǎocóng* 'grass'. Less commonly used situational roles include Reason, Scope, Measure, and State. Reason explains why the action happens and develops. For example, 家长 *jiāzhǎng* 'parents' holds their breath due to the 波动 *bōdòng* 'fluctuation' of the college entrance examination. Scope indicates the extent to which the action happens, such as 禁锢 *jìngù* 'imprisonment'. Measure denotes how many times the action happens, such as 又一次 *yòu yī cì* 'again'. State represents the condition of the action when it happens, such as 痛楚 *tòngchǔ* 'pain'.

Suffocate verbs usually appear in two kinds of event relations: a coodination event (eCOO) and a succession event (eSUCC). A coordination event indicates ceasing to breathe occurs simultaneously with another event, while a succession event signifies an occurrence that happens later in time. In Table 6, 发狂 *fākuáng* 'crazy' is a coordination

Table 5. Situational roles of *suffocate* verbs

Situational roles		Examples
Frequently used situational roles	Manner	这种新经学严重窒息了我们民族的思维能力和创造活力。 Zhè zhǒng xīn jīngxué **yánzhòng** _zhìxī_ le wǒmen mínzú de sīwéi nénglì hé chuàngzào huólì. this_kind_new_Chinese classics_seriously_suffocate_ASP_our_nation_DE_thinking_ability_and_create_energy 'This kind of new Chinese classics have seriously suffocated the thinking ability and creative energy of our nation.'
	Time	喝下去一两分钟就断气。 Hē xiàqù yī_liǎng **fēnzhōng** jiù _duànqì_. drink_go down_one_two_minute_then_stop breathing 'Stop breathing after drinking for a minute or two.'
	Location	希莉丝在草丛里屏息凝视着火光。 Xīlìsī zài **cǎocóng** lǐ _bǐngxī_ níngshì zhe huǒguāng. Hillis_in_grass_inside_hold one's breath_stare_ASP_firelight 'Hillis stared at the firelight in the grass while holding her breath.'
Less used situational roles	Reason	家长们为高考的每个细小波动屏气凝神。 Jiāzhǎngmen wèi gāokǎo de měi gè xìxiǎo **bōdòng** _bǐngqì_ níngshén. parents_for_the college entrance examination_DE_every_Classifier_small_fluctuation_hold one's breath_focus 'Parents hold their breath and focus on every small fluctuation in the college entrance examination.'
	Scope	你的恋爱才不至于在禁锢中窒息。 Nǐ de liàn'ài cái bùzhìyú zài **jìngù** zhōng _zhìxī_. you_DE_love_just_not to the extent of_in_confinement_inside_suffocate 'Your love will not suffocate in confinement.'
	Measure	又一次屏气、扬臂、翻腾。 Yòu yī cì _bǐngqì_, yáng bì, fānténg. again_one_Classifier_hold one's breath_raise one's arm_toss 'Hold your breath, raise your arms, and toss again.'
	State	他在一阵剧烈的痛楚中咽气了。 Tā zài yī zhèn jùliè de **tòngchǔ** zhōng _yànqì_ le. he_in_one_burst_sharp_DE_pain_inside_stop breathing_ASP 'He stops breathing in a burst of sharp pain.'

event of 窒息 *zhìxī* 'suffocate', while 死 *sǐ* 'death' is a succession event of 窒息 *zhìxī* 'suffocate'.

Table 6. Event relations of *suffocate* verbs

Event relations	Examples
eCOO	这种局势使人民窒息和发狂。 Zhè zhǒng júshì shǐ rénmín *zhìxī* hé **fākuáng**. this_kind_situation_make_people_suffocate_and_crazy 'This situation suffocates people and drives them crazy.'
eSUCC	婴儿很快就会窒息而死。 Yīng'ér hěn kuài jiù huì *zhìxī* ér **sǐ**. baby_very_quick_then_will_suffocate_a conjunction_die 'Babies will quickly suffocate and die.'

In terms of event relations, 窒息 *zhìxī* 'suffocate' differs from 屏息 *bǐngxī* 'hold one's breath' and 屏气 *bǐngqì* 'hold one's breath' in terms of the types of events. The coordination events associated with 窒息 *zhìxī* 'suffocate' mostly exhibit negative characteristics, such as 呕吐 *ǒutù* 'vomit', 失明 *shīmíng* 'blindness', 发狂 *fākuáng* 'crazy', etc. Succession events of 窒息 *zhìxī* 'suffocate' are predominantly 死 *sǐ* 'death'. In contrast, events related to 屏息 *bǐngxī* 'hold one's breath' or 屏气 *bǐngqì* 'hold one's breath' tend to be more static and stationary, such as 凝神 *níngshén* 'concentrate', 静听 *jìngtīng* 'listen', 等待 *děngdài* 'wait', and 注视 *zhùshì* 'watch'. According to *The Contemporary Chinese Dictionary (7th Edition)* [22], 屏息 *bǐngxī* 'hold one's breath' and 屏气 *bǐngqì* 'hold one's breath' mean "temporarily restraining breathing", emphasizing that the agent of breathing does it intentionally. 窒息 *zhìxī* 'suffocate' is passively caused by "insufficient oxygen" or "obstruction of the respiratory system".

In sum, *suffocate* verbs selected in this paper demonstrate certain differences in agent-like semantic roles, patient-like semantic roles, situational roles, and event relations. In comparison to [4], the results indicate that among the five *suffocate* verbs, only 窒息 *zhìxī* 'suffocate' occurs in the causative alternation.

3 The Semantic Entry for a *Suffocate* Verb

Based on the above analysis, this paper summarizes the semantic usage of 窒息 *zhìxī* 'suffocate' as an example, as presented in Table 7. *The Knowledge Base of Content Words* [21] provides entries for four *suffocate* verbs (屏气 *bǐngqì* 'hold one's breath' is considered as a synonym for 屏息 *bǐngxī* 'hold one's breath'). Concerning 窒息 *zhìxī* 'suffocate', it has listed the semantic role *Experiencer* and the pattern *Experiencer* + 窒息. This paper further expands on the semantic roles and patterns in which it can occur.

Table 7. The entry of 窒息 *zhìxī* 'suffocate'

Entry	窒息
Meaning	People or animals have difficulty in breathing or even stop breathing due to insufficient oxygen or obstruction in the respiratory system.
Semantic roles:	【Agent-like semantic roles】 **Experiencer:** 我快～了。 **Wǒ** kuài *zhìxī* le. I_soon_suffocate_ASP 'I'm suffocating.'
	苦闷与困惑～着每一个人。 Kǔmèn yǔ **kùnhuò** *zhìxī* zhe měi yī gè rén. depression_and_confusion_suffocate_ASP_every_one_Classifier_people 'Depression and confusion are suffocating everyone.' 【Patient-like semantic roles】 **Content:** 监狱和镇压不能～人民拥护和平与民主的**愿望**。 Jiānyù hé zhènyā bùnéng *zhìxī* rénmín yōnghù hépíng yǔ mínzhǔ de **yuànwàng**. prison_and_repression_can not_suffocate_people_support_peace_and_democracy_DE_desire 'Prisons and repression cannot suffocate people's desire to support peace and democracy.' **Patient:** 德国人民被～在法西斯血腥的恐怖统治中。 Déguó **rénmín** bèi *zhìxī* zài Fǎxīsī xuèxīng de kǒngbù tǒngzhì zhōng. Germany_people_Passive Marker_suffocate_at_fascism_bloody_DE_terrifying_rule_inside 'The German people were suffocated by the bloody and terrifying rule of fascism.' 【Situational roles】 Manner:

(continued)

Table 7. (*continued*)

	这种新经学**严重室**息了我们民族的思维能力和创造活力。 Zhè zhǒng xīn jīngxué **yánzhòng** _zhìxī_ le wǒmen mínzú de sīwéi nénglì hé chuàngzào huólì. this_kind_new_Chinese classics_seriously_suffocate_ASP_our_nation_DE_thinking_ability_and_create_energy 'This kind of new Chinese classics have seriously suffocated the thinking ability and creative energy of our nation.' Time: 后来母亲在短**时**间内～而死。 Hòulái mǔqīn zài duǎn **shíjiān** nèi _zhìxī_ ér sǐ. later_mother_at_short_time_in_suffocate_a conjunction_die 'The mother later suffocated to death within a short time.'
Semantic Collocations:	【Experiencer + 室息 _zhìxī_ 'suffocate'】 我快～了。 Wǒ kuài _zhìxī_ le. I_soon_suffocate_ASP 'I'm suffocating.' 【Experiencer + 室息 _zhìxī_ 'suffocate' + Content】 监狱和**镇压**不能～人民拥护和平与民主的**愿望**。 Jiānyù hé **zhènyā** bùnéng _zhìxī_ rénmín yōnghù hépíng yǔ mínzhǔ de **yuànwàng**. prison_and_repression_can not_suffocate_people_support_peace_and_democracy_DE_desire 'Prisons and repression cannot suffocate people's desire to support peace and democracy.' 【Experiencer + 使 _shǐ_ 'make'/让 _ràng_ 'make'/令 _lìng_ 'make' + Content + 室息 _zhìxī_ 'suffocate'】 沉闷的**空气**让人～。 Chénmèn de **kōngqì** ràng rén _zhìxī_. dull_air_make_people_suffocate 'The dull air makes people suffocate.'

In a second language classroom, multimodal teaching can fully mobilize students' senses (such as vision and hearing) to improve the teaching effect [24]. Additionally, multimodal teaching is applicable to different kinds of Chinese teaching, such as vocabulary teaching in elementary Chinese courses [25] and Chinese song teaching [26]. Breathing, unlike running, jumping and other actions, can hardly be displayed through pictures, so a video is more suitable for teaching these verbs. For example, to better explain 窒息 zhìxī 'suffocate' and 屏息 bǐngxī 'hold one's breath', teachers can choose some medical-related videos to show different kinds of breathing.

4 Conclusion

Breathing is a basic behavior of living things. Verbs related to breathing are ubiquitous in languages. Among these verbs, *suffocate* verbs have been paid little attention to in the fields of linguistics and language teaching. This paper has selected five Chinese *suffocate* verbs and analyzed their semantic usage. It shows the differences in semantic roles of *suffocate* verbs: 窒息 zhìxī 'suffocate' can have both agent-like roles and patient-like roles, whereas the other four verbs only involve agent-like roles. Only 窒息 zhìxī 'suffocate' appears in the causative alternation. Common situational roles of these verbs include Manner, Time, and Location. Regarding event relations, the meaning of verbs affect their combination with other events. This study not only enriches *The Knowledge Base of Content Words*, but also serves as a reference for language teaching.

Acknowledgement. This study is supported by the University of Macau (MYRG2022-00191-FAH).

References

1. Wang, C., Qian, Q., Xun, E., Xing, D., Li, M., Rao, G.: Construction of semantic role bank for Chinese verbs from the perspective of ternary collocation [Sānyuán dāpèi shìjiǎo xià de hànyǔ dòngcí yǔyì juésè zhīshìkù gòujiàn]. J. Chin. Inf. Process. **34**(9), 19–27 (2020). (in Chinese)
2. Hanban: The Syllabus of Graded Words and Characters for Chinese Proficiency (revised) [Hànyǔ shuǐpíng cíhuì yǔ hànzì děngjí dàgāng (xiūdìng běn)]. Economic Science Press, Beijing (2001). (in Chinese)
3. Levin, B.: English Verb Classes and Alternations. The University of Chicago Press, Chicago (1993)
4. Guo, Y.: A cognitive-functional approach to Chinese and English causative alternations [Hàn yīng zhìshǐ jiāotì xiànxiàng de rènzhī gōngnéng yánjiū]. PhD. Shanghai International Studies University, Shanghai (2011). (in Chinese)
5. Yuan, Y.: The fineness hierarchy of semantic roles and its application in NLP [Yǔyì juésè de jīngxì děngjí jíqí zài xìnxī chǔlǐ zhōng de yìngyòng]. J. Chin. Inf. Process. **21**(4), 10–20 (2007). (in Chinese)
6. Liu, T., Che, W., Sheng, L.: Semantic role labeling with maximum entropy classifier [Jīyú zuìdà shāng fēnlèiqì de yǔyì juésè biāozhù]. J. Softw. **18**(3), 565–573 (2007). (in Chinese)
7. Liu, H., Che, W., Liu, T.: Feature engineering for Chinese semantic role labeling [Zhōngwén yǔyì juésè biāozhù de tèzhēng gōngchéng]. J. Chin. Inf. Process. **21**(1), 79–84 (2007). (in Chinese)
8. Yu, S., Zhu, X.: Comprehensive language knowledge base and its preliminary application in international Chinese language education [Zōnghé xíng yǔyán zhīshìkù jíqí zài guójì hànyǔ jiàoyù zhōng de yìngyòng chūtàn]. Int. Chin. Lang. Educ. 174–180+203 (2013). (in Chinese)
9. Munir, K., Zhao, H., Li, Z.: Neural unsupervised semantic role labeling. Trans. Asian Low Resour. Lang. Inf. Process. **20**, 1–16 (2021)

10. Xu, K., Wu, H., Song, L., Zhang, H., Song, L., Yu, D.: Conversational semantic role labeling. IEEE/ACM Trans. Audio Speech Lang. Process. **29**, 2465–2475 (2021)

11. Liu, Y., Yang, H., Li, Z., Zhang, M.: A lightweight annotation guideline of Chinese semantic role labeling [Yīzhǒng qīngliàng jí de hànyǔ yǔyì juésè biāozhù guīfàn]. J. Chin. Inf. Process. **34**(4), 10–20 (2020). (in Chinese)

12. Tesnière, L.: Comment construire une syntaxe. Bullet de la Facultédes Lettres de Strasbourg **7**, 219–229 (1934)

13. Tesnière, L.: Eléments de Syntaxe Structurale. Klincksieck, Paris (1959)

14. Nugues, P.: An Introduction to Language Processing with Perl and Prolog. Springer, Berlin (2006). https://doi.org/10.1007/3-540-34336-9

15. Schuler, K.K.: VerbNet: A Broad-Coverage, Comprehensive Verb Lexicon. University of Pennsylvania, Pennsylvania (2005)

16. Wang, S., Liu, X., Zhou, J.: Developing a syntactic and semantic annotation tool for research on Chinese vocabulary. In: Dong, M., Gu, Y., Hong, J.F. (eds.) CLSW 2021. LNCS, vol. 13250, pp. 272–294. Springer, Cham (2022). https://doi.org/10.1007/978-3-031-06547-7_22

17. Wang, S.: Investigating verbs of confession through a syntactic and semantic annotation tool. In: Dong, M., Gu, Y., Hong, J.F. (eds.) CLSW 2021. LNCS, vol. 13249, pp. 198–211. Springer, Cham (2022). https://doi.org/10.1007/978-3-031-06703-7_15

18. Che, W., Li, Z., Liu, T.: LTP: a Chinese language technology platform. In: Liu, Y., Liu, T. (eds.) Proceedings of the Coling 2010: Demonstrations, pp. 13–16. Chinese Information Processing Society of China, Beijing (2010)

19. Liu, T., Che, W., Li, Z.: Language technology platform [Yǔyán jìshù píngtái]. J. Chin. Inf. Process. **25**, 53–62 (2011). (in Chinese)

20. Yuan, Y.: On the hierarchical relation and semantic features of the thematic roles in Chinese [Lùnyuán juésè de céngjí guānxì hé yǔyì tèzhēng]. Chin. Teach. World (3), 10–22+12 (2002). (in Chinese)

21. Yuan, Y., Cao, H.: An introduction to the syntactic-semantic knowledge-base of Chinese verbs [《Dòngcí jùfǎ yǔyì xìnxī cídiǎn》zhīshí tǐxì jíqí jiansuo jièmiàn]. J. Chin. Inf. Process. **36**(8), 29-36+45 (2022). (in Chinese)

22. Dictionary Editing Office: Chinese Academy of Social Sciences: The Contemporary Chinese Dictionary, 7th edn. [Xiàndài hànyǔ cídiǎn (dì qī bǎn)]. The Commercial Press, Beijing (2016). (in Chinese)

23. Su, X.: A Thesaurus of Modern Chinese [Xiàndài hànyǔ fēnlèi cídiǎn]. The Commercial Press, Beijing (2013). (in Chinese)

24. The New London Group: a pedagogy of multiliteracies: Designing social futures. Harv. Educ. Rev. **66**, 60–92 (1996)

25. Wang, S., Liu, J.: The application of multimodal discourse analysis in international Chinese vocabulary teaching [Guójì hànyǔ cíhuì jiàoxué zhōng de duōmótài huàyǔ fēnxī]. Chin. Lang. Learn. **6**, 85–96 (2020). (in Chinese)

26. Wang, S., Wang, S.: A study of incidental vocabulary acquisition based on Chinese popular songs [Jīyú huáyǔ liúxíng gēqǔ de cíhuì fùdài xídé yánjiū]. Chin. Second Lang. J. Chin. Lang. Teach. Assoc. **57**(1), 21–57 (2022). (in Chinese)

From Blame to Exclamation: On the Lexicalization Mechanism and Syntactic-Semantic Function of Cross-Layer Sequence Form "guài zhǐ guài"

Xuting Zhan[✉]

School of Literature, Shandong University, No. 27 Shanda South Road, Licheng District, Jinan 250100, China
zhanxuting00@163.com

Abstract. Guài zhǐ guài(怪只怪) is a relatively common and special fixed phrase in modern Chinese oral expressions, which is actually a cross-layer lexical product obtained by intercepting and condensing on the basis of hypothetical conditional complex sentences. About it's part-of-speech function, guài zhǐ guài is a component between verbs and conjunctions, or a verbal fixed phrase with a connect function. From the perspective of semantic function, the basic semantic function of guài zhǐ guài is the meaning of blame. After the pragmatic function has been expanded, a sigh function has been added to convey the speaker's subjective stance and emotion. In addition, by comparing some similar structures, for example guài zhǐ guài, yào guài zhǐ guài(要怪只怪) and yào guài zhǐ néng guài(要怪只能怪), zhǐ guài(只怪), dōu guài(都怪), quán guài(全怪), jiù guài(就怪), we found that guài zhǐ guài and jiù guài have a higher degree of lexicalization, which can convey more prominent subjective meanings.

Keywords: Guài Zhǐ Guài · Cross-layer Lexicalization · Blame Meaning · Exclamation Tone

1 Introduction

In modern spoken Chinese, there is a relatively common but somewhat unique word combination sequence —— guài zhǐ guài. At first glance, it appears to be a phrasal verb formed by the repetition of the verb guài(怪). V zhǐ V(V只V) construction seems very similar to verb reduplication for example V yì V(V一V) and V bù V(V不V). He (1958) regarded it as a sub-type of verb reduplication [1]. We believe that V zhǐ V is actually a product of cross-layer sequence form lexicalization. Based on this understanding, this paper will take guài zhǐ guài as a case study to explore the following four questions:

I. What is the mechanism and process of lexicalization of guài zhǐ guài? What is its lexical and syntactic identity after lexicalization?

II. What are the limitations of guài zhǐ guài in terms of syntactic position and discourse distribution?

© The Author(s), under exclusive license to Springer Nature Singapore Pte Ltd. 2024
M. Dong et al. (Eds.): CLSW 2023, LNAI 14514, pp. 466–479, 2024.
https://doi.org/10.1007/978-981-97-0583-2_36

III. What are the semantic and pragmatic functions of guài zhǐ guài, and how are they related to each other?

IV. How is guài zhǐ guài different from other semantically similar constructions or fixed phrases in terms of meaning and function?

2 The Syntactic Effects of Cross-Layer Lexicalization of guài zhǐ guài

2.1 Cross-Layer Lexicalization of guài zhǐ guài

Internal Structure Analysis of guài zhǐ guài. From the perspective of lexical meaning combination, guài zhǐ guài consists of the intentional verb guài and the scope adverb zhǐ(只). Both guài mean blame and reproach. For convenience, we will refer to the first and second guài as guài$_1$(怪$_1$) and guài$_2$(怪$_2$), respectively. [2] points out, zhǐ means only or nothing but. From the perspective of syntactic structure, the adverb zhǐ modifies guài$_2$, which means that guài$_2$ is the predicate center, and correspondingly, guài$_1$ can only be analyzed as the subject. However, this subject-predicate structure has its peculiarities: firstly, although guài$_1$ should be analyzed as the subject syntactically, its semantic role is ambiguous, or in other words, it is difficult to clearly define the event semantic relationship between guài$_1$ and guài$_2$; secondly, guài$_2$ is a transitive verb that serves as the predicate center, but there is no object following it, which means that the scope restriction function of zhǐ has no operating object, which is obviously inconsistent with the conventional expression of subject-predicate structure.

The fundamental reason for these peculiarities is that guài zhǐ guài is actually a cross-layer sequence form that is still in the process of lexicalization. From the perspective of language decoding, there is a hypothetical conditional reasoning behind guài zhǐ guài:

(1) If there is blame, it can only be blamed on a specific person or thing.

However, when using this hypothetical conditional reasoning, certain contextual premise conditions are required:

Premise 1: A negative situation has occurred in the context;

Premise 2: The cause of the situation has multiple possibilities.

Therefore, the hypothetical conditional reasoning activated by guài zhǐ guài in a specific context can be fully expressed as:

(2) For a negative situation that has already occurred, there are multiple possible causal factors. If one wants to investigate the responsibility, one can only attribute it to one or more specific factors among the causal factors.

From the real corpus, we can see that many examples present the above hypothetical reasoning process in a typical way. For example:

(3) 唉, 怪制度怪不上, 怪那些人也怪不上, <u>千怪万怪只怪</u>自己灵魂肮脏了、污染了, 在诱惑面前没有把持住自己.

Alas, there is no one to blame but myself, for the dirty and polluted soul, for not being able to control myself in the face of temptation. (科技文献).

(4) "小飞, 你是怎样的人, 我是明白的, 若要怪, <u>只怪</u>你运气不好".

"Xiaofei, I know what kind of person you are. If you want to blame someone, blame your bad luck." (黄鹰 《天蚕变》).

Therefore, this special subject-predicate structure of guài zhǐ guài is essentially based on a hypothetical conditional reasoning sentence, which is truncated and simplified. Guài₁ is extracted from the conditional clause, zhǐ and guài₂ are extracted from the conclusion clause, and the combined product guài zhǐ guài is a lexical sequence form that crosses different relationship clauses.

Diachronic Examination of the Cross-Layer Lexicalization of guài zhǐ guài. In the corpus of ancient Chinese, there are very few examples of guài zhǐ guài, with only 11 instances, and even the verb guài used to express the meaning of blame is not commonly used. From the retrieved corpus, guài zhǐ guài may have first appeared in the late Yuan and early Ming dynasties in the jìng jiāng bǎo juàn(《靖江宝卷》), and increased in usage during the Ming and Qing dynasties. For example:

(5) ...千怪万怪, 只怪我祖上缺德。怪只怪, 我祖上, 不曾积德, 苦得我, 这一生, 草木无根.

...blaming this and that, only blaming my ancestors for being wicked. Blame only my ancestors for not accumulating virtue, leaving me with a rootless life.(元末明初《靖江宝卷》).

It is worth noting that yuàn zhǐ yuàn(怨只怨), which is basically equivalent to guài zhǐ guài, appeared earlier and may have first appeared in Yuán Qǔ(元曲). It is commonly used in works of sǎn qǔ(散曲) and drama, with a total of 20 instances, for example:

(6) 谁惯经, 害相思病, 怨只怨枕闲衾剩。.

Who is used to chanting sutras, causing lovesickness. Blame only the leftover pillow and quilt. (《全元曲——散曲》).

Furthermore, we found one sentence that contains both guài zhǐ guài and yuàn zhǐ yuàn, which is:

(7) 怪张三并李四, 只怪我苦命一个人. 怪只怪, 我苦命, 不曾生养, 怨只怨, 我妾身，破血不生。.

Blame Zhang San and Li Si, only blame my unfortunate fate. Blame only my unfortunate fate for not being able to bear children, and blame only my concubine body for being unable to conceive. (元末明初《靖江宝卷》).

In comparison, in the communicative use of modern Chinese, guài zhǐ guài is more colloquial and the meaning of blame is more obvious, which better meets the speaker's pragmatic needs. It appears more frequently, with nearly 200 instances found in the modern Chinese corpus. On the other hand, yuàn zhǐ yuàn is more commonly seen in poetry, songs, and essays, with a stronger sense of rhythm, and there are only 7 instances found in the modern Chinese corpus. Therefore, we speculate that in the diachronic evolution of Chinese, guài zhǐ guài may have replaced yuàn zhǐ yuàn to some extent.

The Mechanism of Cross-Layer Lexicalization of guài zhǐ guài. Regarding this question, we believe that there are three main factors.

Firstly, there is a need for the reanalysis of the semantic structure of guài zhǐ guài. [3] believes that under the conditions of equivalent truth-value semantics and dual analysis of the structure, the understanding of language structure will naturally tend towards the direction of being more unmarked, i.e., more dominant. The natural result is reanalysis, where the unmarked analysis replaces the originally more marked analysis. This kind of reanalysis can be achieved in two ways: structural simplification, including a reduction in structural hierarchy and a downgrade of grammatical units; and natural matching, where the form and semantics are configured in a more unmarked way. [4, 5] We believe that guài zhǐ guài has achieved structural simplification from a hypothetical conditional sentence to a fixed phrase, while maintaining its original attribution meaning, thus enabling it to be reanalyzed and generating new pragmatic functions.

Secondly, the syllabic rhythm of guài zhǐ guài is driven by echoic copying. [6] defines echoic copying structure as the echo in language communication, which refers to the same-voice response of a subsequent discourse to a certain linguistic component in a preceding discourse, and copying refers to the copying of a certain linguistic component to another syntactic position in the same sentence. guài zhǐ guài intercepts the guài in the conditional clause to express a hypothetical mood, and combines with the zhi and guài in the conclusion clause to form a V zhǐ V structure. The latter V can be seen as a response and copy of the previous V, thereby strengthening the syllabic rhythm of the word and enhancing the language's sense of rhythm.

Thirdly, the structural compression of guài zhǐ guài is an inevitable choice of the principle of linguistic economy. [7] introduced the principle of linguistic economy. This principle refers to the forces within speech activities that promote the development of language movement from within. These forces can be attributed to the basic conflict between the need for human communication and expression and the natural inertia of humans in terms of physical and mental abilities. The conflicting results of these two factors keep language in a state of constant development, and it can always achieve relative balance and stability under the premise of successfully completing communicative functions. Therefore, under the premise of saving energy consumption and ensuring smooth communication, people naturally choose language structures that are more concise, efficient, familiar, and more universal. Moreover, if one wants to express a hypothetical conditional sentence similar to "if (something) is to be blamed", one can either directly say "not to blame someone (something)" or "just blame someone (something)". The use of such a hypothetical sentence is often for politeness, to gently remind the listener of the content of the subsequent discourse. However, in reality, the use of guài alone is sufficient to cover the semantic and attitudinal meaning that the speaker wants to attribute. Therefore, we believe that the use of guài zhǐ guài saves the speaker's energy and improves communicative efficiency.

In summary, guài zhǐ guài is undoubtedly the result of the cross-layer lexicalization of hypothetical conditional sentences, influenced by the gradual loss of yuàn zhǐ yuàn, and the combined effects of semantic reanalysis, verb echoic copying, and the principle of linguistic economy. It has ultimately become a common fixed phrase in modern Chinese communication.

2.2 The Syntactic Identity and Position of guài zhǐ guài

The Part-of-Speech Features of guài zhǐ guài. Firstly, from the part-of-speech features of guài zhǐ guài, it retains certain verb-like features and can take an object. For example:

(8) "唉!怪只怪你阿弟, 当日轻信那老杂工的话……".

"Ah! It's only your younger brother's fault. He believed the words of that old handyman…" (商魂布《孽缘》).

(9) "怪只怪你辜负了他一片苦心。".

It's only your fault for letting him down. (兰京《情牵贝勒》).

In example (8), guài zhǐ guài is followed by a definite object, and example (9) is followed by a predicate clause.However, guài zhǐ guài is different from typical verb copying structures, for example V yì V and V bù V. As shown in (10a-e), guài zhǐ guài cannot be preceded by a subject or modified by a negated modal element. It can be followed by a pause marker ",", but cannot be immediately followed by tense-aspect markers for example zhe(着), le(了), and guo(过).

(10) a. 怪只怪你运气不好。

　　It's only your bad luck that's to blame.

b. *我们怪只怪你运气不好。

　　We blame only your bad luck.

c. *不能怪只怪你运气不好。

　　It's not just your bad luck that's to blame.

d. 怪只怪，你运气不好。

　　It's only your bad luck, nothing else.

e. *怪只怪着/了/过你运气不好。

It's only because of you that your bad luck persists.

Moreover, guài zhǐ guài often implies a causal relationship between the preceding and following clauses and can be analyzed as a conjunction, for example example (9).

According to [8]: Conjunctions connect words, phrases, clauses, and sentences, indicating relationships for example coordination, selection, progression, contrast, condition, and cause and effect. Guài zhǐ guài not only serves as a conjunction to connect clauses, but sometimes its omission does not affect the overall semantics and structure of the sentence. The sentence meaning can still be understood through semantics to identify the real cause of blame. For example:

(11) 不能去怪那个买鸡蛋的城里人，更不能去怪要鱼吃的孩子，怪只怪那时候我们的国家还很穷，家家都为生计发愁.

We cannot blame the city people who buy eggs, nor can we blame the children who want to eat fish. It's only because our country was poor at that time, and every family was worried about their livelihood. (《人民日报》1997).

If we delete the guài zhǐ guài in example (15), its meaning has no change. However, sometimes guài zhǐ guài cannot be casually omitted, otherwise the semantic of blame will be lost, and the sentence structure will be incomplete. For example:

(12) 白剑在井底弄了个啼笑皆非，这不能怪李老头，怪只怪自己粗心大意，自愿化名易凡.

Bai Jian made a funny scene in the well, which cannot be blamed on Lao Li, only on his own carelessness and voluntary change of name to Yi Fan. (东方英 《霹雳金蝉》).

In example (12), after deleting guài zhǐ guài, the sentence connection is incomplete, and the object projected by the reflexive pronoun zìjǐ(自己) is not clear, which may refer to lǐ lǎo tóu(李老头) or bái jiàn(白剑). However, if we replace guài zhǐ guài with yīnwèi(因为), the sentence becomes valid, and has no ambiguity. Therefore, sometimes guài zhǐ guài and yīnwèi can be interchangeable, and it has the function of a conjunction.

The conjunction attribute of guài zhǐ guài gives it the pragmatic function of discourse cohesion. Cohesion is an important component of discourse coherence, playing a role in linking and transitioning between sentences. [9] mainly classified cohesion into five categories: reference, substitution, ellipsis, conjunction, and lexical cohesion. guài zhǐ guài mainly focuses on ellipsis, conjunction, and lexical cohesion, making the sentence and discourse coherent and natural, enhancing the rhythm and prosody of the language as a whole. For example:

(13) "你错了, 小梁, 你真的错了!怪只怪他太少与你沟通, 怪只怪他老是只做不说, 怪只怪苍天作弄."".

"You're wrong, Xiaoliang, you're really wrong! It's only because he communicates with you too little, only does but doesn't say, and it's only because the heavens are playing tricks on you." (紫琳《咕噜月亮》).

Example (13) uses three guài zhǐ guài to connect the reasons for the speaker's blame, forming a parallelism in rhetorical devices, with a strong sense of rhythm and prosody. Therefore, guài zhǐ guài is actually a component between a verb and a conjunction, and can also be understood as a verb phrase with a connecting function.

The Sentence Component Status of guài zhǐ guài. Sometimes, guài zhǐ guài can be separated from the following text by a pause mark "," and can express some subjective meaning of the speaker beyond the proposition. Can it be regarded as an interjection?

[8] regard interjections as a subordinate type of independent language, believing that independent language is a special component in the sentence, independent of the eight paired components, does not form a structural relationship with other components in the sentence, has no paired components, and has a specific and important role in meaning, which can meet the needs of sentence pragmatics or expression.

(14) 怪只怪, 他龙湖是个有热血、有感情的好男儿.

It is only because Longhu is a passionate and emotional good man. (谢上薰《名花与枭雄》).

Firstly, from the collected corpus, there are only five instances of guài zhǐ guài followed by a pause mark ",", which is relatively rare. Most sentences cannot have a pause in pronunciation or be followed by modal particles. Secondly, guài zhǐ guài has the actual semantic meaning of blame, which is different from typical interjections for example nǐ kàn(你看). Although it can also express the speaker's emotional tone beyond the proposition, it also retains a more practical propositional meaning. Finally, guài zhǐ guài is usually not easily omitted in most cases, and it has a relatively important impact on the semantics and completeness of the sentence. Therefore, we believe that guài zhǐ guài cannot be considered as an interjection in the sentence.

Syntactic Position of guài zhǐ guài. From a syntactic perspective, guài zhǐ guài usually only appears at the beginning of a sentence. It can only be placed in the middle of a sentence in more colloquial and casual situations, but there is only one example of this:

(15) 我不能这样, 我真的好无奈, 这一切怪只怪我的被动, 你的晚到, 又能怎么样, 我不会后悔了, 只是还有点不舍.

I can't do this. I'm really helpless. It's all because of my passivity and your lateness. What can you do? I won't regret it, but I still feel a little reluctant. (微博).

However, guài zhǐ guài can appear in two positions in a turn. Firstly, it usually appears at the beginning of a turn, directly connected to the subsequent statement, and can also be followed by a pause mark. From the proportion of real examples, the former is more common, and the latter only has two examples.

(16) 怪只怪足协条例解释不清, 让大家看花了眼.

There is no one to blame but the Football Association's unclear interpretation, which has confused everyone. (《文汇报》2003-1-5).

(17) 她勉强的说:"怪只怪, 我们相遇的时间, 从来没有对过了!".

She reluctantly said, "It's only because the time we met has never been right!" (琼瑶《聚散两依依》).

In some examples, there are some modal particles, address terms, and exclamation elements around guài zhǐ guài. Since these elements do not affect its syntactic identity, they are omitted and do not affect the sentence.

(18) "哼! 怪只怪你太笨了, 早在我往前跨步的时候, 便瞧出草丛中有银光一闪.".

"Hmph! It's only because you are too stupid. I had already seen a flash of silver in the grass when I took a step forward." (叶崴 《娇妻看招》).

Secondly, it is located in the middle of a turn, usually connecting two clauses, as in (19); it can also be followed by a pause mark, as in (20), with only three examples.

(19) 雅晴相信, 宜娟决无任何恶意, 怪只怪她对桑桑的事了解得太少又太多……

Yaqing believed that Yijuan had no malicious intent. It's only because she knew too little and too much about Sangsang's affairs… (琼瑶《梦的衣裳》).

(20) 她比谁都深刻, 怪只怪, 她是方仲卿的人.

She felt this emotion more deeply than anyone else. It's only because she is Fang Zhongqing's person. (常欢《失落卿心》).

In summary, guài zhǐ guài is a verb phrase with a connecting function, with a word class between a verb and a conjunction. It does not function as an interjection in the sentence. It usually appears at the beginning of a sentence and can be at the beginning or middle of a turn, connecting clauses expressing causal relationships.

3 Semantic Function Analysis of guài zhǐ guài

After undergoing lexicalization, guài zhǐ guài has formed a fixed phrase with a specific meaning and pragmatic function. Influenced by the semantic components of its composition, its basic semantic function is to express the meaning of blaming. Based on this, guài zhǐ guài incorporates the speaker's subjective stance and emotions, and in certain contexts, adds the pragmatic function of expressing a tone of lamentation.

3.1 Basic Semantic Function of guài zhǐ guài - Blaming

The basic semantic function of guài zhǐ guài is to express blame, that is, to blame someone for the negative situation in the previous context.

(21) 怪谁呢, 谁会为他退出江湖而前哭失声?怪只怪夏彭年本人爱名贪利.

Who can blame him? Who would cry so loudly for him to quit the martial arts world? It's only because Xia Pengnian himself loves fame and fortune. (亦舒《叹息桥》).

The surface meaning of guài zhǐ guài is blaming. In the above examples, what follows guài zhǐ guài is usually the thing or behavior that the speaker wants to blame, which is usually a noun referring to a person. It expresses the speaker's evaluative stance, and in most contexts, the blame is attributed to a third party, implying the speaker's helplessness.

It is particularly important to note that in typical examples of expressing blame, guài zhǐ guài is essentially a verb phrase with a person noun as its object argument. Therefore, even in example (21), where a complete clause follows guài zhǐ guài, a pause mark "," can be added after the person noun.

The basic semantic function of guài zhǐ guài is blaming, which gives it a pragmatic function of expressing the speaker's subjective stance. There are many linguistic means that reflect the speaker's stance and attitude in language, and different languages have their commonalities and differences. The key elements are subjectivity, evaluation, and interaction [10]. guài zhǐ guài is commonly used in spoken and written language, in monologues and dialogues, fully embodying the three main features mentioned above, and clearly conveying the speaker's subjective stance. Subjectivity is a characteristic of language, and the speaker expresses their stance, attitude, and emotions towards the words they are saying [11, 12]; evaluation refers to the speaker's judgment and evaluation of someone's speech or behavior; interactive interaction is generally only reflected in the conversation structure, with its specific response types and patterns. For example:

(22) 怪只怪我当时年轻懵懂, 全不明白姑娘家的心事.

It's only because I was young and ignorant at the time, and didn't understand the girl's thoughts. (应天鱼《鬼啊!师父》).

3.2 The Pragmatic Expansion of guài zhǐ guài - Expressing a Lamenting Tone

After the pragmatic expansion of guài zhǐ guài, it can express a lamenting tone, which expresses a helpless and blameless emotion towards the unsatisfactory reality in the preceding context.

(23) "怪只怪命运捉弄人吧!".

"It's fate that played a trick on me!" (蓝嫣 《花过雨》).

In the above sentences, the object following guài zhǐ guài is generally words for example fate, heaven, reality, and society, expressing the speaker's dissatisfaction with the current situation. It is a helpless and blameless lament. It is worth noting that compared with the guài zhǐ guài expressing attribution, the logical object of the guài zhǐ guài expressing a lamenting tone is the event clause, while the former's logical object is mostly a person's name, which is the key difference between the two pragmatic functions. Therefore, in example (24), we cannot add a pause after the subject noun of the following clause after guài zhǐ guài.

When guài zhǐ guài expresses a lamenting tone, exclamation words or phrases for example "ài, qí and àiya(唉, 嗷, 哎呀)" may appear before it, which can further highlight the speaker's emotional tone, as shown in (25):

(24) 只听他一声叹息, 唱歌一样叫起苦来: "哎呀, 陈总监!难呀!怪只怪中国经济发展得太快, 如今这世道, 你都知道的啦, 人才难求!".

He sighed and sang out his bitterness like a song: "Aiya, Director Chen! It's difficult! It's just that China's economy has developed too fast. You know how it is these days, talent is hard to find!" (李可《杜拉拉升职记》).

In addition, when guài zhǐ guài expresses a lamenting tone, the semantic meaning of blaming will be weakened. The speaker does not really want to blame someone or something, but rather expresses a subjective emotion of helplessness and a mismatch between their thoughts and reality.

[6] analyzed the basic functions of echo copy structures in discourse. For the echo copy structure A jiù A(A就A), the echo component A serves as the old information and takes on the topic role, while the copy component A combined with the adverb jiù(就) serves as the predicate, conveying new information and expressing the speaker's subjective attitude and viewpoint, which is a subjective evaluation and recognition of the event or the people and things involved in the event expressed in the preceding discourse. Similar to the echo copy structure V jiù V(V就V), guài zhǐ guài expresses the speaker's subjective position of blaming and helplessness towards the behavior or ideas of the object that follows it in the sentence. For example:

(25) 因此错不在她, 一切纯属巧合, 怪只怪那个倒霉男今天运气欠佳。.

Therefore, it's not her fault, it's all just a coincidence. It's just that the poor guy's luck is bad today. (左晴雯 《近君情怯》).

The anonymous reviewer suggested, Comparing the connective words bú guài(不怪) and guài zhǐ guài in the prepositional clause may be more comprehensive and appropriate. According to corpus statistics, when guài zhǐ guài expresses the semantic meaning of blaming, only a small number of examples have explicit words for example bú guài, bú néng guài(不能怪), and wú fǎ zé guài(无法责怪)in the preceding discourse, with only 8 examples out of a total of 77. Therefore, guài zhǐ guài is not a common combination of connective words. However, because the prepositional clause generally implies the meaning of not blaming others, and the semantic function of guài zhǐ guài is weakened when it expands, the insertion of bú guài in the prepositional clause can be used as a test standard to judge whether the pragmatic function of guài zhǐ guài has expanded.

4 Several Comparisons of Similar Structures

The semantic meaning of the verb guài is blame, and it often produces different semantics and pragmatic effects when used with different adverbs. Based on specific language facts, this section will compare and analyze the similarities and differences in meaning and usage of the semantically similar terms or fixed phrases, such as guài zhǐ guài, yào guài zhǐ guài, yào guài zhǐ néng guài, zhǐ guài, dōu guài, quán guài and jiù guài.

4.1 guài zhǐ guài vs. yào guài zhǐ guài and yào guài zhǐ néng guài

As mentioned earlier, guài zhǐ guài is a contracted form of the hypothetical conditional sentence "yào guài, zhǐ guài(要怪, 只怪)" after cross-layer lexicalization. From this perspective, guài zhǐ guài, yào guài zhǐ guài and yào guài zhǐ néng guài can be replaced with each other. For example:

(26) 怪只怪/要怪只怪/要怪只能怪 生活自有自己的轨迹, 它总使我很难舍弃那脑海里的空中楼阁.

It's just that life has its own trajectory. It always makes it difficult for me to give up the castles in the air in my mind. (冯苓植 《雪驹》).

However, this kind of equivalent substitution is not applicable to all contexts.Firstly, from a syntactic position, guài zhǐ guài and yào guài zhǐ guài can only be placed at the beginning of a sentence, while yào guài zhǐ néng guài can be preceded by a subject, a demonstrative pronoun or an adverb, for example:

(27)a.但那要怪只能怪我自己。

But I can only blame myself.(南强《稀世古钱》)

b.但那*怪只怪/*要怪只怪我自己。

but I can only blame myself.

Secondly, from the nature of the post-verbal elements, as mentioned earlier, guài zhǐ guài and yào guài zhǐ guài cannot be followed by a single personal pronoun, reflexive pronoun, or a bare noun, but yào guài zhǐ néng guài can.

(28) a.她说要怪只怪自己的妹妹，她恨死她了。

She said she could only blame her sister, and she hated her to death.

(《都市快讯》2003-7-25)

b.*她说要怪只怪妹妹，她恨死她了。

She said she could only blame her sister, and she hated her to death.

(29) a.要怪只能怪自己，怪自己没眼睛，不能识别骗子。

You can only blame yourself for not having eyes and not being able to identify scammers.(艾米《山楂树之恋》)

b*怪只怪/*要怪只怪自己，怪自己没眼睛，不能识别骗子。

Blame yourself, for not having eyes and not being able to identify scammers.

In example (28a), yào guài zhǐ guài followed by "zìjǐ de mèimèi(自己的妹妹)" is a definite phrase. If we replace it with mèimèi(妹妹), (29b) becomes invalid. Example (29a) indicate that yào guài zhǐ néng guài can be directly followed by personal pronouns, reflexive pronouns, and common nouns, indicating a broader context of use.

Through comparative analysis, we found that guài zhǐ guài, yào guài zhǐ guài and yào guài zhǐ néng guài can be equivalently replaced in some cases, but there are significant differences in syntactic position, post-verbal elements, and pragmatic function. Compared with the other two expressions, yào guài zhǐ néng guài is more flexible and less restrictive in actual use.

4.2 guài zhǐ guài vs. zhǐ guài, dōu guài, quán guài and jiù guài

When guài is combined with different range adverbs for example zhǐ guài, dōu guài, quán guài and jiù guài, what are the similarities and differences in their usage compared to guài zhǐ guài?

Firstly, we need to clarify the structure and function of the above combination forms. [13] proposed that zhǐ is a range adverb that indicates limitation; dōu(都) is a typical range adverb that indicates summarization, covering various aspects for example subject, object of action, time and place of action, and conditions; quán(全) can also summarize the subject and object of action, but generally cannot summarize the latter two. Dōu can also be used in indefinite sentences to summarize the range of the indefinite element, while quán cannot. Zhǐ guài limits the object of blame by the speaker, while dōu guài and quán guài reflect the summarized range of the object and reason for blame by the speaker. In jiù + V, as mentioned in [2], jiù can strengthen affirmation, emphasize determination, and indicate that the action only applies to the object and not to other things outside the object. Jiù guài can also limit the object of blame when expressing the speaker's strong will to blame.

Secondly, from a syntactic perspective, what are the differences between them? Let's take a look at the distribution conditions and syntactic features of the following sentences (Table 1):

Table 1. Summary of Distribution Conditions for guài zhǐ guài, zhǐ guài, dōu guài, quán guài and jiù guài

Distribution Conditions	guài zhǐ guài	zhǐ guài	dōu guài	quán guài	jiù guài
Followed by a pause marker ","	+	-	-	-	-
Followed by a personal pronoun	-	+	+	+	-
Followed by a reflexive pronoun	-	+	-	+	-
Followed by a predicate element	+	+	+	+	-
Followed by a nominal element	-	+	+	+	-
Preceded by a subject	-	+	-	+	-
Preceded by a demonstrative pronoun	-	+	+	+	-
Preceded by a demonstrative pronoun, followed by bù dé(不得)	-	-	+	-	+
Preceded by a negative modal element, followed by a personal pronoun	-	+	+	+	-
Preceded by a negative modal element, followed by a predicate element	-	+	+	+	+

(Note: " +" represents that the word has this distribution condition; "-" represents that it does not.)

Therefore, we can summarize the distribution characteristics of guài zhǐ guài: there are usually no elements before it, and it can be followed by a pause marker "," to indicate a pause in tone. It can be followed by a predicate element or a partially limiting phrase, but cannot be used in negative sentences.

Furthermore, we can clearly see that the distribution conditions of guài zhǐ guài and jiù guài are very limited, with only two conditions, while zhǐ guài, dōu guài, and quán guài have up to seven or eight conditions. Therefore, we can classify these similar structures into two categories:

Group A: guài zhǐ guài and jiù guài.

Group B: zhǐ guài, dōu guài and quán guài.

Regarding this phenomenon, we cannot help but wonder why there is such a significant dichotomy. What is the underlying reason for this? We can use the criterion whether it can be modified by negative modal elements to examine the specific usage of these words. According to the retrieved corpus and manual statistics, the following data summary table is obtained:

Table 2. Statistics of the Number of Cases where guài zhǐ guài, zhǐ guài, dōu guài, quán guài and jiù guài are Modified by negative modal elements

Comparison Item	Group A			Group B	
	guài zhǐ guài	jiù guài	zhǐ guài	dōu guài	quán guài
Total Number of Examples	189	266	937	1782	589
Number of Examples Modified by Negative Modal Elements	0	1	16	28	286
Proportion of Examples Modified by Negative Modal Elements	0	0.38%	1.71%	1.57%	48.56%

From the Table 2, it confirms the dichotomy of these words. Group A are almost impossible to be modified by negative modal elements, while Group B are the opposite, especially quán guài. Nearly half of the examples show that there are negative modal elements before it, and even if there are not, some sentences use rhetorical questions to express the speaker's negative tone, for example "zěn me néng quán guài tā ne? (怎么能全怪他呢? = how can it all be blamed on him?)", which actually conveys that it can't blame him entirely".

We believe that the main reason for this significant difference is that the degree of lexicalization or grammaticalization of the two groups of words is significantly different. The words of Group A have a higher degree of lexicalization and have a relatively concrete propositional meaning, making it almost impossible to be modified by negative modal elements. The words of Group B have a lower degree of lexicalization, and their underlying deep structure is a adverb indicating a limited range and guài, and they have not yet developed a typical lexical meaning. When Group B words are modified by negative modal elements, their underlying structure is not a negation of guài, but a negation of the adverb indicating a limited range.

In addition, we found that the elements that precede and follow guài zhǐ guài and jiù guài cannot form disyllabic words with guài and jiù, while zhǐ guài, dōu guài and quán guài can. This also proves that the former has a higher degree of lexicalization and has formed a more fixed phrase that cannot be further separated. For example:

(30) a. 因此, 我们决不能 <u>只/都/全</u> 怪罪无辜的青年, 更不能由此得出"思想工作无能为力"的悲观论点.

Therefore, we must not only blame the innocent young people, nor should we draw the pessimistic conclusion that ideological work is powerless. (福建日报: 1980-09-25).

b. 因此, 我们决不能 <u>*怪只怪/*就 怪罪</u>无辜的青年……

Therefore, we cannot blame only the innocent young people…

Finally, let's analyze the expressive effects of these words. Although they all have the meaning of blame, their implicit semantics and emotions are different. Guài zhǐ guài and zhǐ guài mean blame on the surface, but they actually convey a sense of helplessness and not blame on others. Zhǐ guài and dōu guài tend to express introspection, and the object of blame is usually me/myself, him/her (himself/herself), oneself, you or third person, expressing the speaker's complaint to the listener or third person. Quán guài is mostly used in negative sentences, expressing the speaker's evaluation and attitude that we cannot blame someone (something) entirely. Jiù guài is mostly used in sentence pattern like "zhè/nà jìu guài bù dé sb./sth. Le"(这/那就怪不得某人/某事了, it's not sb./sth.'s fault), expressing the speaker's disagreement with the reason or object of blame in the previous context, helping someone (something) shirk responsibility.

In summary, while expressing the meaning of blame, these similar structures also have specific grammatical features and modalities, reflecting different lexical functions in actual communication, conveying the speaker's subjective stance, evaluation, and emotional attitude.

5 Conclusions

The guài zhǐ guài is a relatively common vocabulary in Chinese communication. From the perspective of internal structure and generation mechanism, it is a cross-layer lexicalized phrase formed by intercepting and suppressing hypothetical conditional clauses. From the perspective of syntactic identity and status, compared with words like cuò zhǐ cuò zài(错只错在) and duō zhǐ duō le(多只多了), its degree of grammaticalization is higher, between a verb and a conjunction, and it has the function of connecting causal subordinate clauses. From the perspective of semantic and pragmatic functions, its basic semantic function is to express the meaning of blame, and its pragmatic function expansion covers the tone of helplessness and lamentation of the speaker, conveying subjective stance and emotional functions.

Comparing guài zhǐ guài with structures for example yào guài zhǐ guài, yào guài zhǐ néng guài, zhǐ guài, dōu guài, quán guài and jìu guài, we found that the typical grammatical feature of guài zhǐ guài is that it usually appears at the beginning of a sentence, can be followed by a comma, and is followed by a predicate. No other components can appear before it. In comparison, guài zhǐ guài and jìu guài have a higher degree of lexicalization, with a stronger propositional meaning, and are difficult to be further separated or combined with other components.

Acknowledgement. I would appreciate professor Li Xiang(Xiamen University) and professor Kou Xin (Shandong University) for their guidance and assistance about this article. And I am grateful to the anonymous reviewers of CLSW 2023 for helpful suggestions and comments. All errors and misinterpretations remain entirely my responsibility.

References

1. He, R.: A preliminary study on the reduplication of verbs in Chinese. J. Sun Yat-sen Univ. (Soc. Sci. Edn.) **4**, 137–163 (1958). (in Chinese)
2. Lv, S.: Eight Hundred Words in Modern Chinese. The Commercial Press, Beijing (1999). (in Chinese)
3. Liu, D.: Unmarked explanations reanalyzed. Chin. Teach. World **1**, 5–18+2 (2008). (in Chinese)
4. Liu, H.: Structural simplification and lexicalization. Stud. Lang. Linguist. **5**, 497–511 (2014). (in Chinese)

5. Kou, X.: The polylexicalization and grammaticalization of zhiyu. In: Wu, Y., Hong, J., Su, Q. (eds.) Chinese Lexical Semantics, vol. 10709, pp. 235–242. Springer, Cham (2017). https://doi.org/10.1007/978-3-319-73573-3_20

6. Wang, C.: An analysis of echo copying structure in modern Chinese. Chin. Lang. Learn. **6**, 14–18 (2002). (in Chinese)

7. Zhou, S.: Martinet's theory of language function and the principle of linguistic economy. Foreign Linguist. **4**, 4–12 (1980). (in Chinese)

8. Huang, B., Liao, X.: Modern Chinese: Volume 2. Higher Education Press, Beijing (2017). (in Chinese)

9. Halliday, M.A.K., Hasan, R.: Cohesion in English. Longman, London (1976)

10. Yao, S.: Review of "stance in talk: subjectivity, evaluation, interaction." Foreign Lang. Teach. Res. **1**, 145–148 (2011). (in Chinese)

11. Lyons, J.: Semantics, vol. 2. Cambridge University Press, Cambridge (1977)

12. Shen, J.: Subjectivity and subjectivization of language. Foreign Lang. Teach. Res. **4**, 268–275+320 (2001). (in Chinese)

13. Ma, Z.: Methodology of Research on Function Words in Modern Chinese. The Commercial Press, Beijing (2016). (in Chinese)

A Research on the Manchu-Chinese Bilingual Comparative Characteristics of the *Yu Zhi Zeng Ding Qing Wen Jian* Dictionary

Yao Zhang[✉]

The College of Chinese Language and Literature, Hunan University, Changsha 410012, China
254375986@qq.com

Abstract. *Yu Zhi Zeng Ding Qing Wen Jian* was the first official Manchu-Chinese bilingual dictionary of the Qing Dynasty. It added Chinese translation to the entries, employed Chinese characters to indicate the pronunciation of Manchu words, and utilized Manchu words to mark the pronunciation of Chinese words based on *Yu Zhi Qing Wen Jian*. *Yu Zhi Zeng Ding Qing Wen Jian* added 6,904 new entries, accounting for 37.05% of the total number of words. After the dictionary changed from Manchu monolinguals to Manchu-Chinese bilingual mode, it brought about great changes in the editing classification pattern and word collection, which not only inherited ancient Chinese dictionaries, but also had a profound impact on the editing of later Minority-Chinese bilingual and multilingual dictionaries.

Keywords: *Yu Zhi Zeng Ding Qing Wen Jian* Dictionary · Manchu-Chinese Bilingual · Comparative Mode · Characteristics and Function

1 Introduction

Yu Zhi Zeng Ding Qing Wen Jian was the first official revised Manchu-Chinese bilingual dictionary written in the 36th year of the Qianlong reign (1771). It was based on the official revised Manchu monolingual dictionary *Yu Zhi Qing Wen Jian* in the 47th year of the Kangxi reign (1708). Both were dictionaries compiled by the imperial edict of the Grand Master, and the entries and definitions in the *Yu Zhi Zeng Ding Qing Wen Jian* were written in Manchu monolingual language, citing Chinese classics such as the Four Books and Five Classics; The entries in the *Yu Zhi Zeng Ding Qing Wen Jian* had been changed to be written in both Manchu and Chinese languages, with the addition of mutual phonetic notation between Manchu and Chinese entries. On the basis of retaining the monolingual interpretation of Manchu, the original Chinese classic example sentences had been deleted. The *Yu Zhi Zeng Ding Qing Wen Jian* included 18651 sets of entries, including words, phrases, and other forms. The bilingual comparison model between Manchu and Chinese for entries was very distinctive, with an increase of 6904 entries compared to the *Yu Zhi Qing Wen Jian*, expanding nearly one-third of its capacity. This was not only an innovation in the official Manchu dictionaries of the Qing Dynasty, but also a inheritance and development of ancient Chinese dictionaries.

© The Author(s), under exclusive license to Springer Nature Singapore Pte Ltd. 2024
M. Dong et al. (Eds.): CLSW 2023, LNAI 14514, pp. 480–494, 2024.
https://doi.org/10.1007/978-981-97-0583-2_37

Among the large number of dictionaries compiled in the Qing Dynasty that were preserved today, there were roughly three types: fractal order, semantic order, and phonetic order. Among the semantic order dictionaries, the number of classification dictionaries was the highest. Whether it was an official or non-official classification dictionary, the *Qing Wen Jian* series had the highest number [1]. The *Qing Wen Jian* series held an extremely important position in the Qing Dynasty dictionaries. As the first official revised Manchu-Chinese bilingual dictionary, *Yu Zhi Zeng Ding Qing Wen Jian* had a profound impact on the compilation of Manchu language dictionaries for future generations.

2 The Characteristics of the Collection of Bilingual Manchu-Chinese Entries in *Yu Zhi Zeng Ding Qing Wen Jian*

2.1 Dictionary Changed From Manchu Monolingual to Manchu-Chinese Bilingual Comparison Mode

Yu Zhi Zeng Ding Qing Wen Jian was the only bilingual comparison dictionary between Manchu and Chinese in the Qing Wen Jian series. This form of bilingual translation between Manchu and Chinese was a manifestation of the purpose of Emperor Qianlong's order, and it was also an important feature of this dictionary.

Both the translation of Manchu entries using Chinese word meanings and the phonetic annotation of Chinese characters were using bilingual comparison to establish standardization of Manchu writing and pronunciation. Since then, the translation and phonetic annotation between Manchu and Chinese were based on this standard, which provide a unified standard for bilingual comparison between Manchu and Chinese. Moreover, the method of bilingual translation and phonetic annotation between Manchu and Chinese can effectively avoid word ambiguity and obscure abstract descriptions of word meanings and pronunciations. From the perspective of establishing vocabulary norms and interpreting meanings and pronunciations of vocabulary, the processing method of bilingual comparison between Manchu and Chinese was far superior to that of monolingual of Manchu.

2.2 Standardize Entries by Using Three Methods: Adding, Replacing, and Deleting

There were three standardized ways to add, replace and delete new entries in *Yu Zhi Zeng Ding Qing Wen Jian*. Among them, the number of new entries was absolutely dominant, some of the entries were retained in the dictionary after changing their expression forms and only a small number of entries deleted.

Adding New Entries
New Added Entries in the Main Edition
From the above data, we can more accurately see the changes of the entries from the *Yu Zhi Qing Wen Jian* to *Yu Zhi Zeng Ding Qing Wen Jian*. The top five volumes with the highest proportion of newly added entries and the largest number of changes in the volumes are edict volume, official position volume, residence volume, monk volume

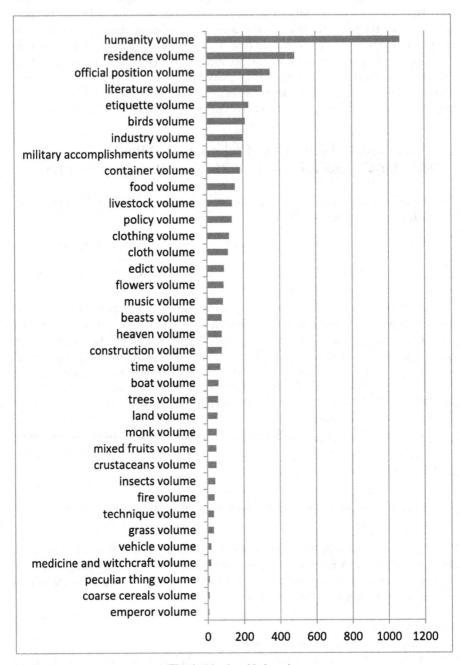

Fig. 1. Newly added entries

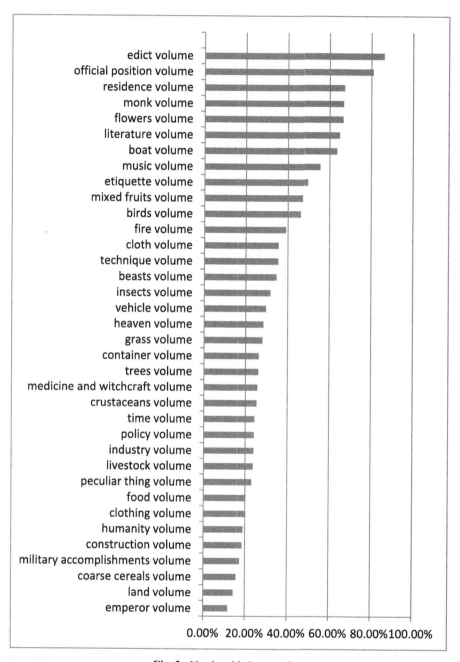

Fig. 2. Newly added proportion

and flowers volume. The emergence of new things often comes with the standardization of their expression methods. Incorporating new entries into dictionaries is an effective measure to fix the expression methods of new things. Adding new entries was also a microcosm of regulating the expression methods of new things at that time. It covered all the manifestations of the development and changes of the Manchu vocabulary system from the early Qing Dynasty to the middle Qing Dynasty. Therefore, understanding the proportion of newly added entries in each volume can not only grasp the key points of revising and standardizing this dictionary, but also demonstrate the focus of vocabulary changes in the Manchu vocabulary system at that time (Figs. 1 and 2).

New Added Entries in the Supplement. The supplement included a total of 1636 words, divided into 26 categories. The specific distribution of word categories is as follows:

Part 1: Heaven Volume (including Heaven Category): 5; Time Volume (including Time Category): 38; Land Volume (including Land Category): 44; Official Position Volume (including ancient official's names Category, Promotion Category): 25; Policy Volume (including Ancient Punishments Category): 6; Etiquette Volume (including Ancient Sacrificial Vessels Category and Ancient Crowns Category): 83; Music Volume (including Music Category): 21; Literature Volume: (including Books Category): 119; Military Accomplishments Volume (including Military Category) 34;
Part 2: Monk Volume (including Gods Category): 48; Resident Volume (including Government Offices Category) 9;
Part 3: Industry Volume (including Measurement Category, Finance Category): 23; Food Volume (including Pastries Category): 9; Fruits Volume (including Exotic Fruits Category): 97; Trees Volume (including Trees Category, Exotic Trees Category): 56; Flowers Volume (including Flowers Category, Exotic Flowers): 113;
Part 4: Birds Volume (including Birds Category, Finches Category): 374; Beasts Volume (including Beasts Category, Exotic Beasts Category): 225; Livestock Volume (including Various Livestock Category): 46.

These supplementary entries illustrated the continuous deepening of people's understanding of nature, and the various names of exotic fruits, flowers, plants and trees were also a manifestation of the continuous trade and contact between countries at that time.

Replacing Entries. The replaced Manchu entries can be divided into six situations. These are transliteration changing into free translation forms, synonym replacement, adding category information, deleting category information, transforming original vocabulary and differentiating original loanwords.

Transforming Chinese Transliterated Loanwords Into Free Translation Forms. Loan words refer to the words borrowed from one language to another. And it also known as foreign words or alien words. Zhang Bo (2019) believed that free translation referred to expressing the meaning of foreign languages in one's own language, which was pure translation and cannot be borrowed at all. As for literal translation, if measured by the standard of translation and borrowing, it did not belong to borrowing [2]. According to this standard, Chinese transliterated words in Manchu were determined as loan words, and the words that replaced Chinese transliterated words with free translation or literal translation were determined as Manchu words.

After statistics, it was found that there were 180 Chinese transliterated entries in *Yu Zhi Qing Wen Jian*, which were revised and replaced with Manchu words in free translation form. These 180 entries were basically in a one-to-one form, with only three examples being one-to-two or two-to-one forms. One was the "黏干子(sticky rod)", which originally only had the Chinese transliteration form of "niyan g'an dzi", corresponding to two free translation forms of "latubukū" and "dalhūwan" in Manchu. One was the "漆(paint)", which originally had two Chinese transliteration forms of "ci" and "cile", corresponding to a free translation forms of "šugile" in Manchu. There was also a military weapon category called "纛(a big army banner)", which originally had two entries of "tu" and "wadan", and "tu" was transformed into "turun". This approach can reduce the impact of Chinese vocabulary on the original Manchu vocabulary system, standardize the use of Manchu and activate the vitality of the Manchu vocabulary system.

Synonym Replacement. By comparing two dictionaries, it was found that some entries had the same category positions and Manchu definitions, but had different written forms in Manchu. There were 12 such words, which were not Chinese transliterated loan words. Therefore, they did not belong to the situation of replacing Chinese transliterated loanwords to Manchu free translation words. However, they had the same definitions, so they were classified as synonym replacement. The specific entries are as follows (Table 1):

Most of these entries existed simultaneously, some of which may be mixed up during using them, and their usage was fixed in the form of standardized dictionaries during the revision process. "Weilembi" and "uilen" both had the meaning of serving, but in the dictionary, it was stipulated that "uilen" was used for serving elders, while "weilembi" was mostly used for labor and work. The "sound of chewing gristle" belonged to imitative words, which were generally achieved by adding suffix "-sum" or having a harmonious sound of repetition. From "kifur seme" to "kifur kifur", it just changed the grammatical means of forming imitative words with unchanged semantics, and the two forms can still be used interchangeably.

Adding Some Words. The words used to add some content involve different parts of speech, and nouns, verbs or adjectives can all be added as supplementary content.

For example, "meeting etiquette of embracing when meeting" had changed from "tebeliyembi" (embrace) to "tebeliyeme acambi"(embrace+meet), which added the verb "meet". "Alliance" had changed from "culgan" to "culgan acambi" (alliance+meet), which also added the verb "meet". "Standing in line" had changed from "sehuleme" to "sehuleme ilimbi" (stand out+stand), which added the verb "stand". These entries, regardless of whether they were preceded by a verb or a noun, were supplemented with the verb part of the phrase to limit the described behavior or action, which can make the content of the entry more completely and the description more clearly.

Deleting Some Words. Some entries were deleted from the original entries, which may serve the purpose of expressing more concisely. For example, there were three entries that were originally in the form of a phrase. The phrase "juhe wengke" (ice thaw) deleted the original noun "juhe" (ice) after revision. The phrase "makarame sakdaka" (old) and the phrase "lalanji oho" deleted the original verb "fatigue" (become old) and "oho" (become) after revision. Because "wengke" means "ice thaw", there was no need to add

Table 1. Synonyms replacement in *Yu Zhi Zeng Ding Qing Wen Jian*

Yu Zhi Qing Wen Jian	Yu Zhi Zeng Ding Qing Wen Jian	Chinese Meaning	Location	
šun tuheke	šun dosika	日入 (sunset)	Heaven Category	Volume·Heaven
jai jidere aniya	cargi aniya	后年 (the year after next)	Time Category	Volume·Time
cifahan	lifahanahabi	成了泥 (turned into mud)	Land Category	Volume·Land
gūsai fujin	beise i fujin	贝子福晋 (Beizi Fujin)	Emperor Category	Volume·Emperor
gosicuka	giljacuka	可矜 (pitiful)	Policy Category	Volume·Waive
hengkilengjimbi	hargašanjimbi	来朝 (come up to court)	Etiquette Category	Volume·Meeting
gūnin be ujimbi	mujin be ujimbi	养志 (cultivate aspirations)	Humanity Category	Volume·Support
weilembi	uilen	侍奉 (wait upon)	Humanity Category	Volume·Support
kifur seme	kifur kifur	嚼脆骨声 (sound of chewing gristle)	Humanity Category	Volume·Sound
furgi	kakū undehen	闸板 (flashboard)	Construction Volume·Streets Category	
misun boco	misuru	酱色 (dark reddish brown)	Clothing Category	Volume·Colours
kuwecihe boco	kuren	古铜色 (bronze)	Clothing Category	Volume·Colours

other "juhe" (ice). Similarly, "makarame" already means "aging", and "lalanji" already means "limping body", so there was no need to add "sakdaka" and "oho".

Transforming the Original Vocabulary of Manchu.   In the process of revising, in addition to standardizing Chinese transliterated loanwords, the original vocabulary of Manchu had also been standardized, which was in line with the principle of economic language usage. Manchu vocabulary had developed from phrases and compound words to proprietary nouns and simplex words.

There were two entries that were originally compound words, but later underwent Manchuization and added suffixes to become derivative words, which was more in line with the usage habits of Manchu vocabulary. It was generally believed that the suffix "-si" was used to represent people engaged in this type of work. The "farmer" was originally named as "usin i haha", which translated directly to the field's man, and was used to refer to the person who cultivated the field. Later, it was revised to "usisi", which was the word of "usin" removed the noun suffix "-n" and added the occupational suffix

"-si". "The person who is in charge of cattle and sheep" was "ulha tuwakiyara niylma," which translated directly as a person who lookd after livestock. It referred to people who make a living by grazing. It was later revised to "ulebusi", which was the word of "ulembi" (feeding) removed the present-future tense suffix "-mbi" of verb and added the occupational suffix "-si".

Changing Writing Caused by the Changes of Pronunciation. There were 5 entries that change their writing caused by the change of pronunciation. "White" was wrote as "šanggyan", later removed the preposition "-gi-" and became to "šanyan", at the same time, the entry with this word as the root also changed, so "the slightly white" also changed from "šanggiyakan" to "šanyakan", "wild wormwood" changed from "šanggyan suiha" to "šanyan suiha", "a piece of wormwood" changed from "šanggyan selbete" to "šanyan selbete".

Deleting Entries. By comparing *Yu Zhi Qing Wen Jian* and *Yu Zhi Zeng Ding Qing Wen Jian*, it was found that some Manchu entries were deleted during the revising process. There were four main situations (Table 2):

Table 2. Table of deleting Chinese transliterated loan words

Deleted transliteration	Reserved free translation	Chinese Meaning	Location in *Yu Zhi Qing Wen Jian*
giyang	ula	江(river)	Land Volume·Land Category
ing	kūwaran	营(camp)	Military accomplishments Volume·Conquest Category
be wang asu	jargiyalakū asu	把网(net)	Industry Volume·Hunting tool Category
giowanse	ceceri	绢(silk)	Clothing Volume·Clothing Categoty
pun	kotoli	篷(canopy)	Boat Volume·Boat Category

Deleting Transliterated Entries. There were 5 pairs of Chinese translated entries in *Yu Zhi Qing Wen Jian* that had two forms of Manchu expression simultaneously, one was Chinese transliterated loan words, and the other was Manchu inherent words. After revision, the transliterated loan words was deleted and the inherent Manchu words were retained. The specific situation is as follows:

Except for these 5 pairs of entries that deleted the Chinese transliterated loan form during the revising process, there was one entry with the opposite situation. There was an entry which means 纛(a big army banner), which included the Chinese transliterated word "tu" and the Manchu inherent word "wadan". However, during the revising process, Chinese transliterated loan words were retained, but the Manchu inherent words was deleted.

Deleting Some Verbs With Different Tense Forms. There were four pairs of entries in *Yu Zhi Qing Wen Jian* that both had the original verb form and nouns derived from verbs or verbs with other tense forms, but they were not included in *Yu Zhi Zeng Ding Qing Wen Jian.* The specific situation is as follows (Table 3):

Table 3. Deleting specific entries for verb derivations or different tense forms

Deleted transliteration	Chinese meaning	Reserved verbs	Reserved Chinese meaning	Location
dū	打 (beat)	dūmbi	打 (beat)	Policy Volume·Punishment Category
sahadabumbi	使打小围 (allow to hunting)	sahadambi	秋狝 (hunting in autumn)	Military accomplishments Volume·Hunting Category
dekjimbi	兴旺 (become prosperous)	dekjike	兴旺 (prosperous)	Humanity Volume·Rich Category
masilame	尽量 (try one's best)	masilambi	输着 (input)	Humanity Volume·Giving Category

Removed the Meaning of Polysemous Words. There were 8 entries that belonged to polysemy and had two meanings in *Yu Zhi Qing Wen Jian.* Therefore, they appeared twice or three times in different categories in *Yu Zhi Qing Wen Jian.* However, during the revising process of *Yu Zhi Zeng Ding Qing Wen Jian,* one of the meanings was deleted. The specific situation is as follows (Table 4):

Although the meaning of "knee" for the word "buhi" had not been retained, two new entries had been added, which was "buhi adame" (sitting with closing knees) and "buhi arambi" (sitting with bending knees). "Hangzhou silk" and "Qing Ming" had the same pronunciation "Hangsi" in Manchu. And as a solar term, Qing Ming had a long history and was also known as "Hangsi" in the folk. This term was deeply rooted in people's hearts and irreplaceable. Therefore, the more commonly used term "Qing Ming" was retained and the meaning of "Hangzhou silk" was removed. There were also duplicate entries, like "hasihimbi" "hūwakšahan" "uden", with the same Chinese meaning in two categories, so one of them were deleted.

Deleting Some Phrases or Proper Nouns. In addition to the above situations, there were also some phrases or proper nouns that had not been included in *Yu Zhi Zeng Ding Qing Wen Jian,* as follows (Table 5):

Table 4. List of deleting partial meanings of polysemous words

Entries in *Yu Zhi Qing Wen Jian*	Deleted location and Chinese meaning	Retained location and Chinese meaning
sambi	Humanity Volume·Intelligence Category：有见识(knowledgeable)	Humanity Volume·Listening Category：知道(know) Humanity Volume·Taking out and expanding Category：伸开(unfold)
jirgahabi	Humanity Volume·Happiness Category：安逸了(became comfortable)	Humanity Volume·Sleeping Category：安寝了(slept)
buhi	Humanity Volume·Sitting and Standing Category：膝(knee)	Humanity Volume·Body Category：马面(horse face) Cloth Volume·Leather Category：去毛鹿皮(buckskin without down)
hasihimbi	Humanity Volume·Walking Category：希图侥幸(hoping to luck)	Humanity Volume·hoping Category：希图侥幸(hoping to luck)
hūwakšahan	Residence Volume·House Category：周兰立柱(handrail)	Construction Volume·Gap Category：周兰立柱(handrail)
uden	Food Volume·Food Category：中火处(kitchen)	Residence Volume·Streets Category：中火处(kitchen)
šenggin	Residence Volume·House Category：檐(cooking beach)	Land Volume·Land Category：山额(top of a mountain) Humanity Volume·Body Category：额(forehead)
hangsi	Clothing Volume·Clothing Category：杭州绸(Hangzhou silk)	Time Volume·Time Category：清明(Qing Ming)

Some of these deleted entries belonged to proper nouns, and they appeared in *Yu Zhi Man Meng Wen Jian*. Jiang Qiao (2018) believed that "Emperor Qianlong compiled *Yu Zhi Man Meng Wen Jian* to strengthen the connection between Manchu and Mongolian languages and help learn to each other" [3]. The deleted entries can reflect the different focus of word selection between the *Yu Zhi Zeng Ding Qing Wen Jian* and *Yu Zhi Man Meng Wen Jian,* and *Yu Zhi Man Meng Wen Jian* payed more attention to including entries related to the culture, production and life of the two ethnic groups.

Table 5. Specific entries of deleting phrases or proper nouns

Entries in *Yu Zhi Qing Wen Jian*	Chinese meaning	Location
forgon i yargiyan ton	时宪万日 (calendar day)	Emperor Volume·Imperial Edict Category
susai nadan gūsa	五十七旗 (57 Banners)	Official Position Volume·Leaders of banners Category
alban jafame hengkilenjire ūlet	进刊头来的厄鲁特人(The ūlet people who kowtowed and paid tribute)	Official Position Volume·Leaders of banners Category
yuwanšuwai	元帅 (marshal)	Military accomplishments Volume·Conquest Category
kūwaran i da	营长 (battalion commander)	Military accomplishments Volume·Conquest Category
gusingga gucu	仁慈朋友 (kind friend)	Humanity Volume·Friends Category
nonggibure gucu	益友 (helpful friend)	Humanity Volume·Friends Category
ekiyedere gucu	损友 (bad friend)	Humanity Volume·Friends Category
funfulambi	吩咐 (command)	Humanity Volume·Speeches Category
tengnembi	腾 (prance)	Humanity Volume·Walking Category
mušu algan	捕猎鹑的网 (the net of hunting quail)	Industry Volume·Hunting tool Category
funde weilembi	替工 (work as a substitute)	Construction Volume·Construction Category
coko umagan i toholiyo	鸡蛋饼糕 (egg fried cake)	Food Volume·Cakes Category
ajilaha	糙米 (brown rice)	Coarse cereals Volume·Rice Category
šanggiyan niongniyaha	白雁 (white goose)	Birds Volume·Birds Category
buluntumbi	蛇类动物交配 (snake mating)	Livestock Volume·Breeding livestock Category
hiyabsa enggemu	小木鞍 (small wooden saddle)	Livestock Volume·Tools of feeding livestock Category

3 The Influence of Manchu-Chinese Bilingual Comparison Model on the Translation of Dictionary Vocabulary

Yu Zhi Qing Wen Jian was divided into 36 volumes, 280 categories and 400 items. Based on this, *Yu Zhi Zeng Ding Qing Wen Jian* still had 36 volumes as the main edition, while the number of categories increased to 292, and the number of items increased to 538. The classification of categories and items were more detailed, with the number of included entries was increasing. Some names of volumes and categories changed, and the names of items did not changed, while the number of items increased. Through careful statistical comparison, we can see the changes in volumes' setting and words' classification in *Yu Zhi Zeng Ding Qing Wen Jian*.

3.1 Changes in Category Names After Chinese Translation

Change in Names of Volumes. The names of the volumes and categories in Yu Zhi Zeng Ding Qing Wen Jian had changed since it became bilingual expression. There were four changes in the names of 36 volumes, which were "dorolon i šošohon" (etiquette volume), "oktosi saman i šošohon" (medicine and witchcraft volume), "tuwa šanggiyan i šošohon" (fire volume) and "jahūdai i šošohon" (boat volume).

Changes of Category Names

Adding Category Name. On the basis of the original categories, there were 11 categories were newly added, which were "funnere temgetulere hacin" (canonizing category), "faidan de baitalara jaka i hacin" (guarding category), "bithei tacin de baitalara jakai hacin" (literary artifacts category), "durunga tetun i hacin" (instrument category), "fiyelere hacin" (gelding category), "mukdehun juktehen i hacin" (altar and temple category), "jurgan yamun i hacin" (government office category), "gurgu i aššara arbušara hacin" (animals category), "esihengge hurungge i be i hacin" (scaly animals category), "umiyaha i aššara hacin" (insects category), "fucihi i hacin" (buddha category) and "enduri i hacin" (god category).

Replacing Category Name. There were 12 category names that had changed, which were "wesire forgošoro hacin"(upgrade category), "hargašara isara hacin" (meeting category), "banin buyenin i hacin" (temperament category), "bibure unggere hacin" (stay and dispatch category), "budun eberi i hacin" (weakness categoty), "heolen calgari hacin" (slow category), "oktosilame dasara hacin" (medical categoty), "gurung deyen i hacin" (palace category), "gūlha fomoci i hacin" (boots and socks category), "nirure simnere hacin" (oil painting category), "jahūdai i hacin" (boat category), "gasha i aššara arbušara hacin" (birds category).

3.2 Changes in the Genus of Some Entries

In the process of revising, the positions of some original entries were adjusted. There was a total of 48 entries were changed their position. The following Table 6 gives some examples of this situation.

Table 6. Comparison table of the entries which were changed their positions in *Yu Zhi Zeng Ding Qing Wen Jian*

Manchu entries	Chinese meaning	present location	previous location
janggiyūn	将军 (general)	Official Position Volume·Minister Category	Military accomplishments Volume·Hunting Category
hebei amban	参赞大臣 (counsellor)	Official Position Volume·Minister Category	Military accomplishments Volume·Hunting Category
dolmombi	撒酒 (pour wine)	Etiquette Volume·Banquet Category	Food Volume·Spooning Category
nirugan	画图 (painting)	Literature Voluem·Literary artifacts Category	Construcition Volume·Oil painting Category
fiyelembi	骟马 (ride a horse)	Military accomplishments Volume·Riding horse Category	Humanity Volume·Walking Category
dubik	熟练 (skilled)	Humanity Volume·Kindness Category	Birds Volume·Sparrows Category
dosombi	耐得住 (afford)	Humanity Volume·Brave Category	Livestock Volume·Horses Category
suihumbi	醉闹 (get drunk)	Humanity Volume·Frivolity Category	Food Volume·Diet Category
ibembi	添草料 (feed fodder)	Livestock Volume·Raising Category	Livestock Volume·Livestock tools Category
dundambi	喂猪 (feed pig)	Livestock Volume·Raising Category	Livestock Volume·Livestock tools Category

The changes in the category of these original entries reflected the editor's new understanding of the attribution of objective things, which was also a new understanding and induction of the meaning of the entries.

4 The Effect and Influence of Manchu-Chinese Bilingual Comparison Model on the Compilation Style of Dictionary

Yu Zhi Zeng Ding Qing Wen Jian was an extremely valuable material for the inheritance and development of the entire history of Chinese dictionaries, as well as for the study of ancient Chinese encyclopedias and classical dictionaries of Chinese ethnic minorities.

4.1 Semantics and Pronunciation of Entries Were Fixed Through Bilingual Comparison Mode

Yu Zhi Zeng Ding Qing Wen Jian was an official revised Manchu-Chinese bilingual dictionary, which was different from traditional monolingual dictionaries or ancient encyclopedias. The entries achieved the coexistence of written and spoken words. In terms of vocabulary collection, it not only collected words of people's daily production and life, but also included a large number of proper nouns in various fields. Hence, it not only reflected the role of interpretation, but also added an encyclopedic function to explain the phenomena and things represented by the entries.

Moreover, due to the background of its official revising dictionary, the use of proper nouns had a mandatory binding effect on the entire social population. Therefore, in addition to a large number of collected words, rich types and comprehensive content, the vocabularies was highly standardized and practical.

The correction of characters and pronunciation was an important goal of the revising the dictionary, which was also a need for the development of the Manchu vocabulary system and a policy demand for protecting the national language. *Yu Zhi Zeng Ding Qing Wen Jian* retained the original entries of the *Yu Zhi Zeng Wen Jian*, and after some appropriate adjustments, adding a large number of entries to enrich Manchu vocabulary system. The official and authoritative entries achieved the standardization in forms, meanings and pronunciations, and provided a unified model for the use of Manchu vocabulary.

4.2 Inheriting Ancient Chinese Dictionaries and Influencing the Compilation of Bilingual Dictionaries in Later Generations

"*Yu Zhi Zeng Ding Qing Wen Jian* was a dictionary that systematically classifies Manchu vocabularies based on inheriting ancient classification encyclopedias. This classification system was an understanding of the concept of semantic categories and a new attempt to study the core meaning and field of semantics, including the arrangement order within categories. It can be explained by using relevant semantic knowledge, etymological knowledge and cognitive linguistics theory." [5]

In addition, as the first official revised Manchu-Chinese bilingual dictionary, *Yu Zhi Zeng Ding Qing Wen Jian* had a profound impact after publication. Many dictionaries were compiled based on it, which follow the writing and usage standards of the dictionary entries and added or deleted content or added languages on this basis.

5 Conclusion

Yu Zhi Zeng Ding Qing Wen Jian was the first official Manchu-Chinese bilingual dictionary in the Qing Dynasty. The biggest role of its Manchu-Chinese bilingual comparison model was to standardize the corresponding Manchu vocabulary's forms, meanings and pronunciations by using official selected meaning and pronunciation of Chinese as compared standard. It also provided an official model for editing Manchu dictionaries in the future.

The bilingual comparison mode between Manchu and Chinese in *Yu Zhi Zeng Ding Qing Wen Jian* had been widely applied in the volumes' setting and entries' classification of the dictionary. From the macro structure of the dictionary editing, the dictionary was changed from monolingual mode to bilingual mode. And under the Chinese comparison, some names of categories in Manchu were changed. From the micro structure of the dictionary editing, the collected entries were changed from Manchu monolingual to Manchu-Chinese bilingual with the help of the bilingual mode. And it adjusted the classification position of some Manchu entries to reduce the frequency of the same entries' appearance in different categories. At the same time, the semantics and phonetics of the original Manchu entries were fixed by using meanings and pronunciations of Chinese characters. By using Chinese to correct the expression of Manchu entries, it can help replace a large number of Chinese transliterated loan words and other phrases during the revising process.

Acknowledgments. This study is supported by 2021 Hunan Provincial Philosophy and Social Sciences Project: Compilation and Language Research of Four Manchu and Han Combined "Four Books" Literature in the Qing Dynasty (21YBL001); Project of the China Postdoctoral Science Foundation: Research on the Contact between Manchu and Chinese Languages in the Eight Manchu "Four Books" of the Qing Dynasty (2022M711118).

References

1. Chun, H.: Research on Manchu and Mongolian Dictionaries in Qing Dynasty. Liaoning Ethnic Publisher, Shenyang (2008). (in Chinese)
2. Zhang, B.: The definition principles and judgment methods of Chinese loanwords. Chin. J. 03, 67–77 (2019). (in Chinese)
3. Jiang, Q.: Research on *Yu Zhi Qing Wen Jian*. Beijing Yanshan Publisher, Beijing (2008). (in Chinese)
4. Zhang, Y.: Research into the additional meanings of the words of Shaanxi-Gansu-Ningxia border region consultative council—taking the Shaanxi-Gansu-Ningxia border region consultative council literature as a corpus. In: Hong, J.F., Zhang, Y., Liu, P. (eds.) CLSW 2019. LNCS, vol. 11831, pp. 249–254. Springer, Cham (2020). https://doi.org/10.1007/978-3-030-38189-9_26
5. Hu, N.: Research on Classification and Words of Yu Zhi Zeng Ding Qing Wen Jian. Xiamen University (2017). (in Chinese)

A Study on the Combination of the "Artificial/Natural" Semantics in the Chinese NN Attributive-Head Compounds

Tengteng Du and Jiapan Li[✉]

Teachers College, Beijing Language and Culture University, Beijing, China
lijiapan@blcu.edu.cn

Abstract. The semantic combination within a compound word affects the characteristics of the whole word. This paper focuses on Chinese noun-noun attributive-head compounds, using "natural/artificial" as classification criteria, and utilizing the theory of qualia structure to explore the qualia relationship between components of compound words and their implicit predicates under consistent and inconsistent modes of semantic classification. The research indicates that there is a selection tendency between the qualia role played by attributive components in compound words and their implicit predicates. Additionally, the semantic type of constituents in a compound word can influence its overall semantic type; this in turn restricts the qualia relationship between constituents within a word and selection for implicit predicates.

Keywords: Noun-noun compound words · Consistent semantics classification · Inconsistent semantics classification · Qualia structure theory · Implicit predicates

1 Introduction

The semantic characteristics of components within a compound word can constrain its formation. For example, Chinese diphthongal attributive-head compounds, whether an attributive component's functional meaning is conventional or not will affect the choice of NN or VN structural form [9]. Noun-noun compounding is a typical method of creating new words in languages such as Chinese and English. Most previous studies have explored the complex relationships between two components in NN attributive-head compounds from a semantic perspective [6, 15]. Semantic relations are closely related to constituent semantics and find key semantic features that constrain human language construction has become academic hotspots over recent decades such as WordNet's or HowNet's divisions into different classes based on semantics [1, 5, 10], qualia structure Theory's division into natural/artificial noun categories [3, 11–13]. Studies show that "artificial/natural" semantic features play important roles in constraining words constructions across many languages including English and Chinese [6–8, 14]. To systematically explore how "artificial/natural" semantic features affect words construction

M. Dong et al. (Eds.): CLSW 2023, LNAI 14514, pp. 495–510, 2024.
https://doi.org/10.1007/978-981-97-0583-2_38

in Chinese language, this study mainly bases on Qualia Structure Theory [11] along with research [7, 14] and takes whether something was intentionally created by humans or if it has utility as distinguishing criteria for "natural/artificial". After exhaustively extracting data from Modern Chinese Dictionary (7th edition) [16] about NN attributive-head compounds, we analyze their "natural/artificial" property of internal components and the whole word. The statistical results are shown in Table 1.

Table 1. Semantic Modes of "Natural/Artificial" within Chinese NN attributive-head Compounds.

Semantic Modes	Art. + Art.	Nat. + Nat.	Art. + Nat.	Nat. + Art.	Total
Artificial	2936	278	641	1573	5428
Natural	10	1813	155	170	2148
Total	2946	2091	796	1743	7576

It could be seen that under the criteria "natural/artificial", there exist significant discrepancies between numbers of natural class and artificial class compounds which indicates the productivity of these two semantic features are not equal. (from the Table 1) What interactive and constraints exist between "natural" and "artificial" features when constructing words? Quantitative results support that in modern Mandarin mostly NN attributive-head compounds are consisted in semantically consistent structures (the whole-word category is consistent with the head constituent category), but also many compounds where these are consisted in semantically inconsistent structures. How do natural class and artificial class differ in terms of how they semantically combine under consistent or inconsistent modes? Are there any differences in terms of semantic expression? What sort of interactive and constraining rules exist when combining constituent properties with whole-word properties? After determining specific combination conditions within NN attributive-head compounds, we further describe and categorize semantic relations between constituents to explore these questions.

2 Principles of Semantic Description in Chinese NN Attributive-Head Compounds

The semantic classification of the internal components of compound words usually suffers from the effects of ambiguity and subjectivity. The qualia structure theory is based on the noun-centered perspective, which provides clear standards for the semantic structural relationship of nominal compounds and enhances the objectivity of classification. The qualia structure theory has hold great significance for the research of noun-noun attributive-head compounds. It divides the semantic relationships between the components of nouns into four basic types: the "formal role" describes the relationship between the object and other objects; the "telic role" describes the utility and function of the objects; the "constitutive role" describes the relationship between the whole and the part; and the "agentive role" describes how the object is formed or produced [3]. Predicates play a very important role in the judgment of qualia structure, and predicates are often implied in attributive-head noun-noun compounds. By exploring the implicit predicates, we can determine the qualia structure more accurately and explore the sub-types of relationships further. Previous studies have summarized different types of implicit predicates based on different research objectives. For example, nine types [2] and eleven types [4]. Although the specific types are summarized differently, implicit predicates have similarities. This paper draws on the research results of previous scholars, based on the objective of this paper, summarizes the categories of implicit predicates in attributive-head noun-noun compounds into nine: EXISTENCE, POSSESSION, GENUS, SIMILARITY, FORM, FUNCTION, CAUSALITY, DEPENDENCE, and CONTENT.

(1) 存在关系 (Existence relationship) refers to the positional relationship within time and space dimensions. For example, "壁纸 (wallpaper)" means "paper" - at the location – "wall", "午饭 (lunch)" - "meal" - at the time – "noon".

(2) 领属关系 (Possession relationship) refers to a general "whole-part" relationship. For example, "花萼 (calyx)" means "flower" - has "calyx", "车头 (headstock)" - "car" - has "head (the front part)".

(3) 系属关系 (Genus relationship) refers to a hierarchical relationship. For example, " 鲤鱼(carp)" means "carp" is a type of "fish", "仓房 (warehouse)" means "warehouse" is a type of "house".

(4) 相似关系 (Similarity relationship) refers to the similarity in appearance or properties between two things. For example, "僚机 (wingman)" means "plane" (attribute) likes "assistant", " 鳞茎(bulb)" means "stem" (shape) like "scale".

(5) 方式关系 (Form relationship) refers to the state of existence or stable characteristics of objects. For example, "汉流 (tributary)" means "flow", which exists in the form of "tributary", "敌人 (enemy)" means "person", which exists in the form of "enemy".

(6) 功用关系 (Function relationship) refers to the fact that the existence of one object is aimed to serve another object. For example, "音叉 (tuning fork)" means "fork" has the function of (making) "sounds", " 蔗农(sugarcane farmer)" means the "farmer" has the purpose of (obtaining) "sugarcanes".

(7) 因果关系 (Causality relationship) refers to the premise that the existence of one object is based on the existence of another object. For example, "姻亲 (in-law relatives)" means "relatives" due to "marriage", "风害 (wind damage)" means "damage" caused by "wind".

(8) 凭借关系 (Dependence relationship) refers to the existence or operation of something that requires the assistance of another thing. For example, " 蔗糖(sucrose)" means "sugar" (production) - depends on "sugarcane", "油灯 (oil lamp)" means (the light of the) "lamp" depends on "oil".

(9) 关涉关系 (Relevance relationship) refers to a general "theme – content" relationship between things. For example, "乐理 (music theory)" means the "theory" is about "music", "病案 (medical record)" means the "case" is about a "disease".

After determining the principles of semantic description, we will explore the qualia structural characteristics and implying predicates of artificial and natural compounds, along with the implicit situations of predicates semantic consistent patterns and semantic inconsistent patterns. In addition, we will also explore the corresponding rules between the qualia structure and the implicit predicates.

3 Semantic Combination Features of NN Attributive-Head Compounds in Artificial Category

Artificial NN attributive-head compounds include two consistent modes of semantic classification: [artificial + artificial] art. and [natural + artificial] art., as well as two inconsistent modes: [artificial + natural] art. and [natural + natural] art.. The specific cases of their semantic combinations are shown in Table 2.

Table 2. Qualia Role and Predicate Implication Situations for Attributive-Head Noun- Noun Compounds in Chinese Artificial Category.

	[Art.+Art.] art.				[Nat.+Art.] art.				[Art.+Nat.] art.				[Nat.+Nat.] art.				Total
	F	T	C	A	F	T	C	A	F	T	C	A	F	T	C	A	
Function	—	845	—	—	—	284	—	—	—	117	—	—	—	35	—	—	1281
Existence	388	—	—	—	454	—	—	—	78	—	—	—	63	—	—	—	983
Possession	348	—	140	—	56	—	82	—	204	—	6	—	56	—	21	—	913
Dependence	—	—	136	93	—	—	212	163	—	—	30	16	—	—	38	32	720
Relevance	390	—	—	—	105	—	—	—	75	—	—	—	9	—	—	—	579
Form	404	—	—	—	85	—	—	—	39	—	—	—	4	—	—	—	532
Similarity	125	—	—	—	127	—	—	—	58	—	—	—	17	—	—	—	327
Genus	51	—	—	—	—	—	—	—	12	—	—	—	—	—	—	—	63
Causality	—	—	—	16	—	—	—	5	—	—	—	6	—	—	—	3	30
Total	1706	845	276	109	827	284	294	168	466	117	36	22	149	35	59	35	5428

Overall, the implicit predicates in the artificial NN compounds present a clear hierarchy: function, existence, possession relationships > dependence, mode, relevance relationships > similarity, causality, genus relationships. There is a strong regularity between qualia roles and implicit predicates. The telic role corresponds entirely with function relationship; the constitutive role corresponds to possession and dependence relationships; the agentive roles correspond to dependence and causality relationships; the formal roles are more complex—apart from possession relationship—they complementarily imply predicates with the other three types of qualia roles.

3.1 Analysis on Semantic Combination for Consistent Mode NN Attributive-Head Compounds

Consistent modes NN attributive-head compounds refer to those where the whole compounds' semantic property consistent with the head component's semantic property— namely [artificial + artificial] art. mode and [natural + artificial] art. mode.

(i) N_1 as the telic role of N_2. People always create specific artifacts for some purpose to satisfy their needs. Thus, from its beginning an artifact carries human intent—it inherently has a functional attribute. When implying predicate of "function" relationship, N_1 is the object that artifact N_2 acts on. The artifacts can act upon both artifacts or natural objects which corresponding respectively to two compound modes. For example:

案饭(incense table): A long table <u>for</u> placing incense burners.
鸟枪 (bird gun): A gun <u>used for</u> bird hunting.
风衣 (windcheater): A type of coat designed <u>against</u> wind.

The function relationships between "案" (table) and "香" (incense), "枪" (gun) and "鸟" (bird), "衣" (coat) and "风" (wind) are constructed through human activities like "placing" "hunting" or "designing".

(ii) N_1 as the formal role of N_2. The formal role distinguishes things in broader scope and the stronger stability distinguishing features are, the greater advantage they gain during compounding process. In both [artificial + artificial] $_{art.}$ and [natural + artificial] $_{art.}$ modes, when N_1 as the formal role of N_2, they often imply predicates of existence and mode relationships.

After creating certain implements, humans usually place them within natural or artificial spaces to utilize it better, therefore, existence relationship holds certain advantage during word formation process. When implying predicate of existence relationship, N_1 represents time or space where artifact N_2 works. For example:

盒饭 (boxed meal): A meal sold <u>in</u> a box.
地铁 (subway): A passage <u>underneath</u> a busy road.
军法 (military law): Criminal law <u>in</u> the military.
内饰 (interior trim): The <u>interior</u> decoration of a car, building, etc.
节礼 (Festival gift): A gift given <u>at</u> Festivals.
夜班 (night shift): The work <u>during</u> the night.

Existence relation presents typicality difference due to specificity degree difference between objects and places. In prototype existence relationship, the existing objects "饭" (meal) and "铁" (rail), and existing places "盒" (box) and "地" (underground) are all concrete and visible which present the existence relationship clearly. In sub-prototype, the existing objects "法" (law), "饰" (decoration) are more general and the existing places "军" (military), "内" (interior) are more abstract. In marginal existence relationships, the words represent time such as "节" (festival) "夜" (night) have higher abstraction degree than space which makes the clarity of the existence relationship lower and decreases the typicality.

The use or operation mode of an artificial object is usually clearly defined from its beginning with strong stability and it generally won't change easily, so highlighting usage manner is also an advantageous choice for word formation. [artificial + artificial] $_{art.}$ compounds tend to indicate that an artifact operates according to man-made rules, while [natural + artificial] $_{art.}$ compounds tend to indicate that an artifact operates according to the standards of a natural object. For example:

歌剧 (opera): Drama that <u>primarily involves singing</u>.

月刊 (monthly): A publication published <u>once a month</u>.

The "drama" is primarily presented in the form of songs and the "publication" are published in the form of "once a month". The ways of "song" and "monthly" are generally not easily changed after being determined by people, so their stability is strong enough to distinguish them from other things on a larger scale.

(iii) N_1 as the constitutive role of N_2. The constitutive role explains the composition of an object, which can either refer to its overall material or its individual parts. This determines whether it implies predicates of dependence or possession. The cognitive prominence of the overall material is higher than that of individual parts, therefore attributive-head compounds implying predicates of dependence are more numerous than those implying predicates of possession.

Humans cannot create something from nothing and they always need certain materials either directly obtained from nature or processed from natural objects before they can be used to make things. For example:

蜡像 (wax figure): An image of a person or object <u>made of</u> wax.
棉线 (cotton yarn): Yarn spun <u>from</u> cotton.
漆布 (lacquer cloth): Cloth coated <u>with</u> lacquer.
毛笔 (writing brush): Pens <u>with</u> nibs made of wool skunk.

"Wax figures" and "cotton yarn" imply predicates of dependence, the "figure" and "yarn" are formed by depending on homogeneous artificial substances "wax" and naturally obtained "cotton". And "lacquered cloth" and "brushes" imply predicates of possession which means the artificial substances "lacquer" and naturally obtained "hair" constitute a part of the "cloth" and "pen".

(iv) N_1 as the agentive role of N_2. The agentive role explains how an object is formed or produced. The production requires certain motivations or specific reasons which determine whether it implies predicates of dependence or causality relationships. The dependence of the motivations or tools are chosen by people independently which can present clearly and the causality relationship is a logical relationship that cannot be clearly presented. Thus attributive-head compounds usually have more compounds implied dependence relationship than causality relationship. For example:

笔供 (written confession): A confession written <u>by</u> the interrogator with a pen.
风车 (windmill): A wind-<u>powered</u> mechanical device...
仇家 (foe): Enemy (a person who is hostile <u>because of</u> hatred).
地缘 (Geography): A relationship formed <u>by</u> geographical proximity.

The "written confession" and "windmill" imply predicate of dependence relationship: pen and wind respectively serve as tool and motivation for creating confessions and windmills. While "enemy family" and "geographical relation" imply predicate of causality relationship: "hatred" and "location" respectively act as reasons behind the "enemy" and "relation".

3.2 Analysis of Semantic Combination for Inconsistent Mode NN Attributive-Head Compounds

Inconsistent NN attributive-head compounds refer to compound words where the semantic classification of the whole word is inconsistent with that of the head component, namely [artificial + natural] $_{art.}$ and [natural + natural] $_{art.}$ modes.

(i) N_1 as the formal role of N_2. In [artificial + natural] $_{art.}$ and [natural + natural] $_{art.}$ compounds, predicates of possession and existence relationships are often implied when N_1 as the formal role of N_2. The possession relationship is a "whole-part" relationship and it is often metaphorically understood through part component or whole word. For example:

钱眼 (money's hole): The square hole in the middle of a coin.
猫眼 (cat eye): The colloquial name for door viewers.

"Square hole" is a part of the "coin" which is similar to the "eye" in shape, "door viewer" is similar to the "eye" of a cat in overall shape. In order to refer to a particular part of an object or to help people understand the whole of an unfamiliar thing, people will choose the metaphors to assist their understanding.

When inconsistent semantic classification compounding patterns imply the existence relationship, N_1 still represents the time or space where artificial object N_2 acts on. For example:

眼影 (eye-shadow): A makeup painted on the eyelids during makeup....
垄沟 (ridge): The lower place (like ditch in shape) between two adjacent ridges.
边地 (border area): Areas located in remote border.
行距 (interior trim): The distance between two adjacent rows.
末日(doomsday): Christianity refers to the last day of the world...
烛泪(candle oil): The wax oil that drips down when a candle burns.

The typicality of the natural compounds is same with the artificial compounds. When the existence objects and existence location are more concrete and visible, the existence relationships are more typical.

(ii) N_1 as telic role of N_2. When the artificial compounds in the inconsistent semantically classified imply predicate of function, they often represent "pseudo-artificial classes" [14], namely, people utilize natural objects to satisfy their needs. By endowing natural objects N_2 with social attributes, human beings forcefully reverse the semantic property of the whole word, causing the inconsistency of semantically classified. For example:

军马 (Military horses): Horse used by military forces.
肉牛 (Beef cattle): Cattle bred specifically for meat production.

(iii) N_1 as constitutive role of N_2. In artificial compounds of inconsistent semantic classified, predicates of dependence and possession relationships are implied when N_1 as the constitutive role of N_2. Which represent overall materiality and partial components due largely cognitive differences between wholes and parts. The overall material has a higher cognitive salience compared to partial components, so the number of compounds implying predicate of dependence relationship is more than the number of possession relationship. The artificial compounds of inconsistent semantically classified mostly occur metaphorically, which is an important reason for their inconsistency. It is impossible for humans to create something out of nothing. They always depend on certain materials which directly obtain from nature or some kinds of processing on natural objects. For example:

面筋 (gluten): Food, use the flour and water…
雪人 (snowman): A humanoid figure made of snow.
窝头 (steamed bread of corn): Food made from cornmeal, sorghum flour, or other kinds of mixed grain flour…slightly conical, with a hole underneath…
汽水 (soft drink): A drink made by dissolving carbon dioxide in water and adding sugar, juice, and spices…

Artifacts similar in property of plastic to "tendon" and in shape to "man" are made up of homogeneous, visible "flour" and "snow", which are clearly present the relationship of dependence. The "hole" and "vapor" are parts of the bottom or inside of the artifacts similar to "head" and "water", which cannot be directly observed. The clarity of the possession relationship is weaker than dependence relationship, the number of compounds is therefore less than compounds implying predicate of dependence relationship.

(iv) N_1 as agentive role of N_2. In artificial compounds of inconsistent semantic classification, they imply predicate either of dependence relationship or of causality relationship. For example:

棒疮(sore): Skin disease caused by being hit with poles or cudgels.
果汁 (juice): Beverage made from fresh fruit juice…
外患 (foreign trouble): Scourge from abroad, mostly referring to foreign invasions.
妖风(demon wind) The winds that rise up from the demons in mythology.

The "sore" is formed by using the tool "stick", the "juice" is formed by using the raw material "fruit". Both the tool and the raw material are chosen by human beings, and the dependence relationship is clear. The "scourge" is produced because of the activity of "foreign", "wind" is produced because of the activity of "demons". However, not every "foreign" brings "scourge", and the causality relation between "demon" and "wind" exists only in specific contexts, so the causality relation in this subcategory is instable and that's why the number of compounds implying predicate of causality is less than that of predicates of dependence relationship.

Inconsistent NN attributive-head compounds refer to compound words where the semantic classification of the whole word is inconsistent with that of the head component, namely [artificial + natural] $_{art.}$ and [natural + natural] $_{art.}$ modes.

4 Semantic Combination Features of NN Attributive-Head Compounds in Nature Category

The attributive-head compounds of nature category include two consistent modes of semantic classification: [natural + natural] $_{nat.}$ and [artificial + natural] $_{nat.}$, as well as two inconsistent modes: [natural + artificial] $_{nat.}$ and [artificial + artificial] $_{nat.}$. The specifics regarding their semantic combinations are shown in Table 3. Overall, attributive-head compounds in nature category exhibit distinct hierarchy concerning predicate implications: Existence, Possession relationship > Similarity, Genus and Dependence relationship > Form, Relevance, Function and Causality relationship. The qualia roles correspond to predicate implications is same with the artificial compounds.

Table 3. Qualia Role and Predicate Implication Situations for Attributive-Head Noun- Noun Compounds in Chinese Natural Category

	[Nat.+Nat.] $_{nat.}$				[Art.+Nat.] $_{nat.}$				[Nat.+Art.] $_{nat.}$				[Art.+Art.] $_{nat.}$				Total
	F	T	C	A	F	T	C	A	F	T	C	A	F	T	C	A	
Existence	543	—	—	—	28	—	—	—	38	—	—	—	—	—	—	—	609
Possession	350	—	99	—	35	—	6	—	37	—	6	—	—	—	—	—	533
Similarity	230	—	—	—	46	—	—	—	44	—	—	—	4	—	—	—	324
Genus	219	—	—	—	—	—	—	—	—	—	—	—	—	—	—	—	219
Dependence	—	—	45	52	—	—	—	10	—	—	10	5	—	—	—	—	122
Form	97	—	—	—	15	—	—	—	2	—	—	—	—	—	—	—	114
Relevance	96	—	—	—	10	—	—	—	—	—	—	—	—	—	—	—	106
Function	—	29	—	—	—	3	—	—	—	28	—	—	—	6	—	—	66
Causality	—	—	—	53	—	—	—	2	—	—	—	0	—	—	—	—	55
Total	1535	29	144	105	134	3	6	12	121	28	16	5	4	6	—	—	2148

4.1 Analysis on Semantic Combination for Consistent Mode NN Attributive-Head Compounds

The consistent mode of semantic classification, namely, the [natural + natural] $_{nat.}$ and [artificial + natural] $_{nat.}$ compound word patterns, is a prevalent pattern observed in attributive-head compounds.

(i) N_1 as the Formal Role of N_2. The compounds in [natural + natural] $_{nat.}$ and [artificial + natural] $_{nat.}$ modes often imply predicates of existence and possession relationships when N_1 as the formal role for N_2.

When implying the predicate of existence relationship, it usually denotes that natural entity N_2 resides within a natural or "semi-artificial" environment (the natural environment was transformed by human activities while retaining much of its property) N_1. This is consistent with Downing's research [6] findings. For example:

海藻 (seaweed): Algae that grow in the ocean...
田鸡 (sora): Birds that look slightly like chickens...live in grasslands and rice fields...
肝炎 (hepatitis): inflammation of the liver...
盆腔 (pelvis): The cavity inside the pelvis...
暮霭 (twilight): clouds and mist in the evening.

In the case of "Seaweed" and "Sora", the object "seaweed" "bird" and the location "sea" "field" are both concrete and visible objective realities, and the relationship of existence represents the environment in which natural creature grow or live, which cannot be changed by human beings. The stability of the relationship is the strongest and it is the most typical existence relation. In the case of "Hepatitis" "Pelvis", although the location "liver" "pelvis" is concrete, the objects "inflammation" "cavity" are abstract, the relation is stable but the clarity of the relationship is reduced, so it is a sub-typical existential relationship. The marginal existential relation still represents the temporal relation which represents the time of the appearance of natural phenomena which is quite explicit but happens sporadically hence lacks stability, so the relation is not very stable and the typicality of existence relation is the lowest.

When implying the predicate of possession relationship, it often represents some structural feature or inherent sentiment related to a certain natural entity which humans can't influence thus exhibiting stable possession relations. For example:

花梗 (pedicel): The stalk of a flower...
母性 (Maternity): The mother's instinct.

In "flower stem" and "maternal instincts", "stem" is a part of inherent structure of "flower "while "instinct" represents the innate nature of "mother" - both being immutable natural relations beyond human intervention. In [natural + natural] $_{nat.}$ compounds both possessor and possessed item are concrete and visible objects with clear relationship. Due to representation of biological structure, the stability of the relationship is stronger hence the typicality is higher. In [artificial + natural] $_{nat.}$ compound words possessor generally represents sociological identity while possessed item refers abstract nature quality which resulting weaker clarity and lowering its typicality.

(ii) N_1 as the agentive role of N_2. When N_1 as the agentive role of N_2, [nature + nature] $_{nat.}$ compounds often imply predicates of dependence which indicating the motivations for something to form. For instance:

阳光 (sunlight): The light emitted by the sun.
风力 (wind power): Force generated by wind...

In "sunlight" and "wind power", "sun" and "wind" are the sources of power for the formation of "light" and "power" respectively, which is an objective relationship of dependence.

(iii) N_1 as the constitutive role of N_2. In attributive-head compounds of the consistent mode of semantic classification, when N_1 as the constitutive role of N_2, there are more compounds imply predicate of possession than predicate of dependence and highlights a certain component part of natural objects. For example:

毛豆 (soybean): Young pods of soybeans <u>with</u> hairy outer skin......
沙碛(sand dunes): The ground completely <u>covered with</u> sand......
钩虫 (hookworm): Parasite worm...... <u>with</u> hooks in the mouth......

In "soybean" and "hookworm," "hairy" and "hook (metaphorical)" respectively form parts of "pod" and "worm," demonstrating the relationship between part and whole. In "sand dunes," "dune" is formed with the homogeneous, singular natural material "sand," which suggests a dependence relationship of natural material. In [artificial + natural] $_{nat.}$ compounds, when N_1 as the constitutive role of N_2, it does not imply predicate of dependence because it's impossible that any homogeneous artificial object can constitute any natural object.

(iv) N_1 as the telic role of N_2. Natural objects do not contain functions; people highlight their properties or behavioral characteristics during research to infer their roles. For example:

海峡 (strait): A narrow waterway <u>connecting</u> two seas or oceans between two pieces of land.
工蜂 (Worker bee): ...Responsible <u>for</u> constructing beehives, collecting pollen and nectar, feeding larvae and queen bees etc...

The "strait" refers to just the naturally occurring waterway located between two seas or oceans; however, people analyze its function as "connecting". The "bee" refers to just a natural creature; but human research discovering its inherent behavioral characteristics and infer its function as being responsible for certain tasks.

4.2 Analysis on Semantic Combination for Inconsistent Mode NN Attributive-Head Compounds

Compound words in inconsistent modes of semantic classification, namely [natural + artificial] $_{nat.}$ and [artificial + artificial] $_{nat.}$ are not dominant during word formation so they produce fewer compound words.

(i) N_1 as the formal role of N_2. In [Natural + Artificial] $_{nat.}$ and [Artificial + Artificial] $_{nat.}$ compounds, when N_1 as the formal role of N_2, it often implies predicate of similarity relationship and mostly represents some organs inside biological bodies that cannot be directly observed by human. Without corresponding background knowledge, people cannot understand the meaning of the words, so the familiar artificial objects are chosen to assist understanding. For example:

脊柱 (spinal): The main support on the back part......it looks <u>like</u> column.
贲门 (cardia): Part where stomach connects with esophagus, it's upper end mouth-like opening through which food enters from esophagus into stomach.

The main support on backside and the place where stomach connects with esophagus are inside of body, hence without medical knowledge these concepts may be hard to understand. Humans chose familiar artificial objects like column or door which are similar in functions to assist understanding while forming these words.

(ii) N_1 as the constitutive role of N_2. When N_1 as the constitutive role of N_2, it is always interpreted metaphorically.

土包 (mound): A large pile of earth.
泽国 (land of lakes): Region with many rivers and lakes.

In the terms "mound" and "land of lakes, the mound-like structure formed by homogeneous soil constitutes a mound and soil is the generalized material for "mound. The region similar to a country consists of numerous "lakes." In [artificial + artificial] $_{nat.}$ compounds, N_1 does not play a constitutive role of N_2.

(iii) N_1 as the telic role of N_2. When N_1 as the telic role of N_2, it often describes physiological characteristics or tissues in human body. Functions are inferred from observations, and all the compounds are understood through metaphors. For example:

筛管(urethra): The tube that expels urine from body.
子宫 (uterus): Female reproductive organ in women and female mammals. It looks like sac......fetus develops inside uterus.

The organs in human body similar to function of transport like channel, and containment like palace perform functions on urine and fetus during normal functioning. This is natural physiological process which humans have summarized based on their research, and used metaphors to assist understanding.

(iv) N_1 as the agentive role of N_2. When attributive-head compounds imply derived predicates where N_1 represents generalized tools that facilitate formation of N_2, there is only one example implying causal predicate relationship: "bloodstain."

耳音 (hearing ability): Ability to perceive sound using ears (ears perceive and distinguish sounds).
血迹 (bloodstain): Mark left by blood on objects.

"Ear" is an auditory organ and as a tool to assist people to perceive "sound". The "blood" is the reason why the "mark" formed.

5 Interaction Between Whole-Word Semantic Classification and Component Semantic Classification

5.1 The Influence of Component Semantic Classification on Whole-Word

(i) Tendency for Metaphor Occurrence. The different combinations of component semantic classifications within NN attributive-head compounds can affect the tendency for metaphor occurrence in the whole word. As shown by our analysis, metaphor situations are complex and not always directly correlated with similarity relationships. Statistical results on metaphor situations are shown in Table 4.

Table 4. Distribution of Metaphor Situations under Different Combination Modes.

	[N+A] n.	[N+N] a.	[A+N] n.	[A+A] n.	[A+N] a.	[N+N] n.	[N+A] a.	[A+A] a.
Metaphor	131/170	170/278	82/155	4/10	224/641	254/1813	189/1573	235/2936
Proportion	77%	61%	53%	40%	35%	14%	12%	8%

Table 4 reveals that among artificial NN attributive-head compounds, the sequence of metaphor tendency is [natural + natural] art. > [artificial + natural] art. > [natural + artificial] art. > [artificial + artificial] art.. That is, when semantic classification of the head component differs from semantic classification of the whole-word, there will be a significant increase in the proportion of metaphors occurring. The rate of metaphor occurrence in natural NN attributive-head compounds is higher than that in artificial ones, with a sequence being [natural + natural] nat. > [artificial + natural] nat. > [natural + artificial] nat. > [artificial + artificial] nat.. That is, when semantic classification of the head component is same with the semantic classification of the whole-word, there will be a significant increase in the proportion of metaphors occurring.

(ii) Tendency for Semantic Consistency. When semantic classifications of component within NN attributive-head compounds are identical, most the semantic classifications of whole-word remain consistent with their components' semantic classifications. Therefore, counts for both [artificial + artificial] art. and [nature + nature] nat. make up 63% of all NN attributive-head compounds. However, very few instances exhibit inconsistent semantics such as those two "natural" components result into an "artificial" category compound word (e.g., [nature + nature] art.). These types represent "pseudo-artificial" objects indicating human subjectivity can force changes to object attributes under certain conditions which is reflected via words where compound's overall semantics differ from its internal head component's semantic classification. For instances out of all NN attributive-head compounds only 10 compounds were found where two "artificial" components resulted into a "nature" category (e.g., [artificial + artificial] nat.), suggesting this type does not align well with Han nationality's conceptualization patterns.

In contrast to both semantically consistent "[natural + artificial]" art. and semantically inconsistent "[natural + artificial]" nat., the former has ten times more compounds than latter which further proving the artificial components are less likely to change their overall attributes due to influence by natural components. On the other hand, in comparison between semantically consistent "[artificial + natural]" nat. and semantically inconsistent "[artificial + natural]" art., the latter has four times more compounds than former which further illustrating how easily natural components change the overall semantics when modified by artificial components.

In summary, the combination state inside the NN Attributive - Head Compounds influences different tendencies towards metaphoric transference. Generally speaking, the greater difference inside components' semantic classifications, the more evident tendency towards metaphoric transference. At the same time, artificial component significantly influences natural component during word formation and when acting as the attributive component, it often forces changes in the semantics of the natural head component. On the contrary, natural component do not have significant influence on artificial components during word formation.

5.2 The Influence of Whole-Word Semantic Classification on Component Semantic Classification

(i) Tendency for Qualia structure. The whole-word semantic classification exerts constraints on component semantic classification mainly through the telic role in word formation. In artificial compounds. Since artificial objects inherently possess functional attributes, N_1 as the telic role of N_2 playing an important part in forming artificial NN compounds. However, natural objects don't inherently have functions hence their numerous of compounds are almost the minimal when N_1 as the telic role of N_2 within natural NN attributive-head compounds.

Furthermore, artificial and natural attributive-head compounds differ in the semantic sub-classification highlighted by their causality and constitutive roles. When constructing an object, humans often consider materiality first. Therefore, when N_1 as the constitutive role of N_2 in artificial NN attributive-head compounds, it generally emphasizes the whole and indicates the material. In contrast, in natural NN attributive-head compounds, objects are naturally occurring and self-contained; therefore, when N1 as the constitutive role of N_2, it tends to highlight a certain inherent or attached part of the whole more prominently. In artificial NN attributive-head compounds where N_1 serves the agentive role of N_2, it is often the energy sources that provide power for specific targets; whereas in natural ones where N_1 plays the agentive role are typically nature's own energy intrinsic such as wind or water which effect on natural objects.

(ii) Modes of Semantic Relation Realization. Due to differences in overall semantic categories, implicit predicates of relationships within artificial compound words all constructed by human activities. Conversely, those within natural compounds do not change according to human activities will but exist objectively in nature. When N_1 as the formal role of N_2 within these two types of compounds: features chosen during word formation of artificial compounds tend to be assigned or stipulated by humans while those distinguishing features within natural ones arise from objective traits exhibited by nature itself or innate properties. When N_1 as the telic role of N_2, the artificial objects explain the transformed objects through human activity which indicating subjective intention behind creating certain tools, while the artificial objects depict physiological characteristics of various structures with functionality being an attribute extracted after research into them—essentially reflecting inherent capabilities. When N_1 as the constitutive role of N_2, the artifacts indicate materials or components chosen during object creation while the natural objects objectively present components inherent. When N_1 as the agentive role of N_2, the artifacts refer to tools or energy sources relied upon for normal operation while the natural objects refer to energy sources from the nature.

6 Conclusion

Modern Chinese NN attributive-head compounds exhibit different qualia structural relations and tendencies towards implicit predicates due to varying internal compositional patterns between artificial/natural semantics and between different qualia structures and implicit predicates present the fairly consistent correspondence. The formal role primarily selects distinctive characteristics allowing differentiation on larger scales with diverse perspectives available thus resulting complex predicate implications. The telic role is purer aligning perfectly with predicate of function relationship. The constitutive role illustrates relationships between wholes/parts also showing implicit predicates of dependence relationship which means homogeneous material of the whole and of possession relationship which means the single parts of the whole. The agentive role explains how things form always requiring some specific powers or reasons and if emphasis lies on power during word formation then predicate of dependence relationship is implied while if reasons are highlighted then the predicate of causality relationship is implied.

Moreover, interactions and constraints exist among components and components, component and whole influencing the qualia structure and the tendencies of implicit predicates. And the semantic classification also affecting occurrence of metaphors.

Acknowledgments. This paper was supported by Major Project of Key Research Institute of Humanities and Social Sciences (22JJD740014); Humanities and Social Sciences Planning Fund of the Ministry of Education of China (23YJC740031); International Chinese Language Education Project of Center For Language Education and Cooperation (22YH65D); the Science Foundation of Beijing Language and Culture University (supported by "the Fundamental Research Funds for the Central Universities") (23YCX184).

References

1. Fellbaum, C.: Wordnet: A Electronic Lexical Database, 1st edn. MIT Press, Mass (1998)
2. Levi, J.N.: The Syntax and Semantics of Complex Nominals, 1st edn. Academic Press, New York (1978)
3. Pustejovsky, J.: The Generative Lexicon, 1st edn. The MIT Press, Cambridge (1995)
4. Zhu, Y.: Semantic Word Formation of Chinese Compound Word, 1st edn. Beijing University Press, Beijing (2016)
5. Dong, Z.D., Dong, Q.: Construction of a knowledge system and its impact on Chinese research. Contemp. Linguist. **1**, 33–44 (2001)
6. Downing, P.: On the creation and use of English compound nouns. Language **4**, 810–842 (1977)
7. Levin, B., Lelia G., Dan J.: Systematicity in the semantics of noun compounds: the role of artifacts vs. natural kinds. Linguistics (3), 1–43 (2019)
8. Li, J.: The development trend and form-meaning features of contemporary Chinese lexical patterns. In: Dong, M., Gu, Y., Hong, J.F. (eds.) CLSW 2021. LNCS, vol. 13249, pp. 391–401. Springer, Cham (2022). https://doi.org/10.1007/978-3-031-06703-7_30
9. Meng, K.: Semantic interpretation and selective rules on the means of telic expressions in compound nouns. Lang. Teach. Linguist. Stud. **6**, 83–93 (2020)
10. Miller, G.A., Richard, B., Christiane, F., Derek, G., Katherine, J.M.: Introduction to WordNet: a on-line lexical database. Int. J. Lexicogr. **4**, 235–244 (1990)

11. Pustejovsky, J.: Type construction and the logic of concepts. In: Bouillon, P., Busa, F. (eds.) The Language of Word Meaning, pp. 91–123. Cambridge University Press, Cambridge (2001)
12. Pustejovsky, J.: Coercion in a general theory of argument selection. Linguistics **6**, 1401–1431 (2011)
13. Pustejovsky, J.: Type theory and lexical decomposition. In: Pustejovsky, J., Bouillon, P., Isahara, H., Kanzaki, K., Lee, C. (eds.) Advances in Generative Lexicon Theory. Text, Speech and Language Technology, vol. 46, pp. 9–38. Springer, Dordrecht (2013). https://doi.org/10.1007/978-94-007-5189-7_2
14. Song, Z.Y.: The role of telic features in the lexical meaning and word formation of nouns: from the perspective of language values and linguistic values. Stud. Chin. Lang. (1), 44–57 (2016)
15. Zhou, R.: A qualia structure analysis on mandarin trisyllabic noun-noun compound. Lang. Teach. Linguist. Stud. **6**, 70–80 (2020)
16. The Dictionary Editing Room of Institute of Linguistics, CASS, Modern Chinese Dictionary, 7th edn. The Commercial Press, Beijing (2016)

Author Index

A

Ahrens, Kathleen II-209
Allassonnière-Tang, Marc II-91
Annaer II-331

B

Bai, Linqian I-160
Bao, Lingxiong II-139

C

Chai, Xingsan I-426
Chang, Hui I-11
Chen, Bingxian II-486
Chen, Jia-Ni II-216
Chen, Jing II-116
Chen, Juqiang I-11
Chen, Shunting II-234
Chen, Si II-435
Chen, Tengfei II-180
Cheng, Ken Siu-kei I-90
Chung, Chih-Hsuan I-34, I-225

D

Dabhurbayar II-15
Dahubaiyila II-139, II-331
Dai, Dongming II-76
Dou, Jinmeng I-254, I-278
Du, Tengteng I-495
Duan, Xun I-426
Dulan II-15

F

Fan, Juanjuan I-239
Feng, Yaolin I-317

G

Gábor, Parti II-274

H

Han, Yingjie II-180
He, Tianqi I-211
Ho, Ho Kuen I-187
Ho, Ka-wai I-90
Hong, Jia-Fei I-60, I-146, II-216, II-377
Hsiao, Huichen S. I-3, II-423
Hsu, Yu-Yin I-130, II-301, II-486
Hu, Xingyu II-126
Huang, Chu-Ren I-130, II-116, II-209,
    II-274, II-316
Huang, Lue II-435
Huang, Wei II-286
Huang, Xiyue I-46
Huang, Yishan II-101

J

Jiang, Menghan II-209

K

Kang, Jung-Jung I-74
Ke, Yonghong II-469
Kim, Chaeri I-370
Kou, Xin I-23

L

Lee, Chainwu II-91
Leung, Ka-Hang I-146
Li, Hanmeng I-23
Li, Jiapan I-116, I-495
Li, Jie II-76
Li, Junlin II-316
Li, Quan I-440
Li, Yi II-42
Lin, Yi-Jia II-377
Liu, Meichun I-254, I-278, II-458
Liu, Xiaomei II-76
Liu, Yi II-192
Liu, Ying II-342

Long, Yunfei   II-52
Lu, Chia-Rung   I-74
Luo, Xin   II-274
Lv, Xiaoqing   I-266

M
Mou, Li   II-257

N
Ning, Xiaodong   II-180

P
Peng, Bo   II-116
Peng, Weiming   II-3

Q
Qiu, Bing   I-302, II-243
Qiu, Le   II-116

R
Rao, Gaoqi   II-27, II-126, II-153, II-192
Rao, Yujing   II-357
Rui, Jingying   I-60

S
Shan, Qingcong   I-343
Shao, Tian   II-192
Shen, Yuqi   I-116
Shih, Meng-hsien   II-173
Song, Jihua   II-3
Song, Yu   II-76
Sun, Ao   I-386
Szeto, Ka Hei   II-393

W
Wan, I.-Ping   II-91
Wang, Enxu   I-266
Wang, Guirong   II-153
Wang, Hongzhu   I-358
Wang, Shan   I-454
Wang, Shaodong   II-3
Wang, Shaoming   I-454
Wang, Weili   I-196
Wang, Yunhan   I-3
Wang, Zhimin   II-406
Wei, Wei   II-406
Wei, Zuntian   II-3
Wen, Han   I-400
Wen, Xueyi   II-42

Wu, Jiun-Shiung   I-34, I-225
Wu, Pengcheng   II-76
Wuyoutan   II-139

X
Xia, Yuhan   II-52
Xie, Siqi   II-498
Xie, Yonghui   II-286
Xiong, Jiajuan   II-447
Xu, Ge   II-52
Xu, Hantao   I-332
Xu, Hongzhi   II-42
Xu, Yifa   I-173
Xu, Yiwei   II-27
Xu, Yue   II-406
Xun, Endong   II-153, II-192

Y
Yang, Erhong   II-286
Yang, Heguo   II-180
Yang, Jianguo   I-239
Yang, Shanshan   I-160
Yang, Yike   I-187, II-393
Ye, Yaoru   II-301
Yi, Jia   I-302
Yi, Zilin   II-126
You, Hao   I-288
Yu, Anwei   I-3, II-423
Yuan, Yulin   I-101

Z
Zan, Hongying   II-61
Zeng, Jinghan   I-101
Zhan, Xuting   I-466
Zhang, Chenghao   II-61, II-76
Zhang, Hengxing   II-76
Zhang, Junping   I-415
Zhang, Kai   I-196
Zhang, Kunli   II-61, II-76
Zhang, Lei   I-160
Zhang, Wenxuan   II-61
Zhang, Xiaopei   II-458
Zhang, Yao   I-480
Zhang, Zhixiong   II-192
Zhang, Zhuo   I-254, I-278
Zhao, Mengyu   II-3
Zhao, Qingqing   II-52
Zhao, Xinlan   I-130
Zhao, Yuanbing   II-42

Zheng, Shuwen I-400
Zhong, Qian I-211
Zhong, Yin I-358, II-357
Zhou, Jianshe I-196
Zhou, Qihong II-257

Zhou, Shufan II-153
Zhu, Qi I-415
Zhu, Shucheng II-342
Zhu, Ting I-415

Printed in the United States
by Baker & Taylor Publisher Services